FROM THE ADRIATIC TO THE ALPS

Archaeopress Roman Archaeology 125

From the Adriatic to the Alps

Transport and Trade Networks in Roman and Late Antique Northern Italy

James Page

Archaeopress Archaeology

ARCHAEOPRESS PUBLISHING LTD
First and Second Floors
13-14 Market Square
Bicester
OX26 6AD

www.archaeopress.com

ISBN 978-1-80327-973-2
ISBN 978-1-80327-974-9 (e-Pdf)

Cover: View over Verona (photograph by Caitlin McMenamin).
Dressel 6A amphorae.

This book is available direct from Archaeopress or from our website www.archaeopress.com

Contents

List of Figures

Introduction

Transport and Infrastructure: The Backbone of Economic Networks

'The Richest District'. Production and Exports from Northern Italy

Amphorae: Containers and Consumables

Red-Slipped Finewares: Local and Long-Distance Consumption

Decorative Stone: Indulgence and Compromise

List of Tables

Acknowledgements

It goes without saying this book would not have been possible without a great deal of help and support from a variety of people and places. The research that forms the basis of this volume began as my PhD thesis, undertaken at and funded by the University of Edinburgh between 2018 and 2022. My primary supervisor, Ben Russell, gave innumerable hours of feedback and support throughout the thesis, constantly pushing me to apply myself in new ways and grow as a researcher. I owe a lot to his wisdom and advice over the course of my studies, and especially for his putting up with me through not one, not two, but three degrees. My evolving team of secondary supervisors, Xavier Rubio-Campillo, Andrew Dufton, and Louise Blanke all brought invaluable new perspectives to the thesis. Special thanks must go to Xavier, whose help was vital in developing the methodology used in the quantitative analysis and patience with QGIS and RStudio knew no bounds. My two examiners, Andrew Wilson and Eberhard Sauer also provided detailed feedback on the thesis and gave key suggestions for its publication.

The award of a Rome Fellowship at the British School at Rome between 2023 and 2024 gave me the time and resources to transition my work from thesis to monograph. The BSR will forever hold a special place in my heart, and the community of staff, award holders, and guests all helped shape the final form of this volume. In particular, I wish to thank Fannie Caron-Roy, Aaron Ford, Oren Margolis, Caitlin McMenamin, Emma Merkling, Tura Olivera, Željka Oparnica, and Angela Trentacoste for their friendship and support during my time in Italy. Invaluable feedback also came from presenting sections of this work at events amongst the wider academic community of the foreign academies and institutes in Rome.

Away from the University of Edinburgh and the British School at Rome, two other people have been instrumental in shaping the trajectory of my career and work. The first is Candace Rice, whose mentorship and supervision during my undergraduate and Master's degrees couldn't have given a better foundation for pursuing the PhD and subsequent research career. The second is Tyler Franconi, who read and commented on sections of this work, and has been a constant source of support and encouragement during my Master's, PhD, and beyond. Words can't express my gratitude for their help, advice, and friendship over the years.

Beyond the academic side of things, I am grateful to all the friends who helped support me along the way and certainly made the PhD and monograph writing process more bearable during the toughest times. At the University of Edinburgh, I would like to thank Sam Ellis, Ambra Ghiringhelli, Dot Longely-Cook, Andrew McLean, Rory Nutter, and Madison Rolls for their friendship during our time in the HCA. In particular, I wish to thank Rory Nutter for always being available for an afternoon coffee, and his ability to allay any worries or fears I had about the PhD. Amongst the wider doctoral community around Edinburgh and St. Andrews I would also like to thank Zofia Guertin, Briana King, and Lucia Michelin for their friendship and all the amazing food we shared together during our studies. Outside of the university, I would like to thank Tilly Adcock, Sophie Cronshaw, David Currey, Victoria Francois, Molly Greasley, Mikey Kotts, Carolina Krödel, Alice Latchford, Sasha Malik, Shaun Massie, Katherine May, Shannon McAllister, Kevin Morrow, Callum Nevett, and Blair Wilson for their friendship and support, alongside their (sometimes not so) gentle reminders that there was a world outside of academia.

Finally, none of this would have been possible without my parents, Philip and Carole Page. Thank you for always encouraging me to pursue my interests, your sage advice, unwavering support, and all the love you have given me over the years. This is for you.

List of Abbreviations

AMINI – Amphora in Northern Italy
ARS – African Red Slip
CBM – Ceramic Building Materials
CITS – Central Italic Terra Sigillata
DESTINI – Decorative Stone in Northern Italy
ETS – Eastern Terra Sigillata
GTS – Gallic Terra Sigillata
LRA – Late Roman Amphora
MADINI – Material Data in Northern Italy
MATS – Middle Adriatic Terra Sigillata
MNI – Minimum Number of Individuals
NITS – Northern Italic Terra Sigillata
OCK – Oxé, Comfort, and Kenrick 2000
RBH – Rims, Bases, and Handles
REFINI – Red-Slipped Finewares in Northern Italy

Introduction

The eleventh region receives from the river the name of Transpadana; it is situated entirely inland, but the river carries to it on its bounteous channel the products of all the seas.
Pliny the Elder, *Natural History* 3.123.1[*]

The waterways of Northern Italy were a busy sight during the 1st century AD. Laden with traffic, the rivers and canals of the Po-Veneto Plain formed the main transport arteries of the region. Slow-moving barges, towed by panting men and loaded with produce from the Adriatic and Eastern Mediterranean dwarfed smaller, faster craft, ferrying passengers to their destination. Fishermen plied their trade along the banks and on the water, while the land around the rivers, recently reclaimed from marsh, hosted herds of cattle and other livestock. Within the great cities that lay along the rivers' path, cargoes were loaded and unloaded from bustling wharves and well-stocked *horrea*. Imported wine amphorae from Crete and coloured marble from Asia Minor competed for space with locally produced terra sigillata, oil, and wine destined for the great ports of Ravenna, Altinum, and Aquileia. This vista represents the culmination of over two centuries of development and investment in Northern Italy's economy, creating the circumstances where the Po truly did carry upon it all the products of the seas.

Despite being located hundreds of kilometres from the nearest seaport, the upper reaches of the Po Valley were integrated into the wider Roman economy. The Po, also known as the Padus or the Eridanus in Antiquity, is the largest river in Italy, host to dozens of tributaries, and was said to be navigable as far as Turin in the Roman period.[1] The wide, flat plain of its valley consisted of an urbanised landscape that included the great cities of Milan, Turin, and Bologna, and contained extensive agricultural wealth. Ancient writers unanimously agree on the prosperity of the region. Tacitus called it 'the richest district of Italy', while Polybius claimed the Po Plain, 'surpassed in fertility any other in Europe'.[2] Yet the Po Valley, and Northern Italy more widely, have at times been written off in modern scholarship as 'marginal' or 'isolated', a border zone between Italy proper and the northern provinces that was economically insignificant.[3] Although there have been moves to challenge perceptions of Northern Italy's

isolation, this important region remains severely neglected within economic scholarship.[4]

Inland areas made significant contributions to the Roman economy, yet inland regions, such as Northern Italy, have not seen the same focused attention as coastal areas when it comes to studying ancient trade networks.[5] The large production centres of Gallic sigillata at La Graufesenque and Lezoux, and African Red Slip (ARS) production sites between Kairouan and Sbeitla in Tunisia, were all located inland.[6] Great quantities of *pavonazzetto* marble were extracted from Dokimion in central Anatolia and exported across the Roman world.[7] Many less archaeologically visible products, such as perishable foodstuffs, livestock, timber, charcoal, and textiles, were also cultivated and extracted from inland areas.[8] However, inland regions were not solely producers; they also consumed significant quantities of imported goods. The Rhenish Limes imported large sums of Baetican olive oil, Gallic wine, and terra sigillata.[9] The Ebro Valley consumed large quantities of wine produced along the Iberian Coast, and the discovery of Iberian Dressel 20 and Dressel 2-4 amphorae at the Temple of Jupiter atop the summit of the Gran San Bernardo Pass in the Alps demonstrates that imported goods could reach even the most remote parts of the Roman world.[10]

Although their distance from the sea did not exclude them from wider markets, inland regions faced additional obstacles to trade when compared with

---

[*] See bibliography for translations used.
[1] Plin. *HN* 3.123; Polyb. 2.16.
[2] Polyb. 2.15; Tac. *Hist.*, 2.17.
[3] Chilver 1941; Brunt 1971; Harris 1985; 2011; Häussler 2007; 2013; Patterson 2006; Scheidel 2014.

[4] Broadhead 2000; Campbell 2012: 302-7; Roncaglia 2013; 2018. These studies take a more positive view of the region's economy and connectivity during the Roman period.
[5] Major studies of maritime trade and coastal regions include: Brandon *et al.* 2014; Horden and Purcell 2000, in particular chapters IV and V; Keay 2012; Leidwanger *et al.* 2014; Morley 2007; Rice 2012; 2016; Tchernia 2011; 2016; Wilson 2009a; 2011a; 2011b; Wilson and Bowman 2018; Wilson, Rice, and Schorle 2011.
[6] Bonifay 2003; 2016; Lewit 2015; Mackensen and Schneider 2002.
[7] Russell 2013: 170-75; 2018: 140. See also the extraction of *giallo antico* at Chemtou in North Africa.
[8] Diosono 2009: 258-76; Liu 2009: 29-31, 75-77; Lavan 2015; Meiggs 1982; Roncaglia 2018: 89-95.
[9] Remesal-Rodriguez 1986; 1997; 2002. Although it might be argued that these imports were driven by state action to feed the frontier armies, Franconi (2014: 103-06) argues that there was also significant civilian demand for foreign goods which would eventually outstrip that of military. Indeed, civilian sites often show a greater diversity of imports than military ones.
[10] Beltrán Lloris 1987: 51-74; 2008: 271–318; Castillo 2016: 132-33; Paccolat, Joris, and Cusanelli-Bressenel 2008: 149.

those on the coast. Maritime transport was the cheapest and the fastest way of moving goods across the Roman world, but costs could rapidly increase as goods began to move inland.[11] River transport, although more expensive than maritime, provided a cheaper alternative to overland travel.[12] However, not every town was located on a navigable river, necessitating the completion of most journeys via overland transport.[13] The transhipment of cargo between maritime, fluvial, and overland transport also incurred additional costs.[14] The low cost of fluvial transport, when compared with overland travel, means river valleys have often played an important role in the development and functioning of inland trade networks, forming corridors of commerce and communication between the coast and the interior.

Beyond transportation and connectivity, river valleys form important economic zones. Valley floors offer flat, fertile land for settlement and agriculture, with the rivers that flow through them presenting a source of water and, if they are navigable, a method of transportation. Even in the absence of a navigable river, a valley floor offers a level or gently sloping path inland, far easier, cheaper, and faster than traversing hills or mountains. The optimum conditions presented by river valleys would result in the development of several major productive landscapes across the Roman world. The Tiber Valley produced food, oil, wine, and building materials for the city of Rome, resulting in an intensively cultivated landscape stretching from the city's hinterland to the river's torrential upper course.[15] The Guadalquivir Valley saw the creation of a landscape orientated around the production of olive oil for export. This included both the olive oil itself and the transport apparatus in the form of Dressel 20 amphorae.[16] The Nile Valley formed one of the most important agricultural landscapes in the Roman world, with its produce responsible for supplying the *annona* in Rome.[17] The river also formed an artery for the transport of stone from the Imperial quarries in the Eastern Desert and goods arriving at Red Sea ports to the Mediterranean coast.[18] The economic impact of rivers has received increasing attention in Roman archaeology, however,

not all rivers have been given equal consideration.[19] Italy itself contained several major river valleys, most notably the Tiber Valley which has been researched extensively. The Tiber Valley has been the subject of intensive study for the past seventy years, beginning with the South Etruria Survey and most recently the Tiber Valley Project, which resulted in a series of major publications that significantly changed understanding of the region.[20] In comparison, the lack of investigation into the Po and its impact on Northern Italy's economic development stands out.

Northern Italy's location and unique geography make it a perfect case study to explore questions related to inland trade during the Roman period. The region forms a transitional zone, a meeting point between the Eastern and Western Mediterranean, and the Italian Peninsula and Northern Europe. How did goods and people move through the region between these places? How did the valley's geography aid or hinder the distribution of goods and people? What was being produced in this fertile region and where was it being consumed? Examining the zones of production from which Northern Italy was importing goods, how they entered the region, and how they circulated, has the potential to shed light on the factors governing inland trade and consumption.

At first glance, Northern Italy appears difficult to access via overland routes. To the south of the Po Valley, the Apennines form a physical separation between the region and the rest of the Italian Peninsula. Bordering the north and west, the Alps create a formidable barrier to movement, beyond which lay the north-western provinces of the Empire. These mountains presented a significantly larger obstacle than the Apennines to overland trade but one that was not necessarily insurmountable. Despite the assumption that the cost of overland transport, particularly over steep gradients, would have been too great for any meaningful trade to have occurred through mountains, in some circumstances the opposite appears to have been true.[21] The potential of the Alps and the Apennines as connective spaces, rather than barriers to movement, warrants investigation.

---

[11] Russell 2018a: 140.

[12] DeLaine 1992; de Soto 2019; Erim and Reynolds 1970; Fernández 2021; Scheidel 2014. Upstream river travel was more expensive than downstream, although still significantly cheaper than overland travel. It is worth noting that many factors, such as weather, seasonality, terrain, and competition between traders would have affected prices.

[13] While it is easy to view terrestrial and fluvial transport networks as independent from one another, Laurence (2005: 138), emphasises that 'to discuss water and land transport as competing systems ... is to misunderstand the economics of transport in the Roman world'. See also Fernández 2021.

[14] Franconi 2014: 58; Russell 2013: 137.

[15] Braconi 2009b; DeLaine 1997; Diosono 2009; Graham 2002; McCallum 2004; Patterson, Di Giuseppe, and Witcher 2020; Vidal 2009.

[16] Ponsich 1974; Remesal Rodríguez 1980; 1997; 1998.

[17] Adams 2018; Erdkamp 2012.

[18] Adams 2001; 2007; Peña 1989.

[19] Campbell's (2012) *Rivers and the Power of Ancient Rome* was the first book to synthesise much of the evidence on ancient rivers. While an essential study, its wide coverage led to a lack of depth in some areas. It has also been criticised for its predominantly western focus, reliance on literary evidence, and dismissal of the role that palaeoclimatological and palaeohydrological data can play in the analysis of ancient rivers. On these points, see Franconi 2013.

[20] Coarelli and Patterson 2009; Patterson 2004; Patterson, Giuseppe, and Witcher 2020. It should be noted, however, that the majority of research has taken place in the lower and middle Tiber Valley. The economy, population, and settlement in the upper valley is understood to a far lesser extent.

[21] Bell, Wilson, and Wickham 2002; Bruno 1998; Carreras, de Soto, and Múñoz 2019; Gabucci 2017.

Looking to maritime routes, Northern Italy's two coastlines on the Adriatic and the Ligurian seas offered competing entry points for extra-regional imports. The Adriatic Coast offered access to the Eastern Mediterranean, while the Ligurian Coast was integrated into Western Mediterranean markets. The Po Valley's connection to the Adriatic and its proximity to the Ligurian Sea allows the opportunity to examine the potential effect that two alternate maritime entry points, located at opposite ends of the region, had on material distribution. Indeed, ports on the Adriatic and Ligurian Coasts were not equally accessible from inland areas. Although the Ligurian ports were in close vicinity to sites in the south-west of the Po Valley, their goods had to cross the Apennines to enter the region. Conversely, goods arriving via the Adriatic ports had a greater distance to travel to reach the west of the valley, yet the flatter terrain and fluvial connections may have resulted in an easier and cheaper journey compared to the goods crossing the Apennines.

The Po Valley itself comprises a great alluvial plain through which flowed one of the largest navigable rivers in the Roman world. The dense network of waterways meant that one was rarely more than fifteen kilometres from a navigable river, the extents of which were further expanded and enhanced through ambitious engineering projects. In tandem with the region's rivers, an extensive network of roads criss-crossed the valley and climbed into foothills and mountains ringing it. Investment in significant infrastructure allowed goods to efficiently move between terrestrial and fluvial transportation, leading to an expansive, interconnected transport network. This provided the means of conveying large quantities of goods from the coast inland and vice versa.

Transport networks and the costs associated with moving cargo have heavily shaped the thinking behind the mechanics of inland trade. It has been hypothesised that there would be a steep drop-off in the distribution of imported goods as one moved further inland due to the high cost of terrestrial transport.[22] This would contrast with the far more extensive distribution of imports in coastal areas due to the low cost of maritime transport. However, this model is somewhat simplistic. For example, Fulford highlights the sustained inland distribution of Dressel 20 amphorae across inland regions, from their production and filling in the Iberian Peninsula to the Empire's northern frontier.[23] State actors may have formed an important driving force behind this pattern, leading to differences in distribution between trade facilitated by the state and that conducted by private

individuals. Fentress further discusses the impact of political and economic geography on inland economies in North Africa, where she highlights how the dual economic systems of the inland city of Sétif allowed some of its produce to be traded over long distances, while other produce remained uncompetitive outside of local markets.[24] Indeed, not all goods would have been traded inland in the same way. African cookwares were widely distributed in coastal regions yet had very little penetration inland.[25] This is in stark contrast to fine African Red Slip ware (ARS) which had far greater inland distribution.[26] The relatively cheap cookware was less able to absorb transport costs in comparison to the more expensive ARS. Stone and marble cargoes could also move in an atypical way. Imported stone, in the form of revetment, sarcophagi, sculpture, or architectural elements, was able to travel great distances inland in some circumstances.[27] The expense and financing behind stone and marble items (especially for monumental architecture and sarcophagi) might mean that transport costs were something the commissioner could readily afford. The picture that emerges of inland trade is far more complex than a simple drop-off of imported goods as distance from the coast increased, with myriad factors besides transport costs affecting material distribution.

A study of inland trade in Northern Italy, one that is grounded in the archaeological evidence, is long overdue. To this end, published assemblages of amphorae, finewares, and decorative stone and marble from across the region have been compiled together in a series of databases. Together they form the Material Data in Northern Italy (MADINI) dataset, a powerful tool to answer chronological and spatial questions on the nature of trade and the economy within Northern Italy during the Roman and Late Antique periods. Containing over 50,000 individual entries, MADINI forms one of the largest quantified datasets applied to the study of the Roman economy, and the largest body of Roman material data compiled for Northern Italy. The analysis presented in this book reappraises prior assumptions about the region's isolation and explores the mechanisms governing the movement and consumption of goods within Northern Italy. Archaeological data forms the heart of the investigation. Utilising the MADINI dataset, long-term chronological and geographic trends in the circulation and consumption of locally produced and imported materials are charted. The patterns exposed by the

---

[22] Bonifay 2018; Fulford 2009: 253; Laven 2016: 3; Vaccaro and MacKinnon 2014.
[23] Fulford 2009: 254. See also Carreras 1994. Gallic terra sigillata would see a similar sustained inland distribution across the northern provinces (Mees and Polak 2013).

[24] Fentress 1990. See also Fentress 2015 on inland textile production in North Africa, alongside Fentress 1979 for inland military supply.
[25] Leitch 2011; 2013.
[26] Bonifay 2003; 2004; 2018.
[27] It is important to note, however, that the long-distance trade of stone and marble constituted an exceptional phenomenon. The majority of stone in the Roman world travelled over very short distances, (Russell 2013: 143; 2018b: 240-42).

material analysis are used to examine the interplay and co-dependency of terrestrial and fluvial transport and demonstrate that, despite their distance from the coast, inland sites were strongly connected to Mediterranean markets through long-distance trade. While transport costs played an important part in the distribution of goods and materials in inland regions, they did not remove choice. The consumer played a significant role in the provenance and type of imports consumed across the region. The study's conclusions have wider applications to the study of inland economies and trade and provides a methodology for future analyses.

Past Research on Trade in Northern Italy

Although Northern Italy holds significant promise as a case study of inland trade, most prior regional scholarship has focused on examining social exchanges and connections, rather than economic ones. Roman expansion into Cisalpina and Transpadana during the mid-Republic, and their eventual incorporation into Italy in 42 BC, has seen significant engagement.[28] Far less attention has been given to the Imperial and Late Antique history of the region.[29] As a result, the Po Valley is often viewed as a frontier region, a border between the Roman south and the barbarian north rather than an area strongly interconnected with the wider Roman world.

As Northern Italy contains Italy's border with the rest of Europe, it has always been the point of entry for land invasions of the Italian Peninsula, with the region being no stranger to conflict during the Roman period. The Po Valley would serve as the theatre for the opening engagements of the Second Punic War, with the major battles of Trebia and Insubria taking place alongside dozens of minor actions.[30] Marius, at the Battle of Vercellae, would defeat the Cimbri and Teutones in 101 BC and the Emilian Plain hosted the first major engagements of the civil war that followed Caesar's death.[31] Beyond that, Augustus would campaign against the Salassi in the Alps, who revolted in 34 BC, and again in 25 BC.[32] Northern Italy would see further

conflict throughout the Imperial and Late Antique Periods. The Po Valley would be the location of several battles in the Year of the Four Emperors in AD 69, most notably that of Cremona but also actions at Piacenza and along the Po itself.[33] Northern Italy would also be invaded during the Marcomannic Wars of the 2nd century AD, with Aquileia besieged and Oderzo razed to the ground.[34] Further conflict would follow during the civil wars of the 3rd century, and the region would see repeated incursions from the Alemanni, Juthungi and Marcomanni during this time.[35] This unrest would see the increasing militarisation of Northern Italy, culminating with the stationing of permanent military garrisons at Milan and Pavia, and the movement of an imperial capital to Milan in AD 286 to allow the emperor to be closer to the frontier.[36] After the fall of the Western Empire, the Po Valley would form a major battleground in the Gothic Wars of the 6th century.[37] The perception of Northern Italy as a buffer zone between Northern Europe and the Italian Peninsula has served to promote narratives of assimilation, either through conquest or 'Romanisation', which in turn reinforces the idea of the region as geographically and socially distinct from Central Italy.

The view of Northern Italy as separate or cut off from the rest of the Italian Peninsula has helped to foster concepts of isolation amongst some scholars, proving an especially common theme amongst the limited discussions of the region's geography and economy.[38] This perception of isolation, both social and geographic, can be traced back as far as the middle of the 20th century when the first regional studies were undertaken. The first to examine the valley in detail was that of Chilver in 1941. Chilver covered the entirety of the Cisalpine Gaul from the enfranchisement of the Transpadani in 49 BC up to the death of Trajan in AD 117, specifically concentrating on the social and economic development of the region. Writing at a time before any large-scale archaeological investigation had taken place, he concluded that the Cisalpine economy could have been of little more than regional significance due

---

[28] See Brunt 1971; David 1997; Dyson 1985; Harris 1985; Häussler 2007; 2013; Lomas 2017; Purcell 1990; Peyre 1979; Roncaglia 2018: Part I; Salmon 1982; Williams 2001. Caesar would grant the inhabitants of Gallia Cisalpina Roman citizenship in 49 BC via the *lex Roscia*, but it would not be until 42 BC that the province was incorporated administratively into Italy.
[29] Chevallier's influential 1983 work *La Romanisation de la Celtique du Pô. Essai d'histoire provincial* remains the most comprehensive history of Northern Italy during the Imperial period, although Roncaglia 2018: Part II provides several important reassessments.
[30] The major Roman defeat at Trebia near Parma was preceded by several skirmishes, notably around Pavia and Piacenza (Livy 21.47-58.).
[31] These were the battles of Forum Gallorum and Mutina in 43 BC (App. *B. Civ.* 3.67-72; Dio Cass. 46.37-39).
[32] On the 35 BC campaign see Dio Cass. 49.34, 49.38. For the 25 BC campaign, see Dio Cass. 53.25. Aosta would be founded on territory confiscated from the Salassi. Campaigns were also undertaken

between 17 and 14 BC against the Cammuni, the Vennii, and the Rhaetians in the area of Trentino (Dio. Cass. 54.20-22; Suet. *Aug.* 21; *Tib.* 7; Velleius Paterculus, 2.95). Their subjugation, along with other Alpine peoples, is recorded on the Tropaeum Alpinum at La Turbie (*CIL* V 7817) and commemorated by triumphal arches at Aosta and Susa. Client kingdoms, such as that of that of the Cottiae in the Western Alps in the territory of Susa, would also survive into the latter half of the 1st century AD (Roncaglia 2013: 334-35).
[33] Suet. *Vit.* 10; *Vesp.* 7; Tac. *Hist.* 2.1-51; 3.1-25.
[34] SHA. *Marc. Aur.* 14.
[35] Aur. Vic. *Caes.* 28.10; 33.1-18; Zos. 1.22. The emperors Philip the Arab, Decius, Gallienus, all fought in Northern Italy. Roncaglia (2018: Chapter 8) contains a good summary of the history of the region between the 3rd and 6th centuries AD.
[36] Aur. Vic. *Caes*, 33; *Epit.* 34.
[37] Procop. *Goth.* 5.
[38] See Chilver 1941; Brunt 1971; Harris 2011; Millar 1995; Patterson 2006; Purcell 2012; Scheidel 2014.

to its inability to export its produce.[39] Brunt, in his *Italian Manpower 225 B.C.-A.D. 14*, would reach a similar conclusion, describing Northern Italy as 'largely cut off from trade with other parts of Italy, Gaul, or the Mediterranean at large'.[40] One of the main issues that both Chilver and Brunt highlighted as an obstacle to the economic development of the Po Valley was the perceived absence of a large port at the mouth of the Po Delta, an argument that would be further developed by Harris in his 1989 paper, *Trade and the River Po: A Problem in the Economic History of the Roman Empire*.[41] Harris believed this to be a result of the Po's regime being too difficult to navigate, the valley having nowhere to trade a surplus to, and the region's cities having little interest in importing large quantities of foreign goods.[42] Notions of the region's geographic isolation have persisted well into the 21st century. To give an example, Scheidel, in his 2014 article on modelling connectivity across the Roman Empire, singles out the 'isolation' of Northern Italy from the rest of the Italian Peninsula.[43] However, Scheidel's model maps connectivity specifically from Rome across the Empire. Does this also mean that the Po Valley was isolated from markets in Germany, Gaul, Illyria, or the Eastern Mediterranean? Taking a Rome-centric viewpoint is unhelpful when discussing regional connectivity. Nevertheless, it has proved surprisingly common in Anglophone scholarship concerned with the Po Valley. In fact, a growing body of evidence suggests Northern Italy formed an important zone of supply for the Danubian *Limes*, providing consumables and commodities to communities on and around the frontier.[44]

The most recent regional study, Roncaglia's 2018 book *Northern Italy in the Roman World*, forcefully challenges perceptions of the social, geographic, and economic isolation of Northern Italy from the rest of the Italian Peninsula and the wider Roman world.[45] Roncaglia's work contains the most complete synthesis of information on the development of the region's economy to date, including information on agricultural production, more

specialised economic activity, and trade.[46] Whereas prior studies have tended to concentrate solely on the early Roman history of the valley, specifically during the Republic, Roncaglia integrates the region's pre-Roman and Late Antique history into her analysis, giving a far more comprehensive overview of the area's development than has been previously available. While Roncaglia's study is a welcome addition to the body of literature on Northern Italy, a considerable amount of work on the region's economy remains to be done. Crucially, engagement with the archaeological evidence in most regional studies often remains superficial.[47] The Adriatic ports, especially Aquileia, are often the main focus, with evidence for inland trade often reduced to distribution maps of amphorae and other goods.[48]

Although the majority of regional scholarship available for the economy of Northern Italy remains grounded in literary and epigraphic evidence, a half-century of archaeological investigation has provided a wealth of new data.[49] At site level, there has been extensive investigation by Italian archaeologists working under the jurisdiction of the *soprintendenze* or academic institutions. Under their guidance, hundreds of excavations have been carried out in the region, including major investigations at important Roman cities such as Aquileia, Brescia, Milan, and Verona.[50] While not every excavation has been published, many have been studied to a high standard. Material specialists have produced catalogues of quantified data for individual excavations, offering detailed insight into the sites under investigation. Unfortunately, this material is rarely analysed in a wider context. There have been some attempts to compare material from sites located within the same *soprintendenza* jurisdiction, alongside several discussions surrounding individual artefact types at a regional level, (for example the distribution of Dressel 6A and Lamboglia 2 amphorae across Northern Italy), but these are seldom integrated into wider discussions on the Roman economy.[51] Analysis of both short and long-distance

---

[39] Chilver 1941: 29-35, 135.

[40] Brunt 1971: 180-81.

[41] Harris 2011: 115. The essay would be edited and republished as part of the 2011 volume, *Rome's Imperial Economy: Twelve Essays*. Harris and his predecessors were writing at a time before the advent of widespread geomorphological investigations. These would later show that the main mouth of the Po during the Roman period was located close to the port of Ravenna.

[42] Harris 2011: 196-97. Harris' analysis was principally based on literary, artistic, and epigraphic evidence and whilst the ideas are well presented, its argument was weakened by a lack of access to archaeological evidence.

[43] Scheidel 2014: 21.

[44] Assirelli 2023; Bekljanov Zidanšek, Vojaković, and Žerjal 2022; Duch 2017: 195-97; Egri 2007; Ehmig 2010: 155-156.

[45] Roncaglia 2018. Her study is primarily focused on the eastern and central valley, specifically the areas to the east of Lake Como and Milan, and the route of the via Aemilia. Whilst this area has produced some of the most detailed scholarship in the region, the western valley, specifically the territory of Piedmont, warrants further attention.

[46] See, in particular, textile production (Roncaglia 2018: 90-94).

[47] Studies that have included archaeological evidence (e.g. Broadhead 2000; Chevallier 1983; Garnsey 1998; Garnsey and Sallar 1987; Roncaglia 2018), have taken a far more positive view of trade within the region.

[48] Broadhead 2000: 156-57; Garnsey 1998: 53-58; Roncaglia 2018: 101-15.

[49] A lack of engagement with archaeological evidence when discussing economic history is not something unique to Northern Italy. The inaccessibility of many material studies and their lack of engagement with broader economic questions, has often led to them being side-lined in wider economic discussions. See, for example, Bang 2009; 2012; Finley 1973; Lo Cascio 2009; Morley 2007; 2012; Morris, Saller, and Scheidel 2007; Whittaker 1993; 1994.

[50] See Brogiolo 1999; Caporusso 1991; Cavalieri Manasse 2008; Filippi 1997; Fontana 2017; Maggi *et al.* 2017.

[51] Betori, Gomez Serito, and Pensabene's (2009) analysis of stone and marble types used in Roman monuments in the western Alps or Bruno (1998) and Melli's (2004) studies on trans-Apennine trade. For examples of studies focusing on single artefact types, see Bruno's (2005) gazetteer of amphora types found within Northern

trade within Northern Italy has seldom passed beyond the use of distribution maps of material. While these are useful for observing the spread of artefacts, they fail to map the intensity of trade by distinguishing between what might be termed 'one-off' imports and more sustained trade.[52] Furthermore, few studies adopt a long-term approach when examining trade networks, choosing instead to focus on a single chronological period.[53] The majority of quantified material analysis remains limited to a site-by-site basis, resulting in a huge amount of excavated material that has never been studied outside of its find context. Only rarely has this body of evidence been applied to broader regional and economic questions.

Towards a Quantitative Approach

One of the key objectives of Roman economic scholarship over the past 20 years has been to promote a more rigorous analysis of existing archaeological data, with an emphasis on moving towards quantified studies of economic activity.[54] Over a century of excavation across the Mediterranean world has produced a vast quantity of Roman material, yet only recently have the technology and methodologies to host and analyse these data become available.[55] An increasing number of studies have used quantified material evidence to analyse and reconstruct economic activity, challenging prior perceptions and drawing new conclusions about the Roman economy and trade.[56] A study that unites individual, quantified material datasets from across Northern Italy has the potential to answer complex questions about the region's economy.[57] By comparing and contrasting the quantity and concentration of material from different sites, geographical and chronological patterns and trends in trade and consumption can be brought to light. An analysis of material distribution across the entirety of Northern Italy will provide new insight into the relationship between the coastal regions and inland zones which

have been previously assumed as marginal and difficult to access.[58]

The analysis performed here goes beyond that carried out by pre-existing quantified studies, which traditionally only examine a single material type. Mapping the spread and provenance of different materials serves to highlight the multiple levels and directions of trade occurring within Northern Italy, exposing the role that cost and choice played in the selection of goods within assemblages. Therefore, this study compares and contrasts three separate material types: amphorae, finewares, and decorative stone (marble and stone flooring and revetment). These materials represent three distinct types of consumption within the Roman world, being traded through different mechanisms and consumed in different ways. Amphorae primarily carried consumables, items such as oil and wine that were essential to the day-to-day diet and would be purchased repeatedly. In contrast, finewares, though widely represented across the strata of Roman society, were a non-essential item rather than a necessity. Decorative stone and marble were luxury items, bulky and expensive one-off purchases that were the preserve of the wealthy or civic projects. The different patterns in the geographic and chronological distribution of these goods serve to contrast the varying levels of trade within Northern Italy and the different supply mechanisms behind them.

Before the analysis could take place, the data, taken from a diverse range of publications, had to be synthesised and prepared for study. To accomplish this, a series of databases were created, one for each of the material types. The result is MADINI, one of the largest and most diverse corpora of material evidence gathered in Roman archaeology, a powerful resource for the analysis undertaken in this book and for future studies.

The MADINI Dataset

The Material Data in Northern Italy (MADINI) dataset consists of three relational databases, one for each of the material types discussed in the analysis: amphorae, finewares, and decorative stone. In total, 58,743 individual entries are recorded across the dataset from 39 urban sites within the region (see Figure 1).[59] The design of the MADINI databases was influenced by other

Italy; Zara's (2018) study of the quarrying, distribution, and use of Euganean trachyte; or Cipriano and Mazzocchin's (2018) analysis of the development of Dressel 6A amphorae.

[52] For example, Kenrick 2000; Lindhagen 2009; Mazzocchin 2009.

[53] Notable exceptions include Auriemma and Quiri 2004; Auriemma, Degrassi, and Quiri 2012; Quiri 2009.

[54] Brughmans 2022; Bowman and Wilson 2009a; Peña 2007; Wilson 2022.

[55] Brughmans 2022; Wilson 2022. See also the work of Project MERCURY, which aims to equip scholars with the skills needed to undertake computational analysis by supplying tutorials, datasets, and a model library, has been instrumental in raising the profile of network and statistical modelling as an analytical tool amongst classical archaeologists (Brughmans 2020).

[56] Bes 2015; Brughmans, Poblome, and Pots 2016; De Callataÿ 2014; Franconi et al. 2023; Rubio-Campillo et al. 2017; Rubio-Campillo and Coto-Sarimento 2022; Romanowska et al. 2021; Taelman 2022.

[57] An array of proxy data has been applied to the study of the Roman economy, some more successfully than others. For a discussion of proxies, their potential, and their shortcomings, see Scheidel 2009; Verboven 2021; Wilson 2009a; 2009b; 2014.

[58] Horden and Purcell's (2000) The Corrupting Sea helped to establish a movement of thought that emphasised the role of ports and coasts in connecting the disparate regions of the Mediterranean, with Rice describing ports as the 'pinnacle of market connectivity' in the Roman world, (Rice 2012: 60, n. 187). See also, Bonifay 2004: 451-2; Leitch 2011: 185-86; Morley 2007: 27-29; Russell 2013: Chapter 5; Tchernia 2016: 90-94.

[59] In Version 1 of the MADINI databases, only urban and suburban sites are included, with rural sites such as farms and villas to be added in future iterations.

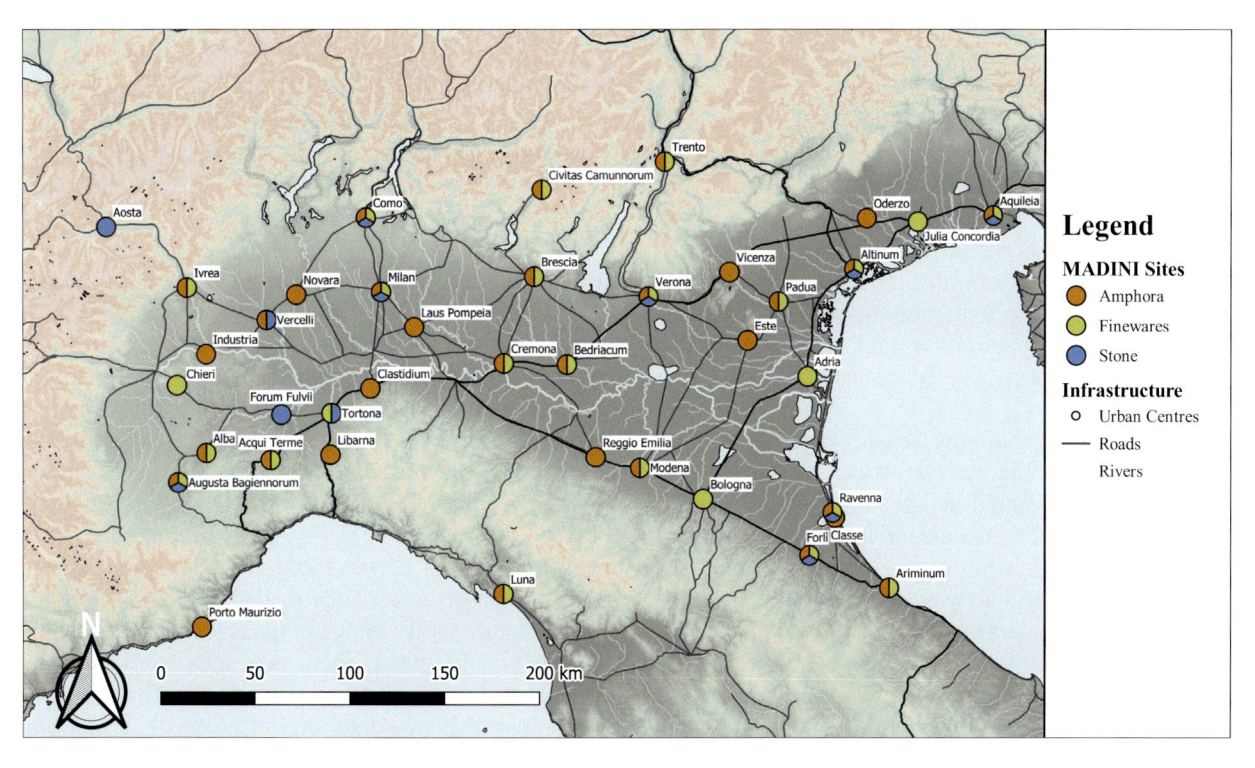

Figure 1. A map of sites within the MADINI dataset and the material assemblages originating from them.

synthetic databases of Roman material, particularly the RAAD (Roman Amphora Assemblage Database) and ICRATES (Inventory of Crafts and Trade in the Roman East) datasets.[60] The incorporation of overlapping design elements ensures a level of compatibility, promoting comparison and the application of pre-existing research methodologies to the data. Each database within MADINI, alongside a full layout and metadata, is hosted online and available to end users.

Although the rise of quantified studies has improved understanding of the Roman economy, they are not without their problems. The survival and publication of the ceramic data are not uniform across the Roman era, with some artefact types and periods better preserved or favoured for study over others. Data from the 1st and 2nd centuries AD are the best studied and published, and were available across all 39 sites within MADINI. Unfortunately, intact Republican deposits of ceramics are rare, with most assemblages returning under ten fragments. The situation is similar for data from Late Antiquity. Assemblages from the 3rd century AD onwards are far less comprehensively studied, with most of the data being described in only a tokenistic manner, if at all. A greater focus is typically given to the earlier Republican and Imperial periods. Where material specialists with Late Antique or Early Medieval experience have examined assemblages, the Late Antique data is presented in greater detail, but such

cases are rare.[61] Consequently, data from the Republican period and the Late Antique are absent for several sites within MADINI. Furthermore, archaeological data contains biases, either inherent (such as survivability) or acquired (such as through excavation practice), and it is important to acknowledge these weaknesses in the data.[62] The MADINI databases are synthetic datasets, combining data from dozens of research publications across Northern Italy. These published assemblages varied in their quality and quantity across the study area. With little to no standardisation, they often reflect the publishing styles and practices of the region and the times in which they were compiled, presenting substantial challenges for synthesisation.[63]

A lack of uniformity amongst the values used to quantify excavation data often forms a significant hurdle to comparing datasets from multiple sites. The unit of quantification is something which often varies from publication to publication, with common methods including minimum number of individuals (MNI), the number of rims, bases, and handles (RBH), sherd weight, and number of sherds (also known as maximum number of individuals). MNI offers the most accurate measure of the quantity of vessels within a

---

60 Bes 2015: 3-5; Franconi et al. 2023.

61 For example, Bruno 2008; 2002; Bruno and Bocchio 1991; 1999; Massa 1999; 2002; Morandini 2008a; 2008b.
62 Heilen and Manney 2023; Orton 2009; Peña 2007b; Wilson 2009a: 229-38; 2009b; 2014.
63 A summary of the challenges and difficulties in synthesising archaeological data for analysis can be found in Franconi et al. 2023: 3-6.

site and would have been the preferential unit to use within MADINI. Unfortunately, while this measurement was present in some publications from Northern Italy, it was absent from the majority. In a significant number of assemblages, the data for specific fragment types (i.e. walls, handles, bases, and rims) was also missing, meaning that it was not possible to calculate the MNI retrospectively for these sites. The number of sherds per vessel was the only measurement available across the entire range of publications and, consequently, this was the measurement selected for analysis.

As with ceramics, there are several possible units of quantification for decorative stone. The preferable comparative unit would be the total weight of each lithotype present in each assemblage, as this offers a more accurate indication of the quantity of material at each site. Unfortunately, weight was only recorded for one assemblage within the study area, that of the *Domus* of 'Bestie Ferite' and 'Titus Macro' at Aquileia.[64] Another possible quantitative measurement available was the total volume of each lithotype. This unit is not without its own problems (namely the difficulty of achieving an accurate volumetric measurement for highly irregular objects) and forms an uncommon method of quantification.[65] For assemblages that solely contained wall revetment or floor panelling, the total surface area of a lithotype might be included in cm^2, but this measurement was also absent from many sites.[66] The final quantitative measurement for stone was the total number of fragments of each lithotype. While providing a starting point for analysis, using the number of fragments as an indication of the total quantities of stone present at a site is problematic. The uneven nature of fragmentation means that two pieces of stone that are vastly different in size are given equal weight in the analysis. As the number of fragments was the only measurement available across all datasets, this was selected as the unit of comparison despite its flaws. However, the possibility of over and underrepresentation of some lithotypes caused by comparing fragments of different sizes remains.

The MADINI dataset of amphorae, finewares, and decorative stone forms a complex, yet powerful tool to analyse trade networks and the economy in Northern Italy. With careful attention to both their strengths and limitations, the material databases will allow a far greater scope of quantified analysis to be achieved than has previously been possible in the region. The following sections provide details on the component MADINI databases (AMINI, REFINI, and DESTINI) and the structure of the data within them.

AMINI: Amphorae in Northern Italy

The first database, AMINI, contains 28,323 sherds of amphora from 32 urban sites across Northern Italy.[67] It comprises five interconnected tables, the contents of which are outlined as follows. The main AMINI Catalogue table contains information on each sherd, including epigraphic data. Where available, the type of sherd (rim, base, handle etc.) was recorded. The AMINI Standard Forms table provides information on the different vessel forms present in the database. This includes details on form name, start and end date of production, provenance, contents, and capacity in litres. Where available, a URL link to the relevant entry on the Southampton University Amphora Project Database is provided.[68] The AMINI Deposits table contains information on the excavation context of the sherds. This includes details on the nature of the deposit and the proposed date of the context. The AMINI Locations table provides information on the site from which the sherd was recovered, including name, coordinates, geography, and topography. Where available, a link to the relevant entry on the Pleiades Database is provided. Finally, the AMINI Publications table supplies information relating to the publications containing the amphora sherds, including author, date, and full bibliographic entry.

Each sherd in the database was assigned a standard vessel form based on the typology of the amphora. The dataset from the Southampton University Amphora Project formed the starting point for standardisation. Vessels were cross-referenced with the Southampton database, with concordances in typologies equated. Across the publications synthesised by AMINI, 127 amphora forms overlapped with the Southampton database. A further 25 amphora forms present in the region were not recorded in the Southampton database and were added to the AMINI dataset. Fragments for which the vessel form was unknown, but whose zone of production could be traced through fabric analysis were grouped together by their origin. This resulted in a total of 165 unique vessel forms.

Each sherd within the database was assigned a zone of production. In total, there were six broad provenances

---

[64] Previato and Mareso 2015. A total weight for the stone assemblage from the Capitolium of Verona was also available, however the weights for individual stone and marble types was not provided (Bocconcello 2008).

[65] The only assemblage to include a measurement of stone and marble volume was the MM3 excavations in Milan (Terraccina 1991). Minato 2018 also included the measurements necessary to work out volume for the architectural elements and sculpture recovered from the Altinum survey.

[66] The stone and marble assemblage from the theatre at Augusta Bagiennorum included these measurements (Gomez Serito and Rulli 2014).

[67] The AMINI dataset is available at https://doi.org/10.5281/zenodo.13745898.

[68] Southampton University Amphora Project, viewed 23 January 2024, http://archaeologydataservice.ac.uk/archives/view/amphora_ahrb_2005/.

for the amphorae circulating in Northern Italy during the Roman period. The first was the 'Adriatic Littoral', encompassing vessels produced in the coastal hinterland of the Adriatic Sea. The second was the 'Eastern Mediterranean', containing vessels from the Aegean, Asia Minor, and Palestine. The third was the 'Iberian Peninsula', encompassing vessels from the provinces of Baetica, Lusitania, and Tarraconensis. The final three origins were for vessels from Southern Gaul, the coast of North Africa, and the Tyrrhenian Littoral. In some cases, a more specific provenance was available for the vessels. Although using these would have obscured the overarching patterns in the data, they are recorded in the database where present.

Two sets of dates were assigned to each fragment. The first were the start and end dates of production for its vessel form. These were taken from each vessel form's typology. The second was the opening and closing dates of the context in which the fragment was deposited. These dates theoretically give a better indication of when a vessel was consumed, rather than simply when it was in circulation. While deposition data were available for many of the sherds in the AMINI database, a large number of publications did not present their material stratigraphically, meaning more refined dating than the overall site chronology (at times covering hundreds of years) was not possible.[69]

Each vessel form was also assigned a broad chronological period reflecting their most prominent era of production and circulation. The longevity of some amphora forms, coupled with uncertainty over the start and end dates of their production, meant that it was necessary to maintain broad dates for these periods. These were the Late Republic (vessels whose main period of production lay between 150 BC and 28 BC), the Imperial period (vessels whose main period of production lay between 27 BC and AD 250), and Late Antiquity (vessels whose main production lay between AD 251 and AD 700). Each vessel was assigned the period which encompassed either the entirety or majority of its production lifespan. While some vessel forms might have seen production outside these parameters, these are exceptional cases.[70]

Finally, a probable content was assigned to each amphora, covering the most likely product to have been transported within the vessel. Possible commodities consisted of wine, oil, fish products, olives, fruit, *defrutum*, and alum. However, expanding evidence for reuse, both within Northern Italy and across the Roman

world, means this data should be approached with caution.[71]

REFINI: Red-Slipped Finewares in Northern Italy

The second database, REFINI, contains 12,112 sherds of red-slipped finewares (terra sigillata and ARS) from 25 urban sites across Northern Italy.[72] As with AMINI, it comprises five interconnected tables. The main REFINI Catalogue table contains information on each sherd. If a stamp was present on a sherd, epigraphic information and its OCK number, if identified, was noted. Where available, the type of sherd (rim, base, handle etc.) was recorded, alongside fabric type (mostly applicable for ARS and ETS sherds). The zone of production of the sherd was also noted. The REFINI Standard Forms table provides information on the different vessel forms present in the database. This includes details on form name, start and end date of production, and vessel type (plate, bowl, cup etc.). The REFINI Deposits, Locations, and Publications tables follow the same format as those in the AMINI database.

Each sherd in the database was assigned a standard vessel form based on the typology of the fineware. Where possible, the vessel form assigned by the publication was used for each fragment. However, some excavations were conducted before updated typologies were available. For example, the MM3 excavations in Milan mainly utilise Goudineau's and Pucci's typologies, rather than the more recent Conspectus series that has become the dominant typology used to identify terra sigillata.[73] Concordances between typologies listed within the Conspectus Series were used to standardise the vessel forms within the REFINI dataset.[74] Fragments for which the vessel form was unknown, but whose zone of production could be traced through fabric analysis were grouped together by provenance. In total 630 unique vessel forms were attested across the publications making up the REFINI database.

Each sherd within the database was assigned a zone of production. In total, there were six broad provenances for red-slipped finewares circulating in Northern Italy during the Roman period. The first was the 'Adriatic Littoral', encompassing finewares produced in the coastal hinterland of the Adriatic Sea. The second was 'Central Italy', applied to terra sigillata produced in workshops located at Arezzo, Pisa, and elsewhere south of the Apennines. The third was the 'Eastern

---

Mediterranean', covering Eastern terra sigillata vessels. The fourth was 'Gaul', encompassing Gallic terra sigillata. ARS was assigned 'North Africa' as its zone of production. Finally, 'Northern Italy' was applied to terra sigillata produced in the Po Valley and Alpine foothills. As with the amphora data, often a more specific provenance was available for a sherd. In particular, sherds equipped with a stamp could often be traced to workshops operating in a limited geographic area. Where available, these more specific provenances have been recorded.

As with the AMINI dataset, each sherd has been provided with a set of production and deposition dates, alongside being assigned to a chronological period.

DESTINI: Decorative Stone in Northern Italy

The third database, DESTINI, contains 18,308 fragments of decorative stone from 13 urban sites in Northern Italy.[75] The stone recorded in DESTINI was primarily revetment, used as paving or cladding, but also contains other small architectural features such as cornices and wainscotting. The main DESTINI Catalogue table contains information on each fragment. Where available, the type of fragment (paving, cornicing, billet etc.) was recorded. The DESTINI Stone Types table provides information on the lithotypes present in the database. This includes name, provenance, and quarry site, alongside whether the stone was white, grey, or polychrome. Where available, a link to the relevant entry on the Corsi Database is provided. The DESTINI Deposits, Locations, and Publications tables follow the same format as those in the AMINI and REFINI databases.

The most common nomenclature (such as *giallo antico*, *africano*, Proconnesian etc.) was used to define the stone or marble present, with a list of concordances found via the Oxford Corsi Collection of Decorative Stone.[76] Each fragment within the database was assigned a zone of production. While specific quarry sites are known for most stone quarried, broad provenances were used to highlight overarching patterns in the data.[77] Stone and marble quarried on mainland Turkey or in the Sea of Marmara was referred to as being extracted from 'Asia Minor'. Stone and marble extracted from south of the Apennines and coastal Liguria were termed as coming from 'Central Italy and Liguria'. Lithotypes from Egypt and North Africa were recorded as being extracted

in 'Egypt and North Africa'. Marble from France was referred to as having a 'Gallic' provenance. Stone and marble extracted from the Aegean islands and Greek mainland was referred to as having originated from 'Greece and the Aegean'. Finally, stone and marble extracted from sites within the Po Valley and the Alps were referred to as having come from 'Northern Italy'. Where possible, the provenance of each fragment was taken from the assemblage publication, however, the exception to this was *greco scritto*. While previously thought to have been sourced from North Africa, recent research has shown that most *greco scritto* quarried in antiquity likely originated from Asia Minor.[78]

When it came to dating the material within the stone and marble assemblages, in some cases the chronology was highly specific. For some structures, especially public buildings, the construction date could be narrowed down to within a few decades or the reign of a specific emperor. Where available, the chronological data for the construction phase of the stone and marble revetment is given. However, in many other cases, chronological data was missing, or the material was predominantly from residual contexts. For example, the publication of the MM3 excavation's assemblage of Roman marble wall revetment and floor panelling did not include a chronological element and its exact origin could not be pinpointed.[79] Consequently, a chronological element is lacking for much of the decorative stone data.

Methods and Approaches

The study presented in this volume represents the largest geographic and chronological examination of trade within Northern Italy during the Roman period so far attempted, offering a unique opportunity to reassess prior thinking on the region's economy and wider connections in the Roman world. Although it hopes to provoke new discussions on the mechanics of inland economies more broadly, it does not seek to create a singular model of trade within inland areas, recognising that the unique geographic and commercial environments within each region resulted in highly individualised economic circumstances. These are circumstances that changed again depending on the materials being exchanged, leading to multiple levels of trade and consumption. The book's conclusions present inland economies and trade in their full breadth and complexity, challenging prior conceptions of isolation and marginality and providing a framework for future regional studies.

---

[75] The DESTINI dataset is available at https://doi.org/10.5281/zenodo.13745898.

[76] Corsi Database, viewed 2 January 2024, http://www.oum.ox.ac.uk/corsi/.

[77] A list of known quarries for each stone and marble type can be found via OXREP database of stone quarries, viewed 2 January 2024, http://www.romaneconomy.ox.ac.uk/databases/stone_quarries_database/.

[78] Attanasio *et al.* 2012. Previously, *greco scritto* was thought to have originated from quarries at Cap de Garde in Algeria. Isotopic and EPR analysis revealed that the quarries at Hasançavuslar, near Ephesus, were in fact the main source during the Roman period.

[79] Terracina 1991. The assemblages from Altinum (Minato 2018), Forum Fulvii, and Tortona (Gomez Serito 2007) also lacked a chronological element in their publication.

The analysis begins with an exploration of Northern Italy's transport infrastructure. Roads, rivers, and canals constituted the backbone of the region's economy, and without them, the complex networks of exchange discussed throughout the volume could not have formed. The development of terrestrial and fluvial transport systems across Northern Italy are charted, demonstrating the significant effort and capital that was expended in the creation of new infrastructure. This extended the transport network into new areas of the region and served to reduce the difficulty of traversing challenging terrains such as low-lying waterlogged ground and steep mountain passes. Evidence for fluvial navigation is also synthesised to create a new catalogue of navigable rivers, revealing many waterways in the region that are no longer navigable did, in fact, support rivercraft during the Roman period.

Although the majority of evidence for trade within Northern Italy comes from imported goods, the role of local production for regional supply and export markets forms an important part of the picture. Evidence for the production of foodstuffs and commodities in Northern Italy is examined, alongside the probable export destinations for these goods. Looking at Northern Italy's agricultural landscape, a wide range of food is shown to have been produced, with sites containing multiple wine or oil presses attested across the region, alongside examples of cereal cultivation, drying, and storage.[80] While exports of foodstuffs have proved hard to trace archaeologically, ceramics from Northern Italy have been found in significant quantities along the Adriatic Coast and the Danubian frontier.[81] It is unknown if Northern Italic ceramics piggy-backed on other goods exported from the region but the frontier and Danubian provinces offered an expansive market in close proximity.[82]

The majority of the volume is dedicated to the analysis of the amphora, fineware, and decorative stone data contained within the MADINI dataset. The MADINI databases present the opportunity to examine long-term patterns and geographic trends in trade across Northern Italy, tracing the evolution of demand and supply within the region. While some superficial patterns can be observed by simply comparing the quantified data, statistical methods form important tools, often revealing underlying patterns not immediately discernible. The potential of statistical studies is readily apparent as they offer ways to scientifically test theoretical models, study large datasets, and overcome flaws or limitations inherent within archaeological data.[83] Such methodologies are especially useful when examining large datasets, providing a way to locate underlying trends hidden by the volume of material contained within them.[84] To examine chronological and geographic patterns, two separate forms of analysis were used. Aoristic analysis was used to examine chronological trends in the data, while geographic changes in consumption and distribution were identified using hierarchical clustering. The code used to run the analysis is openly available to end users online in the form of R Scripts.[85]

Aoristic Analysis

For the ceramic assemblages, long-term chronological changes in the datasets were graphed using aoristic analysis, using the R package \datplot. Aoristic analysis uses a probabilistic approach, selected due to its ability to account for the chronological uncertainty inherent in ceramic data. Ceramic vessels were in production for an extended period of time, with some production timescales lasting for hundreds of years. A vessel may have been produced at any point during its production dates. Likewise, most archaeological contexts are dated to broad periods, often decades-long, and a ceramic vessel may have been deposited at any point within the context's life cycle. Aoristic analysis accounts for this by calculating the probability of an individual sherd being produced or deposited at any point across its production or deposition chronology, distributing it across these timescales.[86] The result is a graph that reflects the level of uncertainty in the archaeological record with greater accuracy than conventional data visualisation techniques.[87] While the advantages of this approach when analysing data with a temporal element are evident, its application remains rare within the field of Roman archaeology.[88]

The aoristic analysis consisted of two main components. First, the frequency of ceramic in a given year was plotted. The data were then subsetted to graph the

[80] Forin 2017: 132-70.

[81] Brusić 1999; Duch 2017: 195-97; Egri 2007; Makjanić 1995; Mercando 1972; Mertens 1972; Schindler Kaudelka 1980; Schindler and Zabehlicky Scheffenegger 1977; Tassaux 2004.

[82] This is a question that concerns fineware ceramics more broadly. Although shipwreck evidence confirms that finewares (both terra sigillata and ARS) piggybacked on the maritime trade of other goods, the mechanics of how it travelled inland are more difficult to track (Dannell and Mees 2013: 175-76; Lewit 2015: 115-18).

[83] Brughmans 2022; Knappett 2013.

[84] Despite their usefulness, the application of network and statistical modelling as tools of analysis has not been without critics. Some have questioned whether modern analytical techniques can be used to rigorously test primitive aspects of the economy without an inbuilt bias against them (See van Oyen's 2017 response to Brughmans and Poblome 2016b, alongside Brughmans and Poblome's 2017 reply).

[85] The code and data used in the analysis can be found at Github Repository: Adriatic-to-the-Alps, viewed 12 September 2024, https://github.com/jamespage15/Adriatic-to-the-Alps.

[86] Crema 2012; Johnson 2004; Orton, Morris, and Pipe 2017: 3-5; Steimann and Weissova 2021: 290.

[87] Steimann and Weissova 2021: 289-290.

[88] Franconi et al. 2023 provides a template for the analysis undertaken in this study. For other examples of studies that have used aoristic analysis, see: Carrignon, Brughmans, and Romanowska 2020; Fentress et al. 2004; Romanowska, Bobou, and Raja 2021; Steimann and Weissova 2021.

frequency of ceramic from each zone of production circulating in a given year. For the amphora data, the frequency of containers carrying wine, oil, or fish products in a given year was also graphed. Second, the number of ceramic vessel types in circulation in a given year was plotted. The data were then subsetted to graph the number of ceramic vessel types from each zone of production circulating in a given year. Each analysis was carried out using both the production dates and deposition dates of each sherd.[89] Sherds without a deposition date or with deposition dates spanning more than 200 years were excluded from the deposition analysis. Due to the lack of chronological data for many fragments in the DESTINI dataset, the stone and marble contained within it were not examined using Aoristic analysis.

Hierarchical Clustering

For both the ceramic and stone assemblages, geographic changes in consumption across the datasets were plotted using hierarchical clustering, using the R packages \dplyr and \reshape2. Hierarchical clustering forms a way of grouping data based on the pairwise distance between assemblages.[90] Pairwise distance measures the separation between values of a dataset (in this case the percentage component of each zone of production). The closer the distance between assemblages, the more likely they are to join a cluster, meaning sites with similar characteristics will group together, mapping zones of consumption.[91] In comparison to other forms of cluster analysis, such as k-means, the number of groups that form are not pre-determined in hierarchical clustering, allowing for more nuanced patterns to emerge.[92]

The clustering analysis was carried out by first sub-setting the material into their broad chronological periods. For each period, the percentage component of each zone of consumption within a site's assemblage was calculated. Sherds or fragments without a known zone of production or date were excluded from the analysis. The percentage totals for each site were then placed in a table, which was then analysed using the UPGMA algorithm (Unweighted Pair Group Method with Arithmetic mean). The analysis created a distance table, recording the pairwise distance between each site assemblage based on the provenance of the vessels or lithotypes within it. This was then used to hierarchically cluster the assemblages based on the similarity of their provenance, which was then plotted as a dendrogram. To ensure a rigorous level of analysis, only assemblages that contained more than thirty sherds or fragments were included.

---

[89] Franconi *et al.* 2023: 9-10, demonstrate the importance of comparing both production and deposition chronologies for ceramic vessels, the distribution of which can vary greatly.

[90] Hodson 1970; Mommsen, Kreuser, and Weber 1988; Shennan 1997: 239–40.

[91] Brughmans 2010: 289-91; Drennan 2010: 79-96.

[92] Baxter 2015: 148; Ducke 2015; Maddison and Schmidt 2020.

Transport and Infrastructure: The Backbone of Economic Networks

In the 2nd century AD, the merchant L. Tettienus Vitalis, born in Aquileia and educated at Julia Emona, would die in Turin.[1] On his grave monument, he complained about the hardships that merchants endured, but would also make reference to the two rivers that were essential to his business: the Po and the Sava.[2] These rivers provided east-west routes into Northern Italy and the Danubian *Limes*, and their inclusion on Vitalis' monument underpins the importance of fluvial networks in regional transport and trade. To successfully move cargoes of amphorae, finewares, stone, and other goods significant distances, an extensive and well-integrated transport network was essential. Northern Italy's waterways were utilised by cargo vessels for much of their length, although the seasonality of the water network and other unpredictable factors, such as low and high flows, might render the riverscape difficult to use at times. Northern Italy also possessed an extensive system of both major and minor roads that connected its principal population centres. The flat, level ground across much of the Po-Veneto Plain allowed for swift and direct connections, taking goods and people to areas where the water network could not reach. They also provided an alternative to fluvial transport when poor conditions made rivers impassable, although it should be noted that periods of high flow could also have impacted terrestrial infrastructure.

It can often be tempting to think of river and road transport as separate, even competing, systems, given that they functioned in vastly different ways and varied greatly in their haulage costs.[3] However, this is misleading.[4] Although river transport had the potential to be cheaper than road transport, it was not necessarily quicker, as moving upstream could take considerable time.[5] Furthermore, roads were crucial for moving goods to areas not in the immediate proximity of a river, meaning that many inland journeys often needed to utilise both forms of transport to reach their desired destination. Both forms of transport involved the creation of major infrastructure, required to overcome obstacles along their routes. On the water network, ports were needed to provide the necessary equipment for the loading and unloading of cargo. Towpaths were essential for providing a continuous surface for the hauling of vessels, and human intervention was often needed to keep river channels open, involving dredging, channel cutting, or canalisation. On the road network, the construction of the road surface, even on level ground, was a substantial task. This could be compounded by the presence of obstacles such as steep slopes and rivers, requiring the creation of embankments and bridges. All required extensive organisation and maintenance. Together, they formed a combined transport network that provided a high level of access across Northern Italy and provided extra-regional connections.

Without the considerable transport infrastructure outlined in this chapter, the economic networks discussed in the rest of this volume could not have formed. Substantial capital and effort were spent on improving transport links across Northern Italy, enabling the conveyance of imported goods from the coast inland and the transportation of local exports in the opposite direction. The physical remains of stone and concrete port infrastructure at sites such as Aquileia, Ivrea, and Tortona, and the monumental cuttings, bridges, and viaducts of the Aosta Valley all attest to the effort involved in reducing the time and cost of moving goods and people from one place to another.

In this chapter the development and extent of Northern Italy's ancient transport network is examined, providing a foundation for the discussion on trade routes and economic networks across the rest of the book. The development of Northern Italy's roads is charted, and the specialised infrastructure created to overcome the obstacles present within the Po-Veneto region, from the sodden ground of the delta to the steep Alpine passes, are analysed. The challenges faced by terrestrial transport and the perception of its feasibility in modern scholarship are also explored. Turning to the river network, evidence for the navigability of the region's rivers is synthesised and a catalogue of navigable rivers produced. Methods of movement and propulsion on the rivers of the Po-Veneto region are analysed, and, for the first time, its inland wreck evidence is presented alongside port infrastructure located on the region's waterscape. Networks of artificial waterways in Northern Italy are also analysed, the crowning jewel

---

[1] Gabucci and Menella 2003: 234.
[2] CIL 5.7047; 5.7127. *Have Vitalis. / L(ucius) Tettienus Vitalis, natus Aquiei(a)e, / edocatus Iulia Emona, titulum pos<u>it / ante aeternam domum Iulia / Augusta Taurinorum. Dicit: / quaerere cessavi numquam, / nec perdere desi(i). Mors intervenit; / nunc ab utroque vaco. / Credite, mortales, astro nato / nihil est sperabile datum / terras nec minus et maria / impuri aqu(a)e Padi nec minus et Savi / ira<m>. Quod optavi mihi tamen pervenit. / Perpetuam requiem pos<c>o.* See also Gabucci and Mennella 2003; Gregoratti 2015.
[3] De Soto 2019; Russell 2013: 96; Scheidel 2014.
[4] Adams 2012; Campbell 2012: 215-17; Laurence 2005: 138.
[5] Cooper 2011; De Soto 2019: 278-81.

of which was a system of para-littoral canals between Ravenna and Aquileia. Combined, these three networks highlight the breadth and diversity of transport routes and connections within the region.

The Road Network

Overland transport has often been assumed to be too expensive or too impractical for the carriage of heavy goods over long distances during the Roman period.[6] Water transport, either fluvial or maritime, was promoted as preferential in all circumstances, exemplified by Horden and Purcell's remark that all roads reflected 'the shortest distance between two prominent seamarks or navigable rivers'.[7] However, this position has been revised over the past two decades, with the growing realisation that fluvial and terrestrial transport necessarily had to work in tandem with one another.[8] The role that roads played in ancient transport networks has been underestimated, in particular their essential part in connecting areas not reachable by water.[9] In some circumstances, it may even have been preferential to transport cargo solely by road rather than utilise available waterways. Heavy, fragile, and high-value cargo with the potential for a high wastage rate, for example, shaped marble, were unwieldy to load and transport. Transhipment between road and water increased the likelihood of damage to the cargo, or in extreme cases its loss entirely (stone elements submerged in a river are difficult to recover, as demonstrated by the Bacchiglione wreck).[10] Transporting the cargo by the same method for the entirety of its inland journey would have minimised the risk, even though it may ultimately have proved more expensive.

The road network could often provide more direct connections between destinations than the water network. Where the roads climbed into the mountains, they were forced to follow the path of the river valleys, but the roadways on the plain had no such constrictions. The flat, even ground was perfectly suited to overland travel and while potentially slower, offered a shorter route than the meandering path of the rivers in many cases. This was especially true between cities along the foothills of the Alps and Apennines, where riverine connections existed north-south as opposed to east-west. For example, the overland journey between Verona and Brescia is 71km, whereas a river journey down the Adige, up the Po, and then up the Oglio was approximately 430km. The long upriver segment of this journey (some 300km) would also have added considerably to the difficulty and cost of its use. The road network was also less weather-prone than other forms of transport. While there was an element of seasonality to the roadways, this was to a far lesser extent than the river network. Although winter rain might turn an unpaved road surface into impassable sludge or snow block mountain passes, many stretches of the network could still be used under the right conditions. Roads were often placed above the level of hydrological hazards and were well-drained, often being flanked by large drainage channels/canals.[11] While not always guaranteed to work (see the flooding of the via Emilia near Modena below) the roads could provide a safer alternative to the often-treacherous winter river regime. Furthermore, as river conditions became more turbulent from the 3rd century onwards, the road network may have become an increasingly important alternative to fluvial travel.

Development of the Road Network

In many respects, the development of the road network is easier to track than that of the water network, with the construction of the major consular roads well-documented by Livy. These main routes were complemented by a system of smaller roads that connected towns, villas, farms, and other sites across the countryside. Most are not named, but their routes are attested to by the *Antonine Itineraries*, the *Peutinger Table*, milestones, and the discovery of their remains in the archaeological record. There have been attempts to reconstruct the path of these roads.[12] However, only an approximation of their route can be traced in the landscape. The construction dates of many minor roads are unknown and their full development, alongside the true extent of the full road network, will likely never be known.[13] Nevertheless, it is possible to sketch out a broad picture of the development of terrestrial transport routes in the region from the surviving evidence.

Roman expansion into Northern Italy began in the 3rd century BC. This was set against a backdrop of road construction in Central Italy, which included the via Flaminia, (completed in 220 BC).[14] The via Flaminia

---

[6] The origin of this movement of thought and the development of scholarly thinking on the issue of overland transport has been extensively covered elsewhere. Laurence (1999: 95-108) contains a good summary of 20th century thinking on the issue. See also Raepsaet 2009.

[7] Horden and Purcell 2000: 126.

[8] Adams 2012; Campbell 2012: 215-17; Laurence 2005: 138.

[9] Hitchner 2012; Quilici 2009; Raepsaet 2009.

[10] Previato and Zara 2014; Russell 2013: 104-05.

[11] Botazzi 1992: 173-75; Ortali 1992: 57-58; Page 2022: 184-90.

[12] For example, Bosio 1991 and Pellegrini 2004. Both use a combination of archaeological and epigraphic evidence to map Roman roads in the Eastern Po-Veneto region and Istria. See also the *Barrington Atlas of the Ancient World* (Talbert and Bagnall 2000).

[13] Discoveries of roadways submerged within the Venetian Lagoon points to a more extensive network in this part of the region than had previously been imagined (Busana and Vacilotto 2022; Madricado et al. 2021).

[14] Livy 20.17; Laurence 1999: 21-25. Many of roads discussed here likely followed the paths of pre-existing connections between places (Hitchner 2012: 223).

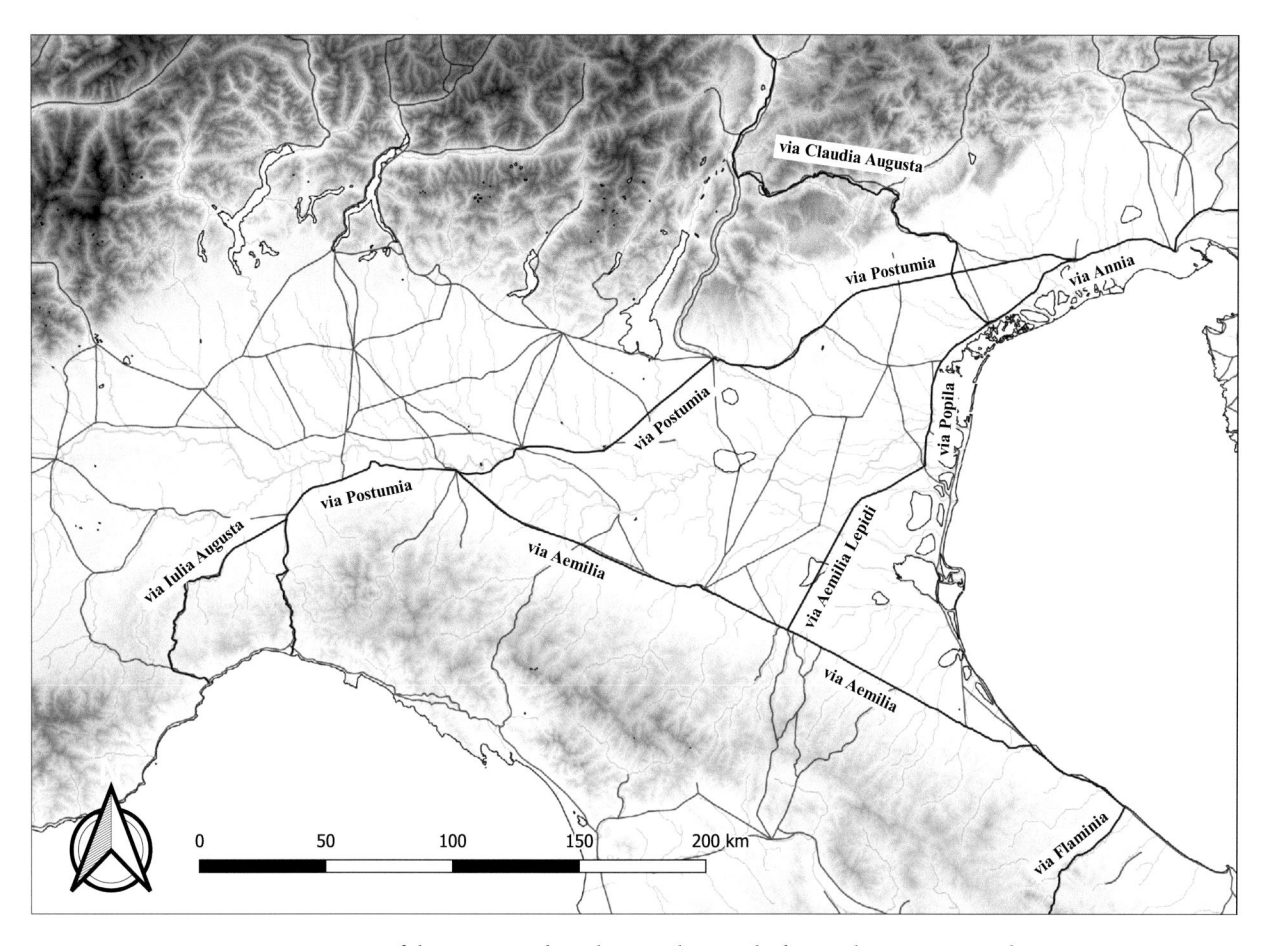

Figure 2. Map of the major roads within Northern Italy during the Roman period.

connected Rome and the colony of Ariminum and provided a jumping-off point for the development of the road network across the Po-Veneto Plain. Roman interests in the area were cemented by the foundation of colonies at Piacenza and Cremona by 218 BC, which would be followed by several decades of regional turmoil that included the Second Punic War and the revolt of the Boii and Insubres.[15] In 187 BC, the via Aemilia was constructed, linking Piacenza and Ariminum.[16] The 180s would see a spate of colony building along the line of this road, including Bologna (189 BC), Modena (183 BC), Reggio Emilia (183 BC), and Parma (183 BC).[17] Another branch, the via Aemilia Lepidi, would connect Bologna and Altinum. The via Postumia would be constructed by 148 BC, connecting Aquileia to Genoa and passing through the important centres of Verona and Cremona. The via Popila, constructed in 132 BC, and the via Annia, constructed in 131 BC, would create important north-

south links along the Adriatic coastline, connecting Aquileia, Padua, and Adria with Ariminum (see Figure 2).[18]

The road building of the 2nd century BC formed the backbone of the terrestrial transport network in Northern Italy. This would be further expanded in the late 1st century BC and 1st century AD, as the development of the region intensified.[19] The foundation of new colonies by Augustus in the far west of the valley, such as Aosta and Turin, necessitated the creation of new roads. In the Aosta Valley especially, significant construction was undertaken to connect the important route over the Great St. Bernard Pass to the wider road network.[20] Other notable works during the Augustan period included the creation of the via Iulia Augusta and the repair of the via Aemilia between Ariminum and the River Trebbia.[21] Many of

---

[15] Livy 21.25, 21.56, 38.11; Polyb. 3.61–71.
[16] Livy 39.2. Only five milestones are dated to the Republican era in Northern Italy. These correspond to the via Aemilia, the via Postumia, and the via Popila, and confirm Livy's dating for the construction of these roads (Basso 2008: 69).
[17] Livy 37.57. The via Aemilia had a significant impact on settlement pattern in Cisalpina, with few major centres south of the Po developing away from the main line of the road (Dall'Aglio 2000).

[18] Basso *et al.* 2004; Pellegrini 2004: 44; Quilici 2009: 558.
[19] In Northern Italy, 24 milestones date from this period, with the main emperors recorded being Augustus, Claudius, Vespasian, and Titus (Basso 2008: 69).
[20] Lucchese 2004: 22; Mollo Mezzana 1992: 70.
[21] Augustan construction or repairs account for 17 milestone. Augustus' repair of the via Aemilia is recorded on a milestone in Bologna (CIL XI.8103 = ILS 9371; Basso 2008: 69).

Table 1. Inscriptions relating to *iumentariorum and collegia iumentriorum* in the Po-Veneto region.

Find Spot	Inscription	Date	Reference
Verona	*V(ivus) f(ecit) / Q(uintus) Spurius Senecio / sibi et Q(uinto) Spurio / Secundo fil(io) et / Spuriae Augustinae / filiae ex permissu* **colleg(ii) / iumentarior(um)** *port(ae) Iov(iae)*	AD 100-200	AE 1987, 552 = AE 2010, 53
Rosegaferro	*D(is) M(anibus) / permiss(u) manc(ipum) /* **iumentarior(um)** */ port(ae) Iov(iae) / [3]sosius / [3]ussem / [3]urno /*	AD 117 - 138	AE 1975, 429 = AE 2007, 576 = AE 2010, 53
Brescia	*Vol<>an(o) Aug(usto) / P(ublius) Antonius / Callistio VI/vir Aug(ustalis) et C(aius) Clod(ius) / Comicus et P(ublius) Post(umius) / Agatho idem / sport(ulis) dedic(averunt) et in / tutel(am) HS CCCC ded(ederunt) /* **coll(egio) iument(ariorum)**	Unknown	CIL V.4294 = AE 2007, 576
Brescia	*Gen(io)* **coll(egii) / [i]umentarior(um)** */ [3]amia Firmia / [T]ertia [3] / [3]iob() C[*	Unknown	CIL V.4211 = AE 2007, 576
Milan	**(c)ollegium (iu)mentario(rum)** *Portae (Ve)rcellinae (e)t Iovae*	Unknown	CIL V.5872

the region's waterways were also bridged in stone for the first time during this period.[22] Furthermore, as the road network grew, pre-existing sections were expanded to accommodate changing vehicle size and increasing traffic. For example, the via Aemilia to the east of Modena was increased from 4.5 m to 6 m in width during the Early Imperial period.[23] Northern Italy's position as a transition zone between Southern and Northern Europe, coupled with the consolidation of Roman expansion in Gaul and Germany, also resulted in the creation of new trans-Alpine roads to connect Italy with the northern provinces. A new road along the banks of Lake Como was constructed during the late 1st century BC, and the via Claudia Augusta, begun by Drusus the Elder, was completed by Claudius *c.* AD 46-47.[24]

By the end of the 1st century AD, the road network seems to have reached its full extent, seeing little notable expansion beyond this point. Alterations or expansions to the network are harder to track from the 2nd and 3rd centuries AD than in the preceding centuries. For example, the via Iulia Augusta seems to have seen extensive repairs under either Antoninus Pius or Caracalla.[25] There is also evidence for the creation of several *collegia iumentariorum* (muleteers) in the region during this time (see Table 1).[26] The connection with specific city gates, for example, the Porta Ioviae and Porta Vercellinae in Milan, suggests that some *collegia* operated or had expertise along specific routes.[27] Echoing the foundation of *collegia nautarum* on the waterways (discussed below), this reflects an increasing

level of organisation in the journeys being undertaken on Northern Italy's road network during this time.

Moving into the 3rd and 4th centuries AD, most evidence for investment and maintenance in the road network comes from milestones. Some 185 of the 250 milestones discovered in Northern Italy date from between the end of the 3rd century AD and the beginning of the 5th century AD.[28] Even accounting for the possibility that many earlier milestones are missing due to their destruction or reuse, this figure seems high. The large increase in milestones may reflect repair work undertaken on the roads during this time. For instance, a string of milestones between Aquileia and Torvicosa refer to the repairing of roads and bridges between AD 235 and AD 238.[29] The greater importance and militarisation of the region during this later period, coupled with the need for quick and efficient transport links in a critical area, could also account for the increase.[30] However, the increase in milestones may also reflect an evolving purpose. Surviving milestones from the Tetrarchy onwards often do not record the number of miles but rather contain honorary language and dedications towards the emperors.[31] Indeed, in times of turmoil, it is not uncommon to see milestones altered in rapid succession in an effort to keep pace with current politics, as is seen on a string of milestones

---

[22] Cera 1996: 193; Marini Calvini 1999: 187; Quilici 2009: 571.
[23] Labate 2019: 198.
[24] CIL, V.8002 = ILS, 208; Bonora Mazzoli 1992: 54; Bosio 1991: 133-47.
[25] Basso 2008: 69.
[26] Data from the Epigraphik-Datenbank, viewed 15 January 2024, https://db.edcs.eu/epigr/epi_ergebnis.php.
[27] Laurence 1999: 134; Perry 2016: 507.

[28] Basso 2008: 69.
[29] CIL V.7989; CIL V.7990; AE 1979.256; AE 1979.257.
[30] Basso 2008: 68; Buonopane and Grossi 2014: 166. Franconi (2014: 54) theorises that the increase in milestones commemorating repairs during this period could reflect a greater drive to repair roads in response to changing climatic conditions. Increased rainfall and flooding may have led to the degradation of sections of the road network, and as fluvial regimes became less suitable for travel, its maintenance increased in importance.
[31] Basso 1987: 80-90; 2011: 67. The relative uniformity of the milestones from the 1st and 2nd centuries AD disappears, with a variety of shapes, sizes, and stone types used. Some milestones were even created using imported coloured marble or from architectural elements such as columns, to monumentalise the markers.

from modern Veneto which were recarved to honour the emperors Valentinian, Valens, and Gratian over a five year period.[32] Consequently, the large increase in milestones during the 3rd and 4th centuries AD may not always represent new investment in the road network but rather reflect the new role milestones played as a medium for local administrators to publicly display loyalty to the emperor.[33] Even so, the choice of milestones as a canvas for these messages suggests there was still significant traffic using the roadways during this time, attesting to their continued importance during this later period.

Road Design

Long-distance overland journeys presented an array of topographical obstacles and challenges to transport, many of which could be reduced or bypassed entirely through the construction of supporting infrastructure. Across Northern Italy, archaeological investigation has shown the great lengths the Romans went to in optimising conditions on the roads. Cuttings, embankments, and bridges brought the road network from the floor of the plain high into the Alps, Apennines, and beyond. The survival of many of these structures to the modern day, and in some cases their continued use in the post-Roman period, attests to their strength and the skill involved in their construction.

Where roads were paved in the east of Northern Italy, the material of choice was often Euganean trachyte, a hard-wearing and exceptionally durable stone. Quarried in the Euganean hills to the north-west of Padua, the stone was transported widely along the road and water network.[34] One of the necessities of using this stone was in part due to a lack of suitable alternatives elsewhere in the region. While local stone was used where possible, on the Apennine side of the Po Valley especially, the local geology is near uniformly limestone and sandstone, too soft for road paving.[35] Mid-level roads in areas close to watercourses often used river pebbles to form a cobble surface.[36] Of course, many roads were not paved at all, such as the axial roads of the centuriation grids that crisscrossed the landscape.[37] While in many cases this was due to the minor nature of the road and the expense involved in paving it, at times this seems to have been a practical choice. For example, when the Alpine roads began to move into the passes, their paved surfaces often switched to that of a beaten earth track or were cut directly into the rock

for large sections.[38] In view of the destructive hazards of the Alpine passes, particularly avalanches, a more easily altered and repaired road surface seems to have been favoured over the monumentality seen on their lower approaches.[39]

Down on the valley floor, the wide, level plain provided efficient transport connections north-south and east-west. However, while the flat, low ground allowed swift travel on a near-even gradient, the marshy ground of the lower areas of the Po-Veneto Plain would have caused difficulties for road construction, requiring technical solutions to overcome them. Any infrastructure following the valley floor would be vulnerable to the high-water table and extreme hydrological events. Indeed, the via Aemilia, in its stretch between Modena and Bologna, was submerged and at times seriously damaged by flood waters.[40] Many roads were flanked by drainage channels, normally ranging between 1 m and 4 m in width, with some of the largest examples reaching 7 m.[41] The widest channels may also have functioned as canals, allowing the road to double as a towpath.[42] In an effort to combat the high-water table and guard against subsidence, one section of the via Aemilia outside of Parma was constructed entirely atop a reclamation deposit of some 20,000 amphorae.[43] In other sections, wooden piling was used to create a foundation for the road surface and stabilise the ground for heavier infrastructure.[44] In particular, piling is often seen in the foundation layers of bridges and bankside infrastructure in the region. For example, the Ponte Vecchio at Ivrea was constructed atop a bed of compacted oak stakes driven deep into the riverbed and consolidated with iron clamps.[45] A similar situation is seen in the foundations of a bridge on the path of the via Annia near Roncade, Treviso.[46] In the low-lying areas near the lagoon system and the Po, it was sometimes necessary to physically raise the height of the roads above the level of flooding and tidal surges. This is seen on the via Annia, where the road runs atop an embankment for long stretches between Altinum and Aquileia, and also in the remains of the via Popilia where it runs near Adria.[47] Finally, it is worth noting that the risk of flooding was not solely limited to lowland areas. In the Alpine valleys, flooding was also a

---

[32] For example, ILS 675, CIL V.8031; CIL V.8032. See also Zanetti 2011: 118-21.
[33] Basso 2018: 107; Buonopane and Grossi 2014: 162-64. See also Sauer 2014, for an Empire-wide discussion of this phenomenon.
[34] Germinario 2017: 426-27; Previato and Zara 2018: 604; Zara 2018: 337-59.
[35] Marini Calvini 1999: 188; Ortali 1992: 150.
[36] Marini Calvini 1999: 189.
[37] Botazzi 1992: 172.

[38] Bonora Mazzoli 1992: 54; Mollo Mezzana 1992: 59, 65.
[39] Mollo Mezzana 1992: 66.
[40] Labate 2019: 199. See also the burial of a major road between Bologna and Padua due to the flooding of the Reno in the late 3rd century AD (Cremonini 2002; 2003).
[41] Botazzi 1992: 173-75. Varr. (R. R. 1.14.2-3) commented that it was common to see 'this type of enclosure ... built along public roads and along streams'.
[42] Botazzi 1992: 172-74; Botazzi and Labate 2017: 18.
[43] Marini Calvini 1999: 190-91.
[44] Calzolari 1992: 162.
[45] Brecciaroli Taborelli 1987a: 147-48; 2007: 130-33.
[46] Busana 2008: 30-31.
[47] Busana and Vacilotto 2022; Calzolari 1992: 165; Page 2022: 184-90; Papisca 2010.

prime concern for engineers in the Valle d'Aosta, where the level of the road between Ivrea and Aosta was kept well above the flood peak of the torrential Dora Baltea.[48]

The heights of the Alps and the Apennines provided a different set of challenges to Roman engineers, in particular the gradient of the road surface. While the deep glacial valleys penetrated deep into the Alps, eventually gradient became more and more of an issue. The grade of a slope has a large impact on the efficiency and feasibility of its traversal. An incline of just 1% required double the number of haulage animals to move at the same speed as over level ground, and slopes of over 5% would likely have been impassable without specialist equipment for heavy loads.[49] This required technical expertise to overcome, resulting in a range of ambitious infrastructure projects. Some of the best-documented examples come from the Valle d'Aosta. Here, a diverse range of bridges, cuttings, embankments, switchbacks, and viaducts were constructed to reduce the gradient and protect travellers from hazards on the road leading to the Great and Little St. Bernard passes. These included the 80 m cutting at Donnas, the retaining wall at Villeneuve, the embankment at Runaz, and the viaduct at Saint Vincent. The road through the valley climbed 517 m between Donnas and Runaz, yet the average gradient was just under 7% and never exceeded 10%.[50] While the Valle d'Aosta contains some of the best-preserved examples of Roman incline engineering, similar examples are seen elsewhere in Northern Italy. In the hills flanking Lake Como, a road was cut through the steep terrain which contained cuttings at regular intervals along its surface, designed to help travellers and beasts of burden cope with the steep gradient, and at Pieve di Tolmezzo in the Tagliamento Valley, an 80 m long cutting allowed the via Iulia Augusta to follow a level path parallel to the river.[51]

Bridges

In a landscape dominated by water, bridges formed a vital component of most roads in Northern Italy. Many were constructed of stone or mixed materials, with roads such as the via Aemilia and via Annia returning evidence for dozens of bridges along their length.[52] Despite this, there is little surviving evidence of bridges constructed on the Po itself. It is possible that bridges on the Po may have been built in wood, accounting for their lack of survival in the archaeological record. Alternatively, circumstances similar to those affecting

the paucity of inland wreck discoveries may also apply to bridges (see below). However, the width of the river, combined with its high volume of discharge and variable path, may have made a permanent structure impractical, especially in the lower reaches of the river. Indeed, the only surviving bridge remains on the Po come from the upper river, at Brusasco near Industria, where the river is less than 150 m in width and the mean discharge rarely exceeds 160 m3/s.[53]

The difficulty of bridge building in the Middle and Lower Po necessitated other ways of crossing the river. Contemporary ancient writers make references to pontoon bridges, often in the context of military campaigns. During the Second Punic War, Cornelius Scipio constructed a pontoon bridge across the Po at Piacenza, retreating across it after being defeated in a skirmish near Pavia. His destruction of the bridge in the aftermath temporarily stranded Hannibal's troops on the north bank, forcing them to take a lengthy detour west to find another crossing point.[54] Later, during the civil wars of AD 69, Tacitus records the construction of a pontoon bridge on the Po by Vitellius, as his forces tried to attack Otho's troops near Cremona.[55] However, the military setting of such encounters suggests these were not permanent features on the riverscape but were constructed as and when needed. Not only would they have been vulnerable to storm and flood damage, but they also would have impeded water transport up and down the river. It seems likely then, that in the absence of bridges, ferries were used to cross the river, such as the one directly mentioned by Seneca and alluded to by Lucian.[56] It is also possible that a *stela* from Augusta Bagiennorum represents a ferryman.[57] Finally, it is worth highlighting that, as bridges are highly technical and expensive feats of engineering, away from major roadways ferries may have provided the only means of crossing isolated stretches of the water network.

While the Po itself seems unlikely to have been bridged for large stretches of its course, there is more evidence for bridges on its tributaries and other waterways within Northern Italy. Substantial remains have been found on the Adige, the Dora Baltea, the Bacchiglione, the Reno, and the Trebbia, to give some examples.[58] It has been noted that some bridges crossing the waterways of the Po-Veneto Plain were designed with the hydrological

[48] Mollo Mezzana 1992: 57.

[49] Raepsaet 2009; Russell 2018: 139.

[50] Mollo Mezzana 1992: 57-62.

[51] Bonora Mazzoli 1992: 54; Bosio 1991: 129. This road is not to be confused with the other via Iulia Augusta, which connected Piacenza to Arles.

[52] See Bosio 1991; Calzolari 1992; Capulli 2023; Catarsi and Dall'Aglio 1993; Cera 1996; Fozzati and Papotti 1996; Labate 2019; Lucchese 2004; Marini Calvini 1999; Ortali 1992.

[53] Fozzati and Papotti 1996: 216. Sidonius Apollonaris (*Epist.* 1.5.3) in the 5th century AD observed that most bridges in the region were constructed on sections of rivers that were not navigable, perhaps helping to account for the lack of evidence for permanent crossings below Turin on the Po.

[54] Livy 21.47.

[55] Tac. *Hist.* 2.34. See also, Plut. *Otho* 10; and Procop. *Goth.* 6.12.30-31 for other military uses of pontoon bridges on the Po.

[56] Sen. *Ben.* 6.19; Lucian, *Electr.* 3.

[57] CIL V, 7679. Medas 2018: 149.

[58] Brecciaroli Taboreli 2007; Catarsi and Dall Aglio 1993; Cera 1996; Fozzati and Papotti 1996.

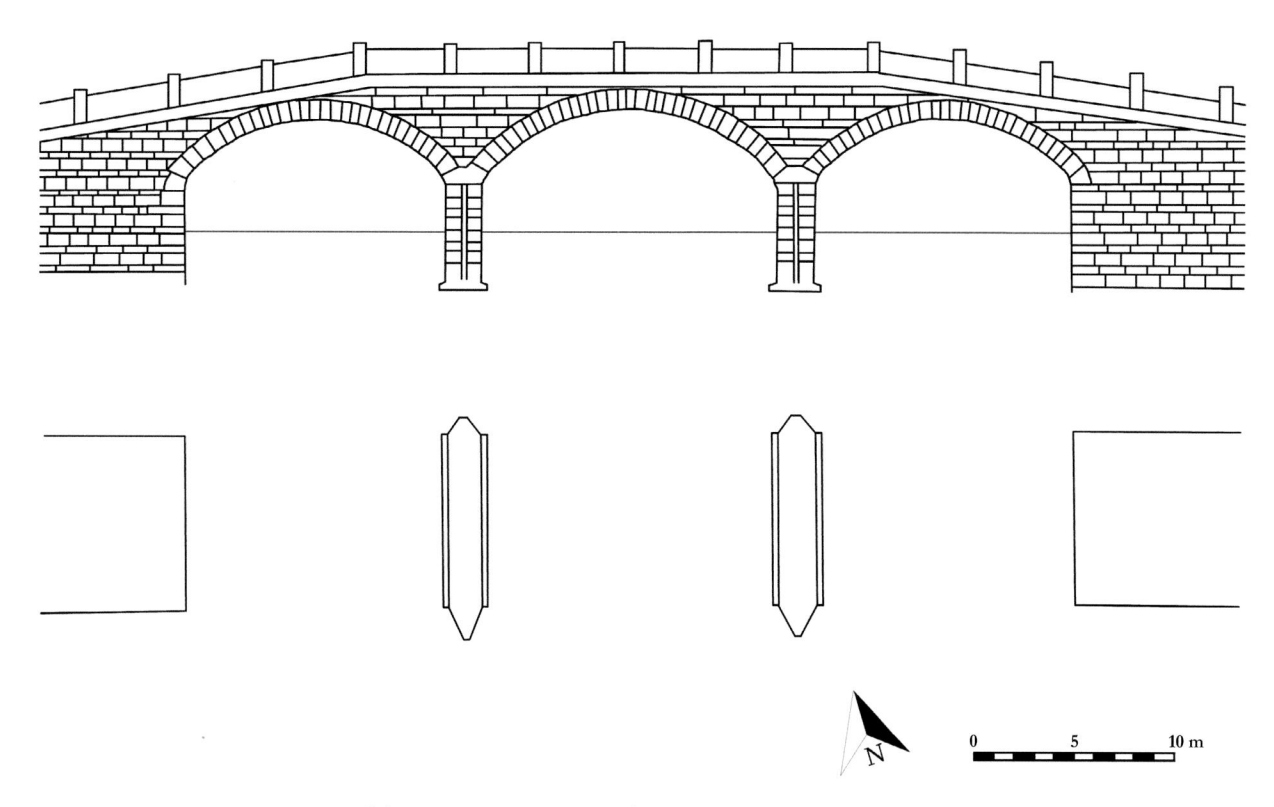

Figure 3. Diagram of the Ponte San Lorenzo, Padua, showing the shallow arches with wide spacing
(redrawn from Cera 1996: Fig. 4).

conditions and human needs of the watercourse in mind. In the Veneto especially, Cera has shown that bridges, for example, the Ponte Pietra in Verona, the S. Lorenzo and Altinate bridges in Padua, and the Ponte degli Angeli in Vicenza, utilised a much wider arch with a shallower angle than was normal (see Figure 3).[59] Reducing the number of pylons subjected to the strong currents of the river would have reduced stress on the structure and created less of an impediment to river traffic passing beneath the bridge.[60] Furthermore, the wide, low arches would have created a shallower gradient for those climbing onto the bridge to cross, an important consideration in the flatter areas of the plain where the height of the roadway on the bridge may have been above ground level. Of course, some bridges were positioned on non-navigable waterways. This is evidenced by their low and narrow arches – impassable to waterborne traffic – such as those seen on the Ponte delle Barche on the Retrone, Vicenza.

Without the creation of extensive terrestrial infrastructure, overland travel in Northern Italy during the Roman era would have been significantly more difficult and labour-intensive. Not all settlements were on the waterways, and no river was navigable all the way to its source. It was here that the roads of the region acted to connect the areas not accessible by water, and, at times, offered an alternative itinerary. In some areas, particularly the low-lying parts of the Po-Veneto Plain and mountainous reaches of the Alps and Apennines, the transportation of heavy loads may have been impossible and the effects of weather and the natural topography more pronounced on travellers and the roadway. Roman engineering allowed the road network to overcome high water tables, steep inclines, rivers, and marshes, enabling routes to extend into remote areas of Northern Italy and beyond. Overland routes thus formed one half of the region's transport network, the other being comprising of Northern Italy's extensive river system.

The River Network

Literary and epigraphic evidence, supported by archaeological finds in the form of wrecks and port infrastructure, all attest to the use of Northern Italy's waterways for transport. The modern geomorphology of its rivers, however, cannot be taken as an accurate reflection of ancient navigability, since alterations to the fluvial landscape of the region mean that many rivers that were navigable in the Roman age are no

[59] Cera 1996: 179. Similar designs can also be seen in the remains of the two Roman bridges at Ivrea (Brecciaroli Taborelli 2007: 131-33).
[60] Cera 1996: 190-91.

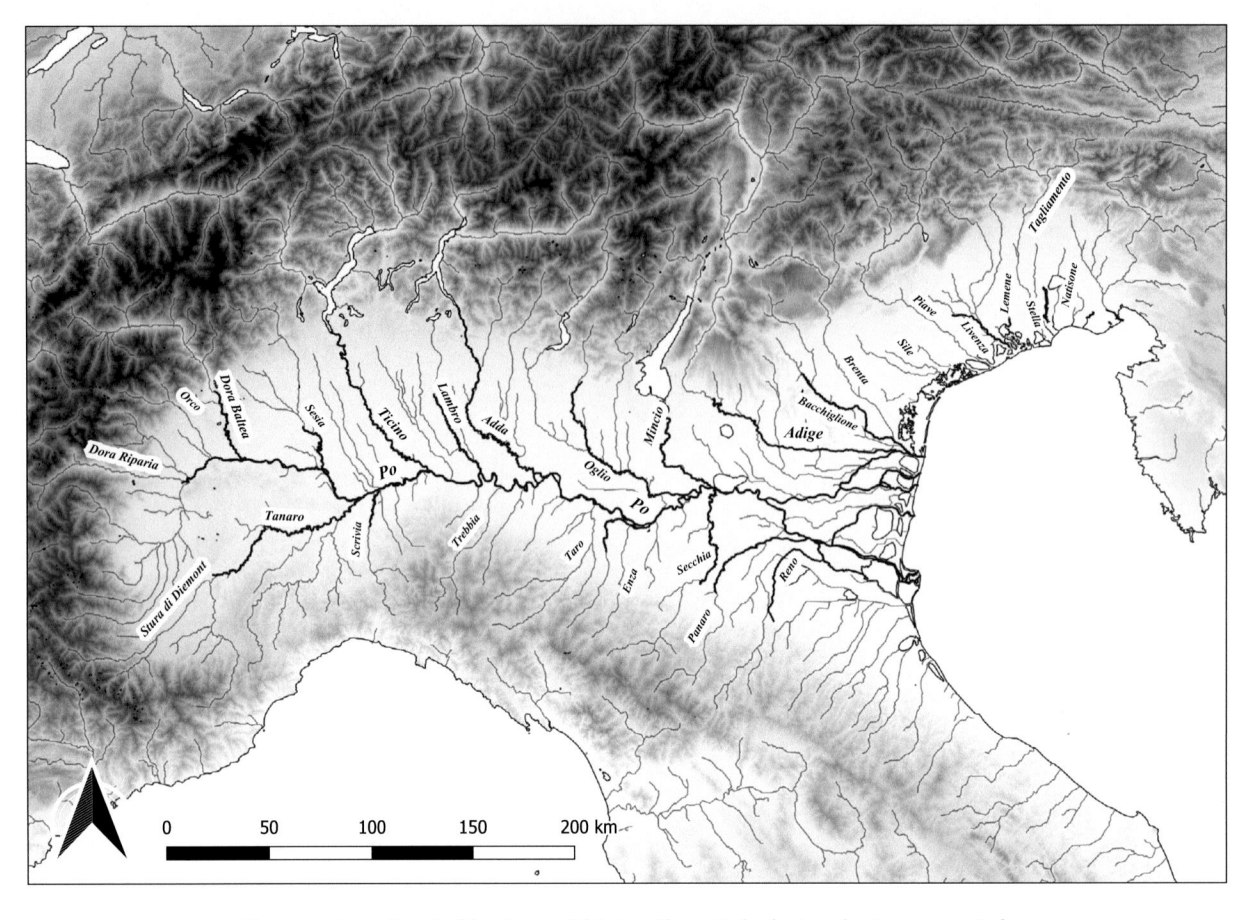

Figure 4. Map of navigable rivers within Northern Italy during the Roman period.

longer usable.[61] For example, several rivers in the Po-Veneto region, such as the Piave and the Scrivia, now exhibit braiding as their dominant geomorphology, making them difficult, if not impossible, to navigate.[62] Nevertheless, both these rivers have produced evidence of port facilities dating from the Roman period.[63] Firm evidence for ancient navigation exists on 26 rivers throughout Northern Italy, although there were probably many more (see Figure 4 and Appendix A). These range from the Po itself to much smaller rivers such as the Enza and the Stella, suggesting a wide utilisation of the water network. Overall, there is little to suggest that the physical characteristics of the ancient Po water network prevented it from being utilised by boats in antiquity, yet this does not mean the entire network should be viewed as equally usable. To do so risks taking a simplistic view of river transport, where rivers can be traversed from source to sea, with no regard to their regime, hazards, or seasonality.[64]

Although there are no complete records of the route and characteristics of the Po in antiquity, the river is mentioned in several ancient geographic texts such as Strabo's *Geography* and Pliny's *Natural Histories*. The Po and its tributaries also appear in several historical works, such as those of Polybius, Livy, Tacitus, and Procopius, and have formed the setting for more literary writing, with Virgil and Lucian both including the Po in their poetry and satire. This corpus of work offers a glimpse into aspects of the region's rivers, which can be combined to create a more complete reconstruction of its water network.

In some aspects, the modern Po shares the same characteristics as the ancient river. The Po, like all rivers, varied substantially along its length and, in its source regions, the Po had torrential qualities, characterised by seasonal periods of high and low water flow. Pomponius Mela described the flow in its upper course as 'scant and meagre', and Pliny the Elder claimed the river's source would dry up under 'the midday summer sun'.[65] As the Po continued downstream its volume was swelled by the addition of multiple tributaries, so by the time it reached Turin, it was navigable according to Polybius

---

[61] See Page 2022 for a discussion of the geomorphology of rivers in the Po-Veneto Plain.

[62] Carton *et al.* 2009; Picco *et al.* 2013; Surian and Fontana 2017.

[63] Cipriano and Sandri 2001; Crosetto 2013b.

[64] See Campbell 2023: 8-9; Franconi 2016: 27, for discussions on the complex array of factors needed to ensure successful fluvial navigation.

[65] Plin. *HN* 2.106; Mela. *Chor.* 2.62.

and Pliny the Elder.[66] Beyond Turin, the river continued to grow, and at its confluence with the Dora Baltea, in the vicinity of the town of Industria, it began to become 'particularly deep'.[67] By the time it reached the plain proper, no longer confined between the Colle di Turin and the Alps, the river seems to have widened. Virgil claimed no other river flowed with a 'mightier force' and the large volume of the river was commented on in antiquity by several authors: Pliny the Elder observed that no 'other river increases so much in volume in so short a distance', while Livy stated that the 'strong current' made the river unfordable in some of its upper sections near the confluence of the Po and the Ticino.[68] Strabo described the river as 'large and swift,' though as it descended from its upper course and onto the plains, it became 'larger and more gentle in its flow'.[69] He observed that the great number of tributaries increased the volume of water in the river, causing 'the stream to widen out in the plain' and resulted in 'the force of its current being dispersed and blunted'.[70] In the river's middle section, its wide meanders, still a characteristic of the modern river despite attempts at channelisation, are commented on by Pliny, who says they added 88 miles to the length of the river.[71]

The Lower Po, in particular the delta region, has changed extensively since the Roman period. The ancient coastline has prograded into the Adriatic by 7km in some places, and the mouth of the Po has moved steadily northwards.[72] Although land drainage schemes were extensive, they did not cover the entirety of the plain. Large areas of marsh and open water remained, particularly around the delta and the coast. The Adriatic lagoon system was once far more extensive, and likely stretched the entirety of the way to Ravenna.[73] Indeed, Strabo recalls that the 'greater part of the (lower) plain is made full of lagoons ... and while some parts have been relieved by drainage and are being tilled, others afford voyages across their waters'.[74] During Antiquity, the Po emptied into the Adriatic through seven mouths, the channel beginning to diverge shortly after the river passed through Hostilia. These seven mouths and extensive adjacent lagoon system resulted in the coastal area being referred to as the Seven Seas.[75] The most southerly mouth and the one closest to Ravenna was called the Padusa, formally known as the Eridanus or the

Spineticus due to its proximity to the former Etruscan city of Spina.[76] The next mouth was the Caprasian, then the Sagis, and then Volane. Further to the north were the mouths of the Carbonaria, the Fossiones, and the Philistina. The paths of these branches have been heavily debated amongst archaeologists, although there is little agreement on their precise locations.[77] Out of the seven mouths, only the Padusa, Carbonaria, the Fossiones, and the Philistina were considered to be deep-water and accessible to large vessels.[78]

Table 2. Mean discharge, length, and basin size of navigable rivers within the Roman Empire (data from Franconi 2014). *Euphrates data only available from the Turkish border (80% total flow).

River	Mean Discharge (m³/s)	Length (km)	Basin Size (km2)
Danube	6500	2860	817,000
Nile	2830	6650	3,400,000
Rhine	2650	1230	185,000
Rhône	1700	810	95,000
Po	1540	650	74,000
Loire	850	1020	117,000
Garonne	630	640	55,000
Euphrates	555*	2780	444,000
Seine	500	770	78,650
Meuse	400	920	34,500
Guadalquivir	229	660	57,530
Tiber	260	400	17,370
Orontes	75	570	35,750
Thames	60	340	12,930
Maeander	35	550	25,000
Medjerda	32	480	23,700

Most navigation on the Po, its tributaries, and the rivers of the Venetian Plain, likely took place on their middle and lower courses, the location of the majority of surviving evidence for fluvial transport. The wide, slower-moving channels of these sections of the river would have been usable by shallow-draft boats such as barges, although sand bars and other navigational hazards may have posed a risk. While the Po's high discharge and volume might be seen as an obstacle to

[66] Plin, *HN* 3.123; Polyb. 2.16.
[67] Plin. *HN* 3.123.
[68] Livy 21.47; Plin. *HN* 3.119; Virgil, *G.* 4.373-74.
[69] Str. 4.6.5.
[70] Str. 4.6.5.
[71] Plin. *HN* 3.118. Ennod. *Vit. Epiph.* 2.1, also mentions the meanders around Pavia.
[72] The evolution of the delta and Adriatic coastline have been well documented using a combination of aerial and satellite photography, LiDAR scans, and sediment coring. See Stefani 2017 for a concise history of the region's coastal evolution.
[73] Marchiori 1990: 197-98; Uggeri 1990: 176-77.
[74] Str. 5.1.5.
[75] Hdn. 8.7; Plin. *HN* 3.119; Mela. *Orbis* 3.2.62.

[76] Plin. *HN* 3.120.
[77] Bosio 1979; Calzolari 2007; Coralini *et al.* 2019; Uggeri 1978; 2016. Numerous paleochannels of the Po have been identified through LiDAR, coring, and aerial survey, but it is difficult to establish a precise chronology of when they were active.
[78] Plin. *HN* 3.121.

navigation, it pales in comparison to other major rivers known to be navigable from the Roman period such as the Danube and the Rhine (see Table 2), and should not be seen as an impediment to waterborne traffic. There is little surviving evidence for navigation on the more variable and torrential upper courses located in the Alps and Apennines.[79] These sections were unreachable by boat, due to the swifter current, lower water level, and greater presence of natural obstacles in the channel.[80] Although the upper courses of the Po and its tributaries were inaccessible to conventional vessels, rafts of logs could likely be floated downstream from relatively high up the watercourse.[81] This is a practice seen elsewhere in Roman Italy, where Pliny describes log rafts being transported downstream from the Tiber's upper course.[82] The above example highlights the bi-directional nature of fluvial navigation. Upstream and downstream travel utilised different methods, with upstream requiring much greater efforts and more favourable conditions. In this case, some parts of the water network may have been usable in one direction but not the other.

Seasonal variation in river flow could often be a governing factor for navigation. Too much or too little water in the river could cause problems for vessels, meaning some parts of the water network may only have been accessible seasonally.[83] Alpine and Apennine discharge regimes affected the river network at different times of the year and in different ways, something that navigators would have needed to be aware of.[84] Extreme hydrological events, themselves often a seasonal factor, would also have prevented the use of the region's waterways. Although Pliny claimed that flooding on the Po caused 'more damage to the fields than to vessels' on the river, watercraft were not immune to the dangers it represented.[85] Indeed, several Roman wrecks recovered in the region, including the Corte Cavanella I, Stella I, and the Santa Maria in Padovetere wrecks, seem to have been lost during flood events.[86] Flooding would have obscured the path of the channel, leaving a vessel vulnerable to hidden underwater hazards or getting stranded as waters receded. The fast current would also have made controlling the path of a vessel difficult, if

not impossible, alongside carrying debris that could strike and damage the craft. Even moored vessels might not have been safe. A vessel secured too tightly to the bank will tilt in a fast current, allowing water to pour in over a low gunwale or any open ports. Alternatively, the stronger current of the flood wave may put stress on already overstressed moorings, causing them to break and leave a vessel floating free in the flood. Periods of low flow could be equally hazardous as flooding for navigation. The volume of water in sections of the river might be severely reduced or dry up altogether, preventing their use or increasing the risk of running aground on hazards such as sandbars in the channel. A dramatic incident involving a period of low water levels on the Po comes from Procopius, during the 6th century AD.[87] He recounts an incident where the Goths had loaded a great number of boats on the Upper Po with grain and other supplies, with the intention of sailing downstream to assault Ravenna. However, as they attempted the journey, water levels in the river fell to such an extent that navigation was impossible, and the vessels ran aground. While the Gothic vessels were stuck, the Romans took the opportunity to capture them and their cargoes. Interestingly, Procopius records that 'as far as we know from tradition, this had never happened to the river before', suggesting that water levels in the Po had previously remained relatively consistent from year to year, or at least reliably deep enough to allow navigation.[88]

Development of the Water Transport Network

Some of the earliest references to Roman navigation on the waterways of Northern Italy come from accounts of the Second Punic War.[89] Polybius describes the Po as being 'navigable for about two thousand *stades* from the mouth called Olana', while Livy records several instances of the Po being used to transport supplies to embattled Roman units between Piacenza and Pavia, demonstrating that even during this early period, the potential of the river as a transport artery was exploited.[90] By the 1st century AD, the waterways of the Po Valley were organised around two axes of travel. The first was the system of para-littoral canals that facilitated north-south travel between the major seaports of the region, Ravenna, Altinum, and Aquileia (see below). The second was the Po river network itself, which provided east-west connections into the interior of Northern Italy. Together these networks enabled merchants such as L. Tettienus Vitalis to distribute

---

[79] Langdon (2006: 80), highlights that even before reaching these unnavigable sections, there would likely have been a tail off in the amount of traffic the further one travelled upriver. Major fluvial ports are unlikely to be located at points of borderline navigability (something that might change seasonally or annually).

[80] Rieth 1998: 33-35.

[81] Uggeri 1987: 333.

[82] Rieth 1998: 54-55; Plin. *HN* 3.53.

[83] The best-known example of seasonal limitations is the Nile, where navigation was often dependent on water levels generated by the annual flood, (Adams 2018: 175-77; Cooper 2011: 195-97).

[84] Benito *et al.* 2015: 17-18; Gumiero *et al.* 2009: 480-81; Nelson 1970: 155; Vezzoli *et al.* 2015: 347.

[85] Plin. *HN* 3.118.

[86] Beltrame *et al.* 2021: 44-46; Castro 2016: 39; Sanesi Mastrocinque, Peretto, and Zerbinati 1985: 15-16.

[87] Procop. *Goth.* 6.28.3-5.

[88] Procop. *Goth.* 6.28.5. Tac. *Hist.* 4.26, records a similar incident on the Rhine frontier where a Roman cargo vessel stranded by low water levels became easy pickings for soldiers on the far side of the river.

[89] The waterways of the Po-Veneto region were already being utilised for transport in the pre-Roman period Ortali 1995: 64; Medas 2018: 146; Roncaglia 2018: 9.

[90] Liv 21.25, 21.57; Polyb. 2.16.

Table 3. Inscriptions relating to *nautae* and *collegia nautarum* in the Po-Veneto region.

Location	Feature	Profession	Reference
Adria	The Po	*Collegia Nautarum*	CIL V.2315
Arco	Lake Garda	*Collegia Nautarum*	AE 1977, 298
Augusta Bagiennorum	The Tanaro	*Nauta*	CIL V.7679
Brescia	Lake Garda/the Oglio	*Collegia Nautarum*	AE 1977,298
Cantù	Lake Como	*Nauta*	AE 2003, 728
Como	Lake Como	*Collegia Nautarum*	CIL V.5295
Este	The Adige	*Nauta*	CIL V.2722
Mantua	The Mincio	*Collegia Nautarum*	ILS 7265
Milan	Lake Como	*Collegia Nautarum*	CIL V.5911 = AE 2014, 440
Milan	The Lambro?	*Collegia Nautarum*	AE 2014, 520
Pavia	River Ticino	*Collegia Nautarum*	AE 1977, 327
Peschiera del Garda	Lake Garda	*Collegia Nautarum*	CIL V.4016 = ILS 8373
Peschiera del Garda	Lake Garda	*Collegia Nautarum*	CIL V.4017 = ILS 8372
Peschiera del Garda	Lake Garda	*Collegia Naviculariorum*	CIL V.4015 = ILS 6711
Ravenna	The Po	*Nauta*	CIL XI.0135
Riva del Garda	Lake Garda	*Collegia Nautarum*	CIL V.4990

extra-regional cargoes from the coast to the interior along the waterways, and vice versa for cargoes originating from inland. This period also saw significant investment in port infrastructure on the banks of the Po and its tributaries, including the construction of new port facilities at Ivrea, Milan, Oderzo, Tortona, and Vercelli (see below).

Literary accounts dating to this period frequently mention sailors, rowers, and boatmen, suggesting there was a strong tradition of working on the waterways of the region. This is supported by the existence of several known *collegia nautarum* that operated on Po, its tributaries, and the lakes of the region, with most dating from the mid-1st century AD to the mid-2nd century AD (see Table 3).[91] *Collegia* are known to have operated out of Adria, Brescia, Como, Milan, Mantua, and Pavia, and their proliferation during this time points to increasing organisation and commerce on the water network. It has been highlighted in the past that for a navigable river system, the water network of Northern Italy has returned remarkably few inscriptions referencing

nautae in comparison to other regions such as Gaul and Germany.[92] While this may be true for inscriptions that only mention *nautae* (Northern Italy contains only three, in comparison to 26 from Gallia Lugudunensis), of the 33 known inscriptions specifically referring to *collegia nautarum* within the Roman Empire, 11 come from the Po-Veneto region – a third.[93]

The 1st and 2nd centuries AD would form the high point of investment on the water network. Between the 3rd and 5th centuries AD, much of the terrestrial infrastructure on the water network would fall into disrepair. Dock infrastructure at Corte Cavanella, Milan, and Ivrea fell out of use at this time, and the artificial channels and drainage schemes undertaken during the Republic and Early Imperial period began to fail or silt up due to a lack of maintenance.[94] In some isolated cases,

---

[91] Broekhart 2013.

[92] Harris 2011: 192.

[93] Many of the Gallic inscriptions relate to the Rhône and the Saône in particular, (see Campbell 2012: 267-70 for more information on *nautae* in Gaul). The number of inscriptions is based on the listings found in the Epigraphik-Datenbank, viewed 24 January 2024, http://db.edcs.eu/epigr/epi_ergebnis.php.

[94] Cera 1995: 186-191; Sanesi Mastrocinque, Peretto, and Zerbinati 1985: 22-23.

this decline was matched by new investment elsewhere. The re-excavation of the harbour channel at Tortona during the mid-3rd century AD prolonged its use (though with a reduced capacity) into the 6th century, and a new port was constructed at Brescia during the 5th century.[95] While evidence for the degradation of physical infrastructure is fairly uniform across the region, there are extensive references to navigation on the Po between the 4th and 6th centuries AD.[96] The travels of Sidonius Apollinaris from Pavia on the region's waterways are well known, and Cassiodorus, writing in the 6th century AD, ordered Pavia to provide the Herulii with boats to sail to Ravenna, suggesting the continuity of this route.[97] Elsewhere, Cassiodorus praises travel on the waterways of the region, specifically the rivers of Veneto, as the keels of ships 'fear no rough blasts (from waves); they touch the earth with the greatest pleasure, and cannot perish however frequently they may come in contact with it'.[98] There are also mentions of the need to remove large quantities of fishing nets from the Mincio and the Oglio that were impeding the passage of boats, suggesting a concern about keeping waterways open.[99] Although changing political and environmental circumstances may have created problems for riparian communities in Northern Italy, it does not seem to have prevented the use of waterways for transport during Late Antiquity and the Early Medieval period.

Moving on the Waterways

While Northern Italy's waterways were extensive, travelling upon them involved a complex array of skills and methods. Fluvial transport is bi-directional, with upstream and downstream travel facilitated in different ways. When travelling downstream, a vessel could simply coast along with the current, needing only simple manoeuvring to maintain direction and avoid obstacles. Of course, additional forms of propulsion, such as sails or oars, could be added to speed up a journey or enhance control over a vessel, something especially important for heavier cargoes. Upstream travel was a different story entirely. Rather than moving with the current, a vessel heading upriver had to actively fight against it, and some form of propulsion was required to overcome the force of the river. Occupying a middle ground between the two was canal transport. Canals mainly consisted of still or very slow-moving water, which meant that, while there was no current to battle against, there was also no source of propulsion for travel. This meant a vessel required a

driving force to move in either direction. In the ancient world, there were three main forms of propulsion used on the waterways: sails, oars, or towing, with evidence for the use of all three coming from Northern Italy.

There are several first-hand accounts of travel on the Po surviving from the Roman era. The poet Gaius Valgius Rufus, writing in the Augustan period, described entering the river from the Adriatic, 'where the mouth of the canal links peaceful Padusa, [the ship] sails the great stream of the Alpine Po'.[100] At some point during the journey, the method of propulsion changed, as he described 'my ship, following a long tow-rope, set me down rejoicing in a delightful place of hospitality'.[101] A second account comes from the satirist Lucian, writing in the 2nd century AD, who set his short work *The Amber, or the Swans* on the Po. During his journey, he asks the boatmen if they have seen any precious amber in the river, to which they reply, 'If we had anything of that sort, do you suppose that for two *obols* we would row or tow our boats upstream'.[102] The final account comes from the 5th century AD, when Sidonius Apollinaris recounts in detail a journey he took downriver from Pavia to Ravenna.[103] Whilst on the Po, Apollinaris used the opportunity to explore several of the river's tributaries and in each case 'cruised a little way upstream from the point of confluence so as to view each actually in the midst of its own waters,' before changing rowers at Brixellum and proceeding the rest of the way to Ravenna.[104] The above accounts reflect the importance of the Po river network in providing transport, not just for cargo, but also for people. Ferry services travelled upstream and downstream, and transport provision provided a living for people who lived along the banks. Strabo documents the existence of a boat service between Piacenza and Ravenna that took two days and nights, while in the 5th and 6th centuries, Cassiodorus records the deployment of naval fast rowers (*dromonarii*) on the river to aid the *cursus publicus*.[105]

The textual evidence suggests a variety of methods were used to move along the waterways of Northern Italy. Rowing proved a popular and versatile form of propulsion along the river, with depictions of ships being moved under oar power featuring prominently on several reliefs from elsewhere in the Western Empire.[106] In addition to rowing as a method of propulsion, both

[95] Cera 1995: 192-94; Crosetto 2013a: 108-110.

[96] For more on the water network of Northern Italy during the Medieval and Early Modern periods see Covini 2010; Galvani and Pellegrini 2007; Greci 2016; and Laven 1989.

[97] Cassiod. *Var.* 4.45; Sid. Apoll. *Epist.* 1.5.

[98] Cassiod. *Var.* 12.24.

[99] Cassiod. *Var.* 5.17. Human additions to the fluvial landscape could often impede navigation as much as natural processes (Jones 2000: 60-69).

[100] Valg. *Frag.* 167 (3 Bl., C.).

[101] Valg. *Frag.* 168 (4 Bl., C.).

[102] Lucian, *Electr.* 3.

[103] Sid. Apoll. *Epist.* 1.5.

[104] Sid. Apoll. *Epist.* 1.5.5.

[105] Cassiod. *Var.* 2.31; Str. 5.1.11. Seneca (*Ben.* 6.19) also records using ferry services to cross the Po.

[106] Campbell 2012: 211. For example, the Neumagen Wine Ship or the vessels depicted on Trajan's Column. Rieth (1998: 103) makes the case that even large or heavily laden vessels could be rowed under the right conditions.

Valgius Rufus and Lucian mention the use of towing, famously represented by a second-century AD relief from Avignon. Towing a vessel requires significant time, energy, and infrastructure. The presence of a towpath is near-essential, as this provides a solid and level surface for the towers, seemingly human instead of animal in these cases. Yet many areas of land directly adjacent to the Po or its tributaries were marshy, despite the intervention of drainage works. Sidonius Apollinarus observed that the river's 'banks and knolls were everywhere clad with groves of oak and maple' for all this growth, 'nourished on the moisture of the spongy soil, had sprouted confusedly along the riverbanks'.[107] This raises the question of whether the construction of a towpath would have been feasible along the entirety of the river. Medas has hypothesised that the embankments and dykes constructed along the Po could have served as a towpath in some areas, but again, they were unlikely to have been constructed along the entirety of the river network.[108] In *The Amber, or the Swans*, Lucian's conversation with the boatmen seems to imply that they were involved in both rowing and towing vessels on the river, and in areas where there was no towpath, those towing could have switched to rowing as an alternative form of propulsion.[109]

Although rowing and towing seem to have been the most common methods of moving on the waterways, the use of sails as a method of propulsion is confirmed by Pliny, who describes them as being woven out of strong rushes in some cases.[110] The Po-Veneto Plain, being surrounded by mountains on three sides, is largely sheltered from the wind. The Alps and Apennines block the majority of northern, westerly, and southerly winds, and as a result, the prevailing wind in the region is an easterly one, coming in over the Adriatic. Consequently, the use of sails, backed by the favourable easterly wind, could have helped counteract the force of the current for boats sailing upstream on the Po.[111] It is worth highlighting, however, that there are practical limitations to using wind power as a form of propulsion. Sails are best suited to large, open expanses of water where there is space to tack (if the wind is not behind the vessel), rather than the narrow confines of the river channel. The curve of a meander might result in the sails being unable to take full advantage of the breeze.

[112] Furthermore, the intermittent nature of the wind makes it a somewhat unreliable form of propulsion, and sails were best combined with other methods. This is reflected in Valgius Rufus' account of his journey on the Po, where his ship begins by sailing up through the mouth of the river, before at an unspecified point alternating to towing as its main form of propulsion.[113] In sum, the surviving literary evidence suggests that watercraft in Northern Italy were propelled by a variety of means. The milieu of river, lake, and canal environments afforded multiple methods of river travel depending on the situation at hand, something that is reflected in the variety of vessels recovered from the Po-Veneto region.

Vessels and Cargos

While most information concerning ancient activity on the water network comes from surviving textual sources, the wreck evidence from Northern Italy has long been overlooked. Indeed, over the past 30 years, the number of wreck discoveries have steadily increased, with the publication of 18 wrecks that can be dated to the Roman period (see Table 4). The wrecks range chronologically from the 1st century BC to the 5th century AD. In size, they vary from small sections of surviving planking (in the case of the wrecks from Aquileia and the Venice Lido) through to the 20 m long hull of the Comacchio wreck which had a displacement of 130 t.[114] They are principally located in the east of the study area, in the coastal region between Ravenna and the Venetian lagoon system, although some have been recovered from further inland (see Figure 5).

It warrants mentioning that, despite the extensive shipwreck evidence in the eastern coastal regions, only a single plank-built vessel from the Roman era (the Santa Maria in Padovetere wreck) has been recovered from the Po and its major tributaries.[115] Given the quantity of surviving Roman organic material in the region, poor preservation conditions do not seem an adequate explanation for the lack of discoveries. Instead, there could be several other possible reasons. First, the Po, alongside many other rivers in the region, has moved extensively since the Roman period, at times up to tens of kilometres from its original bed.[116] This means that any potential wrecks are buried under a deep layer of later alluviation in the river's paleochannels. Second, shipwrecks in rivers, and most importantly their

---

[107] Sid. Apoll. *Epist.* 1.5.4. It is possible that this surge in growth and marshland relates to the degradation of drainage infrastructure in Late Antiquity, but other, earlier authors also relate to their presence during the Late Republic and Early Imperial periods.

[108] Medas 2018: 148-49.

[109] Lucian, *Electr.* 3.

[110] Plin. *HN* 16.70.

[111] Rieth 1998: 100-101. He also highlights the east-west orientation of river basins in Western France as a factor for the widespread use of sail powered craft on them. This orientation is favourable to catch the prevailing western wind of the Atlantic coast as a method of upstream propulsion. See also Cooper 2011: 197-98, for an assessment on the impact of wind on Nile navigation.

[112] Rieth 1998: 101.

[113] Valg. *Frag.* 167 (3 Bl., C.); 168 (4 Bl., C.).

[114] The fragmentary nature of many of the wrecks makes it hard to accurately assess their size.

[115] The Santa Maria in Padovetere wreck was discovered in a Roman era paleochannel of the Po (the *Padus Vetus* – Padovetere) close to Comacchio. By the time the loss of the vessel occurred, the channel (previously some 500 m in width) had become residual as the Po's path shifted north (Beltrame *et al.* 2021: 30-31).

[116] Bridge (2003), 310-11; Corrò and Mozzi 2017: 490; Uggeri 1990: 179.

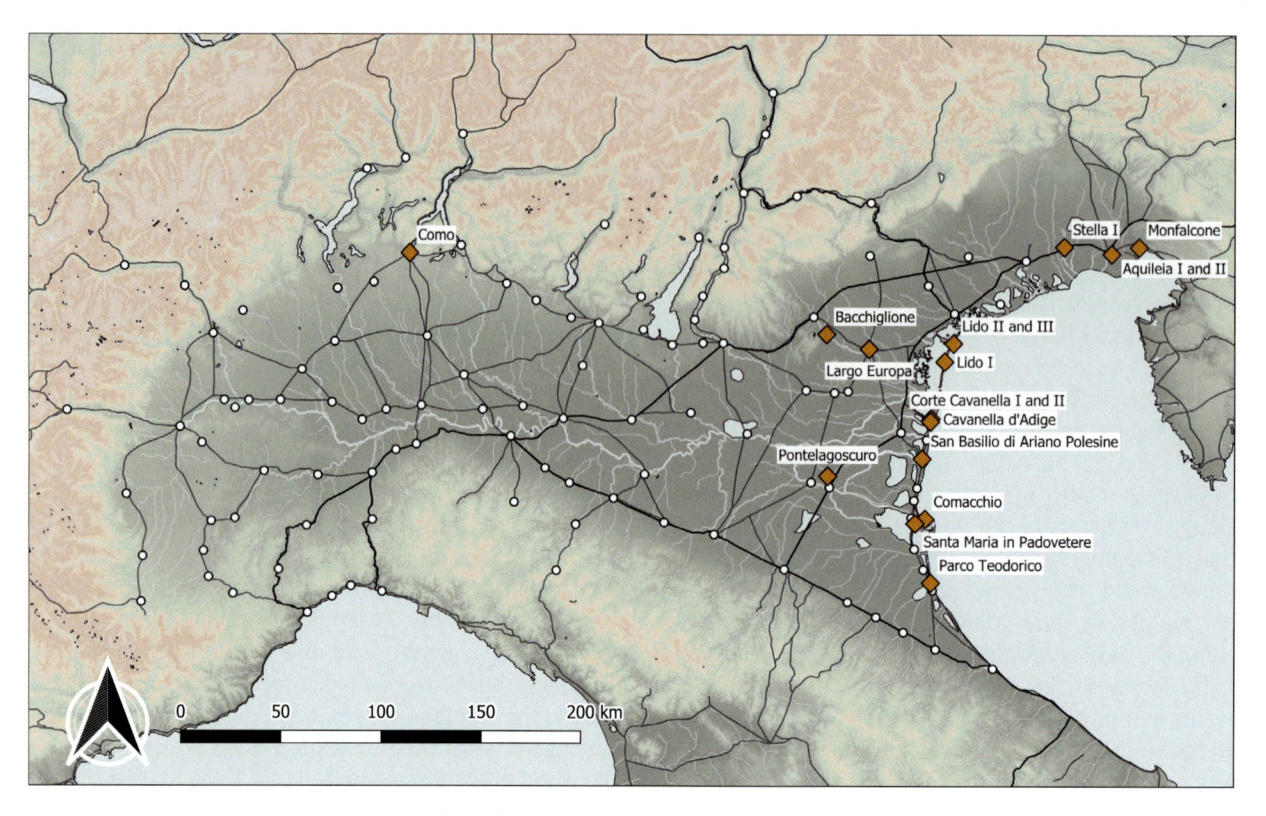

Figure 5. Map of wreck sites in Northern Italy dating to the Roman era.

cargo, are far easier to salvage than those that occur at sea. Whilst a wreck on the seabed would have been permanently out of reach (in most cases) of potential recovery, salvagers would only need to wait for a period of calm or low flow before accessing a river wreck. River wrecks could also have impeded the usability of the channel for other vessels, giving additional impetus for their salvage and removal.[117] Third, few people live near the modern Po channel. The area in the river's vicinity is predominantly rural, with few roads running parallel to the river. This means that any potential wrecks exposed by the river, often during flood events, are unlikely to be spotted immediately. With the exception of the Santa Maria in Padovetere wreck, the only Roman-era vessels so far recovered from the Po itself have been monoxyls (log boats). These are often disturbed during flood events or channel changes, and due to their small size and homogenous construction, once exposed are often carried downstream before being found, often in proximity to bridges or built-up areas.[118] Larger wrecks, inevitably more fragile, do not behave in the same way during flood events and are more likely to be destroyed or broken up by the force of the river. While the above

circumstances contribute to the low discovery rate for wrecks from within Northern Italy, those recovered from the coast can still offer important insights into the vessels travelling on the water network of the Po-Veneto Plain.[119]

Concerning the findspots of the wrecks, the Comacchio, Monfalcone, Parco Theodorico, and Lido I-III wrecks were recovered from areas corresponding to the ancient coastline, which has long since prograded eastwards. The rest were recovered from contexts that were inland during the Roman period, within active rivers or paleochannels. The contexts of other wrecks, such as the Corte Cavanella I and II, the Cavanella d'Adige, the San Basilio di Ariano Polesine, and Santa Maria in Padovatere, match the proposed locations of the para-littoral canals that linked Ravenna and Altinum (see below).[120] This is especially true for the Corte Cavanella wrecks, which were recovered from a settlement, possibly a villa, founded in the early 1st century AD in

---

[117] Wrecks were often recycled, as shown by the recovery of the Largo Europa in Padua and the Corte Cavanella II. Both ships were broken up and reused in later structures, the former as an embankment and the latter as a jetty (Balista and Ruta Serafini 1993; Beltrame 2001; Sanesi Mastrocinque, Bonomi, and Toniolo 1986).
[118] Allini *et al.* 2014: 117-18; Ravasi and Barbaglio 2008: 39-48.

[119] It is also worth considering a significant portion of the traffic on Northern Italy's water network may be invisible in the archaeological record, regardless of survival or not. Rafts might be used to transport goods down a river, with the raft itself comprising part of the cargo (Diosono 2009: 266; Meiggs 1982: 336). Vitr. *De arch.* 2.9.16 records that larch was transported down the Po, and the simplest and most economical method of achieving this would have been to float it down the river, rather than transport it within a vessel.
[120] Beltrame and Costa 2016: 263; Uggeri 1978; 1987.

Table 4. Wrecks dating to the Roman period discovered in inland Northern Italy.

Wreck Name	Date	Cargo	Bibliography
Stella I	1st Century AD	Brick and tile	Castro and Capulli 2016
Bacchiglione	1st Century BC	Stone	Previato and Zara 2014
Corte Cavanella I	1st – 2nd Centuries AD	n/a	Sanesi Mastrocinque, Peretto, and Zerbinati 1985
Corte Cavanella II	1st – 2nd Centuries AD	n/a	Sanesi Mastrocinque, Bonomi, and Toniolo 1986
Monfalcone	1st Century AD	Unknown	Bertacchi 1976
Parco Teodorico	5th Century AD	Unknown, possibly eastern in origin.	Medas 2003
Largo Europa	2nd Century AD	n/a	Balista and Ruta Serafini 1993; Beltrame 2001
San Basilio di Ariano Polesine	Roman	Stone	Dallemulle 1977
Como	Roman	Stone	Montalcini De Angelis D'Ossat 1993
Comacchio	1st century BC	Iberian lead pigs, Adriatic ceramics and amphorae, plus other.	Berti 1999
Cavanella d'Adige	2nd – 1st Centuries BC	Unknown	Tiboni 2009
Santa Maria in Padovetere	4th – 5th Centuries AD	Unknown	Beltrame and Costa 2016; Beltrame et al. 2021
Lido I	1st Century AD	Unknown	Beltrame 1996
Lido II	1st – 2nd Centuries AD	Unknown	Beltrame 2002
Lido III	1st – 2nd Centuries AD	Unknown	Willis and Capulli 2014; 2018
Aquileia I	1st Century AD	Unknown	Bertacchi 1990
Aquileia II	2nd – 3rd Centuries AD	Unknown	Beltrame and Gaddi 2013
Pontelagoscuro	Late Roman-Early Medieval	Unknown	Parker 1992

the delta region near modern Comacchio.[121] The first vessel was discovered in the remains of a boathouse adjacent to a small canal. The boathouse had been covered by a tile roof which had later collapsed in a flood event, sealing the wreck beneath the rubble (see Figure 6).[122] The second vessel was found a short distance away, where the flat bottom of its hull had been recycled as a jetty. Although it is possible that the Corte Cavanella I could have been used as a small cargo barge (7.45 x 2.11 m in its surviving section), the Corte Cavanella II is too small to have fulfilled this function and was probably a personal watercraft.[123] The Bacchiglione and Stella 1 wrecks were found within the rivers from which they take their names, and the Como wreck was recovered from the lake of the same name.[124]

The wrecks of Northern Italy, with the exception of the Monfalcone and the Parco Teodorico wrecks, were constructed using a method called the sewn plank technique. Planks are joined together using cording, which is looped through holes drilled through the wood.[125] These holes are then pegged and sealed with calking. While this practice is seen elsewhere in the Mediterranean during the Roman period, there was a widespread tradition of sewn plank naval construction in the Northern Adriatic.[126] The level of structural elasticity the method afforded may have been advantageous in a shallow water environment where landings and impacts on the hull would have been frequent.[127] The majority of Adriatic examples had flat-bottomed hulls, a design for which sewn plank construction was especially suited.[128] These long,

---

[121] Sanesi Mastrocinque, Peretto, and Zerbinati, 1985; Sanesi Mastrocinque, Bonomi, and Toniolo 1986. The settlement is often equated with the location of a canal side *mansio* on the *Peutinger Table*, however there is little other evidence for this interpretation.
[122] Sanesi Mastrocinque, Peretto, and Zerbinati 1985: 15-16.
[123] Sanesi Mastrocinque, Bonomi, and Toniolo 1986: 27.
[124] Montalcini De Angelis D'Ossat 1993; Previato and Zara 2014.

[125] See Beltrame 1996; 2002a; 2002b; Beltrame and Gaddi 2013.
[126] Beltrame and Gaddi 2013: 303; Beltrame *et al.* 2021: 29; Willis and Capulli 2018: 352-54. There have been several finds of sewn plank vessels off the coast of southern France such as the Cavaliére wreck and the Cap Bear C wreck (Charlin *et al.* 1978).
[127] Medas 2018: 152.
[128] Beltrame 2002a: 358.

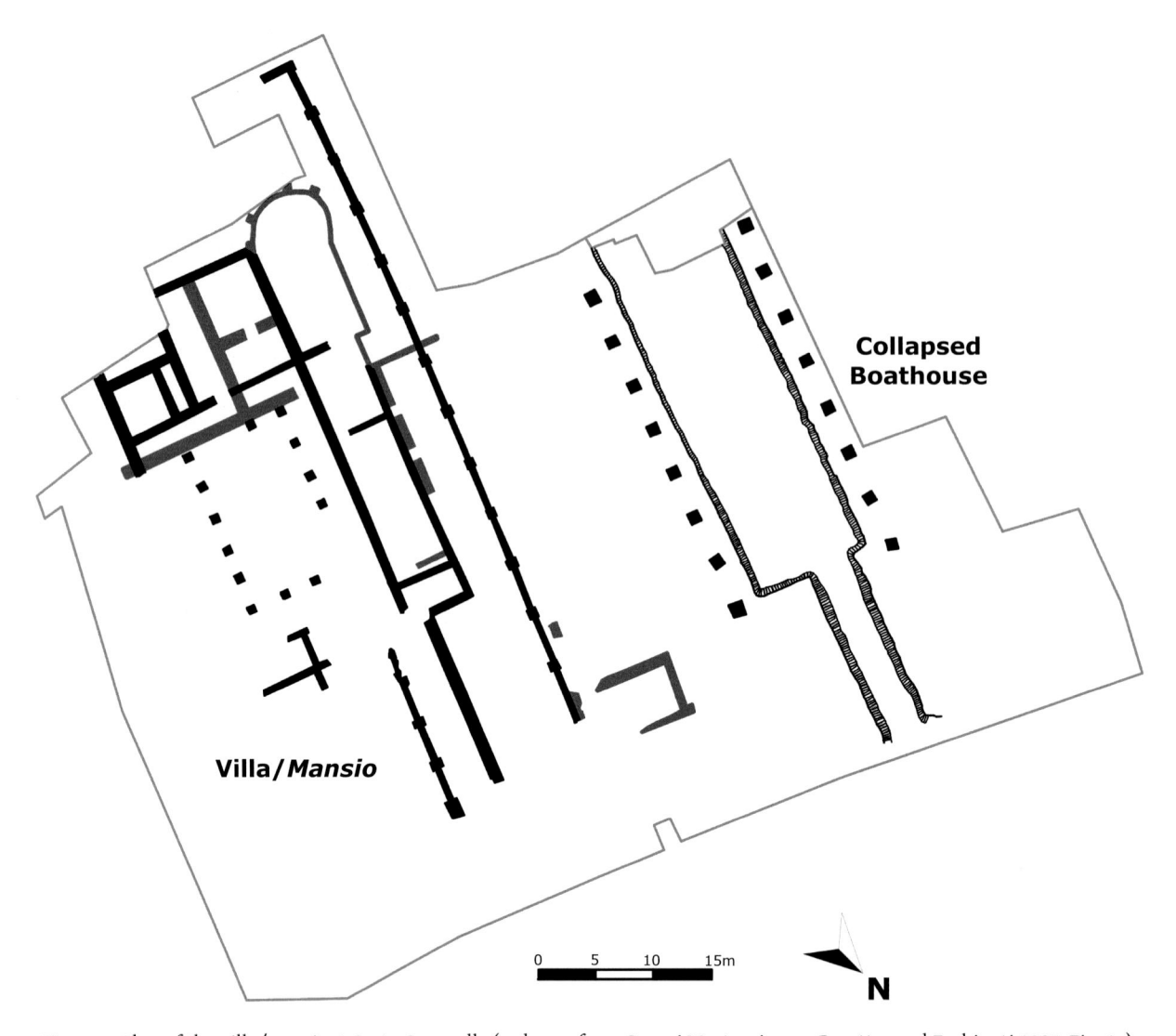

Collapsed
Boathouse

Villa/*Mansio*

0   5   10   15m

N

Figure 6. Plan of the villa/*mansio* at Corte Cavanella (redrawn from Sanesi Mastrocinque, Peretto, and Zerbinati 1985: Fig. 1a).

shallow-draught vessels were perfect for moving on inland waterways and sheltered lagoons, where the absence of waves and currents on the inland waterscape removed the need for a keel.

Although many of the wrecks recovered from the region were flat-bottomed, several belong to a tradition of shipbuilding described as fluvio-maritime. The Comacchio wreck had a shallow, rounded hull with a rudimentary keel, making it suited to both fluvial and maritime operations, a design also seen in the Monfalcone and the Parco Teodorico wrecks.[129] Elsewhere in the empire, the Blackfriars I wreck recovered from the Thames was designed with the same functionality in mind.[130] Given the extensive network of waterways in the Po Valley, it is unsurprising that maritime vessels were designed to take advantage of

the inland routes and the access they offered to the interior.[131] The design would also have allowed the use of the para-littoral canals, avoiding a potentially dangerous voyage along the coast. Indeed, it is striking that all the wrecks recovered from the ancient coastline were discovered near harbour access points. The Comacchio wreck was recovered in proximity to the former mouth of the Po, and the Parco Theodorico wreck was located near the entrance to the harbour of Ravenna. The Lido I-III wrecks were recovered near the access points to the Venice lagoon, and by extension the port of Altinum and the para-littoral canals.

Among the wrecks recovered from further inland or riverine contexts, the Stella I and Santa Maria in Padovetere wrecks have both been identified as flat-

---

[129] Willis and Capulli 2018.
[130] Marsden 1967.

[131] Elsewhere in Italy, the Tiber was also said to be navigable by ocean going vessels up to Ocriculum, (Diosono 2012: 200).

The Santa Maria in Padovetere

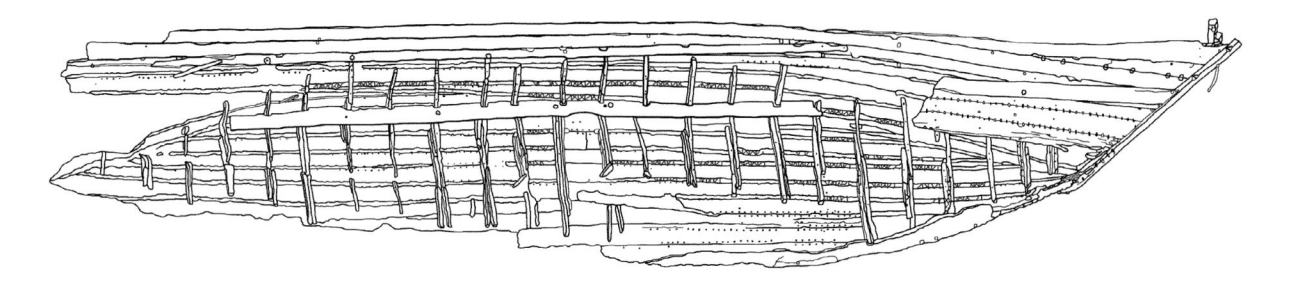

The Stella I

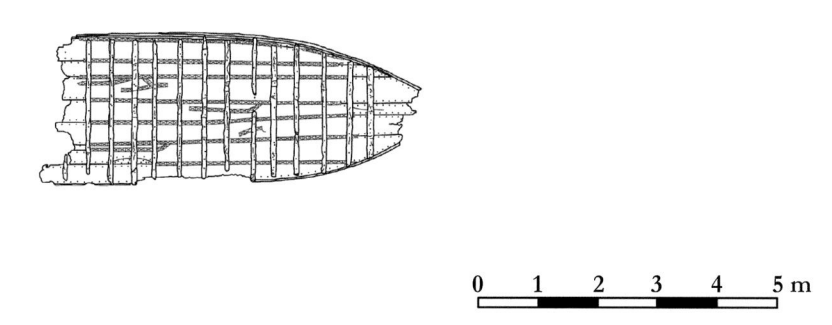

0 1 2 3 4 5 m

Figure 7. The Santa Maria in Padovetere and Stella I wrecks (redrawn from Castro and Capulli 2016: Fig. 3; Beltrame and Costa 2016: Fig. 3).

bottomed cargo barges (see Figure 7).[132] They were both constructed without a keel and have a long, narrow box shape, similar to other barges found in the Western Empire such as the Zwammerdam 2, 4, and 6, the Lyon Parc Saint-Georges 4, or the Arles-Rhône 3.[133] Even fully loaded, barges could have a very low displacement, at times as little as 10 cm.[134] In Northern Italy, the Stella I wreck was carrying a locally sourced cargo towards Aquileia when it sank.[135] The Stella is a small river, a fraction of the size of the Po, the Adige, or any of the other major waterways in the region. The fact that a boat the size of the Stella I, (2 x 4.9 m in its surviving bow section) was able to use the river attests to the versatility of these vessels in operating in restrictive conditions, and the accessibility of even

the smallest waterways to cargo bearing vessels.[136] In contrast, the 5th century AD Santa Maria in Padovetere wreck provides a more complete example of a cargo barge from the region, with its hull surviving to a length of 17m.[137] Its cargo is unknown, but the wreck was located in the remains of a fossilised river channel that connected Ferrara (and the Po) to Ravenna.[138] The proposed path of the *Fossa Augusta* is also less than a kilometre away from the wreck site, although the canal had fallen out of use by the 5th century AD (see below).

The final wreck type recovered from the region are monoxyls, log boats carved from a single tree trunk that could reach up to 18 m in length.[139] They were most likely used for fishing, or other small-scale economic activities and may have also allowed the transport of small groups of people over short distances. While the process of making a basic monoxyl was reasonably simple, some of the recovered monoxyls show considerable sophistication and could carry sails or be combined to form catamarans.[140] They have been recovered from rivers and lakes across Northern Italy,

---

[132] Other fragmentary vessels, such as the Cavanella d'Adige, Aquileia I and II may also have functioned as barges (Beltrame and Gaddi 2013: 301; Bertacchi 1990: 220-26).

[133] Bockius 2004; de Weerd 1978; Rieth 2014; Rieth and Guyon 2011. The Arles-Rhône 3 had a capacity of between 25 and 29 t, with the Bacchiglione (accounting for missing cargo) and the San Basilio di Ariano Polesine wreck sharing a similar capacity (Dallemulle 1977: 123-24; Rieth 2014: 285; Previato and Zara 2014: 72). Outside of the fluvio-maritime vessels, there is so far little evidence to suggest there was anything larger travelling on the waterways of the Po-Veneto region.

[134] Bockius 2004: 109.

[135] The makers stamps present on the roof tiles recovered from the wreck have a distribution across the Upper Adriatic region (Castro and Capulli 2016: 31).

[136] Capulli 2023; Castro and Capulli 2016: 32.

[137] Beltrame and Costa 2016; 2023; Beltrame *et al.* 2021; Ceserano and Corti 2023.

[138] Mozzi and Rucco 2023.

[139] Medas 2003: 162; Uggeri 1990: 188-89.

[140] Ravasi and Barbaglio 2008: 39-48.

and demonstrate that even people without access to larger, more sophisticated vessels were utilising the water network.

As to what goods may have been transported on the waterways, few cargoes have been recovered from inland wrecks within Northern Italy.[141] In some cases, groups of amphorae and other ceramics have been recovered from rivers, but their context is often unrecorded or uncertain.[142] The cargo of the Stella I wreck forms the most complete assemblage recovered so far.[143] This barge was carrying a shipment of at least 120 roof tiles (*imbrices* and *tegulae*), produced by local suppliers along the River Stella.[144] Several Dressel 2-4 and Lamboglia 2 amphorae were also recovered from the wreck, although it is unclear whether these formed part of the cargo or were for use by the vessel's crew. The remains of the Stella I wreck are complemented by the additional discovery of three stone cargoes from across the region (see Table 4). In all cases, the actual remains of the wreck have disappeared, leaving only the remains of the cargo *in situ*. The largest of the three stone cargoes comes from the Bacchiglione wreck, comprising two sets of column bases and column drums, located at the bottom of the Bacchiglione River. The unfinished nature and homogenous grouping of the two sets make it more likely that they formed a cargo as opposed to having been part of a bridge or building adjacent to the river.[145] The Bacchiglione wreck's cargo of stone was 17 tonnes and considering the distribution of the remains it seems likely that the ship was carrying additional cargo, perhaps perishable, that has since been salvaged or decayed.[146] The stone was Euganean trachyte from quarries located less than 10km from the wreck site, which saw common use in Roman construction across Northern Italy.[147] Elsewhere the San Basilio di Ariano Polesine wreck in the delta area was found to be carrying two blocks of limestone from Domegliara near Verona, while the Como wreck's cargo consisted of a 16-tonne load of shaped Musso marble.[148]

The surviving wreck evidence shows a wide variety of craft were active on Northern Italy's water network during the Roman period. The waterways were used by vessels designed solely for inland use and those that could engage in both fluvial and maritime environments. The recovered vessels served a mix of purposes, with wrecks such as the Bacchiglione, Santa Maria di Padovetere, and Stella I suggesting that significant loads were being transported on the riverscape. While the uneven distribution of the evidence allows limited insight into waterborne transport in the western reaches of the Po-Veneto Plain, the extensive remains of port infrastructure uncovered in this area serve to complement the wrecks from the east of the region.

Ports and Harbours

Cargo barges on Northern Italy's water network would have required terrestrial infrastructure to allow the loading, unloading, and storage of their goods. The fluvio-maritime ports of Ravenna, Altinum, and Aquileia, which served as entry points for the inland water network, are well documented (see Chapter 3).[149] Further inland, the situation is more complex. The surviving textual sources indicate the navigability of the river network and its use to transport goods and people far into the valley. Unfortunately, many cities in Northern Italy that are linked to travel on the water network through ancient literature or inscriptions, lack archaeological evidence for a port (see Appendix A). This is not to say that they did not exist, but rather they have been either lost to the erosional forces of the river or are buried too deep and yet to be discovered. There were likely far more ports than the surviving evidence suggests. On the Po itself, there have been limited discoveries of ports or their associated structures. A minor structure that might be identified as a port installation was discovered at Lago Tramonto, a flooded gravel pit on a paleochannel of the river at Gambulaga, near Ferrara.[150] An underwater survey carried out by the Emilia-Romagna *soprintendenza* documented many Roman artefacts exposed by the collapse of the pit's walls, including a line of 11 wooden piles retaining a layer of compacted clay, thought to represent the northern bank of the Po during the 2nd century AD.[151] The quay at Lago Tramonto is complemented by the discovery of a large *horreum* adjacent to the Po in Turin, which the excavators hypothesised was linked to the city's river port.[152] However, no other traces of port infrastructure, such as embankments or wharfing, have been discovered. There is more extensive evidence for ports on the tributaries of the Po and rivers of the Venetian Plain but even this is limited when compared

---

[141] Most ancient literature concerned with transport on the Po water network focuses on passengers being transferred up and downriver in the Roman period. Accounts mentioning material cargoes are less common, but they do exist. Livy (21.57) mentions that during the winter of 218/217 BC, Hannibal's forces were harassing Roman troops in their winter quarters near Piacenza, resulting in 'the cutting off of all supplies from every quarter, save such as were brought up the Po in ships'. Polybius (3.57) records a similar story. Pliny (*N. H.* 3.123) claimed the river 'carried up it all the products of the seas', and Saint Ambrose (*Hexaëm.* 2.3.12), writing in the 4th century, called the Po, 'a trusty conveyer of maritime produce for the support of Italy'.
[142] Zucca 1996: 126.
[143] This is excluding the cargo of the Comacchio wreck, which was discovered in a maritime context. See Bondesan, Dal Cin, and Monari 1990 for details on the cargo.
[144] Castro and Capulli 2016: 31.
[145] Previato and Zara 2014: 61-63.
[146] Previato and Zara 2014: 72.
[147] Previato and Zara 2014: 71.
[148] Dallemulle 1977: 123-24; Montalcini De Angelis D'Ossat 1993: 56.

[149] See Bertacchi 1980; 1990; Grazia Maiolo 1990; Mozzi *et al.* 2016.
[150] Bucci 2015: 55.
[151] Bucci 2015: 59. Several monoxyls were also recovered from the site (Bucci 2015: 57-58; 2018: 11-16).
[152] Barrico and Subbrizio 2007.

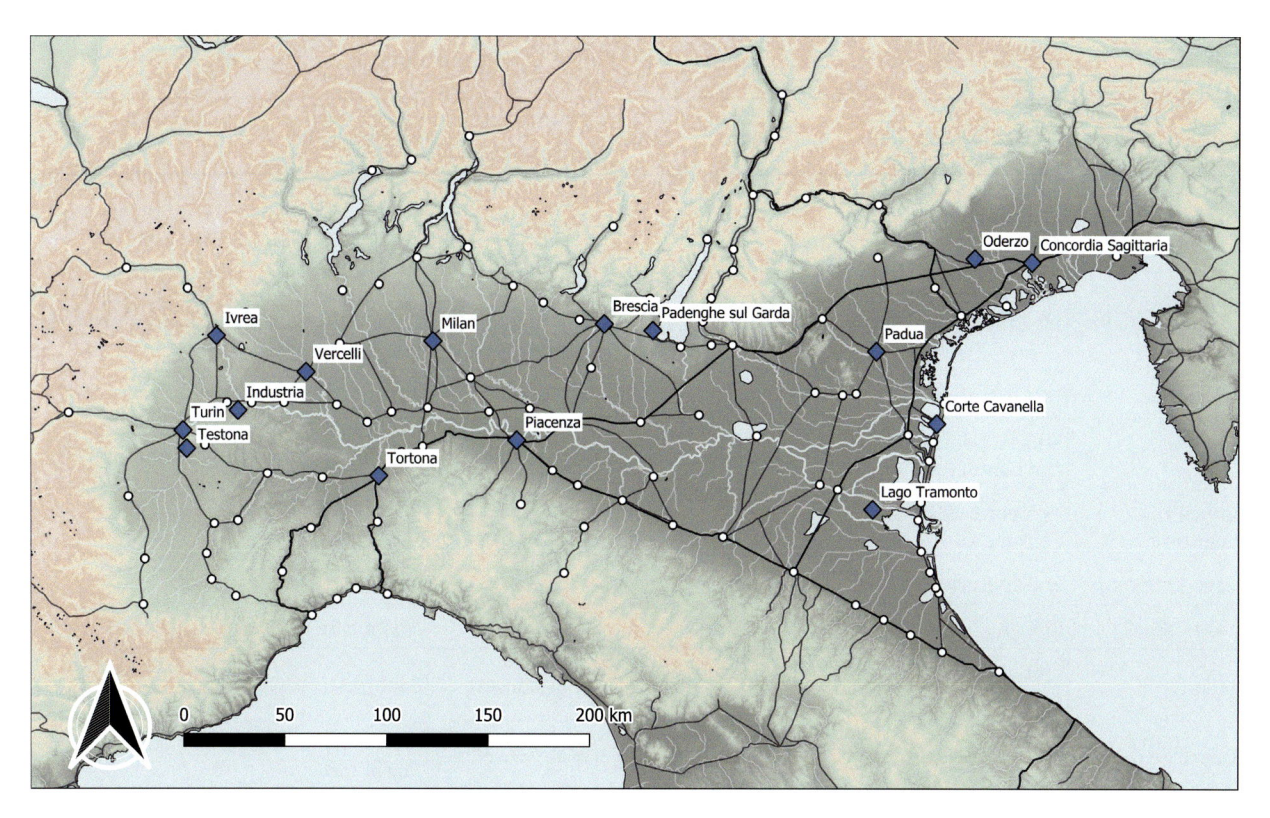

Figure 8. Map of fluvial ports in Northern Italy during the Roman period.

to the supposed extent of navigable rivers in the Roman period. Figure 8 maps the locations of fluvial ports within the Po-Veneto region, with the surviving archaeological evidence compiled in Table 5.

Within Northern Italy, many cities were not located directly on a riverfront, either to avoid flooding or because the channel had subsequently moved away, necessitating the construction of a channel to link the city with the river network. In the south-west of the valley at Tortona, a short canal connected the city's port with the Torrente Scrivia. The canal was formed by diverting part of the Scrivia closer to the city during the 1st century AD and was re-excavated during the 3rd century AD.[153] The port itself consisted of two long masonry docks lining either side of the canal, the channel of which was 9m wide.[154] The dock walls were 1m wide and constructed of river pebbles and concrete, being reinforced with buttresses every 10m to anchor the structure to the banks and counteract lateral thrust from the river. A comparable structure exists on the River Sesia, where the remains of a canal constructed in the 1st century BC linking the river to Vercelli were discovered. The canal was 11m wide and 2m deep, with its sides reinforced by stone retaining walls.[155] To the east

in Milan, a complex network of canals flowed through the city to connect it with the Lambro. This relied on the diversion of the Olona, which eventually flowed out towards the Lambro through the *Canale Vettabbia*, a channel that united the majority of waterways within the city.[156] Finally, at Brescia, in the foothills of the Alps, it seems probable that either the Garza, Mella, or Chiese were channelled to more directly connect the city with the Oglio and the Po.[157] Evidence for canals connecting cities to the Po also exists at Industria and Piacenza. At Industria, the path of the port canal is marked by a 16m wide depression linking the city to a paleochannel of the Po.[158] The evidence for a Roman canal at Piacenza (termed the *Fossa Augusta di Piacenza*), is somewhat more circumstantial.[159] There was certainly a medieval canal in the area of the modern Torrione Fodesta, which is attested to in documentation from AD 1209 onwards and the remains of which were found during an excavation in 1958. It has been suggested that the medieval names of *Foxusta* and *Fodesta* used in this documentation represent an evolution of *Fossa*, consequently linking back to the *Fossa Augusta di Piacenza*. The reason for the construction of this canal was likely the Po shifting its

---

153 Crosetto 2013a: 102-8. The wharfing was exposed for a length of 68m, though likely continued beyond the excavation area.
154 Crosetto 2013a: 101-102; Gamberini *et al.* 2011.
155 Spagnolo Garzoli *et al.* 2007: 112; Panero 2013.

156 Caporusso 1990: 94-96; Cera 1995: 179. Several sections of Roman canal have been excavated within the city. At San Lorenzo, a section of brick lined, 4m wide canal was discovered, and at Seveso and Porta Romana, stretches of docks have been found.
157 Cera 1995: 192-93.
158 Zanda 2011: 42. The canal ran over approximately half a kilometre.
159 Cera 1995: 182-83; Pagliani 1991: 78, note 228.

Table 5. Fluvial port infrastructure dating to the Roman period discovered in Northern Italy.

Site	Chronology	Wharf	Canal	Additional Infrastructure	Bibliography
Brescia	5th Century AD (possibly replacing an earlier structure)	Stone	Yes	Warehouses	Cavalieri Manasse 1990; Mirabella Roberti 1961; Ruggiu Zaccaria 1969
Corte Cavanella	1st Century BC	Wooden	Yes	Boathouse	Sanesi Mastrocinque, Peretto, and Zerbinati 1985; Sanesi Mastrocinque, Bonomi, and Toniolo 1986
Industria	1st Century AD?		Yes		Zanda 2011
Ivrea	Mid-1st Century AD – Early 2nd Century AD	Stone		Warehouses	Brecciaroli Taborelli 2007; Finocchi 1980
Concordia Sagittaria	1st Century BC – 1st Century AD		Yes	Warehouses	Vigoni 2006; Rousse 2013
Lago Tramonto	2nd Century AD	Wooden			Bucci 2015; 2018
Lake Garda	Roman			Jetties	Massensini 1973; Uggeri 1990
Milan	1st Century BC – 1st Century AD	Stone and Wooden	Yes	Warehouses	Caporusso 1990a; 1990b; Frontori 2017
Oderzo	Early 1st Century AD	Stone		Waterwheel	Cipriano and Sandri 2001; Malizia 1986; Tirelli 1987
Padua	1st – 2nd Century AD	Stone and Wooden			Balista and Serafini 1993; Uggeri 1990
Piacenza	3rd Century BC – 1st Century BC		Yes		Cera 1995; Pagliani 1991
Testona	Late Roman	Wooden			Pantò 2009
Tortona	Late 1st Century AD – Early 2nd Century AD	Stone	Yes	Warehouses	Crosetto 2013a; Gamberini et al. 2011
Turin	Late 1st century AD-3rd century AD			Warehouses	Barrico and Subbrizio 2007
Vercelli	1st Century BC	Stone	Yes	Warehouses	Panero 2013; Spagnolo Garzoli et al. 2007

course to the north away from the city between the 3rd and 1st centuries BC.[160]

Urban areas contained the most substantial port infrastructure, and river wharfs have been discovered in cities across Northern Italy. Wharfing was primarily constructed on a foundation of timber piles, with the main structure formed of a concrete core faced in stone on its riverward side. One of the best surviving examples of this comes from Ivrea, where a 100m-long stretch of wharf was uncovered during a flood of the Dora Baltea, in 1977 (see Figure 9).[161] In Milan, the MM3 and several earlier excavations uncovered several sections

of wharfing situated along this canal running to a combined length of approximately 250m, constructed in a similar manner to that discovered at Ivrea.[162] The remains were discovered in the Via Baracchini, the Via S. Clemente, the Via Ore, the Via Larga, and in the Porta Romana area. The quay itself seems to have been constructed during the Augustan period, and finds of ARS suggest it was active until at least the end of the 5th century AD.[163] This was complemented by the remains of a large basin, set beside the canal. At Brescia, a section of quay thought to date from the 5th century AD was discovered beneath the via Mantova, to the south-east of the city walls.[164] The exposed section of the quay ran

[160] Marchetti and Dall'Aglio 1990: 604-40.
[161] Finocchi 1980: 89-90. Brecciaroli Taborelli 2007: 133. Finds from the excavation dated its construction to the mid-1st–early 2nd century AD (Cera 1995: 186).

[162] Caporusso 1990: 94, 1991b: 245-46; Frontori 2017: 41-44, 93-97, 109-13.
[163] Caporusso 1990: 96; 1991b: 246.
[164] The dating of the port itself is uncertain. Although the original excavator suggested a Severan date for its construction, a strong

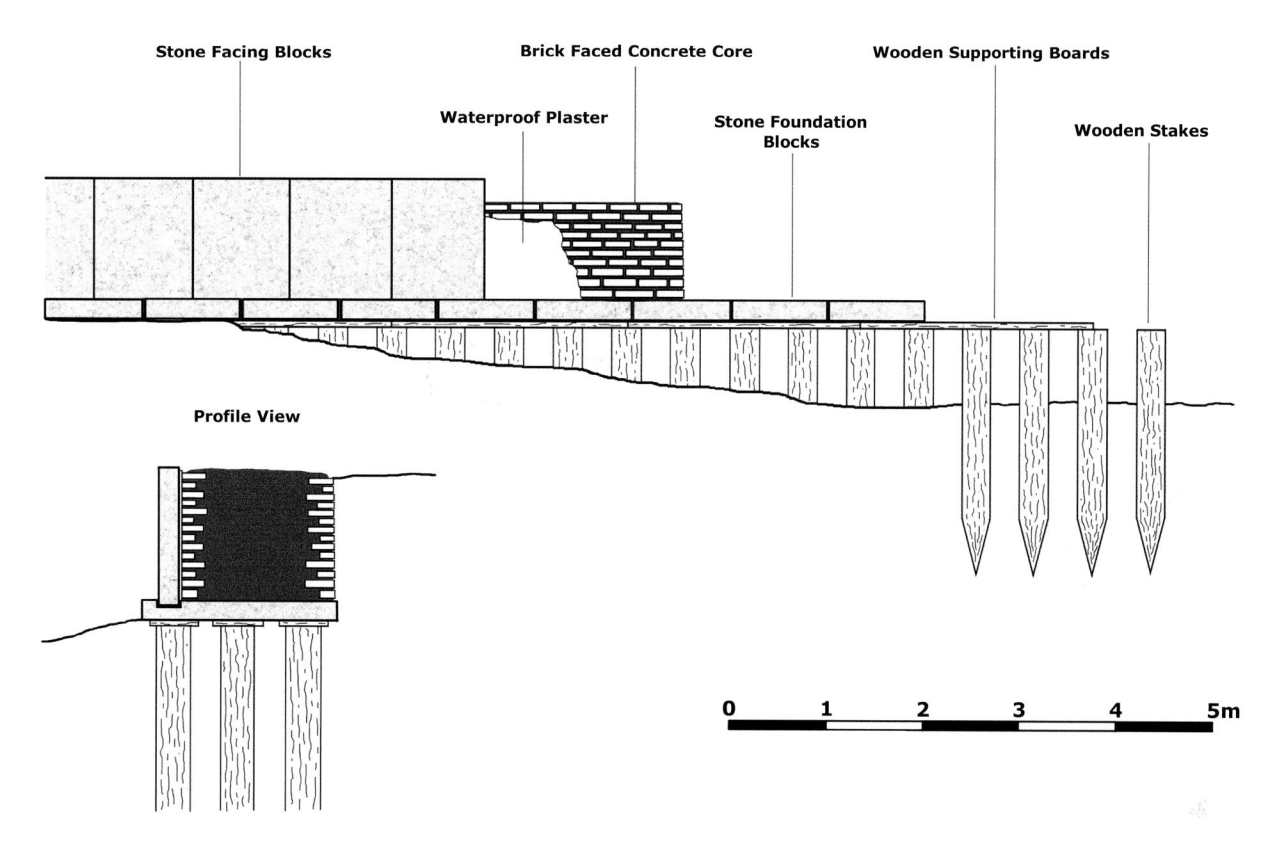

Figure 9. Plan of the fluvial port at Ivrea (redrawn from Finocchi 1980: Tav. XXVIIIb).

for 24m and was constructed using blocks of Botticino marble, recycled from a large funerary monument.[165] The structure seems to be a reconstruction or relocation of an earlier port installation. At Padua, a small section of wooden wharfing was uncovered on the banks of the Bacchiglione, abutting the city walls.[166] More substantially, in the area near the University and the Café Pedrocchi, close to the paleochannel of the Bacchiglione, several ramps were discovered that linked the ancient street level to the lower wharves on the riverbank below.[167]

Port infrastructure did not stop at the wharves but extended into the area immediately behind the riverbank and (at times) into the river itself. At Oderzo, a section of wharfing on the Piave, abutting an area of riverbank reclaimed by an amphora deposit, was discovered during the 1980s.[168] Abutting the quay were the remains of several dolphins (groups of wooden pilings used to moor boats and protect the quay from impact).[169] On Lake Garda, the remains of a set of wooden jetties at Padenghe sul Garda were also discovered. However, the poor state of the remains meant little could be inferred other than that they dated to the Roman period.[170] In the majority of instances where wharfing survives, it has been accompanied by the discovery of *horrea* in areas adjacent to or immediately behind the structure. *Horrea* formed an integral part of dockside infrastructure, enabling the storage of cargo prior to its loading or redistribution.

Away from urban areas, there were smaller rural ports and landing sites, although the evidence is much patchier. The site of Corte Cavanella has already been mentioned above in relation to its accompanying wrecks. The villa and boathouse were located a short

---

case has been made for the 5th century AD based on other reuse of monumental funerary architecture in Lombardy (Mirabella Roberti 1961: 272-80; Ruggiu Zaccaria 1969: 144-46).

[165] Cavalieri Manasse 1990: 11-12.

[166] Balista and Ruta Serafini 1993: 110. While its primary function was to prevent the undermining of the city walls by the river, it has been hypothesised the structure also functioned as a quay.

[167] Uggeri 1990: 184.

[168] Cipriano and Sandrini 2001; Malizia 1986; Tirelli 1987.

[169] Cipriano and Sandrini 2001: 291. The area of the river above the quay seems to have been repurposed in the 2nd century AD, when a rubble filed wooden formwork was laid across the river. This blocked upstream navigation beyond the river port, and a wooden water wheel was installed upon the barrage, alongside other supporting infrastructure (Trovò 1996: 130-32).

[170] Massensini 1973: 44-47; Uggeri 1990: 185. It is also possible that port structures existed near Sirmione, at the Grotte di Catullo, however these were destroyed during the Second World War (Cera 1995: 196). The lake would have been linked into the water network by the River Mincio, which forms a tributary of the Po. The guilds of *nautae* active on the lake and the river have been discussed above, but the journey upriver to the lake is also alluded to by Catullus (4), when he describes taking his boat 'from a foreign sea, here, as far as this limpid lake'.

distance from a canal, its banks reinforced by wooden stakes, which remained active into the 4th century AD.[171] At Lago Tramonto and Testona, small stretches of wooden wharfing extended along the riverbanks.[172] While these sites could certainly have served as landing stages for smaller watercraft, it is also possible that their main purpose was to protect the bank itself from erosion and undermining.[173] Although the facilities at Corte Cavanella, Lago Tramonto, and Testona may have only served an individual site, they demonstrate that smaller settlements were still investing in facilities to access the water network.

The archaeological evidence has shown there was widespread and significant investment in port infrastructure across Northern Italy from the 1st century AD onwards. The size and scope of the surviving port network in the Po Valley suggests navigation was possible on the Po and many of its tributaries to a point well beyond current limitations. Indeed, the construction of significant port infrastructure at Ivrea, some 545km upstream from the modern mouth of the river, suggests that the water network offered far-reaching connections into distant areas of the region. Overall, the surviving textual, epigraphic, and archaeological evidence paints a picture of a sophisticated transport network in place on the waterways of Northern Italy. From ferries to cargo barges, goods and people moved up and down the river in a variety of ways. This was complemented by considerable terrestrial infrastructure, the docks and warehouses necessary for the safe transfer of cargo from vessel to shore and vice versa.

The Canal Network

One of the most ambitious engineering projects the Romans undertook in Northern Italy was the construction of a system of para-littoral canals along the Adriatic Coast. These canals formed an important part of the water network, from both a transport and hydrological standpoint. Canals could join formerly separate river basins together, redirect the flow of water away from areas where it had previously travelled, or connect sections of a river to the sea. The system was composed of three canals, the *Fossa Augusta*, the *Fossa Claudia*, and the *Fossa Flavia*, which connected the ports of Ravenna and Altinum over a distance of 120 Roman miles.[174] The three waterways are recorded in the *Peutinger Table*, and the *Antonine Itinerary* alludes to

them by detailing that the quickest route from Ravenna to Altinum was to sail through 'the Seven Seas'.[175] It is also possible that the canal system had been extended as far as Aquileia by the reign of Diocletian through the remainder of the lagoon system.[176] It would be a mistake to envisage these canals in the traditional sense of a continuous excavated channel. The para-littoral *fossae* connected multiple branches of the Po, at times by diverting them, and utilised the coastal lagoons for large sections of their course.[177] The creation of the canal system allowed vessels to travel between ports along the Northern Adriatic Coast without being exposed to the perils of the sea, and would have enabled maritime ships to bypass the dangerous mouths of the delta to access the Po, which, according to Strabo, 'could only be overcome with experience'.[178]

The *Fossa Augusta* was constructed during the reign of Augustus and connected Ravenna to the southernmost channel of the Po.[179] It was likely created in tandem with the founding of the naval base at Ravenna and Classis, and would have allowed products travelling on the inland waterways to access the port more easily.[180] Excavation has produced evidence of the *Fossa Augusta* in several areas. Extensive coring has revealed its path to the immediate north of Ravenna, and within Ravenna itself, several sections have been excavated.[181] These investigations revealed the canal had a width of 50m in places, and its bank was reinforced with wooden stakes in sections. At several points along the path of the canal, there is evidence for dock facilities constructed in concrete and masonry, in some cases with adjacent warehouses and workshops.[182] A road also ran parallel to the canal and was paved in the areas closest to Ravenna. This may have acted as a towpath for ships using the channel. The route of the *Fossa Augusta* can be mapped with a good degree of accuracy until it reaches the lagoon of the Valli di Comacchio about 15km north of Ravenna, where its path is lost.[183]

In comparison to the *Fossa Augusta*, there is less evidence for the *Fossae Claudia* and *Flavia*. The *Fossa Claudia* was probably constructed during the reign of Claudius, and while its path is uncertain, the modern town of Chioggia

[171] Sanesi Mastrocinque, Peretto, and Zerbinati 1985: 15-16, 19-20; Sanesi Mastrocinque, Bonomi, and Toniolo 1986: 25-27.
[172] Bucci 2015: 59; Pantò 2009: 228.
[173] Page 2022: 180-83.
[174] Plin. *HN* 3.119; Uggeri 1978. The first to excavate navigable artificial channels within the Po-Veneto Plain were supposedly the Etruscans, who excavated a channel to maintain sea access to the port of Atria (Plin. *HN* 3.120).
[175] *It. Ant.* 126.
[176] Hrdn. 8.7.1; Uggeri 1987: 343; 1997: 60.
[177] Using canals to connect rivers is seen elsewhere in the Roman world. The *Fossa Corbulonis* in the Netherlands was constructed in AD 50 to connect the mouths of the Meuse and the Rhine, while the *Fossae Drusianae*, the exact routes of which are unknown, possibly connected the Rhine with Lake Flevo (Franconi 2014: 41-44).
[178] Str. 5.1.5. Parallels are drawn to the mouth of the Rhône, another river whose delta was said to provide difficult passage for ships. Here too, a canal was built, the *Fossa Mariana*, in order to bypass the mouth of the river (Str. 4.1.6). See also Salomon and Rousse 2022; 2023.
[179] Plin. *HN* 119.
[180] Uggeri 2016: 88.
[181] Cirelli 2013: 117-19; Grazia Maiolo 1990: 380-82; 2018: 333-34; Manzelli 2000: 161-62.
[182] Roncuzzi 1992: 725; Roncuzzi and Veggi 1967; 1968.
[183] Mozzi and Rucco 2023; Grazia Maioli 2018: 333; Manzelli 2000: 162.

likely takes its name from the canal and represents the point it entered the Venetian lagoon.[184] The *Fossa Flavia* is thought to have been begun during the reign of Nero and completed by the Flavian dynasty.[185] The *fossa* seems to have revived an older Etruscan canal that was constructed by diverting a branch of the Po across the marshes south of Atria, connecting the Caprisian branch to the Volanian branch.[186] Though no sections of the *Fossae Claudia* and *Flavia* have been excavated, there is circumstantial archaeological evidence for their presence. Foundations of structures interpreted as towers or lighthouses have been discovered along the proposed route of the canals, which could have acted as markers for ships.[187] On clear days, the tower would have acted as a prominent landmark, while during darkness the light would have been able to guide vessels towards the canal entrance. Several stone mooring rings have also been recovered from the Valli di Comacchio, which may indicate docks from either a canal or a channel of the Po.[188] Furthermore, many of the inland wrecks recovered from the coastal regions are located along the proposed path of the canal, most notably the Corte Cavanella I and II wrecks (see above).

The canals themselves seem to have had extraordinary longevity, staying in service for approximately 300 years. In the 3rd century, Herodian described the Emperor Maximus leaving Ravenna and travelling to Aquileia via 'the lagoons into which the River Eridanus and the surrounding swamps empty', suggesting that the para-littoral canals had been extended through the northern lagoon system.[189] An extension of the canals is further supported by the Aphrodisian copy of the Price Edict, which gives a cost of 7500 *denarii* to ship 1000 *kastrenses modii* from Ravenna to Aquileia during the 4th century AD.[190] However, during this later period, there is already evidence of siltation within the *Fossa Augusta* and the surrounding lagoon system, which would have reduced the effectiveness of the channel.[191] This may suggest that the dredging required to keep it operational had ceased or was no longer being carried out as frequently. Its use persisted, but by the end of the 4th century AD, parts of the canal at Ravenna seem to have been abandoned or infilled.[192] The final fate and

abandonment of the three canals remains uncertain due to a lack of records and firm archaeological evidence. However, Procopius' description of being able to transport cargo from Ravenna to Aquileia through the lagoon system using high tides may suggest that a para-littoral route between the two cities persisted into the 6th century AD.[193]

The construction of para-littoral canals represented a significant Roman undertaking during the 1st century AD to alter the water network of Northern Italy to their advantage and enhance the opportunities it offered. The creation and maintenance of these canals was a substantial task, often involving either the redirection of a watercourse or the creation of an entirely new one. During their lifetimes, the para-littoral canals represented a key piece of hydrological infrastructure within the Po-Veneto Plain, one that was used to extend and enhance the water network, alongside opening it up to fluvio-maritime transport along the Adriatic Coast.

Interconnected Infrastructure

The surviving evidence from Northern Italy's water and road networks demonstrates the presence of an extensive and well-integrated transport system. The great consular roads of the 2nd century BC formed the backbone, which soon expanded to include a range of other routes and pathways. The road network allowed more direct connections to be made between the region's urban centres, alongside the redistribution of goods and people to areas not connected by the rivers. Significant investment was made to overcome topographic obstacles in the region and protect the roadways from hydrological hazards. Although all aspects of the network would have been subject to a degree of seasonality, investment in protective infrastructure would have helped to keep the roads open and goods and people moving.

While Northern Italy's roadways saw significant use during the Roman period, this was in conjunction with the water network. In a landscape where water formed a major part of everyday life, it is unsurprising to see the high level of investment in and development of the riverscape. The water network was used extensively, and the combination of navigable rivers and canals offered unprecedented coverage of the region. Literary accounts and wrecks recovered from Northern Italy point to both material and human cargo moving from the coast inland and vice versa. The large ports attached to the region's urban sites, alongside smaller installations at rural sites, allowed goods to be transported to consumption centres directly by water. Urban areas acted as nexus points in the network,

[184] Plin. *HN* 121; D'Agostino and Medas 2010: 288; Uggeri 1987: 341.

[185] This is due to the location of the town of Neronia along the path of the canal, just as there is the town of Augusta along the path of the *Fossa Augusta*.

[186] Plin. *HN* 3.120.

[187] Ceserano and Corti 2023; D'Agostino and Medas 2010: 289-90; Madricadro *et al.* 2021; Uggeri 2006: 145-48.

[188] Uggeri 1990: 185.

[189] Hdn. 8.7.1.

[190] *Edict of Maximum Prices*, XXXVA.33; Laurence 1999: 118; Uggeri 1987: 343; 1997: 60. The journey is assumed to have been via canal due to the total cost being substantially higher than the cost of the maritime route between the two ports when measured using the Price Edict.

[191] Manzelli 2000: 236.

[192] Manzelli 2000: 238; Calzolari 2007: 159.

[193] Procop. *Goth.* 1.1.19-22.

allowing interaction between water and terrestrial transport, and the transfer of goods and people between the two.

Working in tandem, rivers, canals, and roads connected the coast to the mountains, the region to the rest of Italy, and Italy to its northern provinces, creating the necessary links to transport goods and people efficiently between them all. While both the road and water network were in use from the mid-Republic onwards, the 1st century AD saw massive investment that upgraded existing structures and added new ones, with the presence of *collegia* involved in the transport of goods both overland and on the water reflecting an increasing level of organisation. The fact that certain elements of the network saw continued use in the post-Roman era points to its resilience and durability, alongside its ongoing influence over regional travel.

'The Richest District'.
Production and Exports from Northern Italy

As for the excellence of the region, it is evidenced by their goodly store of men, the size of the cities and their wealth, which in all respects the Romans in that part of the world have surpassed the rest of Italy. For not only does the tilled land bring forth fruits in large quantities and of all sorts, but the forests have acorns in such quantities that Rome is fed mainly on the herds of swine that come from there. And the yield of millet is also exceptional, since the soil is well-watered; and millet is the greatest preventive of famine, since it withstands every unfavourable weather, and can never fail, even though there be scarcity of every other grain. The country has wonderful pitch-works, also; and as for the wine, the quantity is indicated by the jars, for the wooden ones are larger than houses; and the good supply of the pitch helps much towards the excellent smearing the jars receive. As for wool, the soft kind is produced by the regions round Mutina and the River Scultenna (the finest wool of all); the coarse, by Liguria and the country of the Symbri, from which the greater part of the households of the Italiotes are clothed; and the medium, by the regions round Patavium, from which are made the expensive carpets and covers and everything of this kind that is woolly either on both sides or only on one.

Strabo 5.1.12

To read ancient writers discuss the landscape of Northern Italy is to be transported to a fertile and productive region, the goods of which were synonymous with quality and available in the greatest quantities. Polybius believed the Po-Veneto Plain 'surpassed in fertility any other in Europe' and recorded that it grew 'an abundance of corn', alongside other crops such as panic, millet, and barley.[1] So plentiful was the region's produce, it was said that innkeepers charged their guests a flat rate per head for dinner, rather than for what they ordered, because of the 'cheapness and abundance' of food.[2] Varro claimed that pigs reared near Milan were so fat that they could not stand, with both Polybius and Strabo stating that Rome was fed 'mainly on the herds of swine' that were reared in Northern Italy.[3] As for wine, Strabo stated that the region's viticulture was of comparable quality with the eminent wines of Central Italy, with Herodian recording it was exported in significant quantities.[4] Away from the fertile valley floor, even the upland areas of the Alps were productive, supplying goods such as cheese, honey, pitch, resin, and wax.[5] It was not just consumables that Northern Italy was famed for. Its textiles were ranked amongst some of the finest in the Roman world, precious metals were extracted from its mountains, strong and flexible wood was felled from its forests, and fine ceramics were fired from its clay.[6] Its thriving economy and flourishing cities would lead Tacitus to describe Northern Italy

as the 'richest district' of Italy, a sentiment shared by other ancient writers.[7]

In a country often characterised by mountains and upland areas, the vast level ground of the Po Plain stands out in stark contrast to the topography of the rest of Italy. Enclosed by the Alps, Apennines, and the Adriatic, the valley floor varies between 100 and 80km in width (roughly north-south), between the Alps and the Apennines, and runs approximately 350km east-west, from the Adriatic to the foothills of the Alps.[8] Although mainly comprised of flat, open country, the Po Plain also contains several small groups of hills. In the west of the plain, the Colline del Po, Monteferrato, Roero, and Langhe Hills rise, forming an undulating landscape that separates the extreme south-western reaches of the Po Valley from the main plain.[9] To the east of the Po Valley lay the Veneto Plain, distinguished by the watersheds of their respective river systems and the transition zone of the Berci and Euganean Hills.[10] Combined, the Po-Veneto Plain covers 46,000km²,

---

[1] Polyb. 2.15.
[2] Polyb. 2.15.
[3] Polyb. 2.15; Str. 5.1.12; Varro, *Rust.* 2.4.11.
[4] Hrdn. 8.2.3-4; Str. 4.6.8.
[5] Str. 4.6.9; 5.1.7.
[6] Vitr. *De arch.* 2.9.16.

[7] Tac. *Hist.* 2.17.
[8] Marchetti 2002: 362. The Po Valley forms part of a massive foreland basin between the fold-and-thrust belts of the Alps and Apennines, a system of deeply buried canyons left over from the collision of the African and Eurasian plates that extends out into the Adriatic. In the Quaternary period, the valley formed a large marine basin that reached as far as Piedmont. Over the past 5-7 million years, this basin has slowly filled with marine and fluvial sediment, forming a layer 8km thick in some places (Bosellini 2017: 23; Bruno *et al.* 2018; Gasperi 2001; Po River Basin Authority 2006: 23).
[9] These hills were likely formed as result of the upthrust of the basin during the Oligocene and Burdigalian epochs, (Faletti, Gelati, and Rogledi 1995; Tiranti *et al.* 2013: 121-23).
[10] Fredi and Lupia Palmier 2017: 50.

constituting 71% of all plain landscapes in Italy, yet only 15% of Italian territory.[11]

The physical landscape of the Po-Veneto Plain is deeply affected by the varied fluvial contexts and geomorphology of the rivers that flow through them. The transition from the Alps and Apennines to the plain of the valley floor is dominated by raised alluvial fans dating from the late Pleistocene and early Holocene.[12] The aggradation of these fans ended in the middle Holocene, at which point rivers and streams began to entrench into them. The alluvial fans and foothills form a transitional piedmont zone between the mountains and the plain. Stretching out beyond these is the flood plain itself, which is criss-crossed by fluvial ridges, some active, some abandoned, which meander out towards the path of the rivers. The result is a landscape of gently undulating, shallow ridges. Depressed areas of backswamp are located between the alluvial fans and ridges, characterised by poorly drained, waterlogged soils of fine sediment and clay.[13] This makes them common hosts to marshland and riparian forests. In the areas closest to the Adriatic Coast, the height of the land falls below sea level in several areas, resulting in waterlogged areas of brackish water and marsh, alongside the formation of lagoons.

The micro-regional variation across Northern Italy supported a variety of agricultural practices, both in the Roman and post-Roman periods.[14] The abundance of flat and fertile land across the Po-Venetian Plain was used for the intensive cultivation of staple and non-staple crops, alongside the rearing of livestock. The pre-Alpine and pre-Apennine piedmonts, although less fertile than the plain, saw intensive cultivation higher up their slopes for olives and vines.[15] The upland areas of the Alps also played a crucial role in the transhumance of livestock, with highland pasture an important source of summer fodder. In addition, Northern Italy was an important region for the extraction of various natural resources in the form of mineral wealth, stone, marble, and timber. The region's output was consumed both within Northern Italy and further afield, distributed across the Roman world via overland routes and through the great commercial ports along the Adriatic Coast. However, the destination and consumption of Northern Italian products have often proved difficult to track archaeologically due to their predominantly organic nature. Nevertheless, even with the limited evidence available, it remains possible to chart the evolution of Northern Italy's productive landscape throughout the Roman period and Late Antiquity. Through careful analysis of the available evidence, the products and produce of Northern Italy can be reconstructed and the routes of its exports tracked, revealing a productive region connected to markets across the Roman world.

Transforming the Landscape: Adaptation and Exploitation

An abundance of level ground, fertile soil, and water has made the Po-Veneto Plain an attractive area for human habitation for millennia and the arrival of humans in Northern Italy saw the beginnings of extensive landscape reorganisation. By the start of the Bronze Age, the Po Plain had already been heavily deforested, and by the Roman period, almost 60% of the region's tree cover had disappeared, mainly confined to mountainsides or riparian forests.[16] Large-scale land clearance went in tandem with the beginnings of intensive agriculture, which led to increasing settlement nucleation and the beginnings of urbanisation during the Late Bronze Age and Early Iron Age.[17] During the Roman period, the Po-Veneto Plain underwent territorial reorganisation in the form of population displacement, settlement foundation, centuriation, land drainage, and land reclamation. This provided the groundwork for an intensive agricultural landscape, responsible for generating much of the regional wealth vaunted by ancient authors.

Landscape and Territorial Reorganisation

While the Roman period saw the widespread exploitation of the natural landscape, agricultural development was preceded by land redistribution and land reorganisation via centuriation.[18] Traces of this land division can still be found in modern field boundaries, roads, and drainage channels, especially

[11] Marchetti 2002: 361. The region is one of the most heavily populated and urbanised areas of modern Italy. The Po Basin alone has over 3,210 recorded settlements in the modern period which contain an estimated 30% of Italy's population, (Po Basin Authority 2006: 12, 47).
[12] Cremaschi, Storchi, and Perego 2018: 53-55. The Veneto Plain along the Northern Adriatic Coast is comprised almost entirely of several large alluvial 'megafans', most notably the Brenta megafan, the Nervesa megafan, and the Tagliamento megafan (Fontana et al. 2008; Mozzi et al. 2010).
[13] Brandolini and Cremaschi 2018: 3.
[14] Bosi et al. 2011: 1629-30; Po River Basin Authority 2006: 14-15.
[15] Str. 5.1.4.

[16] Palynological studies from across the region show a decline in taxa from lowland forests which are replaced with taxa associated with grasslands and cereal crops (Caramiello et al. 2014: 76-77; Caramiello, Fossa, and Arobba 2014: 16-17; Cremaschi 2009: 36-37). Despite heavy deforestation, the region was renowned for its timber, particularly larch, which was brought down the Po to Ravenna. Its properties for construction, especially its fire resistance, were highly valued, with Vitruvius (De arch. 2.9.16) lamenting in the late 1st century BC that there was no provision to transport it to Rome where such qualities were desperately needed.
[17] Zamboni 2021. It has been highlighted that the level of urbanisation in Northern Italy is lower than the rest of the Italian Peninsula during the Roman period, but this is likely due to smaller semi-rural centres (such as Angera and Bedriacum) having a more prominent role in the settlement hierarchy (Maiuro 2017: 116-24).
[18] Cambi and Terranato 1994; Bosio 1984; Gabba 1985; 2001; Prenc 2002. See Muzzioli 2010 for a summary of the centuriation schemes present within Northern Italy with associated bibliography, alongside more recent reappraisals in Dall'Aglio and Franceschelli 2017.

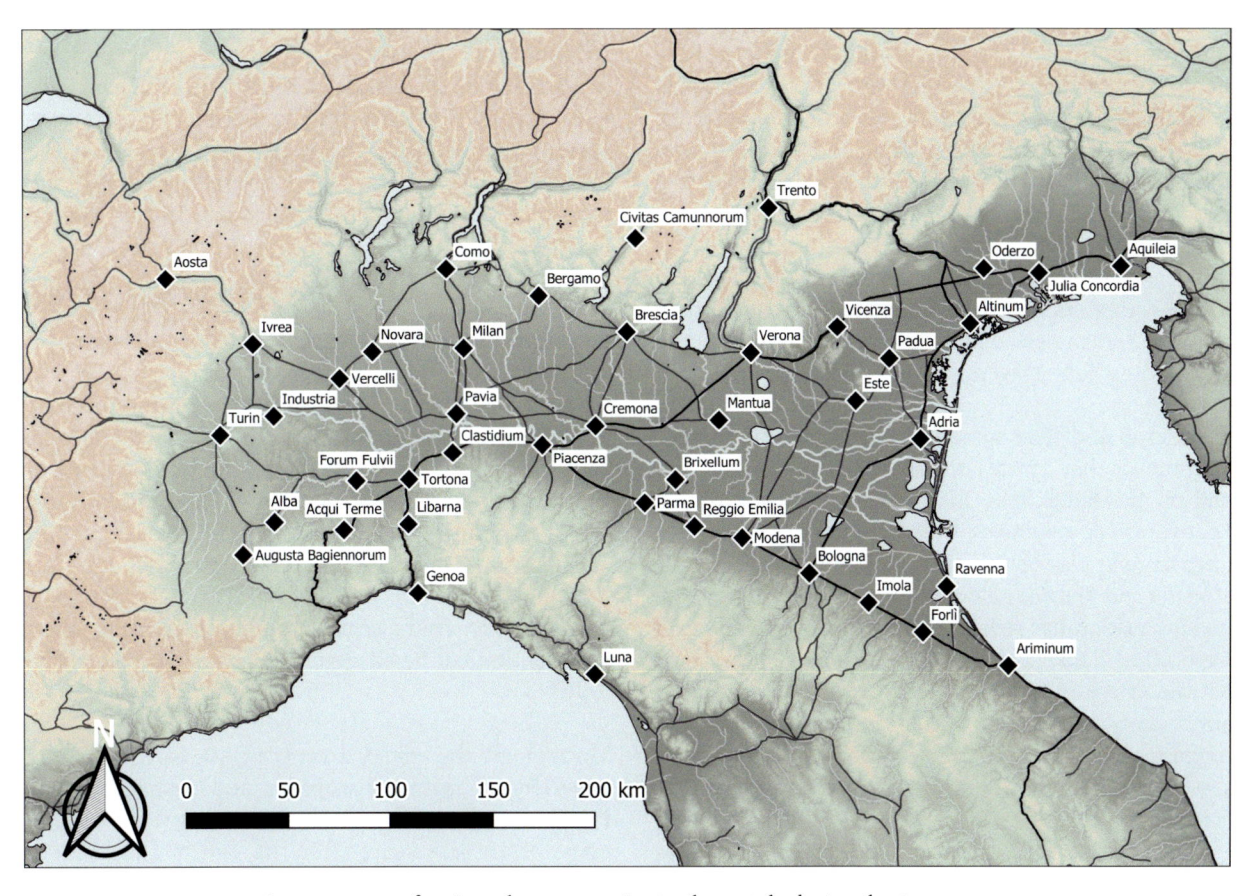

Figure 10. Map of major urban centres in Northern Italy during the Roman era.

in the vicinity of the via Aemilia and in the Veneto Plain north-east of Padua.[19] During the Republic, Roman expansion into Northern Italy resulted in the confiscation of land from tribes such as the Boii and Senones and the eviction of their inhabitants.[20] This land was redistributed amongst Roman colonists and settlers, alongside Veterans during the Triumviral and Early Imperial periods. Between 268 BC and the end of the 1st century BC, over a dozen colonies were founded in Northern Italy. These included Ariminum (289 BC), Piacenza (219 BC), Cremona (219 BC), Bologna (189 BC), Modena (183 BC), Parma (183 BC), Aquileia (181 BC), Luna (177 BC), Tortona (118 BC), Ivrea (100 BC), Como (59 BC), Aosta, Augusta Bagiennorum, and Turin (the Augustan era), (see Figure 10). Settlers in these new foundations or re-foundations were given land as members of the colony. It has been estimated that 559,000 *iugera* of land

were redistributed to colonists during the first half of the 2nd century BC in Cisalpine Gaul alone, attesting to the large quantities of land changing hands during early Roman expansion into Northern Italy.[21] North of the Po, in the areas comprised of modern-day Lombardy and the Veneto, there were fewer colonial foundations and land confiscations, meaning that centuriation schemes in these landscapes may represent territorial reorganisation within existing communities.[22]

The centuriation schemes of the Po-Veneto Plain fulfilled a dual purpose of land division and land reclamation. In an effort to adapt this environment to human needs, large-scale drainage was carried out during the Roman era. As discussed above, water formed an integral part of the landscape of the Po Plain (see Chapter 2 for discussion of the waterscape). The presence of the Alps and Apennines accounts for the high volume of water in the region and the extensive runoff from these two mountain ranges, coupled with the low-lying valley floor, results in a higher-than-average water table. Although important for agriculture

---

[19] Po Basin Authority 2006: 14. Some of the most extensive centuriation occurred along the axis of the via Aemilia where some of Rome's earliest colonies in the region, Ariminium, Bologna, Modena, Parma, and Piacenza, were founded, (Gabba 1985; 2001; Roncaglia 2018: 32-33).

[20] Dall'Aglio and Franceschelli 2017: 263-64. The Senones were evicted from their land during the 3rd century BC, with the confiscated territory distributed as part of the colonial foundation of Ariminum in 268 BC (Livy 15.4-6; Vell. Pat. 1.14.7). The Boii would see half their land taken after their defeat in 191 BC, with the territory distributed as part of the new colony at Bologna in 189 BC (Polyb. 2.35).

[21] Roncaglia 2018: 33.

[22] Dall'Aglio and Franceschelli 2017: 265-66. The chronology of centuriation schemes north of the Po is often difficult to reconstruct, given a lack of corresponding literary evidence. Most agree on a 1st century BC date, either in relation to Sullan interventions or those of the triumvirs in 42-41 BC (Bandelli 1990; Gabba 1985; Tibiletti 1969).

and transport, communities within Northern Italy would try to manage water, both to reduce hydrological risk and expand the availability of arable land in the waterlogged zones.[23] The first documented intervention was undertaken by Marcus Aemilius Scaurus in the late 2nd century BC, where it is recorded that he 'drained the plains by running navigable canals from the Padus as far as Parma.'[24] These interventions would steadily reduce the extent of the marshlands within the Po Plain over the Roman period (although they persisted in the areas closest to the rivers).[25]

Excavation and field survey have revealed the extent and impact that centuriation-based drainage schemes had on the landscape. On the southern bank of the Po, extensive remains of drainage channels have been uncovered as part of the centuriation network between Modena and Piacenza along the line of the via Aemilia, and excavation has revealed that the roads of the grid were often flanked by drainage channels that varied between three and seven metres in width and were often one to two metres deep.[26] The size of these channels suggests they may have been navigable by small craft, serving as an alternate means of transport within the grid. Reconstructions of Modena's centuriation grid estimate it contained approximately 5000km of ditches and canals, which eventually drained into the Po.[27] Field survey between Piacenza, Parma, and Reggio Emilia also shows the expansion of settlement into the territory closest to the river during the Roman period, with the settlement pattern demonstrating a low regard for hydrological risk.[28] These newly reclaimed areas (often consisting of fine sediments) were less suitable for arable farming using Roman agricultural techniques, but may instead have been used for grazing.[29]

The centuriation schemes enacted across Northern Italy during the Republican and Augustan periods resulted in the creation of a well-organised agricultural landscape. Water was controlled and channelled and new land was brought under cultivation. Centuriation schemes in the Adriatic hinterland between Trieste and Ancona alone are estimated to have incorporated between 4800 and 5000km[2] of arable land.[30] Surveys of Northern Italy's rural landscape have recorded an intensification of settlement during the Late Republic that reached its maximum extent in the 1st and 2nd centuries AD.[31] The

1st century BC and 1st century AD also saw significant investment in large-scale productive facilities at villa sites across Northern Italy, pointing to increasing surplus production.[32] The region's economic success and wealth are reflected by a flourishing aristocracy, with increasing numbers of Northern Italian citizens qualifying for the equestrian and senatorial classes under the Early Empire.[33]

Late Antiquity: Restructuring and Self-Sufficiency

In the later Roman period, Northern Italy would become an increasingly important part of the Italian Peninsula. The political separation of the region from the rest of the peninsula into the vicariate of *Italia annonaria* in the 4th century AD, the locating of imperial capitals at Milan (AD 292 – AD 402) and Ravenna (AD 402 – AD 476), and the creation of new administrative, economic, and military frameworks through increasing state intervention, all had a significant impact on Northern Italy.[34]

Throughout the mid-3rd century AD, Northern Italy experienced severe disruption and instability. The region first became a battleground between warring emperors in the years after the end of the Severan Dynasty. In AD 238, Maximinus laid siege to Aquileia in his conflict against the Senate, and elements of the brief civil war between Philip the Arab and Decius in AD 249 may also have been fought near Verona.[35] Political instability was followed by external pressures and incursions, with the Marcomanni invading Italy in AD 254, and the Alemanni in AD 258 and AD 259.[36] They were followed by the Jugurthi in AD 260, who then returned in AD 270, accompanied by the Alemanni.[37] In response to the failure of the *Limes* and the increasing vulnerability of Italy to land invasion, imperial authorities began to fortify towns such as Milan, Pavia, and Verona and placed garrisons within Northern Italy to act as a new line of defence throughout the latter half of the 3rd century AD.[38] Constantine's administrative and territorial reforms of the early 4th century AD, which resulted in Northern Italy being separated from the rest of the Italian Peninsula and incorporated into the new vicariate of *Italia annonaria* (alongside much of

23 See Page 2022 for a discussion of Roman responses to hydrological risk in Northern Italy.
24 Strabo 5.1.11; Dall'Aglio 1995.
25 Brogiolo and Sarabia-Bautista 2017: 150-56; Sarabia-Bautista 2017: 83-85.
26 Botazzi 1992: 172-74; Botazzi and Labate 2017: 18.
27 Botazzi and Labate 2017: 18-19, The excavation of these channels was a serious endeavour, with the network estimated to have taken at least 12,000 man-hours to complete.
28 Brandolini and Carrer 2021: 221; Dall'Aglio and Marchetti 1991: 164.
29 Brandolini and Carrer 2021: 221; Bosi et al. 2015.
30 Ugolini 2021: 90-100; 2023: 96.
31 Bottazzi, Bronzoni, and Mutti 1995; Botazzi and Labate 2017;

Brandolini and Cremaschi 2018; Busana and Forin 2018; Coralini et al. 2019; De Ligt 2017; Franceschelli and Marabini 2007; Launaro 2011; Maiuro 2017; Uggeri 2006.
32 Busana and Forin 2020: 23-25.
33 Roncaglia 2018: 95-100. Strabo (5.1.7) records Padua alone having some 500 equestrians during the Augustan census.
34 Roncaglia 2018: Chapter 8 provides a thorough historical overview of this period in Northern Italy.
35 Aur. Vict. *Caes.* 28.10; Hrdn. 7-8; SHA *Max.* 21-22; Zos. 1.22.
36 Aur. Vict. *Caes.* 33; Eutrop. 9.8; Oros. 7.22; Zon. 12.22; Zos. 1.37.
37 AE 1993: 1231; SHA Aur. 18.3, 21.1; Zos. 1.49.
38 Aur. Vict. *Caes.* 33, *Epit.* 34; SHA *Claud.* 5; Zos. 1.40.1; Cavalieri-Manasse and Bruno 2003: 51; De Bois 1976: 28; Hudson 1993; Roncaglia 2018: 120-21.

Raetia), cemented the region as part of a new frontier zone.[39]

In addition to the political upheaval taking place in Northern Italy during Late Antiquity, the physical landscape of the region also underwent profound changes during this time, especially regarding the management of water. The drainage channels excavated as part of the centuriation and reclamation of the landscape between the 2nd century BC and 1st century AD needed regular maintenance to be effective. With the centuriated landscape in eastern Emilia-Romagna alone having 20,000km of drainage channels, there was a substantial amount of infrastructure to upkeep across the Po-Veneto Plain.[40] If neglected, drainage channels will fill with sediment, reducing capacity, or become blocked by debris, reducing flow. The failure of only a few channels can be enough to compromise the system. Socio-economic and political pressures from the 3rd century AD onwards likely made it increasingly difficult to maintain the complex network of drainage infrastructure required to protect the land.[41] These were further compounded by climatic changes taking place during this time, which led to increasing hydrological instability across Northern Italy's waterways.[42] For example, during the 5th century AD, backswamp areas between Reggio Emilia, Piacenza, and the Po, were reactivated and transformed into two large marshes known as the Valle di Gualtieri and Valle di Novellara as drainage schemes from the Roman era began to fail.[43] Pollen studies record swamp and woodland returned as common landscape features in low-lying areas during this later period.[44] Field survey further suggests a mass restructuring of the landscape in the post-Roman period, with rural settlement retreating to higher ground above inundation level.[45] In contrast to the Roman era, the region's Late Antique and Early Medieval settlement pattern shows a high correlation with zones of low hydrological risk, suggesting this had become an important factor in site placement.[46]

The impact of the political and environmental instability of Late Antiquity on the Northern Italian economy has been the object of much discussion.[47] A contraction of rural settlement across the landscape of Northern Italy has been recorded both by field survey and archaeological prospection. Already from the 2nd century AD onwards, a slowdown in the construction of new rural sites is evidenced in the archaeological record, alongside the beginnings of functional changes in existing structures.[48] By the 3rd century AD, a progressive abandoning of rural sites, especially at the lower end of the settlement hierarchy, is recorded across Northern Italy. A contraction of the Po Plain's agricultural landscape between the 3rd and 4th century AD is also highlighted by palynological data. The amount of land under cultivation decreased and tree cover increased in comparison to earlier periods, a trend that would continue throughout the 5th and 6th centuries AD.[49] While the abandonment of rural sites across the region during the 3rd and 4th centuries AD could represent economic decline and crisis in the landscape, the picture is likely more complex. Although a level of contraction in the rural economy of Northern Italy seems certain, the abandonment of smaller sites in the settlement hierarchy may not necessarily represent a full collapse of the agricultural system. Instead, it may reflect a reorganisation of the countryside, with smaller properties being consolidated into larger estates.[50] This coincided with the movement of production facilities away from the main residential building and the repurposing of small and medium-sized villas and rural sites for productive activities.[51] While the 3rd and 4th centuries AD would see a transformation of the villa system in Italy, with the consolidation and monumentalisation of some large estates demonstrating considerable wealth, the 5th century AD saw an increase in the number of site abandonments as frameworks or aristocratic life changed, leading to the eventual end of the villa system by the 6th century AD.[52]

The political and military importance of Northern Italy during Late Antiquity saw new initiatives by the state to increase the agricultural and manufacturing productivity of the region. In an effort to support the new garrisons stationed in Northern Italy, attempts were made in the 4th century to bring land that had been abandoned back under cultivation. Auxiliaries

[39] Barnes 1982; Bowman 2005; Giardina 1993; 1997.
[40] Cremonini and Mattioli 2017: 22.
[41] Brogiolo 2015: 49-50; Curtis and Campopiano 2014: 95. Many Roman land divisions and drainage works have been discovered beneath deposits formed by the creation of wetlands. See Page 2022 for a discussion of later water management in the region.
[42] Bini *et al.* 2020: 791; Bosi *et al.* 2018; Cremonini, Labate, and Curina 2013: 170–3; Cremaschi, Storchi, and Perego 2018: 59–60; Finné *et al.* 2019: 858–9; Labuhn *et al.* 2016: 74–81; Page 2022: 171-79.
[43] Brandolini and Cremaschi 2018: 4-6; Dall'Aglio and Franceschelli 2017: 270-74. See also the example of the Modenese hinterland discussed above, alongside the floodplain of the Bacchiglione north of Padua, (Sarabia-Bautista 2017: 83-85).
[44] Bosi *et al.* 2019: 11–12; 2020: 692.
[45] Brandolini and Cremaschi 2018: 3; Brandolini and Carrer 2021: 212, 221; Crosetto 2013; Dall'Aglio and Marchetti 1991, 164.
[46] Brandolini and Cremaschi 2018: 7-10. Significant land reclamation would not begin again until the 10th century AD.

[47] Castrorao Barba 2014a; 2014b; 2023; Christie 2006; Roncaglia 2018; Sfameni 2004; Wickham 2005.
[48] Busana and Forin 2020; Castrorao Barba 2014b; Forin 2017: 231-35. These functional changes often involved the conversion of residential spaces into production areas.
[49] Bosi *et al.* 2015: 28-29; 2018; Caramiello, Fossa, and Arobba 2014: 16-17; Marchesini and Marvelli 2017: 294-95.
[50] Brogiolo and Chavarrìa Arnau 2018: 185-86; Sfameni 2004. The consolidation of land holdings during the 3rd and 4th centuries AD amongst the aristocracy is a phenomenon seen across Late Antique Italy (Castrorao Barba 2023).
[51] Forin 2017: 231-36.
[52] Brogiolo and Chavarría Arnau 2014: 230-31; Castrorao Barba 2014a; 2014b; 2023; Wickham 2005: 174-75.

were settled on this unoccupied land, which included a settlement of Sarmatians in AD 334, and the Goths and Taifali in the 370s.[53] New investment in Northern Italian production and manufacturing, such as the creation of so-called 'arms factories' in urban centres that included Cremona, Julia Concordia, Mantua, Pavia, and Verona, further reflect state initiatives to support troops stationed in the region using local resources.[54] The garrisoning of troops in Northern Italy and the placement of an Imperial capital at Milan in AD 289 also provided new markets for existing landowners and producers in Northern Italy during the 3rd and 4th centuries.[55] The construction of new large granaries and storerooms at villas such as Cairate, Mozambano, Somglia, and Strevi points to the continued productivity of these large estates during Late Antiquity.[56] The monumentalisation of villas such as Desenzano, Faustina di Desenzano, and Palazzo Pignano, in the 4th century AD further attests to the success of elite rural landowners during this period.[57] Although Late Antiquity saw agricultural contraction and landscape degradation within Northern Italy, this did not lead to economic collapse in the region. Northern Italy continued to be productive, and while the aristocratic trappings of the Roman countryside may have slowly disappeared, agricultural continuity is evidenced throughout the subsequent Ostrogothic and Lombard Kingdoms.[58]

Staple Goods: Wine, Cereals, and Oil

The Roman economy was first and foremost an agrarian one, and wine, olive oil, and cereals formed three staple products of the Roman world. Wine and cereals accounted for a key part of Northern Italy's agricultural wealth and were consumed both within the region and exported to extra-regional markets. The evidence for oil production is more complex, with its importance to the region's economy difficult to quantify. While many other commodities, such as fruits, vegetables, and animal products were produced in Northern Italy, it goes beyond the scope of this book to examine the evidence for every type of productive activity occurring in the region during the Roman period. In some cases, such as animal husbandry, the production and trade of textiles, and ceramic building materials (CBM), they have been studied in detail elsewhere.[59] Other products,

such as fineware ceramics and stone will be discussed in detail later in this volume (see Chapters 5 and 6). In the following section, a broad overview of the evidence for wine, oil, and cereal production within Northern Italy is outlined.

Wine

Viniculture formed a major part of Northern Italy's agricultural economy, with numerous ancient sources praising the quantity and quality of the region's wine.[60] A wide variety of wines were produced in Northern Italy, intended for both the table and more rarified consumption. Rhaetic wine, grown in the Eastern Alps in the area between Verona and Aquileia, was praised by ancient writers, with Cato and Strabo describing it as being of comparable quality to the wine of Central Italy and Pliny claiming it was a favourite of the emperor Tiberius.[61] Vineyards around Ravenna and Ariminum were also known for their excellence and the quantity of their output.[62] A method of vine cultivation known as *arbustum gallicum* is believed to have been widely used in Northern Italy during the Roman period.[63] Vines were trained to grow alongside trees such as elm and maple, using the branches to support the fruits as part of a mixed arboriculture to maximise the productivity of land under cultivation.[64] Wine production continued to form an important part of the Late Antique agricultural landscape in Northern Italy, with the processes described in detail by later literary sources writing in the region such as Cassiodorus and Zeno of Verona.[65] Substantial facilities for Late Antique wine production are evidenced at the villa sites of San Pietro in Cariano-Ambrosan and San Pietro in Mattonara.[66] The investment in wine making infrastructure at a new and luxurious villa complex at Negar during the 3rd century AD, during a time when rural settlement was undergoing increasing contraction across Northern

---

2018: 89-100), while Forin 2017 catalogues archaeological evidence for sheep rearing and shearing, for example the villa at Roncade-Ca' Tron close to Altinum (Busana *et al.* 2012) and the villa at Dal Molin (Gamba, Raimondi, and Rigoni 2012). The extensive evidence for the production of CBM, especially in the north-east of Northern Italy, is well-documented (Capulli 2023; Glicksman 2005; Wilkes 1979).

[53] Amm. Marc. 31.9; *Exc. Val.* 6.

[54] *Not. Dign. Occ.* 6.

[55] Brogiolo and Chavarría Arnau 2014: 227-28; 2018: 184-86.

[56] Forin 2017: 153-65; Mariotti 2014: 115-20; Quercia, Semeraro, and Barello 2015: 154-55.

[57] Brogiolo and Chavarría Arnau 2014: 230-31; Sfameni 2004.

[58] Castrorao Barba 2023: 33-35; Wickham 2005: 174-75.

[59] For discussions on the Roman impact on animal husbandry in the region, see MacKinnon 2010; Trentacoste *et al.* 2021. The Cisalpine wool and textile trade was the subject of a major conference and book a number of years ago (Busana and Basso 2012). Elsewhere, networks of textile producers in Northern Italy (*collegia centonariora*) have been reconstructed though epigraphy (Liu 2009; Roncaglia

[60] Cato *Orig.* 43; Colum. *Rust.* 3.3.2; 3.13.8; Hrdn. 8.2.3-4; Str. 5.1.12; Varro *Rust.* 1.2.7. See Piccoli 2004 for a summary of the literary evidence. It has been estimated that the coastal hinterland between Trieste and Ancona alone could have produced an annual surplus of 100,000 tonnes of wine (Ugolini 2021: 91).

[61] Cato *Ad Marcum Filium*, c.f. Serv., *In Georg.* 2.95; Mart. *Ep.* 14.100.1-2; Plin. *HN* 14.16, 14.67; Str. 4.6.8; Virgil *G.* 2.95-96.

[62] Plin. *HN* 14.3; 17.35; Varro *Rust.* 1.7.2.

[63] Colum. *Rust.* 3.2.17-24; 5.6.5; 5.6.24; 5.71; Plin. *HN* 14.3; 17.35; Varro *Rust.* 1.7.2; Virgil *G.* 2.217-21; 2.277-78. Cereal crops might also be grown amongst the trees and vines.

[64] Braconi 2009; Marchesini *et al.* 2024: 108-09. Archaeobotanical evidence for *arbustum gallicum* has been recovered from several sites in Emilia Romagna.

[65] Cassiod. *Var.* 12.22.1-3; 12.26.3; Zeno of Verona *Tractatus* 2.27.2; Rossiter 2008.

[66] Busana 2002: 344-50; 2003: 119, 125.

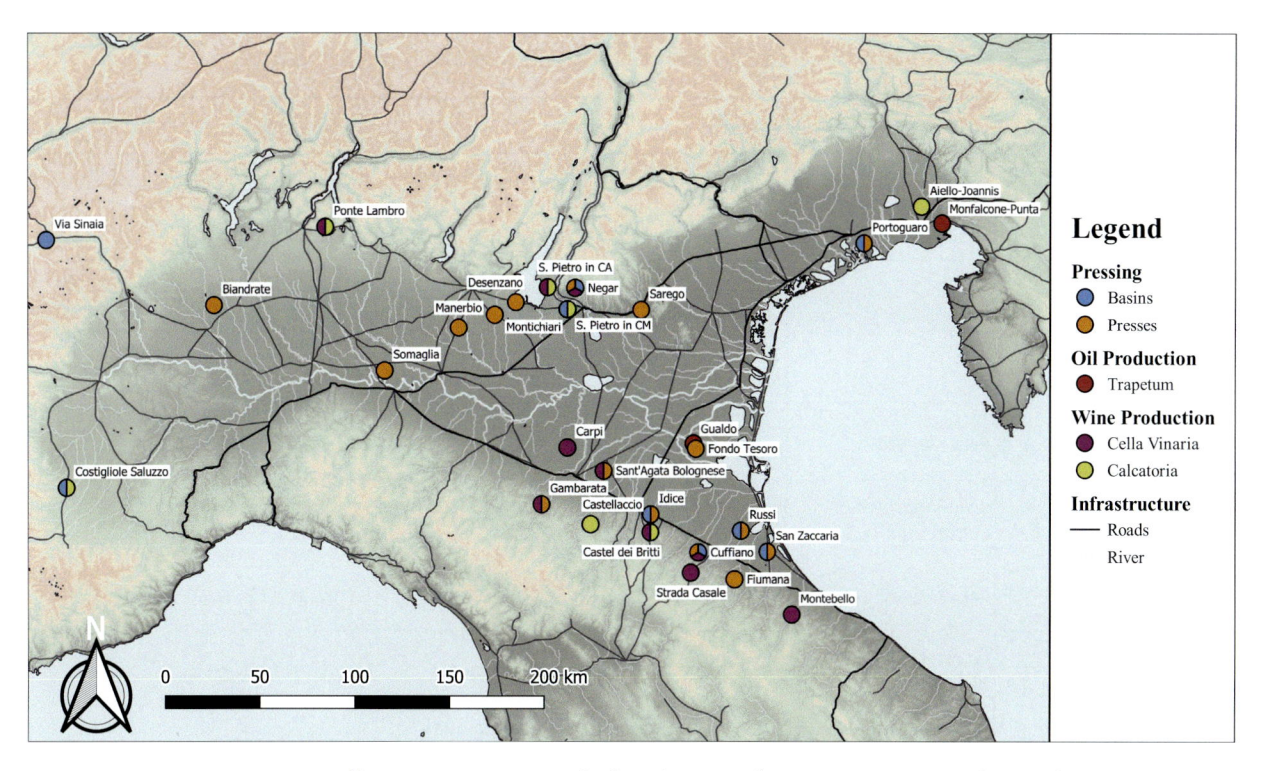

Figure 11. Map of known Roman wine and oil production infrastructure across Northern Italy.

Italy, points to the economic resilience of the wine-producing landscape around Verona.[67]

Despite the importance of viniculture in Northern Italy during the Roman period, the extent and organisation of wine production in the region remain understood to a lesser extent than the rest of the Italian Peninsula. In recent years, there have been attempts to move beyond traditional archaeological approaches in studying wine production.[68] In the past, the physical remains of pressing, settling, and fermentation infrastructure, such as *calcatoria*, *cellae vinariae*, basins, and *torcularia*, formed the primary method of identifying wine production at a site. However, this approach is subject to limitations. The use of organic materials for pressing and fermentation infrastructure means that wine production may not leave traces in the archaeological record. Furthermore, press beds and basins could have been used for either wine or oil production, meaning that without other infrastructure (for example a *cella vinaria* for fermentation or a *trapetum* for olive crushing), it is impossible to assign a function either way. A new range of analytical techniques has opened new avenues of study for ancient viniculture, expanding the available evidence for researchers. Archaeobotany, DNA analysis, palynology, and residue analysis have all increased scholarly understanding of viticulture and viniculture

across the ancient world. Used in combination, a more nuanced picture of wine production in Northern Italy can be developed.

Despite the importance of wine production in Northern Italy amongst literary sources, evidence for the infrastructure involved in wine pressing remains surprisingly limited. In comparison to Central Italy, where hundreds of villa sites are known to have been equipped with presses, only 14 known villa sites from Northern Italy have so-far returned evidence of *torcularia* (see Figure 11 and Table 6).[69] Of these, only four contain other infrastructure (*cellae vinariae*) to confirm they were involved in wine production, leaving open the possibility the others were used for oil pressing. Treading floors scarcely fare better, with only eight known *calcatoria* surviving. Even accounting for factors such as preservation and discovery, the number of villas with surviving wine-making infrastructure seems low in comparison to elsewhere in Roman Italy. In particular, the west of the Po Valley and the area around the Langhe and Monferrato hills, has returned limited examples. Regional production practices and preservation conditions in the archaeological record may help to account for the paucity of visible wine-making infrastructure in Northern Italy. In parts of

---

[67] Basso, Dobreva, and de Zuccato 2024: 97-99.
[68] Dodd 2022; Dodd and Van Limbergen 2024; McGovern 2024; Van Limbergen 2024.

[69] Marzano 2007: Chapter 4. A minimum of 169 sites equipped with presses are known to have existed in the hinterland of Rome alone (Marzano 2013: 88-91), while 55 have been identified in Marche and Northern Abruzzo (Van Limbergen 2019).

Table 6. Rural sites with surviving evidence of wine or oil production in Northern Italy.

Site	Infrastructure	Presses	Dating	Bibliography
Aiello-Joannis	*Calcatorium*		1st Century AD	Busana 2002; Forin 2017: UD-10
Aosta-via Sinaia	Basin		1st Century AD	Forin 2017: AO-01
Bagnacavallo		2	2nd Century BC – 3rd Century AD	Franceschelli and Marabini 2007: 193-94, n.268
Biandrate		1-2 (Lever and Screw)	1st Century AD	Forin 2017: NO-04
Carpi	*Cella Vinaria*		1st Century BC – 5th Century AD	Lenzi 2006: 381-83
Castel di Britti	*Cella Vinaria* and *Calcatorium*		2nd Century BC – 6th Century AD	Lenzi and Nenzioni 2016
Castellaccio	*Calcatorium*		1st Century AD – 4th Century AD	Ficara and Manzelli 2008
Costigliole Saluzzo	*Calcatorium* and Basins		Mid-1st Century AD	Forin 2017: CN-01
Cuffiano	*Cella Vinaria* and Basins	1	2nd Century BC – 6th Century AD	Guarnieri 2007
Desenzano-Borgo Regio		1 (Possible millstone)	Mid-1st Century AD	Forin 2017: BS-18
Fondo Tesoro		1	1st Century AD – 4th Century AD	Uggeri 2002: 238-41, n.201
Gambarata	*Cella Vinaria*	1 (Lever)	25 BC – 2nd Century BC	Maldini 2004
Gualdo	*Trapetum?*		Roman	Uggeri 2002: 228, n.191
Idice (via Castiglia)	Basins	1	1st Century BC – 2nd Century AD	Lenzi and Nenzioni 2016
Manerbio		1 (Lever)	1st Century AD	Forin 2017: BS-03
Monfalcone-Punta	*Trapetum*		1st Century AD	Forin 2017: GO-09
Montebello	*Cella Vinaria*		1st Century BC – 3rd Century AD	Lenzi and Nenzioni 2016
Montichiari-Colombara Monti		1	1st Century AD	Forin 2017: BS-07
Negar	*Calcatorium* and Basin	1	Late Antiquity	Basso, Dobreva, and de Zuccato 2024
Ponte Lambro	*Calcatorium* and *Cella Vinaria*		1st Century AD – 3rd Century AD	Arioldi *et al.* 2016
Portogruaro-Marina di Lugugnana	Basin	1	1st Century AD	Forin 2017: VE-06
Russi	Basin	1	1st Century BC – 4th Century AD	Franceschelli and Marabini 2007: 194, n.270
San Pietro in Cariano-Ambrosan	*Calcatorium* and Basin		1st Century AD – 6th Century AD	Busana 2002; 2003; Forin 2017: VR-04
San Pietro in Cariano-Mattonara	*Calcatorium* and *Cella Vinaria*		1st Century AD – 5th Century AD	Busana 2002; 2003; Forin 2017: VR-05

Site	Infrastructure	Presses	Dating	Bibliography
San Zaccaria	Basins	1	1st Century BC – 3rd Century AD	Ficara and Manzelli 2008
Sarego		1	Roman	Giarolo 1910
Somaglia		1	1st Century BC	Forin 2017: LO-01
St. Agata Bolognese	*Cella Vinaria*	1 (Screw)	1st Century BC – 3rd Century AD	Trocchi *et al.* 2014
Strada Casale	*Cella Vinaria*		1st Century AD – 6th Century AD	Montevecchi 2003

the region, production infrastructure such as pressing floors and settling basins, may have been constructed out of organic materials, making them largely invisible in the archaeological record.[70] The use of wooden barrels for the storage of wine in Northern Italy is also well-attested by ancient literary sources.[71] As wine could be fermented in the barrels themselves, this removed the need for a traditional *cella vinaria* utilising *dolia defossa*. Away from presses, basins, and *cellae vinariae*, infrastructure not traditionally associated with wine production may give further indication of viniculture. Recent work has brought to light evidence of *fumaria* (rooms that were equipped with a heating element) that may have functioned to aid in the fermentation of the wine, keeping it above a certain temperature and producing a product of distinctive taste.[72]

Given the patchiness of surviving production infrastructure, other evidence provides an indication of the extent of viticulture within the region. Archaeobotany has produced evidence of wine production at sites across Northern Italy without surviving pressing and fermenting infrastructure. While in some cases it is impossible to know whether grapes were being grown for consumption or wine production, the archaeobotanical and palynological evidence confirms the extensive cultivation of vines across Northern Italy.[73] At the site of Casteldebole, near Bologna, a large deposit of grape pomace (residue from the pressing) was discovered from a pit at the site, while at the villa of Sant'Agata Bolognese numerous

grape seeds were recovered from the area surrounding its *torcular*, confirming in both cases the presence of wine production at these sites.[74] Grapes rank amongst the most common taxa recovered from Roman sites in Northern Italy and were present across the region from the Adriatic Coast to the far western Po Valley.[75] The distribution of remains further indicates viticulture was not just limited to the hillsides but also took place on the plain. For example, archaeobotanical finds from a storage pit at the Late Antique settlement of Badia Polesine, near modern Rovigo, confirm the presence of grapevines even in the areas closest to the Po.[76] The expanding body of evidence for grape cultivation across Northern Italy, from the coast to the mountains, attests to their importance as part of the region's agricultural economy, confirming the picture outlined by the literary sources of a region where high-quality wine was produced in significant quantities.

Cereals

Along with wine, cereals are one of the main foodstuffs highlighted by ancient authors as a major agricultural output of Northern Italy. The agronomists praise the abundance of cereal crops in Northern Italy, with both Varro and Cicero commenting on the scale of agricultural production in the Po Valley.[77] So great was the region's output, Polybius claims that the price of a single Sicilian *medimnus* (approximately 52 litres) of wheat grown in Northern Italy was a mere four *obols*, and that of barley two *obols*, a considerable bargain.[78] Pliny the Younger, in a letter to his friend Julius Naso (*c.* 100 AD), talks about the rich cereal output of his estates in Northern Italy compared to those of his estates in

---

[70] At the Ponte Lambro Villa, for example, two circular foundations are interpreted to have supported wooden fermentation tanks (Arioldi *et al.* 2016: 178-79).

[71] Plin. *HN* 14.27; Str. 5.1.12.

[72] Busana 2002: 187; (forthcoming); Dodd 2022: 468; Plin. *HN* 14.27. Colum. (*Rust.* 1.6.19) references these rooms as *apothecae*, which could also be located above or adjacent to already heated spaces such as baths and kitchens. *Fumaria/apothecae* that may have been linked to wine production are known at the villa sites of Biandrate, Prasco, and San Pietro in Cariano-Ambrosan, although more work is needed to confirm the extent and mechanisms of their use (Forin 2017: 143-47).

[73] For example, Pliny (*HN* 14.34) records a type of grape called *Spionia* (perhaps the modern Nebbiolo) grown in the hinterland of Ravenna that was particularly suited for preservation in jars.

[74] Bandini Mazzanti *et al.* 1995; Marchesini *et al.* 2024: 109; Trocchi *et al.* 2014.

[75] Bosi *et al.* 2020. Grape taxa were recovered from 67% of 'A' sites and 59% of 'B' sites in their study.

[76] Malaguti *et al.* 2011; Marchesini *et al.* 2024: 109. Pliny (*HN* 14.67) also refers to vines being grown around the territory of Adria in the lower Po Valley.

[77] Cato *Orig.* 43; Cic. *Verr.* 3.110; Colum. *Rust.* 3.3.2; 3.13.8; Varro *Rust.* 1.2.7; 1.44.1.

[78] Polyb. 2.15; Ugolini 2023: 91.

Tuscany which were ruined by bad weather.[79] However, he laments that, despite the bountiful harvest, the price for Northern Italian cereals was no better due to the abundance of the crop available in the region. The prominence of cereal crops in ancient discussions of Northern Italian agriculture is not surprising. It has been estimated that the Cisalpine area of Northern Italy alone contains 42% of the total area suitable for cereal cultivation in the Italian Peninsula.[80] Attempts to quantify a potential surplus in cereal production from the coastal hinterland between Trieste and Ancona alone during the Late Republic and Early Imperial periods have produced figures of between 100,000 and 150,000 tonnes per annum.[81] While such figures should be treated with caution, they provide an indication of the region's agricultural potential.

A growing body of archaeobotanical and palynological evidence from Roman and Late Antique rural contexts has allowed the reconstruction of Northern Italy's agricultural landscape in increasing detail.[82] During the Late Republic, sites in the south-east of the Po Plain already show evidence of intensive farming, with cereals, flax, fruit, hemp, pulses, and vegetables all well-attested by palynological data.[83] Amongst the cereal plants grown in Northern Italy during the 3rd to 1st century BC, wheat (*Triticum aestivum/durum*) and barley (*Hordeum vulgare*) were the most common, followed by varieties of millet (*Panicum miliaceum* and *Setaria italica*).[84] Amongst the pulses, the second most commonly attested crop type, fava beans (*Vicia faba*) and lentils (*Lens*) were predominant.[85] The Early Imperial landscape shows signs of increasing intensification of agricultural activity in both the east and the west of the Po Valley, with cereal crops including wheat and barley dominating palynological assemblages.[86] Millet varieties and other minor cereal types were attested in severely reduced quantities, pointing to increasing homogeneity in agricultural practice.[87] In addition to cereals, fruit, pulses, textile plants, and vegetables remain well-represented palynologically, attesting to the variety of agricultural activities taking place and the breadth of output during this period.[88] In Late Antiquity, shifting climatic conditions may have played

a role in changing cultivation habits. Millet varieties such as *Secale* became increasingly large components of assemblages, perhaps due to their resilience to cold temperatures and waterlogged ground.[89] Although the amount of land under cultivation seems to have decreased, it remained significantly higher than in the pre-Roman and Republican periods.

Beyond archaeobotanical and palynological data, extensive remains of the structures for processing and storing cereals survive in Northern Italy. Large courtyards attached to the productive areas of villas and farms have been interpreted as being used to process agricultural products. For example, a new courtyard constructed at the villa of Brandizzo in Piedmont was interpreted as a threshing floor.[90] *Fumaria*, or cereal dryers, are well known from more northerly contexts in the Roman world such as Britain, Gaul, and Germany, but several possible examples have been discovered in Northern Italy in areas north of the Po.[91] Cereal dryers were used to bulk process grains for a variety of purposes, which included easing the removal of husks, preventing spoilage via germination or insect attack, or hardening grain prior to milling.[92] Structures interpreted as storerooms and granaries have been found at sites across the region and took a variety of forms.[93] Evidence for granaries with wooden floors raised up on pillars, used to insulate the cereals from moisture and protect against pests, comes from sites such as Consolata, Isola Vicentina, Prasco, Pordenone, and Rivignano.[94] Others, such as the granaries at Cairate and Isola Vicentina, used a series of long low parallel walls to support the floors above the ground.[95] Buttresses and thick supporting walls at sites such as Castel di Britti and Strevi point to multiple floors for storing goods.[96] While it is impossible to know if these granaries were used solely to house domestic products, a surplus destined for sale, or a combination of the two, the size of some structures suggests they could have held a significant quantity of cereals.

Oil

In comparison to wine and cereals, oil does not receive the same attention in ancient discussions of Northern

[79] Plin. *Ep.* 4.6.

[80] Maiuro 2017: 105-06.

[81] Ugolini 2023: 105-06.

[82] See, for example: Bosi *et al.* 2011; 2015; 2018; 2020; Caramiello, Fossa, and Arobba 2014; Caramiello *et al.* 2014; Marchesini and Marvelli 2017; Marchesini *et al.* 2024; Mercuri *et al.* 2015.

[83] Bosi *et al.* 2020: 691; Marchesini and Marvelli 2017: 291-92.

[84] Bosi *et al.* 2020: 691. Bosi *et al.* 2020 combines archaeobotanical and palynological evidence from over 100 Roman sites in Northern Italy.

[85] Bosi *et al.* 2020: 691.

[86] Bosi *et al.* 2015: 28; 2020; Caramiello, Fossa, and Arobba 2014: 16; Marchesini and Marvelli 2017: 292-93.

[87] Bosi *et al.* 2020: 691. Decreasing cereal crop diversity is a trend seen elsewhere in the Roman world during the Imperial period, perhaps pointing to increasing agricultural specialisation (Lodwick 2017).

[88] Bosi *et al.* 2011; 2015: 28; Marchesini and Marvelli 2017: 293.

[89] Bosi *et al.* 2019; 2020: 692; Cremonini, Labate, and Curina 2013.

[90] Barello and Le Spada 2004: 209-11; Gambari and Barello 2004: 8-19.

[91] Allen and Lodwick 2017; Van der Veen 1989. Possible cereal dryers have been discovered at the sites of, Biandrate, Brandizzo, Cairate, San Pietro in Cariano-Ambrosan, Villabartolomea, and Pordenone (Forin 2017: 143-47).

[92] Van der Veen 1989: 303-04.

[93] Forin 2017: 153-65 provides a detailed summary of the evidence for granaries and storerooms that could have housed cereals within Northern Italy.

[94] Busana 2002: 302-04, 337-38; Filippi and Roncaglio 1999; Maggi and Prenc 1990: 392-94; Mollo Mezzana 1982: 283-91.

[95] Busana 2002: 302-04; Facchinetti 2014; Mariotti 2014.

[96] Lenzi and Nenzioni 2016; Quercia, Semerano, and Barello 2015.

Italian agriculture.[97] Perhaps the quality of Northern Italian oil did not stand out in the same way as did the region's wine, or perhaps it was not produced in the same quantities as the cereals grown across the Po Plain. The areas of Northern Italy north of the Po are close to the geographic limit of optimum conditions for olive trees.[98] While this does not stop the growth of olive trees, it does make attaining consistently high levels of productivity difficult, leading to suggestions that oil production in Northern Italy may have been primarily for regional consumption, rather than producing a surplus for export.[99] In contrast, Istria, on the eastern coast of the Adriatic, formed a major oil-producing region and was responsible for producing a considerable surplus for export.

Olives are recorded by archaeobotanical data, although the high presence of intact seeds may suggest they were intended for consumption, rather than pressing.[100] In the area of the modern Veneto and Friuli-Giulia, pollen evidence for *Olea europaea* (the European Olive) has been discovered in Roman contexts from the Alpine foothills around Lake Garda and the Veneto Plain, alongside some low-lying contexts near the Venice lagoon system, although it formed a minor part of assemblages.[101] The surviving evidence for oil production infrastructure has been outlined in the previous section (see Figure 11 and Table 6). As with wine production, a similar paucity of physical evidence survives for oil production in Northern Italy. Only two sites securely dated to the Roman period, Gualdo and Monfalcone-Punta, record evidence for *trapeta* for the crushing of olives prior to pressing.[102] More sites contain evidence of presses, but without other infrastructure, it is impossible to determine if they were being used for wine or oil production.[103] Again, as with viniculture, oil production in the region may have made greater use of pressing infrastructure constructed of organic materials that do not survive in the archaeological record, masking the full extent of production.[104]

Although the evidence for the physical production of oil in Northern Italy is somewhat limited, the vessels that may have been used to transport oil have been recovered both within the region and elsewhere. The Dressel 6B, the principal Adriatic oil-bearing amphora during the Early Imperial period, is found widely across Northern Italy, Pannonia, and Moesia. Most Dressel 6Bs were produced in Istria, although archaeometric analysis of Dressel 6B fabrics suggests there was some Northern Italic production in the area of the modern Veneto and Friuli Giulia (although no kiln sites have been found).[105] Prominent Cisalpine aristocratic families and individuals, such as the Apicii, L. Trebius Optatus, the Paetinii, P. Petronius, and the Sepullii are attested by stamps on Dressel 6Bs.[106] Distribution maps of Dressel 6B oil amphora bearing Northern Italian stamps primarily suggest regional consumption within Northern Italy, although some sporadic examples are recorded within Panonnia and along the *Limes*.[107] However, Cisalpine production of the Dressel 6B amphora form seems to have dropped off by the middle of the 1st century AD, leaving Istria as the main production zone.[108] A morphological variant of the Dressel 6B, the so-called 'Anfora con Collo ad Imbuto', would also see widespread circulation across Northern Italy from the mid-1st century AD, with archaeometric analysis of fabrics suggesting a coastal production zone in modern Emilia-Romagna and Marche.[109] However, relying on amphorae as a marker of oil production and distribution can be problematic and is subject to limitations. While the Dressel 6B is traditionally attributed as an oil-bearing amphora, there is no guarantee this was always the primary use of the vessel. Finds of Dressel 6B amphorae marked by *tituli picti* as carrying the fish products *liquamen* and *lymphatum* have been recovered from contexts in Northern Italy and elsewhere.[110] While it is unknown if these fish products formed the primary cargo of the amphorae or if the vessels had been refilled, they serve to demonstrate that amphora forms cannot be taken as an accurate indicator of the contents' production and distribution.

Exports: Northern Italic Produce in the Roman World

The productivity of Northern Italy during the Roman period allowed it to generate a significant surplus of agricultural and manufactured products. These were traded and consumed both within the region and further afield, carried via the region's extensive transport network to points of consumption and redistribution. While the distribution and consumption

---

[97] Buonpane 2009; Busana, D'Inca, and Forti 2009: 35.

[98] Busana, D'Inca, and Forti 2009: 36; Ferusin and Tonutti 2002; Marcaccini 1973.

[99] Van Limbergen 2016: 176.

[100] Bosi *et al.* 2020: 689-91.

[101] Busana, D'Inca, and Forti 2009: 38.

[102] Forin 2017: 700; Uggeri 2002: 228.

[103] Additional uncontexted evidence for *trapeta* and presses exists from Northern Italy. Individual examples of press beds, foundations for *arbores*, and *trapetum* grind stones have been recovered from across the region. However, without contexts they are impossible to firmly assign to the Roman or Early Medieval periods (Forin 2017: 132-33).

[104] Busana, D'Inca, and Forti 2009: 41; Rossiter 1981: 348-49. More extensive fieldwork may uncover new evidence for both oil and wine production in Northern Italy (Van Limbergen 2016: 177).

[105] Maritan, Mazzoli, and Mazzocchin 2019; Cipriano *et al.* 2020. Production seems to have been mainly concentrated along the coastal plain between Emilia Romagna and Friuli-Giulia.

[106] Cipriano and Mazzocchin 2000; 2002.

[107] Cipriano and Mazzocchin 2000; 2002; Cipriano *et al.* 2020.

[108] Cipriano and Mazzocchin 2012; 2019; Cipriano *et al.* 2020.

[109] Maritan, Mazzoli, and Mazzocchin 2019; Mazzocchin 2009; Van Limbergen 2016: 176-77.

[110] Cipriano 2009: 173; Van Neer, Ervynck, and Monsieur 2010: 163-66.

of imports and local produce within Northern Italy itself will be explored in detail over the following chapters, an overview of how regional products were exported, and the markets they were consumed, in provides an important point of comparison.

Export Vectors: By Land and Sea

Surrounded on three sides by mountains and the other the Adriatic, Northern Italy was reliant on trans-mountain and maritime routes to import and export goods to and from the region. Maritime routes provided the cheapest and fastest way of carrying bulk cargoes, with major investment in port infrastructure across the Mediterranean world attesting to the importance of these networks in regional and extra-regional trade.[111] Significant maritime and terrestrial infrastructure was constructed at Adriatic port sites.[112] In Northern Italy, Altinum, Ariminum, Aquileia, and Ravenna formed the region's major commercial ports on the Adriatic Coast, with smaller satellite harbours at Brundulum, Equilium, Grado, Julia Concordia, and Eraclea creating a sophisticated and interconnected port system.[113] Other cities close to the coast, such as Adria, Butrium, Oderzo, and Padua, may also have supported limited maritime trade.[114] Using both maritime and canal routes, Northern Italian produce could be moved between ports within the Adriatic network, before being exported to extra-regional markets. Across the Apennines, there were the major ports of Genoa and Luna, which sat on the Ligurian Coast and were integrated into Western Mediterranean markets.[115] Along the Ligurian coastline, there were other, smaller harbours, at places such as Impera and Savona, but neither formed important commercial hubs during the Roman period. The low quantities of surviving Northern Italic goods present at Ligurian ports suggest they were not the main export vectors for the region's produce, although goods such as textiles destined for Rome may have utilised this route.

Within the Northern Adriatic, Aquileia formed an important regional hub, especially for goods heading north or east. Herodian, writing in the 3rd century AD, described the city as the Adriatic's 'port of entry for Italy', with the city's extensive fluvial and terrestrial infrastructure making it possible for goods 'transported from the interior by land or by the rivers to be traded to the merchant mariners, and also for the necessities brought by sea to the mainland, and goods not produced there because of the cold climate, to be sent to the upland areas'.[116] Aquileia possessed a large fluvial port located on the western and eastern banks of the Natisone River, equipped with monumental quays, warehouses, and other infrastructure necessary for the docking, loading, and unloading, of ships, alongside the storage of goods (see Figure 12).[117] The fluvial port was connected to the sea by both the Natisone and a canal (the so-called 'Canale d'Anfora'), enabling ocean-going vessels to navigate to the port.[118] To the south-west, on the shores of the Venetian Lagoon system, sat the port of Altinum. While recorded as an important harbour town in various ancient sources and forming the northern terminus of the 1st century AD para-littoral canal system (see Chapter 2), the layout and infrastructure of Altinum's port remains relatively unknown.[119] The city's main maritime port may have been located along the edges of the Venetian Lagoon close to Treporti, where remains of quays and harbour walls have been found.[120] The maritime port would have been connected to the main settlement via a system of navigable canals, which are shown to have criss-crossed the city.[121]

Further down the coast, Ravenna, located on a lagoonal basin amongst the coastal mashes, was an important port for produce originating from the Po Valley. Ravenna's connection to the River Po via the para-littoral canal system linked it to Northern Italy's inland waterways, enabling the seamless transition of goods travelling via river to the maritime port without adding an additional overland leg to the journey.[122] The *Fossa Augusta* ran through the middle of the Ravenna, linking to the basin and enabling its use by fluvio-maritime vessels. Extensive evidence for port infrastructure such as quays, moles, canals, and warehouses has been discovered in the area surrounding the modern city.[123] The entrance to the basin was protected by two moles, and to the south of the main city sat Classis, home to a fleet of warships and the main maritime harbour (see Figure 13). Ariminum, located to the south of Ravenna and disconnected from the Po-Veneto water network, was not integrated into Northern Italian trade networks in the same way as Altinum, Aquileia, and Ravenna were. Nevertheless, Ariminum's port likely formed an important export centre for goods such as Forlimpopoli-type amphorae produced in the area of modern Emilia-Romagna.[124]

---

[111] Scheidel 2014.

[112] See Ugolini 2021 for a summary of the archaeological remains of port infrastructure in the Northern Adriatic between Aquileia and Ariminum.

[113] Rousse 2013; Uggeri 1978; Ugolini 2021: 50-54.

[114] Str. 5.1.7-8.

[115] Bruno 1998; Melli 2004; Melli and Pasquinucci 1998.

[116] Hrdn. 8.2.3-4.

[117] Bertacchi 1980; 1990; Reddé 1986: 216-17; Ugolini 2021: 54-62.

[118] Beltrame and Gaddi 2013; Gaddi 2017.

[119] Vel. Pat. 2.76; Mozzi et al. 2016: 30; Ugolini 2021: 74.

[120] Cipriano 1999; Cresci Marrone and Tirelli 2011.

[121] Mozzi et al. 2016; Tirelli 2001: 298-300; Uggeri 1978.

[122] See Chapter 2 for more discussion of the para-littoral canal system.

[123] Augenti 2011; Grazia Maioli 1990; 2018; Manzelli 2000; Ugolini 2021: 62-70.

[124] Ugolini 2015: 245-46; 2021.

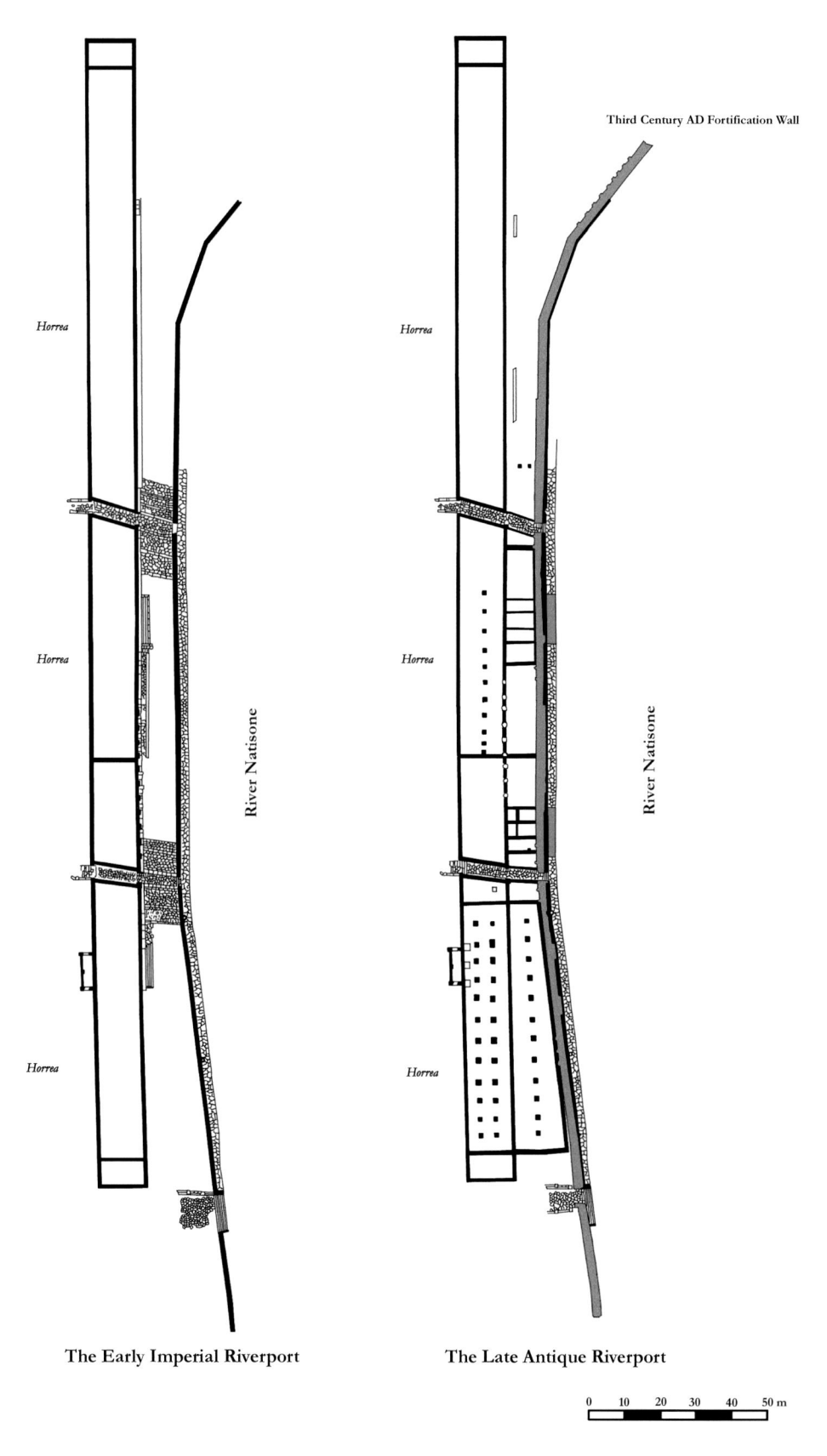

The Early Imperial Riverport

The Late Antique Riverport

Figure 12. Plan of the fluvial port at Aquileia in the Early Imperial and Late Antique periods (redrawn from Bertacchi 1980: Fig. 2).

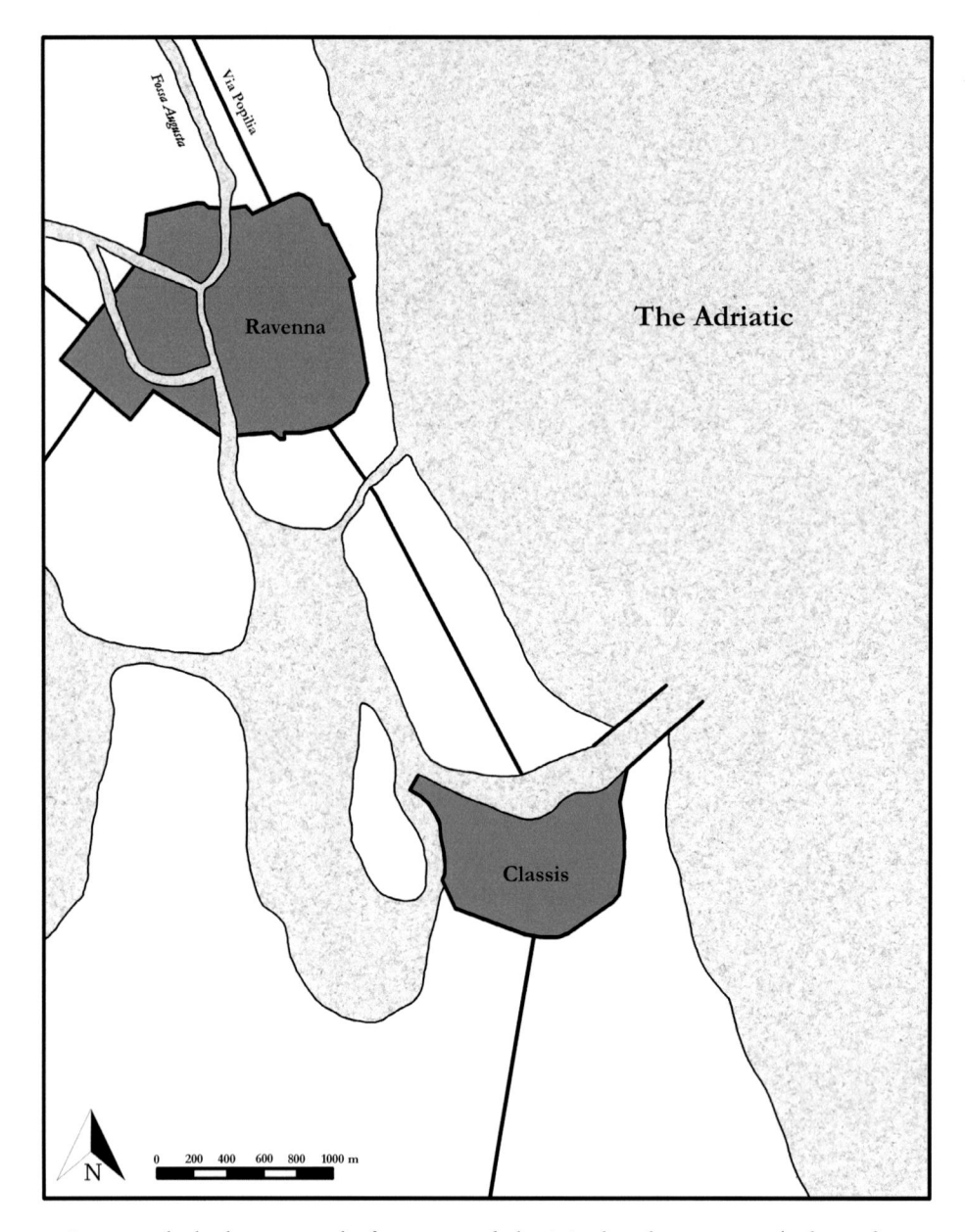

Figure 13. The harbour network of Ravenna and Classis in the 5th century AD (redrawn from Augenti 2011: Fig. 1.1.6).

Of the four major ports outlined above, Aquileia and Ravenna arguably formed the two most important commercial centres on the Northern Adriatic Coast, remaining in operation long after other harbours went into decline.[125] Although Aquileia had been founded in 181 BC and a port at Ravenna is attested from the early 1st century BC, the creation of commercial hubs along the Adriatic Coast intensified during the early principate, in part linked to military operations in Noricum, Pannonia, and Illyricum during the Augustan period.[126]

Aquileia's port, good road connections, and proximity to the conflict made it an important supply base to support these actions. In the same period, Ravenna saw the foundation of its satellite Classis to house a new fleet base and the creation of a new connection to the Po via the *Fossa Augusta*. Both Aquileia and Ravenna would flourish during the Imperial period, seeing growth as urban centres and receiving continued investment in infrastructure.[127] Their importance was not diminished in Late Antiquity. At Aquileia, the use of the river port persisted until at least the 5th century AD, attested by new constructions and renovations of warehouses and a

---

[125] While Altinum is still recorded as being an important urban centre in the 4th century AD, it had already entered into a period of decline by the 3rd century (Dankers 2011; Mozzi *et al.* 2016; Tirelli 2001).
[126] Lilli 1998: 18-35. Aquileia contains the earliest known *portoria* stations in Northern Italy dating to the mid-1st century BC (Cic. *Font.*

---

2), attesting to its growing importance as an entrepôt for goods.
[127] Bertachhi 1980; 1990; Manzelli 2000; Ugolini 2021a.

possible market.[128] The placing of an imperial capital at Ravenna in AD 402 brought the city to new prominence and ensured the continued prosperity of its port. The discovery of warehouses and amphora dumps at Classis dating to between the 5th and 8th centuries AD attests to the strong trade connections the city had with wider Mediterranean markets, especially those in the Eastern Mediterranean and North Africa, highlighting the continued importance of Ravenna and its satellite as regional entrepôts during Late Antiquity.[129]

While maritime routes provided connections across the Mediterranean world and beyond, overland routes from Aquileia into the Danubian provinces formed another significant export vector, both for goods produced within Northern Italy and for import redistribution. Aquileia sat at the intersection of several major roads which included the via Annia, the via Gemina, and the via Postumia, and formed the terminus of the overland Amber Road from the Baltic Sea.[130] The via Geminia in particular formed an important trunk road for products travelling eastwards for Aquileia towards Pannonia and Moesia. The headwaters of the Ljubljanica River were a short journey from Aquileia along the via Gemina, and merchants would transport their goods via wagon to the town of Nauportus (modern Vrhnika in Slovenia), where they could then be transhipped onto river craft.[131] From there, it was a downstream journey to the River Sava, and then onwards to the Danube and the major markets along the *Limes*.[132] Alternatively, goods could continue travelling overland along the via Gemina to reach Emona, either joining the water network there or heading northwards along the Amber Road towards Carnuntum and Vienna. The interest in these overland and fluvial routes amongst Aquileian merchants is confirmed by surviving epigraphy along their paths. The example of L. Tettienus Vitalis has been discussed in the previous chapter, but other prominent Aquileian families such as the Anii, Marcii, and Titii are attested at Nauportus, Emona, and along the road to Carnuntum between the 1st and 2nd centuries AD.[133]

Looking to the south, several overland routes existed between Northern Italy and the rest of the Italian Peninsula, although all involved crossing the Apennines.

Ariminum sat at the northern end of the via Flaminia, which connected Northern Italy with Rome and formed an important conduit for early trade between the capital and the north.[134] Other trans-Apennine roads included the via Postumia, between Tortona and Genoa, a road between Luna and Parma, a road between Bologna and Florence, and a road between Faventina and Florence.[135] While there is evidence for the transport of cargoes of amphorae and fineware ceramics across some of these routes, this was only able to occur under very specific circumstances (discussed in detail in Chapters 4 and 5). In many cases, maritime routes may have been quicker and more economical to move produce either elsewhere in Italy, or to extra-provincial markets.

Export Destinations: Mediterranean Markets

Northern Italian products saw export and consumption across the Roman world, carried upon intra and extra-provincial trade networks. Consumables and commodities were distributed in areas close to Northern Italy and further afield, supplying a variety of needs and demands across the Empire. The best surviving evidence for Northern Italic exports comes from ceramics, especially amphorae, NITS, and CBM, which have been recovered in large quantities. Despite their attested importance in the literary sources, the lack of surviving archaeological evidence for perishable products such as cereals and textiles makes it difficult to trace their export. However, tracking the distribution of other, more archaeologically visible Northern Italic exports such as NITS, Forlimpopoli-type amphorae, and CBM can serve as a proxy for perishable goods, providing an indication of how other products travelling alongside them may have been distributed and consumed.

The wider Adriatic area formed an immediate market for Northern Italic produce, and analysis of maritime sailing routes and shipwreck data has revealed evidence for sophisticated networks of direct trade and redistribution between major and minor ports in the region.[136] Cargoes of CBM from production sites in Northern Italy, such as the one carried by the Stella 1 wreck, formed a significant product destined for regional consumption and were compiled for export at major ports such as Aquileia.[137] Brick stamps from workshops located in the area of modern Friuli-Giulia have been discovered at sites across Istria, Dalmatia, and in maritime wrecks within the Northern Adriatic.[138]

128 Bertacchi 1990; Carre and Maselli Scotti 2001: 218; Ugolini 2021a: 60-62.
129 Augenti and Cirelli 2010; 2012: 207; Cirelli 2013b; Grazia Maioli 1986: 162.
130 Bekljanov Zidanšek, Vojaković, and Žerjal 2022; Donev 2024.
131 Str. 4.6.10; 7.5.2. Strabo implies that this route was active as early as the 2nd century BC. Nauportus seems to have come under Roman control by the mid-1st century BC, and extensive remains of the river port and associated *horrea* have been discovered (Horvat 2008; 2017).
132 The remains of two Roman barges, one of which (the Lipe) had a cargo capacity of approximately 40 tonnes, have been discovered along the Ljubljanica. The barges date from between the late 2nd century BC and early 1st century AD (Čufar, Merela, and Erič 2014; Gaspari 1998; 2021: 126-27).
133 Gabucci and Mennella 2003; Gregoratti 2012; 2014; 2015.

134 Curina *et al.* 2015.
135 Gori 2003: 374; Gottarelli 1988.
136 McLean 2022; McLean and Rubio-Campillo 2022; Ugolini 2021a: 81-85.
137 Castro and Capulli 2016; Capulli 2023; Mondin 2022.
138 Glicksman 2005; Wilkes 1979. Indeed, a third of all stamped bricks in Dalmatia are thought to have come from Northern Italy. See Jurišić 2000 for a catalogue of CBM wrecks from the Adriatic, alongside more recent findings from the Illyrian Coastal Exploration Program in

Based on the distribution of exported material, McLean theorises a triangular maritime trading system in Northern Adriatic, where ships carrying cargoes of CBM and other Northern Italic products first travelled to ports in Istria, where they were partially unloaded and took on additional cargo.[139] They then travelled south to Dalmatia, where remaining Northern Italic and Istrian products were exchanged for local or extra-regional products compiled at major Dalmatian emporia, before completing their journey by returning to Northern Italian ports. Alongside CBM, Northern Italic wine, cereals, and other products were likely traded along these routes, both as singular and mixed cargoes.[140]

Further afield, Rome also formed an important destination for Northern Italic produce, the growing demands of the city pulling in goods from across the Roman world. Textiles, which Northern Italy produced in a variety of styles and qualities, are emphasised as a major export to the capital.[141] Strabo praises 'the quantities of manufactured goods which Patavium sends to Rome to market – clothing of all sorts and many other things'.[142] Consumables also represented important exports to the capital. It has been estimated that Northern Italy and the Adriatic area more widely may have contributed as much as 17% of Rome's annual wine supply in the years leading up to the Antonine plague.[143] Northern Italic wine amphorae are well-attested in Rome archaeologically.[144] In the Emporium district, hundreds of complete Northern Italian and Adriatic amphorae (mainly Dessel 6As) were recycled in the construction of a series of warehouses dating to the 2nd century AD.[145] Pork also seems to have been a major Northern Italian export, with both Strabo and Polybius concurring that large quantities of Cisalpine pork were consumed in Rome and other areas of Italy.[146] Zooarchaeological data has shown Cisalpine swine to have increased in size between the Iron Age and Roman period, and to have been larger than Central Italian pigs during Late Antiquity.[147] Northern Italian swine may have been butchered and preserved before transport to the capital, or herds may have been driven overland before slaughter at the point of consumption.

One of the largest markets for Northern Italian exports were the armies and communities located along the Danubian Limes to the east. The garrisons along the frontier required food, raw materials, and

commodities, many of which Northern Italy was in a position to provide. The most archaeologically visible Northern Italic export along the Limes is NITS, which is found in significant quantities at military and civilian sites in Pannonia and Moesia.[148] Although both maritime and overland routes could be used to reach the frontier, the distribution of NITS between Northern Italy and the Danubian Limes suggests that an overland and fluvial route, rather than a maritime one, was used to export fineware from the region. Findspots of NITS are located along the primary roadways and rivers that cross the Julian Alps and the Nanos Plateau (see Chapter 5 for more details). Alongside NITS, the main Northern Italian product that may have been consumed in significant quantities along the Limes was cereals. Although tracing the export and consumption of cereals in antiquity requires a degree of guesswork, the armies stationed along the Danubian Limes represented a large potential market for Northern Italian food products.[149] Frumentarii are attested at Aquileia, and these soldiers may have been involved in the procurement of cereals to feed garrisons stationed in the vicinity of Northern Italy.[150] While frontier areas saw agricultural exploitation and formed an important source of food for the garrisons and communities within them, extra-regional production still represented a significant part of military and civilian supply. In the wider Mediterranean, the Adriatic naturally orients Northern Italy's maritime connections towards the Eastern Mediterranean, something reflected in the wider distribution of Northern Italic goods across the Roman world. Strong ties are evidenced between the Eastern Mediterranean and Northern Italy through the amphora data (see Chapter 4), and Northern Italic products may have formed return cargoes for vessels transporting Aegean wine to the Northern Adriatic during the late 1st and 2nd century AD. Forlimpopoli-type amphorae have been found at sites across the Eastern Mediterranean such as Athens and Knossos, as well as the Danube Basin and the wider Black Sea region.[151]

'The Excellence of the Region'

Northern Italy, despite its late incorporation into the Italian Roman sphere, saw extensive agricultural exploitation and investment, becoming an important productive zone of the peninsula. The economic potential of the region was identified and capitalised upon early during Roman expansion, leading to the creation of an intensively farmed agricultural landscape by the end of the 1st century BC. This would

---

Royal 2012.

[139] McLean 2022: 240-41.

[140] McLean 2022: 223-42.

[141] Colum. *Rust.* 7.2.3; Plin. *HN* 8.190.

[142] Str. 5.1.7.

[143] De Sena 2005: 135-49; Marzano 2013: 85-90; Ugolini 2021: 87.

[144] D'Alessandro 2013; 2024; Rizzo and Molari 2023; Tempesta 2011.

[145] Sebastiani and Serlorenzi 2008: 141-46.

[146] Polyb. 2.15, Str. 5.1.12.

[147] Trentacoste *et al.* 2021.

[148] Brusić 1999; Leleković 2018; Makjanić 1995; Mercando 1972; Mertens 1972; Schindler-Kaudelka 1980.

[149] Egri 2007; Reed *et al.* 2022; Tonc and Filipović 2020.

[150] CIL 2.2865; 5.941.

[151] Aldini 1978; Dycezk 2001; Panella 1989: 153; 2002: 195-96; Ugolini 2015: 245.

be complemented by the development of specialised production in commodities such as textiles and ceramics, with Northern Italy achieving a reputation for the quality and quantity of its goods. Although the changing political and military situation throughout the Roman era would see the region adapt to meet new needs and requirements, Northern Italy remained an important agricultural and manufacturing zone, supplying the needs of both its inhabitants and those further afield well into Late Antiquity.

Praised by ancient writers, wine and cereals formed the principal agricultural exports from Northern Italy, alongside pork. Textiles and fineware pottery also saw widescale extra-regional distribution. Carried to ports and redistribution centres on the back of Northern Italy's extensive transport network, exported goods travelled on overland and fluvial networks to reach markets in Pannonia, Moesia, and the frontier, while maritime routes enabled Northern Italic products to reach zones of consumption in the Aegean and Black Sea region. Through these networks, Northern Italy was linked into markets in the Mediterranean and Northeastern Provinces. However, exports only tell one side of the story. Northern Italy also imported and consumed a wide variety of goods from across the Roman world that complemented the products produced within the region. Over the following chapters, the trade in amphora-borne goods, red-slipped fineware ceramics, and decorative stone and marble within Northern Italy will be examined, revealing complex, multi-tiered networks of distribution and consumption.

Amphorae:
Containers and Consumables

As one of the most durable, recognisable, and heavily typologised forms of ceramic from the Roman period, amphorae have long been used as a proxy for the study of long-distance trade, primarily in foodstuffs and other consumables.[1] A wide range of goods were moved across the Roman world using amphorae. Wine and oil were amongst the most common, but fish products, fruit, and cereals were also transported alongside other, more unusual contents such as alum. The widespread distribution of amphorae across the Roman world and their high rate of survival in the archaeological record have made them an obvious choice for tracking patterns in trade and connections between producers and consumers. Northern Italy has proved no exception, with assemblages at individual sites having seen detailed quantitative analysis and discussion.[2] The chronology and development of individual vessel forms, such as the Anfora con Collo ad Imbuto, Dressel 6A, Dressel 6B, and Lamboglia 2, have also seen sustained scholarly interest.[3] However, the findings are rarely integrated into wider discussions on trade or compared with other sites.[4] A wealth of data exists in Northern Italy that has the potential to answer complex questions on inland amphora-borne trade, but they have not been combined and studied at a regional level until now. The AMINI dataset analysed in this chapter synthesises 62 published amphora assemblages, the contents of which span nine centuries of trade and exchange within the region.[5] It contains 28,423 sherds of amphora from 32 urban centres in Northern Italy, with 167 unique vessel forms represented.

Within Northern Italy, amphorae have been recovered from a variety of urban contexts. Some are found where they were discarded while others originate from disturbed contexts, recorded as residual finds in excavation reports. The largest quantities of amphorae, often surviving as complete or near-complete vessels, have been recovered from so-called 'reclamation deposits'. In these contexts, recycled whole amphorae were placed to stabilise, aerate, or drain damp and unstable soils during the Roman period.[6] Reclamation contexts are found across the Roman world, the most notable being at the Castro Pretorio in Rome, which gave rise to the Dressel typology.[7] Most discoveries have come from Northern Italy and Southern France, where high water tables and marshy ground saw the need for more extensive foundation and stabilisation work. The contexts of reclamation deposits vary, ranging from domestic townhouses to large-scale rural infrastructure projects.[8] Hundreds of vessels might be used even in small projects, with the largest, such as a deposit found beneath the via Aemilia near Piacenza, having the potential to contain tens of thousands of vessels.[9] Larger amphorae were favoured for this task, particularly the Lamboglia 2, Dressel 6A, and Dressel 6B forms in Northern Italy.[10] Although these vessel types may be overrepresented within the dataset, comparison with other assemblages from the region which do not include reclamation deposits, such as those from Brescia, Civitas Camunnorum, and Industria, demonstrates similar trends in provenance and vessel forms.[11] The high number of reclamation deposits across the Po-Veneto Plain has resulted in a significant survival bias towards vessels from the Early Imperial period. The deliberate burial of these amphorae below occupation levels has helped to ensure their existence in the archaeological record, providing a much larger dataset for examination. The majority of reclamation deposits were created during the late 1st century BC and mid-1st century AD, with limited reclamation works continuing into the 2nd century. This coincides with a time when large-scale landscape intervention and new construction was being undertaken across the Po-Veneto Plain (see the previous chapter). Consequently,

---

[1] For a discussion on the role of proxies in analysing Roman trade; see Bonifay 2018; Scheidel 2009, with Wilson's (2009a) response; Wilson 2009b; 2014.

[2] For example, Auriemma and Degrassi 2017; Biondani 2005a; Bruno 1997; 2005a; 2008; Bruno and Bocchio 1991; 1999; Dobreva 2013; Gaddi and Maggi 2017.

[3] See Cipriano 2009; Cipriano and Mazzocchin 2012; Mazzocchin 2009. Bruno 2005b gives a brief overview of the regional chronology of the most common amphora forms found within Northern Italy.

[4] For example, Gabucci and Quiri 2008; Spagnolo Garzoli et al. 2007; 2008.

[5] The AMINI dataset can be found at https://doi.org/10.5281/zenodo.13745898. The code and data used in the analysis can be found at Github Repository: Adriatic-to-the-Alps, viewed 12 September 2024, https://github.com/jamespage15/Adriatic-to-the-Alps.

[6] For a discussion on the mechanisms behind reclamation deposits and their distribution within Northern Italy, see Antico Gallina 2011; 2014; Cipriano and Mazzocchin 1998; Pesavento Mattioli 1998. For examples of reclamation deposits elsewhere within the Western Empire, see Antico Gallina 2011: 193-96; Laubenheimer 1991; Laubenheimer, Béraud, and Gébara 1992.

[7] Dressel 1872.

[8] Cipriano and Mazzochin 1998; 2020; Pesavento Mattioli 1998.

[9] Marini Calvini 1999: 190-91. Unfortunately, the assemblage was not quantified beyond the total number of vessels, leading to its exclusion from the AMINI database.

[10] Pliny (HN 35.161) praises Adriatic amphorae for their *firmitas*, a desirable characteristic for their use in foundations and stabilisation.

[11] The Lamboglia 2, Dressel 6A, and Dressel 6B remain the most common vessel forms in their respective periods and the Adriatic Littoral continues to be the dominant provenance for amphora imports across sites both with and without reclamation deposits.

amphora assemblages from the 3rd century AD onwards appear in much lower quantities.

Of course, amphorae represent only one possible form of transport container circulating during the Roman era. Other containers, such as barrels and skins, only survive under certain preservation conditions and are found far less frequently than their ceramic counterparts.[12] Although the waterlogged contexts of Northern Italy should provide optimum preservation conditions, surviving examples have yet to be recovered from the region.[13] Consequently, the contribution of locally produced consumables travelling in perishable containers to Northern Italy's food supply cannot be quantified. There is also the uncertainty surrounding what amphorae may have been carrying and where they may have originated. Studies using amphorae as a proxy for trade operate on the assumption that their provenance was from the area where the vessel was produced. However, over the past 20 years, evidence for the reuse and recycling of amphorae has steadily increased.[14] A Dressel 6A wine amphora manufactured on the Adriatic Coast may not necessarily have travelled from there when it entered Northern Italy, nor may it have been carrying wine.[15] Unfortunately, without specialist testing such as residue analysis, it is often impossible to tell what amphorae were carrying and where they originated from before they entered into the archaeological record.[16] As such, there remains a degree of assumption in their provenance and contents.

Zones of Production

During the Roman era, Northern Italy was supplied with amphorae from six main zones of production. These were the Adriatic Littoral, Eastern Mediterranean, Gaul, the Iberian Peninsula, North Africa, and the Tyrrhenian Littoral. When the AMINI dataset is viewed as a whole, the Adriatic Littoral dominates assemblages, with other provenances supplying vessels in much lower quantities (see Figure 14). In the following section, a

brief summary of the amphora forms present from each zone of production is laid out.

The Adriatic Littoral

Amphorae from the Adriatic Littoral formed the main component of the AMINI dataset. Adriatic vessels were amongst some of the earliest amphorae circulating in the region, primarily the Greco-Italic type during the 3rd and 2nd centuries BC.[17] By the 1st century BC, the Lamboglia 2 wine amphora accounted for the majority of Adriatic vessels circulating in Northern Italy (see Figure 15). Production seems to have mainly taken place on the eastern coast of Italy in the area of Picenum, with some kilns also documented in Northern Italy near Modena and Aquileia.[18] Other Adriatic vessels circulating within Northern Italy during the 1st century BC included the Brindisian, late-form Greco-Italic, and Ovoidale Adriatica forms, all in much lower quantities than the Lamboglia 2.[19]

By the end of the 1st century BC, the form of the Lamboglia 2 had begun to morph into the Dressel 6.[20] The two sub-forms of this amphora, 6A and 6B, were amongst the most widely circulated and commonly found vessels in Northern Italy during the Early Imperial period. The Dressel 6A was predominantly a wine-carrying amphora and its main zone of production mirrored that of the Lamboglia 2, concentrated around the Central Italian Adriatic Coast and the eastern Po Valley.[21] In contrast, the Dressel 6B was an oil-bearing vessel. Dressel 6Bs seem to have been predominantly manufactured in Istria, with known kiln sites at Fažana and Loron.[22] Although archaeometric analysis of Dressel 6B fabrics suggests there was some Northern Italic production, no kiln site has been found.[23] Furthermore, Cisalpine production of the Dressel 6B form seems to have dropped off by the middle of the 1st century AD, leaving Istria as the main production zone.[24] A morphological variant of the Dressel 6B, the so-called 'Anfora con Collo ad Imbuto', would also see widespread circulation across Northern Italy from the

---

[12] The majority of surviving examples come from France, Germany, and Britain (Marlière 2001).

[13] Barrels are, however, attested to in the region by Pliny and Strabo, alongside funerary stele recovered in Piedmont (Plin. *HN* 14.27; Str. 5.1.12; Tchernia 1986: 286-88.). The closest example to Northern Itay was a barrel recovered from the Grado wreck off the Adriatic Coast, containing recycled glass (Giacobelli 1997). For a history of containerisation in the Mediterranean, see Bevan 2014.

[14] Abdelhamid 2013; Brughmans and Pecci 2020; Pecci *et al.* 2017; Peña 2007b.

[15] For example, Mazzocchin and Wilkins (2013) have found examples of Dressel 6A wine amphorae being reused to carry fish products, while Dressel 6B oil amphorae have been found labelled as carrying *liquamen* and *lymphatum* (Cipriano 2009: 173; Van Neer, Ervynck, and Monsieur 2010: 163-66).

[16] Maritan, Mazzoli, and Mazzocchin 2019; Pecci *et al.* 2017. Even with residue analysis, it can be difficult to conclusively determine an amphora's contents or distinguish separate multiple contents using the same individual vessel (Brughmans and Pecci 2020: 200-01).

[17] Biondani 2005a; Iandoli 2006; Komar 2021: 58-60; Van Limbergen 2018.

[18] Carre, Monsieur, and Pesavento Mattioli 2014: 419-22. A Dalmatian origin has been argued for the Lamboglia 2 in the past (see Lindhagen 2009), but this is no longer widely accepted.

[19] For information on the amphora Ovodiale Adriatica, see: Carre and Pesavento Mattioli (2003), 454-60; Carre, Monsieur, and Pesavento Mattioli 2014: 419-22. The Ovoidale Adriatica form remains one of the least understood forms from this region and period.

[20] Cipriano 2009; Cipriano and Mazzocchin 2012; 2018; 2019.

[21] Maritan, Mazzoli, and Mazzocchin 2019.

[22] Carre and Pesavento Mattioli 2018: 8; Cipriano 2009: 176; Cipriano and Mazzocchin 2012: 244.

[23] Maritan, Mazzoli, and Mazzocchin 2019. Analysis of stamps and *tituli picti* on Dressel 6s also suggests the involvement of prominent Cisalpine families in their manufacture (Cipriano and Mazzocchin 2000; 2002).

[24] Cipriano and Mazzocchin 2012; 2019; Cipriano *et al.* 2020.

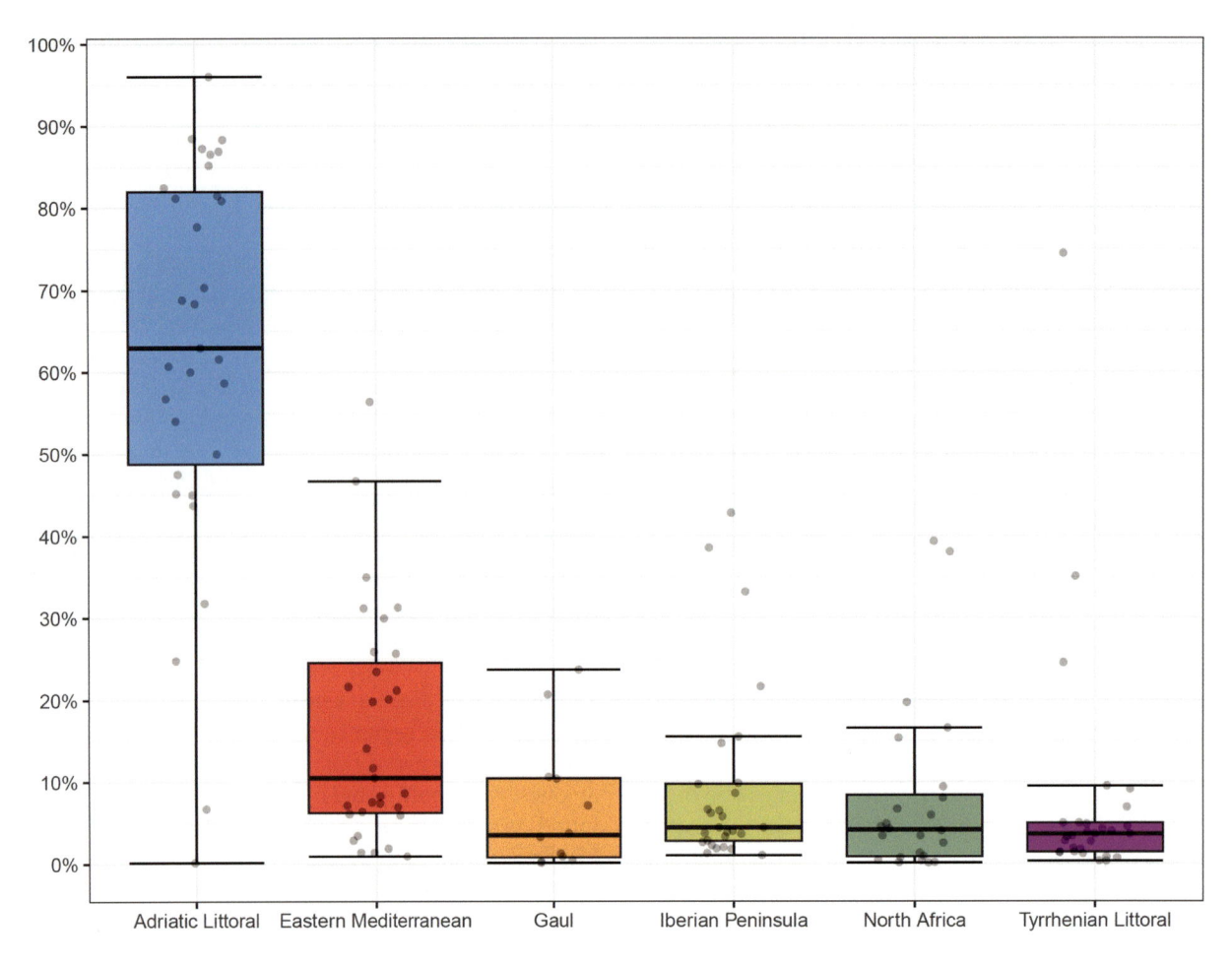

Figure 14. Box and whisker plots showing the percentage of each zone of production within each site assemblage.

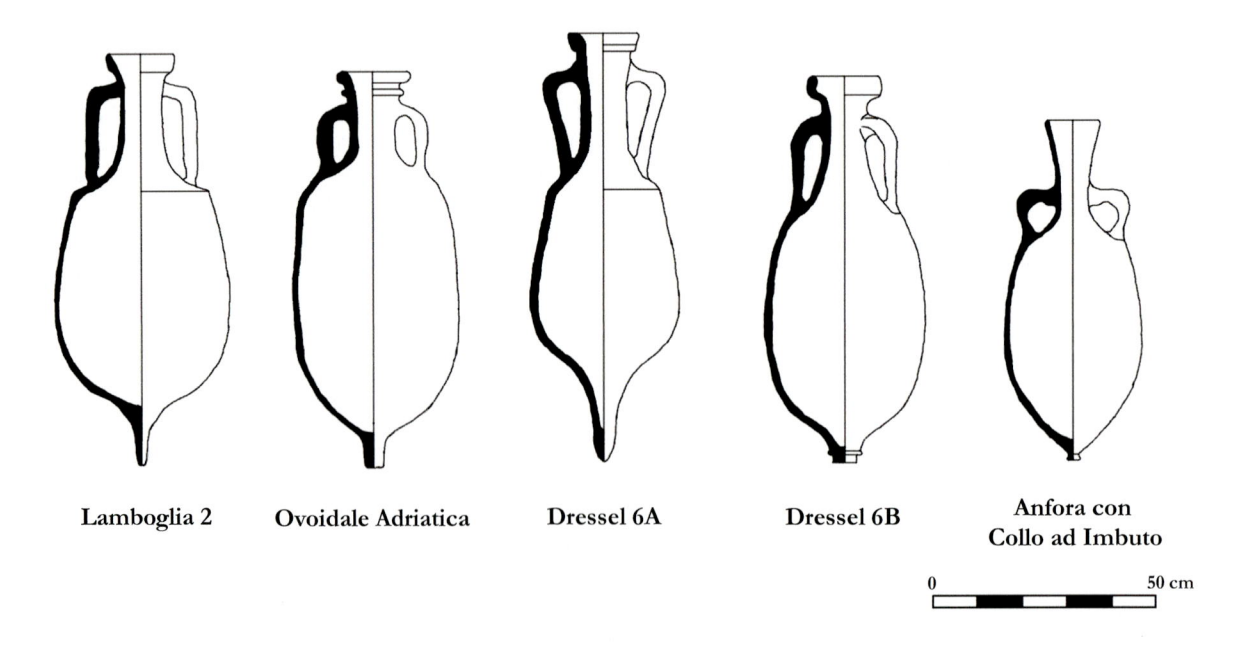

Lamboglia 2   Ovoidale Adriatica   Dressel 6A   Dressel 6B   Anfora con Collo ad Imbuto

0   50 cm

Figure 15. Adriatic amphorae represented in the greatest quantities within the AMINI dataset.

mid-1st century AD, alongside Dressel 2-4s produced in the Adriatic area.[25]

The Dressel 6A and Dressel 6B were predominantly in circulation throughout the 1st century AD, with most production having ceased by the early 2nd century.[26] The Anfora con Collo ad Imbuto would survive longer, with production tailing off towards the late 2nd-early 3rd century AD.[27] As production of the Dressel 6A began to decline from the mid-late 1st century, the Forlimpopoli type (divided into sub-types A-E) would replace it as the dominant wine-carrying amphora in Northern Italy.[28] Produced in the coastal zone of modern Emilia-Romagna, the amphora was flat-bottomed, making it ideal for transport on the region's waterways.[29] Despite this, the distribution of the Forlimpopoli type seems to have been mainly limited to the coastal hinterland, with the form seeing a minimal distribution further inland. It is, however, recovered in comparatively large quantities at port sites on the Adriatic Coast, particularly Aquileia.[30] The Forlimpopoli type was mainly in circulation during the 2nd century AD, although its later variants (D and E) would continue to be produced until the end of the 3rd century.[31] The 2nd century AD would also see the circulation of other types of Adriatic amphorae across Northern Italy in small quantities. These were the Grado 1, Anforetta Adriatiche da Pesce, and Schörgendorfer 558 types, principally used for the transport of fish products or, in the case of the latter, olives.[32] Amphora production along the Adriatic littoral declined significantly from the middle of the 2nd century AD, disappearing entirely by the end of the 3rd.

The Eastern Mediterranean

Amphora-borne imports from the Eastern Mediterranean did not appear in Northern Italy until the end of the 1st century BC. Eastern Mediterranean imports were initially represented by early forms of the Camulodunum 184, alongside Dressel 2-4s with an eastern provenance.[33] The Camulodunum 184, originating from the Aegean and Asia Minor, would be imported in significant quantities during the 1st and 2nd centuries AD, becoming the dominant Eastern Mediterranean vessel in circulation. Wine seems to have been the principal contents of Eastern Mediterranean amphorae, and the Camulodunum 184 was joined by other vessels such as the Cretoise 1-3, Dressel 43, and Kingsholm 117.[34] Cretan wine (such as *passum* or *athalassios*) seems to have been especially popular, its generally sweeter taste perhaps offering a contrast to the more widely available wines of the Adriatic Littoral.[35] Imports besides wine from the Eastern Mediterranean are attested by the Melos-type amphora, which carried alum, and the Camulodunum 189 which is believed to have transported dried fruit.[36]

A wide variety of amphorae from the Eastern Mediterranean continued to circulate within Northern Italy throughout the 3rd century AD and into Late Antiquity. These appeared in significant quantities, with the Eastern Mediterranean (particularly the Levant) forming an increasingly important zone of supply for Northern Italy and the wider Adriatic.[37] The most commonly attested belong to the Late Roman Amphora series (in particular the LRA 1, 2, 3, and 4) which achieved a high level of penetration in Northern Italy, although a wide range of other vessels were in circulation.[38] The LRA 1 was produced in Cilicia and Cyprus, the LRA 2 in the Aegean, the LRA 3 in Asia Minor, and the LRA 4 in Palestine. Amphorae from the Eastern Mediterranean are attested in Northern Italy into the 8th century AD, making it one of the longest operating zones of production supplying the region.

The Iberian Peninsula

Amphorae originating from the Iberian Peninsula began to appear in Northern Italy in the final quarter of the 1st century BC. Initially, these were Dressel 7-11 amphorae, alongside Dressel 2-4s produced in Iberia. The Dressel 7-11 would be the most prolific Iberian amphora to circulate in Northern Italy during the 1st

---

[25] Mazzocchin 2009; Van Limbergen 2016. The contents of the Anfora con Collo ad Imbuto was probably oil. Archaeometric analysis of fabrics suggests a coastal production zone in modern Emilia-Romagna and Marche (Maritan, Mazzoli, and Mazzocchin 2019).

[26] Cipriano and Mazzocchin 2012; 2019.

[27] Mazzocchin 2009: 196-97. While the majority of Anfore con Collo ad Imbuto date to the early 1st to mid-2nd century AD, some variants seem to last into the late 2nd to early 3rd century AD.

[28] Aldini 1978; 1989; 1995; 2000; Panella 2002. Although fish products have been argued as the contents for several Forlimpopoli sub-types (A and D), wine is now the most accepted principal cargo.

[29] Although the production site at Forlimpopoli is best studied, flat-bottomed amphora of the Forlimpopoli type or similar were also produced at Riccione, Rimini, Ronta di Cesena, and Santarcangelo di Romagna-Sant'Ermete in Emilia-Romagna (Auriemma, Degrassi, and Quiri 2012: 270).

[30] Auriemma, Degrassi, and Quiri 2012: 271; Rizzo and Molari 2023: 250-56.

[31] Iandoli 2006: 114-15; Rizzo and Molari 2023: 253-54.

[32] Carre, Pesavento Mattioli, and Belotti 2009: 228-30; Carre and Pesavento Mattioli 2003: 471; Pesavento Mattioli 2011: 168-69.

[33] Auriemma 2007: 139; Auriemma and Quiri 2007: 48; Komar 2021: Chapter 3.

[34] Auriemma and Quiri 2006: 234; Auriemma, Degrassi, and Quiri 2012: 274-76; 2015: 145-47. Goods produced in the wider Aegean seem to have been popular amongst Northern Italic consumers during the 1st and 2nd centuries AD (Quiri 2015: 164).

[35] Dodd 2020: 59–64; Gallimore 2023; Quiri 2015: 165. *Passum* and *athalassios* were not diluted, leading to their sweet taste.

[36] Quiri and Spagnolo Garzoli 2015.

[37] Auriemma, Degrassi, and Quiri 2012: 285-87; 2015: 153-54; Komar 2021: 272. This something reflected in Late Antique amphora assemblages along the Adriatic Littoral, where Eastern Mediterranean amphorae frequently form the largest group.

[38] Auriemma and Quiri 2007: 38-42; Quiri 2015: 164-65. Other Eastern Mediterranean amphorae attested in Northern Italy during this late phase include the Agora M273, Agora M334, and the Samos Cistern Type.

century AD, seeing distribution across the region.[39] Produced along the southern coast of Iberia, the main contents of the Dressel 7-11 were fish products, such as *garum* and *liquamen*. Indeed, most Iberian amphorae imported into Northern Italy during the Roman period are presumed to have been carrying fish products (see below). In the 1st century AD, these included the Beltràn 2A and 2B, Dressel 12, 14, and 17, all present in much lower quantities than the Dressel 7-11.

Despite the ready availability of locally pressed oil and imports from the Adriatic Littoral, there is evidence for imports of Iberian oil into Northern Italy during the 1st and 2nd centuries AD. Iberian oil predominantly entered the region in Dressel 20 amphorae, produced in Baetica, although some limited instances of the Dressel 18 and 24 are also present.[40] The Dressel 20 is present in comparable quantities to the Dressel 7-11 and Iberian Dressel 2-4s, although its circulation is mainly limited to the south-west of the Po Valley.[41] Although its globular shape made it difficult to transport overland, the vector of entry for Dressel 20s into Northern Italy was likely over the Apennines from the Ligurian Coast. Beyond the Dressel 2-4, Iberian wine is attested via limited examples of the Pascual 1A and Oberaden 74 forms during this period, almost uniformly on the Ligurian Coast.[42]

By the 3rd century, fish products from the Iberian Peninsula were predominantly circulating in Almagro 50, Almagro 51A-B, and Almagro 51C amphorae. These were produced on the southern coast of Lusitania (the modern Algarve), exporting the output of the province's fish salting and preserving industries.[43]

Gaul

Amphorae from Gaul did not appear in Northern Italy before the final quarter of the 1st century BC. Despite Gaul's proximity to the region, Gallic amphorae do not form a substantial component of the AMINI dataset, only appearing in significant quantities in assemblages from sites in the south-west of the Po Valley (such as Alba, Acqui Terme, and Augusta Bagiennorum).[44] The most common Gallic imports were the flat-bottomed Gauloise 2 and Gauloise 4 wine amphorae, produced in

the region of Gallia Narbonnensis. Other forms in the Gauloise typology are also attested in small quantities. Dressel 2-4 and Dressel 7-11 amphora produced in Southern Gaul are also moderately attested at the sites of Alba and Acqui Terme.[45]

North Africa

Amphorae from North Africa are rare in assemblages from the 1st century BC and the 1st century AD. They are initially limited to sporadic examples of Late Punic amphorae, with singular finds of the forms Dressel 18, Van der Werff 2 and Van der Werff 3. Dressel 2-4 amphorae with North African fabrics are also present in small quantities, especially in the south-west of the Po Valley. However, from the 2nd century AD onwards, an increasing variety of North African amphora forms began to circulate in Northern Italy.[46]

The Africana 1, attested by both subtypes A and B, was the first North African amphora to appear in significant quantities in Northern Italy. Produced in Africa Proconsularis from the mid-2nd century AD onwards, the form saw widespread diffusion across the Roman world and likely carried oil.[47] Between the mid-2nd century and mid-4th century AD, the Africana 2, with its sub-forms A B, C, and D, account for some of the best-attested North African vessel forms in Northern Italy. There has been uncertainty surrounding the contents of the Africana 2, with wine and fish products alternatively suggested.[48] Most consensus, however, rests with sauces such as *garum* or *salsamenta* being the likely cargo. Tripolitanian amphorae also circulated in Northern Italy. Of these, the oil-bearing Tripolitania 3 form, produced on the southern coast of modern Tunisia, is the most attested, alongside smaller quantities of the Tripolitania 1 and Tripolitania 2.[49]

During the 3rd and 4th centuries AD, an increasing variety of North African amphorae are attested in Northern Italy.[50] Although there is a high level of vessel diversity, many forms are only minimally attested, such as the Keay 1A and 1B, Keay 41, Keay 50, Keay 61, and Keay 62Q. The Africana 3, with its sub-forms A, B, and C, are amongst the North African amphorae present in the highest quantities during this period. Of all the North African amphorae recovered from Northern Italy, the Spatheion 1 was attested in the greatest quantities.[51]

---

[39] Cipriano and Mazzocchinn 2016; Gonzalez Vilches *et al.* 1998; Modrzewska-Pianetti and Pianetti 1994.

[40] Carre and Pesavento Mattioli 2003; Modrzewska-Pianetti 2017.

[41] Bruno 1997; Modrzewska-Pianetti 2017: 402-04; Quiri 2014; Secchi 2017.

[42] Parodi 2013. These limited examples likely reflect the movement of people, rather than sustained trade.

[43] Auriemma, Degrassi, and Quiri 2012: 272-73; Pedro Bernadas and Vietas 2016.

[44] Bruno 1998. Although Gallic amphorae are present at other sites across Northern Italy, their small quantities (often only a fragment or two) are probably more indicative of one-off purchases or the movement of people, rather than sustained trade (Cipolato and Indino 2022).

[45] Bruno 1997: 521; Pettirossi and Pistrano 2008: 61.

[46] Auriemma, Degrassi, and Quiri 2012: 282-85; Bonifay and Capelli 2019; Dobreva 2023: 292-94.

[47] Bonifay 2004: 107; 2021: 282-83.

[48] Bonifay 2021: 282-83.

[49] Auriemma, Degrassi, and Quiri 2012: 283; Dobreva 2023: 294. The Tripolitania 3 is well-attested across the Adriatic area, with Triptolitanian oil containers present in greater quantities than those from Africa Proconsularis.

[50] Auriemma and Quiri 2007: 32-34; Bonifay and Capelli 2019: 77-78.

[51] Most excavation reports from Northern Italy do not make the

Produced between *c.* AD 375 and AD 450, the contents of this vessel are unknown, although may have included wine, olives, or fish products.[52] As with the Eastern Mediterranean, amphorae from North Africa continued to circulate in Northern Italy into the 8th century AD, with the Spatheion 3 being the latest vessel form so far attested.

The Tyrrhenian Littoral

Tyrrhenian imports to Northern Italy are initially represented by the Dressel 1 amphora, a wine-carrying vessel mainly produced in Campania and Tuscany, alongside limited examples of Greco-Italic amphorae produced on the Tyrrhenian Coast.[53] In the late 1st century BC, the Dressel 1 would be superseded by Dressel 2-4 wine amphorae produced along the Tyrrhenian Littoral, which circulated until the end of the 2nd century AD. During the 1st and 2nd centuries AD, a variety of other Tyrrhenian amphorae would circulate, albeit in small quantities. These included the Dressel 21-22, Richborough 527, and Late Campanian type. Moving into the Late Antique period, only the Keay 52 amphora circulated in appreciable quantities. Produced in Calabria, this small vessel transported wine and was predominantly distributed in the Western Mediterranean.[54]

Chronological Trends

Mapping chronological trends in the frequency of amphorae across Northern Italy reveals important patterns in the trade and consumption of these vessels. Graphing changes in overall quantities, contents, and zones of supply reveals information on the evolution of trade networks and consumer preferences, which can then be studied against the region's historical context. In the following section, the AMINI dataset is subjected to aoristic analysis. Both production chronologies (the date range within which a vessel is believed to have been manufactured) and deposition chronologies (the date range of the deposit within which the vessel was found) are graphed, enabling detailed comparison and analysis.

Overall Trends: Production vs. Deposition Chronologies

The chronological distribution of amphorae within the AMINI database was initially analysed using both the production chronology of the vessel form and the deposition chronology of the site in which it was deposited (if these data were available).[55] At an initial glance, there are marked similarities between both production and deposition chronologies, although key differences remain (see Figure 16). Using production chronologies saw the distribution curve start in 300 BC, 32 years before the foundation of the first Roman colony in the region at Ariminum in 268 BC. This is a reflection of amphora forms with long production chronologies, such as the Greco-Italic type (*c.* 300 - 100 BC) or Dressel 2-4 (*c.* 50 BC-AD 250), which in some cases outstrip the occupation dates of the sites they were recovered from.[56] Both production and deposition chronologies reveal a rapid spike in the frequency of amphorae during the 1st century BC, leading to a peak in the late 1st century AD. Each set of dates also suggests a second peak in amphorae during the 5th century AD (Graphs A and B). This second peak, however, is problematic, formed due to the inclusion of the amphora assemblage from Classis. Classis' assemblage originated from a Late Roman warehouse complex and was comprised of 7525 sherds, accounting for a quarter of the entire AMINI dataset.[57] As such, its inclusion in the analysis significantly warps the curve, and when Classis' data are removed the 5th century AD peak in amphorae disappears from both analyses (Graphs C and D). Consequently, Classis' assemblage has been excluded from the subsequent chronological analysis.

Returning to Graphs C and D, after the 1st century BC rise in vessel frequency, production and deposition chronologies begin to differ. Production chronologies suggest a continuous rise in the frequency of amphorae, leading to a peak in the late 1st century AD. While deposition chronologies reflect a similar overall pattern, they also suggest a dip in the number of amphorae between *c.* AD 50 and *c.* AD 75. As noted above, a significant number of amphorae contained within the AMINI database originate from reclamation deposits.[58] These contexts are often well-defined stratigraphically, with Northern Italian examples overwhelmingly dating from 25 BC to AD 50.[59] This is

---

distinction between sub-types 1A and B.

[52] Excavation and archaeometry has revealed evidence for oil, olives, fish products, and wine being carried in the Spatheion 1, suggesting the vessel may have been used interchangeably (Bonifay 2021: 282).

[53] Tyrrhenian Greco-Italic amphorae seem to have been predominately produced in the Bay of Naples and Sicily (Olcese 2006). Dressel 1 kiln sites are more concentrated in Campania (Olcese 2020). The appearance of Dressel 1 amphorae in Northern Italy coincides with the intensification of production and exportation of Tyrrhenian wine in the Western Mediterranean in the late 2nd century BC.

[54] Corrado and Ferro 2012.

[55] Contexts dating to the post-Roman period containing residual material were excluded from the depositional analysis.

[56] A similar issue was highlighted by Franconi *et al.* 2023 in their aoristic study.

[57] Augenti *et al.* 2011; Cirelli 2014; Grazia Maioli 1991.

[58] For example, Acari 1996; Buchi 1973; Cipriano and Ferrarini 2001; Cipriano and Mazzocchin 1998; Dobreva and Ravasi 2018; Francesconi 2020; Mazzocchin 2011; Michelini and Mazzocchin 1998; Mongardi 2014; Pesavento Mattioli 1992.

[59] Antico Gallina 2011; Cipriano and Mazzocchin 2020; Pesavento Mattioli 1998; Quilici Gigli 1998.

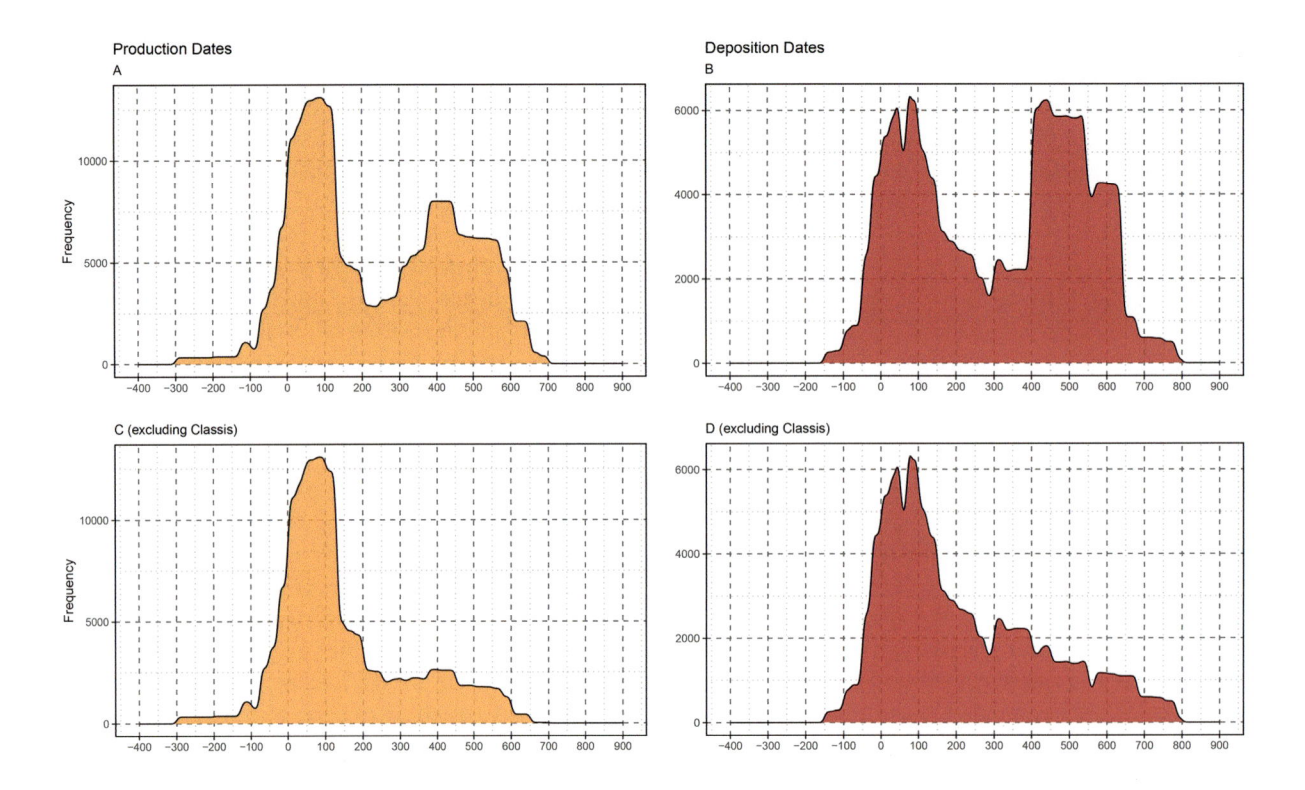

Figure 16. Comparison of Production and Deposition chronologies for amphora consumption in Northern Italy. Note that the Y axes are not constant.

reflected when the distribution of amphorae found in reclamation deposits is graphed (see Figure 17). The frequency of vessels recovered from reclamation contexts peaks *c.* AD 50, before dropping sharply and disappearing almost entirely by the 2nd century. Consequently, the dip in amphorae during the latter half of the 1st century AD suggested by deposition chronologies is likely a reflection of a decline in the use of amphorae in reclamation deposits, rather than a drop in consumption. Furthermore, as reclamation deposits represent a form of reuse and deliberate deposition of amphorae after their initial purpose was fulfilled, it remains unknown when the vessels were initially in circulation. Their contents were consumed prior to the point the amphorae were placed within the reclamation deposit, and it is impossible to estimate the length of time between these two events. As a result, it is likely the spike in amphora frequency caused by the use of reclamation deposits between AD 25 and AD 50 cannot be used as an accurate indicator of consumption.

After the late 1st century AD peak, production chronologies suggest a continuous decline in the frequency of amphorae throughout the 2nd century and into the 3rd, before numbers begin to stabilise through the 4th and 5th centuries. In comparison, although deposition dates also record a sharp drop in frequency in the 2nd century AD, the decline becomes more gradual throughout the 3rd and 4th centuries,

before another sharp drop in the mid-5th century AD. After this, the decline in frequency continues gradually throughout the 6th to 9th centuries AD, forming a long tail. This tail is, in part, a by-product of the post-Roman continuity in occupation across most urban sites in the AMINI dataset, which sees the re-use and redepositing of amphorae into the Early Medieval period and beyond.[60] This leads to the appearance of vessels, such as the Dressel 6A, Dressel 6B, and Lamboglia 2 from the Adriatic Littoral, in contexts long after their production chronology had ceased.[61] A similar problem is caused by deposits with large distances between their opening and closing dates, which can distribute vessels earlier and later than their probable point of consumption.[62]

---

[60] Goodson 2020: Chapter 2, highlights the transformation of many urban cities in Late Antiquity and the Early Medieval period, with the deliberate creation of spaces and deposits suitable for cultivation. These deposits could contain a mix of contemporary ceramics and those from earlier periods.

[61] Adams 2003; Cessford 2017: 167-70. For example, in the MM3 excavations in Milan, the majority of Adriatic amphorae were recovered from Late Antique and Early Medieval contexts, where they formed residual finds (Bruno and Bocchio 1991). A similar example also comes from a deposit of so-called 'Dark Earth' in Milan, dating between the 4th and 8th centuries AD, which saw the redepositing of broken amphora sherds and earth to raise the ground level (Corrado 2003; Massa 2003).

[62] In some cases, this is due to the condensing of stratigraphic units in excavation reports to create a more coherent narrative. In others, such as the Canale d'Anfora in Aquileia, the formation process of the deposit itself prevents a narrower chronology from being recognised. See Franconi *et al.* (2023: 27-28) for a discussion of the problems of

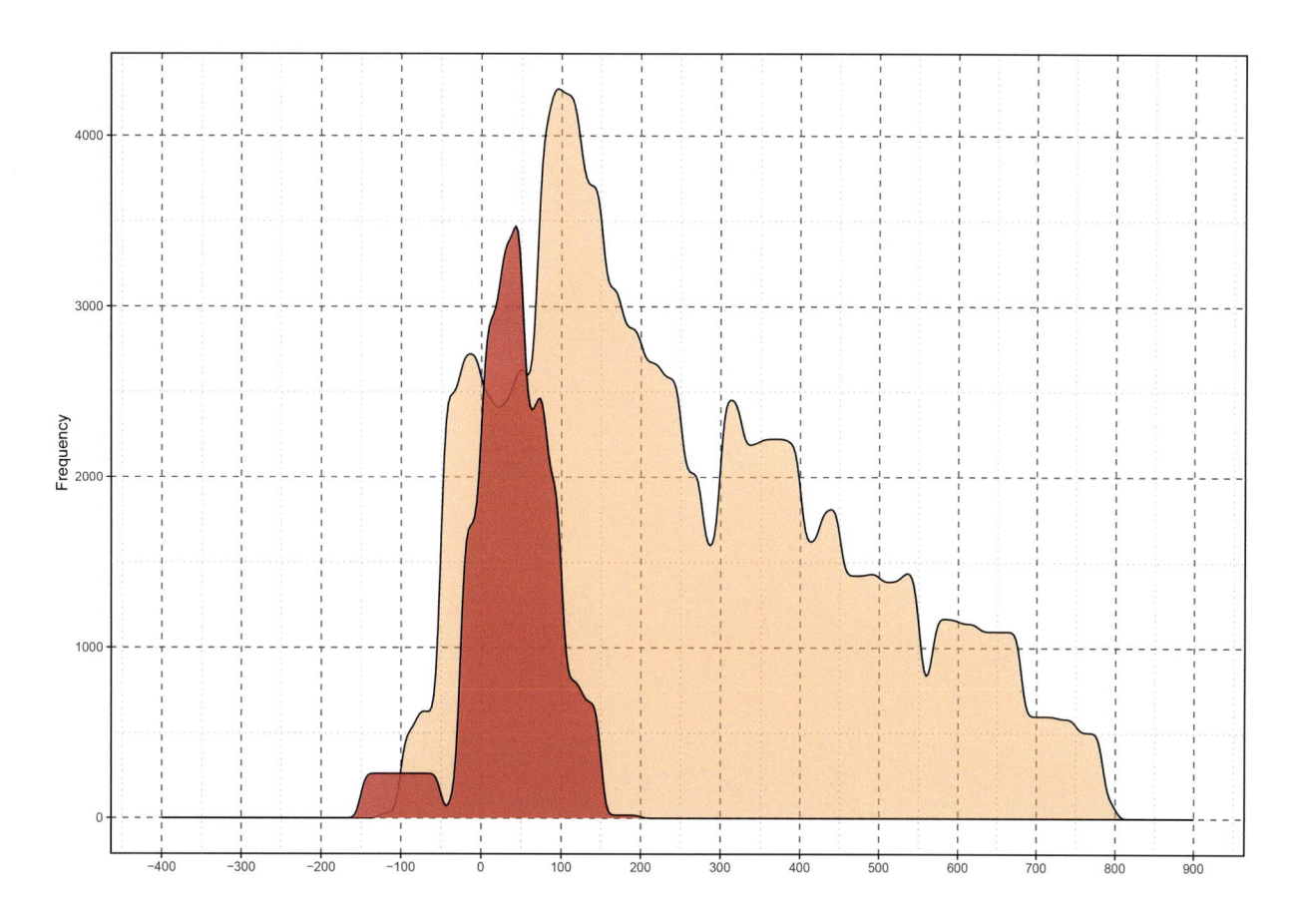

Figure 17. Frequency of amphora placed in reclamation deposits compared to non-reclamation deposits.

As such, the distribution curve presented by deposition chronologies somewhat stretches consumption patterns.

Both production and deposition chronologies suggest a significant reduction in the number of amphorae circulating in Late Antiquity. Increasing instability in Northern Italy, especially from the mid-3rd century AD onwards, may also have served to disrupt trade networks supplying amphora-borne goods, reducing the number of vessels imported to the region. The civil wars, especially those between Philip the Arab and Decius, alongside new incursions from the Alemanni, Jugurthi, and Marcomanni during the 250s and 260s, caused significant damage and upheaval in the region.[63] Although both graph curves suggest significantly fewer amphorae were circulating in Northern Italy from the 3rd century AD onwards, it is important to note that this pattern may also be influenced by publication practices. Late Antique amphora assemblages are published to a far lesser extent than vessels from earlier periods, and

this neglect may serve to artificially deflate the number of vessels in circulation during this period.

Moving away from the quantities of amphorae consumed over time, analysing diversity via the number of amphora forms circulating in a given year offers a different perspective on the data (see Figure 18). Production chronologies in Graph A show a sharp, continuous rise in vessel diversity from the mid-1st century BC onwards, leading to a peak in *c.* AD 90. This is followed by a sudden dip, then a gradual and continuous decline in the number of forms circulating in the region over the following centuries. The curve for deposition chronologies is substantially different. In Graph B, diversity steadily climbs from the mid-2nd century BC onwards. The number of forms plateaus in the first half of the 1st century AD, before sharply rising to an initial peak in *c.* AD 90. Diversity moderately declined throughout the 2nd century AD before plateauing in the 3rd century. However, the number of vessel forms sharply increases at the end of the 3rd century, leading to a second peak in *c.* AD 310. Diversity remains high over the following century, before sharply declining in the mid-5th century followed by a more gradual decrease in the number of vessel forms.

---

long deposition chronologies.
[63] Aur. Vict. *Caes.* 33; Eutrop. 9.8; Oros. 7.22; SHA *Aur.* 18.3, 21.1, *Gall.* 14; Zon. 12.22; Zos.1.37. See Roncaglia 2018 for a detailed summary of the period.

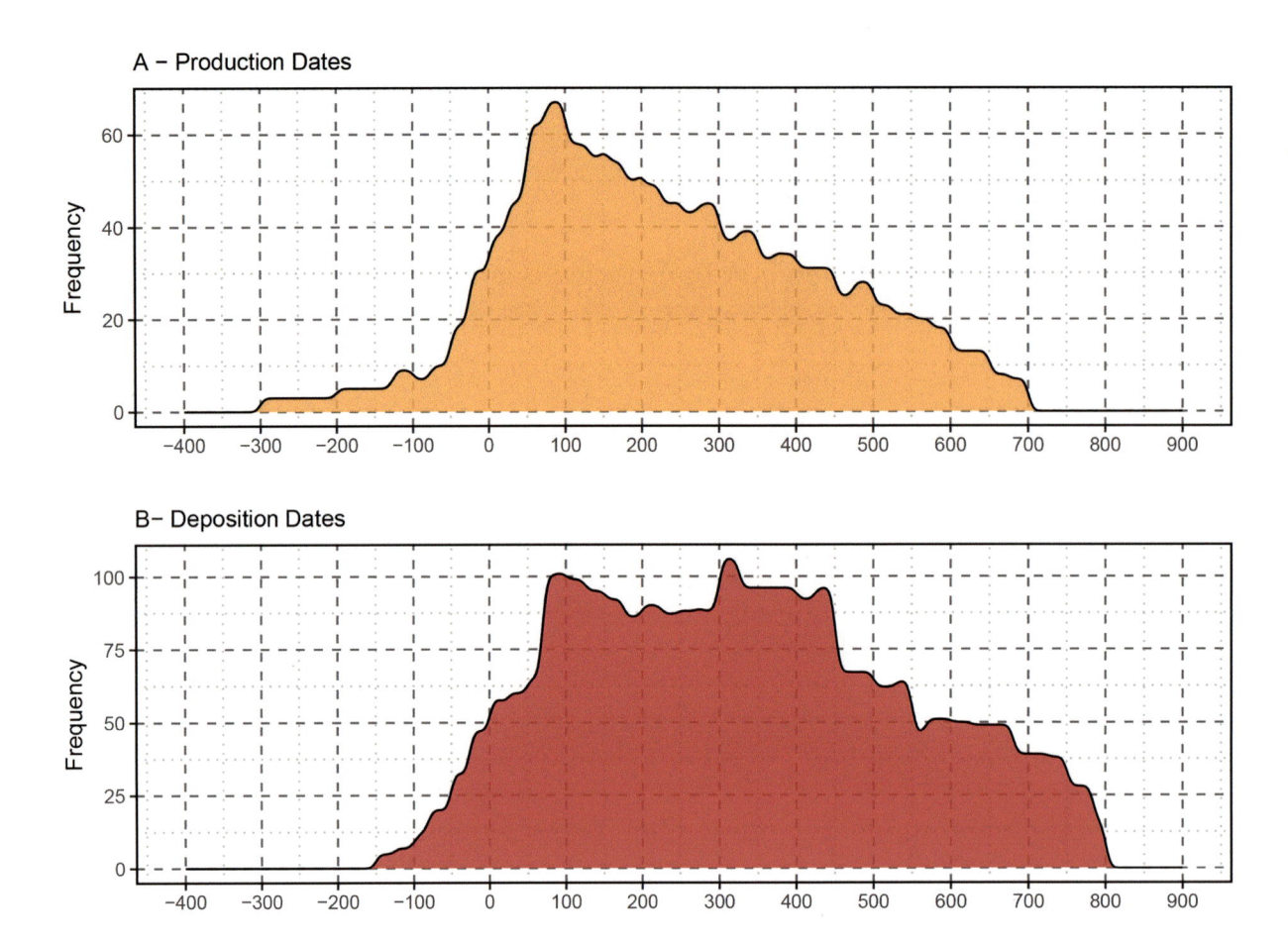

Figure 18. Comparison of Production and Deposition chronologies for vessel diversity in Northern Italy. Note that the Y axes are not constant.

Although there are limitations to both production and deposition chronologies, when studied in tandem they can provide a more nuanced interpretation of amphora distribution. The overall picture that emerges from Northern Italy suggests the number of amphorae peaked in the 1st century AD, followed by a significant decline from the 2nd century onwards. This pattern is not dissimilar to other regions in the Roman world, although in many cases the drop in the frequency of vessels occurs slightly later towards the end of the 2nd century to the start of the 3rd century.[64] While overall quantities of amphorae significantly decreased after the 1st century AD, the number of forms in circulation remained high, with deposition chronologies even suggesting an increase in vessel diversity during Late Antiquity.

Trends in Provenance: Changing Suppliers

Further insights into consumption patterns of amphora-borne goods are gained by separating the AMINI dataset by vessel provenance (see Figure 19). In Graph A, production chronologies a clear dominance of amphorae from the Adriatic Littoral, which first appeared in the late 2nd century BC, before rising sharply in frequency during the 1st century BC. Adriatic amphorae peak c. AD 75, followed by a small drop in the late 1st century AD, followed in turn by a pronounced sharp decline in frequency throughout the mid-2nd century. The decline is somewhat arrested by the introduction of the Forlimpopoli-type amphora, but Adriatic vessels completely disappear by the late 3rd to early 4th century AD. Amphorae from the Eastern Mediterranean form the second most prominent group. Arriving in Northern Italy later than amphorae from the Adriatic Littoral, Eastern amphorae rise in frequency from the 1st century BC, with the curve shallowing throughout the 1st and 2nd centuries AD. This is followed by a dip in frequency during the late 2nd and 3rd centuries AD, before rising and plateauing through the 4th, 5th, and 6th centuries AD to replace the Adriatic Littoral as the dominant provenance. The Eastern Mediterranean would form the most enduring zone of production for amphorae in Northern Italy, supplying the region for over 800 years.

---

[64] For example, in Roman Britain (Carreras 1994), Germany (Franconi *et al.* 2023), and North Africa (Fentress *et al.* 2004).

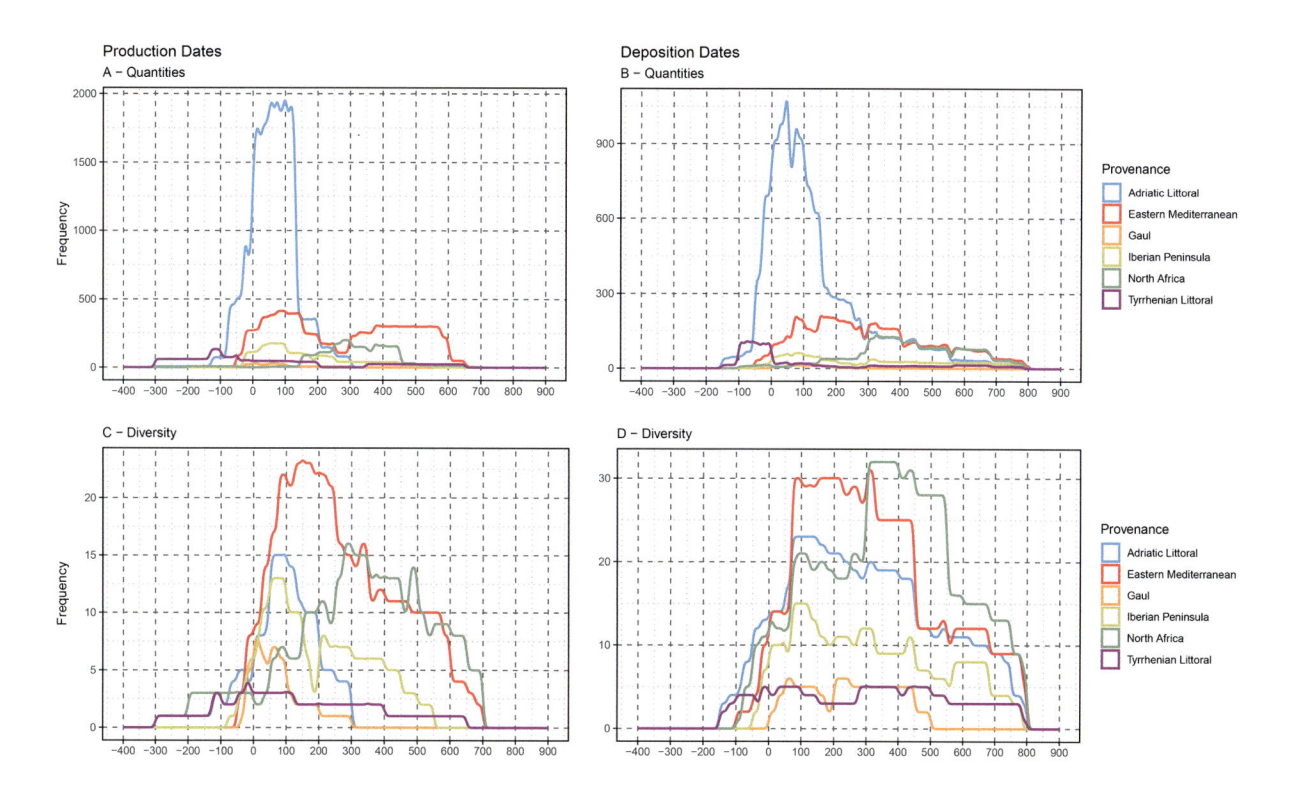

Figure 19. Comparison of Production and Deposition chronologies for the quantity and diversity of amphora from each zone of production in Northern Italy. Note that the Y axes are not constant.

Other zones of production contributed to Northern Italy's supply of amphora-borne goods to varying degrees. Production chronologies show the frequency of North African vessels gradually increased from the early 2nd century AD, going on to form the second most common provenance of amphorae in the Late Antique period. North African vessels would entirely disappear by the early 6th century AD, leaving the Eastern Mediterranean as Northern Italy's sole supplier of amphora-borne goods. Iberian amphorae increase in frequency during the second half of the 1st century BC, before peaking in the 1st century AD. Iberian vessels continue to appear in appreciable frequencies throughout the following centuries, slowly declining until their disappearance at the end of the 4th century AD. Tyrrhenian vessels appear in low frequencies throughout the Republican era, before rising and peaking in the late 2nd-early 1st century BC. They then decline, appearing in limited quantities throughout the Imperial and Late Antique periods. The chronology of Gallic vessels is limited, only appearing in low frequencies during the 1st century AD.[65]

The picture changes somewhat when using deposition chronologies, although the broad trends remain the same. Both the Adriatic and Eastern Mediterranean maintain their dominant positions, however, the decline in Adriatic amphorae is less severe and these vessels continue to appear in low frequencies into the 8th century AD. Meanwhile, vessels from the Eastern Mediterranean still make their first appearance c. 50 BC, rising at a shallower rate than in Graph A and only becoming the dominant provenance in the late 3rd century AD. Eastern Mediterranean amphorae still peak in the late 1st century AD but then plateau in frequency over the following centuries. This is followed by a dip in frequency in the early 4th century, with numbers stabilising again after c. AD 460. The role of North African amphorae in regional supply is more pronounced in deposition chronologies. North African vessels arrive earlier and peak later in the early 4th century AD. It is at this point that frequencies of North African amphora closely match those of Eastern Mediterranean amphorae, with both zones of production attested in near equal quantities. Vessels from the Tyrrhenian Littoral create a marked bump in the 1st century AD, before disappearing almost entirely over the following centuries. The frequency of Iberian and Gallic amphorae closely matches that of their production chronologies.

Further insight is provided when analysing the vessel diversity of each provenance chronologically. Although the Adriatic Littoral formed the dominant

---

[65] It remains possible that Western Mediterranean goods transitioned to perishable containers such as barrels, rather than amphorae, during the 2nd and 3rd centuries AD, obscuring their full extent in Northern Italy (Marlière 2001; Wilson 2011a: 37; 2011b: 228-29).

zone of production for amphorae in terms of quantity, the range of vessels transporting Adriatic goods was limited in comparison to other provenances. In Graph C, production chronologies suggest the Eastern Mediterranean exported the highest number of vessel types, with the diversity of forms in circulation peaking in the mid-2nd century AD. After this point, the diversity of Eastern Mediterranean amphorae declined, although remained significantly higher than other provenances. The diversity of North African amphorae in Northern Italy steadily increased throughout the 1st and 2nd centuries AD, before rising sharply in the mid-3rd century. The diversity of African vessels over the following centuries remained high, with similar numbers of North African and Eastern Mediterranean forms attested during this time. For deposition chronologies in Graph D, the reuse of amphorae and the residual nature of many contexts serve to distort the picture somewhat (as discussed above). After an initial rise in diversity during the 1st century BC and the 1st century AD, the number of vessels circulating from most zones of production remains relatively constant. The Eastern Mediterranean and North Africa stand out, with Eastern vessels sharply increasing in diversity in the late 1st century AD, plateauing, and then declining in variety from the early 4th century onwards. North African vessels show high levels of diversity from the late 1st century AD onwards, before the number of amphora forms circulating rapidly jumps in the early 4th century. At this point, the diversity of North African vessels in circulation outstrips other zones of production, remaining so for the rest of the period.

Northern Italy was supplied with amphora-borne goods from a range of production zones throughout the Roman period. Both production and deposition chronologies demonstrate the importance of Adriatic Littoral to the region's overall supply of amphorae, especially between the 1st century BC and the 2nd century AD. The graphs suggest that the greatest diversity in the provenance of amphora-borne goods occurred during the 1st and 2nd centuries AD, after which the regions supplying Northern Italy became more limited. However, there is a marked difference between the quantities of amphorae and the diversity of vessel forms in circulation. Although the Adriatic Littoral formed the dominant provenance for quantity, Adriatic products were travelling in a limited selection of amphorae. While the number of amphorae circulating in the region declined significantly in the 2nd century AD, the number of vessel forms in distribution remained high and, for some zones of production, increased in diversity. The change in provenances and the increased variation amongst amphorae from the 3rd century AD onwards suggests that Northern Italy's supply networks had changed significantly from earlier periods. The collapse of old trade routes and production zones led to the creation of new supply networks, originating from areas that had previously played a marginal role in the provisioning of the region. The dominance of North African and Eastern Mediterranean amphora, alongside the presence of Iberian vessels in significant quantities, demonstrates Northern Italy's continued integration into extra-provincial economies.

Trends in Contents: Varied Appetites

There is a high degree of assumption regarding amphora contents, with evidence for the reuse of containers and the use of containers for multiple product types continuing to grow.[66] The true quantities of wine, oil, and fish-products, alongside other contents in circulation, are impossible to accurately track. The following section serves as an exploratory analysis but cannot be taken as a fully accurate representation of amphora-borne cargoes in Northern Italy during the Roman period.

The three dominant amphora-borne goods circulating in Northern Italy were wine, oil, and fish products. Other contents are also attested, such as alum, *defrutum*, fruit, and olives, but these were present in minimal quantities, leading to their exclusions from the following graphs. The distribution curves charting wine and oil mirror those charting the overall trends in amphora across Northern Italy (see Figure 20). There are spikes in frequency occurring in the 1st century BC leading to a peak in the 1st century AD, followed by a decline in the 2nd century. The curve for fish sauce is less pronounced, also peaking in the 1st century AD but then plateauing over the following centuries, with frequency only marginally changing. Ratios between the three contents remain relatively consistent.

Wine forms the dominant product in both production and deposition chronologies, with circulation starting earlier and ending later than oil and fish products. In Graph A, Wine rises rapidly in the 1st century BC, before frequency drops sharply *c*. AD 130, a date that coincides with the end of the production lifespan of the Dressel 6A. The frequency of wine-bearing vessels then plateaus in the mid-3rd century, remaining near-constant until their final decline and disappearance in the 7th century. Deposition chronologies in Graph B suggest a more gradual fall in wine amphorae, with frequency halving across the 2nd century AD before beginning a steady decline. Late Roman wine amphorae are also often significantly smaller than their earlier predecessors, making it likely that even less product by volume was reaching Northern Italy via amphorae during the Late Antique.[67]

[66] Abdelhamid 2013; Brughmans and Pecci 2020; Pecci *et al.* 2017; Peña 2007b.
[67] Komar 2021: 250-56; Panella 1993: 668.

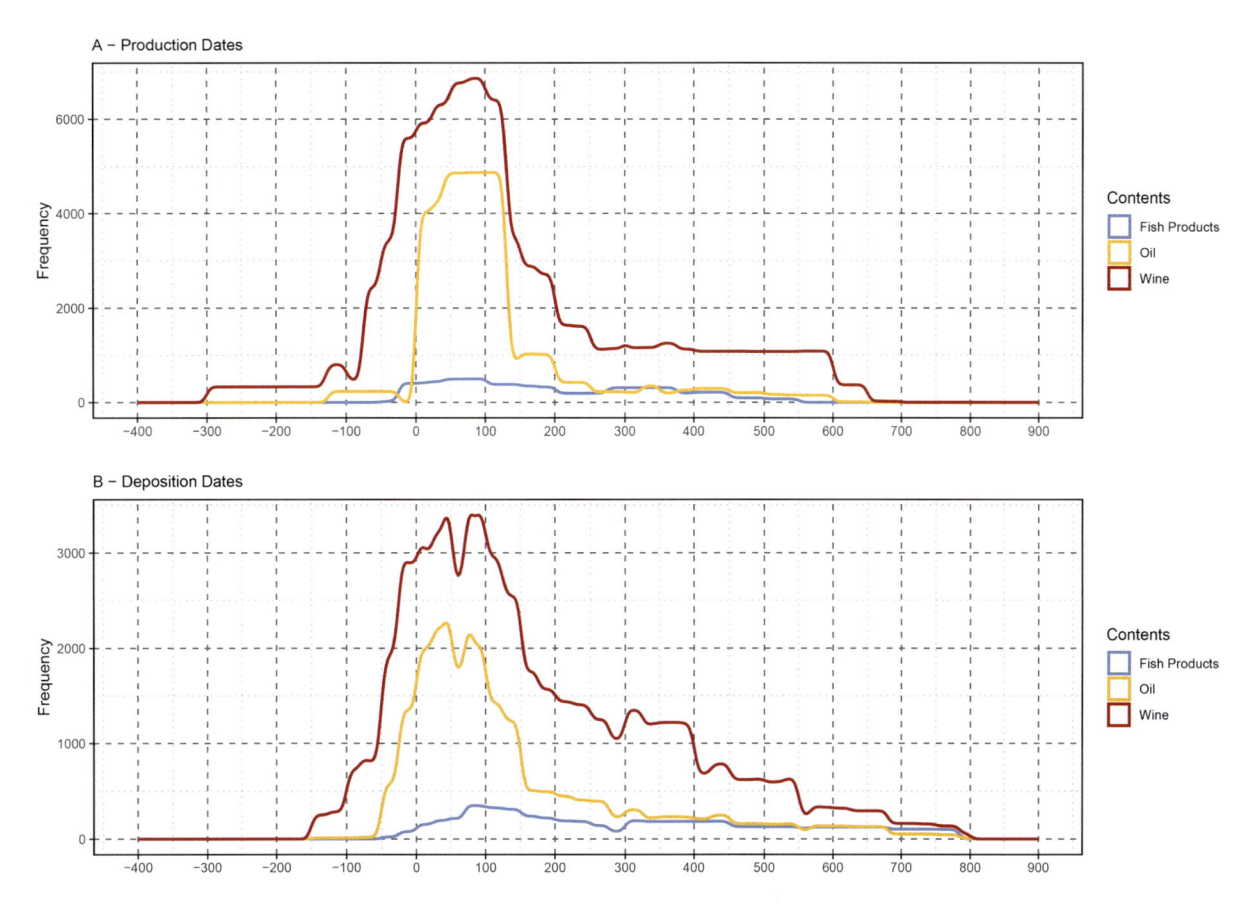

Figure 20. Comparison of Production and Deposition chronologies for the quantities of wine, oil, and fish product amphorae. Note the Y axes are not continuous.

The second most common amphora contents was oil, which appears in significant quantities. Although there was a relatively constant demand for amphora-borne wine over time in Northern Italy, the curve for oil tells a different story. Production chronologies suggest a rapid spike and decline in oil that perfectly matches the production lifespan of the Dressel 6B, the principal oil-bearing vessel attested in the region. This is followed by a plateau in the frequency of oil amphora throughout the following centuries. In contrast, deposition chronologies imply a more gradual (although still significant) rise and fall in frequency, followed by a similar plateauing of oil amphorae. Finally, fish product amphorae appear in significantly lower frequencies than those for wine and oil. After their initial peak towards the end of the 1st century AD, fish products remained relatively constant across the following centuries, a pattern represented by both production and deposition chronologies.

Moving beyond the overall picture, separating supplies of wine, oil, and fish products by their provenance provides a more detailed understanding of how consumption patterns changed (see Figure 21). Imports of wine were present in the highest frequency and had the greatest diversity in their provenance. Production

chronologies in Graph A show initial imports of wine arrived from the Tyrrhenian Littoral, with an early peak *c.* 125 BC. These vessels would see a moderate decline throughout the 1st century BC, before plateauing throughout the 1st and 2nd centuries AD. Tyrrhenian wine amphorae were absent between the 3rd and mid-4th centuries before imports of the Keay 52 appeared from *c.* AD 350 onwards. Adriatic wine was present in the highest frequencies, dominating imports during the 1st century BC and 1st century AD, before falling sharply through the first half of the 2nd century and disappearing completely by the end of the 3rd century. Wines from the Eastern Mediterranean also appeared in high frequencies, arriving in increasing quantities from the mid-1st century BC onwards. After an initial peak *c.* AD 150, they declined, yet at the same time replaced the Adriatic as the dominant provenance for wine. Quantities increased again at the start of the 4th century, leading to a second peak and stable frequency until their disappearance in the 7th century. North African wines are represented in limited quantities from the mid-2nd to 4th century AD and Gallic and Iberian wines are barely present, confined to the 1st century AD. Deposition chronologies in Graph B tell a similar story, with some refinements. The chronology of wine from the Tyrrhenian Littoral is more confined,

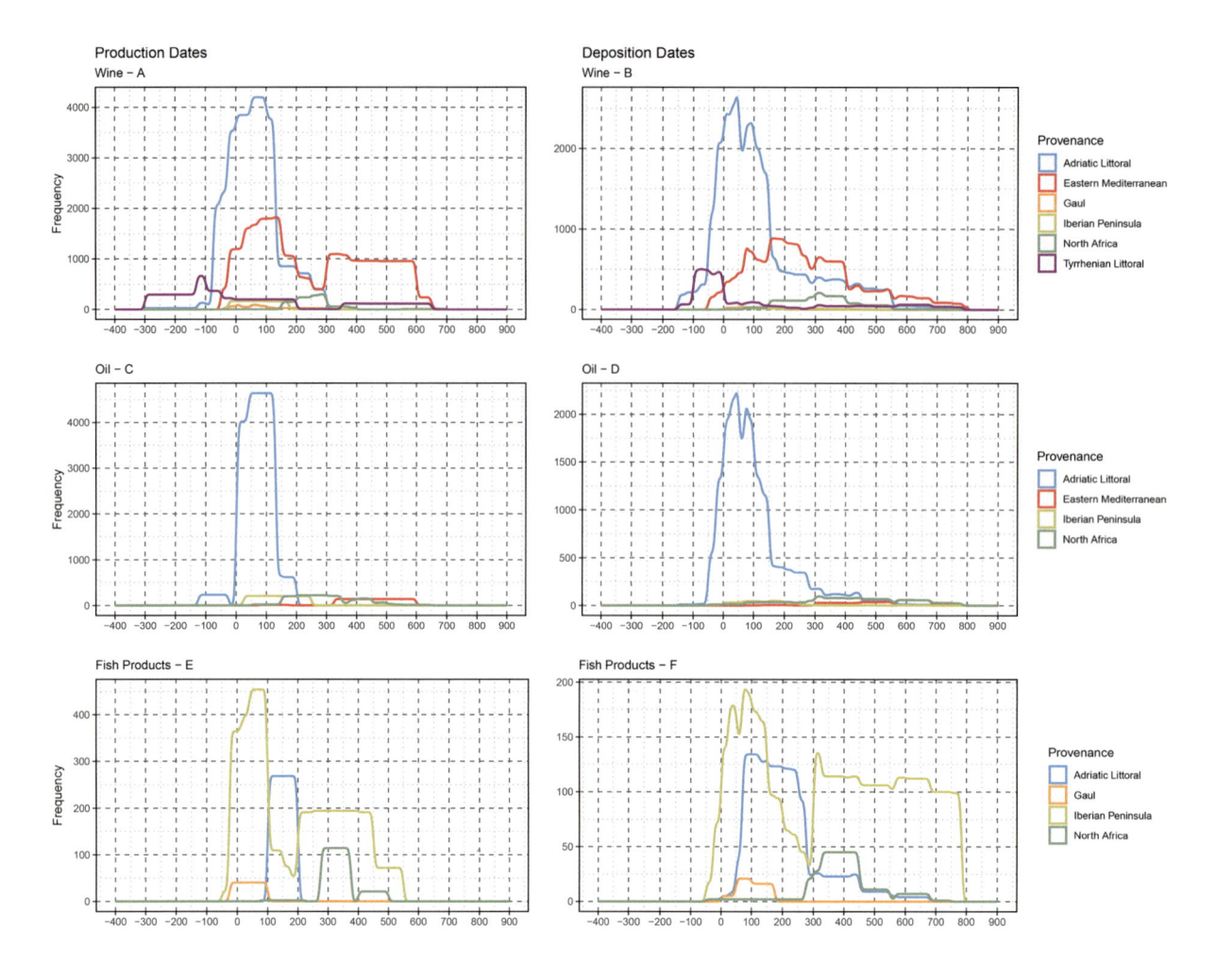

Figure 21. Comparison of Production and Deposition chronologies for the frequency of each zone of production supplying wine, oil, and fish product amphorae. Note the Y axes are not continuous.

with a pronounced peak in the 1st century BC, before their near total disappearance. Adriatic wine amphorae peaked and declined earlier, although continued to appear in appreciable quantities into the 6th century. The curve for Eastern Mediterranean wine is also more pronounced, with a single peak in the mid-2nd century AD.

In contrast to wine, only four oil-producing regions are represented within Northern Italy. These were the Adriatic Littoral, the Eastern Mediterranean, the Iberian Peninsula, and North Africa. Out of these, the dominance of the Adriatic Littoral in the supply of oil is striking. Production chronologies in Graph C show that, after an initial rise between c. 130 BC and 30 BC, the frequency of Adriatic oil increased sharply in the late 1st century BC, before plateauing between AD 50 and AD 125. This is followed by an equally sharp drop, leading to a final disappearance of Adriatic oil by the end of the 2nd century. Other oil-producing regions are barely present in the graph, even after the cessation of Adriatic supply. The distribution is similar when

measured using deposition chronologies in Graph D. Although Adriatic oil appears and disappears from the region later than in Graph C, the Adriatic Littoral remains the overwhelmingly dominant provenance for oil.

The picture that emerges for fish products is significantly different to that of wine and oil. Of the major contents so far examined, fish products are the only ones not dominated by amphorae from the Adriatic Littoral. When measured using production chronologies in Graph E, the Iberian Peninsula stands out as the dominant supplier, with an initial sharp rise in the latter half of the 1st century BC. The frequency of Iberian vessels reaches its peak between AD 50 and AD 100, before dropping sharply at the beginning of the 2nd century. This dip in Iberian fish products is matched by a spike in amphorae from the Adriatic Littoral, namely the Grado 1 and Anforetta da Pesce Adriaticha. Fish products from the Adriatic are only in circulation for approximately 100 years, disappearing entirely by the beginning of the 3rd century AD. However, this pattern should be viewed with caution, considering the known reuse of Dressel 6A wine amphorae and Dessel 6B and Africana 1 oil amphorae as containers for fish sauce and preserved fish originating from the Adriatic Coast.[68] Adriatic fish products may well have formed a higher percentage of consumption than is currently visible. Indeed, extensive evidence for the production of fish products and fish breeding along the Adriatic Coast is visible in the Po delta (for example at the villas of Argine d'Agosta, Bocca delle Menate, Corte Cavanella di Loreo, and Dosso dei Sassi) and Istria (for example at the villas of Katoro, Kupanja, and Svršata).[69] Unfortunately, without widespread residue analysis, the scale of the trade in Adriatic fish products in recycled vessels remains unknown, although it has the potential to have made a significant contribution to regional supply.[70]

This disappearance of Adriatic fish product amphorae is coupled with a revival of Iberian vessels, the frequency of which rises again before plateauing until the 5th century. North African fish products appear in the region from *c.* AD 250 onwards, forming two peaks, and amphorae from Gaul are attested in minimal frequencies. Imports of fish products disappear entirely by the middle of the 6th century AD. The view presented by deposition chronologies in Graph F is significantly different, with zones of supply being far more evenly distributed. The initial spike in Iberian imports in the mid-1st century AD remains but Adriatic and North African amphorae subsequently appear much earlier and endure far longer. The size of their curves is also much larger in relation to Iberian vessels than in Graph E.

The analysis of amphora contents, and the provenance of the individual goods across the zones of production, highlighted evolving patterns of consumption within Northern Italy across the Roman period. Booming demand for wine and oil saw imports of both rise to a pronounced peak in the 1st century AD, with the Adriatic Littoral acting as their principal zone of production. Demand for fish products remained relatively constant across the Roman period, with the Iberian Peninsula forming their main origin. Of all the products in circulation, wine was the most common. Imported wine arrived earlier and declined later than oil within the region. There was sustained demand for wine in Northern Italy across the Roman period and

wine was always imported in higher quantities than both oil and fish sauce. The ability of wine to serve as both a staple and luxury product ensured it remained a desirable and competitive import, something that does not seem to have applied to oil. Eastern Mediterranean wines, initially travelling in the Camulodunum 184, Cretoise 1-3, and Dressel 43, had different attributes to Italian wine, being generally sweeter.[71] Many Eastern Wines were also held in high repute amongst ancient writers.[72] This enabled them to compete against the more numerous local products and Adriatic wine travelling in the Dressel 6A under the Early Empire. After the 3rd century AD, when wine from other zones of production began to disappear in the region, Eastern Mediterranean wines (principally from the Levant) continued to circulate in similar quantities, remaining competitive import against a backdrop of expanded local wine production (see Chapter 3).

Although the total frequency of vessels carrying fish products as their primary contents remained low in comparison to wine and oil, demand for fish products does not seem to have been subject to the same fluctuations in imports. As with wine, fish products were both a staple and a luxury, with some products praised for attributes and taste.[73] Iberian fish products were especially prized and had a reputation for high quality, making them a worthwhile and desirable product for traders.[74] Depletion of fish stocks around Italy may also have resulted in a continued reliance on imported fish products.[75] While Iberia would dominate Northern Italic fish product imports, the evidence for the reuse of other amphorae as transport containers for Adriatic fish products discussed above also opens the possibility that far more fish products were in circulation than suggested by the current analysis.

In comparison to the continued import of wine and fish products after their late 1st century AD peak, the near total collapse of amphora-borne oil imports to Northern Italy during the 3rd century AD is striking. The region heavily relied on Adriatic amphorae, mainly the Dressel 6B and Anfora con Collo ad Imbuto for its oil imports, to the exclusion of almost all other zones of production. When these vessel forms ceased production, North African became the principal supplier of amphora-borne oil to the region, but in significantly lower

[68] Auriemma 2000: 42-45; Carre and Pesavento Mattioli 2021; Cipriano 2009; Mazzocchin and Wilkins 2013. Bones recovered from the interior of the Dressel 6A consisted of a mixture of freshwater and saltwater fish, suggesting production was taking place in the lagoon system or a river mouth.

[69] Buonopane 2009; Busana, D'Inca, and Forti 2009; Carre and Auriemma 2009. Most of this evidence dates to the 1st and 2nd centuries AD.

[70] Van Neer, Ervynck, and Monsieur 2010: 163-66. Dressel 6A and 6B amphorae marked as carrying fish products have been found as far afield as Magdalensberg and Salzburg.

[71] Dodd 2020: 59–64; Komar 2021: 100-102.

[72] See Komar 2021: Chapter 2 for a summary of ancient attitudes towards Eastern Mediterranean wines.

[73] See Grainger's (2021: 253-56) discussion about the status of Iberian fish products as a higher quality alternative to locally produced sauces in Early Imperial Italy. See Ettienne 1970 and Curtis 1991 for prior interpretations.

[74] Hor. *Sat.* 2.8.42; Plin *HN* 31.94. The consistent use of large, high-quality mackerel in Iberian fish sauces, as opposed to the more widely used smaller, miscellaneous, and cheaper fish in other sauce production, served to set it apart (Grainger 2021: 27-31; Morales-Muñiz and Roselló-Izquierdo 2016).

[75] Curtis 1991: 59.

quantities. The contribution of locally produced oil travelling in perishable containers to regional supply during this later period was probably considerable.

Geographic Trends

So far, analysis of the AMINI dataset has demonstrated significant variation in the quantities and provenance of amphorae chronologically across Northern Italy. This variation is mirrored geographically across the region. To explore spatial trends, the assemblages of the regional urban centres in the AMINI dataset were analysed using hierarchical clustering based on their assemblage provenance. Sites with similar assemblage provenances are grouped by the analysis, allowing geographic clusters to form (see Figure 22). The site assemblages are subdivided by chronological period based on vessel production chronologies.[76] To ensure a rigorous level of analysis, a minimum sample size of 30 sherds per period was necessary for a site to be included. Port sites are excluded from the analysis, as their role as entrepôts results in assemblages significantly different in composition to other inland sites in their geographic vicinity (discussed in further detail below).

The Late Republic

Nine sites from the Late Republican dataset met the minimum threshold of 30 sherds for analysis. When these sites were hierarchically clustered based on the provenance of their assemblages, a single main geographic group was identified (see Figure 23). This cluster contained eight sites located in the central and eastern Po Valley, alongside the coastal plain, the assemblages of which were dominated by amphorae from the Adriatic Littoral. Adriatic vessels comprised between 81.2% and 100% of assemblages in the cluster, with other provenances minimally attested (see Appendix B for a breakdown of each site's assemblage). The only inland site not to join the main cluster was Ivrea in the western Po Valley, which placed independently. The composition of Ivrea's assemblage was very different from other Late Republican sites.[77] Only 59.2% of its assemblage derived from the Adriatic zone of production, and it contained the highest quantity of Tyrrhenian amphorae out of the Late Republican dataset (40.1% of Ivrea's assemblage). This served to set it apart from other regional centres.

The geographic distribution of amphorae in Northern Italy during the Late Republic suggests that the mechanisms and infrastructure needed to transport large quantities of goods inland were already in place during this early period. The Adriatic Coast likely formed the main entry point for goods entering the region, with the Po forming the main axis of trade from east to west. Amphora imports from the Adriatic Littoral, overwhelmingly the Lamboglia 2 form, were found in large numbers at sites across the study area. The Tyrrhenian Littoral, near uniformly represented by the Dressel 1, formed the next most common provenance, although, for the most part, made minor contributions to each assemblage. Imports from other provenances appeared in negligible quantities. Such limited diversity reflects the lack of choice available to consumers during this period, with zones of production in Gaul and Iberia yet to be fully established and Eastern Mediterranean amphorae only just beginning to penetrate the Adriatic.[78]

The dominance of Adriatic production and the limited number of vessel forms circulating during the Late Republic resulted in greater uniformity, rather than diversity, in the provenance of amphora assemblages across Northern Italy. Even Tyrrhenian amphorae only appeared in significant quantities at urban centres in the west of the Po Valley such as Ivrea, the only sites well-placed to take advantage of Tyrrhenian goods. The low number of Tyrrhenian vessels recovered from the eastern Po Valley suggests that Dressel 1 amphorae were mainly entering the region over the Apennines, with the via Postumia (constructed in 148 BC) being the obvious route. The costs and logistics of transporting these vessels across the mountains would have made it prohibitive to transport them further east than the areas nearest the Apennine passes. The geopolitical situation present in Liguria for much of the Republican era would also form a barrier to substantial trade across trans-Apennine routes. The hostility of its inhabitants to Roman intervention and the presence of pirates operating from Ligurian ports served to hinder the creation of stable economic networks until the 1st century BC.[79]

The Late Republican assemblages demonstrate that amphora-borne goods in Northern Italy were almost exclusively supplied by areas in the region's immediate vicinity during this period. Northern Italy was strongly integrated into the Adriatic economy and its predominant imports travelled a very short distance to reach their destination. There were fewer connections to Western Italy, but significant quantities of Tyrrhenian amphorae were able to supply the western Po Valley. The penetration of significant quantities of Adriatic amphorae into the far west of the Po Valley suggests that the region's networks of transport and redistribution were already relatively sophisticated during this period, especially considering most infrastructure investment would take place in

---

[76] This was to maximise the amount of data available for the analysis, as not all assemblages included deposition dates.
[77] Brecciaroli Taborelli 1987; Gabucci and Quiri 2008.

[78] Auriemma and Quiri 2004; Auriemma, Degressi, and Quiri 2015.
[79] Diod. Sic. 5.39; Livy 40.18.4; Sall. *Hist.* 3.5-7; Plut. *Aem.* 6.2-3.

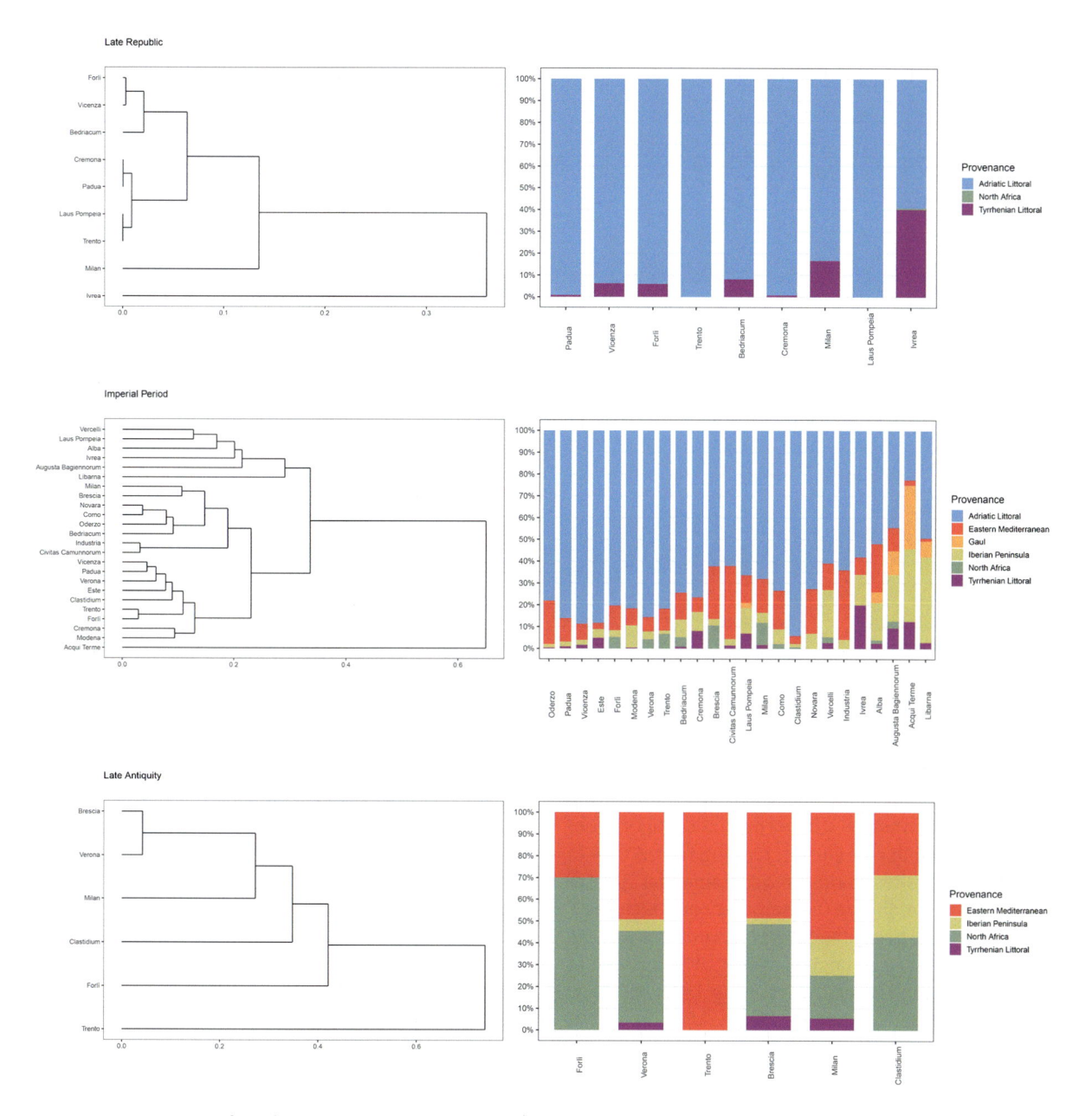

Figure 22. Percentages of amphora provenance at each site divided by period, with subsequently formed hierarchical clusters. See Appendix B for exact percentages and n numbers for each assemblage.

the following century. Connections to wider extra-provincial economies located in the Western and Eastern Mediterranean were overall limited during this period, but the networks that future imports would travel along were already in place by the Late Republic.

The Imperial Period

From the Imperial period dataset, 24 sites met the minimum threshold of 30 sherds for analysis. When these sites were hierarchically clustered, three geographic groups were identified (see Figure 24).[80] The first cluster was comprised of nine sites dominated

by Adriatic amphorae. Sites within this cluster were mainly located on the coastal plain, eastern and central Po Valley, and the Adige Valley. They were uniformly in lowland, rather than upland areas. Amphorae from the Adriatic Littoral ranged from 76.6% to 94.6% of assemblages and were complemented by very low numbers of other imports, principally from the Eastern Mediterranean. These ranged from 2% to 12.8% of assemblages. Some Iberian and North African vessels were also attested, but Gallic and Tyrrhenian vessels were present in minimal quantities.

The second cluster was comprised of eight sites, located further inland within the north-west and centre of the Po Plain, alongside the Alpine foothills and valleys.

---

[80] Some overlap exists between the groups, but the overall pattern is consistent.

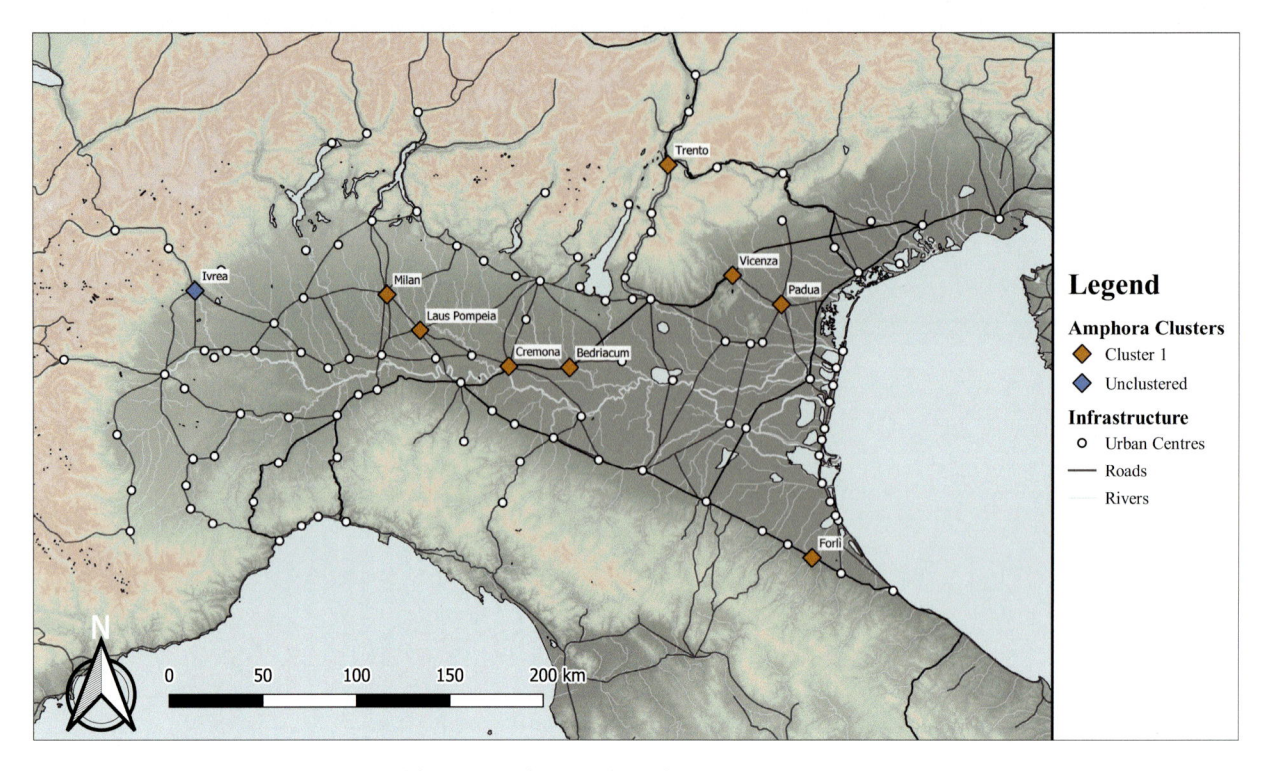

Figure 23. Late Republican site clusters, based on amphora assemblage provenance.

Oderzo formed an outlier, located on the coastal plain.[81] Adriatic vessels still formed the majority of each assemblage in this cluster, ranging from 67.9% to 78.1%. However, sites in cluster 2 contained far greater quantities of amphorae from other provenances.[82] Eastern Mediterranean amphorae accounted for the second largest group, ranging from 12.3% to 33.5% of assemblages. Iberian vessels made up the next most common provenance, ranging from 1.3% to 20.5%. Tyrrhenian and North African imports remained low, generally under 4%. The exceptions to these were Brescia and Milan, where North African vessels made up over 10% of each assemblage.[83]

The third and final cluster contained sites located in the west and south-west of the Po Valley, the areas closest to the Ligurian Apennines and the Western Alps, and furthest away from the Adriatic Coast. Laus Pompeia formed an outlier, located in the central Po Valley.[84] The Adriatic Littoral still formed the dominant zone of production, ranging between 44.1% and 48.5%

of each site assemblage. However, the Adriatic Littoral was complemented by a much greater diversity in the provenance of the remaining vessels present at each site, including significant quantities of Western Mediterranean amphorae.[85] No single provenance formed the second largest across the cluster, with quantities differing across the sites. Eastern Mediterranean vessels accounted for between 2.8% and 22.1% of assemblages; Iberian vessels ranged from 11.6% to 39.1%; Gallic vessels ranged from between 0% and 10.8%; and Tyrrhenian imports between 2.8% and 9.5%. North African imports, however, remained in quantities below 2% of each assemblage.

The site of Acqui Terme did not join a cluster, instead placing independently. The composition of Acqui Terme's assemblage was significantly different to other sites in the Imperial dataset, being mostly comprised of Western Mediterranean amphorae.[86] The Iberian Peninsula formed the dominant zone of production (33.3%), closely followed by Gaul (29.1%). Amphorae from the Adriatic Littoral comprised only 22.5% of Acqui Terme's assemblage, the lowest within the Imperial sample. Although it did not group with other sites, the high quantities of Western Mediterranean vessels in Acqui Terme's assemblage echo wider trends of Gallic

[81] Cipriano and Ferrarini 2001. It is possible that Oderzo's assemblage, due to its proximity to the major ports of Aquileia and Altinum, might reflect a different axis of trade, one geared towards the Danubian *Limes*, rather than the Po Valley. However, the quantity of Adriatic vessels in Oderzo's assemblage were also the highest in the cluster, accounting for 78.1% and putting it on par with sites in cluster 1.

[82] Bocchio 2004; Bruno 2005a; Facchini and Leotta 2005; Masseroli 1997; Quiri and Spagnolo Garzoli 2015; Volonte 1996; Zanda 2011.

[83] Bruno 2002; 2003; Bruno and Bocchio 1991; 1999; Contessi 2014; Corrado 2003; Panazza and Brogiolo 1998.

[84] Francesoni 2020.

[85] Brecciaroli Taborelli 1987a; 1987b; Bruno 1997; 1998; Gabucci and Quiri 2008; Quiri 2014, Spagnolo Garzoli *et al.* 2007.

[86] Bruno 1998; Pettirossi and Pistarino 2008; Secchi 2017.

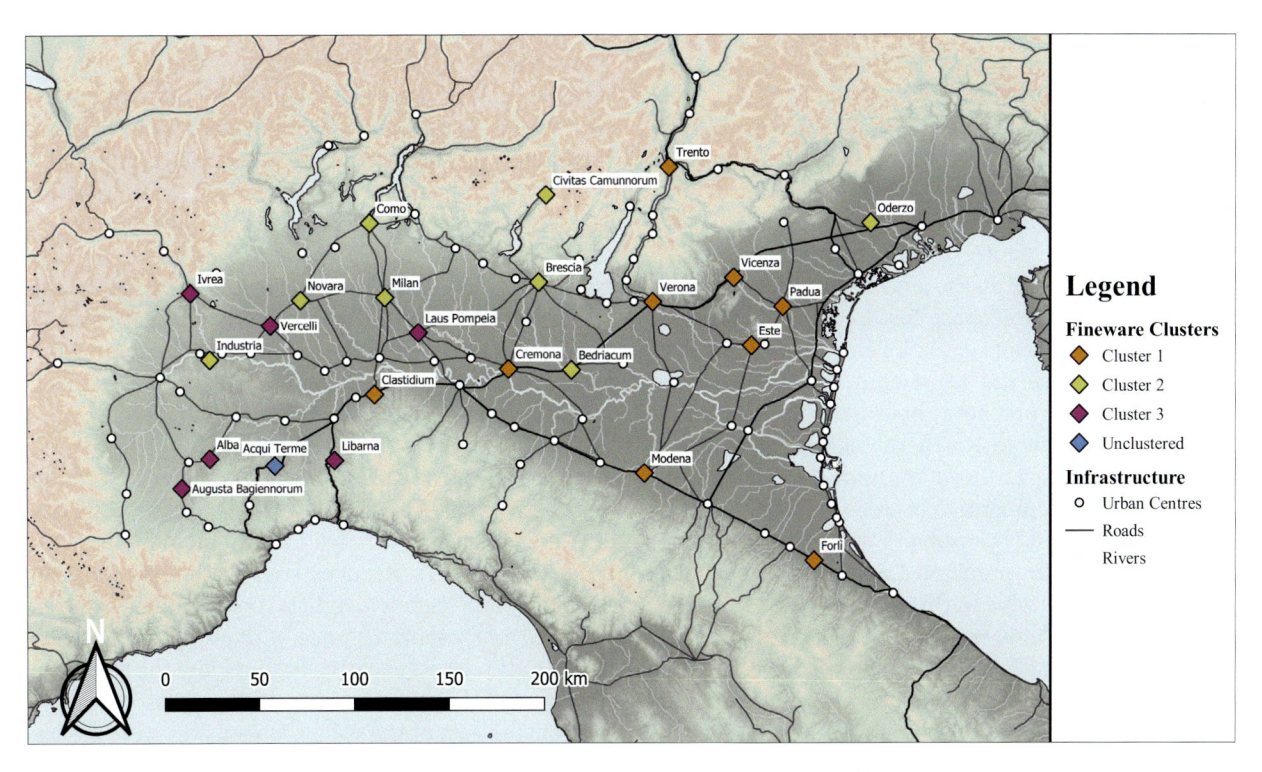

Figure 24. Imperial period site clusters, based on amphora assemblage provenance.

and Iberian consumption seen in the geographically adjacent cluster 3.

The Imperial period saw an increase in the number of zones of production supplying Northern Italy. Although amphora assemblages across the region continued to be dominated by goods produced along the Adriatic Littoral, as new productive landscapes were brought under cultivation and inter-provincial trade increased, communities were presented with a greater choice in the goods they consumed. Amongst the continuity of pre-existing trade routes, new networks of supply were created, leading to the formation of distinct zones of consumption within Northern Italy.

The first zone of consumption is represented by assemblages from sites in the Adriatic coastal hinterland, alongside those that lay directly on the Po itself. Site assemblages in this zone consisted almost entirely of Adriatic amphorae, with vessels of other provenances appearing in minimal quantities. Given the proximity of these urban centres to the Adriatic ports, or their placement on the river network (the region's main transport artery), the low quantities of other imports present in these assemblages are at first somewhat surprising. Coastal hinterlands have been promoted as some of the best-connected areas in the Roman world due to their proximity to maritime trade routes.[87] However, this greater connectivity does

not seem to have translated into a greater variety of imports for sites near the coast. Instead, the available quantity and presumably lower prices of Adriatic imports may have been favoured over more exotic or unusual goods on the market, with specific product choice less of a concern. Sites in the central and eastern Po Valley and the coastal plain had initial access to Adriatic imports, which had travelled the least distance to reach consumers.[88] Low transport costs afforded by the density of the river and road networks in this part of the region allowed large quantities of Adriatic goods to penetrate significant distances inland, explaining why sites in the centre of the Po Valley, such as Cremona and Clastidium, had similar assemblage compositions to those on the coastal plain.[89]

The second zone of consumption was formed of sites mainly located in the Alpine foothills and north-west of the Po Valley. Its sites were at a greater distance inland than those on the coastal plain and central valley and were placed in peripheral locations in the foothills off the valley floor. Although Adriatic amphorae were still present in the greatest quantities, other goods travelling inland from the Adriatic Coast seem to have become more competitive. The Po Valley's geography

---

[87] Horden and Purcell 2000: 115-22; Scheidel 2014: 14; Wilson, Schörle, and Rice 2009: 384.

[88] Dressel 6A and 6B amphorae produced in eastern Emilia-Romagna and the Veneto Plain would have travelled the least distance of all, making them the most competitive (Carre, Monsiuer, and Pesavento Mattioli 2014; Cipriano and Mazzocchin 2019; Martin, Mazzoli, and Mazzocchin 2019).

[89] Acari 1996; Dobreva and Ravasi 2018; Marrioti, Massa, and Ravasi 2008; Vecchi 1999; Volonte, Ravasi, and Nicodemo 2008.

naturally facilitated access to markets in both the Adriatic and Eastern Mediterranean, and Eastern wine amphorae appear in increasing quantities within this zone of consumption. The reduction in the quantities of Adriatic vessels seen at sites in the Alpine foothills and north-west of the Po Valley may be related to price. These urban centres, at a greater distance from the coast or located at the end of navigable rivers, incurred a greater transport cost to reach than those in the central valley and coastal plain. Rising transport costs may have served to remove the comparative advantage Adriatic amphorae held due to the proximity of their production to Northern Italic markets. This may have served to make Eastern Mediterranean amphorae more competitive in price as distance from the coast increased.[90] Consumers may have made the deliberate choice to purchase Eastern Mediterranean wine over Adriatic wine in this case. In contrast to the diversification of wine suppliers, it is interesting that the zones of production supplying oil to this area of Northern Italy did not expand. Perhaps other supplies of oil (mainly from the Iberian Peninsula during this period) remained uncompetitive from a cost standpoint, resulting in the Adriatic Littoral remaining the principal supplier. While Eastern Mediterranean vessels were travelling along the same trade routes as Adriatic amphorae within Northern Italy, goods from Iberia would need to travel across the Apennines before entering the region. This trans-Apennine crossing, followed by further transport stages to reach sites in the north and central Po Valley, may have ensured their price remained uncompetitive in comparison to Adriatic oil.

The final zone of consumption was comprised of sites in the west and south-west of the Po Valley, where the provenance of amphorae assemblages diverged significantly from those in the previous two zones and contained high quantities of Western Mediterranean amphorae. While the geography of Northern Italy naturally orientates its connections east, the south-west of the valley is located a short distance from the Ligurian Sea. Separated by the Apennine mountains, Ligurian ports such as Genoa offered an alternative entry point for goods to enter the region.[91] By the time Adriatic and Eastern amphorae had travelled into the west and the south-west of the Po Valley, prices may have risen to such an extent that Western Mediterranean goods crossing the Apennines became competitive.[92]

The existence of trans-Apennine trade and the presence of Western Mediterranean goods in the south-western Po Valley has been commented on before, but the intensity of this traffic has never been quantified.[93] During the Imperial period, Western Mediterranean imports comprised between 23.1% and 48.5% of assemblages within this zone, suggesting significant trans-Apennine trade despite the obstacle posed by the mountains. At Acqui Terme, the percentage of Western Mediterranean amphorae rose to 74.9%, indicating the level of intensity connections with Ligurian ports, and through them, western markets, could achieve.

The amphora data from the Imperial period demonstrates the various levels of economic activity and networks of exchange present across Northern Italy. The region's strongest ties were with areas in its immediate vicinity and its predominant imports travelled a very short distance, with production areas in the Adriatic almost exclusively supplying the Northern Italian market with oil and wine. This was especially true for the east of the valley, where sites were almost entirely dominated by Adriatic vessels. However, inland areas show increasing integration with other extra-provincial economies, particularly those in the Eastern Mediterranean. This reached its greatest extent in the west and south-west of the Po Valley, which recorded the lowest quantities of Adriatic goods and saw integration into Western Mediterranean markets, despite the barrier posed by the Apennines. Overall, amphora-borne trade in Northern Italy during this period seems to have been import-orientated, mostly consisting of vessels produced outside the region with strong connections to extra-provincial markets.[94]

Late Antiquity

Late Antiquity saw significant spatial reorganisation across Northern Italy. The region was first divided into provinces within the diocese of *Italicana* by Diocletian's reforms, and then split from the rest of Italy under Constantine I, being incorporated into the new vicariate of *Italia annonaria* in the early 4th century AD.[95] Unfortunately, due to the small sample size in the dataset, it is impossible to see whether the division of Northern Italy impacted the movement of amphora-borne goods within it. The low number of assemblages containing Late Antique material in sufficient quantities for analysis severely limited the effectiveness of the hierarchical clustering in this final period. Only six sites made the threshold for analysis, hampering interpretation. When sites in the Late Antique dataset

[90] Gallimore (2023: 375-78) suggests that the high quality of some Eastern Mediterranean wines (especially Cretan ones) may have made them more competitive in inland markets.

[91] Imports of Gallic amphorae were likely traded along the coast and over the Apennines, rather than across the Alps. Although some goods did cross the Alps in significant quantities (see Gabucci 2017 and Chapter 5 of this volume), these were mostly smaller than amphorae and were traded for their items themselves, not their contents.

[92] See Page 2023; 2024, for a discussion of transport costs across Northern Italy during the Roman era.

[93] Bruno 1998; Melli 2000.

[94] Cipriano and Mazzocchin 2019: 240-43. The majority of Dressel 6A and Dressel 6B vessels identified as being produced in Northern Italy were distributed either within the region itself or in the vicinity of trans-Alpine routes near Magdalensberg.

[95] Barnes 1982; Bowman 2005; Giardina 1993; 1997.

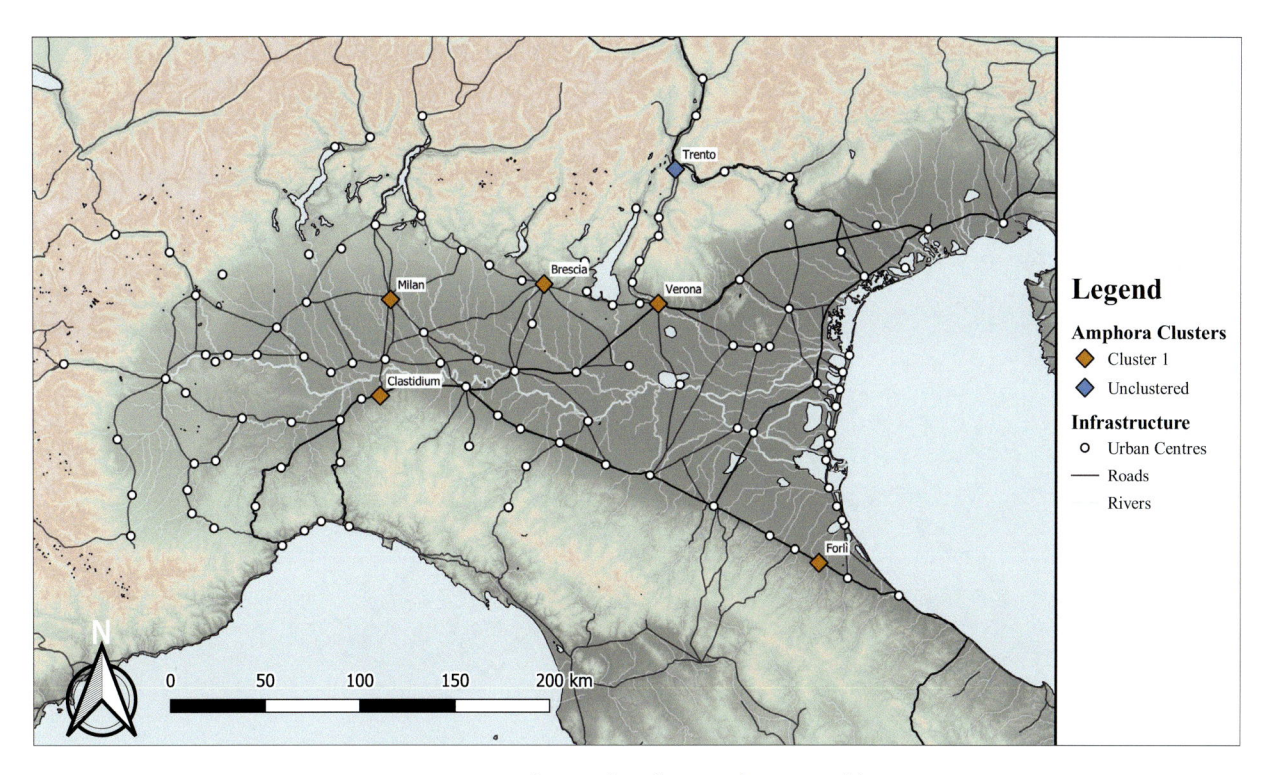

Figure 25. Late Antique site clusters, based on amphora assemblage provenance.

were hierarchically clustered based on the provenance of their assemblages, only a single cluster formed (see Figure 25). This cluster was comprised of five sites: Brescia, Clastidium, Forlì, Milan, and Verona.[96] No one zone of production dominated the site assemblages, with Eastern Mediterranean and North African vessels comprising the two main zones of production. Eastern Mediterranean amphorae comprised between 58.1% and 28.5% of assemblages in the cluster, while North African vessels consisted of between 70% and 19.8%. Quantities of Iberian amphorae varied between 0% and 28.5%, while vessels from the Tyrrhenian Littoral were present in minimal quantities. The site of Trento did not join the cluster, as its assemblage was entirely composed of Eastern Mediterranean amphorae.[97]

Amphora-borne trade in Late Antiquity saw major changes from the preceding periods and, despite the limited sample size, some tentative patterns can be inferred. Assemblages from across Northern Italy demonstrate greater uniformity in their composition during this period than in the preceding two centuries. The split between Eastern Mediterranean and North African vessels remains fairly even across site assemblages during this period, with both zones of production making substantial contributions to regional imports. The domination of Eastern Mediterranean and North African amphorae across

Northern Italy during this period demonstrates a strong level of integration into markets in the Eastern and Southern Mediterranean. However, the uniformity in the provenance of Late Antique assemblages in comparison to the preceding period may suggest that the factors governing the distribution of amphora-borne goods had changed. The placement of an imperial capital at Milan in AD 289, and the increasing militarisation of Northern Italy during the 3rd century, created new demand for foodstuffs.[98] The state may have played a role in organising the movement of Eastern Mediterranean and North African goods to provision the armies now operating in Northern Italy.[99] It is also possible that imported amphorae contributed towards Late Antique military supply or piggy-backed on other goods intended for the *annona militaris*.[100] Such state action could have helped to determine the quantities of Eastern Mediterranean and North African amphorae arriving in Northern Italy. Equally, the decline of other zones of production meant that North African imports were needed to make up a shortfall in goods previously supplied from the Adriatic and Western Mediterranean.[101]

---

[96] Bruno 1988; 2002; 2008; Bruno and Bocchio 1991; 1999; Biondani 2008; Vecchi 1999.
[97] Maurina 1995.

[98] Roncaglia (2018: 119-26) argues that *Italia annonaria* was envisioned as a vicariate that could both host and provision the armies defending Northern Italy.
[99] Reynolds 1995: Chapter 3; 2018: 381. This particularly evident from the Severan period onwards with the introduction of the *annona militaris*.
[100] McCormick 2001: 87-92; Tchernia 2011: 345-48.
[101] Dobreva 2023; Pieri 2012. The overall frequency of Eastern Mediterranean vessels remains relatively similar to earlier periods (something also highlighted by Komar 2021: 268-70). However,

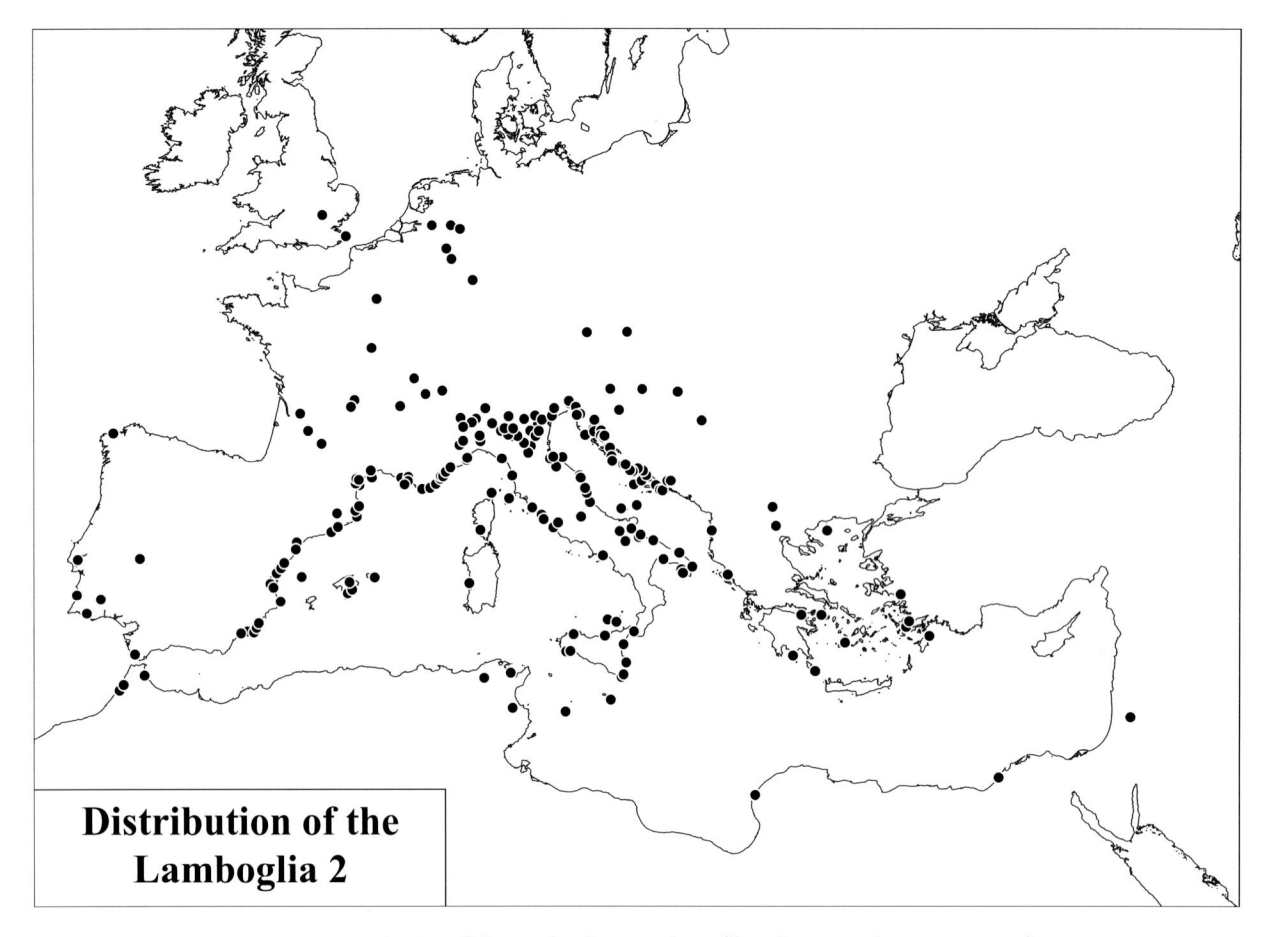

Distribution of the Lamboglia 2

Figure 26. Distribution of the Lamboglia 2 amphora (data from Van den Bergen 2012).

The dominance of Eastern Mediterranean and North African imports suggests the Adriatic Coast continued to be the main entry point for goods coming into the valley, especially given the increased political and strategic importance of Aquileia and Ravenna during Late Antiquity.[102] While Eastern Mediterranean and Northern African imports travelled up the Po, the limited data from the west of the study area may suggest that trans-Apennine trade remained important during this period. The highest quantities of Iberian amphorae were recovered from Clastidium and Milan in the western Po Valley, with Iberian imports appearing in minimal quantities at sites elsewhere in the region.[103] Forlì, the eastern most site in the Late Antique sample, contained no Iberian amphorae.[104] Unfortunately, without the publication of more assemblages from the western end of the valley, it is difficult to make conclusive judgements on the intensity of trans-Apennine trade during the Late Antique period.

Amphora-borne Trade in Northern Italy

Analysis of the AMINI dataset outlined numerous trends in amphora-borne trade in Northern Italy between the 3rd century BC and the 8th century AD. The following section explores a series of case studies identified through the analysis, enabling a greater depth of understanding behind the chronological and spatial trends so-far highlighted.

The Adriatic Littoral: Evolving Containerisation and Specialisation

Of all the zones of production supplying Northern Italy during the Roman era, it was the Adriatic Littoral that had the greatest impact on amphora-borne trade within the region. Adriatic amphorae were the most numerous and widespread of all vessels within the AMINI dataset, with the shape of many graphs overwhelmingly influenced by the frequency of vessels from the Adriatic Littoral across Northern Italy.

Adriatic amphora imports began to circulate during the initial Republican expansion into Northern Italy. These vessels were overwhelmingly the Lamboglia 2 form, which were found in large numbers at sites across the

---

the paucity of Late Antique data may obscure the true quantity circulating.
[102] Komar 2021: 269-70; Roncaglia 2018: 136-41.
[103] Bruno and Bocchio 1991; Vecchi 1999.
[104] Tempesta 2013.

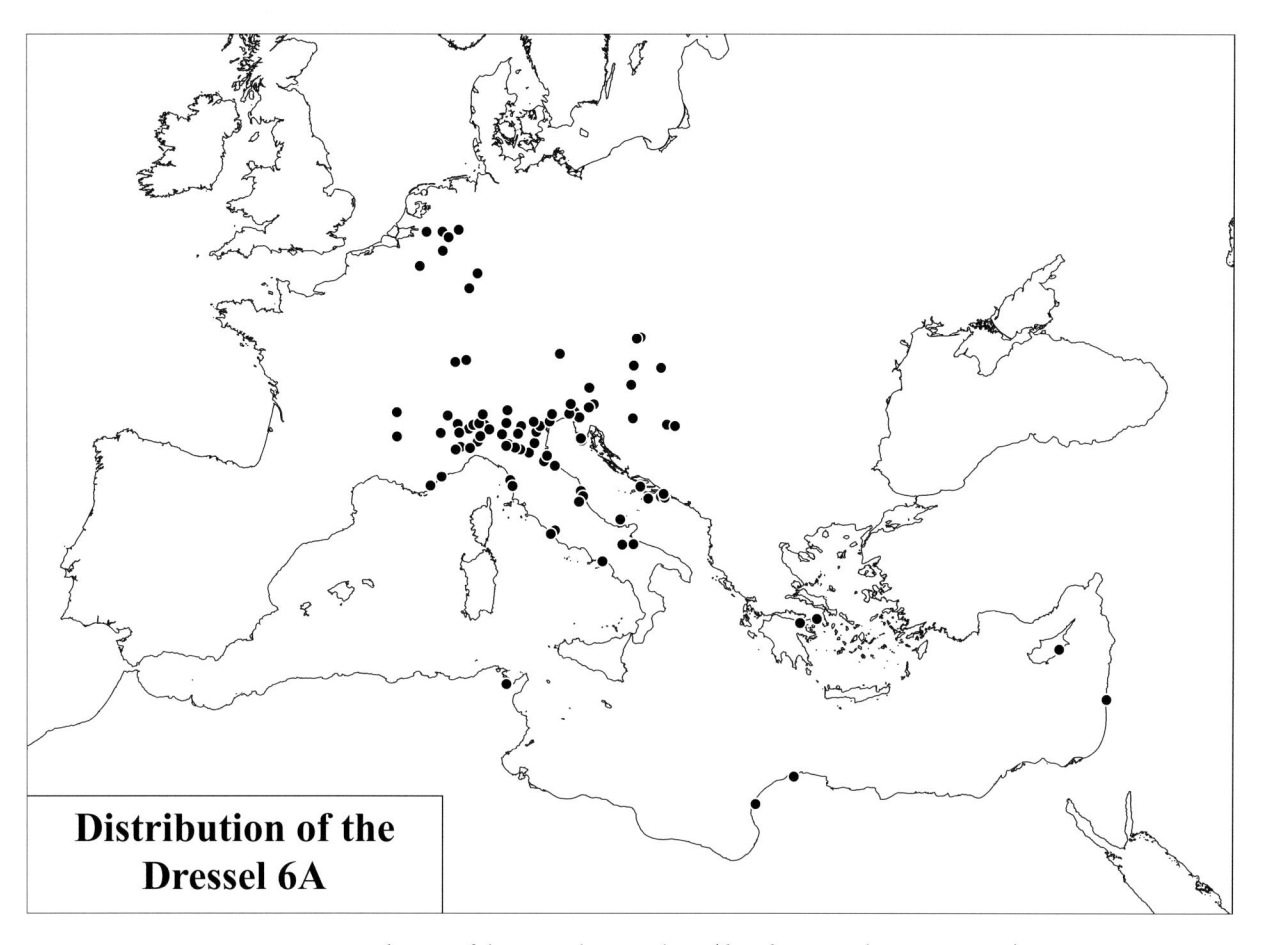

Distribution of the Dressel 6A

Figure 27. Distribution of the Dressel 6A amphora (data from Van den Bergen 2012).

region. While the Po-Veneto Plain formed a principal market for the Lamboglia 2, its wider distribution was not limited to Northern Italy, and the form is found extensively not just in the Adriatic, but also along the western coast of Italy, in Southern Gaul, and Western Iberia (see Figure 26).[105] In the late 1st century BC, the Lamboglia 2 would be replaced by the Dressel 6A as the dominant Adriatic wine-carrying vessel. The majority of Dressel 6A production seems to have been concentrated in the area around Picenum in the Middle Adriatic during the early 1st century AD.[106] However, production sites expanded as far north and as far inland as far as Parma during the late 1st century BC–early 1st century AD.[107] Adriatic oil also became increasingly important during this time, with the Dressel 6B transporting vast quantities of oil across Northern Italy. Fabric analysis suggests there was some Dressel 6B production in the area around the Euganean and Berici hills, alongside the area around Verona, although the kiln sites have yet to be found.[108] The production of

Dressel 6Bs in this area seems to have tailed off by the mid-1st century AD, with most examples originating from Istria beyond this point.[109] The Anfora con Collo ad Imbuto, the morphological successor to the Dressel 6B, was also produced in Emilia-Romagna, Istria, and the Middle Adriatic, making an important contribution to oil imports.[110]

In comparison to the Lamboglia 2, which saw widespread dispersion beyond its area of production, the Dressel 6A and Dressel 6B saw very limited distribution. Circulation was divided between Northern Italy, the Central and Southern Adriatic, and the Danubian *Limes*, with Northern Italy having the greatest concentration of findspots (see Figures 27 and 28). As wine production expanded into new areas such as Southern Gaul and the Iberian Peninsula during the Early Empire, rising connectivity and political stability allowed the mass transport of wine export to new markets, especially

[105] Lindhagen 2009: 95-97; Righini 2004: 240-44.
[106] Cipriano and Mazzocchin 2018: 261-62; 2019: 242-43.
[107] Cipriano and Mazzocchin 2019: 235-36; Marini Calvini 1981: 127-29.
[108] Cipriano and Mazzocchin 2000; 2002; 2004: 108-10; Martin, Mazzoli, and Mazzocchin 2019. Oil production in general is poorly

attested in this part of Northern Italy. See Busana, D'Incà, and Forti 2009: 35-41, for a synthesis of the available archaeological evidence from the region, alongside wider discussion in Chapter 3 of this volume.
[109] Cipriano 2009: 183; Cipriano *et al.* 2020.
[110] Martin, Mazzoli, and Mazzocchin 2019; Mazzocchin 2009: 198-200. Likely production zones for the Anfora con Collo ad Imbuto have been reconstructed on the basis of archaeometric and stamp data.

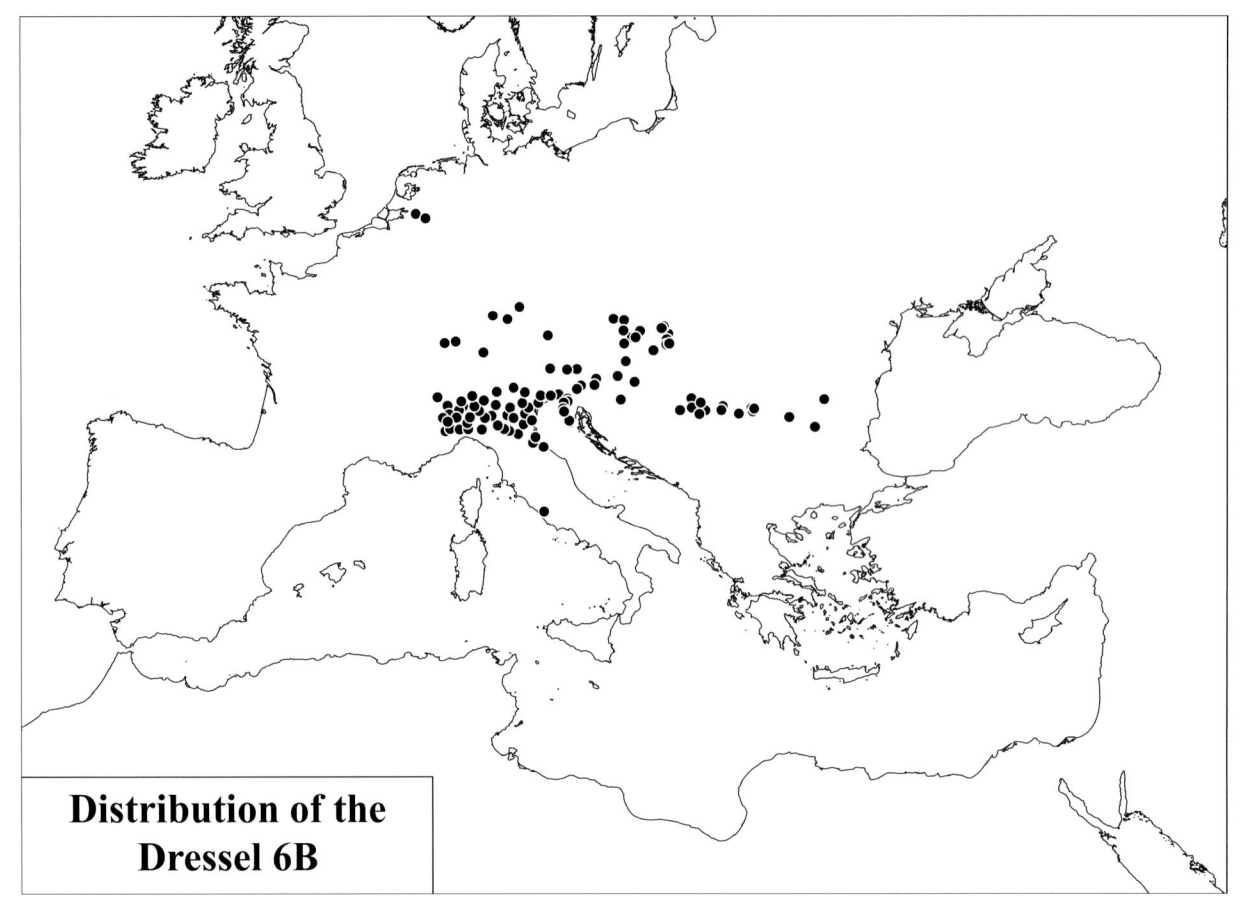

Distribution of the Dressel 6B

Figure 28. Distribution of the Dressel 6B amphora (data from Van den Bergen 2012).

those in Rome and the northern provinces.[111] The comparative advantage that these new producers enjoyed made the Dressel 6A uncompetitive over the long distances the Lamboglia 2 had previously travelled. Instead, Adriatic wine production seems to have responded to these market changes and refocused on supplying Northern Italy, with the period also seeing a massive expansion in Adriatic oil production to meet similar demand both within Northern Italy and on the Danubian *Limes*.[112] The concentrated distribution of Adriatic amphorae in significant quantities within Northern Italy during the Imperial period points to increasing market specialisation amongst Adriatic oil and wine producers. This was especially true for oil, where the Adriatic formed the region's main supplier to the near total exclusion of other zones of production during the 1st and 2nd centuries AD.

From the late 1st to the early 2nd century AD flat-bottomed Italic forms, such as the Forlimpopoli type,

would start being produced in the area south of Ravenna to carry wine. Although these replaced the Dressel 6A as the main wine-carrying vessel produced on the Adriatic Coast, their intended market was significantly different, and they were produced in much lower quantities. There was minimal distribution of Forlimpopoli amphorae inland and they are barely attested at sites in their immediate vicinity such as Forlì.[113] They instead seem to have travelled primarily along the coast and the para-littoral canal system towards Aquileia where they saw overseas distribution.[114] There is also the possibility this wine was used to support the increased troop presence in the north-east of Northern Italy during this time, responding to external pressures such as the Marcomannic incursions. However, the final sub-types of the Forlimpopoli amphora would also disappear by the end of the 3rd century AD, leading to a complete cessation of Adriatic amphora production.

---

[111] Rice 2016: 17-18, 199-200; Scheidel 2015: 24-26; Tchernia 2016: 90-95.

[112] Cipriano and Mazzocchin 2000; 2002; Carre and Pesavento Mattioli 2018. Van Limbergen 2018 tracks the evolution of Central Adriatic wine production during the Late Republic and Early Empire. See Egri 2007 on the consumption of Adriatic oil on the Danubian *Limes*.

[113] This is perhaps unsurprising, as amphorae were primarily designed for long distance transport. Wine travelling over shorter distances may have been stored in other containers, such as skins (Tchernia 1986: 285-92).

[114] Aldini 1999; 2000. This was mainly concentrated in the Central and Northern Adriatic, alongside some distribution to the Black Sea region, the Eastern Mediterranean, and to Rome (Dyczek 2001: 80; Panella 2002: 195-96; Rizzo and Molari 2023: 253-70).

The disappearance of Adriatic amphorae during the 3rd century AD has been noted across wider Adriatic Italy, where they are predominantly replaced by Eastern Mediterranean containers.[115] The Northern Adriatic and Northern Italy show a slightly different pattern, where North African imports gain an equal/greater share of the market than their Eastern counterparts.[116] The rapid decline in the production of Dressel 6A and Dressel 6B amphorae, responsible for transporting the overwhelming majority of Adriatic oil and wine consumed within Northern Italy, is particularly striking.[117] While the rapid decline and subsequent disappearance of Adriatic vessels could indicate a collapse of wine, oil, and fish sauce production in the region, this seems a somewhat simplistic interpretation of the available evidence. It is more probable that the archaeological record reflects a cessation of production of the vessels previously used to transport these products, with a gradual switch to containers such as barrels and skins during the mid-2nd to early 3rd century.[118] Unfortunately, the paucity of surviving examples of these containers makes it difficult to establish a chronology for their use within the region. Barrels are already mentioned as having an important role in the maturation and transport of wine within Northern Italy from the late 1st century BC.[119] Other evidence points to a rise in their use in Northern Italy from the 2nd century AD onwards. Multiple reliefs depicting the transport of barrels and skins have been recovered from the area around Picenum, the principal production area for amphora-borne wine in the Adriatic. A second-century AD funerary monument celebrates the life of a cooper at Cupra Marittima, while a third-century relief from Ancona depicts a transaction involving barrels of wine.[120] Two mid-1st century AD urns from Firmum also depict the storage and transport of wine in skins.[121] In the 4th century AD, references to *vinum Picenum* appear in Diocletian's Price Edict and the *Expositio totius mundi et gentium,* suggesting Adriatic wines were still circulating (and finding new markets) during this late period.[122]

Beyond the evidence for changes in containerisation, a collapse of Adriatic oil and wine is not supported by evidence from the production sites themselves. A survey of production sites along the Adriatic Coast

of Italy demonstrates the continuation of oil and wine production at rural sites between the 3rd and 5th centuries AD.[123] While the area's rural economy does seem to have contracted during the 2nd century AD, several wine and oil-pressing sites, such as Cupra Marittima San Basso, Pollenza Santa Lucia, and Tortoreto Muracche, see repairs or expansion during the subsequent centuries, suggesting continuity of production.[124] Similar continuity is also seen within oil-producing Istria.[125] Within Northern Italy itself, the period of the 3rd and 4th centuries AD also saw a consolidation and reorganisation of villa estates in the Po Plain and Alpine foothills, especially in the area surrounding Milan (see Chapter 3).[126] In the absence of another mass-produced Adriatic amphora form during this period, the productive output of villas and other rural units must have travelled in barrels or skins, obscured by their lack of survival archaeological record. Consequently, the true contribution of Adriatic and regional goods to Northern Italian consumers during the Late Antique remains unknown but was likely considerable.

The View from the Ports

While the majority of analysis has focused on the inland circulation of amphora-borne goods, port assemblages offer a point of comparison. As the principal point of entry for the majority of Northern Italy's amphora-borne goods, port sites had access to the greatest range of imports. Consequently, the provenance of port assemblages was significantly different to the sites surrounding them, often showing far greater variety. Figure 29 provides a breakdown of amphora frequency from each zone of production at Northern Italian maritime ports.[127] Quantified data from port sites from the 4th century AD onwards was present in limited quantities at Ariminum, Luna, and Ravenna, as was Imperial data for Classis.[128] However, comparisons between ports and inland sites, and between the ports themselves, can still be made.

At Adriatic ports between the 1st century BC and the 1st and 2nd centuries AD, amphora from the Adriatic Littoral appeared in the greatest frequencies. Indeed,

---

[115] Auriemma, Dregrassi, and Quiri 2015: 153.

[116] Auriemma, Dregrassi, and Quiri 2012: 285-90; Cirelli 2022: 476.

[117] Łoś and Pietruszka 2016: 525–26.

[118] Marlière 2002; Mille and Rollet 2020; Panella and Tchernia 1994: 159-60; Tchernia 1986: 285-92; Wilson 2011a: 37; 2011b: 228-29. There also remains the possibility that goods were circulated over short distances in locally produced ceramic containers that have not been typologised.

[119] Plin. *HN* 14.27; Str. 5.1.8; 5.1.12.

[120] Paci 2009; Profumo 2005.

[121] Marengo 2003.

[122] *Edict of Maximum Prices* 2.1-19; *Exp.* 55.4-5. See Rizzo and Molari 2023 for a discussion of evidence for Adriatic wine exports in Late Antiquity.

[123] Van Limbergen 2018: 77, 87.

[124] See Busana and Forin 2020; Van Limbergen 2011; 2019, for a discussion of the evidence for continued agricultural production in the Late Antique Adriatic. Larger production units in Picenum, such as those at Chiarino de Ricanti, Colombara, La Pineta, Paese Alto, Piana dei Cesari, San Pellegrino, Tortoreto Muracche, and Villamagna, seem to have been more resilient to the economic and political upheaval than smaller sites, continuing to operate throughout the 3rd and 4th centuries AD (Van Limbergen 2019: 116-18).

[125] Matijašić and Bulić 2023.

[126] Brogiolo and Chavarría Arnau 2018: 184-85; Forin 2017: 231-42.

[127] Production dates are used due to the absence of deposition data for several port assemblages.

[128] In comparison, Aquileia's assemblage formed one of the largest in the AMINI dataset, containing 3114 sherds of amphora.

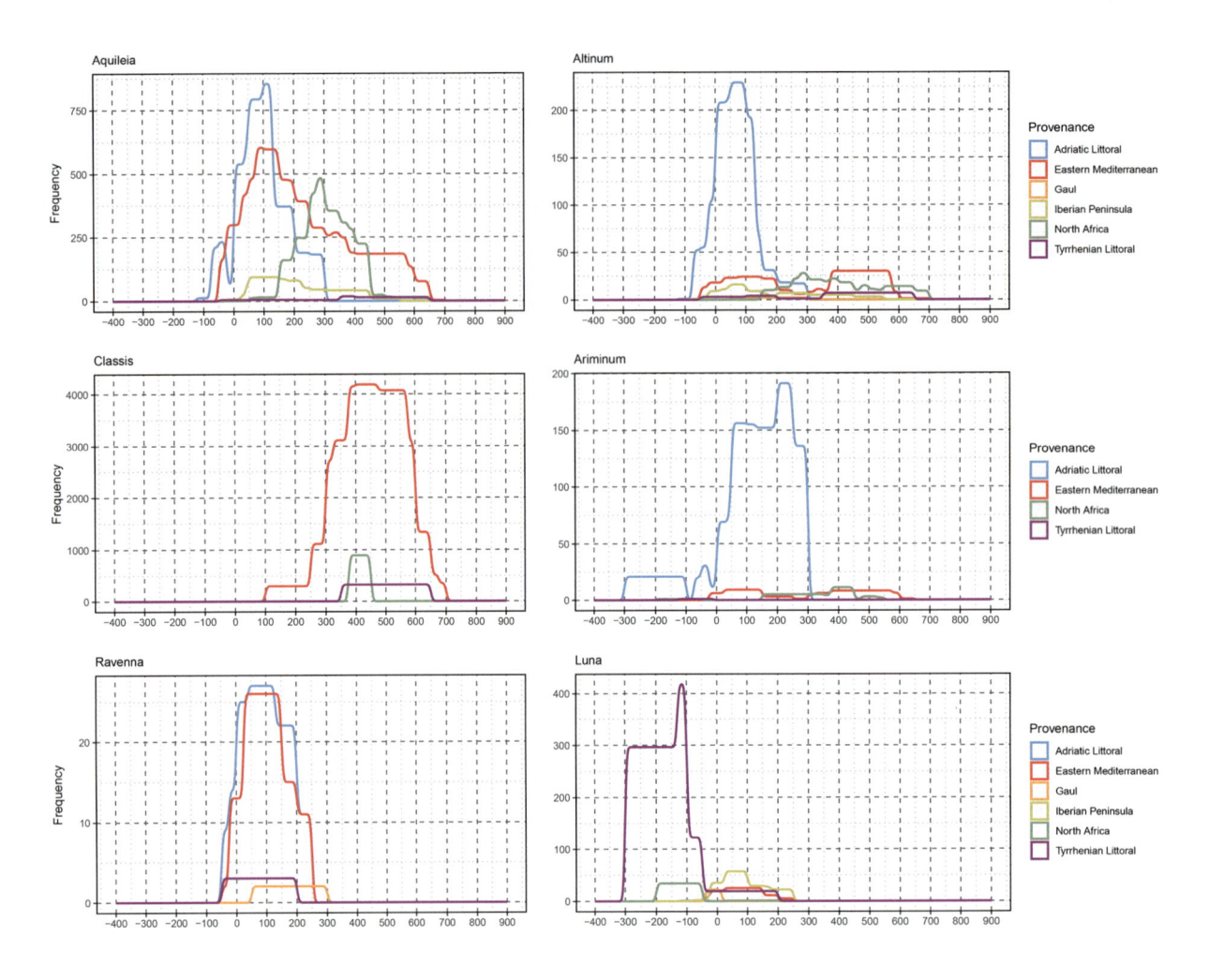

Figure 29. The quantities of amphora from each zone of production at maritime ports in Northern Italy. Note the Y axes are not continuous.

Ariminum's assemblage was almost entirely dominated by Adriatic amphorae, a composition similar to inland sites in its geographic vicinity, such as Forlì.[129] Ariminum was the maritime port closest to production zones for Adriatic wine in Picenum, and the Forlimpopoli type was produced in its hinterland, making it uniquely placed to take advantage of these goods.[130] Furthermore, although Ariminum was situated on important overland routes at the junction of the via Emilia and the via Flaminia, it did not sit on the Po-Veneto river system, the main network of inland distribution across Northern Italy. Consequently, the dominance of Adriatic amphorae in Ariminum's assemblage may reflect its integration into networks primarily for the export of regional produce, rather than imports to supply inland areas.[131]

The situation is different at the ports of Ravenna, Altinum, and Aquileia. These three sites were connected via the para-littoral canal system (see Chapter 2), integrating them into the Po-Veneto water network. Ravenna, lying close to the Po, offered direct access to the interior, while Aquileia served both markets in the Veneto and the northeastern provinces.[132] The importance of these ports as major trade hubs is demonstrated by the variety of amphorae from each zone of production, some of which appeared in high quantities.[133] At Aquileia and Ravenna, quantities of Eastern Mediterranean amphorae rival vessels from the Adriatic Littoral from the mid-1st century BC to the 1st century AD.[134] At Altinum, Adriatic vessels still dominated the assemblage, but Eastern Mediterranean and Iberian amphorae appeared in significant

[129] Biondani 2005a; Iandoli 2006; Tempesta 2013.
[130] Stoppiono 2021; Ugolini 2015; 2021b.
[131] Biondani 2005a; Rizzo and Molari 2023: 255; Stoppioni 2021.

[132] Carre *et al.* 2007; Donat *et al.* 2023; Grazia Maioli 2018; Manzelli 2000.
[133] Bonivento and Vecchiet 2017a; 2017b; Cipolato 2018; Gaddi 2017a; Pizzolato 2018b. The low quantities of amphorae from some zones of production, such as Gaul and the Tyrrhenian Littoral, may point to opportunistic, one-off deliveries of cargoes, or specific orders, rather than sustained trade connections.
[134] Auriemma and Degrassi 2017; Bonivento and Vecchiet 2017b; Cipolato 2018; Gaddi and Maggi 2017; Tempesta 2018.

quantities, alongside lesser numbers of Gallic and Tyrrhenian vessels.[135] As sites in the coastal hinterland surrounding Aquileia, Altinum, and Ravenna had low quantities of Eastern Mediterranean amphorae within their assemblages, these imports were either consumed within the ports themselves, or were destined for distribution further inland to areas where their price became competitive.

The composition of Adriatic port assemblages between the 3rd and 7th centuries AD more closely mirrors those of inland sites during this period. However, a comparison between port and inland assemblages reveals that port sites continued to have greater vessel diversity in this later period, enjoying a wider range of amphora-borne goods thanks to their privileged position as entrepots.[136] Eastern Mediterranean amphorae continued to form the bulk of imports, and the rise in North African goods can be seen at Aquileia, Altinum, and Ariminum throughout the 2nd and 3rd centuries AD.[137] Unfortunately, quantified data for Ravenna is missing between the 4th and 7th centuries AD. Nonetheless, the assemblage from nearby Classis serves to indicate the importance and vibrancy this harbour zone continued to have in Late Antiquity.[138] The continued prominence of Eastern Mediterranean wines in the Late Antique is especially apparent at Classis, where they appear almost to the total exclusion of all other provenances.

In comparison to ports on the Adriatic Coast, Luna, on the Ligurian Coast, had an assemblage entirely different to sites within the Po-Veneto Plain. Tyrrhenian amphorae, starting with the Dressel 1 and then moving to the Dressel 2-4, made up the majority of Luna's assemblage in the 3rd to 1st centuries BC.[139] By the 1st century AD, Iberian imports had begun to circulate in significant quantities, as did Eastern Mediterranean amphorae. The near total absence of vessels from the Adriatic Littoral at Luna suggests that the movement of amphora-borne goods between the Ligurian Coast and the western Po Valley was one-directional. Wool products and other textiles from the western Po Valley may have formed the return cargoes for trans-Apennine traders.[140]

Trans-Apennine Trade: Enabling Choice

During the hierarchical clustering analysis, three clusters formed based on the provenance of amphorae assemblages. Of these, the third cluster, comprised of sites in the west and the south-west of the Po Valley, stood out due to the large quantities of Western Mediterranean amphorae it contained (see Figure 30). The contribution of Gallic, Iberian, and Tyrrhenian goods to the supply of sites in cluster 3, zones of production which were almost entirely absent from clusters 1 and 2, raises questions not only about the role transport costs played in determining material distribution but also the impact of consumer choice in deciding what goods to buy.

It is clear that the cost of overland transport through the Apennines did not prohibit the movement of staple goods in significant quantities between the Ligurian ports and the Po Valley. Although carts and mule trains would have needed to traverse routes through mountain zones, investment in road infrastructure served to reduce the impact of gradient on transport.[141] On the via Postumia, the main trans-Apennine route between Genoa and the Po Valley, efforts were made to follow the natural topography of the valleys and passes where possible, in an attempt to reduce large elevation changes.[142] The quantities of Western Mediterranean goods suggest they were not moving speculatively and that there was a ready market for them at sites in the south-west of the Po Valley. The large numbers of Iberian, Gallic, and Tyrrhenian imports at urban centres in this part of the region suggest they were competitive cost-wise against Adriatic and Eastern Mediterranean amphorae. Modelling of transport costs in Northern Italy during the Roman period has suggested that the cost of moving cargo between the Adriatic and Ligurian ports to this area was similar, reducing the advantage enjoyed by Adriatic amphorae elsewhere in the region.[143]

As prices for Adriatic goods travelling up the Po Valley began to match those for goods coming from the Eastern Mediterranean or over the Apennines, buyers may have chosen to make purchases based on the quality of a product, rather than simply choosing the provenance of the lowest cost.[144] For example, the majority of Iberian imports in the south-western valley were of fish sauce.[145] The higher presence of Iberian imports in the west of Northern Italy may be a result of fish sauce producers on the Adriatic Coast being unable to compete with Spanish products on either quality

---

[135] The high number of Adriatic vessels in Altinum's assemblage stems from the discovery of a reclamation deposit composed almost entirely of Dressel 6A and 6B amphorae (Toniolo 1991), increasing the prominence of Adriatic amphorae in the frequency curve.
[136] Auriemma and Quiri 2007; Komar 2021: 269-70.
[137] Bonivento 2017; Gaddi 2017a; Pizzolato 2018a.
[138] Augenti 2011; Cirelli 2013a; 2014; Stoppioni 1990.
[139] Bruno 1998.
[140] Roncaglia 2018: 89-100.

[141] Cera 2000; Repetto 2021.
[142] The via Postumia followed the path of the Torrente Scrivia for large sections of its course, taking advantage of the river valley's route.
[143] Page 2023; 2024. See also Chapter 7 in this volume.
[144] For discussions on consumer choice in the Roman period through the application of material studies, see Allison 2004; Greene 2008; Laurence and Trifilò 2015; Pitts 2013; 2015.
[145] Some oil, travelling in Dressel 20 amphorae, is also attested (Carre and Pesavento Mattioli 2003; Modrzewska-Pianetti 2017).

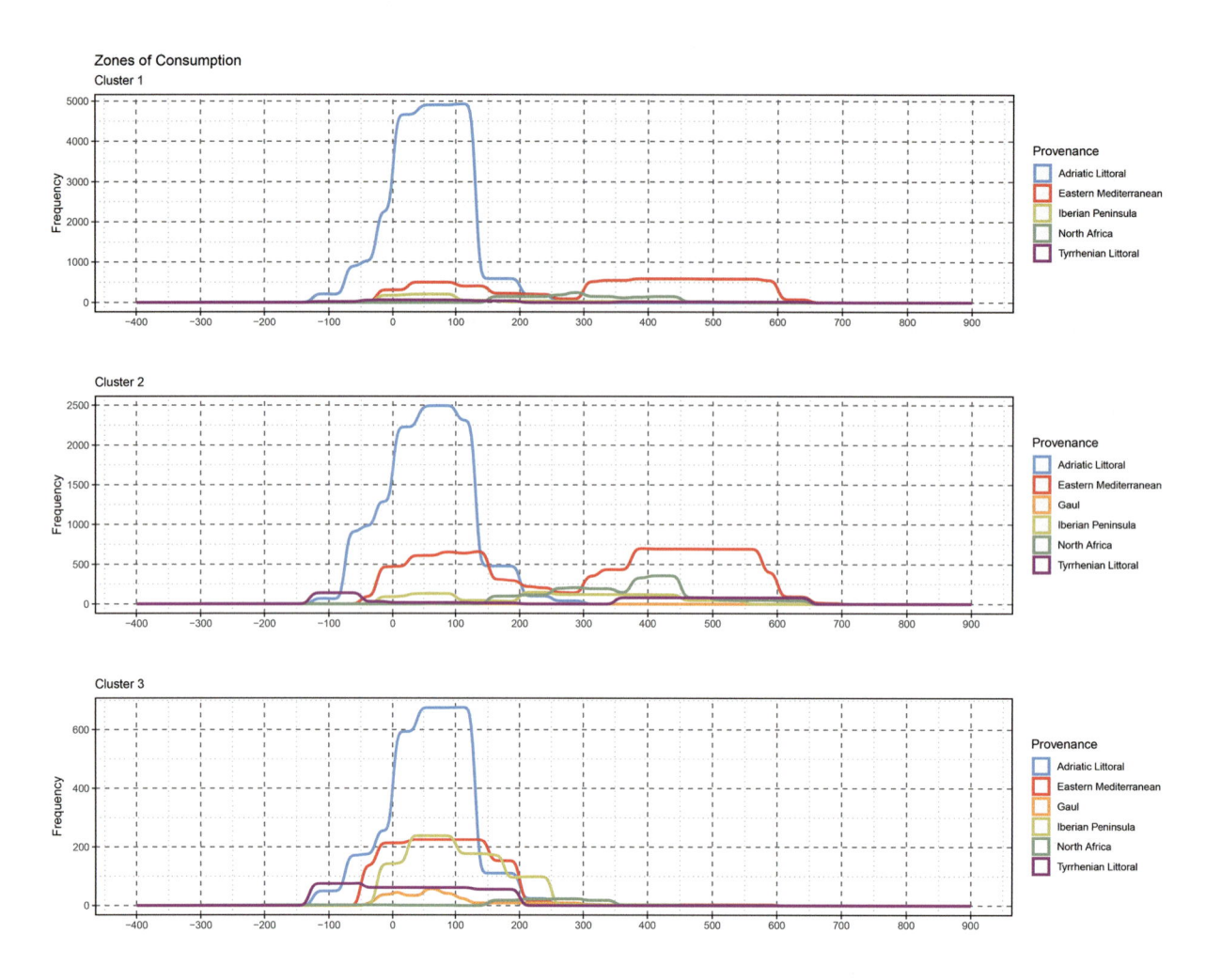

Figure 30. The quantities of amphora from each zone of production identified by the hierarchical clusters. Note the Y axes are not continuous.

or cost of product.[146] Iberian fish sauces, famed for their quality, were a desirable product, and consumers in the south-west chose to capitalise on the relative affordability in comparison to alternative products. In contrast to Iberian imports, Gallic and Tyrrhenian amphorae were mainly carrying wine. Both zones of production were prized for their output, and their presence, alongside very limited quantities of Iberian wine, suggests a wide range of styles were on offer to consumers in this part of the region.[147] In a similar vein, the continued presence of Adriatic wine in the west of the Po Valley area may, in part, be due to it being able to compete with Gallic and Tyrrhenian wine on taste.[148] It is also possible that Western Mediterranean imports

instead represent opportunistic buying in response to fluctuations in production or price in the Adriatic. While the location of sites in the west and south-west of the Po Valley, at the end of the Po transport corridor, left them especially vulnerable to such changes, their proximity to ports on the Ligurian Coast meant they were better placed to take advantage of alternative extra-provincial markets in the event of such a scenario. This situation would be reliant on free-market forces, with buyers and sellers having the requisite knowledge to capitalise on price changes.[149]

Although Western Mediterranean amphorae played an important part in supplying the west and southwestern Po Valley, it is worth emphasising that these goods were only competitive in a small area of Northern Italy. The transport costs incurred during their overland journey from the Ligurian Coast put them at an increasing disadvantage the further inland they progressed, especially in areas connected to the Po-Veneto water

---

[146] Pliny, *HN* 31.43, suggests that some specific producer's fish sauces were esteemed for their high quality, and mentions several areas of the Iberian Peninsula as producing some of the best.

[147] Strabo (5.3.6; 5.4.3) discusses the high quality of several wines produced along the Tyrrhenian Littoral, especially those made in Campania.

[148] Van Limbergen 2011: 85-86. See Str. 5.4.2 and the *Anthologia Graeca*, 6.257, 9.232, which suggest some styles produced in the area of Picenum were of high quality.

[149] Brughmans and Poblome 2016: 402-04; Temin 2013: 13-15.

network. As highlighted above, they achieved minimal penetration at sites further to the north and east of the Po Valley and Veneto Plain. Even in the south-west, for the most part, assemblages were composed of a combination of Adriatic and Eastern Mediterranean amphorae, with the Po Valley and Adriatic remaining the main axis of trade. Northern Italy did not form a principal market for western amphorae, with their production largely directed towards other areas of consumption. For Gallic amphorae, the Rhône Valley and the German *Limes* likely formed the predominant axis of trade, with some distribution across the Western Mediterranean.[150] In a similar vein, Tyrrhenian wine production saw distribution into Southern Gaul and the northern frontier, while Rome also formed a major market for both Gallic and Tyrrhenian production.[151] For Iberian imports, Rome and the *Limes* were the main markets for Spanish oil, although wrecks such as the Culip IV point to a trading triangle that included the Eastern Iberian Peninsula, Southern France, and Western Italy.[152] While Iberian, Gallic, and Tyrrhenian vessels may have made their way along the Ligurian Coast in significant quantities, the direction of trade seems to have para-littoral, rather than inland.

Conclusions

Amphora-borne trade in Northern Italy saw continuous evolution over the Roman period, both in the variety and the provenance of imported staples and commodities. Both production and deposition chronologies suggest that amphora-borne imports peaked during the late 1st century AD, followed by a continuous decline over the following centuries. The Adriatic Littoral formed the most important zone of production for amphora-borne goods circulating in Northern Italy, supplying the majority of imported oil and wine. Although the rapid decline, followed by the total disappearance of Adriatic amphorae in the 3rd century AD is a striking development, this is likely a reflection of changes in containerisation, rather than a collapse of production. Evidence from the production sites themselves suggests Adriatic goods continued to make an important contribution to Northern Italy's supply throughout the 4th and 5th centuries.

While the majority of its amphora-borne imports originated from within its immediate vicinity, Northern Italy was also integrated into the wider Mediterranean economy, with Eastern Mediterranean, Iberian, and North African vessels making important contributions throughout the Roman period. The Adriatic would dominate in the Late Republic and Imperial period, with both Western and Eastern Mediterranean imports assuming an increasingly important role in the 1st and 2nd centuries AD. By the 3rd century AD, North Africa, a previously minor contributor, had gone on to become an important supplier of amphorae to the region, although Eastern Mediterranean vessels remained prominent amongst assemblages. A wide range of amphora types continued to circulate during this later period, attesting to the diversity of choice available to consumers.

Analysing the spread of different amphora provenances and vessel types produced some surprising results, challenging the perception of inland areas as being disconnected and isolated. By the 1st century AD, the political and economic stability afforded by the principate had enabled clear zones of consumption to develop across Northern Italy. A wide variety of amphorae-borne imports were often available further inland, in contrast to the greater uniformity demonstrated in coastal regions. The results highlight the role of both cost and choice in determining import provenance, and the sophistication of the networks of transport and exchange within the valley that enabled the circulation of amphora-borne trade. The Adriatic Coast would form the principal entry point of imports into Northern Italy throughout the Roman period, but the amphora analysis also demonstrated the important role trans-Apennine trade played in supplying the west and south-west of the Po Valley. The picture of amphora-borne trade that emerges from Northern Italy is of a complex interplay between cost and choice influencing the spread of goods during the Roman period and Late Antiquity.

---

[150] Remesal Rodríguez and Revilla Calvo 1991; Rice 2012: 251-57.
[151] De Sena 2015: 8-9; Iavarone and Olcese 2013; Olcese 2020; 2022.
[152] Nieto *et al.* 1989: 239-44.

Red-Slipped Finewares:
Local and Long-Distance Consumption

Factoring amongst the most widespread artefacts recovered from the Roman era, red-slipped finewares, such as terra sigillata and African Red Slip (ARS), have long been used to examine patterns in trade and distribution. The increasingly comprehensive study and identification of sigillata workshops, the creation of typologies, the discovery of production sites, and an ever-growing body of data from across the Roman world, have enabled the detailed reconstruction of consumption and export patterns.[1] While their ubiquity makes fineware datasets an obvious choice for analysis, they also provide a valuable point of comparison to amphora-borne trade. Amphorae were primarily traded for their contents, whereas finewares were consumed as a singular product. As a non-essential commodity, patterns of fineware distribution reflect different mechanisms of consumption and exchange compared to the foodstuffs that formed the most common amphora-borne cargoes.[2] Furthermore, the fact that there was significant production of terra sigillata within Northern Italy itself (in comparison to the limited evidence for amphora production), offers greater insight into networks of local distribution present within the region during this period. The REFINI dataset analysed in this chapter synthesises 61 published fineware assemblages, the contents of which span nine centuries of trade and exchange within the region.[3] It contains 12,112 sherds of fineware from 25 urban centres in Northern Italy, with 630 unique vessel forms represented.

Both terra sigillata and ARS have seen intensive study over the past century and the chronology of the production and consumption of Roman red-slip tablewares in Italy is well established. Italian terra sigillata began to appear during the late Republic and quickly replaced Black Gloss ceramics, which had previously been the dominant form of tableware in Italy.[4] Production is assumed to have begun at Arezzo

but quickly expanded to include other sites in Central and Northern Italy by the end of the 1st century BC. This was followed by the establishment of workshops first in Southern, and then Central Gaul, which produced sigillata between the late 1st century BC and 2nd century AD.[5] The development of ARS in the mid-1st century AD saw it rise to become the dominant tableware in the Mediterranean from the 3rd century AD into the Early Medieval period.[6] Against this backdrop, other forms of tableware such as Eastern Terra Sigillata and Middle Adriatic Terra Sigillata also circulated in the market, but none achieved the same prominence within Northern Italy as the types mentioned above.

While the development of fineware production and imports in Northern Italy is (reasonably) well-understood at a macro-level, the ways in which finewares entered and were distributed across the region are less so. Numerous hypotheses have been put forward over how red-slipped finewares circulated within Northern Italy, yet most of these have focused on the regional diffusion of vessels from individual potters or the provenance of sigillata at individual sites.[7] A region-wide study of quantified fineware assemblages will allow underlying patterns and trends present in the data to be brought to the fore, allowing engagement with broader questions about inland trade in Northern Italy.

Fineware Types and Zones of Production

During the Roman era, Northern Italy was supplied with finewares from six main zones of production. The first three zones were located within Italy and consisted of the Adriatic Littoral, which supplied Middle Adriatic Terra Sigillata (MATS), Central Italy, which produced Central Italic Terra Sigillata (CITS) at sites including Arezzo and Pisa, and Northern Italy, which produced Northern Italic Terra Sigillata (NITS). Outside of Italy, Eastern Terra Sigillata (ETS) came from production sites within the Eastern Mediterranean and Gallic Terra Sigillata (GTS) was produced within Southern

[1] Ettlinger *et al.* 1990; Oxé, Comfort, and Kenrick 2000.

[2] Although the term 'finewares' suggests a level of expense and exclusivity, fine tablewares achieved a remarkable level penetration across all social strata. The Roman Peasant Project found evidence for the consumption of finewares at even the lowest sites in the settlement hierarchy (Arnoldus *et al.* 2021a: 190-94; 2021b: 559-61).

[3] The REFINI dataset can be found at https://doi.org/10.5281/zenodo.13745898. The code and data used in the analysis can be found at Github Repository: Adriatic-to-the-Alps, viewed 12 September 2024, https://github.com/jamespage15/Adriatic-to-the-Alps.

[4] Mazzeo Saracino 2000: 38; Mantovani 2013: 143. It is worth highlighting that red-slipped Eastern Terra Sigillata A had already begun to appear in the Eastern Mediterranean by the latter half of the 2nd century BC and was already circulating in Italy prior to the

development of Italian Terra Sigillata (Van Oyen 2016: 13).

[5] Desbat, Genin, and Lasfargues 1996; Picon and Lasfargues 1974.

[6] Bonifay 2003; 2004.

[7] See, for example, Kenrick's (2000) mapping of the distribution of *Sarius* and *Serius* stamps in Northern Italy; Gabucci and Quiri's (2008) discussion on the evolution of ceramic imports to Ivrea, or Gabucci's (1995) discussion of sigillata consumption in Tortona in the Early Imperial period. Such an approach has been criticised in the past by those studying sigillata who have called for greater integration of data between sites (see Della Porta 1998; Olcese 1999).

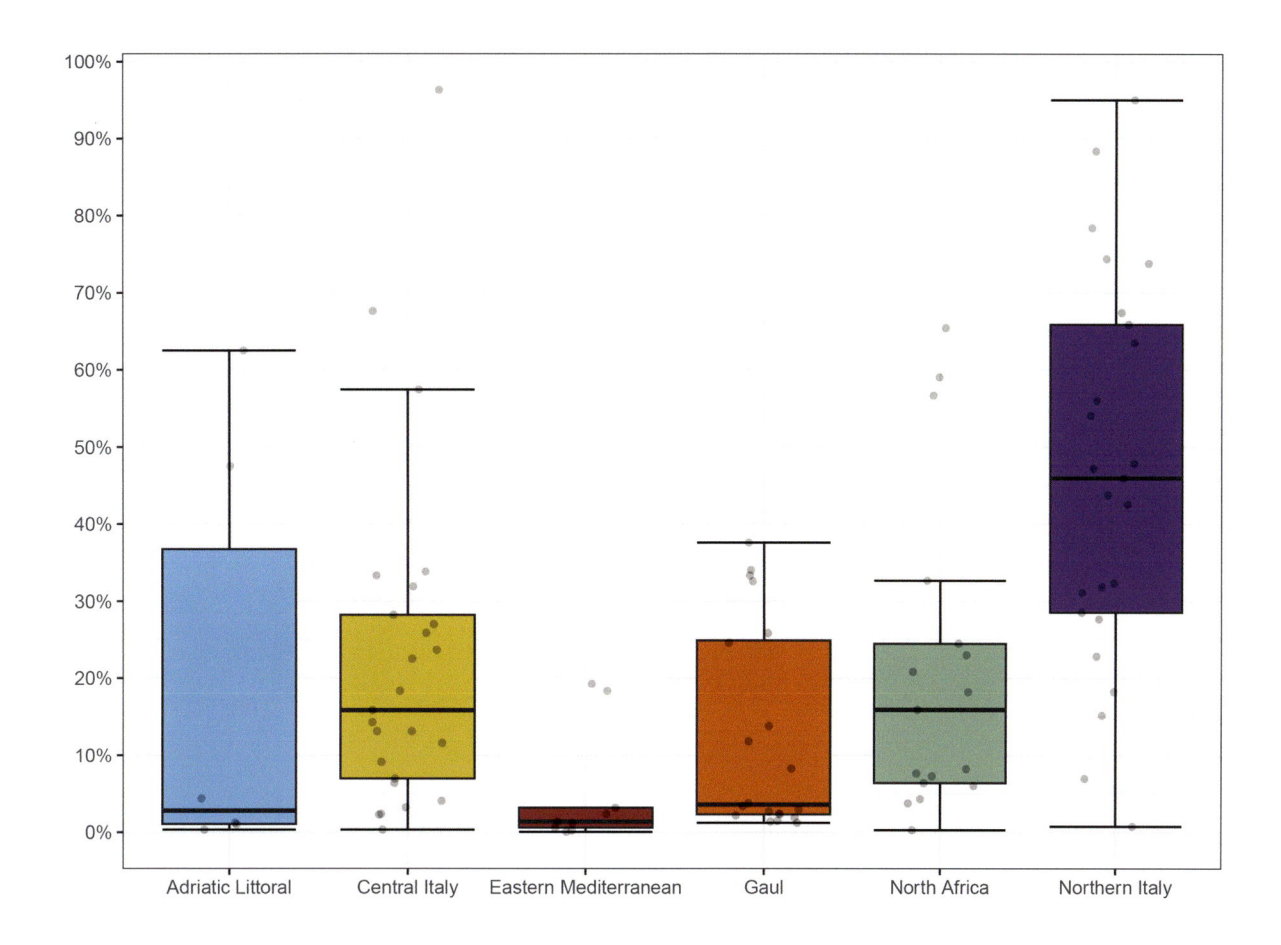

Figure 31. Box and whisker plots showing the percentage of each zone of production within each site's fineware assemblage.

and Central Gaul.[8] Finally, African Red Slip (ARS) was produced at sites in North Africa. When the REFINI dataset is viewed as a whole, sigillata from Northern Italy formed the largest component of assemblages (see Figure 31). Central Italy and North Africa also made significant contributions to assemblages, while the quantities of finewares supplied by the Adriatic Littoral and Gaul saw considerable fluctuation between sites. The amount of Eastern Mediterranean finewares in circulation was minimal. In the following section, a brief summary of the different fineware types supplied from each zone of production is laid out.

African Red Slip

Mainly produced in the area of modern Tunisia, ARS constitutes one of the most important and widespread finewares circulating during the late Roman period. ARS formed the principal successor to terra sigillata, having become the dominant red-slipped fineware in the Western Mediterranean by the 3rd century AD. Production began in the late 1st century AD

and continued until the end of the 7th century.[9] ARS production is often divided amongst several main fabric or 'production' groups, labelled A, C, D, and E, to which can be added A/D, C/D, and C/E.[10] Archaeometric analysis has allowed these classifications to be further subdivided (for example C1, C2 etc.) and even the locations of workshops to be traced, providing a more nuanced picture of regional ARS production.[11] Within the REFINI dataset, fabric D appears in the greatest quantities, although C is also well-represented (see Figure 32).

ARS Production A seems to have originated in the area around Carthage.[12] It represents the earliest production of ARS and was predominantly in circulation between the 1st century AD and the 3rd century AD. Production A/D is thought to have been based in Western Libya from the area surrounding Leptis Magna, although a

---

[8] Minimal quantities of other red-slipped finewares produced in the Eastern Mediterranean, such as Late Roman C and Late Roman D, were also present in the REFINI dataset.

[9] Bonifay 2004: 155; Fentress *et al.* 2004: 150; Hobson 2015: 117-19.
[10] Bonifay 2003; 2004: Chapter 2; Carandini *et al.* 1981; Hayes 1972: 287-92. ARS productions F and G are also recognised to have existed, although no examples are present within the REFINI dataset.
[11] Bonifay 2016: 519-28; 2018: 329; Bonifay, Capelli, and Brun 2012; Mackensen 1993; Mackensen and Schneider 2002.
[12] Bonifay 2016: 520-22; Mackensen and Scheider 2006: 168-69.

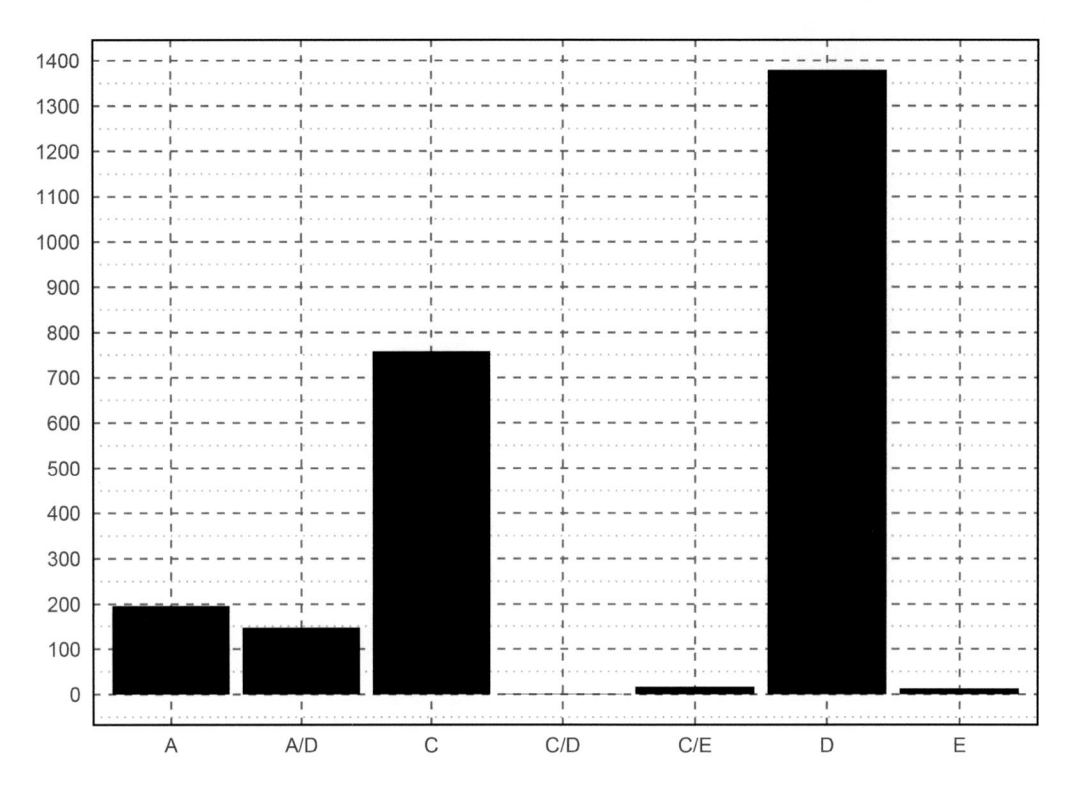

Figure 32. Quantities of each ARS production type within the REFINI dataset.

Central Tunisian provenance cannot be ruled out.[13] It mainly circulated between the mid-2nd and late 3rd century AD. Production C was in circulation between the beginning of the 3rd century AD and the second half of the 5th century AD and was produced in Central Tunisia in the area surrounding Sidi Marzouk Tounsi.[14] Productions C/D and C/E are also present within the REFINI dataset, although in minimal quantities. They likely originated from Northern and Central Tunisia respectively. Production D was in circulation between the mid-3rd century AD and the middle of the 7th century AD. It was produced in Northern Tunisia, with workshops traced to Borj el-Jerhbi, El Mahrine, and Oudha.[15] Production E, attested in minimal quantities within Northern Italy, was in circulation from the middle of the 4th to the middle of the 5th century AD.[16] It likely originated somewhere in Southern Tunisia.

Central Italic Terra Sigillata

Production of terra sigillata within Italy is thought to have begun at Arezzo (ancient Arretium) in the late 1st century BC.[17] Potters, originally specialising in black glossed ceramics, began to experiment with using red glazes, resulting in the smooth, red-slipped finish that characterises terra sigillata.[18] Arezzo would quickly become a major hub of sigillata production, with multiple workshops operating within its immediate vicinity.[19] Some workshops, such as that of Ateius, would make the move from Arezzo to Pisa at the end of the 1st century BC. Pisa, with its coastal position, was well-situated to take advantage of maritime trade networks connecting Italy's Tyrrhenian Coast to Gaul and the Iberian Peninsula.[20] A wide range of other workshops would also be established across Central Italy at places such as Scoppieto, Siena, and Torrita di Siena. Operating at varying levels of production, these workshops were often well-placed to take advantage of fluvial and terrestrial transport links.[21] CITS circulated in the greatest quantities during the early 1st century AD and saw exportation across the Mediterranean and Rome's northern provinces. However, by the mid-1st century AD, competition from potters in Gaul saw a decline in sigillata production within Central Italy. Late versions of CTS would continue into the 4th century AD, although in significantly lower quantities than during the fineware's heyday.[22]

[13] Bonifay 2016: 522; Mackensen 2006: 111-13.
[14] Bonifay 2004: 46-47; 2016: 523-24.
[15] Barraud *et al.* 1998; Bonifay 2016: 524-26; Mackensen 1993.
[16] Production E is only attested at the sites of Aquileia (Trivini Bellini 2021), Brescia (Massa 1999), Milan (Roffia 1991), and Verona (Morandini 2008a) within the REFINI dataset.
[17] Ettlinger *et al.* 1990; Menchelli 2005; Morel 1981.

[18] Marabini Moevus 2006: 7; Morel 2009: 125-28.
[19] Kenrick 1993; Van Oyen 2015: 281-85.
[20] Kenrick 1997: 186; Menchelli 1997: 191; Menchelli and Sangriso 2017.
[21] Kiiskin 2013: 59-87; Sternini 2019: 487-90; Vaccaro, Capelli, and Ghisleni 2017.
[22] Ettlinger *et al.* 1990: 13-16. This is often referred to as sigillata tardo-italica in Italian publications.

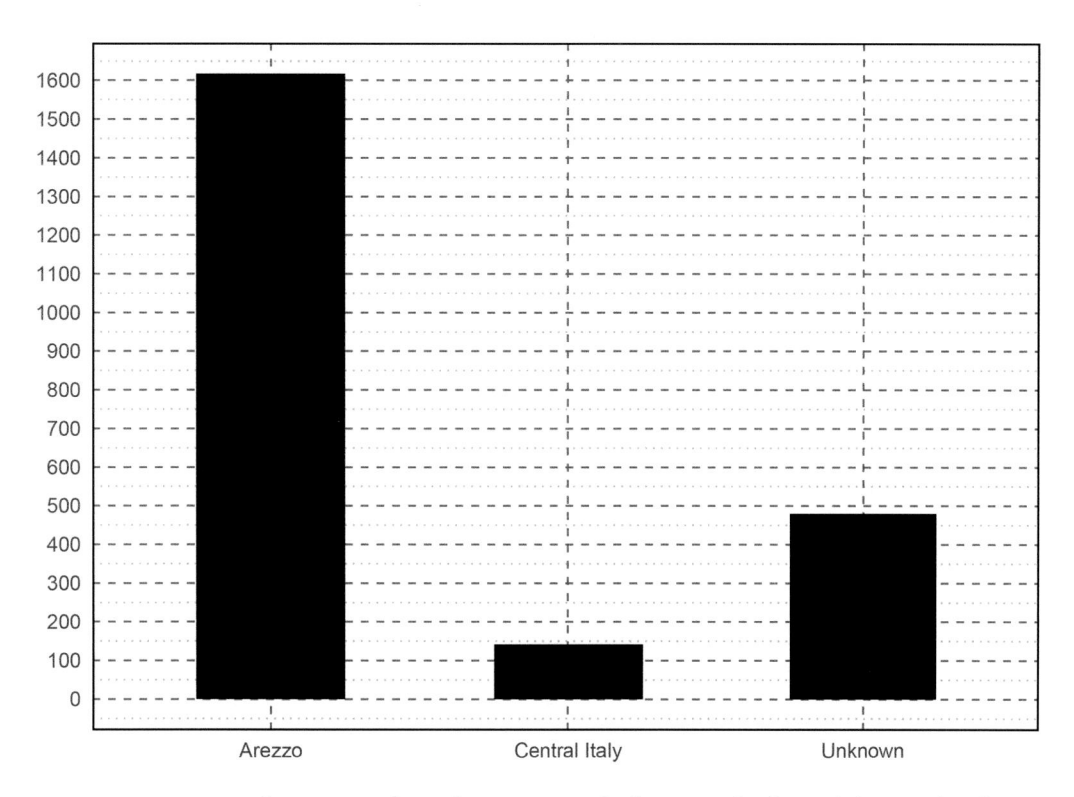

Figure 33. Quantities of provenanced CITS from Arezzo and other Central Italic workshops within the REFINI dataset.

The phenomenon of potters' stamps on terra sigillata has often enabled the provenance of marked vessels to be traced to a single workshop, providing a high level of detail when attempting to reconstruct the distribution and trade in finewares.[23] While a detailed analysis of REFINI's stamp data is beyond the scope of this volume, they can be used to give an indication of the broad zones within Central Italy where sigillata consumed in Northern Italy was produced. Unfortunately, most unstamped sherds of CITS within the REFINI dataset could not be traced to a location beyond 'Central Italy'. Where a more specific provenance is available from stamp data, workshops operating in Arezzo are shown to have supplied the majority of CITS recovered in Northern Italy (see Figure 33). Workshops located elsewhere in Central Italy, such as Pisa, were represented in significantly lower quantities.

Eastern Terra Sigillata

Eastern Terra Sigillata forms the earliest type of red-slipped pottery circulating in Northern Italy and was present in the lowest quantities.[24] Like ARS, ETS has been subdivided into four fabric types, A, B, C, and D, reflecting their zone of origin.[25] Initially produced in

Asia Minor between *c.* 150 BC and *c.* AD 150, Eastern Sigillata A (ESA) forms the earliest type of ETS in circulation.[26] Eastern Sigillata B (ESB) and Eastern Sigillata C (ESC) were also produced in Asia Minor.[27] ESC began circulating during the mid-1st century BC and would see a long production lifespan well into the 2nd century AD.[28] ESB was produced from the late 1st century BC onwards, with quantities peaking towards the end of the 1st century AD. It had disappeared from wider Mediterranean markets by the end of the 2nd century.[29] Eastern Sigillata D (ESD) was produced in Cyprus, with production beginning *c.* 100 BC. The majority of ES recovered from Northern Italy belongs to ESB (see Figure 34). ESA and ESC are found in small amounts, while ESD is attested in minimal quantities.

Gallic Terra Sigillata

Gallic Terra Sigillata, also known as 'Samian Ware' in Anglophone scholarship, was a red-slipped fineware produced in Gaul. It was predominantly in circulation between the mid-1st century AD and the 3rd century AD, although the earliest red-slipped production dates

[23] Oxé, Comfort, and Kenrick 2000.
[24] Airoldi, Cipriano, and Montevecchi 2018; Dobreva and Griggio 2021; Ganzaroli 2017; Maselli Scotti 2017; Pagan 2018; Pettenò 2007.
[25] Bes 2015: 11-12.

[26] Gunneweg, Perlman, and Yellin 1983: 11-14.
[27] Lund 2003: 127-28.
[28] Bes 2015: 27. Earlier, unslipped versions of ESC were in circulation from *c.* 150 BC.
[29] Bes 2015: 27; Lund 2003: 130.

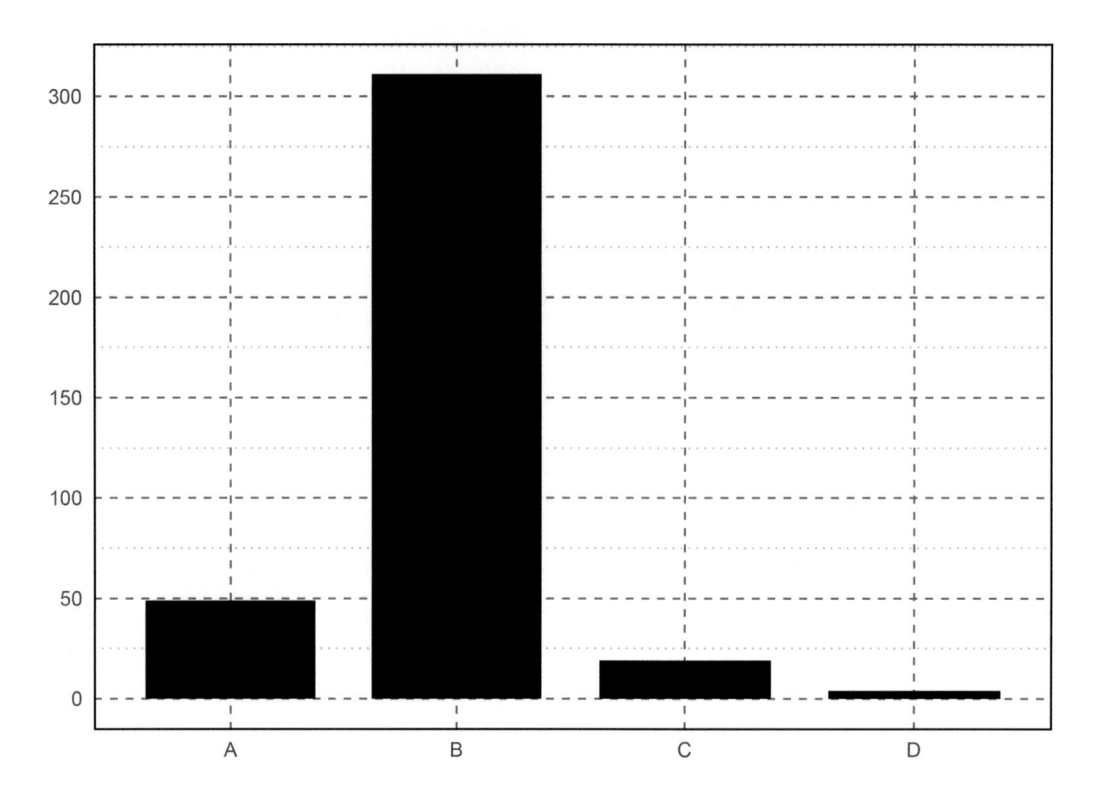

Figure 34. Quantities of each ETS production type within the REFINI dataset.

to the late 1st century BC.[30] Potters from the Italian Peninsula initially sought to establish workshops in Gaul during the Augustan period, bringing with them technical expertise and stylistic preferences influenced by ITS.[31] By the early 1st century AD, Gallic sigillata production was firmly established, with the majority of workshops located in Southern Gaul. Of these, La Graufesenque formed the most important, exporting large quantities of GTS to Britain, Germany, and wider Gaul.[32] Workshops in Central Gaul, such as Lezoux, began to produce sigillata from the late 1st century AD, going on to replace Southern Gaul as the centre of GTS production during the 2nd century.[33] By the late 2nd and 3rd centuries, the focus of production had shifted again, this time to Eastern Gaul and Germany, with workshops such as Rheinzabern achieving prominence.[34] The majority of GTS imported to Northern Italy was produced by workshops in Southern Gaul (see Figure 35). Of these, La Graufesenque and Banassac are the most widely attested among sigillata finds.[35] GTS from Central Gaul is present in much lower

quantities, with most examples coming from Lezoux.[36] Later GTS from Eastern Gaul and Germany is attested in minimal quantities at sites outside of the REFINI dataset, especially in the east of Northern Italy.[37]

Middle Adriatic Terra Sigillata

MATS (or Sigillata Medio-Adriatica as it is otherwise known) is a late form of sigillata produced between the 3rd and 5th centuries AD. First typologised by Luisa Brecciaroli Taborelli during the 1970s, the production and distribution of MATS remains poorly understood.[38] MATS seems to have mainly been produced along the Western Adriatic Coast of Italy between southern Emilia-Romagna and central Marche, and was exported along the Adriatic and Tyrrhenian Coasts of Italy.[39] Sigillata belonging to the group is characterised by an opaque, reddish-brown slip, which is lighter and a deeper orange in colour than other sigillata produced in Italy.[40] In some cases, vessels are additionally decorated with circular patterns added in brown paint over the

[30] Dannel and Mees 2013; Gabucci 2017; Lewit 2015; Mees 2011; Mees and Polak 2013. Some Augustan period experimentation is known in Southern Gaul, but widescale Gallic production would not begin until the Tiberian age (Genin 2007: 178).
[31] Van Oyen 2016: 13-14. These were short-lived and seem to have been focused in the area around Lyon.
[32] Dannel and Mees 2013; Genin 2007; Middleton 1980.
[33] Desbat, Genin and Lasfargues 1996; Gabucci 2017: 2.20-21; Lewit 2015: 232; Picon and Lasfargues 1974.
[34] Lewit 2015: 232; Mantovani 2018.
[35] Gabucci 2017: 2.1-2.

[36] Sigillata produced in Central Gaul was predominantly consumed in Northern Gaul and Britain, with distribution also extending along the Rhenish and Danubian Limes (Brulet, Vilvorder, and Delage 2010: 95; Dannel and Mees 2013: 165-67; Gabucci 2017: 2.18-22).
[37] Donat 2015: 45-46; 2022: 193; Gabucci 2017: 2.1. These assemblages were not quantified, leading to their exclusion from the REFINI dataset.
[38] Brecciaroli Taborelli 1978; Stoppioni 2008: 713-4.
[39] Biondani 2005d; 2014b: 253; Dal Sie 2018b: 105; Tortorella 1996: 325.
[40] Brecciaroli Taborelli 1978.

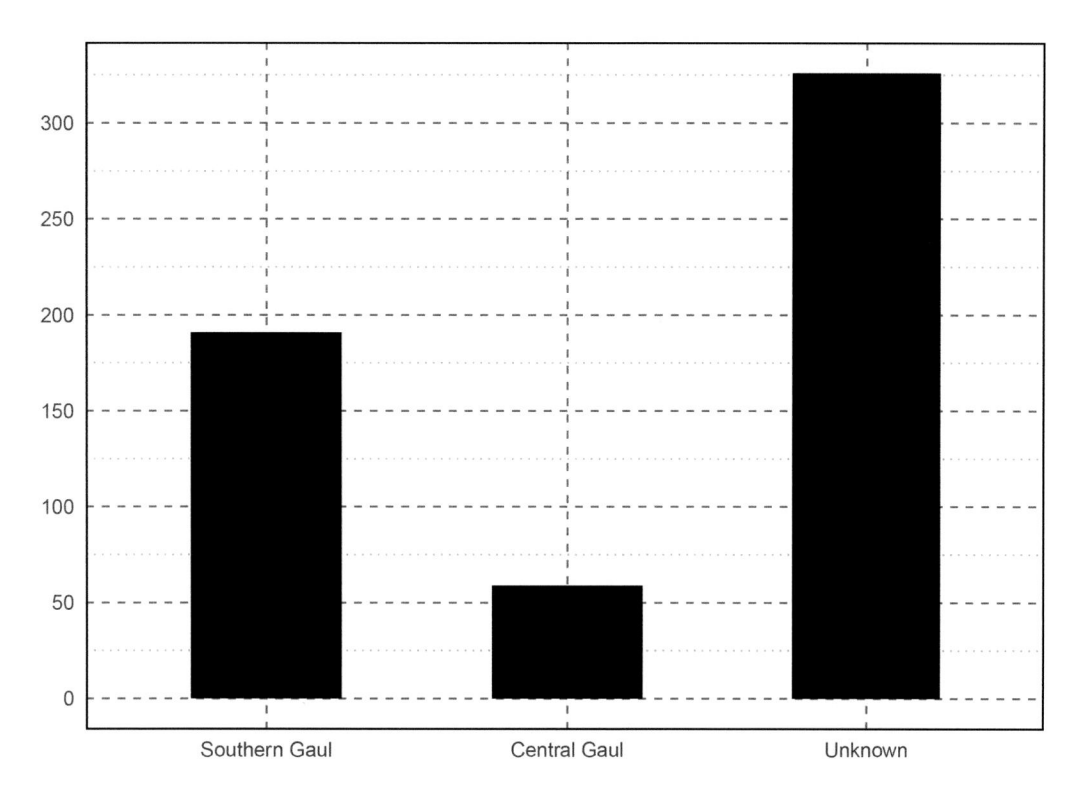

Figure 35. Quantities of provenanced GTS from Southern and Central Gaul within the REFINI dataset.

slip.[41] It appears in significant quantities within the east of the Po-Veneto Plain, particularly in coastal areas and port sites.[42]

Northern Italic Terra Sigillata

In contrast to the amphorae discussed in the previous chapter, there is widespread evidence for the production of terra sigillata across Northern Italy from the latter half of the 1st century BC to the end of the 4th century AD.[43] It is assumed that sigillata production began in Northern Italy during the last quarter of the 1st century BC when workshops that had previously specialised in Black-Gloss ceramics began to emulate red-slip wares originating from Central Italy.[44] The most recent edition of the *Corpus Vasorum Arretinorum* identifies at least 145 potters active in Northern Italy between the mid-1st century BC and the late 2nd century AD.[45] The greatest concentrations of NITS are found within Northern Italy itself, the Adriatic Littoral, and along the Danubian *Limes*, although it also saw wider distribution across the Mediterranean.[46] Despite its widespread circulation, both in Northern Italy and further afield, the production of NITS is far less well-understood than

its Arretine and Central Italic counterparts. While there have been repeated calls for additional study and the creation of a research framework, much of the most influential scholarship on NITS still dates to the 1990s and early 2000s.[47]

Although a large number of potters are known to have been based in Northern Italy, few production sites have been discovered.[48] Some have hypothesised that this is due to most kiln sites being located in urban areas, having been destroyed or buried beneath later structures.[49] Even among kilns that have been located, such as those at Cremona and Padua, there is controversy over whether they were used to produce terra sigillata or other forms of ceramics.[50] Other studies have attempted to distinguish production areas using different methods, with mixed success. Fabric analysis

---

[41] Dal Sie 2018b: 105.
[42] Biondani 2005d; 2014b: 253; Dal Sie 2018b; Ferrando 2008.
[43] Jorio 1998: 125; Mazzeo Saracino 2000: 33.
[44] Mantovani 2013: 143; Mazzeo Saracino 2000: 38.
[45] Oxé, Comfort, and Kenrick 2000.
[46] Brusić 1999; Makjanić 1995; Mercando 1972; Mertens 1972; Schindler-Kaudelka 1980.

[47] Kenrick 2000; Mantovani *et al.* 2022; Mazzeo Saracino 2000; Olcese 1999.
[48] Kenrick 2000: 47.
[49] Della Porta 1998: 82. Another possible reason may be due to kiln sites having been located on the valley floor close to the watercourses, in which case they may be buried beneath later alluvial deposits, too deep to detect by conventional means.
[50] Cipriano and Mazzocchin 2010: 141; Della Porta 1998: 83. While some kilns have been discovered, the low incidence of terra sigillata and absence of sigillata wasters amongst the artefacts recovered makes a firm identification difficult. Mantovani (2013: 143-44) provides a list of possible production sites for Northern Italic Sigillata, which include Adria, Bolonga, Cremona, Faenza, Milan, Mirandola, and Padua. Although Gabucci and Quiri (2008: 51-52) have also identified several possible sigillata wasters at Ivrea that hint at possible mid-Augustan production at the site, the evidence is somewhat inconclusive.

is one such approach, however, the geology of the Po Plain is so homogenous that it is difficult to distinguish the provenance of a vessel from its fabric alone.[51] Indeed, it can often be difficult to distinguish between sigillata originating from Central Italy and the highest quality sigillata produced in Northern Italy in the absence of stamps or laboratory analysis.[52] Archaeometric analysis has helped to isolate some broad areas of production, although narrowing this down to specific locations continues to be reliant on the discovery of kiln sites.[53]

The principal phase of sigillata production in Northern Italy took place between the latter half of the 1st century BC and the first half of the 1st century AD. This phase was characterised by the production of high-quality vessels, many of which were indistinguishable from Arretine and Central Italic vessels. In the latter half of the 1st century AD, the quality of the sigillata being produced in the Po Valley began to decline. This later sigillata is sometimes referred to as Sigillata Tardopadana, 'Late Padan Sigillata', or 'Late Northern Italic Sigillata'; here referred to as late NITS. Its production is primarily dated to between the late 1st century AD and the mid-3rd century AD, although it continued to circulate into the 5th century.[54] What exactly constitutes late NITS is often poorly defined. Some studies distinguish between the earlier NITS of the 1st century BC – mid-1st century AD and the late NITS of the late 1st century AD – 4th century AD, while others treat them as a single evolving style of production without drawing a distinction.[55] This confusion is compounded by the fact that there is no separate typology for late NITS. The style typically mimics vessel forms from earlier periods, as well as some ARS vessel forms which begin to appear in the region during the 2nd century AD.[56] The forms and decoration of the style also seem to be heavily influenced by Gallic wares, combining applied barbotine decoration and wide brims in a style not seen in previous iterations of NITS.[57] Aside from imitating earlier and contemporary vessel forms, late NITS is characterised by a decline in

quality when compared to previous sigillata produced in Northern Italy. This declining quality in production is characterised by the use of poor-quality clay, variable fabric consistency from different firing temperatures, rough textures, and thin, cracked, or blotchy slips.[58] Due to the mixed quality of production, there is very little homogeneity within the style, which can make it hard to identify. Despite this, late NITS seems to have seen similar distribution to earlier sigillata produced in Northern Italy, principally being traded within the Po-Veneto region and the Danubian provinces.[59]

Chronological Trends

Mapping chronological trends in the frequency of finewares across Northern Italy reveals important patterns in the trade and consumption of these vessels. Graphing changes in overall quantities and zones of supply reveals information on the evolution of trade networks and consumer preferences, which can then be studied against the region's historical context. In the following section, the REFINI dataset is subjected to aoristic analysis. Both production chronologies (the date range within which a vessel is believed to have been manufactured) and deposition chronologies (the date range of the deposit within which the vessel was found) are graphed, enabling detailed comparison and analysis.

Overall Trends: Production vs. Deposition Chronologies

The chronological distribution of finewares within the REFINI database was initially analysed using both the production chronology of the vessel form and the chronology of the site in which it was deposited (if these data were available).[60] At an initial glance, there were marked differences between both production and deposition chronologies (see Figure 36). According to production chronologies in Graph A, red-slipped finewares began circulating in Northern Italy during the late 2nd century BC. Initially present in low quantities, the frequency of finewares in the region rapidly spiked c. 50 BC, leading to a peak in the early 1st century AD. However, as quickly as they had risen, the number of finewares began to decline and, although there was a brief plateau in supply during the mid-1st century AD, the quantity of finewares in circulation would only stabilise in the 2nd century. The rise and fall of finewares seen in production chronologies mirrors the main production lifespan of Italian Terra Sigillata, the majority of which was produced between the mid-1st century BC and late 1st century AD.[61] The frequency

---

[51] Della Porta 1998: 82; Jorio 1999: 84. There have also been attempts to subdivide NITS into separate fabric groups in the same way as ETS and ARS, however this has not seen wide adoption amongst researchers (Zabehlicky Scheffenegger and Sauer 2000). The existence of distinct productions of NITS was recognised during the Magdalensberg excavations in the 1970s (Schindler and Zabehlicky Scheffenegger 1977). These were classified as productions A-D. Of the reports in the REFINI dataset, only those for Aquileia (Mantovani 2021), Ivrea (Gabucci and Quiri 2008), and Padua (Rossi 2013) made use of the fabric classifications when referring to their material.

[52] Della Porta 1998: 81; Mazzeo Saracino 2000: 37.

[53] Maritan *et al.* 2013; Olcese 1999.

[54] Mazzeo Saracino 2000: 39; Zabehlicky-Scheffenegger 1990a: 415; 1992.

[55] Of the assemblages analysed below, only Alba (Volonte 1997), Aquileia (Donat and Maggi 2017), Chieri (Vanetti 1987), Cremona (Amadori 1996), and Milan (Jorio 1991) list Sigillata Tardopadana amongst their finewares. The other assemblages treat all Italian material dating from the 1st, 2nd, 3rd, and 4th centuries AD as a single, evolving style of sigillata.

[56] Jorio 1998: 125; Robino 2008: 27.

[57] Ettlinger *et al.* 1990: 50; Mazzeo Saracino 2000: 39.

[58] Jorio 1998: 127.

[59] Makjanić 1995; Zabehlicky-Scheffenegger 1992.

[60] Contexts dating to the post-Roman period containing residual material were excluded from the analysis.

[61] Ettlinger *et al.* 1990: 1-16; Menchelli 2005; Morel 1981.

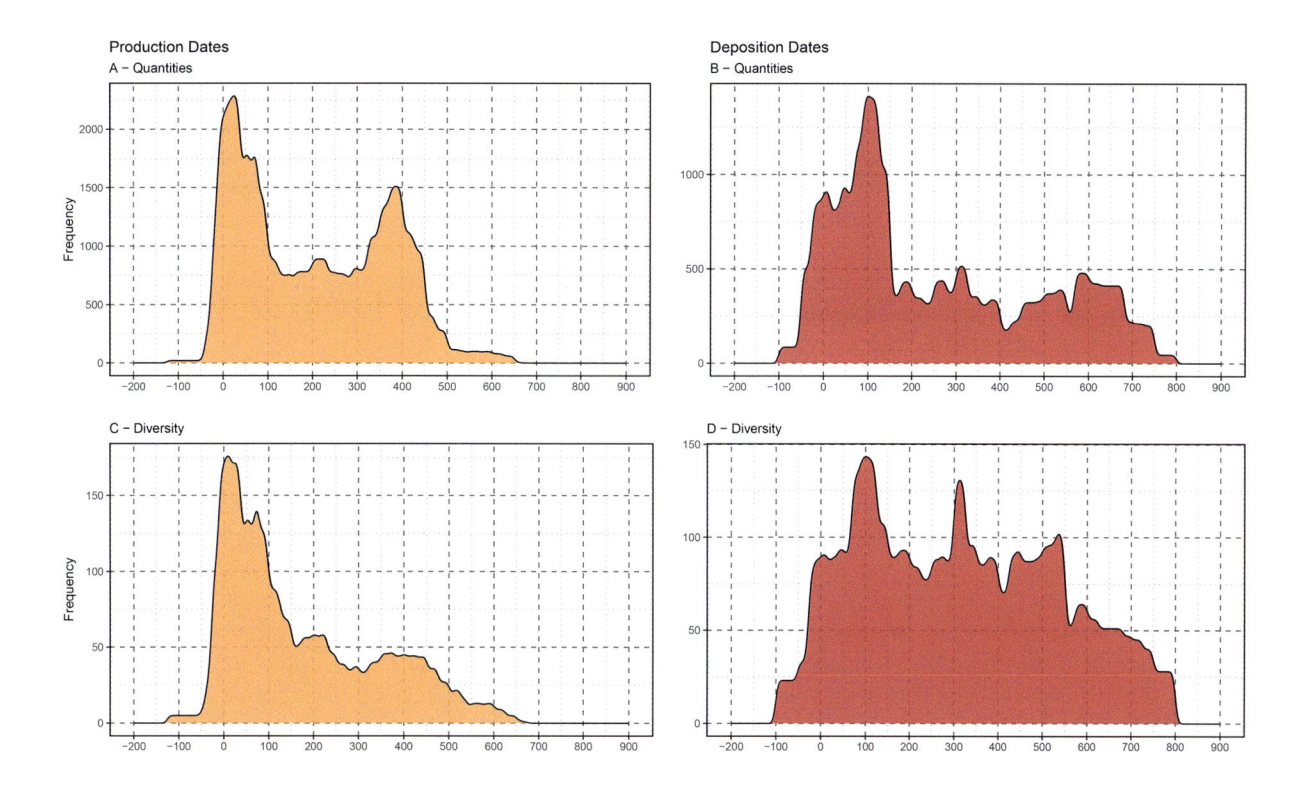

Figure 36. Comparison of Production and Deposition chronologies for fineware quantities and diversity in Northern Italy. Note that the Y axes are not constant.

of finewares in Northern Italy remained relatively unchanged over the following centuries, before rising again to form a second peak *c*. AD 380. After this point, the number of finewares in circulation dropped, declining continuously until the first decades of the 6th century, and disappearing entirely by the mid-7th century.

Deposition chronologies, charted in Graph B, recorded a different story. Initially, deposition chronologies also suggested red-slipped finewares appeared in Northern Italy during the late 2nd century BC, followed by a rapid rise during the late 1st century BC. However, after this initial spike in frequency, the number of finewares in circulation then dipped, only starting to gradually rise again in the mid-1st century AD. This led to a peak in red-slipped finewares *c*. AD 100, followed by a sharp decline throughout the first half of the 2nd century. The frequency of finewares would then fluctuate over the course of the following centuries, dipping then rising again throughout the 5th and 6th centuries AD. Numbers then somewhat plateaued before a final decline began in the late 7th century AD. The deposition chronologies for finewares suffered many of the same difficulties as those for amphorae. The continued presence of red-slipped finewares into the 8th and 9th centuries AD is a reflection of post-Roman continuity in occupation at sites within the REFINI dataset resulting in the reuse and redepositing of ceramics into the

Early Medieval period and beyond.[62] This causes some finewares, such as early ITS, to appear in contexts long after their production chronology had ceased. Deposits with large distances between their opening and closing dates also distribute vessels earlier and later than their probable point of consumption.

Moving away from the quantities of red-slipped finewares consumed in Northern Italy over time, analysing diversity via the number of fineware forms circulating in the region in a given year offers a different perspective on the data. At first glance, there are notable similarities between the quantities and diversity of vessel forms in circulation. In the production chronologies shown in Graph C, the number of fineware forms present within Northern Italy rapidly rose in the late 1st century BC, peaking in the first decades of the 1st century AD. This was followed by an initial decline and brief plateau in vessel diversity during the mid-1st century, after which the decline continued throughout the early 2nd century AD. Between the mid-2nd and mid-5th centuries AD, vessel diversity remained relatively stable, before entering a final, continuous decline *c*. AD 445. The sharp spike and subsequent second peak in frequency seen in the total number of vessels circulating at the start of the

---

[62] Adams 2003; Cessford 2017: 167-70. See Franconi *et al.* (2023: 27-28) for a discussion of the problems of long deposition chronologies.

4th century AD (see Graph A) was not echoed by vessel diversity. Instead, a far shallower rise and decline was recorded.

Deposition chronologies in Graph D suggest a significant number of vessel forms were circulating during the early 1st century BC in Northern Italy. This was followed by a rapid rise in vessel diversity during the mid-1st century BC, followed by the number of vessel forms plateauing throughout the first half of the 1st century AD. Diversity then increased again, leading to a brief peak *c.* AD 100, followed by a decline throughout the early 2nd century AD. This first peak and decline was then followed by a number of rises and falls in diversity over the following centuries. The limited number of published fineware assemblages from the 3rd century AD onwards served to hinder the analysis, causing individual contexts to have a large impact on the shape of the curve. For example, the variety of finewares in circulation rose and declined sharply in the first decades of the 4th century AD, with the number of vessel forms approaching the levels of the late first-century peak. However, this spike is representative of a single, large, well-dated context in Aquileia.[63] Diversity would increase again throughout the 5th and early 6th centuries AD, the impact of Milan's extensive and well-published late assemblage on the curve, before sharply declining.[64] This decline would steadily continue throughout the following centuries. The overall variety of vessel forms in circulation remained higher in comparison to the number suggested by production chronologies, once again a reflection of the re-use and redepositing of ceramics beyond their production lifespans.

As with the amphora data examined in the previous chapter, there were limitations to both production and deposition chronologies when graphing fineware distribution, with each offering a competing picture of the overall trend in fineware trade and consumption in Northern Italy. Both production and deposition chronologies showed an initial spike in the quantity and diversity of finewares circulating during the 1st century AD. This was then followed by a decline in the number of finewares within Northern Italy. However, there was conflict over the trajectory of fineware consumption during the mid-Imperial period and Late Antiquity. While production chronologies recorded a second peak in the quantity of finewares during the late 4th century AD, deposition chronologies instead suggested the number of finewares stabilised in the mid-2nd century AD, fluctuating within narrow margins until a final decline in the late 7th century. Likewise, although production chronologies documented a continuous decline in the number of vessel forms circulating after the early 1st century AD, deposition chronologies instead recorded continued high levels of diversity well into the 6th century.

Trends in Provenance: Local Products vs. Long-Distance Imports

A more nuanced understanding of fineware consumption patterns can be gained by separating the REFINI dataset by vessel provenance (see Figure 37). In Graph A, production chronologies show that red-slipped finewares from the Italian Peninsula dominated Northern Italian markets from *c.* 50 BC to *c.* AD 100. NITS, produced in Northern Italy, would appear in the greatest quantities, with the number of CITS vessels produced at Arezzo, Pisa, and other sites in Central Italy, present in almost comparable numbers. Sigillata from Northern and Central Italy would decline rapidly throughout the latter half of the 1st century AD. CITS would disappear entirely by the mid-2nd century AD, but late NITS continued to circulate, remaining the dominant fineware type throughout the 2nd century and persisting in significant quantities until the end of the 5th century.[65]

Of the other types of sigillata present in Northern Italy, ETS began circulating in minimal quantities from the late 2nd century BC. Appearing in low frequencies, the number of ETS vessels rose sharply in the mid-1st century AD, leading to a peak *c.* AD 100.[66] This was followed by an equally rapid decline, with Eastern Mediterranean finewares disappearing from Northern Italy by the mid-2nd century AD. Sigillata from Gaul began to circulate in minimal quantities from the late 1st century BC. As with ETS, the frequency of GTS vessels rose sharply in the mid-1st century AD, coinciding with the decline of CTS imports and NITS production in Northern Italy. Quantities of GTS then plateaued throughout the 2nd century AD, before rapidly declining during the first half of the 3rd century and disappearing from Northern Italy. Sigillata from the Adriatic Littoral began circulating during the mid-2nd century AD, with quantities gradually rising to form a late third-century peak. Numbers then plateaued, before declining during the mid-5th century AD. North African finewares began to circulate in Northern Italy during the late 1st century AD, with quantities gradually increasing over the following century.[67] The frequency of ARS vessels rapidly rises in the early 3rd century

---

[63] Gaddi 2017b: 27-34; Zulini 2017. At Aquileia, the deliberate infilling of the so-called 'Canale d'Anfora' at the beginning of the 4th century AD preserved a diverse range of fineware forms, leading to the sudden spike seen in the deposition chronologies.

[64] Jorio 1991; Roffia 1991. The scale of the MM3 excavations at Milan resulted in a wide variety of fineware forms being recovered, many from closely dated Late Antique contexts.

[65] Mazzeo Saracino 2000: 39; Zabehlicky-Scheffenegger 1992: 415.

[66] This reflects wider distribution chronologies of ESB, the dominant ETS fabric found within Northern Italy (Bes 2015: 27-28; Cipriano and Sandrini 2003).

[67] Biondani 2005c; Rossi 2013; Trivini Bellini 2021; Zulini 2017. See also Cirelli 2022: 469-70; Dobreva 2023a; 2023b.

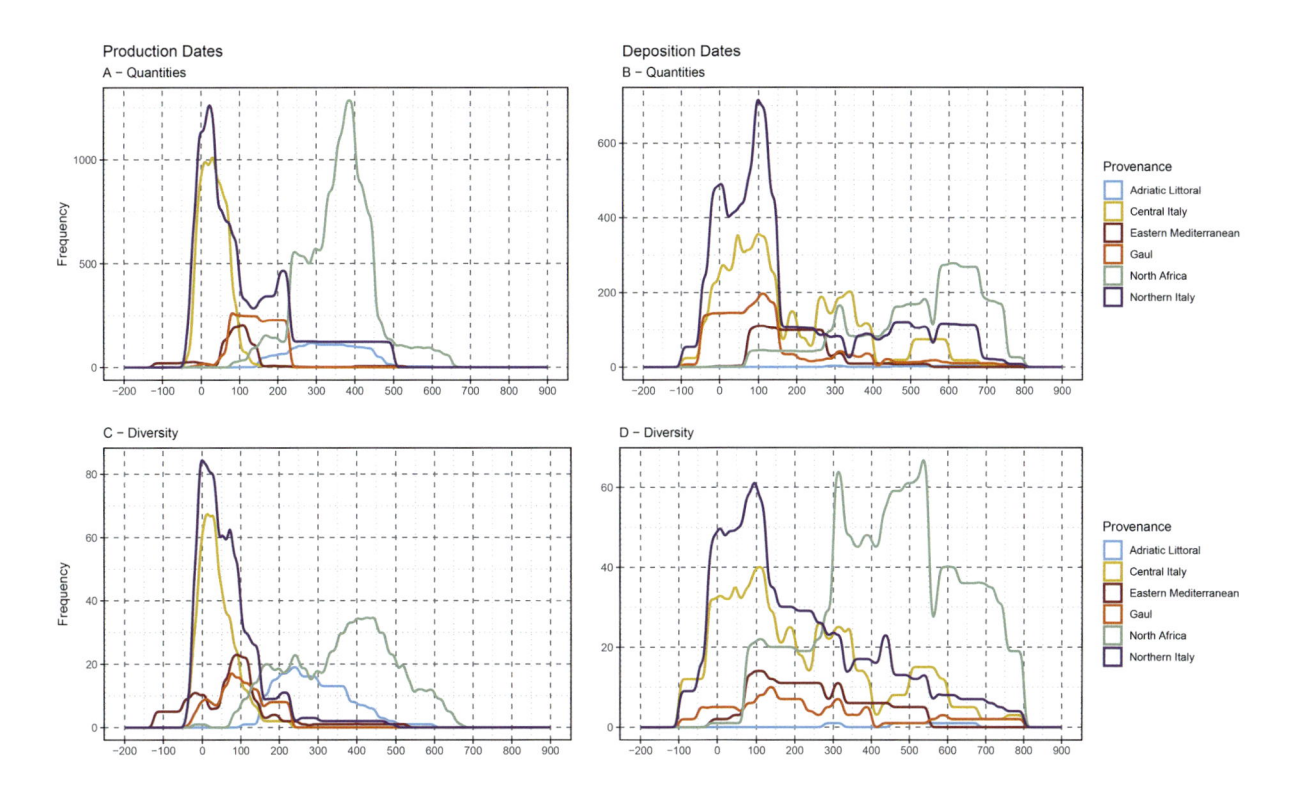

Figure 37. Comparison of Production and Deposition chronologies for the quantity and diversity of finewares from each zone of production in Northern Italy. Note that the Y axes are not constant.

AD, coinciding with a sharp decline in the quantity of NITS in the region. The amount of ARS in circulation stabilised during the latter half of the 3rd century AD, before rising rapidly to form a peak in the late 4th century, exceeding the peak of NITS in the early 1st century AD. Quantities of ARS then declined sharply *c.* AD 390, with frequency continuously falling throughout the 5th century.[68] Numbers would somewhat stabilise in the 6th century AD, before the final disappearance of ARS in the mid-7th century.[69]

The picture presented by deposition chronologies in Graph B is significantly different to that suggested by production chronologies. The large range between the opening and closing dates of some contexts resulted in Gallic and Italian sigillata appearing before the start of their production lifespans in the early 1st century BC. Quantities of CTS, GTS, and NITS, increased together during the mid-1st century BC, all peaking *c.* AD 100, before declining in the mid-2nd century. NITS remained the most dominant fineware, with CITS also circulating in significant quantities. From the mid-2nd century AD onwards, the low number of securely dated Late

Antique contexts once again hampered interpretation.[70] Throughout the 3rd, 4th and 5th centuries AD, no single provenance dominated, with significant quantities of ARS, CITS, and NITS in circulation.[71] By the 6th century AD, North Africa had become the main supplier of finewares to Northern Italy, with the frequency of ARS remaining stable throughout most of the 7th century AD. By the end of the 7th century, the number of North African finewares in circulation began to decline, with ARS disappearing by the beginning of the 9th century AD. The low number of stratigraphically published assemblages containing MATS meant that they were almost entirely absent from deposition chronologies.

Further insight is provided when analysing the vessel diversity of each provenance chronologically. In the production chronologies charted in Graph C, spikes in vessel diversity often closely correspond to peaks in the quantity of finewares circulating. The diversity of both CITS and NITS vessel forms peaked in the early

---

[68] Quantities of ARS in circulation seem to have dropped across the Mediterranean world from the mid-5th century onwards (Bes 2015: 91-92; Bonifay 2018: 337; Fentress and Perkins 1988; Fentress *et al.* 2004: 140-50; Hayes 1972: 423).

[69] Most ARS production had ceased by the mid-7th century AD (Bonifay 2004: 207-10; Hayes 1972: 423-24).

[70] This led to fineware from the Adriatic Littoral appearing in negligible quantities in the deposition chronologies, despite MATS having a significant Late Antique circulation according to production chronologies. Large assemblages published with deposition dates from single sites, such as Aquileia, Brescia, and Milan, were also able to have a large impact on the shape of the Late Antique graphs.

[71] Late production of CITS and NITS, often difficult to identify, may account for the continued circulation of finewares from Central and Northern Italy during Late Antiquity (Jorio 1999: 83; Morandini 2008b: 332; Robino 2017: 71; Volonte 1997: 443).

1st century AD, while the greatest variety of ETS and GTS forms were in circulation *c.* AD 100. The diversity of ARS vessels would also be at its maximum in the late 4th and early 5th centuries AD. However, peaks in the quantity and diversity of finewares did not match up for every zone of production. The greatest diversity of MATS vessels occurred during the early 3rd century AD, with the variety of forms already in decline by the 4th century AD when it was circulating in the greatest quantities. The sharp decline in the quantity of ARS forms during the 5th century AD was also not mirrored by a drastic drop in diversity. Instead, the variety of ARS forms declined more gradually. Furthermore, although the peak quantity of ARS in Northern Italy would exceed that of NITS, the number of ARS vessel forms in circulation never approached a similar level of diversity to NITS vessels, suggesting a more limited selection of finewares was available.

The overview suggested by deposition chronologies in Graph D was somewhat different. As with production chronologies, deposition chronologies saw overlap between the quantity and diversity of vessel forms in circulation. The diversity of CITS, ETS, GTS, and NITS vessel forms closely matched the quantities of these finewares circulating, with form variety peaking in *c.* AD 100. However, after their initial peaks in diversity, the variety of CITS, ETS, GTS, and NITS vessels remained high over the following centuries, declining slowly. This is partly a result of the long continuity in occupation at urban centres within the REFINI dataset, resulting in the disturbing of earlier stratigraphy and the redepositing of ceramics from these contexts. However, as functional items, fine tablewares saw continual use until they broke, meaning vessel forms may have remained in active circulation long after their production had ceased.[72] Both these factors contributed to the slow decline in vessel diversity suggested by deposition chronologies. The variety of ARS forms in circulation saw little relation to the quantities present in Northern Italy recorded by deposition chronologies. The diversity of ARS vessel forms initially peaked in the early 4th century AD, with the number of types exceeding those of NITS. A second peak would occur during the early 6th century AD before diversity declined. While the variety of ARS vessel forms remained high during the 7th century AD, the period of peak quantities circulating according to deposition chronologies, diversity was considerably lower than in the preceding centuries.

Northern Italy was supplied with finewares from a range of production zones throughout the Roman period. Both production and deposition chronologies demonstrate the importance of Central Italy, North Africa, and Northern Italy to the region's overall supply of red-slipped finewares. The graphs suggest that the greatest diversity in the provenance of finewares occurred during the 2nd century AD, where the arrival of finewares from new zones of production, such as ETS, GTS, and early ARS, coincided with the rapid decline of Central and Northern Italic sigillata in production chronologies. The paucity of stratigraphically published assemblages from the 3rd century AD onwards once again hindered analysis of Late Antique trends. Although production chronologies documented a rapid spike in the quantity of ARS during the early 3rd century AD, coinciding with a decline in NITS, deposition chronologies suggested that a mix of finewares from various zones of production were circulating in Northern Italy during this time. The overwhelming dominance of North African finewares from the mid-3rd century AD onwards, recorded by production chronologies, demonstrates Northern Italy's continued integration into and reliance on extra-provincial economies during Late Antiquity. However, deposition chronologies suggest the picture is more complex. While North Africa proved to be the main provenance of red-slipped finewares in Northern Italy during Late Antiquity, tableware produced in earlier periods, such as CITS and NITS, may have continued to circulate alongside new imports.

Geographic Trends

So far, analysis of the REFINI dataset has demonstrated significant variation in the quantities and provenance of finewares chronologically across Northern Italy. As with the amphora data analysed in the previous chapter, this variation is mirrored geographically across the region. To explore spatial trends, the assemblages of the regional urban centres in the REFINI dataset were analysed using hierarchical clustering based on their assemblage provenance. Sites with similar assemblage provenances are grouped by the analysis, allowing geographic clusters to form (see Figure 38). The site assemblages are subdivided by chronological period based on vessel production chronologies.[73] To ensure a rigorous level of analysis, a minimum sample size of 30 sherds per period was necessary for a site to be included. The low quantities of red-slipped finewares circulating in the Late Republic meant that only the Imperial and Late Antique periods were subjected to clustering. Port sites are excluded from the analysis, as their role as entrepôts results in assemblages significantly different in composition to other inland sites in their geographic vicinity.

---

[72] Adams 2003; Cessford 2017: 167-70. Alternatively, broken fragments of fineware vessels may have continued to circulate, changing use and function as they were reworked into items such as pendants, keepsakes, spindle whorls, stoppers, or counters (Nieuwhof 2020).

[73] This was to maximise the amount of data available for the analysis, as not all assemblages included deposition dates.

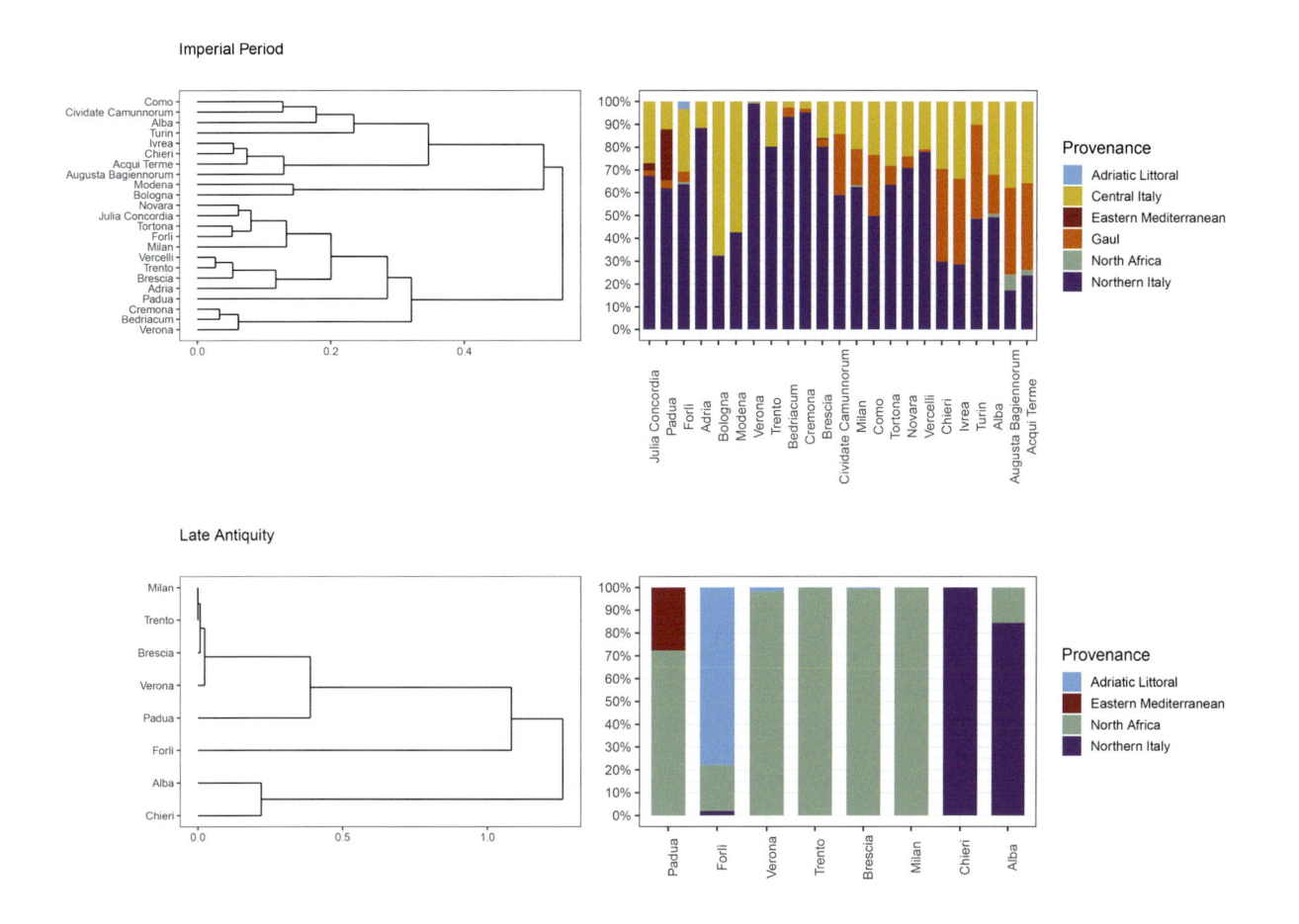

Figure 38. Percentages of fineware provenance at each site divided by period, with subsequently formed hierarchical clusters. See Appendix B for exact percentages and n numbers for each assemblage.

The Imperial Period

From the Imperial period dataset, 20 inland sites met the minimum threshold of sherds for analysis. Outside of the REFINI database, the percentage composition of three unquantified assemblages from Novara, Turin, and Vercelli was also available, bringing the total number of sites to 23.[74] When these sites were hierarchically clustered, three geographic groups were identified (see Figure 39). The first cluster was comprised of 13 sites, mostly located in the Po-Veneto Plain. Urban centres in this cluster had the highest levels of NITS in their assemblages, which ranged from 61.8% to 99%. Most hypothesised production sites for NITS are located in the Po-Veneto Plain and include sites such as Adria, Bologna, Cremona, Faenza, Milan,

Mirandola, and Padua.[75] Consumers seem to have taken advantage of the breadth of NITS producers operating in their immediate vicinity, with most assemblages in this cluster exhibiting low levels of finewares from other provenances. Other finewares, which had to travel from further afield to reach Northern Italic markets, may have struggled to compete with NITS. CITS often formed the second largest component of assemblages in cluster 1, ranging from <1% to 27.2%. However, urban centres located near port sites in the coastal hinterland did contain a greater variety of fineware types. Julia Concordia and Padua both recorded Eastern Terra Sigillata B in their assemblages, while Forlì's assemblage contained small quantities of early MATS.[76]

The second cluster contained two sites, Bologna and Modena. Both sites contained high quantities of CITS, which comprised 67.6% of Bologna's assemblage and 57.4% of Modena's. NITS made up the remainder of both sites' assemblages. From production centres in Arezzo and elsewhere in Central Italy, CITS would have travelled overland across the Apennines to

---

[74] Data for Novara and Vercelli came from a series of urban excavations published in Spagnolo Garzoli *et al.* 2008. The provenance of the imperial assemblages at Novara and Vercelli were provided as percentages, without a total number of fragments provided. Both assemblages lacked a full-breakdown of vessel forms. Data for Turin came from the excavations of the city wall and the theatre, published in Brecciaroli Taborelli and Gabucci 2007. Turin's assemblage also lacked identified vessel forms, but the overall number of fragments from each zone of production was given, allowing the provenance of the assemblage to be broken down as percentages.

[75] Mantovani 2013: 143-44; Maritan *et al.* 2013.
[76] Cipriano 2013; Cipriano and Sandri 2003; Pettenò 2007; Rossi 2013.

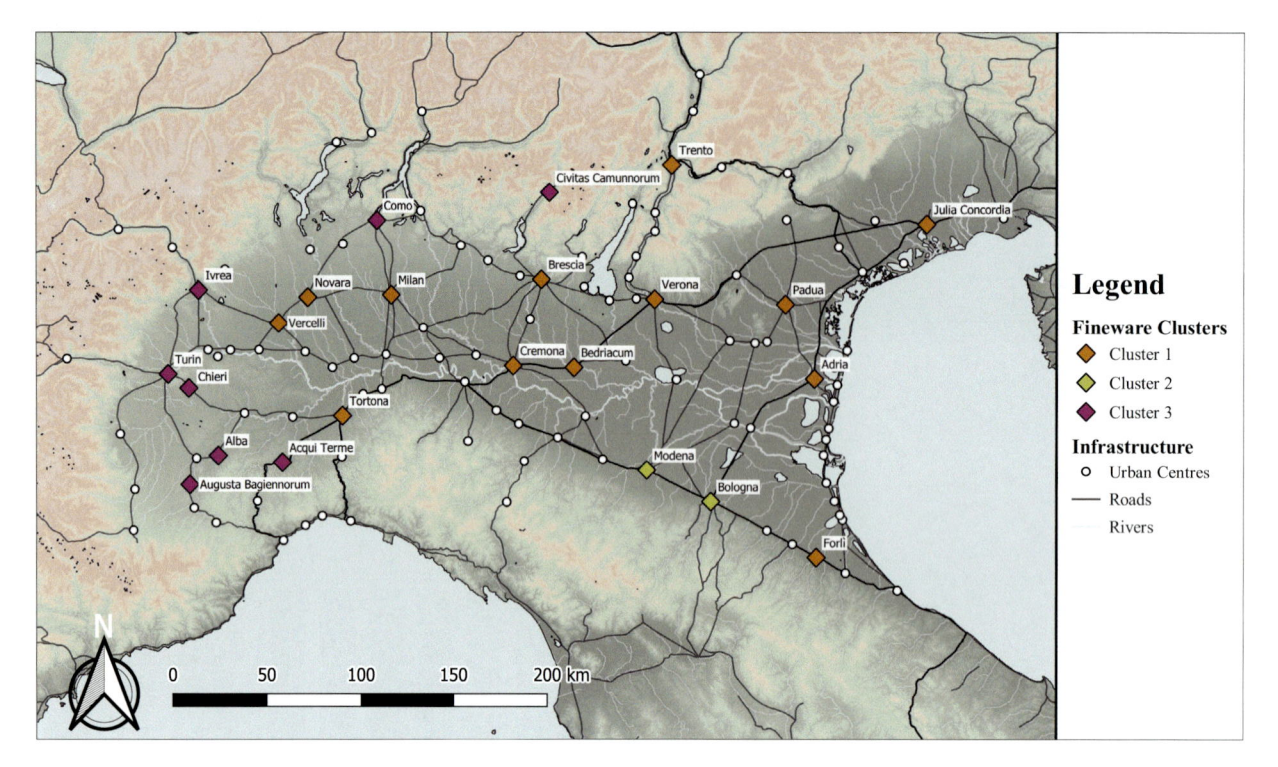

Figure 39. Imperial period site clusters, based on fineware assemblage provenance.

reach markets in central and eastern Northern Italy. Bologna was located at the terminus of the main trans-Apennine road that connected the eastern Po Valley with Florence, and beyond it, CITS production centres at Arezzo.[77] The high quantities of CITS at Bologna and Modena likely reflect their position as the initial entry point and redistribution centres for Arretine sigillata into Northern Italy.

The third cluster was composed of eight sites. These urban centres were located in the west and south-west of the Po Valley, alongside the northwestern Alpine foothills. Although NITS continued to form a major component, assemblages in this cluster also contained the highest quantities of GTS, which ranged from 17.1% to 41.1%.[78] The concentration of Gallic sigillata within this part of the region, at urban centres closest to the Alps and Alpine passes, is indicative of trans-Alpine trade between production centres in Gaul and Northern Italy. As GTS formed a minor component of fineware assemblages within the central and eastern Po Plain, Gallic sigillata seems to only have been competitive in the areas closest to its point of entry into Northern Italy. CTS also appeared in appreciable numbers within the third cluster, constituting between 14% and 31.9% of assemblages. Sites in this cluster closest to the Ligurian Coast (Acqui Terme, Alba, Augusta Bagiennorum, and

Turin), also contained small quantities of early ARS in their assemblages.[79] ARS imports to this area of Northern Italy may have travelled with North African or other Western Mediterranean amphorae crossing the Apennines during this period (see the previous chapter).[80]

The fineware data from the Imperial period demonstrates that red-slipped tablewares circulated in significantly different ways to the amphorae explored in the previous chapter. During this era, Northern Italy primarily consumed sigillata that had been produced within the region. NITS was present in every site assemblage, often forming the major component. Other finewares from different zones of production were also in circulation, but they were concentrated in specific areas of Northern Italy. Although assemblages in the coastal hinterland and Po Valley were composed almost entirely of NITS, sites in the far west of the region and those in the Alpine foothills, located closest to Gaul, saw imports of GTS take up a greater portion of their assemblage. In a similar vein, Bologna and Modena, located on the main road between Arezzo and the Po Valley, saw CITS make up the majority of their

---

[77] Gori 2003: 374; Gottarelli 1988.
[78] Brecciaroli Taborelli 1987; 2007; Fabbri, Gualtieri, and Massa 2004; Gabucci 2017; Pisano Briani 2016; Ratto 2014; Robino 2008; 2017; Vanetti 1987; Volonte 1997.

[79] Brecciaroli Taborelli 2007; Ratto 2014; Robino 2008; 2017; Volonte 1997.
[80] See Fulford 1987: 59–62; Reynolds 1995: 128–29; 2018; and Tomber 1993, for discussion on how finewares travelled. Bonifay and Tchernia (2012: 322-24) highlight that it is rare to find cargoes of ARS travelling with North African amphorae, although it may have piggy-backed on other maritime goods crossing the Apennines (see also Bonifay 2018: 334-36).

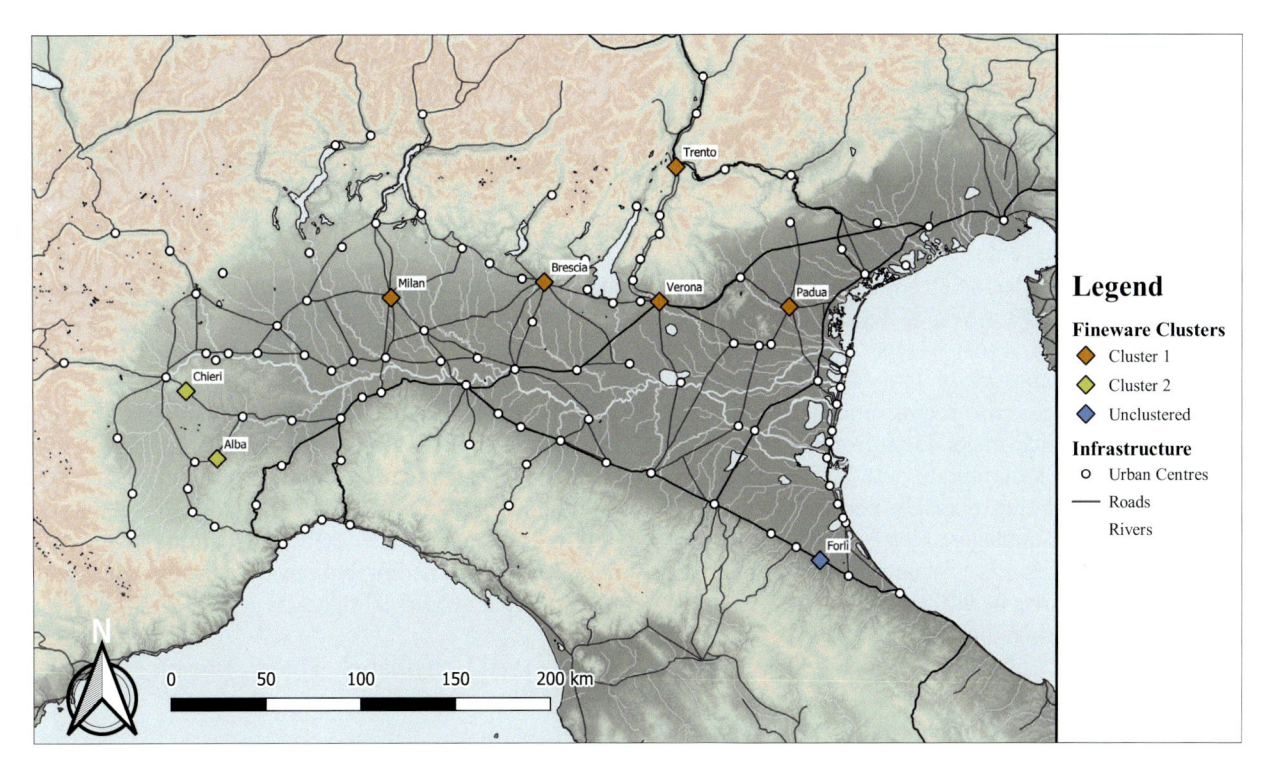

Figure 40. Late Antique site clusters, based on fineware assemblage provenance.

assemblages.[81] This resulted in the creation of distinct zones of consumption within Northern Italy, closely linked to the initial point of entry for extra-regional finewares.

Late Antiquity

As with the amphora data in the previous chapter, the low number of assemblages containing Late Antique material in sufficient quantities for analysis limited the effectiveness of the hierarchical clustering. Only eight inland sites from the Late Antique period dataset met the minimum threshold of sherds for analysis. When these sites were hierarchically clustered, two geographic groups were identified (see Figure 40). The first group was composed of five sites, the assemblages of which were almost entirely composed of ARS.[82] Quantities of North African fineware ranged from 72.2% to 100% of assemblages in the cluster. Padua formed an outlier as a result of having significant quantities of the fineware Late Roman C, produced in Asia Minor, within its assemblage (27.7%).[83] Marginal quantities of MATS from the Adriatic Littoral were also present at Brescia and Verona.[84] The dominance

of ARS in fineware assemblages from the 3rd century AD onwards is a pattern seen across Late Antique Italy, where it replaces terra sigillata.[85] The sites in cluster 1, primarily located in the central and eastern Po Valley, were either close to the Adriatic Coast or integrated into inland trade networks connected to Adriatic ports. ARS, alongside other North African goods, was circulating in the upper Adriatic area in increasing quantities from the mid-2nd century AD onwards and was primarily distributed inland from Aquileia, Classis, and Ravenna.[86] Consequently, urban centres in cluster 1 were well-placed to take advantage of new ARS imports as the production of other fineware types began to decline.

The second cluster was composed of two sites, Alba and Chieri, located in the south-west of the Po Valley. The assemblages at these urban centres were almost entirely comprised of late NITS, which ranged from 84.4% at Alba to 100% at Chieri.[87] ARS formed the remainder of Alba's assemblage. Against the backdrop of widespread ARS imports during Late Antiquity, the evidence from Alba and Chieri suggests regional fineware production continued in some capacity.[88] The late NITS found at these sites shared many characteristics: thin or opaque slip, variable colouring, imitation of Gallic

---

[81] Curina 1986; Mongardi 2014.

[82] Jorio 1999; 2002; Morandini 2008b; Massa 2002; Oberosler 1995; Roffia 1991.

[83] Also known as Phoenician Red-Slip Ware, Late Roman C was mostly produced in the vicinity of Phokaia on the western coast of Turkey (Bes 2015: 25-26; Hayes 1972: 323). It was produced between the 4th and 7th centuries AD.

[84] Jorio 1999; 2002; Morandini 2008b.

[85] Bes 2015, 122-28; Bonifay 2003; 2004. ARS has been found in significant quantities across sites in the Upper Adriatic area but has yet to be studied at a regional level (Biondani 2014b: 229).

[86] Auriemma, Degrassi, and Quiri 2015; Dobreva 2023a: 298; 2023b.

[87] Vanetti 1987; Volonte 1997.

[88] Della Porta 1998; Jorio 1998: 125-27; Olcese 1998.

and North African vessel forms, and friability (due to being fired at sub-optimal temperatures).[89] Late NITS was absent from all other sites apart from Forlì, where it appeared in marginal quantities (2%). The quantities of late NITS present at sites in cluster 2 may be reflective of their somewhat isolated position at the end of inland trade routes from the Adriatic, resulting in an increased reliance on locally produced finewares to meet demand. However, a sudden cessation of sigillata production across Northern Italy, suggested by the apparent absence of late NITS in most Late Antique assemblages, also seems unlikely. The lack of typologies, difficulty in its identification (especially regarding vessels that imitate ARS and GTS), a lack of specialists, and the relatively poor publication of later fineware assemblages, means that the scale of later NITS production is probably under-represented in the sites discussed here.[90] This makes it impossible to determine whether the high quantities of late NITS found at Alba and Chieri are an isolated phenomenon or are representative of wider late NITS production obscured by the archaeological record and publication practices.

The final site in the Late Antique assemblage, Forlì, did not join a cluster. Forlì instead placed independently due to the majority of its assemblage being composed of MATS. The high quantities present are likely reflective of Forlì's proximity to MATS production sites in Emilia-Romagna.[91] Although it was found in low quantities at Brescia and Verona, it seems that MATS failed to penetrate further inland and was uncompetitive against ARS in areas further away from its zone of production. In a similar matter to NITS produced during this later period, the difficulty of identifying MATS and a lack of specialists may mean that this fineware is under-represented in assemblages in the eastern Po Valley and Adriatic coastal regions.

The trade in finewares during Late Antiquity saw significant changes from earlier periods and, despite the limited sample size, some tentative patterns can be inferred. The decline in CITS, NITS, and GTS production saw a major reorientation in the locations supplying fineware to Northern Italy during Late Antiquity, with North Africa forming its main provenance. Assemblages in the Po-Veneto Plain were comprised of ARS to the exclusion of almost all other fineware types, resulting in greater uniformity in their composition. Some production of NITS continued in the south-west of the Po Valley, and MATS saw significant circulation in the coastal hinterland closest to its production sites, but their contribution to wider fineware consumption

in Northern Italy is hard to quantify. The dominance of ARS, and reliance on North African production to satisfy demand, represents a shift from predominantly short-distance to long-distance trade in the supply of finewares to Northern Italy. Rather than arriving in the region via overland routes, ARS cargoes initially entered Northern Italy through its maritime ports, before being redistributed inland.

Trade in Red-Slip Finewares in Northern Italy

Analysis of the REFINI dataset outlined numerous trends in the red-slipped fineware trade in Northern Italy between the 2nd century BC and the 9th century AD. The following section explores a series of case studies identified through the analysis, enabling a greater depth of understanding behind the chronological and spatial trends so far highlighted.

Italic Terra Sigillata: Short Distance Trade, Desirability, and Choice

Between the 1st century BC and the early 3rd century AD, the Italian Peninsula formed the largest zone of production for red-slipped finewares consumed in Northern Italy. Compared to the amphora data analysed in the previous chapter, which saw the majority of Northern Italy's demand fulfilled by extra-regional imports, one of the most striking results from the analysis of the REFINI dataset was the prominence of locally produced NITS within site assemblages. Ceramicists in Northern Italy seem to have enjoyed a high degree of regional and extra-regional success, with NITS dominating fineware assemblages across the Po-Veneto Plain between the 1st century BC and the 2nd century AD and seeing large-scale export to the Danubian *Limes*.[92] It is perhaps unsurprising that sites in Northern Italy predominantly consumed fineware produced within the region. Vessels were of a comparable, if not equal quality, to imports of CITS, which would also have travelled further and accumulated additional costs before entering Northern Italy. Sites in the centre and east of the region, close to possible sigillata production sites such as Adria, Bologna, Cremona, Faenza, Milan, Mirandola, and Padua, returned the highest quantities of NITS in their assemblages, demonstrating the impact of locally produced finewares on regional consumption habits.[93]

Although helpful for highlighting broad geographic trends, NITS is not a particularly useful definition of provenance, considering the geographic extent of the area. A pot produced in the hinterland of Aquileia

[89] Jorio 1999: 83; Morandini 2008b: 332; Robino 2017: 71; Volonte 1997: 443.
[90] Massa 2000; Morandini 2000: 165-66; 2008b: 332-33; Olcese 1998: 18-19.
[91] Biondani 2005b: 117-78; Tortorella 1996: 325.

[92] Mercando 1972; Mertens 1972; Brusić 1999; Schindler Kaudelka 1980; Makjanić 1995.
[93] Amadori 1996; Ceri 1991; Jorio 1991; 2002; Mantovani 2013: 143-44; Morandini 2008a; Volonte 1996.

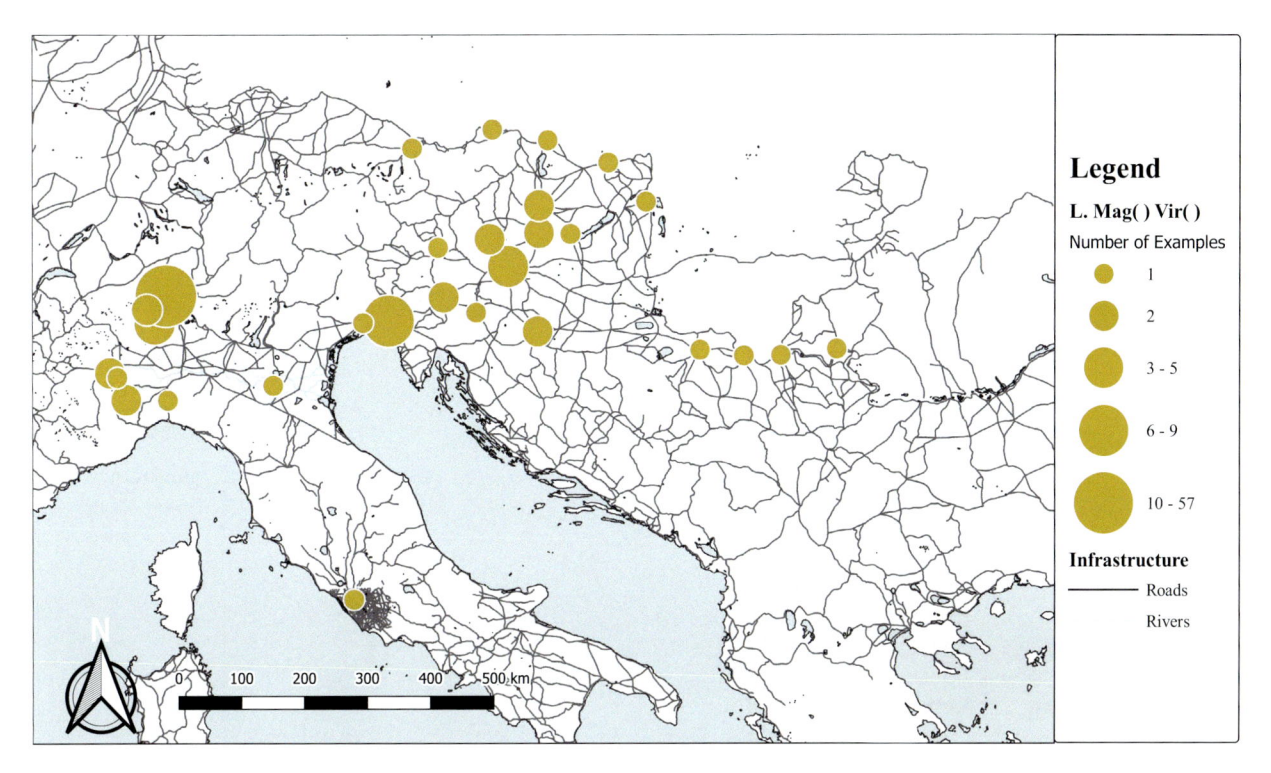

Figure 41. Distribution of western Po Valley NITS producer *L. Mag( ) Vir ( )* across the Roman Empire (data taken from the RGZM Samian Database, viewed 7 May 2024, www1.rgzm.de).

found at Turin, for example, may have travelled just as far as one produced in Arezzo or in Southern Gaul to reach Northern Italy. Unfortunately, in the absence of confirmed production sites, it is impossible to attribute a more accurate provenance for Northern Italic vessels, frustrating attempts at more nuanced interpretations of short-distance trade in the region. Looking at sigillata stamp data can be of some help in this regard, with the distribution of a workshop's stamps giving an indication of where its finewares were consumed.[94]

At first glance, a clear east-west split is observable in the distribution of potters' stamps across Northern Italy. NITS made by producers in the west, such as the workshops of *L. Mag( ) Vir ( )* and *Q. S( ) P( ))*, was primarily consumed in the western Po Valley (see Figure 41 and Figure 42).[95] However, these potters are almost entirely absent in the eastern Po Valley, with vessels attributed to them only reappearing at Aquileia, and then along the main roads to the Danube and *Limes* themselves.[96] A similar situation is seen amongst workshops in the eastern Po Valley and the Veneto Plain. Sigillata made by

workshops in the east, such as those of *A. Terentius* and *Agatho*, was primarily consumed in the eastern Po Valley and Veneto Plain, alongside major roads and urban centres in the Balkans, before reaching the Danubian *Limes* (see Figure 43 and Figure 44).[97] Northern Italic terra sigillata seems to have been primarily consumed within a short radius of the workshop that produced it. With such a diverse range and quantity of potters present in the region, consumers seem to have been content with the choice of vessels in their immediate vicinity. Transport costs incurred as sigillata moved away from their production areas may have further served to reduce the competitiveness of Northern Italic vessels outside of local contexts.

While NITS circulation within Northern Italy was limited to the areas closest to its production zones, the products of both eastern and western NITS workshops would see similar distribution along the Danubian *Limes*, pointing to a distinction between how sigillata was consumed and traded over short and long distances. The widespread production of NITS across Northern Italy meant there was little reason for sigillata made in the eastern Po Valley to travel west. It was unable to compete with NITS vessels produced

---

[94] For example, Annibaletto *et al.* 2007; Buora 2001; Kajanto 1982; Kenrick 2000.

[95] *L. Mag( ) Vir( )* (OCK = 1085), *Q. S( ) P( )* (OCK = 1765). Similar distribution patterns can be seen for potters such as *C. T( ) Suc( )* (OCK = 2028), *T. Turius* (OCK = 2271), *Q. S( ) C( )* (OCK = 1763) and *Q. Sen( ) P( )* (OCK = 1851). Many of these workshops seem to have been located in the area around Lago Maggiore (Biaggio Simona and Butti Ronchetti 1999; Schulthess 2020: 142-43).

[96] Brecciaroli Taborelli and Gabucci 2007; Gabucci and Quiri 2008; Spagnolo *et al.* 2008.

[97] *A. Terentius* (OCK = 2066), *Agatho* (OCK = 54). Similar distribution patterns can be seen for potters such as *Albanus* (OCK = 61), *Amicus* (OCK = 86), *Ingenuus* (OCK = 981), *Maepates* (OCK = 1083), *Primus* (OCK = 1535), *Secundus* (OCK = 1842), and *Serius* (OCK = 1898). See also Annibaletto *et al.* 2007; Buora 2001: 243-44, Mongardi 2014: 248-50.

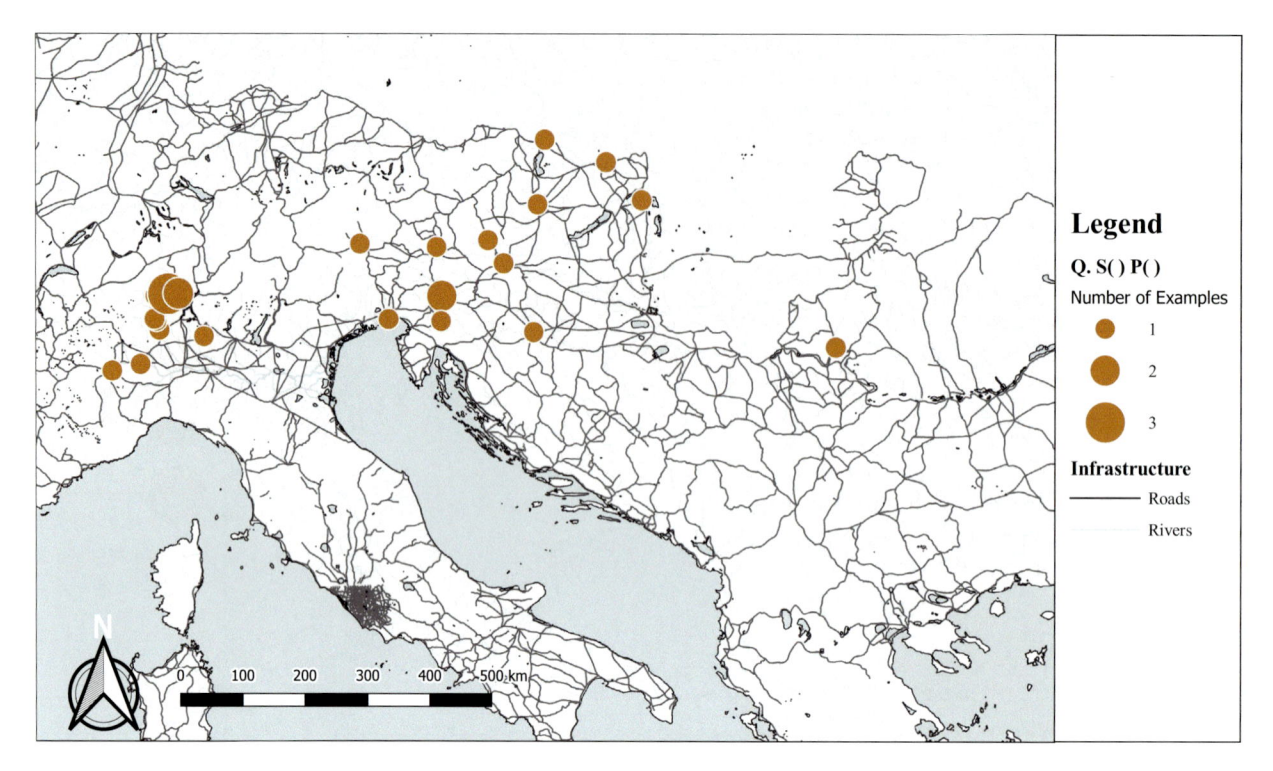

Figure 42. Distribution of western Po Valley NITS producer *Q. S( ) P( )* across the Roman Empire (data taken from the RGZM Samian Database, viewed 7 May 2024, www1.rgzm.de).

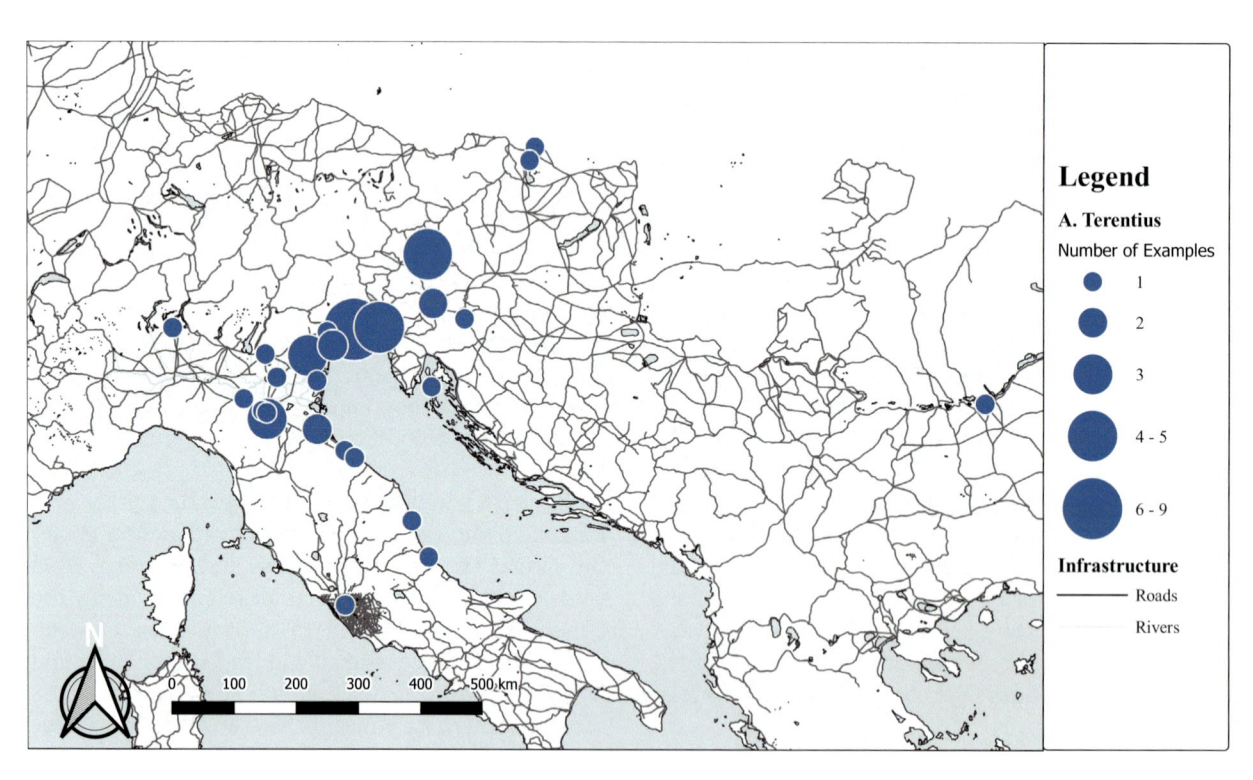

Figure 43. Distribution of eastern Po Valley NITS producer *A. Terentius* across the Roman Empire (data taken from the RGZM Samian Database, viewed 7 May 2024, www1.rgzm.de).

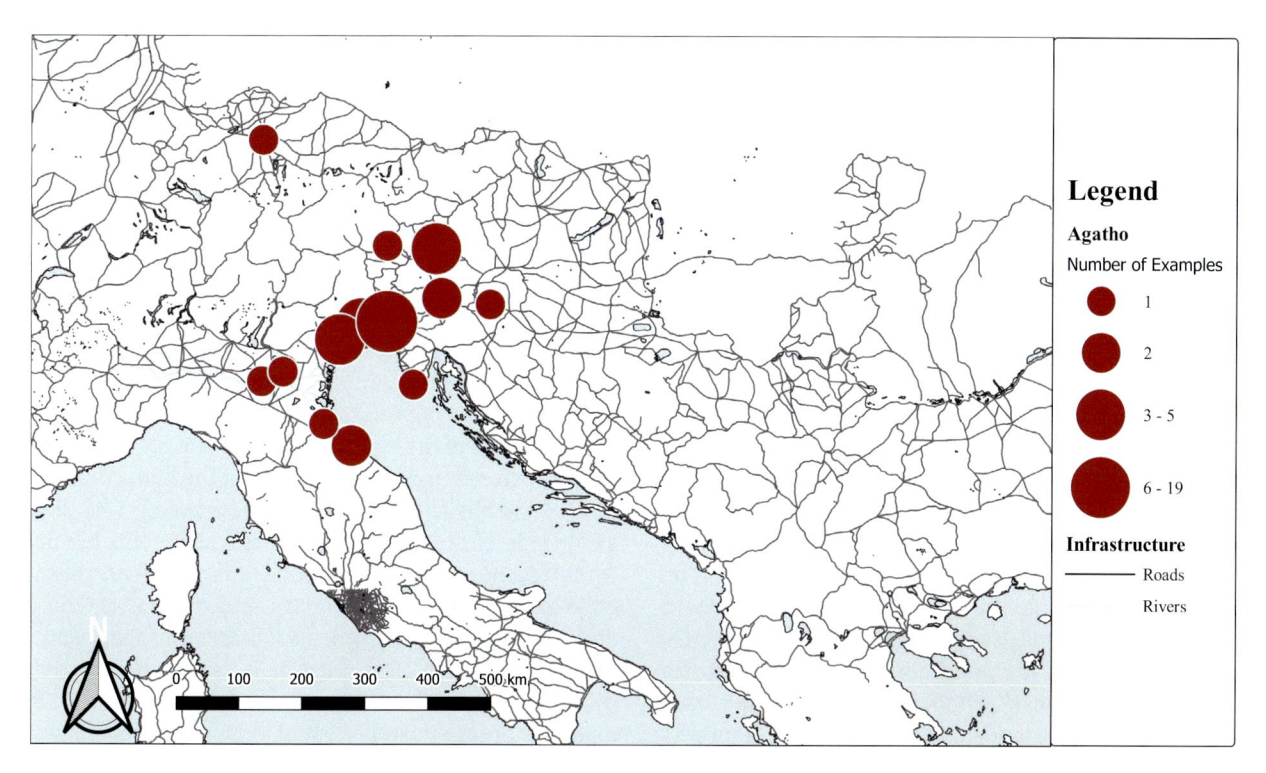

Figure 44.Distribution of eastern Po Valley NITS producer *Agatho* across the Roman Empire (data taken from the RGZM Samian Database, viewed 7 May 2024, www1.rgzm.de).

in the western Po Valley, but it also did not need to. The large market created by the Danubian *Limes* lay to the east. Meanwhile, NITS produced in the western Po Valley seems to have passed over markets in the eastern Po Valley and Veneto, travelling directly to Aquileia for export towards the Balkans and Danube. The Danubian *Limes* was the main export market for NITS, where vessels were consumed in significant quantities by both the military and civilian populations.[98] Overland routes such as the via Gemina, departing from Aquileia over the Julien Alps, formed the principal path for goods produced in Northern Italy and the wider Adriatic area to reach the Danube and the *Limes*.[99] The importance of this trade route is well-attested in antiquity, with the Aquileian merchant L. Tettienus Vitalis citing the Po and the Sava (a tributary of the Danube with its headwaters close to Aquileia) as the two most important rivers to his business.[100] The division between the local and long-distance consumption of NITS suggests it was traded through different intermediaries. Local traders who operated in the immediate area surrounding NITS workshops were likely responsible for the short-distance distribution of sigillata in Northern Italy.[101] In contrast, traders who specialised in supplying

Moesia, Pannonia, and the Danubian frontier were probably responsible for the long-distance movement of Northern Italian finewares. For such long-distance movement, several traders may have been involved across different stages of the journey, with the product changing hands multiple times between its area of production and its final destination.[102]

The division between the east and west of the region suggested by the NITS stamp data raises questions over how finewares were transported within Northern Italy. Although river transport was a more cost-effective way of moving cargo long distances, even when considering transhipment costs, the stamp data implies that most NITS initially moved short distances overland to markets in the immediate vicinity of production sites. Furthermore, given the inland location of production sites, cargoes of NITS would have needed to travel overland for at least some of their journey before being transhipped onto a fluvial or maritime vessel if they were destined for export. However, overland transport may have been preferable to fluvial regardless of the extra costs incurred, especially considering the high risk of breakages involved with each transfer of cargo.[103] Prior work on tracing stamp distribution further indicates the importance of road over water transport, with the via Aemilia and via Popila forming the main

[98] Arioli 2019: 152; Makjanić 1995.
[99] Istenič 2009; Zidanšek, Vojaković, and Žerjal 2022.
[100] Gabucci and Mennella 2003; Gabucci, Mennella, and Pejrani Baricco 2000; Gregoratti 2015.
[101] See Kiiskinen (2013: 88-93) for a discussion of the market mechanisms behind the movement of terra sigillata and the role of regional markets in its distribution.

[102] Rice 2012: 100-102; Tchernia 2016: 261; Terpstra 2013; 2019.
[103] See Harris 2000: 716; Lewit 2015: 240; and Middleton 1980, for discussions of overland vs. fluvial distribution.

transport routes for the finewares of potters such as *Sarius, Serius*, and *A. Terentius*.[104]

Although many assemblages in central and eastern Northern Italy were dominated by NITS during the Imperial period, two sites bucked this trend. The cities of Bologna and Modena returned high levels of CITS within their assemblages, forming a separate cluster of two sites. These urban centres, located at the terminus of the main trans-Apennine route connecting the eastern Po Valley with CITS production centres in the Arno Valley, were uniquely positioned to take advantage of Central Italic finewares.[105] Unfortunately, the limited number of sites with quantified assemblages in the south-west of the Po Valley makes it difficult to determine the impact of CITS on consumption patterns in other areas close to trans-Apennine routes. The assemblage of Forlì, the next closest REFINI site to Bologna and Modena, was primarily composed of NITS, although CITS was also present in significant quantities (27.27%).[106] A trans-Apennine crossing would have been an expensive endeavour in terms of transport costs, even before taking into account the additional overland transport cost from their original production site to the foot of the pass. The costs accumulated by crossing the Apennines may have reduced the competitiveness of CITS against locally produced NITS in the Po Valley, possibly accounting for the drop-off in the quantity of Central Italic finewares recovered from assemblages across the rest of the region. Furthermore, if Bologna and Modena were acting as the initial point of redistribution for CITS arriving in Northern Italy via trans-Apennine routes, the large quantities of Central Italic finewares passing through these sites may have served to reduce the market for Northern Italic finewares.[107]

Of course, transport costs may not have been the only factor affecting the distribution of finewares in Northern Italy. Although they never exceeded 50% of an assemblage outside of Bologna and Modena, CITS still appeared in significant quantities across the region into the late 1st century AD, despite the ready availability of locally produced vessels. Consumer choice may have played a role here, with CITS deliberately chosen despite its higher cost. The desirability of Arretine sigillata is reflected by several Northern Italic vessels at Ivrea stamped with the word *ARRET[IUM]*, possibly in an attempt to pass off their origin as Arretine or exposit their comparable quality.[108] Trade connections

between workshops in Central Italy and Northern Italy also pre-dated the foundation of Northern Italic workshops. Established connections between Northern Italic consumers and Central Italic producers may have allowed them to better weather new competition from local finewares.[109]

Gallic Terra Sigillata and Trans-Alpine Trade

The hierarchical clustering analysis demonstrated that GTS formed a significant component of some fineware assemblages during the 1st and 2nd centuries AD. Sites in the far west of the Po Valley, such as Turin, Chieri, and Ivrea, clustered together as a result of the high quantity of GTS within their assemblages (between 17% and 41%). This cluster further extended along the Alpine foothills and into the Alpine valleys along the northern edge of the Po Plain, with urban centres such as Como and Civitas Camunnorum also returning significant quantities of GTS. The pattern is further supported by the limited data from Aosta, which suggests GTS made up approximately 39% of fineware assemblages in the city during the 1st and 2nd centuries AD.[110] The site of Trento forms an exception to this distribution; returning no evidence of GTS in its assemblage despite being located within the Alpine valleys.[111]

Beyond the western reaches of the Po Valley and the Alpine foothills, GTS seems to have had low penetration into the central and eastern Po-Veneto Plain, where it is present in minimal quantities (generally <5% of the assemblage). In some cases, such as at Adria, Bologna, Modena, and Verona, it is entirely absent. Given the limited quantities in east Northern Italy, it seems unlikely that GTS was entering the region through the Adriatic ports.[112] Equally, the low quantities of GTS present at Luna suggest that the Ligurian ports were not its main entry point into Northern Italy.[113]

---

[104] Kenrick 2000: 49-51.
[105] Gori 2003: 374; Gottarelli 1988.
[106] Cipriano 2013: 189-96.
[107] The prominence of NITS at sites to the east of Bologna and Modena suggests that the via Flaminia was not the main overland route via which CITS entered the region.
[108] Gabucci and Quiri 2008: 51. See also Jorio 2000: 102-16; Wiseman *et al.* 2022.

[109] There is also the possibility that distribution was linked to military deployments, with Central Italic workshops contracted to supply the army with fineware vessels (Menchelli and Sangriso 2017; Sternini 2019: 493.
[110] Gabucci 2017: 4.6. The Aostan data presented here was not included in the main analysis within this volume as it failed to distinguish between a Central Italic and Northern Italic provenance for Italic sigillata.
[111] The absence of GTS from the Trento assemblage is unusual, especially considering that it has been recovered in significant quantities from sites within the city's hinterland (Oberosler 1995: 324-26). It is possible that, in the absence of stamp data or archaeometric analysis, some GTS was misidentified as coming from an alternate provenance in Trento's assemblage.
[112] GTS is also mostly absent from the wider Adriatic area. See Dannell and Mees 2013 for distribution maps of GTS in the Roman world.
[113] Lavizzari Pedrazzini 1973a; 1973b; 1977. In the past, Liguria has been put forward as the main entry point for GTS into the Po Valley (Lavizzari Pedrazzini 2003). The absence of other coastal assemblages in the dataset makes it difficult to know if Luna is reflective of wider trends on the Ligurian seaboard. However, the low quantity of GTS recovered from Tortona (8.1% of the assemblage), a site on the via Postumia and the main overland route from Genoa and Savona into the Po Valley, further suggests that the Ligurian ports were not the main entry point.

Consequently, the most likely routes via which GTS was transported were over the Alpine passes.[114] Although transporting loads of finewares, not just overland but also over the steep gradients of the Alpine passes, would have carried with it numerous risks, it may not have been as prohibitively expensive as has often been assumed. Network modelling of trans-Alpine routes in the Roman period has suggested that it could have been just as expensive to transport a one-tonne cargo to Aosta from the upper Rhône Valley as it would have been to transport it from the upper Po valley.[115] The steep and mountainous terrain of the Alps would have been most suited to pack animals (such as mules and donkeys) carrying loads in paniers, as opposed to wagons.[116] It is estimated pack animals could carry loads of between 80 kg and 150 kg, which would have been sufficient for moving finewares in significant quantities.[117] Pack animals may also have reduced the likelihood of breakages, their cargo not at the mercy of a wagon's suspension and the road surface.

The quantities of GTS present in the western Po Valley and Alpine foothills seem indicative of sustained trans-alpine trade, rather than one-off imports. Conversely, the marginal quantities of GTS in the eastern Po Valley and Veneto Plain may reflect more sporadic purchases, or relate to the movement of people.[118] For example, the homogeneity of the assemblage of GTS found at Brescia suggests that it was bought as a single lot, rather than accumulated over time.[119] In a similar manner to the CITS discussed above, mounting transport costs may help to account for the sudden drop-off in the quantity of GTS recovered from the centre of the Po Valley, where it seems unlikely GTS was able to compete with

locally produced ceramics (that would have travelled much shorter distances).[120] It warrants mentioning, however, that even though GTS was able to compete with locally produced ceramics in some parts of the region, it never comprised more than 41% of an assemblage. Furthermore, GTS would only form the main component at one of the nine sites in the cluster, with NITS remaining the dominant fineware in seven out of the eight sites.

In addition to the high level of GTS present in their assemblages, many sites within cluster 3 also returned significant quantities of CITS. Central Italic finewares were present in some of the highest levels outside of Bologna and Modena, comprising more than 30% of the assemblages at Alba and Augusta Bagiennorum. CITS producers, especially those from Arezzo and Pisa, would have been well-placed to take advantage of fluvial and maritime connections to transport their wares along the Tyrrhenian and Ligurian Coasts. These connections may also have served to help reduce transport costs accumulated before crossing the Apennines. Stamps from non-Arretine potters producing on the Tyrrhenian Coast at sites such as Livorno, Pisa, and the Isola di Migliarino are widely attested in the western Po Valley.[121] Urban centres such as Alba, Augusta Bagiennorum, and Tortona, close to the Ligurian ports and the via Postumia, were well-positioned to take advantage of ceramic trade networks along the Ligurian and Tyrrhenian Coasts, reflected in the high quantities of stamps from non-Arretine workshops in the REFINI dataset.[122] The position of sites in the western Po Valley meant that CITS, and GTS had to travel similar distances to reach them. Transport costs between the two zones of production may have been similar, enabling these urban centres such as Alba, Augusta Bagiennorum, and Chieri, to draw upon more varied provenances for their fineware consumption.

African Red Slip: Evolving Consumption

During the early 3rd century AD, production chronologies suggest that the quantities of ARS circulating in Northern Italy sharply increased, becoming the dominant fineware in the region. Many Late Antique assemblages from the REFINI dataset were almost entirely composed of ARS, with other red-slipped finewares appearing in minimal quantities. The shift from finewares predominantly produced within the Italian Peninsula to extra-regional imports

---

[114] Artru 2016: 109-43; Donat 2015: 42-43; Gabucci 2017: 11.20; Mantovani 2018: 180-81.

[115] Page 2023; 2024.

[116] Pack animals were probably the most common way of transporting goods in the Roman period (Adams 2007; Chevallier 1976). Strabo (4.6.7) would also state that the road over St. Bernard Pass was impassable to wagons.

[117] Adams 2007: 77–81; 2012: 230; Raepsaet 2009. Evidence for the transport of sigillata using mules also comes from La Graufesenque, where they were hired to move the site's output to a redistribution centre (Middleton 1980: 188–89).

[118] Gabucci (2017: 11.22) has argued that the Po formed a major trade corridor for GTS from the west to the east of the region, however, the small quantities recovered from sites in the eastern Po Valley and coastal plain suggest against large-scale, organised trade. GTS is certainly present in contexts further east than the Po-Veneto region, and the Danubian Limes were an important market for sigillata produced in Southern and Central Gaul at sites such as Le Graufesenque, Bassanac, and Lezoux, alongside later German centres such as Rheinzabern (Lewit 2015: 230; Leleković 2018; Radbauer 2013: 152-4). Whether Gallic sigillata was transported via maritime routes to Aquileia and into Pannonia, or utilised the Rhône Valley to reach the Danube, both methods would have bypassed the Po Valley (Dannell and Mees 2013; Donat 2020; Gabler 1982: 51).

[119] Gabucci 2017: 9.11. Gabucci examines the GTS from a wide range of assemblages (both published and unpublished) from a variety of urban and rural sites within the eastern Po Valley and the Veneto Plain. Where quantification was available, rural sites returned very low quantities of sigillata from their assemblages. See also, Donat 2015; 2020.

[120] The drop-off in the quantity of GTS was far more abrupt than that seen for CITS in the central and eastern Po Valley, perhaps suggesting a sudden jump in price.

[121] For example, the workshops of *Euhodus, L. Rasinus Pisanus, Xanthus*, and *Zoilus*. See Sternini 2019: 485-90 for a summary of CTS production centres.

[122] Bruno 1998; Melli 2000; Melli and Pasquinucci 1998. Arretine potters continued to be the best represented, attesting to the high output and extensive distribution of sigillata from Arezzo.

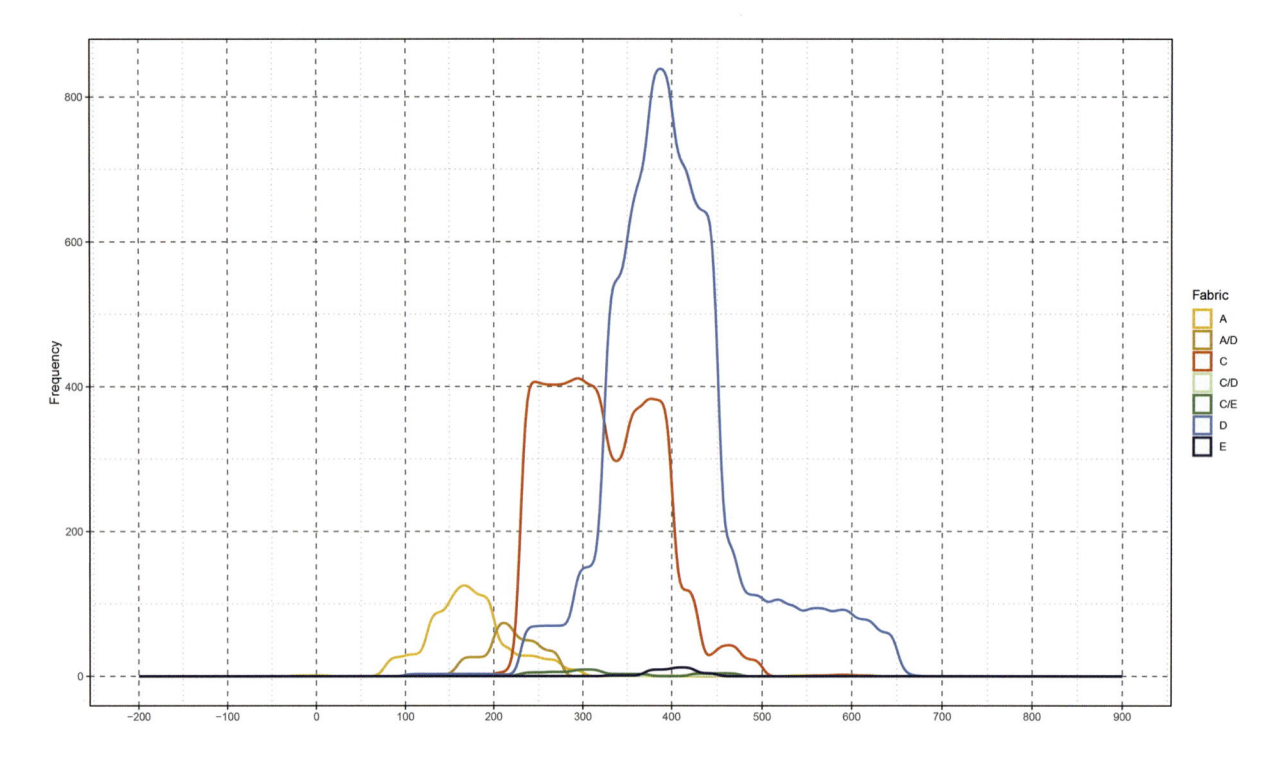

Figure 45. Quantities of ARS production types circulating in Northern Italy using Production chronologies.

is striking, but the adoption of ARS within Northern Italy is more complex than a simple replacement of ITS with North African products. Although many studies choose to treat ARS as a single, continuously produced fineware type, the rise and fall of fabrication areas means it can be more fruitful to view it as a sequence of different productions (see Figure 45).[123]

Separating ARS fragments in Northern Italy by fabric type immediately reveals a more complex picture of the North African fineware trade. Initial imports of ARS into Northern Italy during the late 1st century AD consisted of Production A, manufactured in the area surrounding Carthage.[124] The quantities of Production A in circulation peaked in the latter half of the 2nd century AD, before declining and disappearing around the end of the 3rd century. Production A/D was the next to appear in Northern Italy, circulating between the mid-2nd century AD and the late 3rd century AD. Produced in the area around Leptis Magna, Production A/D appeared in lower numbers than Production A.[125] Productions C and D were present in the greatest quantities, appearing within a few decades of each other in the early 3rd century AD. Quantities of Production C, originating from Central Tunisia, rapidly spiked in the early 3rd century before plateauing until the early

4th century.[126] The frequency of Production C ARS vessels would then dip and recover, before declining throughout the late 4th and early 5th centuries AD. In contrast, quantities of Production D, manufactured in Northern Tunisia, would initially rise gradually throughout the 3rd century AD.[127] Numbers would then rapidly spike at the beginning of the 4th century and peak c. AD 390, before experiencing an equally rapid decline. Quantities stabilised in the late 5th century AD, with Production D persisting until the mid-7th century. Minimal quantities of Productions C/D, C/E, and E were in circulation between the early 3rd century AD and the end of the 5th century AD.

The earliest instances of ARS A within Northern Italy arrived at a time when North African imports remained a relatively minor component of regional assemblages.[128] Distribution of ARS Production A seems to have been mainly limited to Adriatic maritime ports, with the greatest quantities seen at Aquileia and sites in its hinterland.[129] During this period, CITS and NITS continued to form the majority of assemblages, with varied quantities of ETS and GTS also appearing at urban centres across the region. A similar picture

---

[123] Fentress and Perkins 1988: 208; Fentress et al. 2004: 150; Hobson 2015: 117-18.
[124] Bonifay 2016: 520-22; Mackensen and Scheider 2006: 168-69.
[125] Bonifay 2016: 522; Mackensen 2006: 111-13.

[126] Bonifay 2004: 46-47; 2016: 523-24.
[127] Bonifay 2016: 524-26; Mackensen 1993.
[128] See Dobreva 2023a for an overview of early North African imports into the Upper Adriatic area.
[129] Biondani 2005c; Rossi 2013; Trivini Bellini 2021; Zulini 2017. See also Cirelli 2022: 469-70; Dobreva 2023a; 2023b.

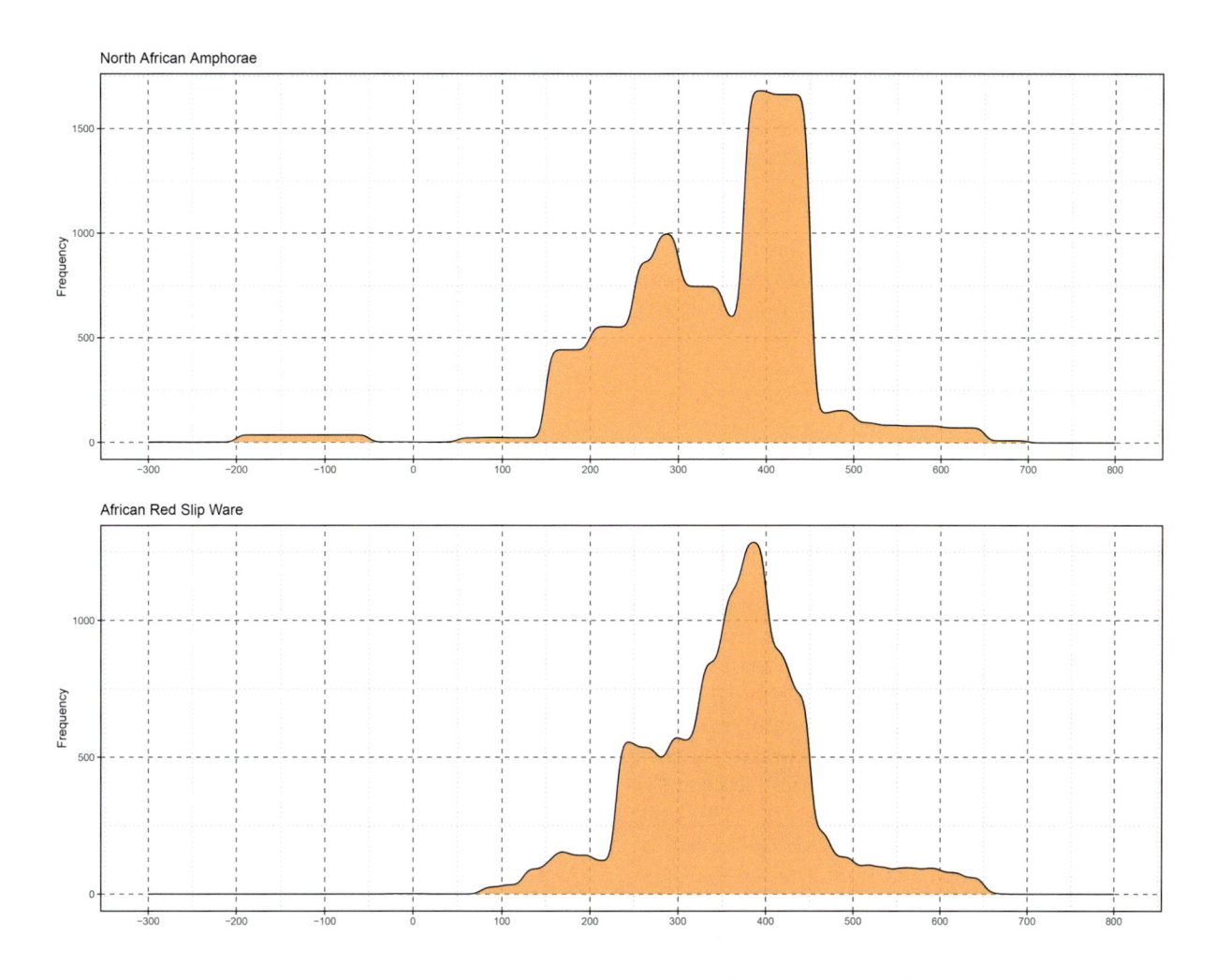

Figure 46. Quantities of North African amphorae and ARS circulating in Northern Italy using Production chronologies. Note the Y axes are not constant.

is seen in the amphora data from the AMINI dataset (see Figure 46).[130] Small numbers of North African amphorae, such as the Ostia 59, Tripolitanian 1, and Tripolitanian 2 were circulating in Northern Italy from *c.* AD 50 onwards, however, the Adriatic Littoral and the Eastern Mediterranean dominated assemblages.[131] The arrival of ARS Production A/D in Northern Italy *c.* AD 150 coincides with a sharp rise in the number of North African amphorae circulating in the region. The Africana 1A and 1B amphora forms, alongside the Africana 2A and the Tripolitania 3, began to appear in significant quantities from *c.* AD 150 onwards.[132]

Tripolitanian oil amphorae were predominantly circulating in the wider Adriatic during this time, mirroring the distribution pattern of ARS A/D.[133] While this period saw a significant increase in the quantities of North African amphora-borne goods present in Northern Italy, the number of ARS vessels in circulation remained relatively low.

ARS productions C and D would appear in Northern Italy during the first decades of the 3rd century AD. Their arrival marked the wider spread of ARS to inland sites within Northern Italy, with urban centres such as Alba, Augusta Bagiennorum, Bedriacum, Brescia, Milan, and Verona recording significant quantities within their assemblages.[134] The appearance and spikes in the

---

[130] While there was a degree of correlation between the frequency of ARS and North African amphora imports to Northern Italy, the variation between the two may further support the notion that ARS and North African amphorae did not travel together. ARS may have travelled with other foodstuffs such as grain, or with goods like textiles, while in contrast, amphorae seem to have comprised the major component of the maritime cargoes that they formed a part of (Bonifay 2007; 2018: 334-36; Bonifay and Tchernia 2012: 322-24; Hobson 2015: 133-35).

[131] Bruno and Bocchio 1991; Gaddi 2017a; Mazzocchin 2011.

[132] This coincides with the founding of the *classis Africana,* in AD 150, by Commodus (SHA. *Com.* 17.7; Rickman 1981: 129-30). If Rome was

operating as the main redistribution point for North African amphora (one of several scenarios for the movement of North African exports) then the increase in foodstuffs travelling as part of the *annona* may have resulted in a greater diffusion of North African amphora-borne goods across the wider Mediterranean (Bonifay 2018: 338-41; Bonifay and Tchernia 2012).

[133] Dobreva 2023a; 2023b.

[134] Jorio 1999; 2002; Morandini 2008b; Ratto 2014; Roffia 1991.

quantities of ARS C and D during the early 3rd and early 4th centuries AD are mirrored by an increase in the number of North African amphorae in Northern Italy. Quantities of North African amphorae continued to gradually increase with the introduction of the Africana 2B, 2C, and 2D, alongside variants of the Africana 3. It was at this time that North Africa rose to become the second-largest supplier of amphora-borne goods to Northern Italy, after the Eastern Mediterranean. The number of African amphorae would reach an initial peak during the late 3rd century AD, before experiencing a modest decline throughout the early 4th century. In contrast, quantities of ARS would plateau during the latter half of the 3rd century AD, before steadily increasing over the 4th century AD.[135] Tunisia formed the dominant provenance for both North African amphorae and ARS during this period.

The number of ARS Production C vessels circulating in Northern Italy would plateau during the 3rd and 4th centuries AD, before seeing a sudden and sharp decline. In contrast, quantities of ARS Production D would continue to rise throughout the 4th century to form a peak c. AD 390. North African amphora would also spike in the late 4th century AD, with quantities subsequently plateauing until the mid-5th century AD.[136] This peak in the late 4th century AD was driven by the arrival of Spatheion-type amphorae from Tunisia, the most common North African amphora type in the AMINI dataset.[137] The Keay 35A and 35B would also circulate in appreciable quantities. In the late 4th and early 5th century AD, the number of ARS Production D vessels would start to decrease, with the decline accelerating c. AD 440. The sharp decline of ARS Production D during the mid-5th century AD corresponds to a similar pronounced drop off in the number of North African amphora circulating in Northern Italy. Although quantities of North African amphorae would decline slightly later than ARS Production D, they both experienced a similar sharpness in the rate of their decrease. Although numbers would subsequently stabilise at a significantly lower frequency than before, ARS and North African amphorae would cease circulating in Northern Italy during the mid-7th century AD.

A sudden decline in North African exports during the 5th century AD is a phenomenon recorded elsewhere across the Roman world.[138] While there remains variation on a region-to-region and site-to-site basis, the overall trend remains consistent.[139] The disruption caused by the Vandal invasion and conquest between AD 429 and AD 439 at first seems an obvious candidate for the rapid decline in North African exports and in the past has been used to explain diminishing ARS quantities during this time.[140] Although the fall in North African amphorae does correspond to the conquest period, the rapid decline of ARS Productions C and D in Northern Italy predates this event by some 40 years (although an acceleration in the rate of decline for Production D does align with the fall of Carthage in 439 AD). The invasion of Northern Italy between AD 401 and AD 403 by the Goths may have served to disrupt supply chains of North African imports.[141] However, this event also post-dates the decline of ARS Productions C and D and seems to have had little effect on the trade in North African amphora-borne goods in Northern Italy.

The reasons behind the decline of ARS exports during the late 4th and early 5th centuries AD, remain poorly understood. It is possible political instability in North Africa during the late 4th century AD, contributed to the decline in output amongst ARS Production D workshops. However, major events such as the revolt of Firmus and subsequent Theodosian suppression do not coincide with the start of the decline in ARS Productions C and D. Alternatively, it has been theorised ARS workshops may have struggled to meet demand, leading consumers to seek out other finewares, such as Late Roman C or D from the Eastern Mediterranean, to fulfil their needs.[142] However, there is little evidence of replacement finewares circulating in Northern Italy at the time ARS numbers decline.[143] As has been highlighted in this volume and elsewhere, the limited availability of quantified Late Antique ceramic assemblages hampers analysis. The publication of new quantified data may help to further refine and define patterns during this late period, both across Northern Italy and the rest of the Roman world.

Conclusion

Analysis of the REFINI dataset highlighted the varied levels and the different factors behind the fineware trade within Northern Italy during the Roman period. As a non-essential item, red-slipped finewares were traded in a markedly different way to the amphorae discussed in the previous chapter, providing a key point of contrast. Fineware markets in Northern Italy between

[135] Fentress and Perkins (1988: 209) have argued the continued rise in quantities of ARS under export during this period reflects increasing political and economic stability in Africa after the end of Firmus' revolt in the 370s AD. See also Fentress et al. 2004: 150.

[136] Increasing quantities of North African goods are recorded at sites across the Mediterranean world during the 3rd and 4th centuries AD (Cirelli 2022: 469; Hobson 2015: 123-46).

[137] Bonifay 2004: 124-25; Donat 1994: 433-36; Pizzolato 2018a: 154-56.

[138] Bes 2015: 125-27; Bes and Poblome 2009; Fentress and Perkins 1988; Fentress et al. 2004; Fulford 1984; Hayes 2008.

[139] See, for example, Cirelli (2022: 476) who highlights peaks and declines during the 3rd and early 4th century AD in the Central and Southern Adriatic.

[140] Bes and Poblome 2009: 69-70; Hayes 1972: 423.

[141] Claud. Bel. Get. 595-645; Zos. 5.37.

[142] Bes 2015: 125-27; Bonifay 2022: 227.

[143] Minimal quantities of Late Roman C in the form of the Hayes 3 (in production c. AD 400-530) are found at Altinum, Aquileia, and Padua (Dobreva and Griggio 2021; Ganzarolli 2017; Pagen 2018).

the 1st century BC and 2nd century AD were primarily dominated by short-distance, rather than long-distance trade, with demand for red-slipped tablewares mostly met by regional production. The majority of finewares recovered from urban centres were produced within Northern Italy, something particularly true for the central and eastern Po Valley, where site assemblages were mainly composed of NITS. Analysis of stamp data suggests NITS was probably traded over short distances within the region, primarily being consumed in the areas adjacent to its production zones. Although Northern Italy formed the primary market for NITS, it was also exported over long distances, with the output of workshops located in the east and the west of the region seeing similar distribution along the Danubian *Limes*. This clear distinction between short and long-distance consumption demonstrates the differing mechanisms and market forces behind the trade of NITS in Northern Italy and the provinces. Although beyond the scope of this publication, a more detailed analysis of stamp assemblages in Northern Italy may be able to highlight further nuances in the consumption of sigillata both within the region and further afield.

While locally produced NITS would dominate many Imperial assemblages in the REFINI dataset, the western valley shows increased integration with extra-regional economies, particularly those in Southern Gaul and Central Italy. Assemblages in the western Po Valley and Alpine valleys contained the greatest quantities of non-NITS finewares. The main method of entry into Northern Italy for finewares and their subsequent distribution seems to have been overland, rather than fluvial or maritime. This formed a stark contrast to amphora-borne goods, most of which had travelled over long distances to reach Northern Italy and were likely redistributed via the water network.

The limited publication of data from contexts dating to the 3rd century AD onwards obscures the true picture of how finewares circulated during Late Antiquity, although several clear patterns were visible. Mirroring the Late Antique amphora data, the decline of zones of production that had previously supplied Northern Italy during the 1st and 2nd centuries AD led to the creation of new trade networks, with most finewares now originating from regions that had previously played a marginal role in supplying Northern Italy. From the 3rd century AD to the 8th century AD, ARS from North Africa formed the main component of fineware assemblages in the region. The dominance of ARS during this later period reflects a shift from short to long-distance trade and a greater reliance on extra-provincial economies to meet the demand for finewares within Northern Italy. In addition, new areas of production, such as the Adriatic Littoral, also contributed to supply but were only competitive in specific contexts (often close to their area of production).

So far, analysis of the AMINI and REFINI datasets has produced a complex picture of inland trade within Northern Italy between the 3rd century BC and the 9th century AD. There were many similarities and differences between the fineware and amphora datasets, ranging from the zones of production from which they were sourced, their distribution across Northern Italy, and the chronological evolution of their supply. In both analyses, the distribution of both amphorae and finewares reflected the compromises buyers made between practicality and choice in the wares they consumed. The final material type analysed is the DESTINI dataset of decorative stone and marble from Northern Italy, materials that were consumed and travelled in vastly different ways from the ceramics studied so far.

Decorative Stone:
Indulgence and Compromise

One of the greatest logistical and commercial feats of the Roman era was the extraction and export of vast quantities of stone and marble across the Mediterranean.[1] As Rome's expansion brought new sources of material under its control, a flourishing trade in decorative stones, principally marble, was established, reflected by their expanding use in the construction and decoration of buildings, statuary, and funeral monuments.[2] In Northern Italy, worked marble objects are ubiquitous finds and are seen in both public and private contexts. They include the monolithic marble columns of Brescia and Verona's *capitolia*, marble and granite sarcophagi in the *necropoleis* of Aquileia, Pavia, and Modena, and polychrome marble wall revetment and paving present in private homes and public buildings from Ravenna to Aosta.[3] The widespread inland circulation of decorative stone is not a situation unique to Northern Italy, yet their distribution represents an oft-overlooked aspect of the Roman economy.[4] Many studies are content to limit their analysis to the more numerous (and often better-published) ceramic assemblages. While these are undeniably important commodities, they represent only part of the picture. The DESTINI dataset analysed in this chapter synthesises 14 published assemblages of decorative stone and marble, complementing the previous ceramic analyses.[5] It contains 18,308 fragments of stone from 13 urban centres in Northern Italy, with 61 unique lithotypes represented.

The inclusion of decorative stone in an analysis of regional inland trade is important for several reasons. First, stone is a heavy material. Cargoes of marble, especially blocks or columns, were more difficult and costly to move than amphorae and finewares, which put limitations on their circulation. Consequently, they represent communal or elite investment, as opposed to widely consumed essentials and commodities. Second, shipments of stone were also specialist cargoes. Consignments of stone, whether for building, decoration,

or sculpture, were normally commissioned for a specific project or purpose. As a result, they primarily represent one-off purchases, rather than intensive and sustained trade between areas. Furthermore, the varying forms of stone products presented different challenges for transport. A monolithic column was far more difficult and dangerous to move than blocks destined to be used as paving or revetment.[6] They were commissioned via separate methods, utilised different supply mechanisms, and do not represent like-for-like investments. Of all the material finds discussed so far, decorative stone is the most indicative of the power of the consumer, principally in public construction but also private projects, in dictating supply and overcoming obstacles in the movement of goods. For these reasons, they form a necessary comparison to the material discussed in the previous chapters.

As highlighted above, the stone trade presented numerous economic and practical limitations not shared by ceramic materials. In the past, the ubiquity of imported decorative stones across the Roman world led to the suggestion that they were imported *en masse* and stockpiled for use in local construction projects.[7] However, on close examination, the evidence for stockpiling has proven unconvincing and patchy, with the exception of a few unique sites such as Portus and the *Emporium* district in Rome.[8] It is more likely that architectural elements, such as columns and capitals, would have needed to have been commissioned from the quarries directly by contractors such as *marmorarii* and *lapidarii*.[9] The same may also have been true for sarcophagi, although the situation is more complex.[10] In most cases, the blank chests that would become sarcophagi were roughed out at the point of extraction, before being shipped to local independent workshops (often located near urban centres), where they would be completed according to regional tastes and the desires

---

[1] Russell's (2013) book *The Economics of the Roman Stone Trade* forms the definitive volume on this topic.

[2] Lazzarini 2019: 367-69; Pensabene 2002; 2013. While imported decorative stone had already been used in Rome for several centuries, Augustus' reign saw a significant increase in the scale of extraction and transport of stone.

[3] Castoldi 2015; Cavalieri Manasse 2008; Framarin and Castoldi 2013; Gabelmann 1973; Guarnieri, Montevecchi, and Pagani 2018; Kleineberg 2021.

[4] Russell 2018b: 237; Taelman 2022.

[5] The DESTINI dataset can be found at https://doi.org/10.5281/zenodo.13745898. The code and data used in the analysis can be found at Github Repository: Adriatic-to-the-Alps, viewed 12 September 2024, https://github.com/jamespage15/Adriatic-to-the-Alps.

[6] Russell 2013: 144.

[7] This is the production-to-stock model proposed by Ward-Perkins (1980; 1992a; 1992b), where he envisioned that increasing demand for stone in the Early Imperial period saw the extraction of marble take place along 'quasi-industrial' lines. This allowed quarries to generate quantities of standardised material for export to stockpiles across the Roman world. For a critique of the production-to-stock model, see Russell 2013: 232-39, alongside Chapter 6 more widely.

[8] Maschek 2023; Russell 2013: 235-36.

[9] See Russell 2013: Chapter 6, particularly pp. 207-28, for an exploration of the relationship between building projects and stone supply.

[10] For a thorough analysis of the mechanics behind the Roman sarcophagus industry, see Russell 2011.

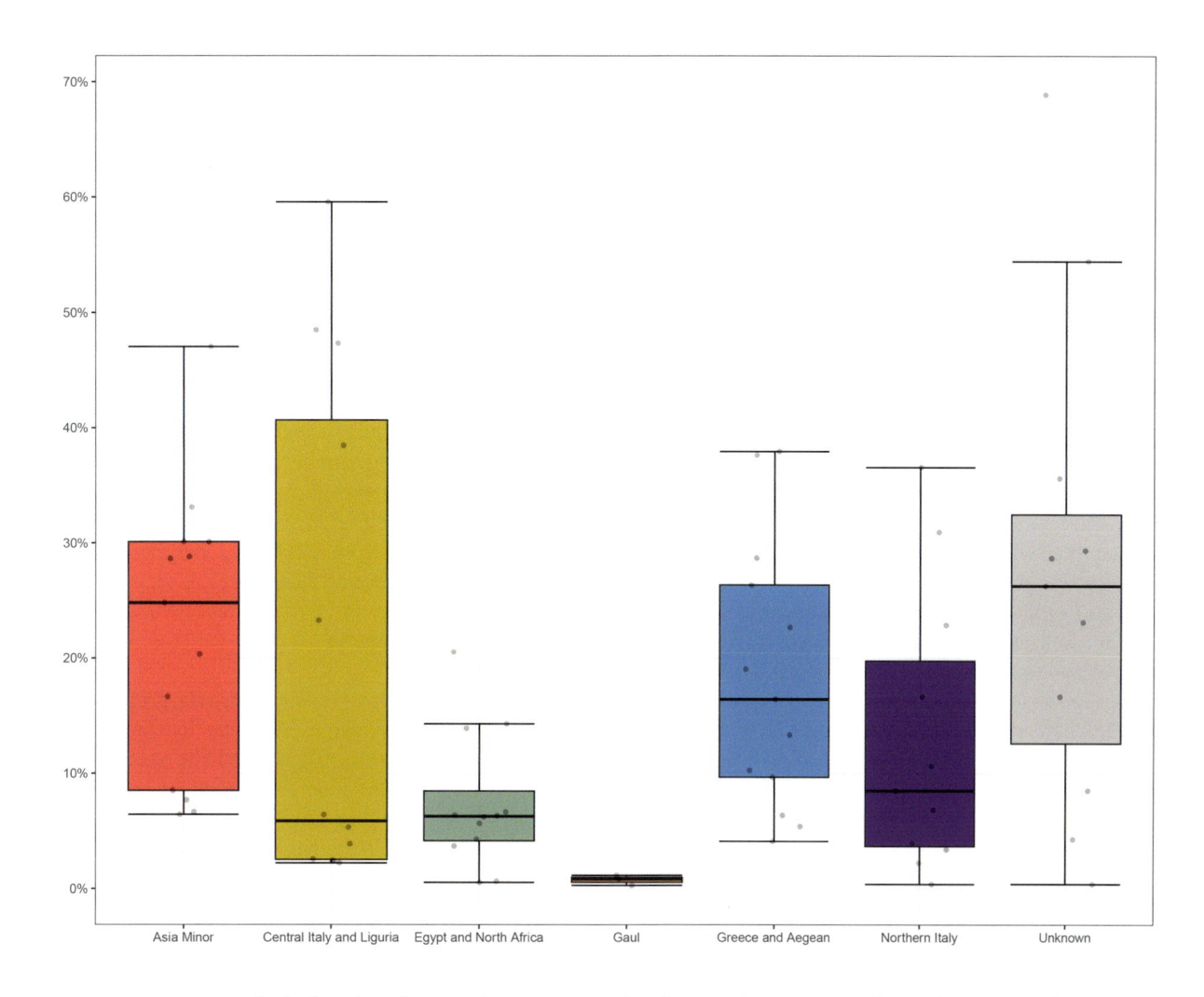

Figure 47. Box and whisker plots showing the percentage of each zone of extraction within each site assemblage.

of the commissioner.[11] Large workshops, with sufficient capital to absorb the risks involved and stable demand, may have been able to stock limited quantities of blank chests.[12] However, most sarcophagi would probably have been produced and shipped in response to a specific commission by a workshop.[13] Wall revetment and floor panelling also represent something of a grey area. Floor panels and revetment, alongside some minor architectural elements, may have been stockpiled by local workshops or craftsmen. The demand for veneer and paving in both public and private contexts, coupled with the high surface area of material that could be extracted from a single block, made them a less risky

investment.[14] Indeed, it seems unlikely that contractors for private construction would have ordered blocks of marble for veneer production from quarries to fulfil individual project requirements. Such an endeavour may have been prohibitively expensive, given the variety of colours often used and the cost of transport.[15] Instead, the veneer used in private projects is likely a reflection of the stock contractors had on hand, rather than a bespoke order. Furthermore, it is unlikely that every city was equipped with the necessary tools and expertise to cut marble blocks into veneer panels; at

---

[11] Russell 2013: 257. Over half of all known sarcophagi are thought to have been produced by such workshops, although the Attic and Dokimeian workshops may have operated in a different way, (Russell 2011: 124-27). In the past, it has been argued that some quarries maintained branch workshops, which were responsible for completing, and selling the finished sarcophagus to local communities, however this has been convincingly challenged by Russell (2011; 2013: Chapters 6 and 7).
[12] Russell 2011: 138.
[13] Russell 2013: 271-72.

---

[14] Stepped blocks that could be cut into veneer panels may also have been kept in stock (whether intentionally or unintentionally) at the quarries themselves, (Peacock and Maxfield 1997: 213–14; Russell 2013: 234-36).
[15] It is worth noting that there is some evidence for the trade of pre-cut veneer panels from the Chrétienne (Joncheray and Joncheray 2002), La Mirande (Descamps 1992), Torre Sgarrata (Throckmorton 1969), and Porto Nuovo (Bernard *et al.* 1998) shipwrecks. See also Beltrame 2021 and Russell 2008. There is also the possibility that some veneer panels may have been bought second-hand after being salvaged from previous projects. On this point, see Fant, Russell, and Barker 2013.

more minor centres, floor and revetment tiles arrived pre-made.[16]

Zones of Extraction

Imported decorative stones, especially white, grey, and polychrome marbles and granites, were widely consumed across the Roman world. Polychrome stone could only be acquired from a select number of quarries. For example, green stone and marble such as *cipollino verde*, *verde di Laconia*, *verde antico*, or *porfido verde Egiziano*, could only be extracted from Greece or Egypt.[17] There was more scope for choice when it came to selecting a supply of white or grey marble, although the majority of extraction sites remained in the Eastern Mediterranean.[18] During the Roman era, Northern Italy was supplied with decorative stone from six main zones of extraction. These were Asia Minor, Central Italy and Liguria, Egypt and North Africa, Gaul, Greece and the Aegean, and Northern Italy itself (see Figure 47). In comparison to the amphora and fineware assemblages, a large portion of the stone and marble assemblage (27.59%) had an unknown provenance. Unprovenanced lithotypes consist almost solely of white marble, the type and origin of which are difficult to securely identify without petrographic and mineralogical analysis. As the Po-Veneto region does not possess any known deposits of pure white marble their provenance is likely extra-regional, however, beyond that, there is little else that can be gleaned from this data.

Asia Minor

Asia Minor would prove to be one of the most important zones of extraction for stone and marble during the Roman period, especially for white Proconnesian marble. Proconnesian marble was intensively extracted from the Island of Marmara and saw extensive distribution across the Mediterranean, becoming one of the most widely traded lithotypes in the Roman period. Although Proconnesian marble had been quarried since the 5th century BC, it was under the Imperial Roman period that its extraction intensified.[19] Initially arriving in Italy during the late 1st century AD, its use continued to expand, peaking in the late 2nd to early 3rd century.[20] The quarries' position, in close proximity to the port of Saraylar, streamlined the loading and transportation process, reducing costs and increasing its competitiveness against other forms of white marble.[21] Indeed, within the DESTINI dataset, Proconnesian marble was the most commonly recorded lithotype, forming 19.2% of all provenanced fragments and attesting to its widespread distribution.

Africano, mined from Teos, and *pavonazzetto,* mined from Iscehisar (ancient Dokimeion), were also well-attested in the DESTINI dataset. *Africano*, introduced to Rome in the 1st century BC, would become so sought after that the quarries at Teos appear to have been exhausted by the end of the 2nd century AD.[22] Pavonazzetto also saw large demand from both imperial and private building projects, with the quarry expected to produce a set output annually.[23] The final lithotype from Asia Minor that appeared in significant quantities was *greco scritto*, extracted from the region surrounding Ephesus.[24] Other lithotypes extracted from Asia Minor included *alabastro fiorito*, *breccia corallina*, and *cipollino rosso*.

Central Italy and Liguria

From quarries in Central Italy and Liguria, grey *bardiglio* formed the most common lithotype in the DESTINI dataset. White Luna marble formed the second most numerous stone type from this zone of extraction, although it appeared in much lower quantities than *bardiglio*. Both came from the same district, extracted from the quarries at Carrara near the ancient city of Luna. The marble deposits at Carrara were discovered in the 1st century BC, with extraction intensifying during the Caesarean and Augustan periods.[25] Heavily used in Rome during the late 1st century BC and 1st century AD, white Luna marble was an important commodity and saw distribution across the Western Mediterranean. However, the increasing availability of Proconnesian marble in the 2nd century AD saw the gradual replacement of Luna as the dominant white marble in Roman markets, with the quarries at Carrara experiencing a significant decline during the 3rd century AD.[26] From quarries further to the south, *selce di Roma* and *alabastro Ghiaccione* are attested in minimal quantities at the sites of Como and Verona.[27]

---

[16] Russell 2013: 253. This would also have made stone and marble easier to transport and handle.
[17] See Lazzarini 2019 for a catalogue of polychrome stone and marble used in the ancient world.
[18] Antonelli and Lazzarini 2016.
[19] Pensabene 2013: 317-20.
[20] Bruno *et al.* 2002; Taelman 2022: 856-60. Proconnesian marble would remain an important architectural material into the 5th century AD.

[21] Barsanti 1989: 93; Russell 2013: 262; Ward-Perkins 1980: 329-34. Proconnesian marble was used in a wide variety of forms, from architectural elements and paving to statuary and sarcophagi.
[22] Fant 1989. Other sources of *africano* may have been found either on Chios or in the territory surrounding Teos (Russell 2013: 195).
[23] Pensabene 2013: 366-69; Russell 2013: 234.
[24] Attanasio *et al.* 2012; Perna, Antonelli, and Lazzarini 2023. Previously, *greco scritto* was thought to have originated from quarries at Cap de Garde in Algeria.
[25] Pensabene 2013: 421-22; Russell 2013: 91. White Luna marble would become the most intensively extracted white marble in the Western Mediterranean during the Roman period.
[26] Pensabene 2013: 320; Taelman 2022: 856-60.
[27] Bocconcello 2008; Bugini and Folli 2016.

Egypt and North Africa

A diverse range of decorative stone originated from North Africa and Egypt. Of these, *giallo antico,* quarried at Chemtou in modern Tunisia, formed the dominant lithotype, to the exclusion of almost all others. The quarries at Chemtou were established in the pre-Roman period, growing to prominence in the mid-1st to 2nd centuries AD.[28] Other decorative stone from North Africa and Egypt appeared in quantities of <1% of the total DESTINI assemblage. Other lithotypes from this zone of extraction included *alabastro egiziano, granito del Foro,* and red and green porphyry.

Gaul

Only two lithotypes from Gaul were recorded in the DESTINI dataset, *bianco e nero antico* and *cipollino mandolato.* Extraction of both lithotypes began much later than in other zones of production, with *cipollino mandolato* appearing in Rome by the start of the 2nd century AD and *bianco e nero antico* predominantly circulating in the 3rd century AD.[29] In Northern Italy, both Gallic lithotypes were primarily found in Aquileia (alongside minimal attestations in Altinum and Milan), a reflection of the variety of revetment passing through the port.

Greece and the Aegean

Stone and marble were extracted from quarries across Greece and the Aegean since the Archaic period, being used in Hellenic sculpture and prestigious architectural projects. The incorporation of Greece into the Roman sphere of influence in the 2nd century BC made a wide variety of white and polychrome marble available to Italian consumers.[30] The expanding appetite for coloured marble led to lithotypes such as *breccia di Settebasi, cipollino verde,* and *rosso antico* being extracted on a scale previously unseen in the region.[31]

Within the DESTINI dataset, green *cipollino* was the lithotype extracted in the greatest quantities from Greece and the Aegean. Quarried in southeastern Euboea, *cipollino* was the most common polychrome marble within the dataset and the second most common lithotype overall, accounting for 9.7% of provenanced fragments. *Cipollino* was not a highly valued stone in the pre-Roman period but saw intensive extraction for use in both revetment and architectural elements from the 1st century BC onwards.[32] *Breccia di Settebasi* from

Skyros, *fior di pesco* quarried near Eritrea, and *marmo Lesbio* from Lesbos constituted the other dominant lithotypes from Greece and the Aegean (all appearing in quantities of greater than 2% of the total DESTINI assemblage). These began to appear in Italy during the 1st century BC and were used in a variety of public and private contexts.[33] Lithotypes that also appeared in significant quantities from Greece and the Aegean included *portasanta, rosso antico, serpentino,* and Thasian marble.

Northern Italy

While finds of imported lithotypes are numerous across Northern Italy, it is worth highlighting that the region itself was not lacking in sources of decorative stone, including marble. These resources could, and did, provide an alternative to imported stones, with Figure 48 displaying the location of stone deposits known to have been quarried in Northern Italy during the Roman period.[34] Given the difficulty and cost of quarrying and transport, the majority of stone used in construction projects would have been locally extracted and transported a minimal distance; imported materials complemented supplies sourced within the region.[35]

Although no stone extracted from the Po-Veneto region saw widespread diffusion across the Mediterranean world, several types seem to have been of sufficient quality (and/or the quarries sufficiently accessible) to enable regional circulation. Studies on the extraction and distribution of decorative stone from Northern Italy remain limited, but substantial progress has been made in tracing the uses and distribution of several prominent lithotypes, such as Aurisina limestone, Candoglia marble, Euganean trachyte, and *Verona rosso.*[36] The cargoes of several inland shipwrecks also attest to the movement of locally quarried stone via water within the region. The best documented is the Bacchiglione wreck, with its cargo of architectural elements in Euganean Trachyte, but the San Basilio di Ariano Polesine wreck with its cargo of Domegliara

---

[28] Hirt 2010: 25-7; Pensabene 2013: 406-13.

[29] Antonelli 2002: 269-70; Antonelli and Lazzarini 2000: 111-28; Russell 2013: 91.

[30] Pensabene 2013: 263-65. The temple of Jupiter Stator in Rome was famously the first temple constructed out of marble (Vell. Pat. 1.11.5.)

[31] Russell 2013: 86-88.

[32] Pensabene 2013: 298-300; Russell 2013: 86-88.

[33] Pensabene 2013: 301-04.

[34] The quarries presented here are by no means a complete list of all quarries operating in Northern Italy during the Roman period.

[35] Russell 2018b: 242-43. See Mosca 2015 for distribution related to stone quarried in the Eastern Alpine area.

[36] Euganean Trachyte was a durable stone quarried in the Colle Euganea near Padua, during the Roman period. The lithotype played an important role in construction projects across the east of Northern Italy, with its distribution suggesting it was primarily transported by water, (Germinario *et al.* 2017; Previato 2023; Previato and Zara 2018; Zara 2018: Part 3). Candoglia marble is still extracted in the present day at the mouth of the Ossola Valley, adjacent to Lago Maggiore, (Poletti Eclessia 2019: 41-43). Aurisina limestone is quarried close to Trieste in the Karst region. Examples of structures and artefacts comprised of Aurisina limestone have been found as far west as Pavia and Milan, (Previato 2018: 937-38). *Verona rosso* was quarried close to Domelgiara, north of Verona, and saw wide diffusion across Northern Italy (Calzolari 2003: 169-70).

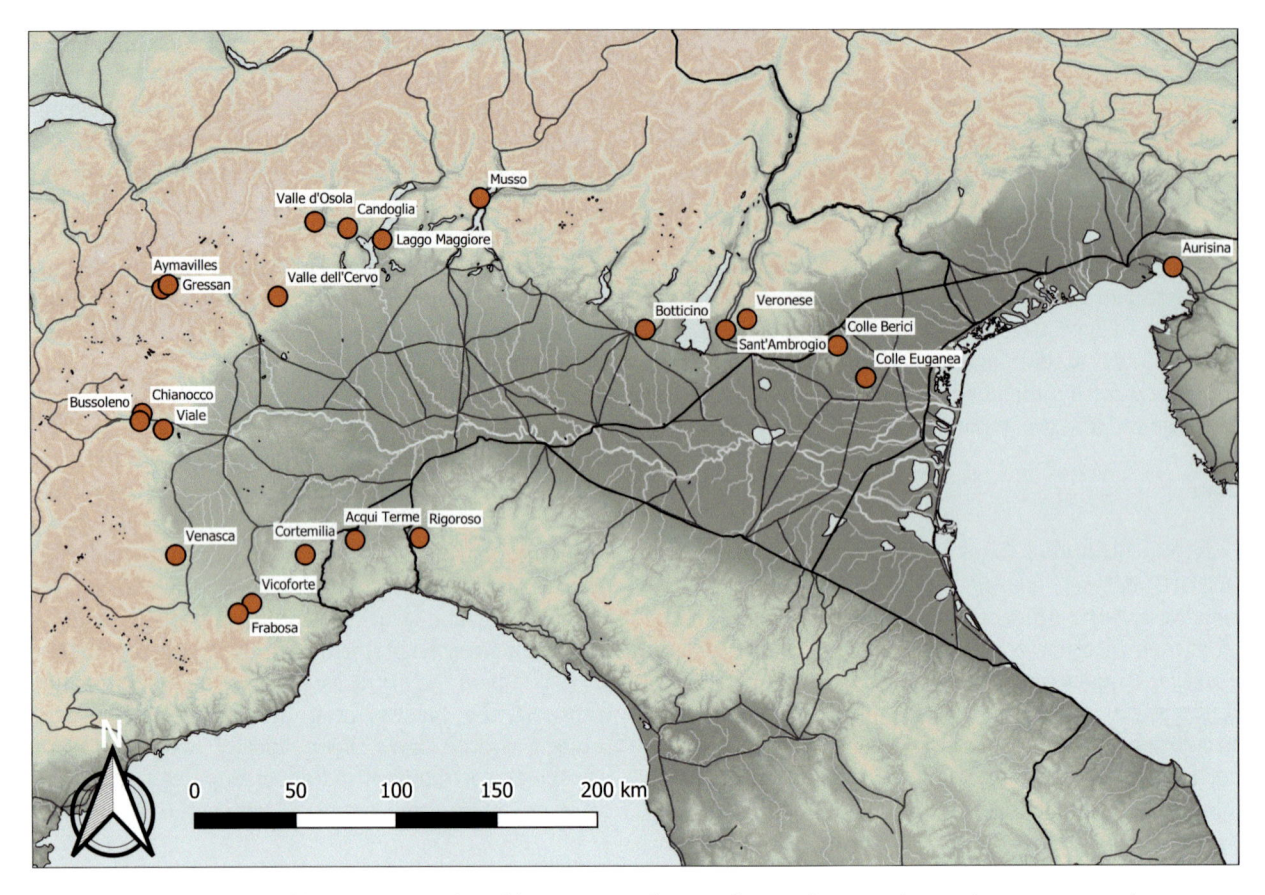

Figure 48. Map of known stone and marble quarries within Northern Italy active during the Roman period.

limestone and the Como wreck with its cargo of Musso marble, are also valuable examples (see Chapter 2).[37]

Exploring Stone and Marble Trends

Although the number of quantified stone assemblages was significantly lower than those in the amphora and fineware datasets, clear trends were still present in its analysis. While the stone data was not analysed chronologically using aoristic analysis, several geographic patterns in both the provenance and diversity of the assemblages were observable.

Trends in Provenance and Colour

Of the six zones of extraction supplying Northern Italy with decorative stone and marble, Asia Minor formed the most common provenance, accounting for 43.2% of revetment fragments within the DESTINI dataset. Mainland Greece and the Aegean formed the second most common (33.3%), followed by Central Italy and Liguria (10.1%), Egypt and North Africa (8.6%), and Northern Italy (4.1%). Lithotypes from Gaul accounted for <1% of the total assemblage. When the lithotypes

in the DESTINI assemblage were separated by their colour (grey, polychrome, or white), it became clear different zones of extraction specialised in providing specific colours (see Figure 49). Grey marble was predominantly sourced from Central Italy and Liguria, with Greece and the Aegean forming the second most common provenance. Polychrome stone and marble mostly originated from Greece and the Aegean, with Asia Minor and North Africa forming the second and third most common provenances. White marble was mainly sourced from Asia Minor, with Central Italy and Liguria forming the second most common provenance. However, as most of the white marble recovered from the region is unprovenanced, this pattern could easily change.

The consumption of different coloured stone and marble also changed from site to site across Northern Italy (see Figure 50). Grey lithotypes formed the smallest component of most site assemblages (with the exception of Forlì). In the centre and east of Northern Italy, polychrome lithotypes were often present in the greatest quantities, often comprising over 60% of assemblages. This pattern changed at sites in the west and south-west of the Po Valley, which had the lowest amount of polychrome stone in their assemblages and sourced white stone and marble in greater quantities.

<hr />

[37] Dallemulle 1977: 123-24; Montalcini De Angelis D'Ossat 1993: 56; Previato and Zara 2014: 61-63.

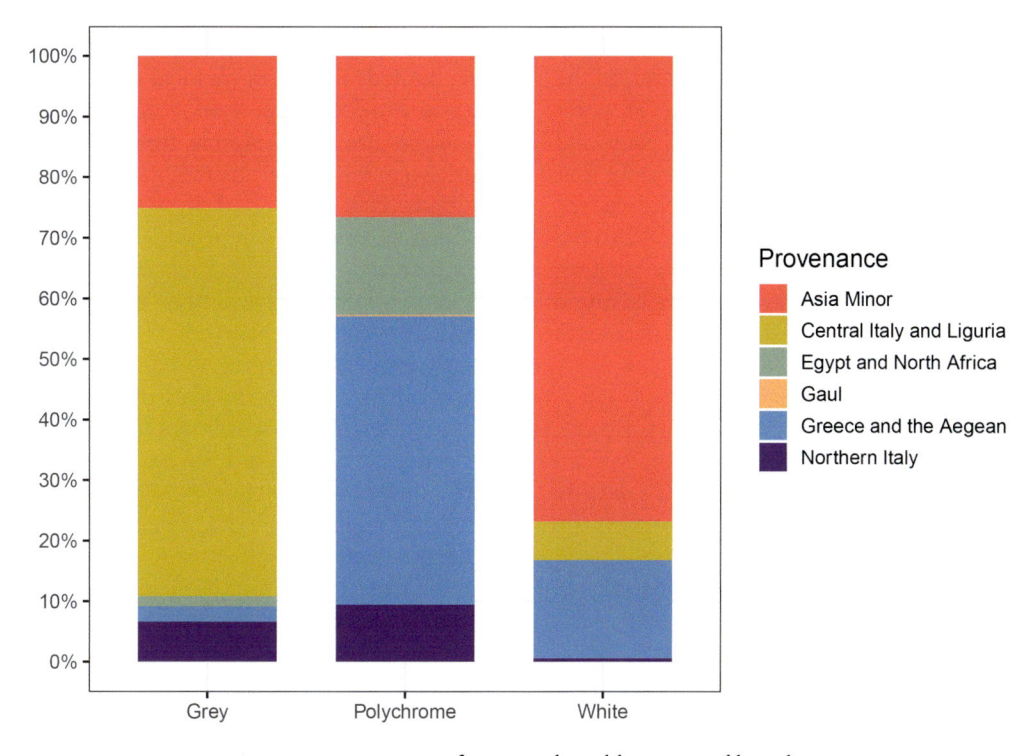

Figure 49. Provenance of stone and marble separated by colour.

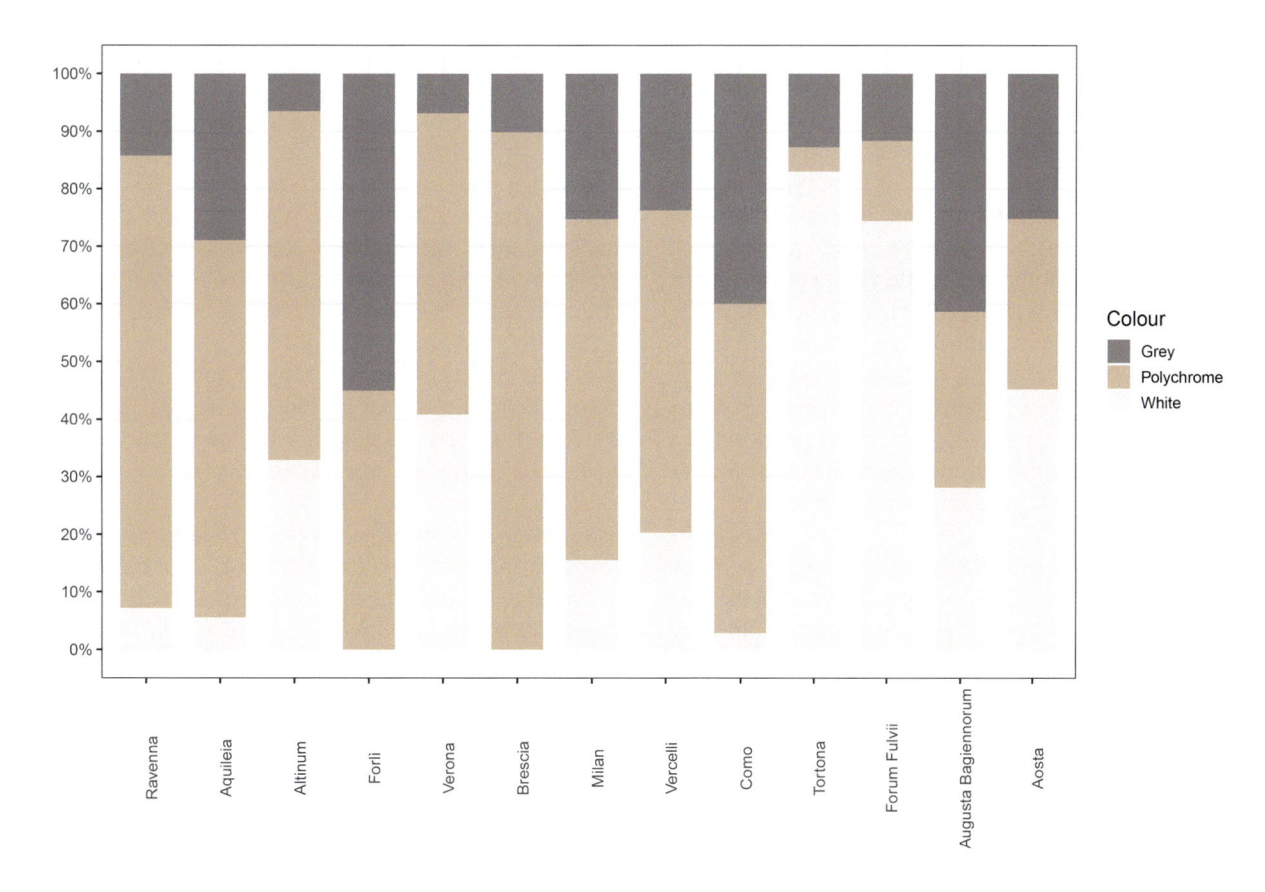

Figure 50. Quantities of white, grey, and polychrome marble at each site.

Polychrome lithotypes were mostly obtained from extra-regional zones of production and had to be imported to Northern Italy, likely arriving at ports along the Adriatic Coast.[38] As stone is a heavy and difficult cargo to transport, it is unsurprising that urban centres in close proximity to ports in the eastern Po Valley had the greatest quantities of polychrome lithotypes in their assemblages.[39] Sites in the western Po Valley, which were further away and more costly to reach, may have had a more limited selection of colours to choose from.

Geographic Trends: Hierarchical Clusters

All urban centres within the DESTINI dataset exceeded the minimum threshold for inclusion in the hierarchical clustering analysis. As only ten inland sites, predominantly located in the western half of Northern Italy, were present in the dataset, the Adriatic ports of Altinum, Aquileia, and Ravenna were included in the cluster analysis to provide perspective from the eastern half of the region.

When the sites were hierarchically clustered based on the provenance of their stone and marble assemblages, three clear groups emerged (see Figures 51 and 52). The first cluster was comprised of five sites, Altinum, Aquileia, Brescia, Ravenna, and Verona. These were all sites in the eastern half of Northern Italy and contained high quantities of imported stone and marble in their assemblages.[40] Asia Minor and Greece and the Aegean formed the main provenances of lithotypes within this cluster. Quantities of decorative stone from Asia Minor ranged from 40.3% to 47.3%, while quantities of decorative stone from Greece and the Aegean ranged from 33.8% to 50%. Lithotypes from Egypt and North Africa also formed significant components of each assemblage in the cluster, constituting between 3.6% and 21.4%. Northern Italian stone and marble were barely present in the assemblages. Maritime ports did not differ significantly from inland sites within the cluster in the make-up of their assemblages.

The second cluster contained three urban centres in the north-west of the Po Valley, Como, Milan, and Vercelli. These sites possessed the highest quantities of Northern Italian stone in their assemblages, which ranged from 15.8% to 41.4%. Other zones of extraction continued to be well-attested, particularly those from the Eastern Mediterranean. In Milan's assemblage, lithotypes from Asia Minor, Greece and the Aegean, and Egypt and North Africa, were all present in quantities over 20%.[41] Como and Vercelli's assemblages were more limited, but extra-regional zones of extraction continued to form important contributors to supply.[42] Decorative stone and marble from Central Italy and Liguria were minimally attested in the cluster.

The final cluster was comprised of five sites: Augusta Bagiennorum, Aosta, Forlì, Forum Fulvii, and Tortona. This cluster contained sites with the highest quantities of Central Italian and Ligurian stone in their assemblages, ranging from 36.1% to 68%.[43] These sites were mainly located in the west of the Po valley, with the exception of Forlì which was located in the south-east. Although lithotypes from Asia Minor appeared in significant quantities at sites within the cluster, stones from Egypt and North Africa, alongside Greece and the Aegean, were present in low amounts. Stone and marble quarried from within Northern Italy also contributed to assemblages, although in smaller quantities than the preceding cluster.

Trends in Diversity

Examining the number of lithotypes present at each site within the DESTINI dataset revealed further geographic patterns (see Figure 53). Urban centres in the centre and east of Northern Italy generally had the greatest diversity in the number of lithotypes present in their assemblages. Verona exhibited the greatest diversity, although this is probably as much a result of the detailed and extensive publishing of the assemblage as it is consumption patterns.[44] Maritime ports, especially Altinum and Aquileia, were amongst the sites with the greatest assemblage diversity, a reflection of their role as the principal entry point for imported stone and marble. In contrast, urban centres in the west and south-west of the Po Valley, furthest away from maritime ports, exhibited lower diversity in the number of lithotypes present in their assemblages. However, this was not significantly lower than inland sites in the central and eastern valley.

In summary, the trade in marble revetment within Northern Italy saw a wide variety of lithotypes from across the Mediterranean distributed within the region. However, as with the amphora and fineware data, there was a clear split between the east and the west of Northern Italy in consumption. Within the eastern Po-Veneto Plain, stone and marble from Asia Minor, Greece and the Aegean, and Egypt and North

---

[38] Gomez Serito and Rulli 2014; Guarnieri, Montevecchi, and Pagini 2018; Minato 2018; Previato and Mareso 2015.
[39] Angelelli 2014; Bocconcello 2008.
[40] Angelelli 2014; Bocconcello 2008; Gomez Serito and Rulli 2014; Guarnieri, Montevecchi, and Pagini 2018; Minato 2018; Previato and Mareso 2015.

[41] Terracina 1991.
[42] Bugini and Folli 2016; Butti 2016; Cardosa 1996.
[43] Framarin and Castoldi 2013; Gomez Serito 2007; Gomez Serito and Rulli 2014; Guarnieri 2013.
[44] Bocconcello 2008. Verona's large and varied assemblage is the largest within the DESTINI dataset, containing 14,390 fragments of stone. As such, most lithotypes that saw large scale extraction and consumption during the Roman period are present within it.

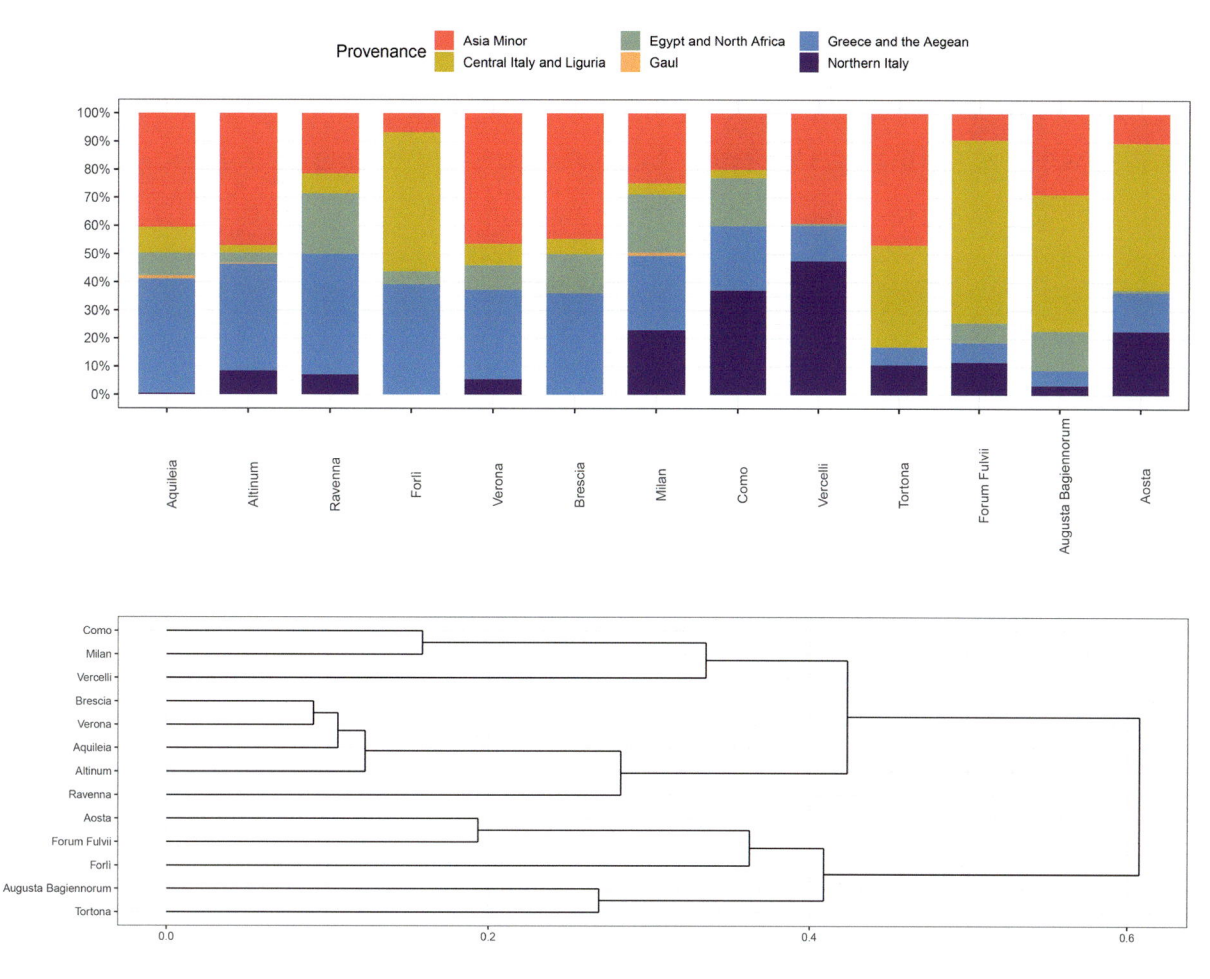

Figure 51. Percentages of the provenance of stone at each site, with subsequently formed hierarchical clusters. See Appendix B for exact percentages and n numbers for each assemblage.

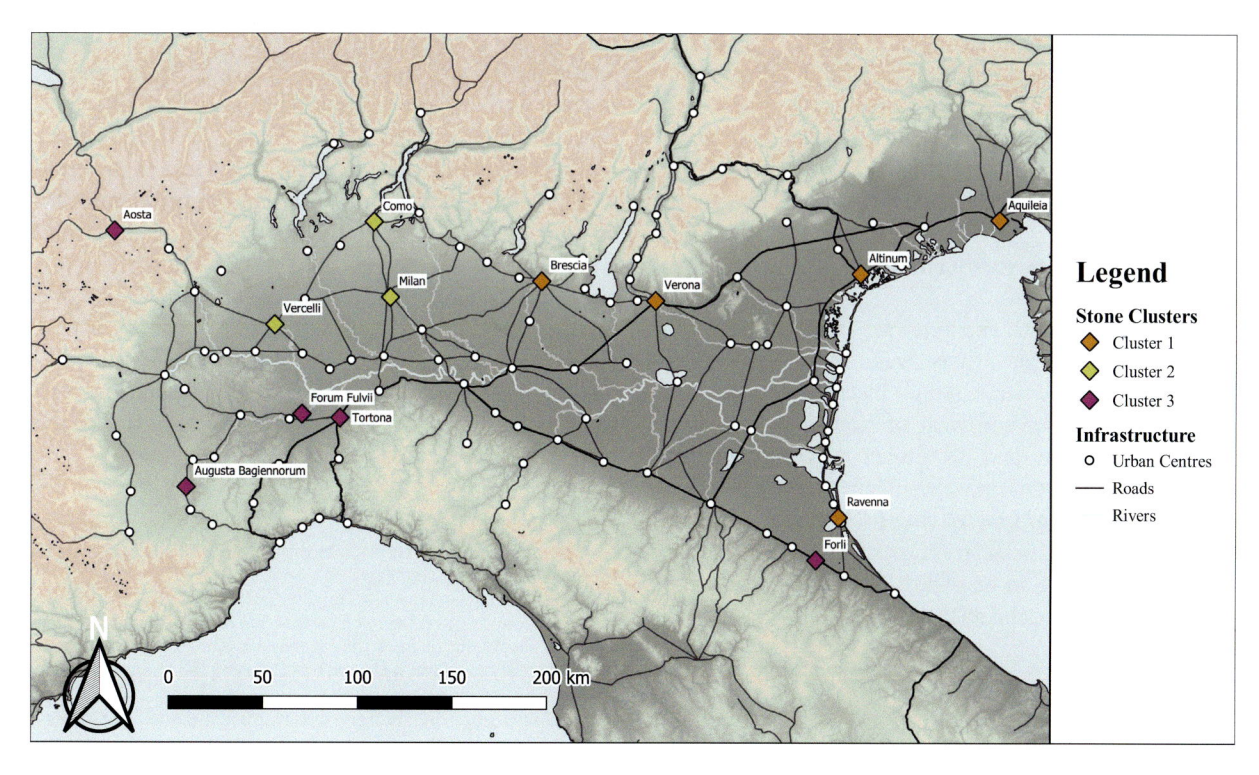

Figure 52. Stone clusters based on assemblage provenance.

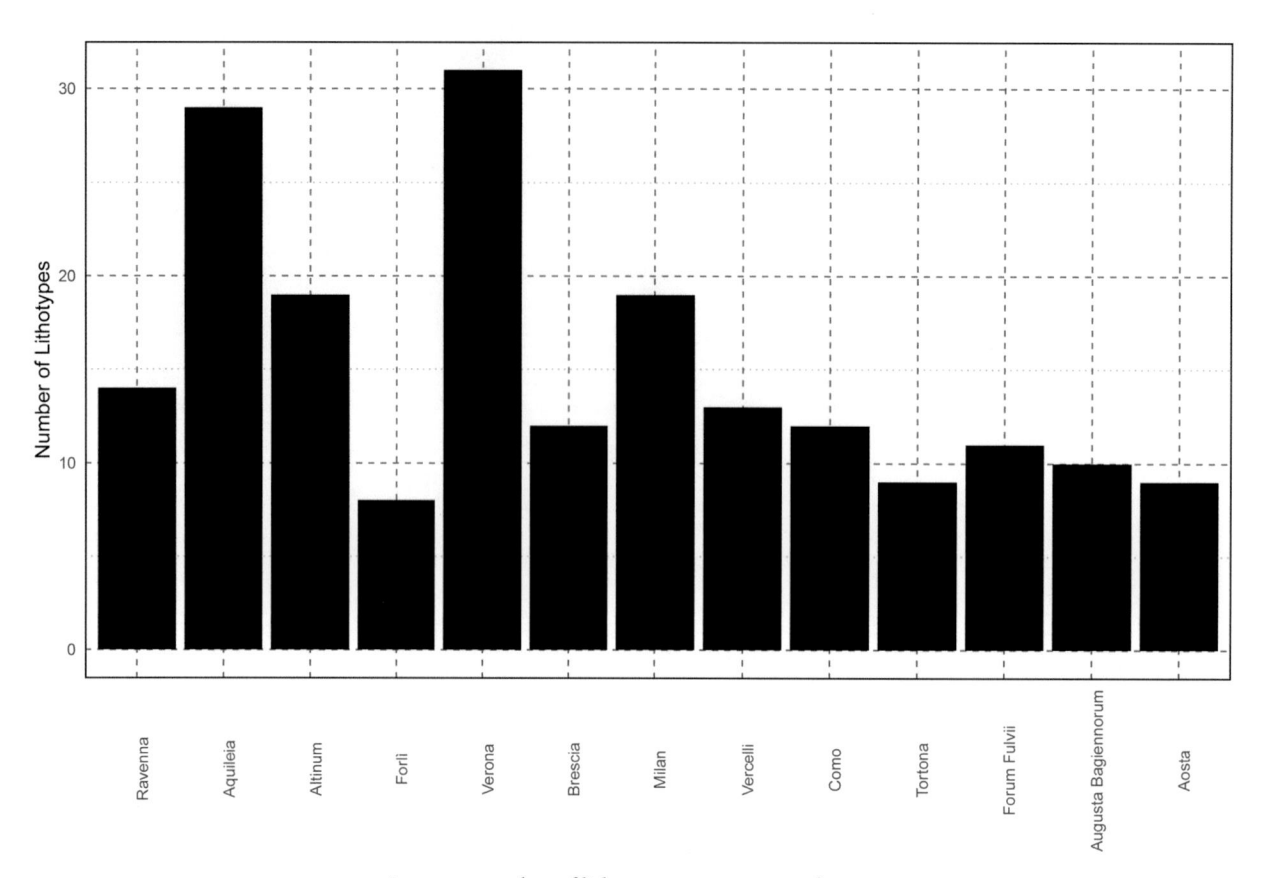

Figure 53. Number of lithotypes present at each site.

Africa comprised the majority of assemblages. Sites in the east of Northern Italy also showed greater diversity in the lithotypes present in their assemblages. At sites in the western Po Valley, Central and Northern Italian lithotypes comprised a much greater part of the assemblages, although white, grey, and polychrome stone from the Eastern Mediterranean, Egypt, and North Africa was still present. The assemblages of these sites exhibited less diversity, particularly sites in the west and south-west of the valley.

The Stone Trade in Northern Italy

As with the amphora and fineware data examined in the previous chapters, there was a clear distinction between the decorative stone assemblages present at sites in the east and west of Northern Italy. The role of topography and its impact on transport was most apparent in the movement of decorative stone, with regional geography having a clear effect on the lithotypes present in different areas of Northern Italy. The following section goes into further detail on the patterns exposed in the analysis.

The Eastern Valley and Asia Minor

The assemblages of most sites in the central and eastern Po-Veneto Plain were defined by high quantities of stone imported from across the Eastern Mediterranean, Egypt, and North Africa, in particular, marble from Asia Minor. The majority of sites in this part of the region (with the exception of Brescia), had a high level of diversity within their assemblages. Furthermore, these sites also contained the greatest quantities of polychrome marble in their assemblages, compared to sites further inland that returned greater quantities of grey and white marble.[45] Proximity to the coast gave these sites access to a greater range of materials and reduced the cost of their distribution to sites in the coastal hinterland and middle valley. Arriving at the Adriatic ports would also have allowed imported stone to be redistributed via the river network, reducing its transport costs as it moved further inland.[46] Furthermore, the relatively flat topography of the valley floor would have served to limit the impact of gradient on overland transport, resulting in lower costs.[47]

---

[45] Ravenna formed an exception to this rule, but this is likely due to the small size of its assemblage.

[46] A similar situation is seen in the distribution of marble in the Ebro Valley (Cisneros 2018). Although as mentioned above, for items that were not revetment or floor tiles, it may have been easier and safer to travel solely overland rather than risk losing the cargo via fluvial transport or transhipment.

[47] For comparison, the unforgiving terrain of the Anatolian coastal hinterland and the absence of navigable rivers served to limit the quantity of imported stone that reached inland sites (Corremans *et al.* 2012; Lazzarini 2004: 107-8).

Of the Eastern marbles attested in Northern Italy, Proconnesian was imported in the greatest quantities, making up the majority of provenanced white marble identified within the region. Pentelic and Thasian marble were barely attested in the DESTINI dataset and Parian, the other Eastern Mediterranean white marble that saw widespread distribution during the Roman period, was absent entirely. The dominance of Proconnesian marble is at first somewhat surprising, given that the closest source of white marble to Northern Italy was the quarries at Luna. However, Luna marble was only present in significant quantities in the south-west and west of the Po Valley (see below). As hypothesised by Russell, the archaeological evidence suggests that, in large parts of the region, it was cheaper to import marble from Proconnesus, rather than geographically closer quarries at Luna.[48] The quarries at Luna, despite their proximity to Northern Italy, were located on the other side of the Apennines, an expensive and arduous journey. Later sources indicate that the 10 km overland journey from the quarry to the port of Luna alone nearly doubled the cost of a block of marble.[49] If a maritime, rather than overland, route was selected to reach the Po Valley, then the marble would have needed to be transhipped from wagon or sledge to ship, before making its way around Italy to the Adriatic ports, adding further costs. In contrast to Luna marble, Proconnesian marble travelled a minimal overland distance from its point of extraction to waiting maritime transport, giving it an edge on cost before it had even arrived within the region.[50]

The distribution of Proconnesian marble, alongside the dominance of Eastern Mediterranean, Egyptian, and North African lithotypes in the east and central Po-Veneto Plain, demonstrates the importance of the Adriatic Coast and its ports in the region's stone trade. Facing the Eastern Mediterranean, the Adriatic Coast offered access into the valley without having to cross the major barrier of the Apennines. The plain's relatively flat topography and the presence of the river network helped imported stone and marble penetrate far inland. However, in a similar manner to the amphora data, assemblages in the far west of the region exhibited very different compositions to their eastern counterparts, as distance and cost began to impact distribution.

Alpine Stone and Marble in the North-West

Moving further inland, sites in the north-west of the region saw decreasing quantities of imported marble in their assemblages and greater reliance on locally quarried lithotypes. This is seen most clearly in the cluster formed by Como, Milan, and Vercelli. The assemblages from these sites contained high quantities of Northern Italic stone and marble, the exact lithotypes of which were often uncertain. Several good sources of Alpine marble were close to Como, Milan, and Vercelli, most notably the quarries at Musso on the cliffs above Lake Como and those along the Val d'Ossala close to Lago Maggiore.[51] From quarries such as Musso and Candoglia, it would have been impractical, if not outright impossible, to transport large quantities of stone overland.[52] The narrow, undulating roads that hugged the hills surrounding the great glacial lakes of Como and Maggiore would have been unsuitable for the transport of heavy loads such as the monolithic Musso columns preserved by the Colonne di San Lorenzo in Milan.[53] The lakes themselves, and the connecting river network, provided a more practical alternative transport route.

Como and Vercelli, located in the north-west of the region, lay at the furthest point from both the Adriatic and the Ligurian Apennines, the two entry points for imported lithotypes in Northern Italy. The distance of these sites from the coast, and the associated transport costs of transporting heavy loads of stone and marble inland, may have served to limit the quantity of imported lithotypes available, forcing a greater reliance on local sources of material.[54] It is, however, important to emphasise that despite the higher quantities of Northern Italic materials present at these sites, imported lithotypes still make up over 50% of each assemblage. Very few Central Italian and Liguruian lithotypes were attested at these sites (4.1% of the assemblage at Milan, 2.8% of the assemblage at Como and absent from Vercelli's assemblage), suggesting a greater reliance on stone traders with Adriatic connections than those dealing in cross-Apennine trade. The overland route from quarries on the Ligurian Coast, followed by either transhipment to river transport or a continuing overland journey to reach sites in the north, seems to have made Central

---

[51] Poletti Eclessia 2019: 41-43.
[52] Although Candoglia marble is not attested in any of the assemblages discussed above, it is present in many rural assemblages in northern Piedmont and western Lombardy (Poletti Ecclesia 2019: 43-44).
[53] Fiorio and Bandera Bistoletti 1985: 409. The columns, originally from a 2nd or 3rd century AD temple and/or bathhouse, were reused in the construction of the Basilica di San Lorenzo during the 4th-5th centuries AD.
[54] A similar situation is seen in the Ebro Valley, with sites in the middle and upper river containing greater quantities of Pyrenean stone that coastal sites, (Andreu Pintado *et al.* 2015).

Italic lithotypes prohibitively expensive compared to their Mediterranean counterparts.

Central Italic and Ligurian Lithotypes. A limited distribution

The final group of sites from the hierarchical clustering consisted mainly of sites in the west and southwest of the Po Valley, alongside Forlì in the southeast. The sites in this cluster contained the lowest levels of stone and marble from the Eastern Mediterranean, Egypt, and North Africa (except Tortona which retained high quantities of stone from Asia Minor). It is possible that the transport costs incurred by heavy cargoes of marble revetment, travelling inland from the Adriatic Coast, began to limit the quantities and selection of stone entering this part of the region. Equally, transporting Egyptian, North African, and Eastern Mediterranean stone and marble across the Apennines may have been prohibitively expensive once prior transport and transhipment costs had been factored in. Aside from low quantities of Egyptian, North African, and Eastern Mediterranean lithotypes, sites in this cluster shared high levels of Central Italian and Ligurian stone and marble within their assemblages. This mainly took the form of white Luna marble alongside grey *bardiglio* marble.[55] The quarries, located near Luna, were approximately equidistant from sites in the eastern and western Po Valley in terms of Euclidean distance, yet Central Italian lithotypes comprised less than 9% of assemblages outside of this cluster.

White Luna marble formed the main Central Italic lithotype present at Augusta Bagiennorum, Aosta, Forum Fulvii, and Tortona. The other white marble appearing in large quantities within Northern Italy, Proconnesian, appears in much lower quantities in the west of the region and was absent from the assemblages of Aosta, Augusta Bagiennorum, and Como. White marble from Luna seems to have been less expensive to transport to sites in the western valley, even after travelling over the Ligurian Apennines, than Proconnesian marble arriving at the Adriatic ports. However, as discussed above, these circumstances did not extend far beyond the west and southwestern Po Valley. Augusta Bagiennorum and Forum Fulvii were close to passes to the Ligurian Coast, as was Tortona. However, despite the high quantity of Central Italic lithotypes present at Tortona, its assemblage contained more Proconnesian than Luna marble, alongside other stone from Asia Minor. Further north, Central Italic and Ligurian lithotypes were also absent from Vercelli and comprised less than 3% of the assemblage at Como. As such, the area around Tortona may represent a

transitional zone, marking an area where Luna and Proconnesian marble began to even out in price, with Luna gaining an edge in areas to the south and the west.

While the high quantities of Central Italic and Ligurian lithotypes in Augusta Bagiennorum's and Forum Fulvii's assemblages can be explained by their proximity to the Ligurian Coast, Aosta's placement in this cluster forms an interesting pattern. Aosta is located further away from supplies of Central Italian stone than Como, Milan, and Vercelli, three sites that contained high quantities of Alpine lithotypes.[56] While the assemblage at Aosta also contained a high percentage of Northern Italian stone (25% of the lithotypes attested), the majority of its assemblage was comprised of Luna marble. The context of Aosta's assemblage, two temples from the forum area, as opposed to a road in Como and a townhouse in Vercelli, may have played a role in the quantity of Central Italian stone present at the site.[57] A project such as a temple, a prestigious architectural undertaking, would likely have been better funded than a domestic property. Given the temple's contemporary date to other Aostan monuments that used imported marble, such as the Porta Praetoria and the theatre, its use on the building may represent an attempt on the part of the city's inhabitants to increase its prestige in the context of a wider architectural program.[58] White marble from local quarries, such as those at Chianocco, Crotte, Foresto, and Tre Piloni, was available during this period (see below), and the decision to instead use the more prestigious (and expensive) marble from Luna, represents a deliberate choice.

The fact that the white marble from Aosta is uniformly Luna, rather than Proconnesian, reinforces the theory that the cost of transporting imported Eastern Mediterranean, Egyptian, and North African marbles from the Adriatic Coast had become either too expensive or comparable in cost to Central Italic and Ligurian imports this far inland. However, the decision to use Luna over Proconnesian marble may also reflect availability. Luna was widely used in the Augustan period, before other sources of white marble were found or systematically exploited.[59] In contrast, the marble at Proconnesus would not see intensive extraction and distribution until the latter half of the 1st century AD, rising to prominence in the Adriatic and Eastern Mediterranean during the 2nd and 3rd centuries AD.[60] Consequently, Aosta's assemblage of decorative stone

---

[55] The true extent of the trade in Luna marble across the region will likely never be known given the amount of unprovenanced white marble contained in the assemblages.

[56] Aosta also had the lowest level of imported Eastern and Egyptian and North African marble of any site within the stone dataset, those provenances forming less than 20% of its assemblage.

[57] The residual context of the majority of Milan's decorative stone fragments makes it hard to identify their original setting (Terracina 1991).

[58] Betori, Gomez Serito, and Pensabene 2009; Vanni Desideri 2001.

[59] Bradley 2006: 2-11; Fant 1999.

[60] Attanasio, Brilli, and Bruno 2008: 747-48; Ward-Perkins 1980.

likely predates the wider availability of Proconnesian marble in Northern Italy.

The contrast between sites in the east and west of Northern Italy, in particular the limitations on variety faced by inland sites, is further reinforced when the contents of assemblages in the west and south-west of the valley are analysed. The sites of Aosta, Augusta Bagiennorum, Forum Fulvii, and Tortona were dominated by large quantities of Luna marble, with low numbers of other lithotypes appearing. This was especially true for material originating outside of Central and Northern Italy. For example, at Augusta Bagiennorum, although almost 50% of the stone and marble assemblage was comprised of material quarried outside of Italy, only six lithotypes made up this total. In comparison, at a coastal site such as Aquileia, where over 90% of the assemblage was comprised of material quarried outside of Italy, 23 lithotypes contributed to the total. Although their inland location did not prevent these sites from accessing imported Eastern Mediterranean, Egyptian, and North African marbles, it does seem to have limited the choice of material on offer.

The inclusion of Forlì within a cluster dominated by Central Italic and Ligurian decorative stone was surprising given its proximity to the Adriatic ports of Ariminum and Ravenna, and the prevalence of imported marbles at other sites in the east of the region. *Bardiglio*, a grey marble, formed the entirety of the Central Italian and Ligurian stone assemblage at the site.[61] Unfortunately, without the publication and quantification of datasets from other sites in the southeast of the Po Valley, it is impossible to know if the high quantity of Italian lithotypes attested in Forlì is reflective of a wider trend in sites along the Apennines or a unique occurrence. As Forlì was well placed to take advantage of the Adriatic coastal ports for imported marble, as shown by the high quantity of lithotypes from Greece in its assemblage, consumer choice may have played a role in the high quantity of Central Italian and Ligurian lithotypes recovered from the city.[62] *Bardiglio* was one of the few grey marbles extracted in significant quantities, the others being *greco scritto* and *marmo Lesbio,* and would have been an understandable choice if grey revetment was key to the building's decoration.[63]

Beyond Veneer. Comparative data from other stone and marble datasets

While the analysis of the DESTIN dataset offers a picture of how decorative stone circulated within Northern Italy, it represents only part of the region's stone trade. Although unquantified, examples of carved stone in the form of architectural elements, building materials, and sarcophagi, form important comparisons.

The fact that most coloured stone recovered from sites in Northern Italy is in the form of veneer is a pattern reflected in other studies on the inland distribution of coloured stone.[64] The cost of transporting material served to limit its applications to flooring and revetment, and slicing a marble block into slabs of panelling maximised its surface area and visibility, allowing more to be achieved for less.[65] Large-scale architectural elements in imported stone and marble are almost entirely absent in the most westerly areas of the region. The Arch of Augustus at Susa, constructed between 9 and 8 BC, was built using mainly local white marble (Tre Piloni, Foresto, and Crotte) from the quarries located within the Susa valley.[66] In contrast, the Arch of Augustus at Aosta, was constructed entirely in local puddingstone. White marble elements at the Palatina Gate and theatre in Turin were carved from Chianocco, quarried a short distance away in the valley of the Dora Riparia.[67] Where larger architectural elements carved from imported marble are present, they are mainly carved from Luna marble. For example, at Aosta, although the main structure of the Porta Praetoria was formed of puddingstone and its front was covered with a veneer of locally quarried Aymavilles marble, the entablature consisted of imported white Luna marble.[68] Further south, at Augusta Bagiennorum, the theatre's *scaenae frons* was also decorated with columns and statues carved from Luna.[69] Although the trans-Apennine journey was economically viable for some larger architectural elements in Luna to be transported into Northern Italy, they are mainly present in the greatest quantities in areas closest to the passes.[70]

In the east of Northern Italy, there is more evidence for the movement of stone for the carving of large architectural elements. Local stones still formed

[61] Guarnieri 2013.

[62] Sites further inland, such as Brescia and Verona, also contained higher quantities of Eastern Mediterranean and North African lithotypes than Forlì.

[63] Leka and Zachos 2015; Russell 2008: 114. The high cost of overland transport for heavy loads of revetment, alongside the proximity of both the quarries and Forlì itself to ports, makes it probable that *bardiglio* was transported via maritime routes. Another possible reason for the supposed high quantity of *bardiglio* at Forlì may be the difficulty of accurately provenancing grey marble without using without petrographic and mineralogical analysis, (Borghi *et al.* 2006:

60; Mariottini 1998: 23). Forlì's assemblage was not subject to such analysis, and *bardiglio* may have been used as the default identification for grey marble (Guarnieri 2013: 87). The site's assemblage could, in fact, have a more varied provenance.

[64] See Russell 2013: Chapter 5 for several case studies of the inland distribution of stone across the Roman Empire.

[65] Russell 2018b: 253-54.

[66] Agostoni *et al.* 2017: 414; Bertori, Gomez Serito, and Pensabene 2009; Borghi *et al.* 2006.

[67] Betori, Gomez, and Pensabene 2009: 96.

[68] Betori, Gomez, Pensabene 2009: 97; Borghi *et al.* 1997.

[69] Ruilli 2008: 14.

[70] Gomez Serito 2019.

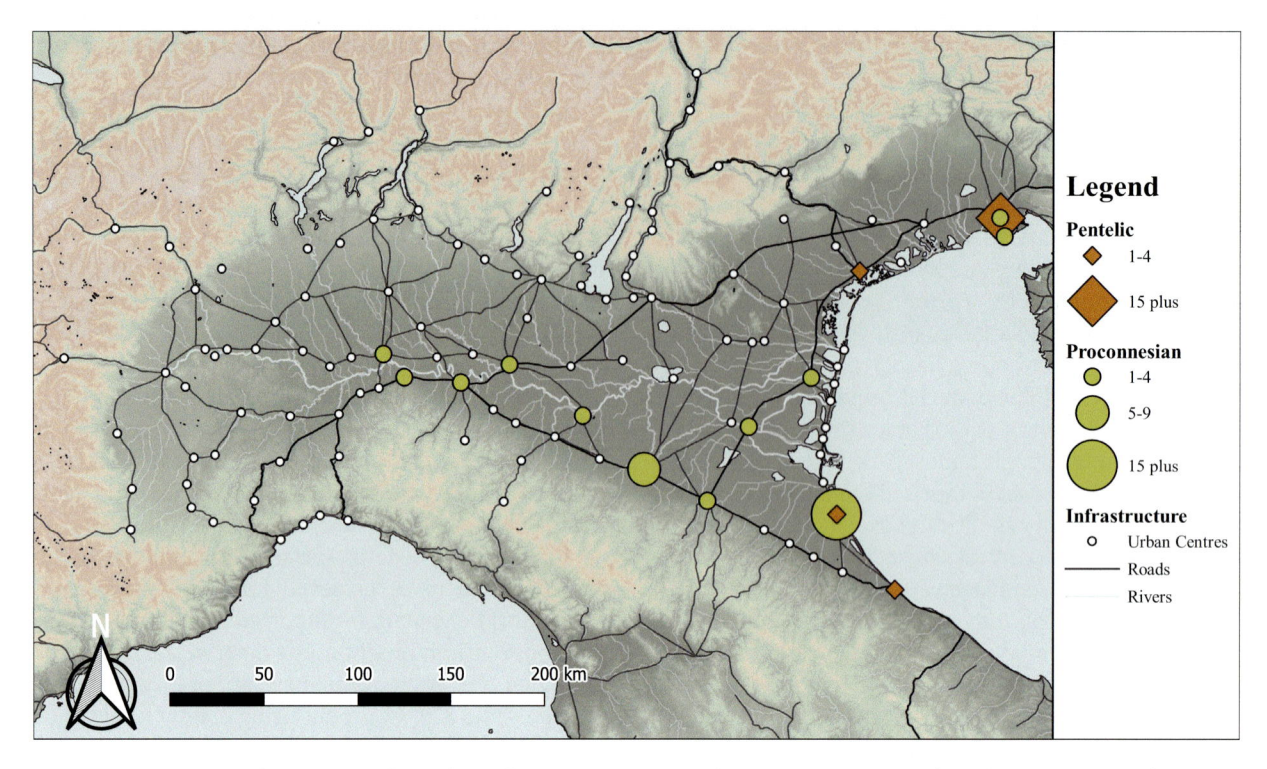

Figure 54. Distribution map of Pentelic and Proconnesian sarcophagi in Northern Italy (data from Russell 2013).

the basis of most structures, for example, the use of Aurisina at Aquileia and Padua or Bottocino at Brescia, but large architectural components that had travelled significant distances took a prominent place in the structural composition.[71] For example, Brescia's forum was bordered by columns of Proconnesian marble, while the columns surrounding the Claudian forum at Verona were carved from a combination of *africano*, *bigio antico*, *cipollino*, and *giallo antico*.[72] Beyond Brescia, however, most prominent architectural elements at sites in the northwest of the Po Valley seem to have been carved from local lithotypes (e.g. the aforementioned Musso marble columns in Milan). The cost of commissioning and transporting such large architectural elements simply seems to have been too expensive for sites furthest inland from the Adriatic Coast.

Aside from architectural elements, sarcophagi of imported white marble form another useful comparative dataset to explore patterns of stone distribution. Gabelmann quantified and mapped the distribution of sarcophagi in Northern Italy.[73] Sarcophagi of Pentelic marble, while well attested on the coast (particularly at Aquileia), had minimal penetration inland (see

Figure 54). In contrast, sarcophagi of the 'Ravenna Type', carved from Proconnesian marble, had much wider inland distribution and have been discovered as far west as Pavia. This mirrors the situation seen with revetment and floor tiles. Pentelic marble was barely attested in the region, while Proconnesian marble was often recovered in significant quantities. Of course, sarcophagi made of imported stone represent the high end of the market. For those who could not afford to be entombed in Proconnesian or Pentelic marble, local alternatives were available. A quantified study of sarcophagi from Pavia shows the reliance of the city's elite on regional materials for its tombs (see Figure 55).[74] Of the 31 sarcophagi recovered, only four were carved from imported marble, three from Proconnesian and one from an unknown source. The rest were made from a mixture of granites and gneisses from Alpine quarries, alongside two 'local' lithotypes from sub-Alpine deposits.[75] It is perhaps unsurprising that there are few examples of imported stone sarcophagi at Pavia, which, being located close to Tortona, seems to have represented the point that imports of Eastern Mediterranean stone and marble began to decline in quantity and diversity.

---

[71] Bonetto and Previato 2013; Destro 2015: 69-75; Kleineberg 2021; Pensabene 2015: 88-90.

[72] For Brescia see Sacchi *et al.* 2011: 122. Although these columns have been alternatively identified as *cipollino* and *pavonazzetto* by earlier publications (see Kleineberg 2021: footnote 17). For Verona, see Bianco 2008: 211-14; Cavalieri Manasse 2008b: 298.

[73] Gabelmann 1970. See Russell 2013: 169-76 for discussion of the data.

[74] Gorrini and Robino 2015.

[75] The Alpine lithotypes present at Pavia were extracted at various points along the River Toce in the Val d'Ossala and at San Fedelino on the shores of Lake Mezzola (Gorrini and Robino 2015: 114). Many of the quarries were in close proximity to a navigable river or lake.

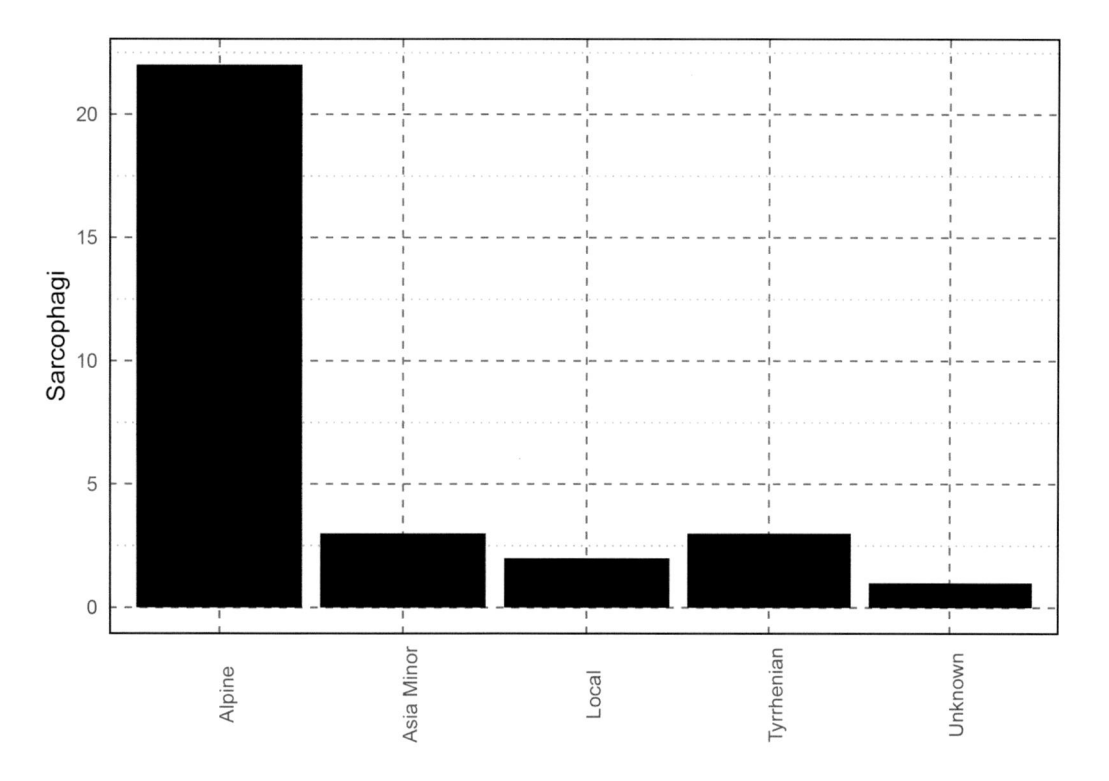

Figure 55. Provenance of sarcophagi from Pavia (data from Gorrini and Robino 2015).

Conclusions

The presence of both imported and regional decorative stone across the Po-Veneto region reflects varying levels of trade and investment in construction, sculpture, and sarcophagi in Northern Italy. The patterns and distribution of decorative stone explored in this chapter form a valuable counterpart to those seen in the amphora and fineware data, allowing a more varied and in-depth picture of inland trade to develop.

Although a very different material from the ceramic assemblages so far analysed, the distribution of decorative stone veneer in Northern Italy bears many similarities to amphora and fineware. The region's geography played an important role in determining the origin of the lithotypes consumed within it, with the different requirements of each consumer balanced against the logistical and economic feasibility of transporting the available material suitable for the project. In the eastern and central parts of the Po Valley, the flat topography and proximity to the coast allowed sites to utilise a wide variety of imported decorative stone, primarily from the Eastern Mediterranean, Egypt, and North Africa. Further inland, the situation became more complex, as mounting transport costs saw an increased reliance on Northern Italic stone in the north-west of the valley, and the dominance of Luna marble from the Ligurian Coast in the west

and southwest. Despite their distance from the coast, inland regions were still able to access a wide range of Mediterranean lithotypes. The fact that sites such as Aosta, which lay more than 650km from the Adriatic Coast, were still able to import Eastern Mediterranean, Egyptian, and North African marble to decorate their buildings shows that cost did not deter consumers from accessing imported marble. However, while cost did not prevent the use of Eastern Mediterranean, Egyptian, and North African lithotypes, it did limit the variety available and its primary application to veneer.

While revetment forms only part of the picture of the stone trade in Northern Italy, the overarching pattern is supported by the distribution of imported architectural elements and sarcophagi. Transport costs formed a major factor in limiting the inland distribution of these items, although some, such as Proconnesian sarcophagi, achieved a remarkable level of penetration. Beyond the confluence of the Ticino and Po at Pavia, there are few examples of such expensive and bulky objects in Eastern Mediterranean, Egyptian, and North African lithotypes, with locally quarried stone and marble utilised to a greater extent. However, it is important to remember that, even in areas with the greatest access to imports, local stone formed the basis of construction projects. Stone and marble retained a decorative function as an expression of wealth and status.

Trade, Transport, and Economy in Northern Italy

Analysis of the MADINI dataset has chronicled the complex development of trade networks and consumption within Northern Italy during the Roman period. On the backbone of an extensive and well-developed transport network, a wide array of goods from varied zones of production and extraction were circulating within the region between the 3rd century BC and the 9th century AD. Cargoes of amphorae from the Eastern Mediterranean, finewares from North Africa, and marble from Asia Minor, to name but a few examples, were carried inland to consumers across the length and breadth of Northern Italy. The distribution of amphorae, finewares, and decorative stone would see chronological and geographical variation over the centuries. Different zones of production rose and fell in importance, reflecting the changing circumstances and wider economic trends seen across the Roman world. From limited beginnings, the quantity and diversity of amphorae, finewares, and decorative stone circulating in Northern Italy would rapidly increase during the 1st century BC, allowing consumers an unparalleled level of choice in the products available to them during the Early Imperial period. Although there would be a contraction in the quantities and provenance of material circulating in Northern Italy after the 2nd century AD, new zones of production would take a prominent role in supplying the region. Northern Italy would continue to be connected to wider Mediterranean markets throughout Late Antiquity.

The contrasting ways in which goods were consumed, especially the distinction between ceramics and stone, had a significant impact in determining the provenance and circulation of each material type within Northern Italy. Staple amphora-borne foodstuffs were consumed in a different way to fine tablewares, which in turn were consumed differently to decorative stone and marble. Consumer taste, product availability, and transport costs all played a role in determining the distribution of local and imported goods across Northern Italy, resulting in distinct zones of consumption. Of these factors, transport costs, especially for amphora-borne foodstuffs and decorative stone, seem to have heavily influenced the geographic spread of imports across the region. To further explore the relationship between transport costs and material distribution, in this final chapter the results of the geographic analysis of the MADINI dataset are combined with an existing network model of Roman transport in Northern Italy.[1]

In many cases, there is a remarkable level of overlap between the distribution of different material types and the cost surfaces generated by the network model. The importance of fluvial networks to inland trade is readily apparent, although this study has also served to highlight their limitations. Overland trade, some of which took place across mountain ranges, seems to have played a major role in supplying certain areas of Northern Italy. While the results of the analyses demonstrate the key role of geography in determining the cost of transport and the subsequent distribution of material within inland regions throughout the Roman period, they also suggest a wider array of other factors played a significant part in how material circulated. These include hidden costs, the vagaries of the market, and consumer choice, alongside availability and supply. Overall, the results of the analyses undertaken in this book challenge long-held orthodoxies that inland sites were geographically isolated and had access to a more limited range of imports than those on the coast.[2] While it is undeniable that inland areas faced additional obstacles to coastal sites when it came to trade, they were not excluded from wider Mediterranean markets; even regions at the furthest distance from the coast could possess imports in significant quantities.

Transport Costs and Networks

Transport costs are thought to have heavily impacted the distribution of goods and materials during antiquity.[3] The figures for transport costs in the ancient world have their basis in Diocletian's Price Edict of AD 301.[4] Although the Edict forms a complex and, at times, problematic source, it provides the most comprehensive and best-surviving evidence for transport cost.[5] The Price Edict text gives the maximum price of transport across 51 maritime routes, with costs ranging between 4 and 26 *denarii* for the transport of

---

[1] The model used in the analysis here can be found in Page 2024, alongside a full methodology behind its creation. See also De Soto 2010; 2019.

[2] Bonifay 2004: 451–2; Hordon and Purcell 2000: Chapters 4 and 5; Tchernia 2016: 90-93; Temin 2001: 179-81.

[3] Adams 2012; Bresson 2005; Horden and Purcell 2000; Laurence 2005; Scheidel 2014; Temin 2013.

[4] Carreras 1994a: 28-33; 1994b: 338-40; DeLaine 1992: 123-126; 1997: 207-20; de Soto 2010; 2019; Schiedel 2014.

[5] Corcoran and DeLaine 1994; Duncan-Jones 1982. The Edict survives in a fragmentary state, and only records maximum prices relevant to the early 4th century AD. There was probably significant variation in costs below this total, and prices may have been higher or lower in the preceding and following periods. Furthermore, the decree seems to have been principally enacted in the eastern half of the empire, giving the potential for regional price variation.

a single *kastrensis modius* (approximately 12.9 litres of wheat).[6] For fluvial transport, only the Aphrodisias copy of the Price Edict distinguishes between upstream and downstream carriage. The Edict gives a price of 1 *denarius* per *kastrensis modius* per 20 Roman miles of downstream travel and 2 *denarii* per *kastrensis modius* per 20 Roman miles of upstream travel.[7] For terrestrial transport, the Edict gives the maximum prices of 2 *denarii* per Roman mile for a passenger in a carriage, 4 *denarii* for a fully laden donkey per Roman mile, 8 *denarii* for a camel carrying 600 Roman pounds per Roman mile, and 20 *denarii* for a wagon carrying 1,200 Roman pounds per Roman mile.[8] As the value of the *denarius* was not consistent throughout Roman history (seeing significant devaluation from the 1st century AD onwards), some scholars have instead sought to express the freight rates contained within the Price Edict in the form of a wheat equivalent.[9] As the value of wheat is thought to have remained relatively stable throughout the Roman period, (with demand and consumption remaining constant), expressing transport costs as a unit of wheat allows them to be used for transport in earlier periods when the *denarius* had greater value.[10] The costs in the Price Edict have led to an accepted hierarchy amongst many scholars in the cost and efficiency of transport types in the Roman world.[11] Maritime transport is viewed as the cheapest and quickest, followed by fluvial transport. Upstream travel is viewed as both more expensive and slower than downstream due to the need to add a means of propulsion (often hauliers or rowers) to counteract the strength of the current. Overland transport is considered the most expensive and least preferable for the transport of large quantities of goods.

Network modelling forms a heuristic tool to explore how ancient transport systems may have operated and the impact of cost on their accessibility. The use of network analysis in archaeology has grown exponentially since the 1990s, as greater interdisciplinary cooperation between statisticians, computer scientists, and archaeologists made the necessary skills and software more available.[12] Network modelling — the mapping of

nodes and connections (also known as edges) between sites, people, or materials – has been used to explore a range of archaeological questions.[13] Spatial network analyses are especially well-suited to analyse real-world transport networks and have been widely applied in the study of Roman trade and transportation.[14] Within a spatial network, the nodes of the model might represent cities, towns, and villages, while the edges between them might represent the routes of the roads, rivers, or sea lanes connecting them. The greater the number of nodes and edges within a set geographic area a model possesses, the more detailed it is. Furthermore, each node and edge can contain data. For an edge, this might relate to the distance of its length, the cost and time it takes to travel along it, or a value to represent connectivity. For a node, values might include delays or penalties in the form of transhipment or customs costs. The values applied to nodes and edges can originate from ancient transport data (such as the costs listed in the Edict of Maximum Prices), or later comparative data.[15] Spatial network analysis can be used to create maps of cost across an ancient transport system or measure complex aspects of the network such as its connectivity (measured using metrics such as betweenness, closeness, or degree centrality).[16] Although network models are not perfect reflections of the ancient world, as long as potential flaws and limitations are acknowledged and engaged with, they form valuable instruments for investigating wider research questions.[17]

Figure 56 maps the incremental cost of transport for a hypothetical 1000 kg cargo from four Adriatic and four Ligurian ports across a network model of Roman transport infrastructure in Northern Italy during the 2nd century AD.[18] The model assumes that transport was taking place during the spring and summer months, at a time of optimum weather and hydrological conditions on the region's rivers. It applies the maximum cost given by the Price Edict to transport, which is expressed as kilograms of wheat, per tonne, per kilometre.

The model largely confirms the importance of waterways in facilitating cost-efficient travel within

---

[6] It is worth noting that the monetary costs for maritime transport given in the Price Edict are probably based on time, rather than distance (Arnaud 2007; Scheidel 2013).

[7] *Edict of Maximum Prices*, XXXVA.31-33.

[8] *Edict of Maximum Prices*, XVII.1-5.

[9] Carreras 1994a: 28-33; 1994b: 338-40; DeLaine 1992: 123-126; 1997: 207-20; de Soto 2010; 2019.

[10] The *kastrensis modius* is assumed to reflect weight, rather than volume, in these figures. See Corbier 1985; DeLaine 1992: 22-23; Duncan-Jones 1978 for further discussion on the use of wheat equivalences and the stability of the price and demand for wheat during the Roman period.

[11] Bonifay 2016; Fulford 2009: 253; Lavan 2015: 3; Vaccaro and MacKinnon 2014.

[12] Brughmans 2010; 2013; Collar *et al.* 2015; Knappett 2013; Mills 2017. The ability of network analysis to handle and visualise large, complex datasets, alongside its compatibility with other, more established tools such as GIS, has helped drive its adoption within the

archaeological community.

[13] Collar *et al.* 2015; Knoke and Yang 2008; Scott 2017; Shafie *et al.* 2020.

[14] See, for example, Brughmans 2013; Carreras and De Soto 2014; De Soto 2019; De Soto and Carreras 2010; Graham 2006; Isaksen 2008; Orengo and Livarda 2016; Page 2024; Preiser-Kapeller and Werther 2018; Scheidel 2014.

[15] Russell 2013: 96.

[16] De Soto 2019: 278-80; Golbeck 2013: 23; Orengo and Livarda 2016: 23-26.

[17] See van Oyen's 2017 response to Brughmans and Poblome 2016, alongside Brughmans and Poblome's 2017 reply, with Knappett 2013: 7-10; Tartaron 2018: 60-61.

[18] The full methodology behind the creation of the network model, alongside a detailed analysis of its results, can be found in Page 2024. The shapefiles used to create the network can be found at https://doi.org/10.5281/zenodo.7937731.

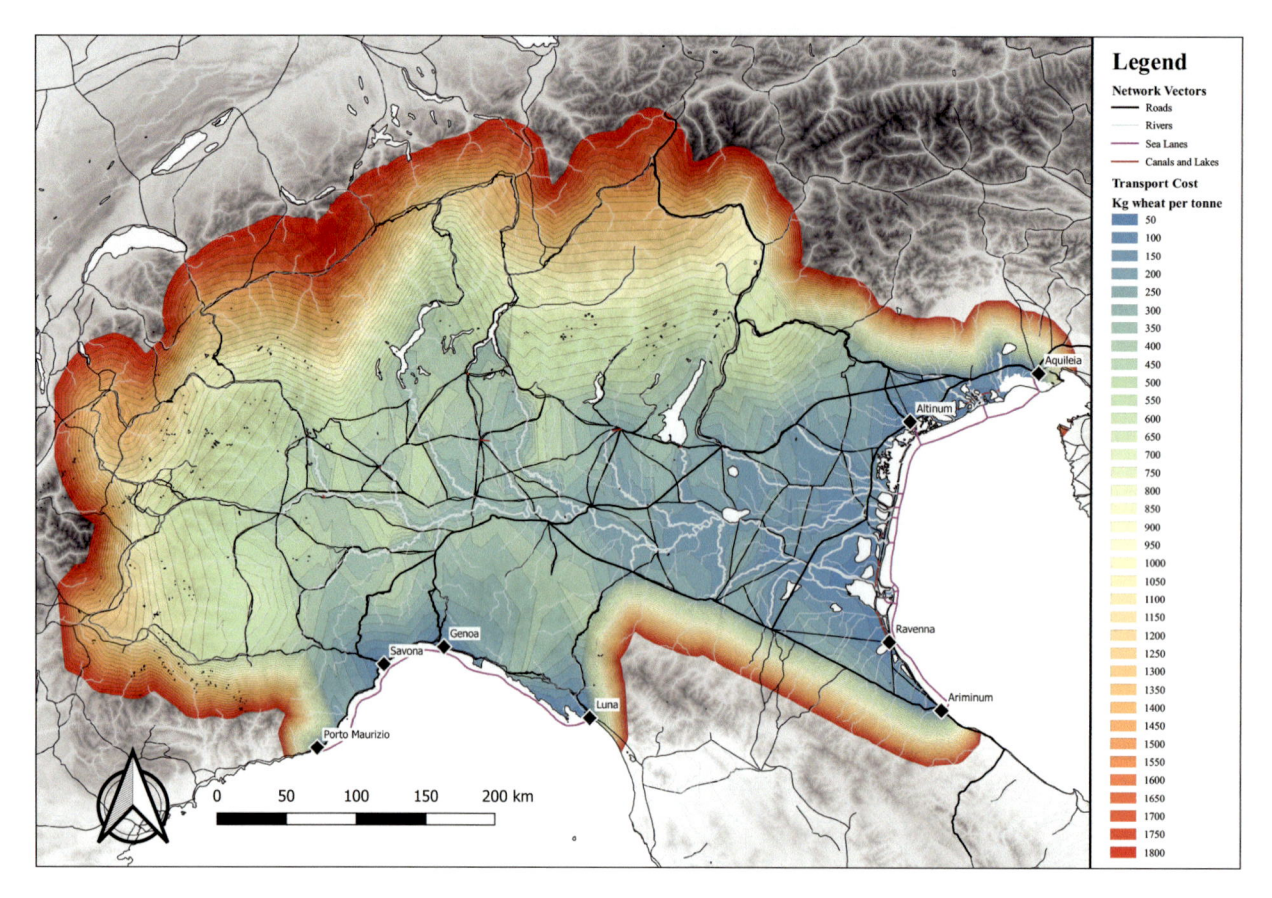

Figure 56. Network model showing the incremental cost of transport from four Adriatic and four Ligurian seaports across Northern Italy.

inland regions, with the Po and its tributaries forming an important axis for transport due to their extent and density across the valley floor. The low cost of upstream transport allowed sites such as Turin, lying in the far west of the valley and at the extreme limits of navigable waterways, to be reached for under 400 kg of wheat from the Adriatic ports. These sites acted as springboards for overland journeys into areas not accessible by water, which may otherwise have been prohibitively expensive to travel to from the Adriatic or Ligurian Coasts utilising solely terrestrial transport. Indeed, upstream transport meant that it was cheaper to reach many sites in the western valley from the Adriatic Coast, despite them being located significantly closer to the Ligurian Coast. However, while it is undeniable that the Po and its tributaries formed cost-efficient routes into the interior of Northern Italy from the Adriatic, it is worth pointing out that, in large areas of the upper valley, there was less than 100 kg of wheat difference in the cost of travel from the Adriatic and Ligurian Coasts. Away from fluvial and maritime routes, the expense of overland transport, compounded by gradient, rapidly increased costs.

While the network model presented here indicates how cost may have affected Roman transport, it exists as a purely heuristic device. Network models, as theoretical representations of past behaviour, cannot form a replacement for archaeological evidence. Instead, they must be used in combination with other materials to test the validity of their results. The results of the geographic analysis of the MADINI dataset provide an opportunity to compare the actual distribution of ancient material with the cost surface generated by the network model, identifying areas of correlation or divergence between the two.

Zones of Consumption

Across the material analyses of the MADINI dataset, when sites were hierarchically clustered based on the provenance of their assemblages, three distinct geographic groups routinely formed (with some overlap between sites). These broadly encompassed the coastal plain and central Po Valley, the northwest Po Valley and the Alpine foothills, and the west and south-west of the Po Valley. This pattern was at its most pronounced during the 1st and 2nd centuries AD, and although the lower quality of data from the Late Republic and Late Antiquity meant that the distribution was less clear, the overall trend remained. The section below outlines each of these geographic zones, the

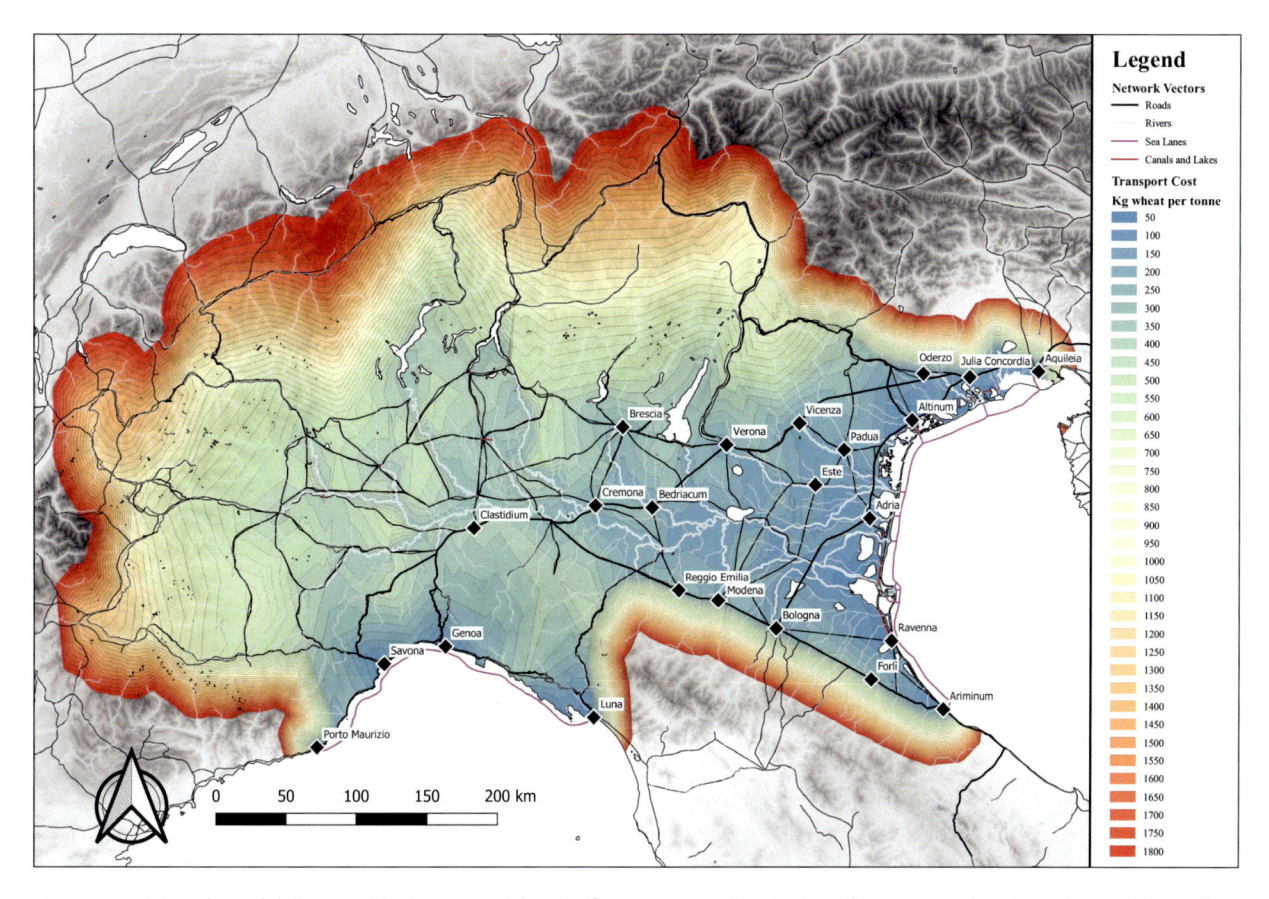

Figure 57. Network model showing the incremental cost of transport to sites in the Adriatic coastal plain and central Po Valley from four Adriatic and four Ligurian seaports.

material trends identified within them, and how their distribution relates to the cost of transport suggested by the network model.

The Coastal Plain and Central Po Valley

The first (and often largest) group of sites to form across the hierarchical clustering consisted of those located in the coastal plain and central Po Valley (see Figure 57). The network model suggested that sites in this area could be reached for an average transport cost of under 300 kg of wheat from the Adriatic Coast, making them the most accessible from a price standpoint (see Table 7).[19] Many urban centres could be reached for far less, with those possessing the best connections, such as Adria, Julia Concordia, and Padua, averaging transport costs of less than 100 kg of wheat from the Adriatic ports. Transport costs to sites in this area of the region from the Ligurian ports, on the other hand, averaged between 500 and 700 kg of wheat. For the sites of Adria, Julia Concordia, and Padua, average transport costs were upwards of 500% more expensive from the

Ligurian, rather than the Adriatic, coast. Even at sites in the centre of the valley such as Bedriacum and Cremona, transport costs were upwards of 100% more expensive to reach from the Ligurian Coast than the Adriatic Coast. This accounts for the relative paucity of material from the Western Mediterranean present in assemblages from the coastal plain and central valley.

For sites in this part of Northern Italy, although their proximity to ports and the density of the transport network should theoretically have afforded them a greater choice of imported amphora-borne goods and finewares, ceramic assemblages were dominated by material from a single provenance. For amphorae, this consisted of vessels produced on the Adriatic Littoral, while for finewares, Northern Italic Terra Sigillata (NITS) formed the main component of assemblages. The dominance of material from a single provenance meant that there was very little diversity in the vessel types present across assemblages within the cluster. This was most noticeable in the amphora data, with Dressel 6A and Dressel 6B vessels forming the major component of assemblages. The ceramic assemblages of Adriatic port sites often exhibited greater diversity in both their provenance and vessel composition than sites in their hinterlands, reflecting their role as centres

---

[19] The costs presented in the tables are averages taken for journeys originating from the four Adriatic and four Ligurian ports within the network model. Transport costs could be lower or higher from individual ports.

Table 7. Average transport costs in kg wheat for a one-tonne cargo from four Adriatic and four Ligurian ports to sites in the Adriatic coastal plain and central Po Valley.

Site	Average cost from Adriatic Ports (kg wheat)	Average cost from Ligurian Ports (kg wheat)	Difference in cost (kg wheat)	Cheapest origin
Adria	88	584	496	Adriatic
Bedriacum	297	661	364	Adriatic
Bologna	143	615	472	Adriatic
Brescia	221	621	400	Adriatic
Clastidium	271	476	205	Adriatic
Cremona	219	512	293	Adriatic
Este	102	612	510	Adriatic
Forlì	267	835	568	Adriatic
Julia Concordia	81	644	563	Adriatic
Modena	170	608	438	Adriatic
Oderzo	121	663	542	Adriatic
Padua	87	608	521	Adriatic
Reggio Emilia	288	653	365	Adriatic
Verona	151	662	511	Adriatic
Vicenza	112	630	518	Adriatic

of import and export.[20] Sites closest to ports, such as Bologna, Forlì, Oderzo, and Padua, do not seem to have shared their diversity in assemblage provenance.[21] The situation was more complex for stone assemblages. Assemblages from the coastal plain and central Po Valley were comprised of decorative stone from multiple provenances, although their main origin could be broadly defined as the Eastern Mediterranean.[22] Stone from Central Italy and Liguria was almost entirely absent from these assemblages (with the exception of Forlì), likely due to the cost of transporting it into Northern Italy.[23] The cost of transporting heavy cargoes from the Ligurian Coast, across the Apennines and then across the valley floor, was significantly more expensive than from the Adriatic ports.

The cluster of ceramic and stone assemblages in the coastal plain and central valley covered a large part of the study area. The level, flat ground and density of the river network enabled goods arriving at the Adriatic ports to penetrate a significant distance inland for comparatively low transport costs. The same was true of ceramics produced within the region, with low transport costs allowing NITS to circulate across the valley floor and coastal plain (although the stamp analysis suggests that the majority of NITS consumed within the region travelled over short distances). The similarity and homogeneity of the ceramic assemblages across this cluster are striking, with sites such as Bedriacum, Clastidium, and Cremona, located several hundred kilometres inland, having near identical assemblages to those on the coast. For ceramic assemblages, vessels produced in the Adriatic and within the region dominated (almost to the exclusion of all other provenances within the amphora data). Northern Italic and Adriatic goods travelled the

[20] The composition of amphora assemblages at Northern Italian port sites are discussed in Chapter 4. For fineware assemblages, see Airoldi, Cipriano, and Montevecchi 2018; Biondani 2005d; 2005e; Bortolamei and Bottos 2017; Dal Sie 2018a; 2018b; Donat 2017; Maselli Scotti 2017; Pagen 2018.

[21] Cipriano 2013; Cipriano and Ferrarini 2001; Curina 1986; Pesavento Mattioli 1992; Tempesta 2013.

[22] Angelelli 2014; Bocconcello 2008; Guarnieri 2013; Guarnieri, Montevecchi, and Pagani 2018; Minato 2018; Previato and Mareso 2015.

[23] See Chapter 6 for a discussion surrounding the quantities of Central Italian and Ligurian stone at Forlì.

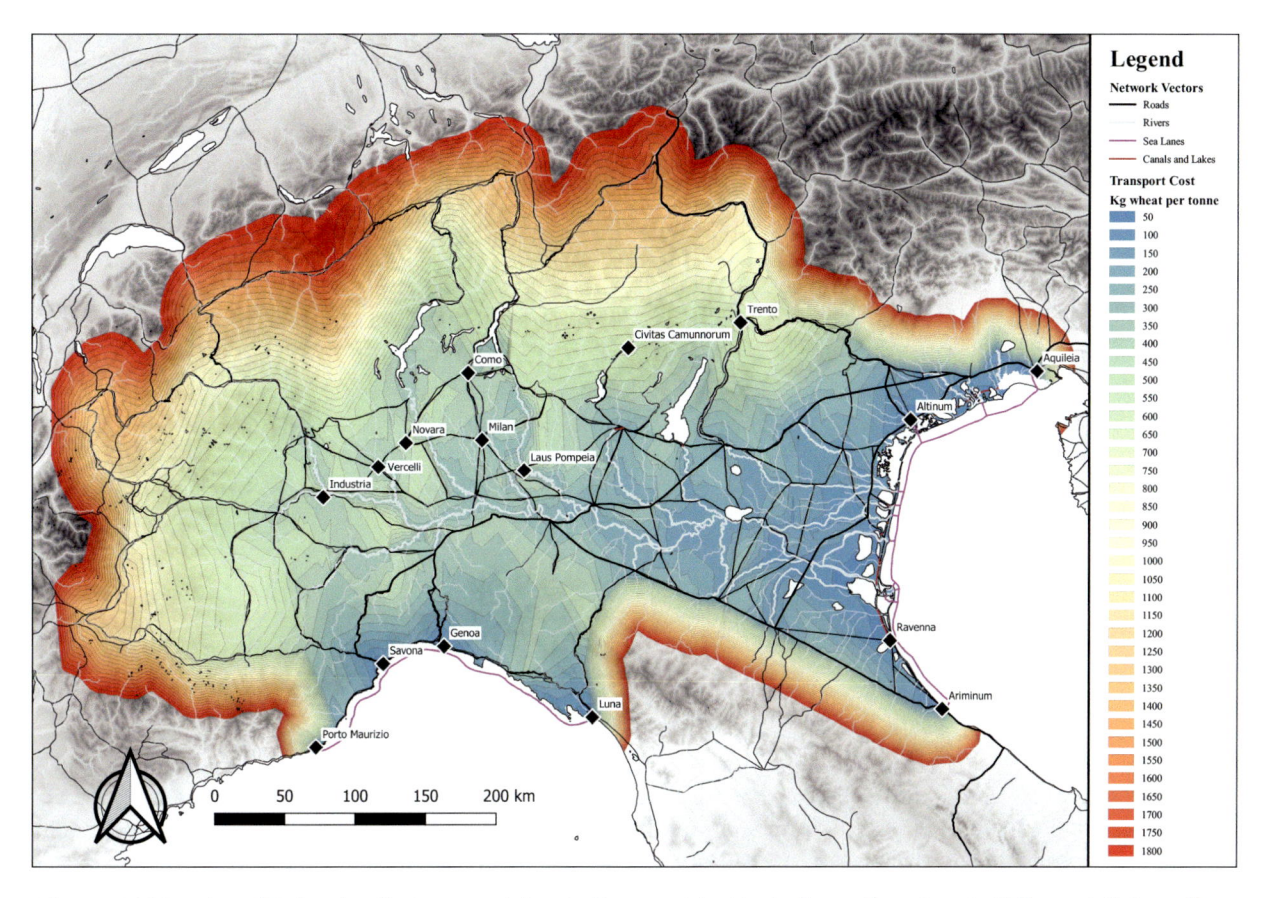

Figure 58. Network model showing the incremental cost of transport to sites in the northwestern Po Valley and Alpine valleys from four Adriatic and four Ligurian seaports.

shortest distance (and presumably incurred minimal additional costs) to reach their point of consumption within Northern Italy. Rather than take advantage of imports from further away, sites in the coastal plain and central Po Valley chose to consume the most readily available (and presumably the cheapest) goods. The opposite was true for stone assemblages, which contained a wide variety of provenances and lithotypes. The diversity of lithotypes found in this part of the region (compared to the more restricted selection seen further inland), reflects the higher cost of transporting heavy cargo, which served to limit its distribution. This ensured the greatest quantities and diversity of imported decorative stone were present closest to their point of entry to the region.[24] As stone was prized for its ornamental qualities, having a greater number of lithotypes allowed a more varied decorative scheme, alongside the prestige this afforded. Consequently, sites in this part of the region made full use of the range of decorative stone available, while locations further inland were forced to contend with less choice.

The Northwestern Po Valley and Alpine Valleys

The second group of sites to form during the hierarchical clustering consisted of those located in the north-west of the Po Valley and the Alpine valleys (see Figure 58). The network model suggested most sites in this part of the region could be reached from the Adriatic Coast for an average cost of under 400 kg of wheat, while average transport costs from the Ligurian ports were mostly under 700 kg of wheat (see Table 8). Although it was still significantly cheaper for goods to travel from the Adriatic Coast, the difference in cost between the Adriatic and Ligurian ports was not as great as it had been for sites further east. Transport costs from the Ligurian Coast, however, still came close to double those from the Adriatic. The network model suggested sites with the most expensive transport costs were those located within the Alpine valleys: Civitas Camunnorum, and Trento. Neither of these sites were located on the navigable segment of the river and the journey to both involved overland transport over medium gradients for large sections of travel.[25]

---

[24] The expertise needed to prepare floor and revetment panels was likely concentrated in these coastal sites, the points where imported decorative stone entered the region (Russell 2013: 167-68).

[25] Although the city was constructed on the banks of the river, there is uncertainty surrounding whether the Adige remained navigable as far as Trento during the Roman period (Bassi 1993: 242). No remains of the river port have been discovered.

Table 8. Average transport costs in kg wheat for a one-tonne cargo from four Adriatic and four Ligurian ports to sites in the northwestern Po Valley and Alpine valleys.

Site	Average cost from Adriatic Ports (kg wheat)	Average cost from Ligurian Ports (kg wheat)	Difference in cost (kg wheat)	Cheapest origin
Civitas Camunnorum	611	1010	399	Adriatic
Como	322	616	294	Adriatic
Industria	368	526	158	Adriatic
Laus Pompeia	371	520	149	Adriatic
Milan	303	527	224	Adriatic
Novara	461	620	159	Adriatic
Trento	631	1143	512	Adriatic
Vercelli	357	516	159	Adriatic

For sites in the north-west of the Po Valley, Adriatic amphorae and NITS continued to form the major components of ceramic assemblages. Although the Adriatic still accounted for the main provenance of amphorae, vessels from this zone of production appeared in lower quantities than at sites from the coastal plain and central Po Valley. Eastern Mediterranean amphorae, particularly the Camulodunum 184, appeared in greater numbers and formed a significant component of assemblages. Amphora-borne goods from the Western Mediterranean, however, continued to appear in only marginal quantities, despite the area's closer proximity to the Ligurian ports. A similar situation is seen with finewares, especially in the Alpine foothills and valleys. At Civitas Camunnorum and Como, although NITS remained the dominant component of assemblages, Gallic Terra Sigillata (GTS) appeared in significant quantities.[26] Stone assemblages in the north-west of the Po Valley exhibited a very different character to those in the central Po Valley and coastal plain. Although Eastern Mediterranean lithotypes were still present, in particular those from Asia Minor, locally quarried stone from the Alps made up a substantial portion of the assemblages at Como, Milan, and Vercelli.[27] The only other site to include Alpine lithotypes in similar quantities was Aosta in the west.[28] Stone assemblages from sites in this part of the region also possessed the highest scores for diversity outside of the Adriatic ports.

The point at which the transport costs for goods originating from the Adriatic Coast began to impact

their distribution seems to have begun in the north-west of the Po Valley. Increased transportation costs saw the assemblages of sites in the northwest begin to take on a different character to those in the coastal plain and central Po Valley, echoing the situation seen in material assemblages at sites in the southwest (discussed below). The network model suggests that the cost of reaching sites in the northwest from the Adriatic ports was almost triple that of sites in the coastal plain and central Po Valley; well over 300 kg wheat per tonne. For sites located away from the river network, although still on the valley floor, such as Novara, this cost rose to over 600 kg wheat. Sites located within the Alpine foothills and valleys, such as Civitas Camunnorum and Trento, had similar assemblage compositions to those in the northwest Po Valley.[29] While theoretically located closer to the Adriatic ports than their western counterparts, their position away from the water network and the gradients faced by overland transport increased the cost of reaching them.

Increasing transport costs seem to have made goods from a wider array of provenances more competitive against those originating from within or directly adjacent to the region, which began to complement Adriatic amphorae and NITS in the ceramic assemblages. For amphorae, vessels from the Eastern Mediterranean began to appear in appreciable quantities, while for finewares, GTS and Central Italic Terra Sigillata (CITS) were present in roughly equivalent quantities to NITS in some sites. Interestingly, the entry point for GTS at sites in the north-west and Alpine valleys seems to have been neither the Adriatic nor Ligurian ports but

---

[26] Fabbri, Gualtieri, and Massa 2004; Pisano Briani 2016.
[27] Bugini and Folli 2016; Cardosa 1996; Terracina 1991.
[28] Framarin and Castoldi 2013.

[29] Bocchio 2004; Fabbri, Gualtieri, and Massa 2004; Maurina 1995; Oberosler 1995.

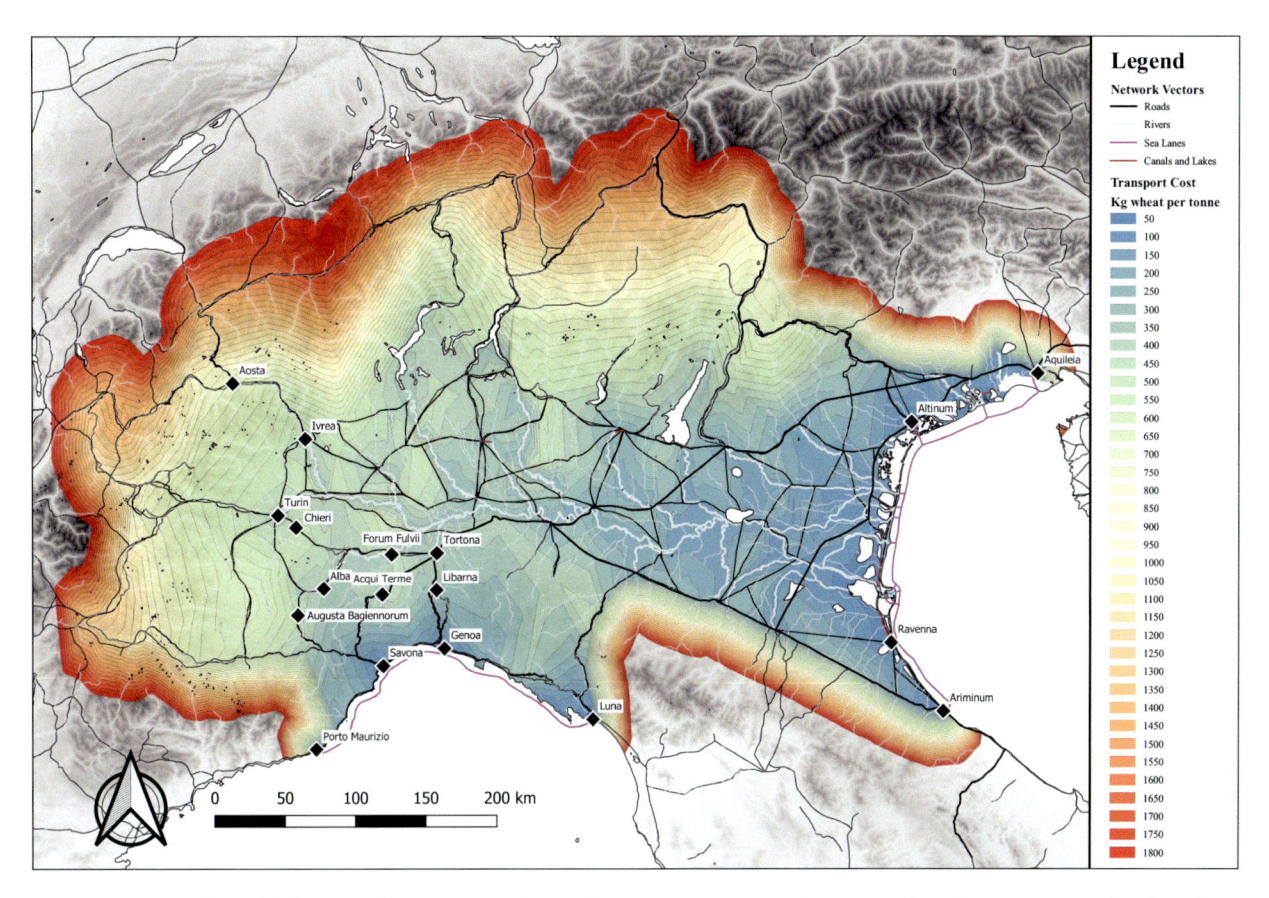

Figure 59. Network model showing the incremental cost of transport to sites in the west and southwestern Po Valley from four Adriatic and four Ligurian seaports.

rather over the Alps from production sites in Gaul. GTS crossing the Alps seems to have been competitive in very specific contexts, as it does not appear in significant quantities on the valley floor. For stone assemblages in the northwestern valley, located at the furthest distance from both the Adriatic and Ligurian ports, the costs and logistics of transporting heavy cargo seem to have resulted in an increased reliance on locally quarried decorative stones. The use of both local stone (not utilised in significant quantities elsewhere in the region), alongside imported lithotypes, was responsible for the high diversity within decorative stone assemblages from this area.

For all the material discussed in this cluster, it is important to highlight that, although transport costs seem to have made goods from extra-regional provenances more (in the case of ceramics) and less (in the case of decorative stone) competitive, they did not drastically change the prevailing trends in material distribution. The Adriatic still formed the main provenance of amphora-borne goods, NITS still appeared in significant quantities, and decorative stone from the Eastern Mediterranean still formed the largest overall component of stone assemblages. The east-west axis of trade along the Po and its tributaries remained dominant and imports from the Western Mediterranean, save GTS in some

unique circumstances, remained uncompetitive given the significant transport costs from the Ligurian ports. It was only in the final cluster of sites in the west and south-west of the Po Valley that the composition of material assemblages radically changed.

The West and Southwestern Po Valley

The final group of sites to form during the hierarchical clustering consisted of those located in the west and south-west of the Po Valley (see Figure 59). The network model suggested most sites in this part of the region could be reached from the Adriatic Coast for an average cost of under 500 kg of wheat, while average transport costs from the Ligurian ports were mostly under 600 kg of wheat (see Table 9). The major exception to this was Aosta, which, like Civitas Camunnorum and Trento in the previous cluster, incurred far greater transport costs due to its position within the upper Alpine valleys. The difference in price between inland transport from the Adriatic and Ligurian Coasts was at its lowest in this cluster. For many sites in this part of the region, the difference in transport price between the two coasts was consistent around the figure of 159 kg wheat.

For the most part, the network model suggests that it remained cheaper to transport goods to the south-

Table 9. Average transport costs in kg wheat for a one-tonne cargo from four Adriatic and four Ligurian ports to sites in the west and southwestern Po Valley.

Site	Average cost from Adriatic Ports (kg wheat)	Average cost from Ligurian Ports (kg wheat)	Difference in cost (kg wheat)	Cheapest origin
Acqui Terme	537	441	96	Ligurian
Alba	393	552	159	Adriatic
Aosta	802	961	159	Adriatic
Augusta Bagiennorum	489	502	13	Adriatic
Chieri	486	645	159	Adriatic
Forum Fulvii	341	500	159	Adriatic
Ivrea	394	553	159	Adriatic
Libarna	442	321	121	Ligurian
Tortona	322	440	122	Adriatic
Turin	390	548	158	Adriatic

west of the Po Valley from the Adriatic, rather than the geographically closer Ligurian Coast. Indeed, it is striking that only two sites in the study area had lower transport costs from the Ligurian ports than the Adriatic ones: Acqui Terme and Libarna. From the Adriatic Coast, transport costs to sites within this cluster were similar to those of sites in the northwest Po Valley (see, for example, Industria, Novara, and Vercelli above), however, ceramic assemblages from this part of the region had a markedly different composition. Products from the Western Mediterranean, such as Gallic, Iberian, and Tyrrhenian amphorae, and CITS and GTS, were concentrated in the west and south-west of the Po Valley.[30] Western Mediterranean amphora-borne goods especially achieved minimal penetration further east and to the north. For amphorae, vessels with an Adriatic provenance dropped below 50% in each of the assemblages, while the combination of CITS and GTS made up a greater portion of fineware assemblages than NITS (echoing the situation seen at sites in the Alpine foothills and valleys in the previous cluster).[31]

As with the ceramic assemblages, the decorative stone present at sites in the west and south-west was primarily extracted from the Western Mediterranean, rather than

the Eastern Mediterranean.[32] In particular, Central Italic and Ligurian lithotypes made up a significant portion of stone assemblages within this cluster but had very little penetration further north and east.[33] This mirrors the situation with the ceramic assemblages. The stone assemblage at Aosta also included the greatest quantity of Alpine lithotypes within the study area, echoing the high proportion seen at Como, Milan, and Vercelli. Assemblages of decorative stone recorded the lowest scores for diversity in this cluster, a result of the high quantities of white Luna marble contained within them.

Sites in the west and south-west of the Po Valley were located close to the navigable endpoints of the region's rivers, within the Langhe, Monferrato, and Colline del Po hills, or, in the case of Aosta, high in Alpine valleys. Urban centres such as Acqui Terme, Alba, Augusta Bagiennorum, Forum Fulvii, Libarna, and Tortona, were among those that could be reached from the Ligurian Coast for the least cost. However, the model suggests that only Acqui Terme and Libarna, the sites closest to the Ligurian Coast, could be reached for a lower cost from the Ligurian, rather than the Adriatic, ports. If cost was the sole factor in determining the distribution of goods, then one would expect to see items with a predominantly Adriatic and Eastern Mediterranean provenance make up the assemblages in this cluster (in

---

[30] Brecciaroli Taborelli 1987; Bruno 1997; 1998; Quiri 2014; Ratto 2014; Secchi 2017; Volonte 1997.

[31] While GTS found at sites in the west of the region likely entered the region via a trans-Alpine route, GTS at sites in the south-west of the Po Valley may have entered via the Alpine or crossed the Ligurian passes after a maritime journey.

[32] Framarin and Castoldi 2013; Gomez Serito 2007; Gomez Serito and Rulli 2014.

[33] The only exception to this was the stone assemblage at Forlì, although the Central Italian and Ligurian provenance of the 'bardiglio' marble found at the site is somewhat suspect.

a similar fashion to sites in the north-west). However, this was not the case. Western Mediterranean imports made up a significant proportion (often more than 40%) of the material assemblages of these sites. The high quantity of stone originating from Central Italy and Liguria appearing in the south-west of the Po Valley, despite costing significantly more to transport across the Apennines than decorative stone travelling from the Adriatic ports, formed a particularly striking pattern. Despite the significant portion of Western Mediterranean goods in their assemblages, the east-west axis of trade from the Adriatic Coast along the Po Valley remained important for sites located in the west and south-west of the region, especially for amphora-borne products. The Adriatic persisted as the single largest provenance of amphora-borne goods followed by the Eastern Mediterranean, even at some sites where the network model suggested transport was cheaper from the Ligurian Coast.

As highlighted above, the difference in transport costs between the opposing seaboards was at its lowest here, consistently around 159 kg wheat for one tonne of cargo. While still a significant difference, fluctuations in cost as a result of other elements (discussed in further detail below) may have reduced this further. Alternatively, factors other than cost may have played a role in the selection of goods in this part of the region (see below). In the case of stone transport, the logistics, particularly distance and time, may have been a more important consideration than cost. A longer journey over a greater distance (potentially including multiple transhipments) increased the risk of breakages or loss of the cargo and may have made the shorter and quicker trans-Apennine route more appealing to traders.[34] Regardless, Western Mediterranean imports were uniquely competitive in the west and south-west of the Po Valley in a way unmatched elsewhere in Northern Italy.

Inland Trade: Costs and Other Factors

The uniting of the network and material analyses demonstrated several things about inland trade within Northern Italy. Firstly, the arrangement of material clusters often corresponded closely to transport cost, suggesting this was the primary factor affecting distribution.[35] Secondly, the region's geography played

a key role in influencing transport costs (both positively and negatively), and the corresponding distribution of goods inland. Finally, the comparison of the MADINI clusters with the network model served to highlight some key differences between the model and material evidence, emphasising that factors beyond transport cost may have also influenced the distribution of goods.

Geography: Rivers and Mountains

The geography of Northern Italy played a crucial role in determining the cost of transport and distribution of material within the region. Geography and cost are intrinsically linked, with the region's topography and fluvial network having some of the greatest impact on transport costs.[36] Analysis of the MADINI dataset demonstrated the impact of the Po river system in the distribution of goods across Northern Italy during the Roman period. The importance of the river network to inland trade was established early, with the Po and its tributaries playing a prominent role in the distribution of Adriatic amphorae and other goods in the Late Republic. The river network's continuing importance into the Imperial period is reflected by the widespread investment in fluvial infrastructure across the region during the 1st century AD. The density of the water network, which through the inclusion of the para-littoral canals and Adriatic lagoon system made the rivers of the Veneto accessible from those in the Po Basin, meant that urban centres on the Po-Veneto Plain were never more than 15 km from a navigable river.

The density of the water network in Northern Italy and its role in shaping inland trade echoes the situation seen in ancient Gaul, in particular along the Rhône and its tributaries. Gaul received extensive praise in the ancient sources for the breadth of its navigable river network, with the Rhône providing the main inland trade corridor from the Mediterranean.[37] Both the Po and the Rhône contained a high volume of water and a fast current, and both possessed large and important tributaries that broadened their navigable range to areas beyond their main channels.[38] Water traffic on the river networks of the Po and the Rhône also saw extensive organisation in the form of *collegia nautarum*, attesting to the importance of transport along these waterways.[39]

---

[34] The proximity of the quarries at Luna to sites in the south-west of the Po Valley would also have made it easier for commissioners to correspond directly with the quarry, removing the need for middlemen.

[35] This is, however, not to say that other factors, such as time, had no bearing on how goods moved. Perishable foodstuffs such as fresh fruit, vegetables, and meat would have a short window for transport before spoiling, making time an important factor in their movement. However, these likely travelled over short distances. See, for example, the concentration of sites engaged in the production of perishables in Rome's *suburbium* (Marzano 2007: 108-09; Patterson, di Giuseppe, and

Witcher 2020: 179-82; Wilson 2009c).

[36] Combes, Mayer, and Thisse 2008: 5-10; Limão and Venebals 2001; McCormick 2001: 64; Rodrigue and Nottebottom 2020.

[37] Plin. *HN* 3.33; Str. 4.1.2-14.

[38] For the Rhône, the largest were the Isere and the Saône, the latter playing a crucial role in accessing the interior and the German *Limes* due to its proximity with the headwaters of the Meuse and Moselle (Campbell 2012: 265, 271; Franconi 2014: 64-66, Chapter 7; Leveau 1999). Both the Po and the Rhône also needed the excavation of canals to bypass the treacherous waters at their mouths.

[39] Broekaert 2013; Schmidts 2012.

At a technical level, the areas furthest 'inland' in Northern Italy, i.e., those equidistant from either coastline, were located in the middle of the Po Valley. Finds assemblages from these sites, despite their distance from both the Adriatic and Ligurian Coasts, continued to be dominated by Adriatic amphorae and decorative stone from the Eastern Mediterranean, with Western Mediterranean goods appearing in minimal quantities. The availability of the Po river network and the barrier of the Apennines to the Ligurian Coast created a scenario of imperfect competition between the Adriatic and Ligurian ports.[40] This allowed imports arriving from the Adriatic ports to penetrate much further upriver in significant quantities before transport costs affected their distribution. Rivers also allowed products manufactured within Northern Italy to widely circulate within the coastal plain and valley floor, facilitating both short and long-distance trade. Aside from the benefits of the river system itself, the level ground of the valley floor also served to reduce overland transport costs. Although the network model suggests there was a noticeable rise in the cost of transport to sites not located directly on rivers (e.g. Chieri or Novara), their material assemblages often did not significantly differ from those with fluvial connections. Sites located on the rivers acted as springboards for trade to sites in their immediate vicinity away from the watercourse. Relatively low transport costs also served to account for the uniformity of assemblages across much of the valley floor and coastal plain, often dominated by goods from a single provenance produced either in Northern Italy or the regions adjacent to it.

Although river transport played a crucial role in facilitating trade between coastal and inland regions, it was not without its limitations. In the north-west, west, and south-west of the region, sites contained material from Western Mediterranean markets that had entered Northern Italy overland via trans-Alpine and trans-Apennine passes. The material analysis confirmed the importance of overland, trans-mountain trade within Northern Italy, with the viability of trans-Alpine routes supported by the presence of significant quantities of GTS at sites within the Alpine passes and the west of the Po Valley. The importance of trans-mountain routes was most apparent in the south-west of the region, where the trans-Apennine passes between the Ligurian Coast and the Po Valley formed a particularly busy trade corridor.[41] The viability of trans-Apennine routes and the quantity of Western Mediterranean material in the

west and south-west is in part a reflection of the unique economic geography of the Po Valley. The upper river valley, the area furthest from the river's mouth on the Adriatic Coast, was only a short distance from another coastline. Although separated by a mountain range, the close proximity provided access to alternative markets via the Ligurian ports and a greater range of choice for consumers. The other river valley in the Roman world that shares these characteristics is that of the Ebro, in the Iberian Peninsula. The river's mouth flows into the Mediterranean but its headwaters are close to the Atlantic, separated from it by the Cantabrian Mountains (see Figure 60). Several ports are known on Spain's northern Cantabrian coast such as *Amanun Portus/Flaviobriga*, *Oiasso*, and *Portus Victoriae* (modern Castro-Urdiales, Irun, and Santander respectively) and the Atlantic formed an important trade route from the Mediterranean to Britain, Northern Gaul, and the Rhine frontier.[42] Sites in the upper Ebro Valley could have utilised these ports to complement trade connections along the river to the Iberian coast and Western Mediterranean, in a similar manner to sites in the west and south-west of the Po Valley.

Unfortunately, the upper Ebro has not seen a similar level of investigation to its lower and middle valley, making comparisons between the coastal and inland sites challenging. The absence of major producers along the Atlantic coast that might leave an archaeologically visible product to trace adds further difficulties in tracking the intensity of this trade, if it existed. Furthermore, many of the amphorae travelling along the Atlantic Façade, such as Dressel 20 and Haltern 70, were produced in Baetica, with the Ebro Valley via the east coast of the Iberian peninsula providing a more direct route to reach the upper valley than going around the western coast.[43] Indeed, sites in the lower and middle Ebro were dominated by ceramic materials produced in its immediate vicinity, principally amphorae and finewares originating from the Iberian coast and within the valley, echoing the situation within Northern Italy.[44] The presence of GTS from the workshop at Montans at sites in the upper Ebro and along the Cantabrian coast provides some tenuous evidence of overland

[40] Combes *et al.* 2008: 31-42; Sheppard 2006: 14-16.

[41] For more information of trans-Apennine trade between the Ligurian Coast and Po Valley see Bruno 1998; Cera 1993; and Melli 2004. The logistical challenges behind transporting goods across these mountains were considerable. All trans-mountain journeys were overland, and many more wagons, hauliers, and beasts of burden would have been needed to transport the equivalent amount of cargo that could be carried by a river vessel.

[42] Fernández Ochoa and Morillo 2010; Morillo, Fernández Ochoa, and Salido Domínguez 2016. It is uncertain whether ships travelling north along the Atlantic façade took a straight route across the Bay of Biscay from Cape Finistere to the Pointe du Raz or hugged the Cantabrian coast and Côte d'Argent. The former would have bypassed ports close to the headwaters of the Ebro.

[43] Carreras and Morais 2012: 429-34. The Dressel 20, however, seems to have achieved minimal penetration along the Ebro Valley from the coast (Beltran Llois 2000: 477-86).

[44] Beltran Llois 1982; 1983; 1987; Castillo 2014. The amphora forms Dressel 2-4, Dressel 28, Tarraconese 1, Tarraconese 2, and Pascal 1 saw widespread diffusion in the Ebro Valley. In terms of finewares, Terra Sigillata Hispanica was produced in the upper Ebro Valley at Tricio and saw widespread distribution both within the Ebro Valley and the wider Iberian Peninsula (Beltran Lloris 1990).

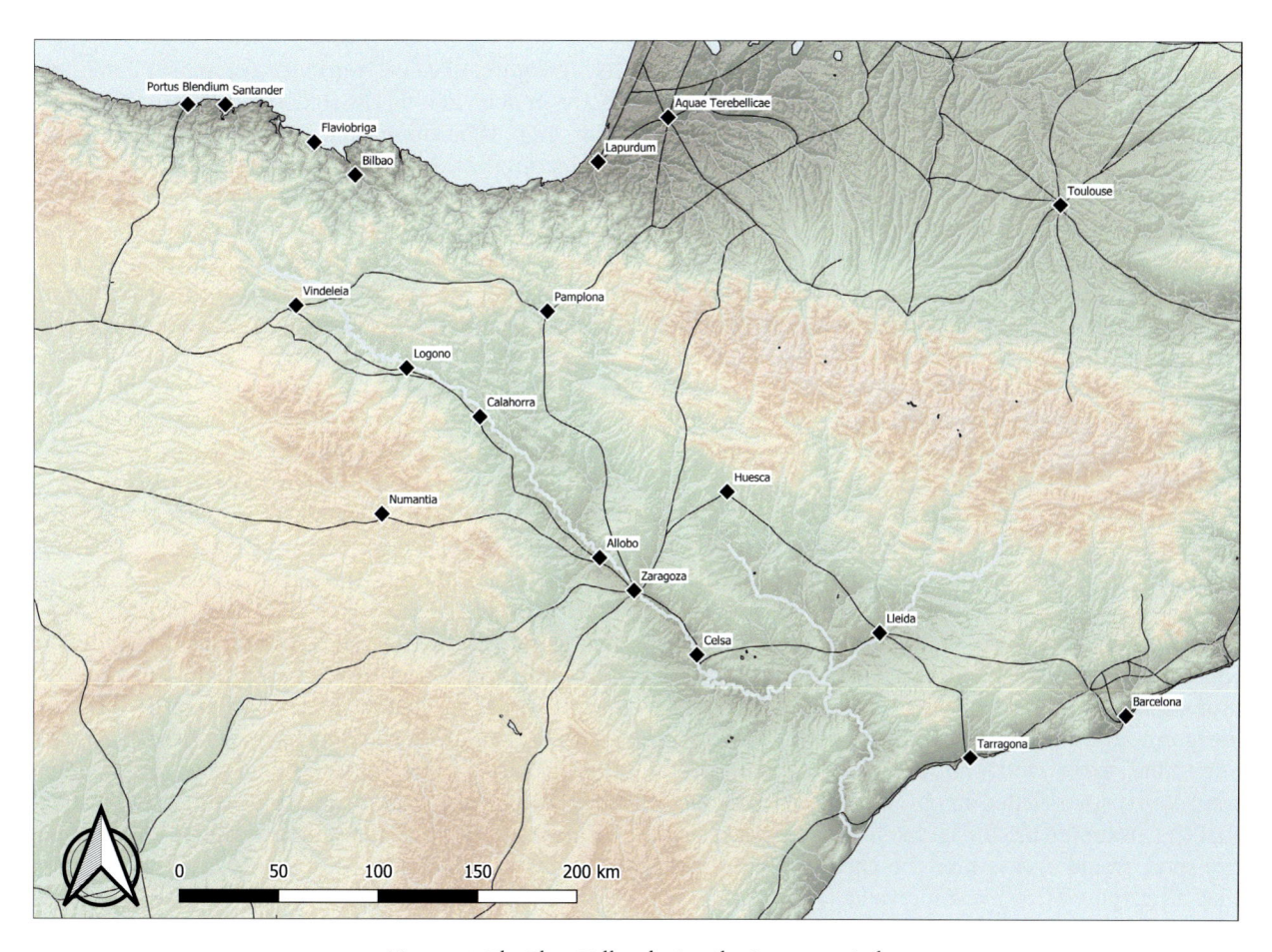

Figure 60. The Ebro Valley during the Roman period.

trade between the two, but without further study and quantification, it is impossible to state its significance.[45]

The importance of an alternate maritime market is readily apparent in the material assemblages of sites in the west and southwestern Po Valley. Despite having similar transport costs from the Adriatic Coast to sites in the north-west of the Po Valley, the availability of an alternate market provided a greater degree of choice to consumers in the south-west. This resulted in a greater proportion of their assemblages being comprised of imports from extra-regional markets in comparison to sites in the north-west. In comparison, without the proximity of a nearby seaboard via which to access maritime trade, the north-west of the Po Valley was forced to rely to a greater extent on goods already circulating in the middle and lower valley, other nearby inland areas, or goods produced or extracted within the upper valley itself.[46] In the north-west of the Po

Valley, assemblages are dominated by goods from a single provenance (Adriatic amphorae and NITS), complemented by the presence of other imported goods either originating from ports located on the coastline at the river mouth (Eastern Mediterranean amphorae), taken from other adjacent inland areas (CITS and GTS) or materials produced in the north-west itself (locally quarried stone). A similar situation to the northwestern Po Valley is seen, for example, in amphora data from the upper Tiber Valley. The majority of amphorae dating the Late Republic and Early Imperial period recovered from the villa at Colle Plinio in the upper Tiber seem to have been produced either locally or regionally, mainly within the middle Tiber.[47] Imports made up approximately 40% of the total amphorae, almost all of them from the Western Mediterranean.[48]

---

[45] Fernández Ochoa and Morillo 1994; Morillo, Fernández Ochoa, and Salido Domínguez 2016.
[46] The situation becomes more complex away from the Mediterranean. In the major river valleys of the northern provinces, the most common goods were often not produced in the immediate vicinity of the region (e.g. GTS and Iberian oil in the Rhine Valley). Military supply and the possibility of state involvement adds an additional layer beyond geography and cost to contend with. See Franconi's

(2014: 212-14) synthesis of amphora material from upper river valleys surrounding the Rhine basin, alongside Franconi *et al.* 2023.
[47] These consisted of locally produced amphorae (e.g. the forms Altotiberine 1-7) or amphorae produced elsewhere within the Tiber Valley such as the Spello type (Vidal 1999; 2009). See also Patterson and Lapadula 1997.
[48] Vidal 1999; 2009. The Iberian Peninsula formed the main provenance of these amphorae. The Western Mediterranean provenance of the amphorae recovered from the upper valley reinforces the importance of markets at the river mouth in determining the provenance of supplies within inland regions.

131

The majority of these imports arrived via Portus and travelled upriver to the upper Tiber.

Rivers and mountains played a key role in shaping the distribution of goods across Northern Italy and the Roman world. Rivers formed corridors of lower-cost transport, and, as the material evidence demonstrated, this allowed goods to achieve greater penetration in greater quantities inland. However, the role of overland trade, in particular trans-mountain trade, seems to have had more importance than previously given credit for, especially in areas furthest from the river mouth.

Theory vs. Reality: Complicating Costs

Although the network model used in the analysis generated a number of interesting patterns in terms of the cost of transport across the region, its simplicity and the incompleteness of the dataset means that there will inevitably be a level of inaccuracy in the picture it presents.[49] The cost surfaces generated by the model represent an idealised scenario, where a hypothetical one-tonne cargo with no previously accumulated transport costs travelled across the region. It assumed that the maximum price was charged for carriage, that transport would always take the cheapest route, and that all cargo was of the same value. When thinking about transport costs, especially through the lens of network models, it can be tempting to imagine that a hard cut-off point existed, beyond which it was prohibitively expensive to travel, and traders did not cross. Yet this absolutist approach does not reflect the reality of ancient commerce.[50] Merchants traded along rivers, as shown by L. Tettienus Vitalis on the Po, and references to the *collegia nautarum* operating on the Lambro, Micino, Po, and Tanaro, while hauliers worked along certain roads, running point-to-point services.[51] If demand existed beyond the line at which transport costs were more expensive than those from an alternate origin point, it seems unlikely that merchants would have passed up the opportunity of additional custom. More expensive does not necessarily equal unprofitable and high costs could be ignored if demand was great enough.[52]

As highlighted above, if transport cost was the dominant factor in determining the inland distribution of goods and cargo, then one would expect to see only goods originating from the Adriatic, Eastern Mediterranean, or within the region to appear within assemblages. However, the overlay of the material evidence shows a more complex situation.[53] Although transport cost was certainly an important factor in the distribution of material within inland regions, the above analysis suggests that in areas subject to the highest costs, several other factors may have come into play that determined the choices made by consumers. The main area where the results of the network model and material analysis do not match up is in the west and south-west of the Po Valley. Material evidence from this part of the region suggested strong trade links with the Ligurian ports, despite the network model indicating that transport was cheaper from the Adriatic Coast. In this section of the valley, where the difference in transport originating from the Adriatic and Ligurian Coasts was at its lowest, small changes to the price of transport or extra costs could have significantly altered the viability of one route over another. Transaction costs, such as negotiations and taxes, could significantly increase the price of cargo and transport costs would also have been accrued before goods reached ports in Northern Italy.[54] Transport may have been charged less than the maximum, pushing back the point at which transport from an alternative origin became cheaper or vice-versa.[55] Goods might also have been bought and sold multiple times by the time they reached their point of consumption, further complicating costs.[56] Finally, the value of the goods may have been able to absorb the transport costs, most notably in the case of decorative stone. Alternatively, demand for specific goods (such as CITS), only available from certain provenances, may have made the cost irrelevant. With this in mind, transport from the Ligurian Coast may have been more cost-efficient for a wider range of sites in the west and south-west of the Po Valley than the network model suggests.[57]

---

[49] The incompleteness of the archaeological record means that reconstructions of ancient transport networks will inevitably be fragmentary. Compromises also need to be made between the scale and detail of a model, ensuring it is sufficiently complex to answer research questions while remaining legible to both researchers and manageable for the tools used to analyse it.

[50] Broekhart 2011; Tchernia 2016, 89-95, 125-28. A single merchant was unlikely to have been responsible for a cargo for the entirety of its journey from source to final sale.

[51] Broekhart 2013; Gabucci and Mennella 2003. See also other *collegia* operating on rivers elsewhere in the Roman Empire (Broekhart 2011; Campbell 2012: 267-70; Schmidts 2012). For hauliers see, Laurence 1999: 134; Perry 2016: 507.

[52] Projecting artificial limitations onto data can obscure the true complexity of Roman trade. See Brughmans and Poblome 2017 and Van Oyen 2017 for a discussion of the difficulties of applying formal modelling to ancient datasets.

[53] Alternatively, the figures used for transport costs within the model may not accurately reflect prices from Northern Italy in the Roman period.

[54] Rodrigue and Nottebottom 2020. See Terpstra 2019: Chapter 4 and accompanying bibliography for a discussion of the various transaction costs that could be incurred in Roman trade, alongside Lo Cascio 2000; 2018.

[55] Contracts may also have included a fixed price for transport that did not reflect the true cost of carriage. For example, a 3rd century AD shipping contract from Fayum implies that the payment to transport the cargo was equivalent to 2% of its value (Adams 2018: 192; *P. Lond.* III. 948 p. 219 (AD 236) = M. Chr. 341).

[56] Rice 2012: 100-102; Tchernia 2016: 261; Terpstra 2013; 2019.

[57] It is also possible that 159 kg wheat, the near uniform difference in transport cost between the Adriatic and Ligurian ports for sites in the west and south-west of the valley, may simply be the margin of error present within the network model.

Amphora, Fineware, and Stone: Contrasting Distribution

Although the discussion above has demonstrated the key role that geography and transport costs played in the distribution of goods, other factors also influenced their circulation. Within the MADINI dataset amphorae, finewares, and decorative stone were imported to Northern Italy from a range of zones of production and extraction. Several zones contributed multiple types of imports, yet the main provenances were not uniform across material types. A zone of production that played a key role in supplying one type of material might be completely absent from the supply of another. For example, Eastern Mediterranean amphorae formed the second largest body of imported vessels in Northern Italy during the 1st and 2nd centuries AD. Eastern Mediterranean amphorae, arriving at Adriatic ports, had good inland penetration and formed a valuable supplement to Adriatic wine. In contrast, ETS is barely attested and is mainly confined to port sites and those in the coastal hinterland. ETS seems to have been unable to compete with NITS, the predominant fineware in the eastern Po Valley and coastal plain.[58]

There is a similar disparity between GTS and Gallic amphorae. Gaul was one of the main provenances for terra sigillata during the 1st and 2nd centuries AD, which was mostly found at sites in the north-west and south-west of the Po Valley. However, Gallic amphorae made up a relatively minor percentage of vessels recovered during this period and were only present in significant quantities in the southwestern valley. At the sites of Milan, Como, and Civitas Camunnorum in the north-west of the valley, Gallic amphorae were entirely absent, despite the comparatively high quantities of GTS within their assemblages. When it comes to Gallic imports, it seems probable that amphorae and finewares travelled by different routes. Gallic amphorae likely entered the region via the Ligurian Apennines, while the distribution of sites with GTS suggests an Alpine route (at least in the north-west). The appearance of GTS in greater quantities than Gallic amphorae may be due to the different ways in which they were consumed. GTS vessels were non-essential items that would be purchased intermittently, whereas wine, in this case, carried in Gallic amphorae, represented a more frequently purchased consumable. The profit margins on wine were likely to have been narrow, making it less able to absorb the cost of a trans-Alpine journey than finewares.[59] This situation was further compounded

by the low number of amphorae able to fit on a wagon or pack animal in comparison to the quantities of fineware.[60] Ultimately, a variety of factors influenced the provenance of goods within inland regions and some zones of production were better suited to provide certain material types over others.

Wider trends in demand seem to have influenced the distribution of material within Northern Italy, with choice playing a key role. This is readily apparent in the case of CITS, which continued to appear in large quantities even after the establishment and success of workshops in the North. Despite travelling further than locally produced NITS (and crossing a mountain range), the desirability of sigillata from Arezzo, Pisa, and other production centres in Central Italy ensured their continued presence in Northern Italy.[61] The extent of demand for Arretine and other Central Italic Terra Sigillata allowed Bologna and Modena, despite being located in the Po Valley, to be dominated by CITS rather than NITS. These two sites, located at the base of trans-Apennine passes that led to CITS production centres to the south, may have formed important distribution centres for CITS elsewhere in the eastern Po-Veneto Plain.[62] For amphora cargoes, the spread and overwhelming quantities of some vessel types, particularly the Dressel 6A and Dressel 6B which saw the majority of their distribution within Northern Italy, also attests to the force of directed trade, the specialisation of production, and the strength of connections between Northern Italy and its adjacent regions.[63]

The ways in which decorative stone was consumed led to it being sourced and distributed in very different ways to the aforementioned ceramic goods. Fine stone and marble were typically put to use as part of broader decorative schemes and some colours (such as yellow *giallo antico*) were only available from single sources, forcing consumers to rely on a select few quarries. The provenance of polychrome decorative stone was remarkably consistent across the study area, and it was only in the north-west of the Po Valley, in the areas furthest from either coast, that communities were forced to rely on locally quarried materials in place of imports. There was more leeway for sourcing white marble, resulting in the split seen between

[58] This is also reflective of a wider failure of Eastern Terra Sigillata to penetrate Western Mediterranean markets, particularly inland regions (Bes 2015; Lund 2003; Papaioannou 2011).

[59] Tchernia (2016: 81-82) highlights that trans-Apennine transport costs likely prevented Pliny the Younger from moving a surplus of cereals from his estate in Northern Italy to markets in Central Italy which were experiencing a shortfall in supply (Plin. *Ep.* 4.6).

[60] Picon (2002) estimates that approximately 1500 fineware vessels could be transported on the average wagon, in comparison to 12 amphorae. On pack animals, see Adams 2007: 77–81; 2012: 230; Middleton 1980: 188–89; Raepsaet 2009.

[61] The desirability of CITS is seen through the imitation of decoration associated with Arretine vessels on some NITS and the stamping of some Northern Italic vessels with *ARRET* to demonstrate comparable quality or pass-off their origin as Arretine. See Gabucci and Quiri 2008: 51-52; Mantovani 2013: 236-41; Mazzero Saracino 2000: 34-38.

[62] Kenrick 2003; Van Oyen 2015: 285-86; Zabehlicky-Scheffenegger 2003: 117.

[63] Auriemma 1997; Carre *et al.* 2007; Rousse 2007; Van Limbergen 2018.

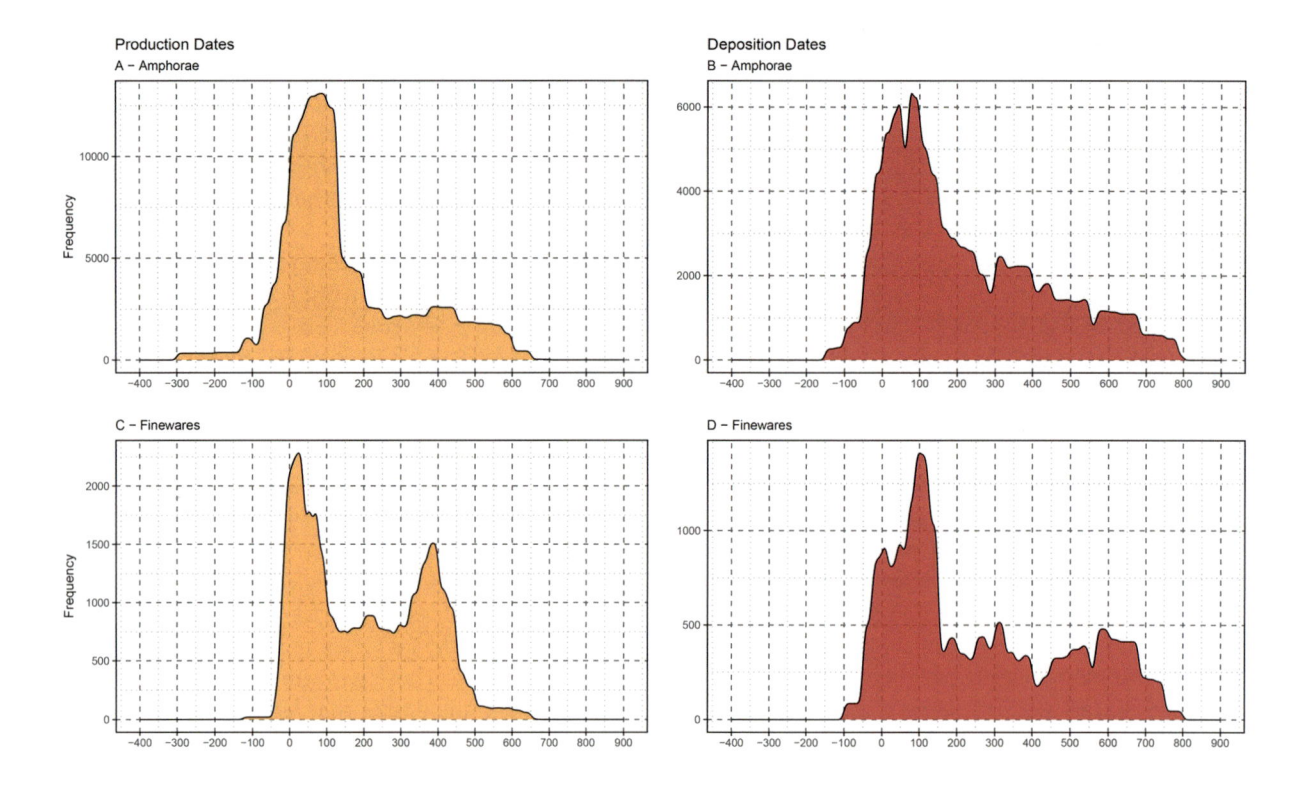

Figure 61. Comparison of Production and Deposition chronologies for overall amphora and fineware consumption in Northern Italy. Note that the Y axes are not constant.

Proconnesian and white Luna marble between the east and west of the region.[64]

The divide between the east and the west of the region was consistent across the Roman period. For the amphora data, across all three chronological periods, sites in the west of the Po Valley had a significantly higher portion of Western Mediterranean vessels in their assemblages than others in the region. For the fineware and stone data, assemblages from sites in the west of the region were also routinely distinct from their eastern counterparts. The continued division between the east and west of Northern Italy across the chronological periods serves to reinforce the important role geography played in the distribution of goods inland. Although the infrastructure projects of the Augustan period and 1st century AD would serve to decrease the point at which geography impacted on cost, this only served to reinforce existing patterns in distribution evident from the Republican period.[65]

Chronological Variation: Amphorae and Finewares

While there was extensive geographic variation in the distribution of material across Northern Italy, analysis of the MADINI dataset demonstrated that the quantities and provenances of ceramic material within Northern Italy also saw significant chronological change across the Roman period. The evolving use of decorative stone and marble, despite often being associated with structures with narrow construction dates, proved the most difficult to track over time. The majority of contexts for stone and marble revetment dated to the 1st century AD, coinciding with a period of expansion in the variety of lithotypes available to consumers.[66] While the residual nature of much of the marble recovered and the limited number of quantified publications made it difficult to track further changes in trade and consumption, the wide range of decorative stones used in Late Antique domestic contexts, like the *Domus* dei Bestie Ferite, *Domus* dei Putti Danzati, and *Domus* of Tito Macro at Aquileia, attests to the

---

[64] Russell 2018a: 139-40.
[65] The expansion of infrastructure across Northern Italy during this period represents a key example of indirect state involvement in economic development. It is uncertain who funded the massive expansion in port infrastructure across Northern Italy between the late 1st century BC and 1st century AD, but these large, civic projects likely had a level of state involvement. The major trans-Alpine extension of the via Postumia between Piacenza and Genoa (the via Iulia Augusta) in 13 BC and the trans-Alpine via Claudia Augusta in AD 46-47 were also both constructed by the state. Without these infrastructure projects, it seems unlikely that the intensity of trade

seen between the south-west of the Po Valley and the Ligurian ports during the 1st and 2nd centuries AD could have occurred, nor could the Po river network have facilitated the mass transport of goods and materials far inland. For comments on state construction of infrastructure and economic development, see Wilson 2009b: 81; Wilson and Bowman 2018: 5-8.
[66] For example, the temples at Aosta (Framarin and Castoldi 2013), the theatre at Augusta Bagiennorum (Gomez Serito and Rulli 2014), and the Capitolium at Verona (Bocconcello 2008).

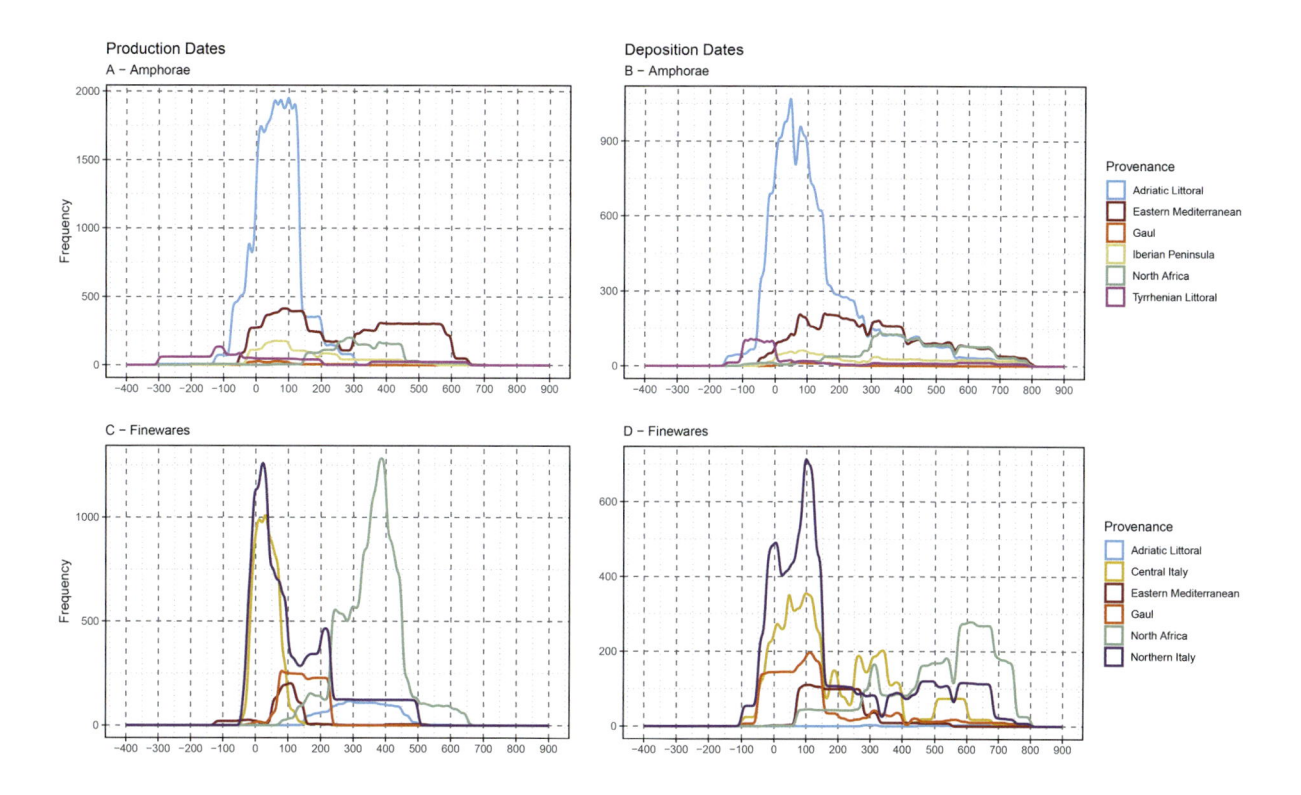

Figure 62. Comparison of Production and Deposition chronologies for the quantities of amphorae and finewares from each zone of production in Northern Italy. Note that the Y axes are not constant.

ongoing importance of marble in display during this later period.[67] In comparison, thanks to the production and deposition date ranges available for ceramic data, detailed long-term chronological trends could be tracked for amphora and fineware consumption across the Roman era.

Production and consumption of amphora-borne goods and finewares did not remain static, with the rise and fall of different zones of production, fluctuating demand, production output, and economic stability all affecting the quantity and type of material circulating. Serving as a proxy, the ceramic data gave important insight into the development and evolution of trade networks across Northern Italy during the Roman period.[68] Various zones of production contributed to the supply of amphora and finewares in Northern Italy, with the importance of different areas rising and falling over time. The importance of zones of production in supply would also differ between amphorae and finewares. The analysis proved the importance of comparing production and deposition chronologies when mapping and interpreting long-term trends in consumption. While there was overlap between both sets of dates in

the amphora and fineware data, significant variation also existed, especially from the 2nd century AD onwards. Although neither chronology is likely a true representation of ancient trade and consumption, comparison between the two allows the creation of a more complex picture with greater nuance than simply utilising one or the other.[69]

During the Late Republic, amphorae and finewares initially circulated in minimal numbers and there seems to have been a limited choice in the variety of extra-regional imports (see Figure 61). Both production and deposition chronologies agree that during the mid-1st century BC, there was a sudden sharp increase in the quantities of amphorae and finewares being consumed in Northern Italy. For amphorae, this reflects an expansion of wine production in the Adriatic and its subsequent consumption within Northern Italy, while for finewares, the introduction of terra sigillata, from workshops in both Arezzo and Northern Italy, rapidly dominated the tableware market.[70] The overwhelming majority of amphorae found in Northern Italy during this period originated from the Adriatic, with minimal quantities of North African and Tyrrhenian vessels also present (see Figure 62). For finewares, ETS was the first

---

[67] Gomez and Rulli 2012; Previato and Mareso 2015.
[68] Although all proxy data is subject to limitations, they remain an important tool in the research of the ancient world, providing they are used sensitively and with an eye to potential flaws (Greene 2005; Van Oyen and Pitts 2017; Wilson 2009a; 2014).

[69] Franconi et al. 2023: 27-28.
[70] Carre, Monsieur, and Pesavento Mattioli 2014; Cipriano 2009; Cipriano and Mazzocchin 2012; 2018; 2019; Ettlinger et al. 1990; Menchelli 2005; Morel 1981.

red-slipped tableware to circulate during this early period, with Black Gloss pottery forming the dominant fineware until the latter half of the 1st century BC.[71] After this point, the minimal quantities of ETS were eclipsed by the large quantities of CITS and NITS arriving in Northern Italy. Although transport costs in the Late Republic may have been more expensive than the totals suggested by the network model (given that most transport infrastructure would not be completed until the Imperial period), the lack of choice forced the bulk of consumers to rely on a limited range of products, regardless of their location within the region.[72]

The 1st century AD would see a peak in the quantities of both amphorae and finewares within Northern Italy. For amphorae, the number of vessels in circulation would peak during the late 1st century AD. In comparison fineware production chronologies suggest numbers peaked in the early 1st century AD, while deposition chronologies suggest it occurred at the end of the century. During the 1st century AD, as new zones of production, such as those in the Iberian Peninsula and Southern Gaul, were established and pan-Mediterranean connectivity improved, a greater range of amphora-borne goods became available in Northern Italy through strong extra-provincial trade links.[73] While the central and eastern Po Valley continued to rely on amphora-borne goods produced in the Adriatic or the eastern Po-Veneto Plain, sites on the north-west, west, and south-west of Northern Italy tapped into new zones of production. The cost of transport to these locations, on the peripheries of the Po Valley, was similar from both the Adriatic and Ligurian Coasts (as well as Gaul and Germany in the case of sites in the north-west). As a result, consumers made the most of the choice of products on offer, diversifying their amphora assemblages. Fineware assemblages were dominated by terra sigillata from Central and Northern Italy, with production chronologies suggesting GTS began to circulate during the mid-1st century AD. Sigillata produced within Northern Italy formed the dominant component of most fineware assemblages during this period with most traded over short distances. However, sites in the north-west and south-west of the Po Valley were able to diversify the provenance of their assemblages thanks to their proximity to other markets.

Following their respective peaks, quantities of both amphorae and finewares both rapidly declined in Northern Italy. For amphorae, this occurred throughout the early 2nd century AD, while for finewares, production chronologies suggest a late 1st century AD date and deposition chronologies record an early 2nd century AD decline. Although a variety of proxies have been used to suggest the 2nd century saw a mass contraction in Roman economic growth, the true picture is more complex.[74] While the rural economy of the Adriatic Littoral saw some level of decline during the 2nd century AD, a complete collapse of Adriatic wine and oil production, suggested by the amphora data, seems an unlikely cause of this marked decrease.[75] Instead, a switch from durable amphorae to perishable containers such as barrels for staple goods is a more likely reason for the sudden fall in the quantity of amphorae in circulation during this time.[76] In contrast, the drop in the finewares recorded in production chronologies perfectly coincides with the end of the main phase of terra sigillata manufacture in Central and Northern Italy. However, although the number of finewares fell throughout the 1st century AD, production chronologies suggest this was not as drastic as the fall seen in the amphora data, with the number of finewares stabilising during the following centuries. Continuing production of late CITS and NITS during the 2nd century AD, alongside the arrival of GTS and MATS, helped to sustain the overall quantity of finewares in circulation.[77]

By the 3rd century AD, the choice in amphorae and finewares presented to consumers saw a significant reduction as the visible market became dominated by a small number of production zones. For amphorae, Eastern Mediterranean and North African vessels made up the majority of imports, while for finewares, ARS from North Africa dominated assemblages. The shift in provenance for material assemblages in Late Antiquity reflects wider economic trends, as new zones of production came to prominence while others declined.[78] While the number of amphorae circulating in Northern Italy never recovered, with production chronologies suggesting a continuous decline over the following centuries, quantities of fineware would see a resurgence during the 4th century AD through the arrival of ARS. ARS dominated later assemblages to the

---

[71] Brecciaroli Taborelli 1988; Buora 2001; Mantovani 2013: 143; Mazzeo Saracino 2000: 38.

[72] The network model represents the transport network at its full extent seen during the 2nd century AD.

[73] Auriemma 2007; Auriemma, Degrassi, and Quiri 2015; Carre et al. 2007; Dobreva 2023a; 2023b; Gabucci 2017; Wilson 2012: 288; Wilson, Schorle and Rice 2012.

[74] See, for example, the use of shipwreck data and faunal remains by Scheidel (2009) to suggest an economic contraction during this period.

[75] Busana and Forin 2020; Van Limbergen 2011; 2018; 2019.

[76] Bevan 2014: 395-97; Marlière 2002: 190-92; Wilson 2009b: 71; 2014: 150. The decline of amphorae in contexts across the Roman world during the 2nd century AD, from shipwrecks to cities, is likely a result of these wider changes in containerisation. These are especially apparent in the Western Mediterranean, where there were extensive resources of timber suitable for barrel making.

[77] Jorio 2000; 2002; Mazzeo Saracino 2000; Zabehlicky-Scheffenegger 1990a; 1992.

[78] Auriemma, Dregrassi, and Quiri 2012; 2015; Lewit 2015; Tchernia 2016: 310-16. Of course, as to whether the archaeological evidence truly reflects the decline of production in some regions or a shift to perishable containers which do not survive is a matter of debate (McCormick 2012: 74-77).

exclusion of almost all other red-slipped tableware, leading to a second peak in finewares during the late 4th century AD. However, this peak would be short-lived, with quantities of ARS sharply declining throughout the 5th century AD. This was mirrored by a similar decline in North African amphorae in Northern Italy at this time.[79] According to production chronologies, Eastern Mediterranean amphorae would continue to circulate until the 7th century AD, disappearing at the same time as ARS. Both amphora and finewares data from Late Antiquity attest to the new importance of North Africa, a previously marginal contributor to regional supply, in the provisioning of Northern Italy.

In comparison to production chronologies, the deposition data for amphorae and finewares from the 2nd century AD onwards highlights the ongoing use and reuse of ceramic vessels long after their production had ceased. Amphorae from the Adriatic Littoral and finewares from Central and Northern Italy produced in the 1st century AD were recovered from deposits dating as late as the 7th and 8th centuries AD.[80] While the long occupation dates for many sites and constant renewal and disturbance of the urban fabric means that some of these finds are probably residual, the quantity of Imperial amphorae and finewares in Late Antique contexts implies a level of ongoing use and reuse did exist.[81] The possibility that a newly imported ARS bowl could share a table with a NITS plate produced a century earlier demonstrates that the lifespan of the Roman ceramic is more complex and long-lived than previously thought. In addition to the widespread recycling of whole amphorae in reclamation deposits during the 1st century BC and 1st century AD, the high quantities of Republican and Imperial amphorae recovered from Late Antique contexts across urban centres within Northern Italy, suggest some continuing level of reuse in these containers.[82]

Although production chronologies suggest the major imported products of the Roman era would cease to circulate in Northern Italy during the 7th century AD, the region remained integrated into wider Mediterranean markets throughout the Early Medieval period. Extensive epigraphic and literary evidence for mercantile activity survives from Aquileia, Grado, and Ravenna, where traders linked to state, private, and ecclesiastical interests continued to operate between Northern Italy and the Eastern Mediterranean.[83]

Goods such as foodstuffs, textiles, raw materials, and enslaved people, invisible in the archaeological record, were traded within the Adriatic during this later period, attesting to the endurance of trade networks established during the preceding centuries.[84] While it may be tempting to frame the material changes seen in the archaeological record as an ending and transition between social cultures, economic systems, and historical epochs, significant continuity remained.[85]

A Disconnected and Isolated Region?

Northern Italy's unique situation and geography have allowed it to function as a case study for exploring wider questions relating to inland trade in the Roman period. The analysis of the MADINI dataset demonstrated that despite their distance from the coast, inland sites in Northern Italy were connected to wider markets in the Eastern and Western Mediterranean. The analysis undertaken here further challenges the long-held assumption (one that has been increasingly confronted over recent years), that overland trade was prohibitively expensive except in very specific circumstances.[86] The limitations placed on transporting staple goods in significant quantities or heavy and difficult cargo to areas not on the coast or a navigable river, have been stated time and time again.[87] The only supposed exceptions to this rule were luxury items, the demand for which (and the high initial purchasing costs) often made transport costs irrelevant.[88] However, as demonstrated by the material analysis, staple goods were travelling inland via difficult overland routes in significant quantities, pointing to sustained trade rather than one-off purchases. The ability of overland transport to make significant contributions has been routinely underestimated and the results presented here serve to reinforce the tandem roles of fluvial and overland transport in supplying inland regions.

Past thinking on inland trade has theorised a steep drop off in imported goods as distance from the coast increased.[89] Although the material analyses do show a clear evolution in the provenance of imports as distance inland from the Adriatic Coast increased, the diversity of assemblages increased rather than declined, in the case of ceramic goods.[90] Although port sites had access to the widest variety of goods and materials through

[79] Cirelli 2014: 541-42; 2022: 469-70.
[80] Bruno and Bocchio 1991; Corrado 2003.
[81] Adams 2003; Cessford 2017: 167-70.
[82] For example, in Milan the majority of Republican and Imperial era amphorae during the MM3 excavations were recovered from Late Antique deposits (Bruno and Bocchio 1991). It is unknown what these amphorae may have been used for, or how many times they may have been used.
[83] Brown 1984: 91; Cosentino 2014: 155-59; 2020: 65-69; Gelichi 2015: 80-89.

[84] Hoffman 1968; Mancassola 2019: 246-47.
[85] Cirelli 2022: 479-81; Cosentino 2020: 72-74.
[86] Gabucci 2017; Laurence 2005: 138; Lewit 2015; Wilson 2012: 228.
[87] Bonifay 2004: 451–52; Hordon and Purcell 2000: Chapters 4 and 5; Previato 2023; Trapero Fernández, Carneiro, and Moriera 2023; Tchernia 2016: 90-93; Temin 2001: 179-81.
[88] Harris 2007: 535; Mattingly 2007: 220-21; Russell 2013: 112.
[89] Bonifay 2016; Fulford 2009: 253; Laven 2016: 3; Vaccaro and MacKinnon 2014.
[90] As highlighted above, the situation was more complex for stone assemblages. Those in the north-west of the Po Valley recorded the highest diversity, while those in the south-west of the valley recorded the lowest diversity.

their maritime connections, the analysis demonstrates that this diversity did not extend to sites in their immediate vicinity when it came to ceramic products. Instead, sites at the greatest cost distance from a seaport often possessed the greatest diversity in the type and provenance of their material. These urban centres drew from both Eastern and Western Mediterranean markets to supply their needs, with Eastern Mediterranean, Gallic, Iberian, and Tyrrhenian goods appearing in quantities not seen elsewhere within Northern Italy. Unfortunately, the quality of the material data prevents an accurate reading of how the overall quantities of material changed from site to site. It may be that the sites furthest inland, while exhibiting a high level of diversity in their imports, received them in overall lower quantities than those closer to the coast.[91] Short-distance trade in perishable containers such as skins may have made a more important contribution in these areas than long-distance amphora-borne goods.[92] Unfortunately, the uneven nature of excavation and the archaeological record makes it unlikely there will ever be a way to satisfactorily measure the quantities of goods circulating within inland regions.

The high diversity in the provenance and diversity of ceramic assemblages at sites in the upper river valley and their distinct composition present interesting questions regarding the cost and logistics of supplying inland regions. It is worth highlighting that goods which had either been produced within Northern Italy or in close proximity to it, those with minimal transport costs before entering the region, made up the majority of ceramic assemblages. However, it is clear that, at some point, these goods either lost their comparative advantage or struggled to fulfil the demand of areas at the end of the supply chain.[93] As a consequence, urban centres in the west and southwestern Po Valley increasingly relied on markets at a greater distance from Northern Italy in order to meet their demand. Whether sites at the greatest distance from the river mouth turned to wider markets out of choice or necessity is open to debate, but it is evident that a complex array of factors, of which transport cost was a significant element, governed the provenance of their material. In contrast to the ceramic evidence, the stone and marble analyses serve to largely confirm pre-existing notions on how heavy cargoes moved within inland regions.[94]

The high costs associated with moving such goods served to limit their distribution. Although some inland sites exhibited lower diversity, transport costs did not stop sites at the greatest distance from the coast from accessing decorative stone sourced from markets in the Eastern Mediterranean and North Africa. Where there was demand, obstacles could be overcome.

The role consumer choice played in the distribution of material in Northern Italy is difficult to answer. The analysis of the MADINI dataset was undertaken at a macro level to explore long-term chronological and geographic trends. The actual artefacts themselves, their specific finds contexts, and the ways in which they were used once they had arrived at their point of consumption were not engaged with. This book has primarily used the MADINI dataset in a representative way (i.e. where material objects are analysed as a substitution for something else, such as identity or cultural practices) to examine broader economic questions, using them as proxies for trade in the Roman period.[95] Representative studies of material culture have been criticised in recent years, particularly by those working along theories of materiality.[96] There can be no doubt that a greater level of complexity was present in the material distribution than explored by this book, and a more focused analysis of the artefacts themselves and the ways in which they were consumed could shed additional light on distribution patterns (for example that of CITS). Furthermore, Pitts rejects the dichotomy that 'distribution patterns must either be explained in terms of local (cultural) choice or the manifestation of bigger (economic) market systems'.[97] However, the analysis of the MADINI dataset suggests that, in some cases, where there is evidence of choice playing a potential role in the distribution of material, this was a by-product of wider economic circumstances. For example, the amphora data from the south-west of the Po Valley implies either traders struggled to meet demand at the end of Adriatic supply chains (forcing consumers to choose goods from other producers), or an evening out of transport costs from the Adriatic and Ligurian ports made a wider array of goods competitive (allowing consumers greater choice). Within this scenario, consumers may have been able to choose individual vessel types based on desirable qualities, but the overall provenances of the materials available were subject to wider economic trends. Price and availability seem to have been the main factors dictating the spread of many goods within the region.[98]

[91] Turin forms a case in point. There are known to be at least ten thousand (currently unpublished) amphora sherds from the Piazza Castello and Giardini Reali excavations in Turin, one of the most westerly sites in the region (Quiri 2009; 2015). Although this is a large number, to what extent is it exceptional, especially given that they were recovered from one of city's main refuse middens? Might comparable, or larger figures be recovered from similar contexts at sites closer to the coast?

[92] Panella and Tchernia 1994: 159-60; Tchernia 1986: 285-92.

[93] For discussions on comparative advantage across and within regions, see Heckscher and Ohlin 1991; Martin 2006: 164-66; Scheidel 2012; Temin 2012: 55-60.

[94] See the arguments outlined in Russell 2018a.

[95] Scheidel 2009; Verboven 2021; Wilson 2009a; 2009b; 2014.

[96] Materiality is defined as the 'cultural nexus between artefact and person' (Taylor 2009: 299). For criticisms of representative studies of ancient material, see Pitts 2017; Van Oyen and Pitts 2017.

[97] Pitts 2017: 64. See also Gardner 2007: 91-96.

[98] This is reflective of Temin's model of an 'instrumental' economy (Temin 2001: 171-72; 2013: 7-9). In this scenario, human actors, driven by array of motivations such as profit, are responsible for material redistribution. See also Poblome 2003; Poblome, Özden Gerçekerand,

Knowledge and exchange of information would have been central to the workings of inland markets.[99] Sites in the upper valley contained high quantities of material not seen in the middle and lower valley, some of which travelled upriver along the Po, and some overland across the Alps and the Apennines. Such large quantities of staple goods did not move speculatively. Traders operating out of the Ligurian ports would have needed an awareness of markets on the other side of the Apennines before moving cargoes across the mountains, with the same being true for trans-Alpine trade. The cost of the journey alone would not have been worth the risk of being unable to sell the cargo on the other side, or indeed the lack of a return cargo. Similar concerns would have affected fluvial traders operating between the lower and upper reaches of the Po water network. Networks of market information extended beyond the region itself and areas in its immediate vicinity to the wider Mediterranean. Cargoes of Eastern Mediterranean amphorae or North African finewares travelling up the Po to supply sites in the north-west of the Po Valley are unlikely to have arrived at ports in the Northern Adriatic, a so-called 'maritime dead-end,' by chance.[100] Knowing the locations of extra-regional markets and the type and style of goods in demand there was crucial for shippers and traders operating between zones of production and consumption. Sites in Northern Italy are unlikely to have dealt with the source regions of these goods themselves (the exception being for architectural stone, as the nature of commissioning large public projects meant that buyers would have needed to liaise directly with a quarry).[101] Merchants and other go-betweens would have instead relayed details between markets and suppliers. Rather than being isolated and disconnected, Northern Italy was integrated into wider Mediterranean networks of supply and information.

Conclusions

Despite the (sometimes considerable) costs involved, inland regions were not excluded from wider Mediterranean markets in the Roman world. The analysis of the MADINI dataset throughout this volume has allowed a greater depth of understanding of how cost, geography, and a host of other factors affected inland trade and exchange. Rivers were important transport arteries and there is no doubt that they allowed goods to travel further inland in greater quantities, and for a lower cost than would otherwise have been achievable via solely overland transport.

Prior concerns over the navigability of the Po river network and the role it played in trade during the Roman period are untenable in the face of the evidence synthesised. There was, however, a limit to the river network's effectiveness. Overland transport could, and did, play a crucial part in supplying inland regions, not just with luxury items but also staple goods. Although the price of transport played an important role in influencing the distribution of material within inland regions, a singular focus on cost risks obscuring the fact that fluvial and overland transport were not competing systems. As demonstrated by the analysis of the MADINI dataset, Northern Italy relied on both forms of transport to supply inland sites.

Statistical analysis, formal modelling, and simulation are becoming increasingly important tools applied to the study of the Roman economy, ones that have the potential to clarify ambiguities and test the validity of past hypotheses.[102] Using data that have previously only been studied in isolation or qualitatively, the aoristic analysis and hierarchical clustering of the MADINI dataset was able to conclusively challenge several prior orthodoxies regarding inland trade in Northern Italy and across the Roman world more generally. Clear zones of consumption could be seen across the region, but there was not a drop off in imports as distance from the coast increased. Most notably, within Northern Italy, sites furthest inland often possessed the greatest diversity in vessel forms, lithotypes, and provenance, an inversion of the expected pattern of coastal areas using their location and connectivity to access a wider variety of goods. Extensive chronological changes in both the quantity and types of goods circulating in Northern Italy were also documented. While data from the 3rd century BC to the 2nd century AD produced strong patterns in chronological and geographic distribution, the low quantity of published Late Antique data hampered the analysis. The gathering and publication of new quantified assemblages from the 3rd century AD to the 9th century AD represents an urgent challenge for future study.

The methodology brought to bear on the material datasets analysed within this volume proved highly successful in answering the questions it was designed to address, opening up further avenues of research. The methodology has the potential to be applied at a similar scale to other inland regions, offering a valuable comparison to the results from Northern Italy. How might the inland distribution of goods differ in a region lacking Northern Italy's unique geography? The methodology can also be applied to other types of material data. While the MADINI dataset utilised widely published amphora and fineware data (alongside more

---

and Loopmans 2017: 96, for a discussion of correlation between economic rational, market-functioning, and the distribution of Roman material.

[99] The importance of the 'information economy' in trade and exchange has been increasingly noted over the past decade. See Bang 2008: 288; Bes 2015: 82. Brughmans 2020; Brughmans and Poblome 2016a; 2016b; 2017; Temin 2013; Terpstra 2013; Van Oyen 2017.

[100] Harris 2011: 196-7; Scheidel 2014: 21.

[101] Russell 2011: 137-38; 2013: 211-14.

[102] Brughmans 2022; Brughmans and Pecci 2020; Brughmans and Wilson 2022.

limited stone and marble assemblages), how far might trends in distribution extend to other materials, such as glass and metal? MADINI remains a powerful tool, one that has the potential to form the basis of other types of analysis. Moving beyond networks towards simulation, such as that performed by Project MERCURY, the MADINI dataset has the potential to test more complex models and hypotheses relating to inland trade.[103] Finally, while this book has deliberately chosen to focus on broader trends within the data at a macro level, a closer analysis of the material itself may bring forth greater nuance as to why certain provenances, vessels, and lithotypes were favoured by consumers.

Far from being disconnected and isolated, Northern Italy has been shown to be connected to wider Mediterranean markets. From the Adriatic Coast to the Alpine valleys, communities were able to access goods from across the Roman world. The results presented in this book do not claim to be a perfect reflection of transport and trading practices in Roman and Late Antique Northern Italy. Patterns can, and will, change as new and greater quantities of data become available. However, it has demonstrated the power of large, quantified datasets in exploring questions related to trade and distribution. The picture that has emerged of inland trade in Northern Italy is far more complex than previous studies have accounted for, and continued analysis of the MADINI dataset will further refine understanding of the spatial and chronological dynamics of inland trade and economic networks within the region.

---

[103] Brughmans 2020. See Brughmans 2022 for a discussion on why simulation will form the next major avenue of research in the study of the Roman economy.

Appendix A:
Fluvial Navigation in Northern Italy

This appendix lays out the evidence for fluvial navigation on the rivers of Northern Italy during the Roman period.

Table 10. Rivers with evidence for navigation during the Roman period in Northern Italy.

River	Ancient Name	Ports	Wrecks	Textual Reference	Epigraphic Reference
Po	*Padus/Eridanus*	Bucci 2015	Beltrame and Costa 2016; Parker 1992 (n. 864)	Ambro. *Hexam.* 2.3.12; App. *B. Civ.* 2.3.17; Cassiod. *Var.* 2.31; Valg. *Frag.* 167 (3 Bl., C.); 168 (4 Bl., C.); Liv. 21.57; Lucian, *Electr*; Plb. 3.57; Plin. *N. H.* 3.20; 16.70; Sid. Apoll. *Epist.* 1.5.4	CIL V.2315; CIL XI.0135
Adda	*Addua*			Plin. *N. H.* 3.20; Sid. Apoll. *Epist.* 1.5.4	
Oglio	*Ollius*	Cavalieri Manasse 1990		Plin. *N. H.* 3.20	
Tanaro	*Tanarus*			Plin. *N. H.* 3.20	CIL V.7679
Ticino	*Ticinus*			Plin. *N. H.* 3.20; Sid. Apoll. *Epist.* 1.5.4	AE 1977, 327
Mincio	*Mincius*			Catull. 4; Plin. *N. H.* 3.20	ILS 7265
Secchia	*Gabellus*			Plin. *N. H.* 3.20	
Dora Baltea	*Duria Bautica*	Finocchi 1980; Brecciaroli Taborelli 2007		Plin. *N. H.* 3.20	
Panaro	*Scultenna*			Plin. *N. H.* 3.20	
Sesia	*Sessites*	Spagnolo Garzoli et al. 2007		Plin. *N. H.* 3.20	
Lambro	*Lambrus*	Caporusso 1990; Cera 1995		Sid. Apoll. *Epist.* 1.5.4	
Dora Riparia	*Duria*			Plin. *N. H.* 3.20	
Trebbia	*Trebia*			Plin. *N. H.* 3.20	
Scrivia	*Iria*	Crosetto 2013a; 2013b; Gamberini *et al.* 2011			
Adige	*Athesis*		Tiboni 2009	Sid. Apoll. *Epist.* 1.5.4	CIL V.2722
Brenta	*Medoacus Maior*	Balista and Ruta Serafini 1993	Beltrame 2001	Plin. *N. H.* 3.20	
Bacchiglione	*Medoacus Minor*		Previato and Zara 2014	Str. 5.1.7	
Sile	*Silis*	Cipriano and Sandri 2001; Tirelli 1987		Str.5.1.7	
Stella	*Anaxum*		Castro and Capulli 2016	Plin. *N. H.* 3.22	
Lemene	*Romatinum*	Rousse 2013		Plin. *N. H.* 3.22; Str. 5.1.7-8	

River	Ancient Name	Ports	Wrecks	Textual Reference	Epigraphic Reference
Natisone	*Natiso*	Bertacchi 1980; 1990	Bertacchi 1990; Beltrame and Gaddi 2013	Plin. *N. H.* 3.22	
Taro	*Tarus*			Plin. *N. H.* 3.20	
Enza	*Incia*			Plin. *N. H.* 3.20	
Orco	*Orgus*			Plin. *N. H.* 3.20	
Stura di Demonte	*Stura*			Plin. *N. H.* 3.20	
Livenza/Piave	*Liquentia*	Cipriano and Sandri 2001; Tirelli 1987		Plin. *N. H.* 3.22	
Reno	*Rhenus*			Plin. *N. H.* 3.20	
Tagliamento	*Tiliaventum Maior*			Plin. *N. H.* 3.22	

Appendix B:
Values Used in the Hierarchical Clustering

This appendix contains a breakdown of the values used to generate the hierarchical clusters of sites seen in Chapters 4, 5, and 6. The percentage of each zone of production or extraction in a site's assemblage, separated by period, is provided for each material type within the MADINI dataset. The N numbers of the values used to calculate the percentages are also given.

Amphorae

Table 11. Percentage of amphora provenance by site during the Late Republic.

Site	N. Sherds	Adriatic Littoral (%)	North Africa (%)	Tyrrhenian Littoral (%)
Bedriacum	98	91.83	0	9.16
Cremona	346	99.13	0	0.86
Forlì	67	94.02	0	5.97
Ivrea	157	59.23	0.63	40.12
Laus Pompeia	50	100	0	0
Milan	678	83.33	0	16.66
Padua	223	99.1	0	0.89
Trento	162	100	0	0
Vicenza	32	93.75	0	6.25

Table 12. Percentage of amphora provenance by site during the Imperial period.

Site	N. Sherds	Adriatic Littoral (%)	Eastern Mediterranean (%)	Gaul (%)	Iberian Peninsula (%)	North Africa (%)	Tyrrhenian Littoral (%)
Acqui Terme	120	22.5	2.5	29.16	33.33	0	12.5
Alba	796	51.88	22.11	4.89	17.08	1.5	2.51
Augusta Bagiennorum	221	44.34	10.85	10.85	21.26	3.16	9.5
Bedriacum	113	74.33	12.38	0	7.96	4.42	0.88
Brescia	376	62.23	24.2	0	2.92	10.63	0
Civitas Camunnorum	137	62.04	33.57	0	2.91	0	1.45
Clastidium	135	94.07	3.7	0	1.48	0.74	0
Como	90	73.33	17.77	0	6.66	2.22	0

Site	N. Sherds	Adriatic Littoral (%)	Eastern Mediterranean (%)	Gaul (%)	Iberian Peninsula (%)	North Africa (%)	Tyrrhenian Littoral (%)
Cremona	370	76.48	6.75	0	8.64	0	8.1
Este	102	88.23	2.94	0	3.92	0	4.9
Forlì	132	80.3	11.36	0	3.03	5.3	0
Industria	72	63.88	31.94	0	4.16	0	0
Ivrea	50	58	8	0	14	0	20
Laus Pompeia	86	66.27	12.79	2.32	11.62	0	6.97
Libarna	69	49.27	1.44	7.24	39.13	0	2.89
Milan	571	67.95	15.58	0	4.55	10.15	1.75
Modena	635	81.57	7.87	0	10.07	0	0.47
Novara	845	72.54	20.47	0.11	6.86	0	0
Oderzo	1014	78.1	19.82	0.29	1.38	0	0.39
Padua	1431	86.09	10.83	0	2.16	0	0.9
Trento	1351	81.71	10.06	0	1.48	6.73	0
Vercelli	74	60.81	12.16	0	21.62	2.7	2.7
Verona	999	85.58	6.6	0	3.5	4.3	0
Vicenza	689	88.67	7.4	0	2.17	0.14	1.59

Table 13. Percentage of amphora provenance by site during Late Antiquity.

Site	N. Sherds	Eastern Mediterranean (%)	Iberian Peninsula (%)	North Africa (%)	Tyrrhenian Littoral (%)
Brescia	693	48.62	2.59	42.13	6.63
Clastidium	10	28.57	28.57	42.85	0
Forlì	10	30	0	70	0
Milan	609	58.12	16.58	19.86	5.41
Trento	339	100	0	0	0
Verona	494	49.19	5.26	42.10	3.44

Red-Slipped Finewares

Table 14. Percentage of red-slipped fineware provenance by site during the Imperial period. * Denotes site for which the number of sherds was not given in the publication but the percentage breakdown of each zone of production was provided.

Site	N. Sherds	Adriatic Littoral (%)	Central Italy (%)	Eastern Mediterranean (%)	Gaul (%)	North Africa (%)	Northern Italy (%)
Acqui Terme	42	0	35.71	0	38.09	2.38	23.8
Adria	1500	0	11.6	0	0	0	88.4
Alba	187	0	32.08	0	17.11	1.6	49.19
Augusta Bagiennorum	30	0	37.93	0	37.93	6.89	17.24
Bedriacum	74	0	2.70	0	4.05	0	93.24
Bologna	34	0	67.64	0	0	0	32.35
Brescia	354	0	16.1	0.56	3.1	0	80.22
Chieri	322	0	29.5	0	40.68	0	29.81
Civitas Cammunorum	56	0	14.28	0	26.78	0	58.92
Como	231	0	23.37	0	26.83	0	49.78
Cremona	340	0	3.23	0	1.47	0	95.29
Forlì	85	3.4	27.27	0	4.54	1.13	63.63
Ivrea	133	0	33.83	0	37.59	0	28.57
Julia Concordia	252	0	26.98	3.17	2.38	0	67.46
Milan	619	0	21	0.16	15.67	0.8	62.35
Modena	141	0	57.44	0	0	0	42.55
Novara	*	0	24	0	5	0	71
Padua	139	0	12.23	22.3	3.59	0	61.87
Tortona	85	0	28.23	0	8.23	0	63.52
Trento	268	0	19.77	0	0	0	80.22
Turin	*	0	10.16	0	41.19	0.06	48.57
Vercelli	*	0	21	0	1	0	58
Verona	1185	0.33	0.5	0.08	0	0	99.07

Table 15. Percentage of red-slipped fineware provenance by site during Late Antiquity.

Site	N. Sherds	Adriatic Littoral (%)	Eastern Mediterranean (%)	North Africa (%)	Northern Italy (%)
Alba	45	0	0	15.55	84.44
Brescia	530	0.56	0	99.43	0
Chieri	80	0	0	0	100
Forlì	50	78	0	20	2
Milan	172	0	0	100	0
Padua	18	0	27.77	72.22	0
Trento	11	0	0	100	0
Verona	593	1.85	0	98.14	0

Decorative Stone

Table 16. Percentage of decorative stone provenance by site during the Roman period.

Site	N. Fragments	Asia Minor	Central Italy and Liguria	Egypt and North Africa	Gaul	Greece and the Aegean	Northern Italy
Altinum	353	47.02	2.54	3.68	0.28	37.96	8.49
Aosta	115	10.43	52.17	0.86	0	13.91	22.6
Aquileia	1122	40.55	9.09	8.02	1.15	40.64	0.53
Augusta Bagiennorum	295	28.81	48.47	13.89	0	5.42	3.38
Brescia	374	44.65	5.34	13.9	0	36.09	0
Como	35	20	2.85	17.14	0	22.85	37.14
Forlì	89	6.74	49.43	4.49	0	39.32	0
Forum Fulvii	43	9.3	65.11	6.97	0	6.97	11.62
Milan	257	24.9	3.89	20.62	1.16	26.45	22.95
Ravenna	14	21.42	7.14	21.42	0	42.85	7.14
Tortona	47	46.8	36.17	0	0	6.38	10.63
Vercelli	143	39.16	0	0.69	0	12.58	47.55
Verona	10,260	46.41	7.49	8.75	0	31.8	5.53

Bibliography

Classical Authors in Translation

Anderson, W.B. 1936. *Sidonius. Poems. Letters: Books 1-2.* Cambridge (MA): Loeb Classical Library.

Bjornlie, M.S. 2019. *Cassiodorus. The Variae: the complete translation.* Oakland: University of California Press.

Cary, E. and Foster, H.B. 1924. *Dio Cassius. Roman History. Vol. 7. Books 56-60.* Cambridge (MA): Loeb Classical Library.

Cook, G.M. 1942. *Ennodius. Vita Epiphani.* Washington (DC): Catholic University of America Press.

Dewing, H.B. 1924. *Procopius. History of the Wars, Volume IV: Books 6.16-7.35. (Gothic War).* Cambridge (MA): Loeb Classical Library.

Duff, J.D. 1928. *Lucan. The Civil War (Pharsalia).* Cambridge (MA): Loeb Classical Library.

Fairclough, H.R. 1999. *Virgil. Eclogues. Georgics. Aeneid: Books 1-6.* Cambridge (MA): Loeb Classical Library.

Foster, B.O. 1929. *Livy. History of Rome. Vol. V. Books 21-22.* Cambridge (MA): Loeb Classical Library.

Harmon, A.M. 1913. *Lucian. Phalaris. Hippias or The Bath. Dionysus. Heracles. Amber or The Swans. The Fly. Nigrinus. Demonax. The Hall. My Native Land. Octogenarians. A True Story. Slander. The Consonants at Law. The Carousal (Symposium) or The Lapiths.* Cambridge (MA): Loeb Classical Library.

Hollis, A.S. 2007. *Fragments of Roman Poetry c.60 BC–AD 20.* Oxford: Oxford University Press.

Hooper, W.D. and Ash, H.B. 1934. *Cato, Varro. On Agriculture.* Cambridge (MA): Loeb Classical Library.

Jones, H.L. 1923. *Strabo. Geography. Vol. 2. Books 3-5.* Cambridge (MA): Loeb Classical Library.

Jones, W.H.S. 1935. *Pausanias. Description of Greece. Vol. 4. Books 8.22-10 (Arcadia, Boeotia, Phocis and Ozolian Locri).* Cambridge (MA): Loeb Classical Library.

Magie, D. 1932. *Historia Augusta. Vol. 3. The Two Valerians. The Two Gallieni. The Thirty Pretenders. The Deified Claudius. The Deified Aurelian. Tacitus. Probus. Firmus, Saturninus, Proculus and Bonosus. Carus, Carinus and Numerian.* Cambridge (MA): Loeb Classical Library.

Moore, C.H., and J. Jackson. 1925. *Tacitus. The Histories. Vol. 1. Books I-III.* Cambridge (MA): Loeb Classical Library.

Paton, W.R. 2010. *Polybius. The Histories. Vol. 1. Books 1-2.* Cambridge (MA): Loeb Classical Library.

Rackham, H. 1942. *Pliny. Natural History. Vol. 2. Books 3-7.* Cambridge (MA): Loeb Classical Library.

Rolfe, J. 1914. *Suetonius. Lives of the Caesars. Vol. 1. Julius. Augustus. Tiberius. Gaius. Caligula.* Cambridge (MA): Loeb Classical Library.

Romer, F.E. 1998. *Pomponius Mela's Description of the World.* Ann Arbour: University of Michigan Press.

Savage, J. 1961. *Saint Ambrose. Hexameron, Paradise, and Cain and Abel.* (The Fathers of the Church 42). New York: CUA Press.

Whittaker, C.R. 1970. *Herodian. History of the Empire, Volume II: Books 5-8.* Cambridge (MA): Loeb Classical Library.

Modern Authors

Abdelhamid, S. 2013. Against the throw away mentality: The reuse of amphoras in ancient maritime transport, in H.P. Hahn and H. Weiss (eds) *Mobility, Meaning and the Transformations of Things*: 91-106. Oxford: Oxbow.

Acari, L. 1996. Un deposito di anfore in via Massarotti a Cremona, in G.M. Facchini, L. Passi Pitcher and M. Volonte (eds) *Cremona e Bedriacum in età romana 1. Vent'anni di tesi universitarie*: 185-203. Milan: ET Edizioni.

Adams, C. 2001. Who bore the burden? The organization of stone transport in Roman Egypt, in D. Mattingly and J. Salmon (eds) *Economies Beyond Agriculture in the Classical World*: 171-193. London: Routledge.

Adams, C. 2007. *Land transport in Roman Egypt a study of economics and administration in a Roman province.* Oxford: Oxford University Press.

Adams, C. 2012. Transport, in W. Scheidel (ed.) *The Cambridge Companion to the Roman Economy*: 218-240. Cambridge: Cambridge University Press.

Adams, C. 2018. Nile River Transport under the Romans, in A.I. Wilson and A.K. Bowman (eds) *Trade, Commerce, and the State in the Roman World*: 175-208. Oxford: Oxford University Press.

Adams, W.H. 2003. Dating Historical Sites: The Importance of Understanding Time Lag in the Acquisition, Curation, Use, and Disposal of Artifacts. *Historical Archaeology* 37: 38-64.

Agostoni, A., Barello, F., Borghi, A. and Compagnoni, R. 2017. The White Marble of the Arch of Augustus (Susa, North-Western Italy): Mineralogical and Petrographic Analysis for the Definition of its Origin: The white marble of the Arch of Augustus (Susa, Italy). *Archaeometry* 59: 395-416.

Airoldi, F., Bona, A., Cattaneo, C., Cesana, D., Fortunati, M., Fossati, A., Grassi, E., Mattia, M., Perassi, C., Sacchi, F., Sannazaro, M. and Uboldi, M. 2016. Ponte Lambro tra età romana and tardoantica: the part rustica of the villa in località Schieppo. *Rivista archeologia dell'antica provincia e diocesi di Como* 198: 172-250.

Airoldi, F., Cipriano, S. and Montevecchi, G. 2018. Suppelletile da mensa, in C. Guarnieri and G. Montevecchi (eds) *Il Genio delle Acque. Scavi nelle piazze di Ravenna*: 107-120. Ravenna: Longo Angelo.

Aldini, T. 1978. Anfore Foropopiliensi. *Archeologia Classica* 30: 236-245.

Aldini, T. 1989. Nuovi dati sulle anfore foropopiliensi. *Studi Romagnoli* 40: 383-418.

Aldini, T. 1995. Elementi per una più corretta classificazzione delle anfore foropopiliensi. *Atti e Memorie della Deputazione di Storia Patria per le province di Romagna* 46: 11-18.

Aldini, T. 1999. Anfore foropopiliensi in Italia, Forlimpopoli. *Documenti e studi* 10: 23-56.

Aldini, T. 2000. Archeologia Bertinorense Forlimpopoli. *Documenti e studi* 11: 23-66.

Allen, M. and Lodwick, L. 2017. Agricultural strategies in Roman Britain, in M. Allen, T. Brindle, A.T. Smith, L. Lodwick and M. Fulford (eds) *New Visions of the Countryside of Roman Britain: The Rural Economy of Roman Britain*: 142-177. London: Society for the Promotion of Roman Studies.

Allini, A., Asta, A., Medas, S. and Miari, M. 2014. Due piroghe rinvenute nel fiume Po presso Monticelli d' Ongina (PC) e Spinadesco (CR), in A. Asta, G. Caniato, G. D. and S. Medas (eds) *Archeologia Storia Etnologia Navale. Atti del II convegno nazionale Cesenatico - Museo della Marineria (13-14 aprile 2012)*: 117-124. Padua: Libreriauniversitaria.it.

Allison, P.M. 2004. *Pompeiian Households: An Analysis of Material Culture*. Los Angeles: Cotsen Institute of Archaeology Press.

Amadori, C. 1996. La terra sigillata proveniente dai "vecchi scavi" di Cremona, in G.M. Facchini and L. Passi Pitcher (eds) *Cremona e Bedriacum in età romana. I. Vent'anni di tesi universitarie*: 99-124. Milan: ET Edizioni.

Andreu Pintado, J., Royo Plumed, H., Lapuente, P. and Brilli, M. 2015. Imported marbles found in three Roman cities of the territory of "Cinco Villas" (Zaragoza), north of Hispania Citerior, in P. Pensabene and E. Gasparini (eds) *ASMOSIA X. Proceedings of the Tenth International Conference of ASMOSIA Association for the Study of Marble and Other Stones in Antiquity Rome, 21-26 May 2012*: 13-22. Rome: L'Erma di Bretschneider.

Angelelli, C. 2014. Materiali lapidei da rivestimento dalle campagne di scavo 2009-2011, in F. Rossi (ed.) *Un luogo per gli dei: l'area del Capitolium a Brescia*: 491-497. Florence: All'Insegna del Giglio.

Antico Gallina, M. 2011. Strutture ad anfore: un sistema di bonifica dei suoli. Qualche parallelo dalle Provinciae Hispanicae. *Archivo Español de Arqueología* 84: 179-205.

Antico Gallina, M. 2014. Dalla Topografia al Diritto. Sistemi ad anfore e mutamenti verticali del suolo. *Atlante tematico di topografia antica* 24: 233-246.

Antonelli, F. 2002. I marmi della Gallia e dell'Iberia importati a Roma, in M. De Nuccio and L. Ungaro (eds) *I marmi colorati della Roma imperiale*: 267-276. Padua: Marsilio Editori.

Antonelli, F. and Lazzarini, L. 2016. An updated petrographic and isotopic reference database for white marbles used in antiquity. *Rendiconti Lincei Scienze Fisiche e Naturali* 26: 399-413.

Arioli, L. 2019. Roman pottery and trade networks. Some notes on Italian sigillata in the lower Danube and in the north-western Black Sea, in P. Schirripa (ed.) *Greci e Romani sulle sponde del Mar Nero*: 129-168. Milan: Ledizioni.

Arnaud, P. 2007. Diocletian's Prices Edict: the prices of seaborne transport and the average duration of maritime travel. *Journal of Roman Archaeology* 20: 321-335.

Arnoldus, A., Bowes, K., Grey, C., Ghisleni, M. and Rattighieri, E. 2021. Podere Terrato, in K. Bowes (ed.) *The Roman Peasant Project 2009-2014: Excavating the Roman Rural Poor*: 237-264. Philadelphia: University of Pennsylvania Press.

Arnoldus, A., Bowes, K., Grey, C., Ghisleni, M. and Rattighieri, E. 2021. Poggio dell'Amore, in K. Bowes (ed.) *The Roman Peasant Project 2009-2014: Excavating the Roman Rural Poor*: 185-206. Philadelphia: University of Pennsylvania Press.

Artru, F. 2016. *Sur les routes romaines des Alpes Cottiennes, entre le Mont-Cenis et col de Larche*. Besançon: Presses universitaires de Franche-Comté.

Assirelli, F. 2023. Economy and trade in the mid-Imperial Adriatic between Classe and the Mediterranean, in I. Borzić, E. Cirelli, K. Jelinčić Vučković, A. Konestra and I. Ožanić Roguljić (eds) *TRADE: Transformations of Adriatic Europe (2nd–9th Centuries AD) Proceedings of the conference in Zadar, 11th–13th February 2016*: 365-369. Oxford: Archaeopress.

Attanasio, D., Brilli, M. and Bruno, M. 2008. The properties and identification of marble from Proconnesos (Marmara Island, Turkey): a new database including isotopic, EPR and petrographic data. *Archaeometry* 50: 747-774.

Attanasio, D., Yavuz, A.B., Bruno, M., J.J., H., Tykot, R.H. and Van Den Hoek, A. 2012. On the Ephesian Origin of *Greco Scritto* Marble, in A.G. Garcia-M, P.L. Mercadal and L. Rodà De Llanza (eds) *Interdisciplinary Studies on Ancient Stone. Proceedings of the IX Association for the Study of Marble sand Other Stones in Antiquity (ASMOSIA) Conference (Tarragona 2009)*: 245-254. Tarragona: ICAC.

Augenti, A. 2011. Classe: Archeologia di una città scomparsa, in A. Augenti (ed.) *Classe. Indagini sul potenziale archeologico di una città scomparsa*: 15-44. Bologna: Ante Quem.

Augenti, A. and Cirelli, E. 2010. Classe: un osservatorio privilegiato per il commercio della Tarda Antichità, in S. Menchelli, S. Santoro, M. Pasquinucci and

G. Guiducci (eds) *LRCW3. Late Roman Coarse Wares Cooking Wares and Amphorae in the Mediterranean. Archaeology and Archaeometry. Comparison between Western and Eastern Mediterranean* (BAR International Series 2185): 605-615. Oxford: Archaeopress.

Augenti, A. and Cirelli, E. 2012. From Suburb to Port: The Rise (and Fall) of Classe as a Centre of Trade and Redistribution, in S. Keay (ed.) *Rome, Portus, and the Mediterranean*: 205-221. Rome and London: The British School at Rome.

Auriemma, R. 1997. Le anfore africane del relitto di Grado. Contributo allo studio delle prime produzioni tunisine e del commercio di salse e di conserve di pesce. *Archeologia Subacquea. Studi, ricerche e documenti* 2: 129-55.

Auriemma, R. 2000. Le anfore del relitto di Grado e il loro contenuto. *Mélanges de l'Ecole française de Rome. Antiquité* 112: 27-51.

Auriemma, R. 2007. Anfore. Produzioni orientali, in C. Morselli (ed.) *Trieste antica. Lo scavo di Crosada*: 136-154. Trieste: Edizioni Quasar.

Auriemma, R. and Degrassi, V. 2017. Anfore del Mediterraneo Orientale, in P. Maggi, F. Maselli Scotti, S. Pesavento Mattioli and E. Zulini (eds) *Materiali per Aquileia: lo scavo di Canale Anfora (2004-2005)*. Trieste: Edizioni Quasar.

Auriemma, R., Degrassi, V. and Quiri, E. 2012. Produzione e circolazione di anfore in Adriatico tra III e IV secolo: dati da contesti emblematici, in S. Fioriello (ed.) *Ceramica Romana nella Puglia Adriatica. Indagini archeologiche a Egnazia. Dallo scavo alla valorizzazione*: 255-298. Bari: SEDIT.

Auriemma, R., Degrassi, V. and Quiri, E. 2015. Eastern amphora imports in the Adriatic Sea: evidence from terrestrial and underwater contexts of the Roman Imperial age, in S. Demesticha (ed.) *Per Terram, Per Mare: Seaborne Trade and the Distribution of Roman Amphorae in the Mediterranean*: 139-160. Uppsala: Astrom Editions.

Auriemma, R. and Quiri, E. 2004. Importazioni di anfore orientali nell'Adriatico tra primo e medio impero, in J. Eiring and J. Lund (eds) *Transport amphorae and trade in the Eastern Mediterranean: acts of the International Colloquium at the Danish Institute at Athens, September 26-29, 2002*: 43-55. Aarhus: Aarhus University Press.

Auriemma, R. and Quiri, E. 2006. Importazioni di anfore orientali nel Salento tra primo e medio impero, in S. Čače, A. Kurilić and F. Tassaux (eds) *Les routes de l'Adriatique antique: géographie et économie. Actes de la Table ronde du 18 au 22 septembre 2001 (Zadar)*: 225-151. Bordeux: Ausonius.

Auriemma, R. and Quiri, E. 2007. La circolazione delle anfore in Adriatico tra V e. VIII sec. d.C., in S. Gelichi and C. Negrelli (eds) *Atti III incontro di studio Cer. Am.Is. sulle ceramiche tardoantiche e medievali. "La circolazione delle ceramiche nell'Adriatico tra tarda antichità e altomedioevo" (Venezia, 24-25 giugno 2004)*:

31-64. Mantua: SAP Società Archeologica.

Balista, C. and Ruta Serafini, A. 1993. Saggio stratigrafico presso il muro romano di Largo Europa a Padova. Nota preliminare. *Quaderni di Archeologia del Veneto* 9: 95-111.

Bandelli, G. 1990. Colonie e municipi delle regioni transpadane in età repubblicana, *La Città nell'Italia settentrionale in età romana. Morfologia, strutture e funzionamento dei centri urbani delle Regiones X e XI, Atti del convegno di Trieste (13-15 marzo 1987)*: 251-277. Rome: École Française de Rome.

Bandini Mazzanti, M., Accorsi, C.A., Curina, R., Gattini, A. and Marchesini, M. 1995. Carpological remains from a pit fill at the Roman villa (1st - 4th century AD) of Casteldebole. *Giornale Botanico Italiano* 129: 221-228.

Bang, P.F. 2008. *The Roman Bazaar: A Comparative Study of Trade and Markets in a Tributary Empire*. Cambridge: Cambridge University Press.

Bang, P.F. 2012. A Forum on Trade: Bazaars, Empires, and Roman Trade, in W. Scheidel (ed.) *The Cambridge Companion to the Roman Economy*: 296-303. Cambridge: Cambridge University Press.

Barello, F. and La Spada, M.G. 2004. Brandizzo, loc. Cascina Bologna. Villa rustica di prima età romana imperiale. *Quaderni della Soprintendenza Archeologica del Piemonte* 20: 209-211.

Barnes, T.D. 1982. *The new empire of Diocletian and Constantine*. Cambridge, (MA): Harvard University Press.

Barraud, D., Bonifay, M., Dridi, F. and Pichonneau, J.-F. 1998. L'Industrie céramique dans l'Antiquité tardive, in H. Ben Hassan and L. Maurin (eds) *Oudhna (Uthina): La redécouverte d'une ville antique de Tunisie*: 139-167. Bordeux: Ausonius.

Barrico, L.P. and Subbrizio, M. 2007. L'indagine archeologica di piazza Vittorio Veneto a Torino. L'età Romana. *Quaderni della Soprintendenza Archeologica del Piemonte* 22: 105-123.

Barsanti, C. 1989. L'esportazione di marmi dal Proconneso nelle regioni pontiche durante il IV-VI secolo. *Rivista dell'Instituto Nazionale d'Archeologia e Storia dell'Arte* 3: 91-220.

Bassi, C. 1993. I trasporti fluviali in Trentino-Alto Adige durante l'età romana. *Atlante tematico di topografia antica* 2: 237-48.

Basso, P. 1987. *I miliari della Venetia romana*. Padua: Società Archeologica Veneta

Basso, P. 2008. I miliari della Cisalpina romana: considerazioni storico-epigrafiche, in P. Basso, A. Buonapane, A. Cavarzere and S. Pesavento Mattioli (eds) *Est enim ille flos Italiae. Vita economica e sociale nella Cisalpina romana, Atti delle Giornate di Studi in onore di Ezio Buchi (Verona, 30 novembre - 1 dicembre 2006)*: 67-76. Verona: QuiEdit.

Basso, P. 2011. I miliari della Cisalpina romana: una lettura archeologica, in P. Basso (ed.) *I miliari lungo le* strade dell'impero. Atti del Convegno (Isola della Scala, 28 novembre 2010): 61-76. Verona: Cierre Editions.

Basso, P. 2018. Cosa raccontano i cippi miliari. Quaderni Friulani di Archeologia 28: 107-121.

Basso, P., Bonetto, J., Busana, M.S. and Michelini, P. 2004. La via Annia nella Tenuta Ca' Tron, in M.S. Busana and F. Ghedini (eds) La via Annia e le sue infrastrutture: 41-98. Cornuda: Fondazione Cassamarca.

Basso, P., Dobreva, D. and De Zuccato, G. 2024. Archaeobotany in the archaeology of wine: Current approaches and future possibilities, in E.K. Dodd and D. Van Limbergen (eds) Methods in Ancient Wine Archaeology. Scientific Approaches in Roman Contexts: 89-104. London: Bloomsbury.

Baxter, M.J. 2015. Exploratory multivariate analysis in archaeology, with a new introduction by the author. Clinton Corners: Percheron Press.

Bekljanov Zidanšek, I., Vojaković, P. and Žerjal, T. 2022. The Amber route between Caput Adriae and Emona basin the ceramic evidence on inner road – and water – communications, in G.L. Vrkljan, A. Konestra and A. Eterović Borzić (eds) Roman Pottery and Glass Manufactures: Production and Trade in the Adriatic Region and Beyond: 36-46. Oxford: Archaeopress.

Bell, T., Wilson, A.I. and Wickham, A. 2002. Tracking the Samnites: Landscape and Communications Routes in the Sangro Valley, Italy. American Journal of Archaeology 106: 169-186.

Beltrame, C. 1996. La sutilis navis del Lido di Venezia. Nuova testimonianza dell'antica tecnica cantieristica 'a cucitura' nell alto Adriatico, in F. Ciciliot (ed.) Navalia. Archeologia e storia: 31-53. Sarona.

Beltrame, C. 2001. Imbarcazioni lungo il litorale altoadriatico occidentale, in età romana. Sistema idroviario, tecniche costruttive e tipi navali. Antichità Altoadriatiche 46: 431-449.

Beltrame, C. 2002a. Le sutiles naves romane del litorale alto-adriatico. Nuove testimonianze e considerazioni tecnologiche., in P.A. Gianfrotta and P. Pelagatti (eds) Archeologia subacquea. Studi, ricerche e documenti III: 353-379. Rome: Poligrafico dello Stato.

Beltrame, C. 2002b. Sewn plank boats of the Roman era in the upper Adriatic sea. New evidence. Tropis 7: 103-113.

Beltrame, C. 2021. The contribution of four shipwrecks to the reconstruction of the trade dynamics of Proconnesian marble in the Roman period. Archeologia Classica 72: 437-462.

Beltrame, C. and Costa, E. 2016. A 5th-Century-AD Sewn-Plank River Barge at St Maria in Padovetere (Comacchio-FE), Italy: an interim report. The International Journal of Nautical Archaeology 45: 253–266.

Beltrame, C. and Costa, E. 2023. Description and analysis of the hull of Santa Maria in Padovetere, in C. Beltrame and E. Costa (eds) The shipwreck of Santa Maria in Padovetere (Comacchio-Ferrara). Archaeology of a riverine barge of Late Roman period and of other recent finds of sewn boats: 67-78. Florence: All'Insegna del Giglio.

Beltrame, C. and Gaddi, D. 2013. Fragments of Boats from the Canale Anfora of Aquileia, Italy, and Comparison of Sewn-Plank Ships in the Roman Era. The International Journal of Nautical Archaeology 43: 296-304.

Beltrame, C., Mozzi, P., Forti, A., Maritan, M., Rucco, A.A., Vavasori, A. and Miola, A. 2021. The Fifth-Century AD Riverine Barge of Santa Maria in Padovetere (Ferrara, Italy): A Multidisciplinary Approach to its Environment and Shipbuilding Techniques. Environmental Archaeology 26: 29-50.

Beltrán Lloris, F. 2000. La vida en la frontera, in F. Beltrán Lloris, M. Martín-Bueno and F. Pina Polo (eds) Roma en la Cuenca Media del Ebro. La Romanización en Aragón: 45-62. Zaragoza: CAI.

Beltrán Lloris, M. 1982. El comercio vinario tarraconense en el valle del Ebro: bases para su conocimiento, in M.D. Cultura (ed.) Concepción Fernández-Chicarro y de Dios, En homenaje a Conchita Fernández Chicarro: 319-330. Madrid: Ministerio de Cultura, Dirección General de Bellas Artes.

Beltrán Lloris, M. 1983. El aceite en Hispania a través de las ánforas: la concurrencia del aceite itálico y africano, in J. María Blázquez and J. Remesal Rodríguez (eds) II Congreso Internacional sobre Producción y Comercio del Aceite en la Antigüedad: 515-545. Madrid: Ministerio de Cultura, Dirección General de Bellas Artes.

Beltrán Lloris, M. 1987. El comercio del vino antiguo en le valle del Ebro, El vi a l'antiguitat. Economia, producció i comerç al Mediterrani occidental. I Colloqui d'arqueologia romana (Badalona, 1985). 51-74. Badalona: Musée de Badalona.

Beltrán Lloris, M. 1990. Guía de la cerámica romana. Zaragoza: Portico Libros.

Beltrán Lloris, M. 2008. Las ánforas tarraconenses en el valle del Ebro y la parte occidental de la Provincia Tarraconense, in A. López Mullor and A. Aquilué Abadías (eds) La producció i el comerç de les àmfores de la "Provincia Hispania Tarraconensis": Homenatge a Ricard Pascual i Guasch. Actes de les jornades d'estudi celebrades al Palau Marc de la Generalitat de Catalunya els dies 17 i 18 de novembre de 2005.: 271–318. Barcelona: MAC.

Benito, G., Macklin, M.G., Zielhofer, C., Jones, A.F. and Machado, M.J. 2015. Holocene flooding and climate change in the Mediterranean. Catena 130: 13-33.

Bernard, H., Bessac, J.-C., Mardikian, P. and Feugère, M. 1998. L'épave romaine de marbre de Porto Nuovo. Journal of Roman Archaeology 11: 53-81.

Bertacchi, L. 1976. L'imbarcazione romana di Montefalcone. Antichità Altoadriatiche 10: 39-45.

Bertacchi, L. 1980. Il Porto Fluviale, in B.F. Tamaro (ed.)

Da Aquileia a Venezia. Una mediazione tra l'Europa e l'Oriente dal II secolo a.C. al VI secolo d.C.: 123-133. Milan: Maremagnum.

Bertacchi, L. 1990. Il sistema portuale della metropoli aquileiese. *Aquileia e l'arco adriatico Antichit`a Alto Adriatiche* 36: 227-253.

Bes, P. 2015. *Once upon a Time in the East: The Chronological and Geographical Distribution of Terra Sigillata and Red Slip Ware in the Roman East.* (Roman and late antique Mediterranean pottery. Oxford: Archaeopress.

Bes, P. and Poblome, J. 2009. African Red Slip Ware on the move: the effects of Bonifay's Études for the Roman East, in J.H. Humphrey (ed.) *Studies on Roman Pottery from Africa Proconsularis and Byzacena (Tunisia). Hommage à Michel Bonifay* (Journal of Roman Archaeology Supplements 76): 67-75. Portsmouth (RI): Journal of Roman Archaeology.

Betori, A., Gomez Serito, M. and Pensabene, P. 2009. Investigations of Marbles and Stones Used in Augustan Monuments of Western Alpine Provinces (Italy), in Y. Maniatis (ed.) *ASMOSIA VII. Proceedings of the 7th International Conference of Association for the Study of Marble and Other Stones in Antiquity. Thassos 15-20 september, 2003*: 89-102. Athens: École française d'Athènes.

Bevan, A. 2014. Mediterranean Containerization. *Current Anthropology* 55: 387-418.

Biaggio Simona, S. and Butti Ronchetti, F. 1999. Les potiers QSP et QSS dans le Canton du Tessin: une mise à jour sur la diffusion des céramiques tardopadanes au Tessin, *SFECAG, Actes du Congrès de Fribourg*: 189-192. Marseille: SFECAG.

Bianco, L. 2008. La decorazione architettonica lapidea e marmorea, in G. Cavalieri Manasse (ed.) *L'area del Capitolium di Verona. Ricerche storiche e archeologiche*: 169-214. Verona: Soprintendenza per i Beni Archeologici del Veneto.

Bini, M., Zanchetta, G., Regattieri, E., Isola, I., Drysdale, R.N., Fabiani, F., Genovesi, S. and Hellstrom, J.C. 2020. Hydrological changes during the Roman Climatic Optimum in northern Tuscany (Central Italy) as evidenced by speleothem records and archaeological data. *Journal of Quaternary Science* 35: 791-802.

Biondani, F. 2005a. Anfore, in L. Mazzeo Saracino (ed.) *Il complesso edilizio di età romana nell'area dell'ex Vescovado a Rimini*: 263-282. Florence: All'Insegna del Giglio.

Biondani, F. 2005b. Terra sigillata africana, in L. Mazzeo Saracino (ed.) *Il complesso edilizio di età romana nell'area dell'ex Vescovado a Rimini*: 197-202. Florence: All'Insegna del Giglio.

Biondani, F. 2005c. Terra sigillata italica, in L. Mazzeo Saracino (ed.) *Il complesso edilizio di età romana nell'area dell'ex Vescovado a Rimini*: 171-174. Florence: All'Insegna del Giglio.

Biondani, F. 2005d. Terra sigillata medioadriatica e tarda, in L. Mazzeo Saracino (ed.) *Il complesso edilizio di età romana nell'area dell'ex Vescovado a Rimini*: 177-196. Florence: All'Insegna del Giglio.

Biondani, F. 2005e. Terra sigillata orientale b, in L. Mazzeo Saracino (ed.) *Il complesso edilizio di età romana nell'area dell'ex Vescovado a Rimini*: 169-170. Florence: All'Insegna del Giglio.

Biondani, F. 2008. Le Anfore Africane, in G. Cavalieri Manasse (ed.) *L'Area del Capitolium di Verona. Ricerche Storiche e Archeologiche*: 387-404. Verona: Soprintendenza per i Beni Archeologici del Veneto.

Biondani, F. 2014a. Terra sigillata africana, in L. Mazzeo Saracino (ed.) *Scavi di Suasa. I. I reperti ceramici e vitrei dalla domus dei Coiedii*: 229-249. Bologna: Ante Quem.

Biondani, F. 2014b. Terra sigillata medioadriatica ed altre ceramiche da mensa medio e tardoimperiali, in L. Mazzeo Saracino (ed.) *Scavi di Suasa I. I reperti ceramici e vitrei dalla Domus dei Coiedii*: 251-292. Bologna: Ante Quem.

Bocchio, S. 2004. Anfore, in V. Mariotti (ed.) *Il teatro e l'anfiteatro di Cividate Camuno: scavo, restauro, e allestimento di un parco archeologico*: 255-65. Florence: All'Insegna del Giglio.

Bocconcello, S. 2008. Il Rivestimento Marmoree, in G. Cavalieri Manasse (ed.) *L'Area del Capitolium di Verona. Ricerche Storiche e Archeologiche*: 233-253. Verona: Soprintendenza per i Beni Archeologici del Veneto.

Bockius, R. 2004. Ancient riverborne transport of heavy loads, in M. Pasquinucci and T. Weski (eds) *Close Encounters: Sea and Riverborne Trade, Ports and Hinterlands, Ship Construction and Navigation in Antiquity, the Middle Ages and in Modern Time*: 105-115. Oxford: Archaeopress.

Bondesan, M., Dal Cin, R. and Monari, R. 1990. L'ambiente in cui si arenò la nave romana di Comacchio: possibili modalità del suo naufragio e seppellimento, in F. Berti (ed.) *Fortuna maris: la nave romana de Comacchio*: 13. Bologna: Nuova Alfa.

Bonetto, J. and Previato, C. 2013. Trasformazioni del paesaggio e trasformazioni della città: le cave di pietra per Aquileia. *Antichità Altoadriatiche* 43: 141-162.

Bonifay, M. 2003. La céramique africaine, un indice du développement économique? *Antiquité Tardive* 11: 113-128.

Bonifay, M. 2004. *Études sur la céramique romaine tardive d'Afrique.* (BAR International Series 1301). Oxford: Archaeopress.

Bonifay, M. 2007. Que transportaient donc les amphores africaines?, in E. Papi (ed.) *Supplying Rome and the Empire* (Journal of Roman Archaeology Supplements 9): 8-32. Portsmouth (RI): Journal of Roman Archaeology.

Bonifay, M. 2016. Éléments de typologie des céramique de l'Afrique romaine, in D. Malfitana and M. Bonifay (eds) *La ceramica africana nella Sicilia romana - La céramique africaine dans la Sicile romaine 507-573.*

Catania: CNR.

Bonifay, M. 2018. Distribution of African pottery under the Roman Empire: evidence vs. interpretation, in A.I. Wilson and A.K. Bowman (eds) *Trade, Commerce, and the State in the Roman World*: 327-352. Oxford: Oxford University Press.

Bonifay, M. 2021. African amphora contents: an update, in D. Bernal-Casasola, M. Bonifay, A. Pecci and V. Leitch (eds) *Roman Amphora Contents: Reflecting on the Maritime Trade of Foodstuffs in Antiquity (In honour of Miguel Beltrán Lloris). Proceedings of the Roman Amphora Contents International Interactive Conference (RACIIC) (Cadiz, 5-7 October 2015)*: 281–298. Oxford: Archaeopress.

Bonifay, M. 2022. The African economy: the ceramic evidence, in R.B. Hitchner (ed.) *A Companion to North Africa in Antiquity*: 220-232. London: Wiley.

Bonifay, M. and Capelli, C. 2019. African amphorae, in T. Bezeczky (ed.) *Amphora Research in Castrum Villa on Brijuni Island*: 71-98. Vienna: Österreichische Akademie der Wissenschaften.

Bonifay, M. and Tchernia, A. 2012. Les réseaux de la céramique africaine (IER-VE siècles), in S. Keay (ed.) *Rome, Portus and the Mediterranean*: 315-333. Rome and London: The British School at Rome.

Bonivento, C. 2017. Anfore di produzione africana, in F. Fontana (ed.) *Aquileia, l'insula tra foro e porto fluviale. Lo scavo dell'Università degli studi di Trieste*: 425-444. Trieste: EUT.

Bonivento, C. and Vecchiet, C. 2017a. Anfore di produzione iberica, in F. Fontana (ed.) *Aquileia, l'insula tra foro e porto fluviale. Lo scavo dell'Università degli studi di Trieste*: 405-410. Trieste: EUT.

Bonivento, C. and Vecchiet, C. 2017b. Anfore di produzione orientale, in F. Fontana (ed.) *Aquileia, l'insula tra foro e porto fluviale. Lo scavo dell'Università degli studi di Trieste*: 411-423. Trieste: EUT.

Bonora Mazzoli, G. 1992. Tecnica Stradale nella Reggio XI: La Via Regina. *Atlante tematico di topografia antica* 1: 51-55.

Borghi, A., Appolonia, L., L., F. and Zoja, A. 2006. The grey marble of Porta Praetoria (Aosta, Italy): a minero-petrographic characterisation and provenance determination. *Periodico di Mineralogia* 75: 59-74.

Borghi, A., Vaggelli, G., Marcon, C. and Fiora, L. 2009. The Piedmont white marbles used in Antiquity: an archaeometric distinction inferred by a minero-petrographic and C-O stable isotope study. *Archaeometry* 51: 913-931.

Bortolamei, F. and Bottos, M. 2017. Terre sigillate e altre ceramiche fini orientali, in F. Fontana (ed.) *Aquileia, l'insula tra foro e porto fluviale. Lo scavo dell'Università degli Studi di Trieste*: 267-269. Trieste: Edizioni Università di Trieste.

Bosellini, A. 2017. Outline of the Geology of Italy, in M. Soldati and M. Marchetti (eds) *Landscapes and Landforms of Italy*: 21-27. Cham: Cham: Springer International Publishing.

Bosi, G., Castiglioni, E., Rinaldi, R., Mazzanti, M., Marchesini, M. and Rottoli, M. 2020. Archaeobotanical evidence of food plants in Northern Italy during the Roman period. *Vegetation History and Archaeobotany* 29: 681-697.

Bosi, G., Labate, D., Rinaldi, R., Montecchi, M.C., Mazzanti, M., Torri, P., Riso, F.M. and Mercuri, A.M. 2018. A survey of the Late Roman period (3rd-6th century AD): Pollen, NPPs and seeds/fruits for reconstructing environmental and cultural changes after the floods in Northern Italy. *Quaternary International*: 1-21.

Bosi, G., Mazzanti, M.B., Florenzano, A., N'siala, I.M., Pederzoli, A., Rinaldi, R., Torri, P. and Mercuri, A.M. 2011. Seeds/fruits, pollen and parasite remains as evidence of site function: piazza Garibaldi – Parma (N Italy) in Roman and Medieval times. *Journal of Archaeological Science* 38: 1621-1633.

Bosi, G., Mercuri, A.M., Bandini Mazzanti, M., Florenzano, A., Montecchi, M.C., Torri, P., Labate, D. and Rinaldi, R. 2015. The evolution of Roman urban environments through the archaeobotanical remains in Modena – Northern Italy. *Journal of Archaeological Science* 53: 19-31.

Bosio, L. 1979. I Septem Maria. *Archeologia Veneta* 2: 33-44.

Bosio, L. 1984. Capure la terra: La centurazione romana del Veneto, in R. Bussi and V. Vandelli (eds) *Misurare le terra: Centuriazione e coloni nel mondo romano. Iil caso Veneto*: 15-21. Modena: Franco Cosimo Panini.

Bosio, L. 1991. *Le Strade Romane della Venetia e dell'Histria*. Padua: Esedra.

Botazzi, G. 1992. Le Vie Pubbliche Centurali tra Modena e Piacenza. *Atlante tematico di topografia antica* 1: 169-178.

Botazzi, G., Bronzoni, L. and Mutti, A. 1995. *Carta Archeologica Del Comune Di Poviglio: 1986-1989*. Poviglio: SN.

Botazzi, G. and Labate, D. 2017. Bonifiche idrauliche e centuriazione nel Modenese in età romana. Roman land drainage and centuriation within Modena and its surrounding territory. *Geologia dell'Ambiente* 25: 16-20.

Bowman, A.K. 2005. Diocletian and the first tetrarchy, AD 284-305, in A.K. Bowman (ed.) *The Cambridge ancient history. Volume 12, The crisis of Empire, AD 193-337*: 67-89. Cambridge: Cambridge University Press.

Bowman, A.K. and Wilson, A.I. 2009. Quantifying the Roman Economy: Integration, Growth, Decline?, in A.K. Bowman and A.I. Wilson (eds) *Quantifying the Roman Economy: Methods and Problems*: 4-69. Oxford: Oxford University Press.

Braconi, P. 2009a. In vineis arbustisque. Il concetto di vigneto in età romana, in H. Patterson and F. Coarelli (eds) *Mercator placidissimus. The Tiber Valley in Antiquity. New research in the upper and middle river valley*: 291-306. Rome: Edizioni Quasar.

Braconi, P. 2009b. Territorio e paesaggio dell'alta valle del Tevere in età romana', in H. Patterson and F. Coarelli (eds) *Mercator Placidissimus: The Tiber Valley in Antiquity. New research in the Upper and Middle river valley. Rome 27 – 28 February 2004*: 87-104. Rome: Edizioni Quasar.

Bradley, M. 2013. Colour and marble in early imperial Rome. *The Cambridge Classical Journal* 52: 1-22.

Brandolini, F. and Carrer, F. 2021. *Terra, Silva et Paludes.* Assessing the Role of Alluvial Geomorphology for Late-Holocene Settlement Strategies (Po Plain – N Italy) Through Point Pattern Analysis. *Environmental Archaeology* 26: 511-525.

Brandolini, F. and Cremaschi, M. 2018. The Impact of Late Holocene Flood Management on the Central Po Plain (Northern Italy). *Sustainability* 10: 39-68.

Brandon, C.J., Hohlfelder, R.L., Jackson, M.D., Oleson, J.P. and Bottalico, L. 2014. *Building for eternity: the history and technology of Roman concrete engineering in the sea.* Oxford: Oxbow Books.

Brecciaroli Taborelli, L. 1978. Contributo alla classificazione di una terra sigillata chiara italica. *Rivista di Studi Marchigiani* 1: 1-38.

Brecciaroli Taborelli, L. 1987a. Per una ricerca sul commercio della Transpadana occidentale in età romana: ricognizione sulle anfore di "Vercellae", in G. Cresci (ed.) *Atti del Convegno di Studi nel centenario della morte di L. Bruzza, 1883-1983, Vercelli. 1984*: 129-208. Vercelli: Maremagnum.

Brecciaroli Taborelli, L. 1987b. Un contributo alla conoscenza dell'impianto urbano di Eporedia (Ivrea): lo scavo di un isolato a Porta Vercelli. *Quaderni della Soprintendenza Archeologica del Piemonte* 6: 97-157.

Brecciaroli Taborelli, L. 1988. *La ceramica a vernice nera da Eporedia (Ivrea). Contributo alla storia della romanizzazione nella Transpadana occidentale.* Turin: Cuorgné.

Brecciaroli Taborelli, L. 2007. Eporedia tra tarda repubblic e primo impero: Un aggiornamento, in L. Brecciaroli Taborelli (ed.) *Forme e tempi dell'urbanizzazione nella Cisalpina (II secolo a.C. – I secolo d.C.). Atti delle Giornate di Studio Torino. 4-6 maggio 2006*: 127-140. Florence: All'Insegna del Giglio.

Brecciaroli Taborelli, L. and Gabucci, A. 2007. Le mura e il teatro di Augusta Taurinorum: sequenze stratigrafiche e dati cronologici, in L. Brecciaroli Taborelli (ed.) *Forme e tempi dell'urbanizzazione nella Cisalpina: II secolo a.C.-I secolo d.C.: atti delle Giornate di studio: Torino, 4-6 maggio 2006*: 243-259. Florence: All'Insegna del Giglio.

Bresson, A. 2005. Ecology and Beyond: The Mediterranean Paradigm, in W.V. Harris (ed.) *Rethinking the Mediterranean*: 94-114. Oxford: Oxford University Press.

Bridge, J.S. 2003. *Rivers and Floodplains: Forms, Processes, and Sedimentary Record.* Oxford: Wiley.

Broadhead, W. 2000. Migration and Transformation in North Italy in the 3rd-1st Centuries BC. *Bulletin - Institute of Classical Studies* 44: 145-166.

Broekaert, W. 2011. Partners in business: Roman merchants and the potential advantages of being a 'collegiatus'. *Ancient society* 41: 221-256.

Broekaert, W. 2013. *Navicularii et negotiantes: a prosopographical study of Roman merchants and shippers.* (Pharos: Studien zur griechisch-römischen Antike Series 28). Rahden/Westf.: Verlag Marie Leidorf.

Brogiolo, G.P. (ed.) 1999. *Santa Giulia di Brescia: gli scavi dal 1980 al 1992: Reperti preromani, romani e altomedievali*, Florence: All'Insegna del Giglio.

Brogiolo, G.P. 2015. Flooding in Northern Italy during the Early Middle Ages: Resilience and Adaptation. *The European Journal of Post Classical Archaeologies* 5: 47-68.

Brogiolo, G.P. and Chavarría Arnau, A. 2014. *Villae, praetoria* e *aedes publicae* tardoantichi in Italia settentrionale: riflessioni a partire da alcune ricerche recenti, in P. Pensabene and C. Sfameni (eds) *La villa restaurata e i nuovi studi sull'edilizia residenziale tardoantica: atti del Convegno internazionale del Centro interuniversitario di studi sull'edilizia abitativa tardoantica nel Mediterraneo (CISEM), (Piazza Armerina, 7-10 novembre 2012)*: 227-239. Bari: Edipuglia.

Brogiolo, G.P. and Chavarría Arnau, A. 2018. Villas in Northern Italy, in A. Marzano and G.P.R. Métraux (eds) *The Roman Villa in the Mediterranean Basin*: 178-194. Cambridge: Cambridge University Press.

Brogiolo, G.P. and Sarabia-Bautista, J. 2017. Land, rivers and marshes: changing landscapes along the Adige River and the Euganean Hills (Padua, Italy). *The European Journal of Post Classical Archaeologies* 7: 149-171.

Brown, T.S. 1984. *Gentlemen and Officers, Imperial Administration and Aristocratic Power in Byzantine Italy, 554-800.* Rome and London: British School at Rome.

Brughmans, T. 2010. Connecting the dots: towards archaeological network analysis. *Oxford Journal of Archaeology* 29: 377-303.

Brughmans, T. 2013. Thinking Through Networks: A Review of Formal Network Methods in Archaeology. *Journal of Archaeological Method and Theory* 20: 623-662.

Brughmans, T. 2020. Evaluating the Potential of Computational Modelling for Informing Debates on Roman Economic Integration, in K. Verboven (ed.) *Complexity Economics. Building a New Approach to Ancient Economic History*: 105-123. Cham: Springer.

Brughmans, T. 2022. Why simulate Roman economies?, in T. Brughmans and A.I. Wilson (eds) *Simulating Roman economies. Theories, methods and computational models*: 3-36. Oxford: Oxford University Press.

Brughmans, T. and Pecci, A. 2020. An Inconvenient Truth. Evaluating the Impact of Amphora Reuse through Computational Simulation Modelling, in C.N. Duckworth and A.I. Wilson (eds) *Recycling and Reuse in the Roman Economy*: 191-234. Oxford: Oxford University Press.

Brughmans, T. and Poblome, J. 2016a. MERCURY: an agent-based model of tableware trade in the Roman East. *Journal of Artificial Societies and Social Simulation* 19: 1-3.

Brughmans, T. and Poblome, J. 2016b. Roman bazaar or market economy? Explaining tableware distributions through computational modelling. *Antiquity* 90: 393-408.

Brughmans, T. and Poblome, J. 2017. The case for computational modelling of the Roman economy: a reply to Van Oyen. *Antiquity* 91: 1364-1366.

Brughmans, T. and Wilson, A.I. 2022. *Simulating Roman economies. Theories, methods and computational models*. Oxford: Oxford University Press.

Brulet, R., Vilvorder, F. and Delage, R. 2010. *La céramique romaine en Gaule du Nord. La vasseille à large diffusion*. Turnhout: Brepols.

Bruno, B. 1988. Anfore, in G. Panazza and G.P. Brogiolo (eds) *Ricerche su Brescia altomedioevale. Vol. 1: Gli Studi Fino al 1978, Lo Scavo di via Alberto Mario*: 77-83. Brescia: Ateneo di Brescia.

Bruno, B. 1997. Contenitori da trasporto: i consumi di olio, vino e di altre derrate, in F. Filippi (ed.) *Alba Pompeia. Archeologia della città dalla fondazione alla tarda antichità*: 516-532. Alba: Omega.

Bruno, B. 1998. Importazione di merci e itinerari commerciali nella Liguria Transappenninica. Alcune considerazioni sulla presenza di anfore tra la fine del II sec. A.C. e il II sec. D.C., in G. Sena Chiesa and A.E. Arslan (eds) *Optima via. Atti delConvegno internazionale di studi Postumia. Storia earcheologia di una grande strada romana alle radicidell'Europa*: 329-343. Venice: Associazione promozione iniziative culturali.

Bruno, B. 2002. Importazioni e consumo di derrate nel tempio: l'evidenza delle anfore, in F. Rossi (ed.) *Nuove ricerche sul capitolium di Brescia. Scavi, studi e restauri*: 277-307. Milan: Edizioni ET.

Bruno, B. 2003. Le anfore della cava di UC VII. Considerazioni sulle anfore nei contesti databili tra la tarda età antonina e la prima età severiana, in S. Lusuardi Siena and M.P. Rossignani (eds) *Dall'antichità al Medioevo, aspetti insediativi e manufatti, Atti delle giornate di studio (Milano, 24 gennaio 2000)*: 85-97. Milan: Vita e Pensiero.

Bruno, B. 2005a. Le anfore da trasporto, in I. Nobile De Agostini (ed.) *Indagini archeologiche a Como. Lo scavo nei pressi della Porta Pretoria*: 129-142. Como: Comune di Como.

Bruno, B. 2005b. Le anfore da trasporto, in D. Gandolfi (ed.) *La ceramica e i materiali di età romana. Classi, produzioni, commerci e consumi*: 353-394. Bordighera: Ist. Studi Liguri.

Bruno, B. 2008. Le anfore di media e tarda età imperiale di produzione italica, egeo-orientale, ispanica e le anfore non identificate, in G. Cavalieri Manasse (ed.) *L'area del Capitolium di Verona: ricerche storiche e archeologiche*: 373-386. Verona: Soprintendenza per i Beni Archeologici del Veneto.

Bruno, B. and Bocchio, S. 1991. Anfore, in D. Caporusso (ed.) *Scavi MM3. Ricerche di archeologia urbana a Milano durante la costruzione della linea 3 della Metropolitana, 1982- 1990*: 259-297. Milan: Edizioni ET.

Bruno, B. and Bocchio, S. 1999. Le Anfore da Trasporto, in G.P. Brogliolo (ed.) *Santa Giulia di Brescia: gli scavi dal 1980 al 1992: Reperti preromani, romani e altomedievali* 231-269. Florence: All'Insegna del Giglio.

Bruno, L., Piccin, A., Sammartino, I. and Amorosi, A. 2018. Decoupled geomorphic and sedimentary response of Po River and its Alpine tributaries during the last glacial/post-glacial episode. *Geomorphology* 317: 184-198.

Bruno, M., Cancelliere, C., Gorgoni, C., Lazzarini, L. and Pallante, P. 2002. Provenance and distribution of white marbles in temples and public buildings of Imperial Rome, in J.J. Herrmann, N. Herz and R. Newman (eds) *ASMOSIA V. Interdisciplinary Studies on Ancient Stone*: 289-300. London: Archetype.

Brunt, P.A. 1971. *Italian Manpower 225 B.C.-A.D. 14*. Oxford: Oxford University Press.

Brusić, Z. 1999. *Hellenistic and Roman Relief Pottery in Liburnia*. (BAR International Series 817). Oxford: Archaeopress.

Bucci, G. 2015. Padus, Sandalus, Gens Fadiena. Underwater Surveys in Palaeo-Watercourses (Ferrara District - Italy). *The International Archives of the Photogrammetry, Remote Sensing and Spatial Information Sciences* XL-5/W5: 55-60.

Bucci, G. 2018. Remote Sensing and Geo-Archaeological Data: Inland Water Studies for the Conservation of Underwater Cultural Heritage in the Ferrara District, Italy. *Remote Sensing* 10: 1-21.

Buchi, E. 1973. Banchi di anfore romane a Verona. Nota sui commerce cisalpine, in S.E.L.D.V. Accademia Di Agricoltura (ed.) *Il territorio veronese in età romana. Atti del convegno 1971* 531-637. Verona: Accademia di agricoltura, scienze e lettere di Verona.

Bugini, R. and Folli, L. 2016. Indentificazione dei frammenti marmorei. *Rivista archeologia dell'antica provincia e diocesi di Como* 198: 74-78.

Buonapane, A. 2009. La produzione olearia e la lavorazione del pesce lungo il medio e l'alto Adriatico: le fonti letterarie, in S. Cipriano and M.-B. Carre (eds) *Olio e pesce in epoca romana: produzione e commercio nelle regioni dell'Alto Adriatico: atti del convegno (Padova 16 febbraio 2007)*: 25-36. Rome: Edizioni Quasar.

Buonapane, A. and Grossi, P. 2014. Costantino, i miliari dell'Italia Settentrionale e la propaganda imperiale. *Antichità Altoadriatiche* 78: 161-177.

Buora, M. 2001. La seconda edizione del Corpus Vasorum Arretinorum e lo studio dei bolli relativi alla Venetia e all'area transalpina. *Aquileia Nostra* 62: 241-300.

Busana, M.S. 2002. *Architetture rurali nella Venetia romana.* Rome: L'Erma di Bretschneider.

Busana, M.S. 2003. La produzione vinaria dalle fonti archeologiche nella Valpolicella di età romana. *Annuario storico della Valpolicella* 19: 117-132.

Busana, M.S. 2008. Indagini nell'agro orientale di Altino: il popolamento in età romana tra Sile e Piave. *Atlante tematico di topografia antica* 17: 27-47.

Busana, M.S. Forthcoming. Wine Production in the Roman West: The Role of Artificial Heating, in D. Van Limbergen, E.K. Dodd and M.S. Busana (eds) *Vine-Growing and Wine Making in the Roman World.* Leuven: Peeters.

Busana, M.S. and Basso, P. (eds) 2012. *La lana nella Cisalpina romana: economia e società. Atti del Convegno - Padova/Verona 18-20 maggio 2011,* Padua: Padova University Press.

Busana, M.S., Bon, M., Cerato, I., Garavello, S., Ghiotto, A.R., Migliavacca, M., Nardi, S., Pizzeghello, D. and Zampieri, S. 2012. Agricoltura e allevamento nell'agro orientale di Altinum: il caso di Ca' Tron, in M.S. Busana and P. Basso (eds) *La lana nella Cisalpina romana: economia e società. Atti del Convegno - Padova/Verona 18-20 maggio 2011*: 127-169. Padua: Padova University Press.

Busana, M.S., D'incà, C. and Forti, S. 2009. Olio e pesce in epoca romana nell'alto e medio Adriatico, in S. Pesavento Mattioli and M.B. Carre (eds) *Olio e pesce in epoca romana. Produzione e commercio nelle regioni dell'alto adriatico*: 37-81. Rome: Edizioni Quasar.

Busana, M.S. and Forin, C. 2018. Interventi agrari e popolamento nella Venetia romana. Alcune considerazioni in merito ai tempi di attuazione (agri di Adria, Padova, Altino, Oderzo, Concordia, Aquileia). *Atlante tematico di topografia antica* 28: 139-154.

Busana, M.S. and Forin, C. 2020. Economy and Production Systems in Roman Cisalpine Gaul: Some Data on Farms and Villae in A. Marzano (ed.) *Proceedings of the 19th International Congress of Classical Archaeology Volume 17: Villas, Peasant Agriculture, and the Roman Rural Economy*: 17-30. Cologne/Bonn: Propylaeum.

Busana, M.S. and Vacilotto, A. 2022. Il sistema itinerario nella periferia dei centri urbani della fascia costiera adriatica: i casi di Aquileia, Altino e Concordia. *Atlante tematico di topografia antica* 32: 207-223.

Butti, F. 2016. La torre di via Parini e le mura di Como *Rivista archeologia dell'antica provincia e diocesi di Como* 187: 47-120.

Calzolari, M. 1992. Le Strade Romane della Bassa Padania. *Atlante tematico di topografia antica* 1: 161-168.

Calzolari, M. 2003. La diffusione dei marmi veronesi in età romana nell'Italia settentrionale: aspetti topografici. *Annuario storico della Valpolicella* 19: 169-184.

Calzolari, M. 2007. Il Delta padano in Età romana: idrografia, viabilità, insediamenti, in F. Berti, M. Bollini, S. Gelichi and J. Ortalli (eds) *Genti nel delta da Spina a Comacchio: uomini, territorio e culto dall'antichità all'alto Medioevo*: 153-172. Ferrara: Corbo.

Cambi, F. and Terrenato, N. 1994. *Introduzione all'archeologia dei paesaggi.* Rome: Nuova Italia Scientifica.

Campbell, B. 2012. *Rivers and the power of ancient Rome.* Chapel Hill: University of North Carolina Press.

Campbell, P.B. 2023. The Archaeology of Rivers. Processes and Patterns, in A. Tibbs and P.B. Campbell (eds) *Rivers and Waterways in the Roman World. Empire of Water*: 3-19. London: Routledge.

Caporusso, D. 1990. La situazione idrografica di Milano romana, in Silvana (ed.) *Milano capitale dell'Impero romano 286-402 d.C*: 94-96. Milan: Vita e Pensiero.

Caporusso, D. 1991. La zona di corso di Porta Romana in età romana e medieval, in D. Caporusso (ed.) *Scavi MM3. Ricerche di archeologia urbana a Milano durante la costruzione della linea 3 della metropolitana. 1982-1990 I*: 237-295. Milan: Edizioni ET.

Caporusso, D. (ed.) 1991. *Scavi MM3. Ricerche di archeologia urbana a Milano durante la costruzione della linea 3* Milan: Edizioni ET.

Capulli, M. 2023. Understanding the Cultural Landscape of the Stella River Through Underwater Archaeology, in A. Tibbs and P.B. Campbell (eds) *Rivers and Waterways in the Roman World. Empire of Water*: 69-84. London: Routledge.

Caramiello, R., Fossa, V. and Arobba, D. 2014. Analisi archeopalinologiche nel sito romano di Pollentia. *Quaderni della Soprintendenza Archeologica del Piemonte* 29: 11-18.

Caramiello, R., Fossa, V., Siniscalco, C. and Arobba, D. 2014. La ricostruzione paleoambientale ad Augusta Bagiennorum in età romana, in M.C. Preacco (ed.) *Augusta Bagiennorum. Storia e archeologia di una città augustea*: 66-77. Turin: Celid.

Carandini, A., Sagui, L., Tortorella, S. and Tortorici, E. 1981. Ceramica africana, in A. Carandini, L. Anselmino, C. Pavolini, L. Sagui, S. Tortorella and E. Tortorici (eds) *Atlante delle forme ceramiche 1: ceramica fine romana nel bacino Mediterraneo (medio e tardo impero)*: 9-183. Rome: Istituto della Enciclopedia Italiana.

Cardosa, M. 1996. I materiali pertinenti all'apparato decorativo della domus, in G. Pantò (ed.) *Il Monastero della Visitazione a Vercelli. Archeologia e storia*: 223-234. Vercelli: Edizioni dell'Orso.

Carre, M.-B. and Maselli Scotti, F. 2001. Il porto di Aquileia: dati antiche e ritrovamenti antichi recenti, in C. Zaccaria (ed.) *Strutture portuali e rotte marittime nell'Adriatico di età romana*: 211-244. Trieste: Edizioni Quasar.

Carre, M.-B. and Auriemma, R. 2009. Piscine e vivaria nell'Adriatico settentrionale: tipologie e funzioni in S. Cipriano and M.-B. Carre (eds) *Olio e pesce in epoca romana: produzione e commercio nelle regioni dell'Alto Adriatico: atti del convegno (Padova 16 febbraio 2007)*: 83-100. Rome: Edizioni Quasar.

Carre, M.-B., Maggi, P., Merlatti, R. and Rousse, C. 2007. L'évolution des importations à Aquilée. V. Quelques réflexions sur les échanges à l'Aquilée. *Antichità Altoadriatiche* 65: 621-632.

Carre, M.-B., Monsieur, P. and Pesavento Mattioli, S. 2014. Transport amphorae Lamboglia 2 and Dressel 6A: Italy and/or Dalmatia? Some clarifications. *Journal of Roman Archaeology* 27: 417-428.

Carre, M.-B. and Pesavento Mattioli, S. 2003. Tentativo di classificazione delle anfore olearie adriatiche. *Aquileia Nostra* 74: 453-476.

Carre, M.-B. and Pesavento Mattioli, S. 2018. The amphorae of the western Adriatic: an update, in G. Lipovac Vrkljan and A. Konestra (eds) *Pottery Production, Landscape and Economy of Roman Dalmatia. Interdisciplinary approaches*: 7-13. Oxford: Archaeopress.

Carre, M.-B. and Pesavento Mattioli, S. 2021. The content of amphorae from Adriatic Italy, in D. Bernal-Casasola, M. Bonifay, A. Pecci and V. Leitch (eds) *Roman Amphora Contents. Reflecting on the Maritime Trade of Foodstuffs in Antiquity. In honour of Miguel Beltrán Lloris. Proceedings of the Roman Amphora Contents International Interactive Conference (RACIIC). (Cadiz, 5-7 October 2015)*: 273-280. Oxford: Archaeopress.

Carre, M.-B., Pesavento Mattioli, S. and Belotti, C. 2009. Le anforette da pesce adriatiche, in S. Pesavento Mattioli and M.B. Carre (eds) *Olio e pesce in epoca romana. Produzione e commercio nelle regioni dell'alto Adriatico: Atti del Convegno (Padova, 16 febbraio 2007)*: 215-238. Rome: Edizioni Quasar.

Carreras, C. 1994a. *A Macroeconomic and Spatial Analysis of Long Distance Exchange: The Amphora Evidence from Roman Britain.* Unpublished PhD dissertation, University of Southampton.

Carreras, C. 1994b. *Una reconstruccion del comercio en cerdmicas: la red de transportes en Britannia. Aplicaciones de modelos de simulacion en PASCAL y SPANS.* Barcelona: Edicions Servei del Llibre l'Estaquirot.

Carreras, C. and De Soto, P. 2013. The Roman transport network: a precedent for the integration of the European mobility. *Journal of Quantitative and Interdisciplinary History* 46: 117-133.

Carreras, C., De Soto, P. and Muñoz, A. 2019. Land transport in mountainous regions in the Roman Empire: Network analysis in the case of the Alps and Pyrenees. *Journal of Archaeological Science: Reports* 25: 280-293.

Carreras, C. and Morais, R. 2012. The Atlantic Roman trade during the principate. New evidence from the western façade. *Oxford Journal of Archaeology* 31: 419-441.

Carrignon, S., Brughmans, T. and Romanowska, I. 2020. Tableware trade in the Roman East: Exploring cultural and economic transmission with agent-based modelling and approximate Bayesian computation. *PLOS ONE* 15: e0240414.

Carton, A., Bondesan, A., Fontana, A., Meneghel, M., Miola, A., Mozzi, P., Primon, S. and Surian, N. 2009. Geomorphological evolution and sediment transfer in the Piave River system (northeastern Italy) since the Last Glacial Maximum. *Géomorphologie: relief, processus, environnement* 3: 155–174.

Castillo, P. 2014. The Navigability of the River Ebro: A Reason for Roman Territorial Planning in the Ebro Valley. *The Journal for Ancient Studies* 3: 129-152.

Castoldi, M. 2015. Il marmo nel Foro di Augusta Prætoria (scavi 2005-2009) e il linguaggio della propaganda augustea. *Anno* 52: 325-330.

Castro, F. and Capulli, M. 2016. A Preliminary report of recording the Stella 1 Roman River Barge, Italy. *The International Journal of Nautical Archaeology* 45: 29-41.

Castrorao Barba, A. 2014a. Le ville romane in Italia tra III e VI sec. d C.: approccio statistico e considerazioni generali. *Amoenitas* 3: 9-24.

Castrorao Barba, A. 2014b. Continuità topografica in discontinuità funzionale: trasformazioni e riusi delle ville romane in Italia tra III e VIII secolo. *The European Journal of Post Classical Archaeologies* 4: 259-296.

Castrorao Barba, A. 2023. The Afterlife of Roman Villas in Italy Between the 5th and 8th Centuries CE, in I. Bavuso and A. Castrorao Barba (eds) *The European Countryside during the Migration Period. Patterns of Change from Iberia to the Caucasus (300–700 CE)*: 33-50. Berlin: De Gruyter.

Catarsi, M. and Dall'aglio, P.L. 1993. I ponti romani dell'Emilia occidentale. *Atlante tematico di topografia antica* 2: 209-221.

Cavalieri Manasse, G. 1990. *Il monumento funerario romano di via Mantova a Brescia.* Rome: Edizioni Quasar.

Cavalieri Manasse, G. 2008. Il contesto urbanistico del santuario: l'area forense, in G. Cavalieri Manasse (ed.) *L'area del Capitolium di Verona*: 293-306. Verona: Soprintendenza per i Beni Archeologici del Veneto.

Cavalieri Manasse, G. (ed.) 2008. *L'Area del Capitolium di Verona. Ricerche Storiche e Archeologiche,* Verona: Soprintendenza per i Beni Archeologici del Veneto.

Cavalieri Manasse, G. and Bruno, B. 2003. Edilizia abitativa a Verona, in J. Ortalli (ed.) *Abitare in città: La Cisalpina tra impero e medioevo*: 47-64. Wiesbaden: Dr. Ludwig Reichert Verlag.

Cera, G. 1995. Scali portuali nel sistema idroviario padano in epoca romana. *Atlante tematico di topografia antica* 4: 179-198.

Cera, G. 1996. Peculiari esempi di architettura strutturale in alcuni ponti della Venetia. *Atlante tematico di topografia antica* 5: 179-194.

Cera, G. 2000. *La via Postumia da Genova a Cremona.* (Atlante tematico di topografia antica. Supplemento 7). Roma: L'Erma di Bretschneider.

Ceserano, M. and Corti, C. 2023. New excavations at Santa Maria in Pado Vetere and in the Po Delta (2014-2015), in I. Borzić, E. Cirelli, K. Jelinčić Vučković, A. Konestra and I. Ožanić Roguljić (eds) *TRADE – Transformations of Adriatic Europe (2nd–9th Centuries AD). Proceedings of the conference in Zadar, 11th–13th February 2016*: 210-219. Oxford: Archaeopress.

Cessford, C. 2017. Throwing away everything but the kitchen sink? Large assemblages, depositional practice and post-medieval households in Cambridge. *Post-Medieval Archaeology* 51: 164-193.

Charlin, G., J.M., G. and Lequément, R. 1978. L'épave antique de Cavaliére *Archaeonautica* 2: 9-93.

Chevallier, R. 1976. *Roman Roads.* (Batsford Studies in Archaeology. London: Batsworth.

Chevallier, R. 1983. *La Romanisation de la Celtique du Pô.* Paris and Rome: École française de Rome.

Chilver, G.E.F. 1941. *Cisalpine Gaul: Social and Economic History from 49 B.C. to the Death of Trajan.* Oxford: Clarendon Press.

Christie, N. 2006. *From Constantine to Charlemagne. An Archaeology of Italy AD 300-800.* Aldershot: Routledge.

Cipolato, A. 2018. Anfore italiche, egeo-orientali e galliche, in L. Sperti, M. Tirelli and S. Cipriano (eds) *Prima dello scavo. Il survey 2012 ad Altino*: 142-153. Venice: Edizioni Ca' Foscari.

Cipolato, A. and Indino, G. 2022. Le anfore galliche nella Regio X: dati preliminari, in G.L. Vrkljan, A. Konestra and A. Eterović Borzić (eds) *Roman Pottery and Glass Manufactures: Production and Trade in the Adriatic Region and Beyond*: 212-221. Oxford: Archaeopress.

Cipriano, S. 1999. L'abitato di Altino in età tardorepubblicana: i dati archeologici, in G. Cresci Marrone and M. Tirelli (eds) *Vigilia di romanizzazione. Altino e il Veneto orientale tra II e I sec. A.C. - Atti del Convegno - Venezia 1997*: 35-65. Trieste: Edizioni Quasar.

Cipriano, S. 2009. Le Anfore Olearie Dressel 6B, in S. Pesavento Mattioli and M.-B. Carre (eds) *Olio e pesce in epoca romana: produzione e commercio nelle regioni dell'Alto Adriatico: atti del convegno (Padova 16 febbraio 2007)*: 173-189. Rome: Edizioni Quasar.

Cipriano, S. 2013. La terra sigillata, in C. Guarnieri (ed.) *Vivere a Forum Livi. Lo scavo di via Curte a Forlì*: 189-198. Bologna: Ante Quem.

Cipriano, S. and Ferrarini, F. 2001. *Le anfore romane di Opitergium, Oderzo (Treviso)*. Cornuda: Alfredo.

Cipriano, S. and Mazzocchin, S. 1998. Bonifiche con anfore a Padova: distribuzione topografica e dati cronologici. *Quaderni di Archeologia del Veneto* 14: 83-87.

Cipriano, S. and Mazzocchin, S. 2000. Considerazioni su alcune anfore Dressel 6B bollate. I casi di 'VARI PACCI' e 'PACCI'', 'APICI' e 'APIC', 'P.Q.SCAPVLAE', 'P.SEPVLLIP.F'. e 'SEPVLLIVM'. *Aquileia Nostra* 71: 149-192.

Cipriano, S. and Mazzocchin, S. 2002. Analisi di alcune serie bollate di anfore Dressel 6B (AP.PVLCRI, FLAV. FONTAN/FONTANI, L.IVNI.PAETINI, L.TRE.OPTATI). *Aquileia Nostra* 73: 305-340.

Cipriano, S. and Mazzocchin, S. 2004. La coltivazione dell'ulivo e la produzione olearia nella Decima Regio. Riflessioni su alcune serie bollate di anfore Dressel 6B alla luce delle analisi archeometriche. *Aquileia Nostra* 75: 93-120.

Cipriano, S. and Mazzocchin, S. 2010. Un quartiere artigianale a Patavium. La fornace per la produzione di terra sigillata tardo-padana. *Rei Cretariae Romanae Fautorum Acta* 41: 141-153.

Cipriano, S. and Mazzocchin, S. 2012. Produzioni anforarie dell'Italia alto e medioadriatica in età romana, in S. Fioriello (ed.) *Ceramica Romana nella Puglia Adriatica*: 241-254. Bari: Sedit.

Cipriano, S. and Mazzocchin, S. 2016. Lusitanian Amphorae in the Northern Adriatic Region: the Western Part of the *Decima Regio*, in I.V. Pinto, R.R. De Almeida and A. Martin (eds) *Lusitanian Amphorae: Production and Distribution*: 429-436. Oxford: Archaeopress.

Cipriano, S. and Mazzocchin, S. 2018. Sulla cronologia delle anfore Dressel 6A: novità dai contesti di bonifica della Venetia. *Rei Cretariae Romanae Fautorum Acta* 45: 261-271.

Cipriano, S. and Mazzocchin, S. 2019. Dressel 6B and Dressel 6A's oil and wine production in North Italy and the Adriatic western coast (1st century BC - 2nd century AD), in J. Remesal Rodríguez, V. Revilla Calvo, D.J. Martín-Arroyo Sánchez and A.M. I Oliveras (eds) *Paisajes productivos y redes comerciales en el Imperio Romano/Productive Landscapes and Trade Networks in the Roman Empire*: 233-246. Barcelona: Edicions de la Universitat de Barcelona.

Cipriano, S. and Mazzocchin, S. 2020. I sistemi di bonifi ca con anfore in area nord adriatica in epoca romana, in M.S. Busana, E. Novello and A. Vacilotto (eds) *Archeologi nelle terre di bonifica. Paesaggi stratificati e antichi sistemi da riscoprire e valorizzare.* Padua: Cleup.

Cipriano, S., Mazzocchin, S., Maritan, L. and Mazzoli, C. 2020. Le anfore Dressel 6B prodotte in area nord adriatica: studio archeologico e archeometrico di materiali da contesti datati, in P. Machut, Y. Marion, A. Ben Amara and F. Tassaux (eds) *Adriatlas 3. Recherches pluridisciplinaires récentes sur les amphores nord-adriatiques à l'époque romaine*: 103-119. Bordeaux: Ausonius Éditions.

Cipriano, S. and Sandrini, G.M. 2001. La banchina fluviale di Opitergium. *Antichità Altoadriatiche* 46: 289-294.

Cipriano, S. and Sandrini, G.M. 2003. Sigillate orientali a Iulia Concordia. Primi dati da un'area campione: lo scavo del piazzale antistante la cattedrale di Santo Stefano. *Aquileia Nostra* 74: 425-452.

Cirelli, E. 2013a. Roma sul mare e il porto augusteo di Classe, in F. Boschi (ed.) *Ravenna e l'Adriatico dalle origini all'età romana*: 109-122. Bologna: Ante Quem.

Cirelli, E. 2013b. L'Adriatico romano e il problema di Ravenna, in F. Boschi (ed.) *Ravenna e l'Adriatico dalle origini all'età romana*: 123-138. Bologna: Ante Quem.

Cirelli, E. 2014. Typology and diffusion of Amphorae in Ravenna and Classe between the 5th and the 8th centuries AD, in N. Poulou-Papadimitriou, E. Nodarou and V. Kilikoglou (eds) *Late Roman Coarse Wares, Cooking Wares and Amphorae in the Mediterranean*: 541-552. Oxford: Archaeopress.

Cirelli, E. 2022. African imports. New scenarios and new agents, in C. Fernández Ochoa, C. Heras, A. Morillo, M. Mar Zarzalejos Prieto, C. Fernández Ibáñez and M. Rosa Pina (eds) *De la costa al interior: las cerámicas de importación en Hispania*: 467-487. Madrid: Comunidad de Madrid.

Cisneros, M. 2018. Use and trade of ornamental rocks in the Mid-Ebro valley (Spain) in the Roman era, in C. Coquelet, G. Creemers, R. Dreesen and É. Goemare (eds) *Roman Ornamental Stones in North-Western Europe. Natural Resources, Manufacturing, Supply, Life and After-Life*: 163-174. Jambes: AWaP.

Collar, A., Coward, F., Brughmans, T. and Mills, B.J. 2015. Networks in Archaeology: Phenomena, Abstraction, Representation. *Journal of Archaeological Method and Theory* 22: 1-32.

Combes, P.P., Mayer, T. and Thisse, J.F. 2008. *Economic Geography. The Integration of Regions and Nations*. Princeton: Princeton University Press.

Cooper, J.P. 2011. No easy option: the Nile *versus* the Red Sea in ancient and mediaeval north-south navigation, in W.V. Harris and K. Iara (eds) *Maritime Technology in the Ancient Economy* (Journal of Roman Archaeology Supplements 84): 189-210. Portsmouth (RI): Journal of Roman Archaeology.

Coralini, A., Cerasetti, B., Cordoni, C. and Vescio, M. 2019. *Ruri*. Forms of living in the Po delta in the Roman age on the basis of remote sensing data, in E. Cirelli, E. Giorgi and G. Lepore (eds) *Economia e territorio. L'Adriatico centrale tra tarda Antichità e alto Medioevo*: 224-39. Oxford: Archaeopress.

Corbier, M. 1985. Dévaluation et évolution des prix, Ier - IIIe siècles. *Revue Numismatique* 27: 69-106.

Corcoran, S. and Delaine, J. 1994. The unit measurement of marble in Diocletian's Prices Edict. *Journal of Roman Archaeology* 7: 263-273.

Corrado, M. 2003. Le anfore tarde del 'dark layer' di UC VII (US 1098), in S. Lusuardi Siena and M.P. Rossignani (eds) *Dall'antichità al Medioevo: aspetti insediativi e manufatti: ricerche archeologiche nei cortili dell'Università cattolica*: 101-30. Milan: Vita e Pensiero.

Corrado, M. and Ferro, I. 2012. Le anfore Keay LII in e dalla Calabria: una prova della rinascita economica dei Bruttii nella tarda Antichità?, in M. D'Andrea (ed.) *Vincenzo Nusdeo. Sulle tracce della storia. Studi in onore di Vincenzo Nusdeo nel decennale della scomparsa*: 175-186. Vibo Valentia: AdHoc.

Corremans, M., Degryse, P., Wielgosz, D. and Waelkens, M. 2012. The import and use of white marble and coloured stone for wall and floor revetment at Sagalassos, in A.G. Garcia-M, P.L. Mercadal and L. Rodà De Llanza (eds) *Interdisciplinary Studies on Ancient Stone. Proceedings of the IX Association for the Study of Marble sand Other Stones in Antiquity (ASMOSIA) Conference (Tarragona 2009)*: 38-53. Tarragona: Institut Catalá d'Arqueologia Clàssica.

Corrò, E. and Mozzi, P. 2017. Water matters. Geoarchaeology of the city of Adria and palaeohydrographic variations (Po Delta, Northern Italy). *Journal of Archaeological Science* 15: 482-491.

Cosentino, S. 2014. Constans II, Ravenna's Autocephaly and the Panel of the Privileges in St. Apollinare in Classe: A Reappraisal, in T.G. Kolias, K.G. Pitsakis and C. Synellis (eds) *Aureus. Volume dedicated to Professor Evangelos K. Chrysos*: 153-169. Athens: National Hellenic Research Foundation.

Cosentino, S. 2020. The Structural Features of Ravenna's Socioeconomic History in Late Antiquity, in S. Cosentino (ed.) *Ravenna and the Traditions of Late Antique and Early Byzantine Craftsmanship. Labour, Culture, and the Economy*: 59-82. Berlin: De Gruyter.

Cosentino, S. 2021. Goods on the move across the late antique Mediterranean: some remarks on shipping, the management of ports and trading places, in V. Caminneci, E. Giannitrapani, M.C. Parello and M.S. Rizzo (eds) *LRCW6. Land and Sea: Pottery Routes (Agrigento, 24-28 maggio 2017)*: 1-12. Oxford: Archaeopress.

Covini, N.M. 2010. Strutture portuali e attraversamenti del Po: alcuni aspetti delle relazioni tra comunità, signori e stato ducale lombardo (secolo XV), in L.S. Olschki (ed.) *La civiltà delle acque tra Medioevo e Rinascimento. Atti del Convegno internazionale, Mantova, 1-4 ottobre 2008.*: 243-259. Florence: All'Insegna del Giglio.

Crema, E.R. 2012. Modelling Temporal Uncertainty in Archaeological Analysis. *Journal of Archaeological Method and Theory* 19: 440-461.

Cremaschi, M. 2009. Foreste, terre coltivate e acque: L'originalita del progetto terramaricolo, in M. Bernarbò Brea and M. Cremaschi (eds) *Acqua e civiltà nelle Terramare*: 34-42. Milan: Skira.

Cremaschi, M., Storchi, P. and Perego, A. 2018. Geoarchaeology in an urban context: The town of Reggio Emilia and river dynamics during the last two millennia in Northern Italy. *Geoarchaeology* 33: 52-66.

Cremonini, S. 2002. Preliminary geomorphological and stratigraphic settings of a large Roman-age village near Maccaretolo (low alluvial plain between

Bologna and Ferrara, Italy). *Mineral Periodical* 71: 125-136.

Cremonini, S. 2003. Contesti stratigrafici del sito archeologico di Maccaretolo Via Setti (S. Pietro in Casale, BO). Problemi geomorfologici e paloambientali, in S. Cremonini (ed.) *Maccaretolo: un pagus romano della pianura.*: 9-106. Bologna: Ante Quem.

Cremonini, S., Labate, D. and Curina, R. 2013. The late-antiquity environmental crisis in Emilia region (Po river plain, Northern Italy): Geoarchaeological evidence and paleoclimatic considerations. *Quaternary International* 316: 162-78.

Cremonini, S. and Mattioli, S. 2017. Geomorfologia e poleogenesi nella VIII Regio augustea. Considerazioni sui siti urbani d'età antica. Geomorphology and poleogenesis in the Augustus' 8th Region. Considerations on ancient urban sites. *Geologia dell'Ambiente* 25: 21-27.

Cresci Marrone, G. and Tirelli, M. 2011. *Altino dal cielo: la città telerivelata. Lineamenti di Forma urbis.* Trieste: Edizioni Quasar.

Crosetto, A. 2013a. Tortona, il porto fluviale nella tarda antichità, in S. Lusuardi Siena, E. Gautierdi Di Confiengo and B. Tarrico (eds) *Il viaggio della fede. La cristianizzazione del Piemonte meridionale tra IV e VIII secolo (Atti del con-vegno, Cherasco - Bra - Alba 2010)*: 101-115. Carru: Comune di Alba.

Crosetto, A. 2013b. Trasformazioni e continuità nel territorio delle antiche diocesi di Acqui, Tortona e Asti, in S. Lusuardi Siena, E. Gautierdi Di Confiengo and B. Tarrico (eds) *Il viaggio della fede. La cristianizzazione del Piemonte meridionale tra IV e VIII secolo (Atti del con-vegno, Cherasco - Bra - Alba 2010)*: 73-103. Carru: Comune di Alba.

Čufar, K., Merela, M. and Erič, M. 2014. A Roman barge in the Ljubljanica river (Slovenia): wood identification, dendrochronological dating and wood preservation research. *Journal of Archaeological Science* 44: 128-135.

Curina, R. 1986. Materiali di Scavo: Strati della fase imperiale, in J. Ortalli, D. Baldoni and R. Curina (eds) *Il teatro romano di Bologna (Documenti e studi (Deputazione di storia patria per le province di Romagna); 19)*: 159-188. Bologna: Deputazione di storia patria.

Curina, R., Malnati, L., Manzelli, V., Rossi, F., Spagnolo Garzoli, G. and Tirelli, M. 2015. La Cisalpina tra III e I secolo a.C. alla luce dell'archeologia, in L. Malnati and V. Manzelli (eds) *Brixia. Roma e le genti del Po*: 42-54. Florence: Giunti.

Curtis, D.R. and Campopiano, M. 2014. Medieval land reclamation and the creation of new societies: comparing Holland and the Po Valley, c.800ec.1500. *Journal of Historical Geography* 44: 93-108.

Curtis, R.I. 1991. *Garum and salsamenta: production and commerce in materia medica.* Leiden: Brill.

D'Agostino, M. and Medas, S. 2010. Roman Navigation in Venice Lagoon: the Results of Underwater Research.

The International Journal of Nautical Archaeology 39: 286-294.

D'Alessandro, L. 2013. Anfore adriatiche a Roma: dati epigrafici dal Nuovo Mercato Testaccio, in D. Bernal, L.C. Juan Tovar, M. Bustamante-Álvarez, J.J. Díaz Rodríguez and A.M. Sáez Romero (eds) *Hornos, talleres y focos de produccion alfarera en Hispania. Actas del I Congreso Internacional del la SECAH-Ex Officina Hispana (Cadiz, 3-4 de marzo de 2011)*: 351-364. Cádiz: Servicio de Publicaciones de la Universidad de Cádiz-SECAH.

D'Alessandro, L. 2024. *Anfore adriatiche a Roma: I dati del Nuovo Mercato Testaccio.* Pessac: Ausonius éditions.

Dal Sie, E. 2018a. Terra sigillata gallica, in L. Sperti, M. Tirelli and S. Cipriano (eds) *Prima dello scavo. Il survey 2012 ad Altino*: 77-81. Venice: Edizioni Ca' Foscari.

Dal Sie, E. 2018b. Terra sigillata medi-adriatica e tarda, in L. Sperti, M. Tirelli and S. Cipriano (eds) *Prima dello scavo. Il survey 2012 ad Altino*: 105-113. Venice: Edizioni Ca' Foscari.

Dall'Aglio, P.L. 1995. Considerazioni sull'intervento di Marco Emilio Scauro nella pianura Padana. *Atlante tematico di topografia antica* 4: 87-93.

Dall'Aglio, P.L. 2000. Geografia fisica e popolamento di età romana, in M. Marini Calvani (ed.) *Aemilia: La cultura romana in Emilia Romagna dal III secolo a.C. all'età constantiniana*: 51-56. Venice: Marsilio.

Dall'Aglio, P.L. and Franceschelli, C. 2017. La centuriazione della pianura padana: criteri ricostruttivi e problematiche storiche in E. Lo Cascio and M. Maiuro (eds) *Popolazione e risorse nell'Italia del nord dalla romanizzazione ai longobardi*: 255-288. Bari: Edipuglia.

Dall'Aglio, P.L. and Marchetti, G. 1991. Settlement Pattern and Agrarian Structures of the Roman Period in the Territory of Piacenza, in G. Barker and J.A. Lloyd (eds) *Roman Landscapes: Archaeological Survey in the Mediterranean Region*: 160-168. Rome and London: British School at Rome.

Dallemulle, U. 1977. S. Basilio (Ariano Polesine). Seconda campagna di scavo, agosto 1978. *Padusa* 12: 113-124.

Danckers, J. 2011. The 2nd-century AD crisis in Altinum (Venetia, Northern Italy): A mixture of historiographical determinism and archaeological scarcity? *Babesch* 86: 143-165.

Dannell, G.B. and Mees, A. 2013. New approaches to samian distribution, in M. Fulford and E. Durham (eds) *Seeing Red: New Economic and Social Perspectives on Terra Sigillata*: 165-87. Chicago and London: University of Chicago Press.

David, J.-M. 1997. *The Roman Conquest of Italy.* Oxford: Blackwell.

De Blois, L. 1976. *The policy of the emperor Gallienus.* Leiden: Brill.

De Callataÿ, F. 2014. *Quantifying the Greco-Roman economy and beyond.* Bari: Edipuglia.

De Ligt, L. 2017. Urbanization and Demographic Developments in North Italy 200 BC-AD 150, in E.

Lo Cascio and M. Maiuro (eds) *Popolazione e risorse nell'Italia del nord dalla romanizzazione al longobardi*: 21-48. Bari: Edipuglia.

De Sena, E.C. 2005. An assessment of wine and oil productionin Rome's hinterland: ceramic, literary, arthistorical and modern evidence, in B. Santillo Frizell and A. Klynne (eds) *Roman Villas around the Urbs. Interaction with Landscape and Environment. Proceedings of a Conference at the Swedish Institute in Rome, September 17-19, 2004*: 135-149. Rome: Swedish Institute in Rome.

De Soto, P. 2010. *Anàlisi de la xarxa de comunicacions i del transport a la Catalunya romana: estudis de distribució i mobilitat.* Unpublished PhD dissertation, Universitat Autònoma de Barcelona.

De Soto, P. 2019. Network Analysis to Model and Analyse Roman Transport and Mobility, in P. Verhagen, J. Joyce and M.R. Groenhuijzen (eds) *Finding the Limits of the Limes. Modelling Demography, Economy and Transport on the Edge of the Roman Empire*: 271-290. Springer Open Access: Springer.

De Soto, P. and Carreras, C. 2014. GIS and Network Analysis Applied to the Study of Transport in Roman Hispania, in J.M. Álvarez, T. Nogales and I. Rodà (eds) *XVIII CIAC: Centro y periferia en el mundo clásico/Centre and periphery in the ancient world*: 733-738. Mérida: Museo Nacional de Arte Romano.

De Weerd, M.D. 1978. Ships of the Roman period at Zwammerdam/Nigrum Pullum, Germania Inferior, in J. Du Plat Taylor and H. Cleere (eds) *Roman Shipping and Trade. Britain and the Rhine Provinces*: 15-21. London: Council for British Archaeology.

Delaine, J. 1992. *Design and construction in Roman imperial architecture: the Baths of Caracalla in Rome.* Unpublished PhD dissertation, University of Adelaide.

Delaine, J. 1997. *The baths of Caracalla: a study in the design, construction, and economics of large-scale building projects in imperial Rome.* (Journal of Roman Archaeology Supplements 25). Portsmouth (RI): Journal of Roman Archaeology.

Della Porta, C. 1998. Terra sigillata di età alto e medio imperiale, in G. Olcese (ed.) *Ceramiche in Lombardia tra II secolo a.C. e VII secolo d.C.: Raccolta dei dati editi*: 81-124. Mantua: All'Insegna del Giglio.

Desbat, A., Genin, M. and Lasfargues, J. 1996. Les productions des ateliers de potiers antiques de Lyon: 1ère partie: Les ateliers précoces. *Gallia* 53: 1-249.

Descamps, C. 1992. L'épave antique de La Mirande a Port-Vendres, in J. Rieucau and G. Cholvy (eds) *Le Languedoc, le Roussillon et la mer (des origines à la fin du XXe siècle)*: 79-97. Paris: Broché.

Destro, C. 2015. *Decorazione architettonica lapidea nella provincia di Padova tra età di romanizzazione ed età giulio-claudia.* Unpublished PhD dissertation, Università degli Studi di Padova.

Diosono, F. 2009. Il commercio del legname sul fiume Tevere, in H. Patterson and F. Coarelli (eds) *Mercator*

Placidissimus: The Tiber Valley in Antiquity. New research in the upper and middle river valley. Rome 27 - 28 February 2004: 251-283. Rome: Edizioni Quasar.

Diosono, F. 2012. Paesaggio rurale, produzioni e commerci nella valle del Tevere in età tardoantica, in A. Bravi (ed.) *Aurea Umbria: Una regione dell'Impero nell'era di Constantinio*: 199-209. Spello: Anno Edizione.

Dobreva, D. 2013. Alcune osservazioni sul commercio e il consumo di derrate a Calvatone-Bedriacum. I dati dei contenitori da trasporto dell'area della Domus del Labirinto (2001-2006), in M.T. Grassi (ed.) *Calvatone-Bedriacum. I nuovi scavi nell'area della Domus del Labirinto (2001-2006)*: 461-470. Mantua: Associazione Postumia di Gazoldo degli Ippoliti.

Dobreva, D. 2023a. Expanding African trade in the Adriatic during the early Imperial age, in I. Borzić, E. Cirelli, K. Jelinčić Vučković, A. Konestra and I. Ožanić Roguljić (eds) *TRADE: Transformations of Adriatic Europe (2nd-9th Centuries AD). Proceedings of the conference in Zadar, 11th-13th February 2016*: 290-302. Oxford: Archaeopress.

Dobreva, D. 2023b. Trade and exchange along the Adriatic Sea in Early Imperial times: the case of African imports. *Rei Cretariae Romanae Fautorum Acta* 47: 63-75.

Dobreva, D. and Griggio, A.M. 2021. Le ceramiche fini orientali, in J. Bonetto, S. Mazzocchin and D. Dobreva (eds) *Aquileia. Cossar funds. 3.3. Ceramic materials*: 189-288. Rome: Edizioni Quasar.

Dobreva, D. and Ravasi, T. 2018. Anfore. Il ruolo di Cremona nei commerci regionali e transregionali tra la fondazione della colonia e il I secolo a.C., in A.E. Arslan (ed.) *Amoenissimis...aedificiis. Gli scavi di piazza Marconi a Cremona. I materiali*: 215-240. Mantua: All'Insegna del Giglio.

Dodd, E.K. 2020. *Roman and late antique wine production in the eastern Mediterranean: a comparative archaeological study at Antiochia ad Cragum (Turkey) and Delos (Greece).* Oxford: Archaeopress.

Dodd, E.K. 2022. The Archaeology of Wine Production in Roman and Pre-Roman Italy. *American Journal of Archaeology* 126: 443-480.

Dodd, E.K. and Van Limbergen, D. 2024. Scientific Approaches to Ancient Wine: Developments, Challenges, and Future Perspectives, in E.K. Dodd and D. Van Limbergen (eds) *Methods in Ancient Wine Archaeology: Scientific Approaches in Roman Contexts*: 1-12. London: Bloomsbury.

Donat, P. 1994. Anfore africane, in M. Verzàr-Bass (ed.) *Scavi ad Aquileia 1994 - L'area ad est del Foro. Rapporto degli scavi 1989-91*: 413-450. Rome: Edizioni Quasar.

Donat, P. 2015. Terra sigillata gallica in Italia nordorientale. Dalle collezioni museali alle scoperte recenti. *Quaderni Friulani di Archeologia* 25: 39-51.

Donat, P. 2017. Terra Sigillata Gallica, in P. Maggi, F. Maselli Scotti, S. Pesavento Mattioli and E. Zulini (eds) *Materiali per Aquileia: lo scavo di Canale Anfora (2004-2005)*: 101-108. Trieste: Edizioni Quasar.

Donat, P. 2020. Nuove testimonianze di terra sigillata gallica dal territorio di Iulia Concordia e di Opitergium nella collezione archeologica di Pasiano di Pordenone. *Quaderni Friulani di Archeologia* 30: 121-129.

Donat, P. 2022. Terre sigillate galliche. La collezione "storica" del Museo Archeologico Nazionale di Aquileia (Friuli Venezia Giulia – Italia), in G.L. Vrkljan, A. Konestra and A.E. Borzić (eds) *Roman Pottery and Glass Manufactures: Production and Trade in the Adriatic Region and Beyond*: 191-202. Oxford: Archaeopress.

Donat, P. and Maggi, P. 2017. Terre Sigillate Italiche, in P. Maggi, F. Maselli Scotti, S. Pesavento Mattioli and E. Zulini (eds) *Materiali per Aquileia: lo scavo di Canale Anfora (2004-2005)*: 71-98. Trieste: Edizioni Quasar.

Donat, P., Maggi, P., Ventura, E. and Zulini, E. 2023. Aquileia, Canale Anfora – finds from 1988: pottery as a marker of trade, in A.E. Borzić, E. Cirelli, K. Jelinčić Vučković, A. Konestra and I. Ožanić Roguljić (eds) *TRADE – Transformations of Adriatic Europe (2nd-9th Centuries AD). Proceedings of the conference in Zadar, 11th-13th February 2016*: 327-332. Oxford: Archaeopress.

Donev, D. 2024. The urban corridors of Roman Pannonia, in J. Horvat, S. Groh, K. Strobel and M. Belak (eds) *Roman urban landscape. Towns and minor settlements from Aquileia to the Danube*: 33-52. Ljubljana: Založba ZRC.

Drennan, R.D. 2010. *Statistics for archaeologists: a commonsense approach* New York: Springer.

Dressel, H. 1879. *Di un grande deposito di anfore rinvenuto nel nuovo quartiere del Castro Pretorio (con tavole litografiche)*. Rome: Salviucci.

Duch, M. 2017. *Economic role of the Roman army in the province of Lower Moesia (Moesia Inferior)*. (Acta humanistica Gnesnensia. Poznań: Instytut Kultury Europejskiej.

Ducke, B. 2015. Spatial Cluster Detection in Archaeology: Current Theory and Practice., in J.A. Barcelo and I. Bogdanovic (eds) *Mathematics and Archaeology*. Boca Ranton: Taylor and Francis.

Duncan-Jones, R.P. 1978. Two possible indices of the purchasing power of money in Greek and Roman antiquity. *Publications de l'École Française de Rome* 37: 159-168.

Duncan-Jones, R.P. 1982. *The Economy of the Roman Empire: Quantative Studies*. Cambridge: Cambridge University Press.

Dycezk, P. 2001. *Roman Amphorae of 1st-3rd centuries AD found on the Lower Danube. Typology*. Warszawa: Wydawnictwa Uniwersytetu Warszawskiego.

Dyson, S.L. 1985. *The Creation of the Roman Frontier*. Princeton: Princeton University Press.

Egri, M. 2007. The Use of Amphorae for Interpreting Patterns of Consumption. *Theoretical Roman Archaeology Journal* 2006: 43-58.

Ehmig, U. 2010. *Dangstetten IV: die Amphoren*. Stuttgart: Konrad Theiss.

Erdkamp, P. 2012. A Forum on Trade: The Grain Trade in the Roman World, in W. Scheidel (ed.) *The Cambridge Companion to the Roman Economy*: 304-308. Cambridge: Cambridge University Press.

Erim, K.T. and Reynolds, J. 1970. The Copy of Diocletian's Edict on Maximum Prices From Aphrodisias in Caria. *Journal of Roman Studies* 60: 120-141.

Etienne, R. 1970. À propos du garum sociorum. *Latomus* 29: 297-313.

Ettlinger, E., Hedinger, B., Hoffmann, B., Kenrick, P.M., Pucci, G., Roth-Rubi, K., Schneider, G., Von Schnurbein, S., Wells, C.M. and Zabehlicky-Scheffenegger, S. 1990. *Conspectus formarum terrae sigillatae Italico modo confectae*. Bonn: R. Habelt.

Fabbri, B., Gualtieri, S. and Massa, S. 2004. Studio delle classi ceramiche: Aspetti archeologici e indagnini archeometriche, in V. Mariotti (ed.) *Il teatro e l'anfiteatro di Cividate Camuno: scavo, restauro, e allestimento di un parco archeologico*: 231-54. Florence: All'Insegna del Giglio.

Facchinetti, G. 2014. Le ville e lo sfruttamento del territorio tra Ticino e Olona in età romana, in V. Mariotti (ed.) *Un monastero nei secoli: Santa Maria Assunta di Cairate. Scavi e ricerche* (Documenti di archeologia 57): 155-165. Mantua: All'Insegna del Giglio.

Facchini, G.M. and Leotta, F.M. 2005. Anfore. *Rivista archeologia dell'antica provincia e diocesi di Como* 187: 147-76.

Faletti, P., Gelati, R. and Rogledi, S. 1995. Oligo-Miocene evolution of Monferrato and Langhe, related to deep structures, in R. Polino and R. Sacchi (eds) *Rapporti Alpi-Appennino*: 1-19. Rome: Accademia Nazionale delle Scienze.

Fant, J. 1989. New Sculptural and Architectural Finds from Docimium. *Araştırma Sonuçları Toplantısı* 7: 111-118.

Fant, J. 1999. Augustus and the city of marble, in M. Schvoerer (ed.) *Asmosia IV. Archéomatériaux. Marbres et Autres Roches. Actes de la IVème Conférence Internationale de l'Association pour l'Etude des Marbres et Autres Roches Utilisés dans le Passé*: 277-280. Bordeaux: CRPAA.

Fant, J., Russell, B. and Barker, G. 2013. Marble use and reuse at Pompeii and Herculaneum: the evidence from the bars. *Papers of the British School at Rome* 81: 181-209.

Fentress, E. 1979. *Numidia and the Roman Army*. (BAR International Series 53). Oxford: Archaeopress.

Fentress, E. 1990. The economy of an inland city: Sétif, *L'Afrique dans l'Occident romain (Ier siècle av. J.-C. - IVe siècle ap. J.-C.)*: 117-128. Rome: École Française de Rome.

Fentress, E. 2015. Diana Veteranorum and the Dynamics of an Inland Economy. *Late Antique Archaeology* 10: 315-342.

Fentress, E., Fontana, S., Hitchner, R.B. and Perkins, P. 2004. Accounting for ARS: fineware and sites in Sicily and Africa, in S.E. Alcock and J.F. Cherry (eds) *Side-by-side survey: comparative regional studies in the Mediterranean world*: 147-162. Oxford: Oxbow.

Fentress, E. and Perkins, P. 1988. Counting African Red Slip Ware, in A. Mastino (ed.) *L'Africa Romana: Atti del V Convegno di studio Sassari, 11-13 dicembre 1987*: 205-214. Sassari: Università degli studi di Sassari.

Ferasin, M. and Tonutti, P. 2002. Al di là dei confini di Toscana: tradizione e sviluppo dell'olivicoltura nei Colli Euganei, in O. Longo and P. Scarpi (eds) *Tutte le sfumature del verde. Qualità dell'olio e purezza del paesaggio*: 59-71. Padua: Sargon.

Fernández Ochoa, C. and Morillo, A. 1994. *De Brigantium a Oiasso. Una aproximación al estudio de los enclaves marítimos cantábricos en época romana*. Madrid: Foro.

Fernández Ochoa, C. and Morillo, C. 2010. Roman lighthouses on the Atlantic coast, in C. Carreras and R. Morais (eds) *The Western Roman Atlantic Façade. A Study of the Economy and Trade in the Mar Exterior from the Republic to the Principate*: 109-118. Oxford: Archaeopress.

Fernández, P.T. 2021. Mobility in ancient times: Combining land and water costs. *Digital Applications in Archaeology and Cultural Heritage* 22: e00192.

Ferrando, F. 2008. La produzione di terra sigillata tarda medioadriatica, II-V secolo d.c., dagli scavi di Sentinum, in M. Medri (ed.) *Sentinum 295 a.C., Sassoferrato 2006: 2300 anni dopo la battaglia: una città romana tra storia e archeologia: convegno internazionale, Sassoferrato 21-23 settembre 2006*: 387-390. Rome: L'Erma di Bretschneider.

Ficara, M. and Manzelli, V. (eds) 2008. *Orme nei campi: archeologia a sud di Ravenna. Atti della giornata di studi sui recenti rinvenimenti archeologici nel territorio Decimano (San Pietro in Campiano, Ravenna, 2006)*, Borgo S. Lorenzo: All'Insegna del Giglio.

Filippi, F. (ed.) 1997. *Alba Pompeia. Archeologia della città dalla fondazione alla tarda antichità*, Alba: Omega.

Finley, M.I. 1973. *The Ancient Economy*. Berkeley and London: University of California Press.

Finné, M., Woodbridge, J., Labuhn, I. and Roberts, C.N. 2019. Holocene hydro-climatic variability in the Mediterranean: A synthetic multi-proxy reconstruction. *Holocene* 29: 847-863.

Finocchi, S. 1980. Banchina Romana su Palificata. Trovata a Ivrea nell'alveo della Dora, in S.a.D. Piemonte (ed.) *Studi di Archeologia dedicati a Pietro Barocelli*: 89-93. Turin: Ministero per i beni culturali e ambientali.

Fiorio, M.T. and Bandera Bistoletti, S. 1985. *Le chiese di Milano* Milan: Electa.

Fontana, A., Mozzi, P. and Bondesan, A. 2008. Alluvial megafans in the Venetian–Friulian Plain (north-eastern Italy): Evidence of sedimentary and erosive phases during Late Pleistocene and Holocene. *Quaternary international* 189: 71-90.

Fontana, F. (ed.) 2017. *Aquileia, l'insula tra foro e porto fluviale. Lo scavo dell'Università degli Studi di Trieste*, Trieste: EUT Edizioni.

Forin, C. 2017. *Ville e fattorie nell'Italia settentrionale in epoca romana (II sec. a.C. – V sec. d.C.): architettura, economia e società* Unpublished PhD dissertation, Università degli Studi di Padova.

Fozzati, L. and Papotti, L. 1996. Nuove scoperte in Piedmont. *Atlante tematico di topografia antica* 5: 213-221.

Framarin, P. and Castoldi, M. 2013. Lo studio dei materiali architettonici dall'area sacra del Foro di Augusta Praetoria. *Bollettino della Soprintendenza per i Beni e le Attività Culturali Regione Autonoma Valle d'Aosta* 10: 32-39.

Franceschelli, C. and Marabini, S. 2007. *Lettura di un territorio sepolto. La pianura lughese in età romana.* (Studi e Scavi 17). Bologna: Ante Quem.

Francesconi, A. 2020. Il potenziale delle risorse invisibili, un caso studio: le anfore e i commerci a Laus Pompeia (LO) tra I sec. a.C. e I d.C. *West and East. Rivista della Scuola di Specializzazione in Beni Archeologici* 5: 16-36.

Franconi, T.V. 2013. Rome and the power of ancient rivers. *Journal of Roman Archaeology* 26: 705-711.

Franconi, T.V. 2014. *The Economic Development of the Rhine River Basin in the Roman Period (30 BC - AD 406)*. Unpublished D.Phil dissertation, University of Oxford.

Franconi, T.V. 2016. Climatic influences on riverine transport on the Roman Rhine, in C. Schäfer (ed.) *Connecting the Ancient World. Mediterranean Shipping, Maritime Networks and their Impact (Pharos 35)*: 27-46. Rahden/Westf: Pharos.

Franconi, T.V., Brughmans, T., Borisova, E. and Paulsen, L. 2023. From Empire-wide integration to regional localization: A synthetic and quantitative study of heterogeneous amphora data in Roman Germania reveals centuries-long change in regional patterns of production and consumption. *PLOS ONE* 18: e0279382.

Fredi, P. and Lupia Palmieri, E. 2017. Morphological Regions of Italy, in M. Soldati and M. Marchetti (eds) *Landscapes and Landforms of Italy*: 39-74. Cham: Cham: Springer International Publishing.

Frontori, I. 2017. *L'acqua a Mediolanum. Controllo e gestione delle risorse idriche in età romana.* Unpublished PhD dissertation, Università degli Studi di Milano.

Fulford, M. 1987. Economic interdependence among urban communities of the Roman Mediterranean. *World Archaeology* 19: 58-75.

Fulford, M. 2009. Approaches to Quantifying Roman Trade: A Response, in A.I. Wilson and A.K. Bowman (eds) *Quantifying the Roman Economy: Methods and Problems*: 250-259. Oxford: Oxford University Press.

Gabba, E. 1985. Per un'interpretazione storica della centuriazione romana. *Athenaeum* 73: 265-284.

Gabba, E. 2001. Plinio Fraccaro e la storia antica. *Athenaeum* 89: 3-40.

Gabelmann, H. 1973. *Die Werkstattgruppen der oberitalischen Sarkophage*. Bonn: Landschaftsverband Rheinland.

Gabler, D. 1986. *Terra sigillata im Barbaricum zwischen Pannonien und Dazien*. Budapest: Akadémiai Kiadó.

Gabucci, A. 1995. Marchi di fabbrica da Tortona. Terra sigillata italica, nord-italica e sud-gallica. *Quaderni della Soprintendenza Archeologica del Piemonte* 13: 29-58.

Gabucci, A. 2017. *Attraverso le Alpi e lungo il Po: importazione e distribuzione di sigillate galliche nella Cisalpina*. Rome: École française de Rome.

Gabucci, A. and Mennella, G. 2003. Tra Emona e Augusta Taurinorum. Un mercante di Aquileia. *Aquileia Nostra* 74: 318-334.

Gabucci, A. and Quiri, E. 2008. Eporedia: Appunti su terre sigillate e anfore tra tarda repubblica e età imperiale. *Quaderni della Soprintendenza Archeologica del Piemonte* 23: 45-78.

Gaddi, D. 2017a. Anfore del Mediterraneo Occidentale, in P. Maggi, F. Maselli Scotti, S. Pesavento Mattioli and E. Zulini (eds) *Materiali per Aquileia: lo scavo di Canale Anfora (2004-2005)*: 373-394. Trieste: Edizioni Quasar.

Gaddi, D. 2017b. Lo scavo e la ricostruzione delle fasi di vita del canale, in P. Maggi, F. Maselli Scotti, S. Pesavento Mattioli and E. Zulini (eds) *Materiali per Aquileia. Lo scavo di Canale Anfora (2004-2005)*: 21-34. Rome: Edizioni Quasar.

Gaddi, D. and Maggi, P. 2017. Anfore Italiche, in P. Maggi, F. Maselli Scotti, S. Pesavento Mattioli and E. Zulini (eds) *Materiali per Aquileia: lo scavo di Canale Anfora (2004-2005)*: 263-328. Trieste: Edizioni Quasar.

Gallimore, S. 2023. Do shape and size matter? The distribution of Amphore Crétoise 4 containers, 1st–3rd c. CE. *Journal of Roman Archaeology* 36: 368-396.

Galvani, I. and Pellegrini, M. 2007. Navigare il Po, tra passato e futuro, in I. Ferrari and M. Pellegrini (eds) *Un Po di carte. La dinamica fluviale dell'Ottocento e le tavole della Commissione Brioschi*: 51-65. Reggio Emilia: Edizioni Diabasis.

Gamba, M., Raimondi, N. and Rigoni, M. 2012. Vicenza, Dal Molin. Indagini sul contesto rustico e l'acquedotto romano (2009–2010). *Quaderni di Archeologia del Veneto* 28: 106-111.

Gambari, M. and Barello, F. 2004. *Brandizzo: Un insediamento rurale di età romana*. Turin: Ministero per i Beni e le Attività Culturali.

Gambari, M., Crosetto, A., Deconca, D., Fravega, V., Ghiringhello, C., Giomi, F., Ippolito, M., Manfredi, A. and Parodi, G. 2011. Tortona, via Saccaggi - corso

Repubblica. Resti del porto fluviale di età romana e impianti artigianali postmedievali. *Quaderni della Soprintendenza Archeologica del Piemonte* 26: 163-169.

Ganzarolli, G. 2017. Ceramiche d'importazione fini e da cucina, imitazioni e ceramiche a colature rosse, in A. Chavarría Arnau (ed.) *Ricerche sul centro episcopale di Padova. Scavi 2011-2012*: 209-224. Mantua: SAP.

Gardner, A. 2007. *An Archaeology of Identity: Soldiers and Society in Late Roman Britain*. London: Routledge.

Garnsey, P. 1998. Economy and Society of Mediolanum under the Principate, in W. Scheidel (ed.) *Cities, Peasants and Food in Classical Antiquity: Essays in Social and Economic History*: 45-62. Cambridge: Cambridge University Press.

Garnsey, P. and Saller, R. 1987. *The Roman Empire: economy, society and culture*. London: University of California Press.

Gaspari, A. 1998. Pontonium" iz Lip na Ljubljanskem barju (A "Pontonium" from Lipe on the Ljubljana moor. *Arheološki Vestnik* 49: 187-224.

Gaspari, A. 2021. Ships and boats of late Prehistoric and Roman Nauportus. New evidence and some remarks on the transfer and innovation in the shipbuilding technologies on the northern fringes of the Mediterranean 2nd century BC – 1st century AD. *Archaeonautica* 21: 123-129.

Gasperi, G. 2001. Schema strutturale dell'area, in G.B. Castiglioni and G.B. Pellegrini (eds) *Note illustrative alla Carta Geomorfologica della Pianura Padana*: 45-54. Turin: Comitato Glaciologico Italiano.

Gelichi, S. 2015. La storia di una nuova città: Venezia nell'alto Medioevo, in V. West-Harling and C. Wickham (eds) *Three empires, three cities identity, material culture and legitimacy in Venice, Ravenna and Rome, 750-1000*: 51-98. Turnhout: Brepols.

Genin, M. 2007. *La Graufesenque (Millau, Aveyron). Sigillées lisses et autres productions*. Bordeux: Editions de la Fédération Aquitania.

Germinario, L., Zara, A., Maritan, L., Bonetto, J., Hanchar, J.M., Sassi, R., Siegesmund, S. and Mazzoli, C. 2018. Tracking trachyte on the Roman routes: Provenance study of Roman infrastructure and insights into ancient trades in northern Italy. *Geoarchaeology* 33: 417-429.

Giacobelli, M. 1997. I vetri del relitto di Grado, in G. Vople (ed.) *Atti del Convegno Nazionale di Archaeologia Subaquea. Anzio, 30-31 maggio e 1 giugno 1996*: 311-313. Bari: Edipuglia.

Giardina, A. 1993. La formazione dell'Italia provinciale, in A. Carandini, L. Cracco Ruggini and A. Giardina (eds) *Storia di Roma III: L'età tardoantica. 2. I luoghi e le culture*: 51-68. Rome: Einaudi.

Giardina, A. 1997. *L'Italia romana: storie di un'identità incompiuta*. Rome: Laterza.

Giarolo, D. 1910. La villa romana di Casa Quinta in Comune di Sarego. *Bollettino del Museo Civico di Vicenza*: 14.

Glicksman, K. 2005. Internal and external trade in the Roman province of Dalmatia. *Opvscvla Archaeologica* 29: 189-230.

Golbeck, J. 2013. *Analyzing the Social Web.* Amsterdam: Wiley.

Gomez Serito, M. 2007. Caratterizzazione petrografica e indicazione delle aree di provenienza dei materiali lapidei, in A. Crosetto and M.V. Gambari (eds) *Onde nulla si perda. La collezione archeologica di Cesare di Negro Carpani*: 335-340. Alessandria: LineLab.

Gomez Serito, M. 2019. I percorsi di pietre e marmi a vall e dell e Alp i occidentali in età romana: uno sguardo di sintesi per la proposta di nuove letture sul territorio, in G.A. Mergozzo (ed.) *Le Vie della pietra: estrazione e diffusione delle pietre da opera alpine dall'età romana all'età moderna. Atti del Convegno in occasione del decennale dell'Ecomuseo del Granito di Montorfano (28-29 Ottobre 2017)*: 105-118. Mergozzo: Gruppo Archeologico Mergozzo.

Gomez Serito, M. and Rulli, E. 2012. I materiali lapidei naturali della domus dei "Putti danzanti": marmi bianchi e colorati, in J. Bonetto and M. Salvadori (eds) *L'architettura privata ad Aquileia in età romana, Atti del convegno di studio, Padova 21-22 febbraio 2011*: 309-316. Padua: Edizioni Quasar.

Gomez Serito, M. and Rulli, E. 2014. Le indagini petrografiche, in M.C. Preacco (ed.) *Augusta Bagiennorum. Storia e archeologia di una città augustea*: 141-147. Turin: Celid.

Gonzalez Vilches, C., Gonzalez Rodriguez, M., Modrzewska-Pianetti, I. and Pianetti, F. 1998. Contenitori per garum e loro paste. Confronti fra Dr 7-12 dei ritrovamenti nel Veneto. *Archaeologia e Calcolatori* 9: 331-342.

Goodson, C. 2020. *Cultivating the city in early Medieval Italy.* Cambridge: Cambridge University Press.

Gori, G. 2003. Instrumentum domesticum, in M. Luni (ed.) *Archeologia nelle Marche dalla preistoria all'età tardoantica*: 371-382. Florence: Nardini Editore.

Gorrini, M.E. and Robino, M. 2015. The Sarcophagi of Ticinum (Pavia) A Preliminary Report, in B. Porod and G. Koiner (eds) *Römische Sarkophage: Akten des Internationalen Werkstattgesprächs, 11.- 13. Oktober 2012 (Graz)*: 112-125. Graz: Archäologiemuseum Schloss Eggenberg.

Gottarelli, A. 1988. La via Claudia di età Imperiale tra Bologna e Firenze: nuove ipotesi per una storia dei collegamenti stradali tra la VII e la VIII Regio, in G. Bertuzzi (ed.) *Vie romane tra l'Italia Centrale e la pianura Padana. Ricerche nei territori di Reggio Emilia, Modena e Bologna*: 71-112. Modena: Aedes Muratoriana.

Graham, S. 2002. *'Ex Figlinis': The Complex Dynamics of the Roman Brick Industry in the Tiber Valley during the 1st to 3rd Centuries AD.* Unpublished PhD dissertation, University of Reading.

Graham, S. 2006. Networks, Agent-Based Models and the Antonine Itineraries: Implications for Roman Archaeology. *Journal of Mediterranean Archaeology* 19: 45-64.

Grainger, S. 2021. *The story of garum: fermented fish sauce and salted fish in the ancient world.* London: Routledge.

Grazia Maioli, M. 1986. Ravenna, Loc. Classe, Podere Chiavichetta, quartiere portuale tardoromano e bizantino, in G. Bermond Montanari (ed.) *Studi e documenti archeologia 2*: 161-164. Bologna: Nuova Alfa.

Grazia Maioli, M. 1990. La Topografica della zone di Classe, in G. Susini (ed.) *Storia di Ravenna I*: 375-414. Ravenna: Marsillo.

Grazia Maioli, M. 1991. Strutture economico-commerciali e impianti produttivi, in A. Carile (ed.) *Storia di Ravenna II: Dall'età bizantina all'età ottoniana*: 223-47. Venice: Marsillo.

Grazia Maioli, M. 2018. Antiche acque di Ravenna, in C. Guarnieri and G. Montevecchi (eds) *Il genio delle acque: scavi nelle piazze di Ravenna*: 331-342. Ravenna: Longo Angelo.

Greci, R. 2016. Porti fluviali e ponti in età medievale. Il Po e l'area padana. *Hortus Artium Mediev.* 22: 238-248.

Greene, K. 2005. Roman pottery: models, proxies, and economic interpretation. *Journal of Roman Archaeology* 18: 34-56.

Greene, K. 2008. Learning to consume: consumption and consumerism in the Roman Empire. *Journal of Roman Archaeology* 21: 64-82.

Gregoratti, L. 2012. Linee privilegiate di contatto ed espansione delle élite dei centri italici nei territori alpini. *Historiká* 2: 55-62.

Gregoratti, L. 2014. North Italic Settlers along the "Amber Route". *Studia Antiqua et Archaeologica* 19: 133-155.

Gregoratti, L. 2015. Aquileian Families in Pannonia and Upper Moesia, in G.R. Tsetskhladze, A. Avram and J. Hargrave (eds) *The Danubian Lands between the Black, Aegean and Adriatic Seas (7th Century BC-10th Century AD). Proceedings of the Fifth International Congress on Black Sea Antiquities*: 219-222. Oxford: Archaeopress.

Guarnieri, C. (ed.) 2007. *Archeologia nell'Appennino romagnolo. Il territorio di Riolo Terme,* Imola: Bacchilega.

Guarnieri, C. 2013. I rivestimenti lapidei, in C. Guarnieri (ed.) *Vivere a Forum Livi. Lo scavo di via Curte a Forlì*: 87-90. Bologna: Ante Quem.

Guarnieri, C., Montevecchi, G. and Pagani, C. 2018. La forma e l'evoluzione della domus, in C. Guarnieri and G. Montevecchi (eds) *Il genio delle acque: scavi nelle piazze di Ravenna*: 88-90. Ravenna: Longo Angelo.

Gumiero, B., Maiolini, B., Rinaldi, M., Surian, N., Boz, B. and Moroni, F. 2009. The Italian Rivers, in K. Tockner, U. Uehlinger and C.T. Robinson (eds) *Rivers of Europe*: 467-495. Amsterdam: Academic Press.

Gunneweg, J., Perlman, I. and Yellin, J. 1983. *The provenience, typology, and chronology of Eastern Terra Sigillata.* (Qedem. Jerusalem.

Harris, W.V. 1985. *War and Imperialism in Republican Rome,*

327-70 B.C. Oxford: Clarendon Press.

Harris, W.V. 2007. The Late Republic, in W. Scheidel, I. Morris and R. Saller (eds) *The Cambridge Economic History of the Greco-Roman World*: 511-539. Cambridge: Cambridge University Press.

Harris, W.V. 2011. Trade and the River Po: A Problem in the Economic History of the Roman Empire, in W.V. Harris (ed.) *Rome's Imperial Economy: Twelve Essays*: 189-197. 2 ed. Oxford: Oxford University Press.

Haussler, R. 2007. At the Margins of Italy: Celts and Ligurians in North-West Italy, in G. Bradley, E. Isayev and C. Riva (eds) *Ancient Italy: Regions without Boundaries*: 45-78. Exeter: Exeter University Press.

Haussler, R. 2013. *Becoming Roman?: diverging identities and experiences in ancient northwest Italy*. Milton: Routledge.

Hayes, J.W. 1972. *Late Roman Pottery*. London: British School at Rome.

Hayes, J.W. 2008. *Roman pottery: fineware imports*. (The Athenian agora: results of excavations conducted by the American School of Classical Studies at Athens). Princeton: Princeton University Press.

Heckscher, E.F. and Ohlin, B.G. 1991. *Heckscher-Ohlin Trade Theory*. Boston: MIT Press.

Heilen, M. and Manney, S.A. 2023. Refining Archaeological Data Collection and Management. *Advances in Archaeological Practice* 11: 1-10.

Hirt, A.M. 2010. *Imperial Mines and Quarries in the Roman World: Organizational Aspects, 27 BC–AD 235*. (Oxford Classical Monographs. Oxford.

Hitchner, R.B. 2012. Roads, Integration, Connectivity, and Economic Performance in the Roman Empire, in S.E. Alcock, J.P. Bodel and R.J.A. Talbert (eds) *Highways, byways, and road systems in the pre-modern world*: 222–234. London: Wiley.

Hobson, M.S. 2015. *The North African boom: evaluating economic growth in the Roman province of Africa Proconsularis (146 B.C. - A.D. 439)*. (Journal of Roman Archaeology Supplements 100). Portsmouth (RI): Journal of Roman Archaeology.

Hoffmann, J. 1968. Die östliche Adriaküste als Hauptnachschubbasis für den venezianischen Sklavenhandel bis zum Ausgang des elften Jahrhunderts. *Vierteljahrschrift für Sozial- und Wirtschaftsgeschichte* 55: 165-181.

Horden, P. and Purcell, N. 2000. *The Corrupting Sea: A Study of Mediterranean History*. Oxford: Wiley.

Horvat, J. 2008. Early Roman Horrea at Nauportus. *Mélanges de l École française de Rome Antiquité* 120: 111-121.

Horvat, J. 2017. The Storehouses and River Port of Nauportus, in P. Scherrer (ed.) *Akten des Symposiums "Horrea" am Institut für Archäologie des Universität Graz, 1.-2. oktober 2015*: 1-11. Vienna: Österreichische Gesellschaft für Archäologie im Selbstverlag.

Hudson, P. 1993. Le mure romane di Pavia, in G.P. Brogiolo (ed.) *Mura delle città romane in Lombardia*:

107-118. Como: Società Archeologica Comense.

Iandoli, M. 2006. Le anfore della domus romana di palazzo Diotallevi a Rimini: alcune riflessioni sui circuiti commerciali. *Ariminum, Storia e Archeologia* 2: 103-133.

Iavarone, S. and Olcese, G. 2013. Le anfore Dressel 2-4 di produzione tirrenica: una proposta di progetto archeologico ed archeometrico, in G. Olcese (ed.) *IMMENSA AEQUORA Workshop, Atti del Convegno, Roma 24-26 gennaio 2011*: 221-226. Rome: Edizioni Quasar.

Isaksen, L. 2008. The application of network analysis to ancient transport geography: A case study of Roman Baetica. *Digital Medievalist* 4.

Istenič, J. 2009. The early Roman military route along the river Ljubljanica (Slovenia), in Á. Morillo, N. Hanel and E. Martín (eds) *Limes XX: Estudios sobre la frontera romana (Roman frontier studies)*: 855-865. Madrid: Merida.

Johnson, I. 2004. Aoristic Analysis: seeds of a new approach to mapping archaeological distributions through time, in K.F. Ausserer, W. Börner, M. Goriany and L. Karlhuber-Vöckl (eds) *Enter the Past The E-way into the Four Dimensions of Cultural Heritage: CAA 2003*. Oxford: Archaeopress.

Joncheray, A. and Joncheray, J.-P. 2007. Chrétienne M, trois épaves distinctes, entre le cinquième siècle avant et le premier siècle après Jésus-Christ. *Cahiers d'Archéologie Subaquatique* 14: 57-130.

Jones, E.T. 2000. River navigation in Medieval England. *Journal of Historical Geography* 26: 60-75.

Jorio, S. 1991. Terra Sigillata, in D. Caporusso (ed.) *Scavi MM3. Ricerche di archeologia urbana a Milano durante la costruzione della linea 3*: 57-87. Milan: Edizioni ET.

Jorio, S. 1998. Terra sigillata di età medio e tardo imperiale, in G. Olcese (ed.) *Ceramiche in Lombardia tra II secolo a.C. e VII secolo d.C.: Raccolta dei dati editi*: 125-132. Mantua: All'Insegna del Giglio.

Jorio, S. 1999. Le Terra Sigillate di Produzione non Africana, in G.P. Brogliolo (ed.) *Santa Giulia di Brescia: gli scavi dal 1980 al 1992: Reperti preromani, romani e altomedievali*: 81-95. Florence: All'Insegna del Giglio.

Jorio, S. 2000. Terra sigillata: manufatture "locali" e importazioni nella documentazione di alcuni scavi milanesi, in R. La Guardia, T. Tibiletti and C. Ridi (eds) *Milano tra l'età repubblicana e l'età augustea, Atti del Convegno di Studi 26-27 marzo 1999, Milano*: 99-109. Milan: Settore cultura musei e mostre, civiche raccolte archeologiche, Commune di Milano.

Jorio, S. 2002. Terra sigillata della media e tarda età imperiale di produzione padana. Contributo alla definizione di un repertorio lombardo, in F. Rossi (ed.) *Nuove ricerche sul Capitolium di Brescia: scavi, studi e restauri*: 323-352. Milan: Edizioni ET.

Jurišić, M. 2000. *Ancient shipwrecks of the Adriatic: maritime transport during the first and second centuries AD*. (BAR International Series 828). Oxford: Archaeopress.

Keay, S. (ed.) 2012. *Portus and the Ports of the Roman*

Mediterranean, Rome and London: British School at Rome.

Kenrick, P.M. 1993. Italian Terra Sigillata: a sophisticated Roman industry. *Oxford Journal of Archaeology* 12: 235-42.

Kenrick, P.M. 1997. Cn. Ateius – the inside story. *Rei Cretariae Romanae Fautorum Acta* 35: 179-190.

Kenrick, P.M. 2000. Stamped Sigillata from Northern Italy: Patterns of Distribution, in G.P. Brogliolo and G. Olcese (eds) *Produzione ceramica in area padana tra il II secolo a.C. e il VII secolo d.C: nuovi dati e prospettive di ricerca: convegno internazionale, Desenzano del Garda, 8-10 aprile 1999*: 47-52. Mantua: All'Insegna del Giglio.

Kiiskinen, H. 2013. *Production and Trade of Etrurian Terra Sigillata pottery in Roman Etruria and beyond between c. 50 BCE and c. 150 CE.* Turku: University of Turku.

Kleineberg, A. 2021. The Capitolium at Brescia in the Flavian Period, in A. Haug and M.T. Lauritsen (eds) *Principles of Decoration in the Roman World*: 71-90. Berlin and Boston: De Gruyter.

Knappett, C. 2013. Introduction: Why Networks?, in C. Knappett (ed.) *Network Analysis in Archaeology: New Approaches to Regional Interaction*: 3-15. Oxford: Oxford University Press.

Knoke, D. and Yang, S. 2008. *Social network analysis.* (Quantitative applications in the social sciences series 154). Los Angeles: SAGE Publications.

Komar, P. 2021. *Eastern wines on western tables: consumption, trade and economy in ancient Italy.* (Mnemosyne Supplements 435). Leiden: Brill.

Labate, D. 2019. Archeologia di una strada consolare: la via Emilia dalla fondazione all'età contemporanea. *Atlante tematico di topografia antica* 29: 195-212.

Labuhn, I., Finné, M., Izdebski, A., Roberts, N. and Woodbridge, J. 2016. Climatic Changes and Their Impacts in the Mediterranean during the First Millennium AD. *Late Antique Archaeology* 12: 65-88.

Langdon, J. 2000. Inland water transport in Medieval England—the view from the mills: a response to Jones. *Journal of Historical Geography* 26: 75-82.

Laubenheimer, F. 1985. *La production des amphores en Gaule Narbonnaise.* Paris: Les Belles Lettres.

Laubenheimer, F. 1991. Les vides sanitarieset les amphores de la Porte d'Oree a Frejus. *Gallia* 48: 229-266.

Launaro, A. 2011. *Peasants and Slaves: The Rural Population of Roman Italy (200 BC to AD 100).* Cambridge: Cambridge University Press.

Laurence, R. 1999. *The roads of Roman Italy: mobility and cultural change.* London and New York: Routledge.

Laurence, R. 2005. Land transport in Roman Italy: costs, practice and the economy, in H. Parkins and C. Smith (eds) *Trade, Traders and the Ancient City*: 129-147. London: Routledge.

Laurence, R. and Trifilò, F. 2015. The Global and Local in the Roman Empire: connectivity and mobility from an urban perspective, in M. Pitts and J.M. Versluys (eds) *Globalisation and the Roman world: world history, connectivity and material culture*: 99-122. Cambridge: Cambridge University Press.

Lavan, L. 2015. Local Economies in Late Antiquity? Some Thoughts. *Late Antique Archaeology* 10: 1-11.

Laven, P. 1989. The Venetian rivers in the Sixteenth Century, in J.F. Bergier (ed.) *Montagnes, fleuves, forêts dans l'histoire: barrières ou lignes de convergence: travaux présentés au XVIe Congrès international des sciences historiques, Stuttgart, août 1985*: 198-217. St. Katherinen: Scripta Mercaturae.

Lavizzari Pedrazzini, M.P. 1973. Ceramica arretina, T.S. tardo-italica, T.S. gallica, in A. Frova (ed.) *Scavi di Luni: Relazione preliminare delle campagne di scavo, 1970-1971*: 698-701. Rome: L'Erma di Bretschneider.

Lavizzari Pedrazzini, M.P. 1973. Ceramica arretina, T.S. tardo-italica, T.S. gallica, T.S. italica (D), in A. Frova (ed.) *Scavi di Luni: Relazione preliminare delle campagne di scavo, 1970-1971*: 283-331. Rome: L'Erma di Bretschneider.

Lavizzari Pedrazzini, M.P. 1977. Terra sigillata italica e sud-gallica (D), in A. Frova (ed.) *Scavi di Luni II: Relazione delle campagne di scavo, 1972-1973-1974*: 118-142. Rome: L'Erma di Bretschneider.

Lavizzari Pedrazzini, M.P. 2003. Osservazioni in margine alla terra sigillata gallica rinvenuta a Torino, in L. Mercando (ed.) *Archeologia a Torino. Dall'età preromana all'Alto Medioevo*: 246-257. Turin: Umberto Allemandi.

Lazzarini, L. 2004. Archaeometric aspects of white and coloured marbles used in antiquity: the state of the art. *Periodico di Mineralogia* 73: 113-125.

Lazzarini, L. 2019. Ancient Mediterranean polychrome stones, in G. Artioli and R. Oberti (eds) *The Contribution of Mineralogy to Cultural Heritage*: 367-392. Twickenham: Mineralogical Society of Great Britain and Ireland.

Leidwanger, J., Knappett, C., Arnaud, P., Arthur, P., Blake, E., Broodbank, C., Brughmans, T., Evans, T., Graham, S., Greene, E.S., Kowalzig, B., Mills, B., Rivers, R., Tartaron, T.F. and Van De Noort, R. 2014. A manifesto for the study of ancient Mediterranean maritime networks. *Antiquity* 342.

Leitch, V. 2011. Location, location, location: characterizing coastal and inland production and distribution of Roman African cooking wares, in D. Robinson and A.I. Wilson (eds) *Maritime Archaeology and Ancient Trade in the Mediterranean*: 167-192. Oxford: Oxford University Press.

Leitch, V. 2013. Reconstructing history through pottery: the contribution of Roman N African cookwares. *Journal of Roman Archaeology* 26: 281-306.

Leka, E. and Zachos, G. 2015. The Marmor Lesbium reconsidered and other stones of Lesbos, in P. Pensabene and E. Gasparini (eds) *ASMOSIA X: proceedings of the tenth International Conference of ASMOSIA, Association for the Study of Marble and Other*

Stones in Antiquity, Rome, 21-26 May 2012: 201-211. Rome: L'Erma di Bretschneider.

Leleković, T. 2018. How were Imitations of Samian Formed? *Internet Archaeology* 50.

Lenzi, F. 2006. *Regio VIII. Luoghi, uomini, percorsi dell'età romana in Emilia-Romagna*. San Giovanni in Persiceto: Aspasia.

Lenzi, F. and Nenzioni, G. (eds) 2016. *Savena - Idex. Due insediamenti rustici nell'ager bononiensis orientale*, Bologna: Ante Quem.

Leveau, P. 1999. Le Rhône romain: dynamiques fluviales, dynamiques territoriales. *Gallia* 56: 1-175.

Lewit, T. 2015. The Lessons of Gaulish Sigillata and Other Finewares. *Late Antique Archaeology* 10: 227-257.

Lilli, M. 1998. Le attrezzature portuali di Ravenna durante l'età romana e bizantina: progettualità e trasformazione del paesaggio. *Atlante tematico di topografia antica* 7: 17-42.

Limão, N. and Venables, A.J. 2001. Infrastructure, Geographical Disadvantage, Transport Costs, and Trade. *The World Bank Economic Review* 15: 451-479.

Lindhagen, A. 2009. The transport amphoras Lamboglia 2 and Dressel 6A: a central Dalmatian origin? *Journal of Roman Archaeology* 22: 83-108.

Liu, J. 2009. *Collegia Centonariorum: The Guilds of Textile Dealers in the Roman West*. Leiden: Brill.

Lo Cascio, E. 2000. The Roman Principate. The impact of the organisation of the empire on production, in E. Lo Cascio and D.W. Rathbone (eds) *Production and Public Powers in Classical Antiquity*: 77-85. Cambridge: Cambridge Philological Society.

Lo Cascio, E. 2009. *Crescita e Declino: studi di storia dell'economia romana*. Rome: L'Erma di Bretschneider.

Lo Cascio, E. 2018. Market Regulation and Transaction Costs in the Roman Empire, in A.I. Wilson and A.K. Bowman (eds) *Trade, Commerce, and the State in the Roman World*: 117-132. Oxford: Oxford University Press.

Lodwick, L. 2017. Arable Farming, Plant Foods, and Resources, in M. Allen, L. Lodwick, T. Brindle, M. Fulford and A.T. Smith (eds) *The Rural Economy of Roman Britain*: 11-84. London: Society for the Promotion of Roman Studies.

Lomas, K. 2017. The Veneti, in G.D. Farney and G. Bradley (eds) *The Peoples of Ancient Italy*: 701-718. Berlin and Boston: De Gruyter.

Łoś, A. and Pietruszka, W. 2016. Le vignoble campanien sous les Antonins. *Mélanges de l École française de Rome Antiquité* 128: 521–558.

Lucchese, L. 2004. I ponti romani di Pont-Saint-Martin, Bard, Saint-Vincent, Châtillon, Aosta e Lévérogne. *Atlante tematico di topografia antica* 12: 7-23.

Lund, J. 2003. Eastern Sigillata B: a ceramic fine ware industry in the political and commercial landscape of the Eastern Mediterranean. *Publications de l'Institut Français d'Études Anatoliennes* 15: 125-136.

M., F. and V., M. (eds) 2008. *Orme nei campi: archeologia a sud di Ravenna. Atti della giornata di studi sui recenti rinvenimenti archeologici nel territorio Decimano (San Pietro in Campiano, Ravenna, 2006)*, Borgo S. Lorenzo: All'Insegna dell'Giglio.

Mackensen, M. 1993. *Die spätantiken Sigillata- und Lampentöpfereien von El Mahrine (Nortunesien). Studien zur nordafrikanischen Feinkeramik des 4. bis 7. Jahrhunderts*. Munich: Beck.

Mackensen, M. 2006. The Study of 3rd Century African Red Slip Ware based on the Evidence from Tunisia, in D. Malfitana, J. Poblome and J. Lund (eds) *Old Pottery in a New Century, Innovating Perspectives on Roman Pottery Studies. Atti del Convegno Internazionale di Studi, Catania, 22-24 aprile 2004*: 105-124. Rome: CNR.

Mackensen, M. and Schneider, A. 2006. Production Centers of African Red Slip Ware (2nd-3rd c.) in Northern and Central Tunisia: Archaeological Provenance and Reference Groups based on Chemical Analysis. *Journal of Roman Archaeology* 19: 163-190.

Mackensen, M. and Schneider, G. 2002. Production centres of African red slip ware (3rd-7th c.) in northern and central Tunisia: archaeological provenance and reference groups based on chemical analysis. *Journal of Roman Archaeology* 15: 121-158.

Mackinnon, M. 2010. Cattle 'breed' variation and improvement in Roman Italy: connecting the zooarchaeological and ancient textual evidence. *World Archaeology* 42: 55-73.

Maddison, M. and Schmidt, S.C. 2020. Percolation Analysis – Archaeological Applications at Widely Different Spatial Scales. *Journal of Computer Applications in Archaeology* 3: 269-287.

Madricardo, F., Bassani, M., D'acunto, G., Calandriello, A. and Foglini, F. 2021. New evidence of a Roman road in the Venice Lagoon (Italy) based on high resolution seafloor reconstruction. *Nature. Scientific Reports* 11: 13985.

Maggi, P. and Prenc, F. 1990. Pirin, comune di Teor, scavo 1990. *Aquileia Nostra* 61: 392-394.

Maggi, P., Maselli Scotti, F., Pesavento Mattioli, S. and Zulini, E. (eds) 2017. *Materiali per Aquileia: lo scavo di Canale Anfora (2004-2005)*. Trieste: Edizioni Quasar.

Maiuro, M. 2017. Northern Italy: urbanization, demography, agrarian output in E. Lo Cascio and M. Maiuro (eds) *Popolazione e risorse nell'Italia del nord dalla romanizzazione ai longobardi*: 99-150. Bari: Edipuglia.

Makjanić, R. 1995. Terra Sigillata, in R. Koščević and R. Makjanić (eds) *Siscia, Pannonia superior: Finds and metalwork production. Terra sigillata*: 56-74. Oxford: Archaeopress.

Malaguti, C., Marchesini, M., Casagrande, L., Cobianchi, V., Gobbo, I., Marvelli, S., Mura, L. and Rizzoli, E. 2011. Il pozzo di Badia Polesine (Rovigo). *Antichità Altoadriatiche* 70: 85-114.

Maldini, A. 2004. Il contrappeso del torcular di

Gambarata. *Orizzonti: Rassegna di Archeologia* 5: 65-75.

Malizia, A. 1986. Oderzo. Rinvenimento nel canale Navisego. *Quaderni di Archeologia del Veneto* 2: 86-88.

Mancassola, N. 2019. Paesaggi tardoantichi e paesaggi altomedievali: alcuni contesti romagnoli a confronto, in E. Cirelli, E. Giorgi and G. Lepore (eds) *Economia e Territorio. L'Adriatico centrale tra tarda Antichità e alto Medioevo*: 245-252. Oxford: Archaeopress.

Mantovani, V. 2013. *Aspetti della produzione e del commercio dell'Instrumentum domesticum di età romana ad Adria, alla luce dei rinvenimenti di via Retratto.* Università degli Studi di Padova.

Mantovani, V. 2018. Recenti studi sulle sigillate galliche in area padana: alcune riflessioni. *Quaderni Friulani di Archeologia* 28: 179-184.

Mantovani, V. 2021. La terra sigillata italica, in J. Bonetto, S. Mazzocchin and D. Dobreva (eds) *Aquileia. Fondi Cossar. 3.3. I materiali ceramici* 145-174. Rome: Edizioni Quasar.

Mantovani, V., Schindler-Kaudelka, E., Stuani, R., Mannocci, E. and Corti, C. 2022. Terra sigillata norditalica decorata a matrice intenzionalmente nera. Alcune considerazioni, in G.L. Vrkljan, A. Konestra and A.E. Borzić (eds) *Roman Pottery and Glass Manufactures: Production and Trade in the Adriatic Region and Beyond*: 222-238. Oxford: Archaeopress.

Manzelli, V. 2000. Documentazione Archeologia. *Atlante tematico di topografia antica* 8: 39-196.

Marabini, M., M.T. 2006. Cosa: The Italian Sigillata. *Memoirs of the American Academy in Rome. Supplementary Volumes* 3: 1-170.

Marcaccini, P. 1973. Il limite dell'olivo nella Romagna e in genere nell'Italia continentale. *Rivista Geografica Italiana* 80: 28-49.

Marchesini, M. and Marvelli, S. 2017. Paesaggio vegetale e agricoltura nella Pianura Padana nell'età romana, in E. Lo Cascio and M. Maiuro (eds) *Popolazione e risorse nell'Italia del nord dalla romanizzazione ai Longobardi*: 289-306. Bari: Edipuglia.

Marchesini, M., Marvelli, S., Muscogiuri, A.C. and Rizzoli, E. 2024. Applicability and Use of Archaeobotany for the Study of Vine Cultivation and Winemaking in the Roman Period, in E.K. Dodd and D. Van Limbergen (eds) *Methods in Ancient Wine Archaeology. Scientific Approaches in Roman Contexts*: 105-113. London: Bloomsbury.

Marchetti, G. and Dall'aglio, P.L. 1990. Parte II: antropizzazione ed evoluzione fisica del territorio, *Storia di Piacenza. I. Dalle origini all'anno Mille*: 604-685. Milan: Fondazione Cassa di Risparmio di Piacenza e Vigevano.

Marchetti, M. 2002. Environmental changes in the central Po Plain (northern Italy) due to fluvial modifications and anthropogenic activities. *Geomorphology* 22: 361-373.

Marchiori, A. 1990. Sistemi portuali della Venetia Romana. *Antichità Altoadriatiche* 36: 197-225.

Marengo, S.M. 2003. Donne e produzione: esempi della regio V., in A. Buonapane and F. Cenerini (eds) *Donna e lavoro nella documentazione epigrafica, Atti del I Seminario sulla condizione femminile nella documentazione epigrafica, Bologna 2002*: 75-86. Faenza: Lega.

Marini Calvani, M. 1981. *Per la Val Baganza, numero unico del Centro Studi della Val Baganza.* Baganza: Centro Studi della Val Baganz.

Marini Calvini, M. 1999. Strade Romane dell'Emilia Occidentale. *Atlante tematico di topografia antica* 8: 187-192.

Mariotti, V. 2014. Dalla villa romana al primo nucleo del monastero. Lettura interpretativa dei dati archeologici, in V. Mariotti (ed.) *Un monastero nei secoli: Santa Maria Assunta di Cairate. Scavi e ricerche* Documenti di archeologia 57): 11-109. Mantua: All'Insegna del Giglio.

Maritan, L., Mazzoli, C. and Mazzocchin, S. 2019. Provenance of wine and oil amphorae in northern Adriatic: archaeometric and epigraphic approaches. *Archéosciences*: 203-210.

Maritan, L., Secco, M., Mazzoli, C. and Mantovani, V. 2013. The decorated Padan terra sigillata from the site of Retratto, Adria (north-eastern Italy): Provenance and production technology. *Applied Clay Sciences* 82: 62-69.

Marlière, E. 2001. Le tonneau en Gaule romaine. *Gallia* 58: 181-201.

Marrioti, V., Massa, S. and Ravasi, T. 2008. Cremona, dal fiume alla città: materiali da due scavi degli Anni Ottanta, *Notarizo 2006, Soprintendenza per i Beni Archeologia della Lombardia*: 193-208. Milan: Soprintendenza per i Beni Archeologia della Lombardia.

Marsden, P. 1967. *A ship of the Roman period, from Blackfriars, in the City of London.* London: Guildhall Museum.

Martin, R. 2006. Economic geography and the new discourse of regional competitiveness, in S. Bagchi-Sen and H. Lawton Smith (eds) *Economic Geography. Past, present, and future*: 159-172. London: Routledge.

Marzano, A. 2007. *Roman Villas in Central Italy: A Social and Economic History.* Leiden: Brill.

Marzano, A. 2013. Agricultural Production in the Hinterland of Rome: Wine and Olive Oil, in A.K. Bowman and A. Wilson (eds) *The Roman Agricultural Economy: Organisation, Investment, and Production*: 85-106. Oxford: Oxford University Press.

Maschek, D. 2023. From Tenney Frank to Janet DeLaine: Roman Architecture and Economic History, in S.J. Barker, C. Courault, J.Á. Domingo and D. Maschek (eds) *From Concept to Monument: Time and Costs of Construction in the Ancient World. Papers in Honour of Janet DeLaine*: 1-14. Oxford: Archaeopress.

Massa, S. 1999. La Ceramica d'Importazione Africana, in G.P. Brogliolo (ed.) *Santa Giulia di Brescia: gli scavi dal*

1980 al 1992: Reperti preromani, romani e altomedievali: 101-117. Florence: All'Insegna del Giglio.

Massa, S. 2000. Le imitazioni di ceramiche mediterranee tra IV e VII secolo in area padana e le ultime produzioni fini da mensa: problemi di metodo e stato della ricerca, in G.P. Brogiolo and G. Olcese (eds) *Produzione ceramica in area padana tra il II secolo a.C. e il VII secolo d.C: nuovi dati e prospettive di ricerca: convegno internazionale, Desenzano del Garda, 8-10 aprile 1999*: 121-128. Mantua: All'Insegna del Giglio.

Massa, S. 2002. La ceramica d'importazione africana, in F. Rossi (ed.) *Nuove ricerche sul Capitolium di Brescia: scavi, studi e restauri*: 371-379. Milan: Edizioni ET.

Massa, S. 2003. Il vasellame fine tardoantico dai livelli di 'dark' del lotto 3 (UC VII, US 1098), in S. Lusuardi Siena and M.P. Rossignani (eds) *Dall'antichità al medioevo: aspetti insediativi e manufatti; ricerche archeologiche nei cortili dell'Università Cattolica*: 131-148. Milan: Vita e Pensiero.

Maselli Scotti, F. 2017. Terra Sigillata Orientale, in P. Maggi, F. Maselli Scotti, S. Pesavento Mattioli and E. Zulini (eds) *Materiali per Aquileia: lo scavo di Canale Anfora (2004-2005)*: 109-14. Trieste: Edizioni Quasar.

Massensini, G. 1973. Note sui resti di un antico porto a Padenghe sul Garda. *Benaco* 1: 518-527.

Masseroli, S. 1997. Anfore, in G. Sena Chiesa, S. Masseroli, T. Medici and M. Volonte (eds) *Calvatone romana. Un pozzo e il suo contesto. Saggio nella zona nord dell'area di proprietà provinciale*: 91-107. Milan: Cisalpino Istituto Editoriale Universitario.

Matijašić, R. and Bulić, D. 2023. Rural landscapes in Istrian Late Antiquity, in A.E. Borzić, E. Cirelli, K. Jelinčić Vučković, A. Konestra and I. Ožanić Roguljić (eds) *TRADE – Transformations of Adriatic Europe (2nd–9th Centuries AD) Proceedings of the conference in Zadar, 11th-13th February 2016*: 175-181. Oxford: Archaeopress.

Mattingly, D. 2007. Supplying Rome and the empire: some conclusions, in E. Papi and M. Bonifay (eds) *Supplying Rome and the empire: the proceedings of an international seminar held at Siena-Certosa di Pontignano on May 2-4, 2004, on Rome, the provinces, production and distribution* (Journal of Roman Archaeology Supplements 69): 219-227. Portsmouth (RI): Journal of Roman Archaeology.

Maurina, B. 1995. Trento – Palazzo Tabarelli. Le anfore, in E. Cavada (ed.) *Materiali per la storia urbana di Tridentum*: 209-270. Trento: Archeoalp.

Mazzeo Saracino, L. 2000. Lo studio delle terre sigillate padane: problemi e prospettive, in G.P. Brogliolo and G. Olcese (eds) *Produzione ceramica in area padana tra il II secolo a.C. e il VII secolo d.C: nuovi dati e prospettive di ricerca: convegno internazionale, Desenzano del Garda, 8-10 aprile 1999*: 31-43. Mantua: All'Insegna del Giglio.

Mazzocchin, S. 2009. Le Anfore con Collo ad Imbuto: Nuovi Dati e Prospective di Ricerca, in S. Pesavento Mattioli and M.B. Carre (eds) *Olio e pesce in epoca romana: produzione e commercio nelle regioni dell'Alto Adriatico: atti del convegno (Padova 16 febbraio 2007)*: 191-213. Rome: Edizioni Quasar.

Mazzocchin, S. 2011. *Traffici commerciali a Vicenza in epoca romana: i dati delle anfore.* Unpublished PhD dissertation, Università degli Studi di Padova.

Mazzocchin, S. and Wilkins, B. 2013. Fish and Crustaceans from a Roman Amphora in Northern Italy. *Archaeofauna* 22: 105-111.

Mccallum, M. 2004. *Tiberis Navigabilis: Commercial Activity Between Rome and the Middle Tiber Basin During the Roman Period.* Unpublished PhD dissertation, University of Buffalo.

McCormick, M. 2001. *Origins of the European Economy: Communications and Commerce AD 300 – 900.* Cambridge: Cambridge University Press.

McCormick, M., Büntgen, U., Cane, M.A., Cook, E.R., Harper, K., Huybers, P.J., Litt, T., Manning, S.W., Mayewski, P.A., More, A.F.M., Nicolussi, K. and Tegel, W. 2012. Climate Change during and after the Roman Empire: Reconstructing the Past from Scientific and Historical Evidence. *Journal of Interdisciplinary History* 43: 169-220.

Mcgovern, P.E. 2024. Ancient Viniculture: A Multidisciplinary Holistic Perspective, in E.K. Dodd and D. Van Limbergen (eds) *Methods in Ancient Wine Archaeology. Scientific Approaches in Roman Contexts*: 13-32. London: Bloomsbury.

Mclean, A. 2022. *A Connecting Sea? Modelling Economic Cohesion in the Roman Adriatic.* Unpublished PhD dissertation, University of Edinburgh.

McLean, A. and Rubio-Campillo, X. 2022. Beyond Least Cost Paths: Circuit theory, maritime mobility and patterns of urbanism in the Roman Adriatic. *Journal of Archaeological Science* 138: 105534.

Medas, S. 2003. The Late-Roman "Parco di Teodorico" Wreck, Ravenna, Italy: Preliminary Remarks on the Hull and the Shipbuilding, in C. Beltrame (ed.) *Boats, Ships, and Shipyards. Proceedings of the Ninth International Symposium on Boat and Ship Archaeology Venice 2000*: 42-48. Oxford: Oxbow.

Medas, S. 2018. La Navigazione Lungo le Idrovie Padane in Epoca Romana, in G. Cantoni and A. Capurso (eds) *On the Road. Via Emilia 187 A.C. - 2017* 146-161. Parma: Grafiche Step.

Mees, A. 2011. *Die Verbreitung von Terra Sigillata aus den Manufakturen von Arezzo, Pisa, Lyon und La Graufesenque: die Transformation der italischen Sigillata-Herstellung in Gallien.* Mainz: Verl. des Römisch-Germanischen Zentralmuseums.

Mees, A. and Polak, M. 2013. Scattered pots. Exploring spatial and chronological aspects of Samian Ware, in M. Fulford and E. Durham (eds) *Seeing Red: new economic and social perspectives on terra sigillata*: 36-48. Chicago and London: University of Chicago Press.

Melli, P. 2004. The role of Genoa in the Mediterranean trade in Antiquity, in M. Pasquinucci and T. Weski (eds) *Close Encounters: Sea and Riverborne Trade, Ports and Hinterlands, Ship Construction and Navigation in Antiquity, the Middle Ages and in Modern Time*: 116-124. Oxford: Archaeopress.

Melli, P. and Pasquinucci, M. 1998. Prospettive di ricerca a Genova e nel suo territorio, in G. Sena Chiesa and A.E. Arslan (eds) *Optima via. Postumia. Storia e archeologia di una grande strada romana alle radici dell'Europa*: 417-433. Venice: Associazione promozione iniziative culturali.

Menchelli, S. 1997. Terra sigillata pisana: forniture militari e 'libero mercato. *Rei Cretariae Romanae Fautorum Acta* 35: 191-198.

Menchelli, S. 2005. La terra sigillata, in D. Gandolfi (ed.) *La ceramica e i materiali di età romana. Classi, produzioni, commerci e consumi*: 155–168. Bordighera: Ist. Studi Liguri.

Menchelli, S. and Sangriso, P. 2017. Pisan sigillata: Augustan ideology with a few images, in M. Flecker (ed.) *Neue Bildwelten zu Ikonographie und Hermeneutik italischer Sigillata*: 53-71. Rahden and Leidorf: Verlag Marie Leidorf.

Mercando, L. 1972. Recenti rinvenimenti nelle Marche di terra sigillata nord-italica, in G. Bovini and G.A. Mansuell (eds) *I problemi della ceramica romana di Ravenna, della Valle Padana e dell' alto Adriatico. Atti del Convegno Internazionale Ravenna, 10 - 12 Maggio 1969*: 203-220. Bologna: Forni.

Mercuri, A.M., Allevato, E., Arobba, D., Bandini Mazzanti, M., Bosi, G., Caramiello, R., Castiglioni, E., Carra, M.L., Celant, A., Costantini, L., Di Pasquale, G., Fiorentino, G., Florenzano, A., Guido, M., Marchesini, M., Mariotti Lippi, M., Marvelli, S., Miola, A., Montanari, C., Nisbet, R., Peña-Chocarro, L., Perego, R., Ravazzi, C., Rottoli, M., Sadori, L., Ucchesu, M. and Rinaldi, R. 2015. Pollen and macroremains from Holocene archaeological sites: A dataset for the understanding of the bio-cultural diversity of the Italian landscape. *Review of Palaeobotany and Palynology* 218: 250-266.

Mertens, J. 1972. Terre sigillée d'Ordona. *Ordona* 6: 221-240.

Michelini, P. and Mazzocchin, S. 1998. Este: la temporanea bonifica ed uso funerario di un spazio lungo il fiume, in S. Pesavento Mattioli (ed.) *Bonifiche e drenaggi con anfore in epoca romana: aspetti tecnici e topografici. Atti del seminario di studi di Padova 19-20 ottobre 1995*: 223–235. Modena: F. C. Panini.

Middleton, P. 1980. La Graufesenque: a question of marketing. *Athenaeum* 58: 186-192.

Meiggs, R. 1982. *Trees and Timber in the Ancient Mediterranean World*. Oxford: Clarendon Press.

Millar, F. 1995. The last century of the Republic: Whose history? *Journal of Roman Studies* 85: 236-243.

Mille, P. and Rollet, P. 2020. Étude de trois grands tonneaux mis au jour à Reims/Durocortorum (Marne): le savoir-faire des tonneliers antiques. *Gallia* 77: 123-155.

Mills, B.J. 2017. Social Network Analysis in Archaeology. *Annual Review of Anthropology* 46: 379-397.

Minato, G. 2018. Marmi, in L. Sperti, M. Tirelli and S. Cipriano (eds) *Prima dello scavo. Il survey 2012 ad Altino*: 191-199. Venice: Edizioni Ca' Foscari.

Mirabella Roberti, M. 1961. Archeologia ed arte di Brescia romana, in G. Treccani Degli Alfieri (ed.) *Storia di Brescia, I*: 278-280. Brescia: Morcelliana.

Modrzewska-Pianetti, I. 2017. Les importations d'amphores Dressel 20 en Gaule Cisalpine. *Études et Travaux* 30: 389-407.

Modrzewska-Pianetti, I. and Pianetti, F. 1994. Anfore spagnole del deposito di Verona (Italia). Interpretazione dei dati analitici. *Archivo Español de Arqueología* 67: 147-55.

Mollo Mezzana, R. 1982. Augusta Praetoria. Aggiornamento sulle conoscenze archeologiche della città, in *Atti del Congresso sul Bimillenario della città di Aosta (Aosta, 5-20 ottobre 1975)*: 205-315. Bordighera: Istituto Internazionale di Studi Liguri.

Mollo Mezzana, R. 1992. La strada romana in Valle d'Aosta: procedimenti tecnici e costruttivi. *Atlante tematico di topografia antica* 1: 58-72.

Mondin, C. 2022. Pottery and brick production in northeastern Italy in the Roman Period: the exploitation of clay quarries, in G. Lipovac Vrkljan, A. Konestra and A. Eterović Borzić (eds) *Roman Pottery and Glass Manufactures: Production and Trade in the Adriatic Region and Beyond*: 56-64. Oxford: Archaeopress.

Mongardi, M. 2014. *L'instrumentum fittile inscriptum della colonia romana di Mutina e del suo territorio.* Unpublished PhD dissertation, Università di Bologna.

Montalcini De Angelis D'ossat, M. 1993. Como: rilettura di una città, in G. Luraschi (ed.) *Novum Comum 2050, Atti del Convegno celebrativo della fondazione di Como romana (Como, Camera di commercio, 8-9 novembre 1991)*: 53-57. Como: Società Archeologica Comense.

Montevecchi, G. (ed.) 2003. *Viaggio nei siti archeologici della provincia di Ravenna,* Ravenna: Longon.

Morales-Muñiz, A. and Roselló-Izquierdo, E. 2016. Fishing in Mediterranean prehistory: an archaeo-ichthyological overview, in T. Bekker-Nielsen and R. Gertwagen (eds) *The Inland Seas: towards an ecohistory of the Mediterranean*: 23-56. Stuttgart: Franz Steiner Publishers.

Morandini, F. 2000. Produzioni ceramiche di media età imperiale a Verona. Impianti produttivi e scarichi da vecchi ritrovamenti e recenti indagini, in G.P. Brogiolo (ed.) *Produzione ceramica in area padana tra il II secolo a.C. e il VII secolo d.C: nuovi dati e prospettive di ricerca: convegno internazionale, Desenzano del Garda, 8-10 aprile 1999*: 165-174. Mantua: All'Insegna del Giglio.

Morandini, F. 2008a. La Ceramica Importazione Africana, in G. Cavalieri Manasse (ed.) *L'area del*

Capitolium di Verona: ricerche storiche e archeologiche.: 405-416. Verona.

Morandini, F. 2008b. Le ceramiche fini e le terre sigillate di produzione non africana, in G. Cavalieri Manasse (ed.) *L'area del Capitolium di Verona: ricerche storiche e archeologiche.*: 330-342. Verona.

Morel, J.-P. 1981. *Céramique campanienne. Les formes.* Rome: École française de Rome.

Morel, J.-P. 2009. Le produzioni ceramiche a vernice nera di Arezzo, in G. Camporeale and G. Firpo (eds) *Arezzo nell'antichità*: 125-134. Rome: Accademia Petrarca di Lettere Arti e Scienze.

Morillo, A., Fernandez Ochoa, C. and Salido Dominguez, J. 2016. Hispania and the Atlantic Route in Roman Times: new Approaches to Ports and Trade. *Oxford Journal of Archaeology* 35: 267-284.

Morley, N. 2007. *Trade in Classical Antiquity.* Cambridge: Cambridge University Press.

Morley, N. 2012. A Forum on Trade, in W. Scheidel (ed.) *The Cambridge Companion to the Roman Economy*: 309-314. Cambridge: Cambridge University Press.

Morris, I., Saller, R. and Scheidel, W. 2007. Introduction, in W. Scheidel, I. Morris and R. Saller (eds) *The Cambridge Economic History of the Greco-Roman World*: 1-12. Cambridge: Cambridge University Press.

Mosca, A. 2015. Marble and stones used in the central Eastern Alpine area and in the Northern area of Benacus: topographical reconstruction of trade routes and aspects of use in the Roman era, in P. Pensabene and E. Gasparini (eds) *ASMOSIA X: proceedings of the tenth International Conference of ASMOSIA, Association for the Study of Marble and Other Stones in Antiquity, Rome, 21-26 May 2012*: 575-584. Rome: L'Erma di Bretschneider.

Mozzi, P., Piovan, S., Mossato, S., Cucato, M., Abba, T. and Fontana, A. 2010. Palaeohydrography and early settlements in Padua (Italy). *Italian Journal of Quaternary Sciences* 23: 387-400.

Mozzi, P., Fontana, A., Ferrarese, F., Ninfo, A., Campana, S. and Francese, R. 2016. The Roman City of Altinum, Venice Lagoon, from Remote Sensing and Geophysical Prospection. *Archaeological Prospection* 23: 27-44.

Mozzi, P. and Rucco, A.A. 2023. The Geoarchaeological Context of the Area of Santa Maria in Padovetere, in C. Beltrame and E. Costa (eds) *The shipwreck of Santa Maria in Padovetere (Comacchio-Ferrara). Archaeology of a riverine barge of Late Roman period and of other recent finds of sewn boats*: 49-55. Florence: All'Insegna dell'Giglio.

Muzzoli, M. 2010. Le ricerche sui resti della centuriazione cinquant'anni dopo. *Atlante tematico di topografia antica* 20: 7-49.

Nelson, B. 1970. Hydrography, Sediment Dispersal, and Recent Historical Development of the Po River Delta. *Deltaic Sedimentation, Modern and Ancient* 15: 152-184.

Nieto, F.J., Puig, A.M., Palau, H. and Nieto, P. 1989. *Excavacions arqueològiques subaquàtiques a Cala Culip.* (Sèrie monogràfica (Centre d'Investigacions Arqueològiques de Girona). Girona: Generalitat de Catalunya.

Nieuwhof, A. 2020. Luxury tableware? Terra sigillata in the coastal region of the northern Netherlands, in A. Rubel and H.-U. Voß (eds) *Experiencing the Frontier and the Frontier of Experience: Barbarian perspectives and Roman strategies to deal with new threats*: 94-110. Oxford: Archaeopress.

Oberosler, R. 1995. Trento - Palazzo Tabarelli. Ceramiche in terra sigillata, in E. Cavada (ed.) *Materiali per la storia urbana di Tridentum*: 271-357. Trento: Archeoalp.

Olcese, G. 1998. Ceramiche in Lombardia, in G. Olcese (ed.) *Ceramiche in Lombardia tra II secolo a.C. e VII secolo d.C.: Raccolta dei dati editi*: 7-19. Mantua: All'Insegna del Giglio.

Olcese, G. 1999. Le ceramiche fini del periodo II e alcuni problemi aperti nell'ambito della produzione ceramica di area padana, in G.P. Brogliolo (ed.) *S. Giulia di Brescia. Gli scavi dal 1980 al 1992: reperti preromani, romani e alto medievali*: 97-100. Florence: All'Insegna del Giglio.

Olcese, G. 2006. The production and circulation of Greco-Italic amphorae of Campania (Ischia/Bay of Naples) The data of the archaeological and archaeometric research. *Skyllis*: 60-75.

Olcese, G. 2020. On Land and Sea. Production and Trade of Wine from Campania (3rd BC – 1st AD): Some New Archaeological and Archeometric Data about Amphorae in J.-P. Brun, N. Garnier and G. Olcese (eds) *Making Wine in Western-Mediterranean. B. Production and the Trade of Amphorae: some new data from Italy, Proceedings of the 19th International Congress of Classical Archaeology - Panel 3.5 (Cologne-Bonn 22-26 May 2018)*: 105-29. Heidelberg: Propylaeum.

Olcese, G. 2022. *Relitti dall'Italia tirrenica nel Mediterraneo occidentale (Fine IV secolo a.C.- I d.C.).* Rome: Edizioni Quasar.

Orengo, H.A. and Livarda, A. 2016. The seeds of commerce: A network analysis-based approach to the Romano-British transport system. *Journal of Archaeological Science* 66: 21-35.

Ortalli, J. 1992. La Cispadana Orientale: Via Emilia e altre Strade. *Atlante tematico di topografia antica* 1: 147-160.

Orton, C. 2009. 'Four pots good, two pots bad': exploring the limits of quantification in the study of archaeological ceramics. *Facta* 3: 65-74.

Orton, D., Morris, J. and Pipe, A. 2017. Catch per Unit Research Effort: Sampling Intensity, Chronological Uncertainty, and the Onset of Marine Fish Consumption in Historic London. *Open Quaternary* 3: 1-20.

Oxé, A., Comfort, H. and Kenrick, P.M. 2000. *Corpus vasorum Arretinorum: a catalogue of the signatures, shapes and chronology of Italian sigillata.* Bonn: Habelt.

Paccolat, O., Cusanelli-Bressenel, L. and Joris, C. 2008. Le mobilier céramique du Grand Saint-Bernard (Plan de Jupiter, Plan de Brasson et Musée de l'Hospice), in L. Apollonia (ed.) *Alpis Poenina: Grand Saint-Bernard: une voie à travers l'Europe: Séminaire de clôture 11-12 avril 2008, Fort de Bard (Vallée d'Aoste)*: 139-206. Aosta.

Paci, G. 2009. Monumento funerario di un bottaio da Cupra Marittima, in C. Marengio (ed.) *Palaia Philia. Studi di topografia antica in onore di Giovanni Uggeri*: 289–294. Galatina: Arbor Sapientiae.

Page, J. 2022. Riverbed, banks and beyond: an examination of Roman infrastructure and interventions in response to hydrological risk in the Po–Venetian plain. *Papers of the British School at Rome* 90: 171-200.

Page, J. 2023. 'Carrying Up It All the Products of the Seas': The Po-Veneto Water Network and Trade in the Roman Period, in A. Tibbs and P.B. Campbell (eds) *Rivers and Waterways in the Roman World. Empire of Water*: 85-99. London: Routledge.

Page, J. 2024. Rivers vs. Roads? A route network model of transport infrastructure in Northern Italy during the Roman period, *CAA 2023 Proceedings*: 1-13.

Pagen, M. 2018. Terra sigillata orientale, in L. Sperti, M. Tirelli and S. Cipriano (eds) *Prima dello scavo. Il survey 2012 ad Altino*: 103-104. Venice: Edizioni Ca' Foscari.

Pagliani, M.-L. 1991. *Piacenza: forma e urbanistica*. Rome: L'Erma di Bretschneider.

Panella, C. 1989. 'Le anfore italiche del II sec. d.C., *Amphores et économie romaine. Actes du Colloque de Sienne 1986*: 139-178. Paris and Rome: École Française de Rome.

Panella, C. 1993. Merci e scambi nel Mediterraneo tardoantico, in A. Carandini, L. Cracco Ruggini and A. Giardina (eds) *Storia di Roma: 3. L'età tardoantica. 2. I luoghi e le culture*: 613-697. Rome: Einaudi.

Panella, C. 2002. Le anfore di età imperiale nel Mediterraneo occidentale. *Céramiques héllenistiques et romaines 3. Publications du Centre Camille-Julien* 28: 177-275.

Panella, C. and Tchernia, A. 1994. Produits agricoles transportés en amphores: L'Huile et surtout le vin. *L'Italie d'Auguste à Dioclétien* 198: 145-165.

Panero, E. 2013. Vercelli, via Pastrengo. Strutture pertinenti a una banchina romana? *Quaderni della Soprintendenza Archeologica del Piemonte* 28: 311-313.

Pantò, G. and Occelli, F. 2009. Moncalieri, frazione Testona, parco di Villa Lancia. Abitato e necropoli di età longobarda. *Quaderni della Soprintendenza Archeologica del Piemonte* 24: 227-231.

Papisca, C. 2010. Tra fiumi e paludi. Dal Livenza ad Altino, in F. Veronese (ed.) *Via Annia: Adria, Padova, Altino, Concordia, Aquileia: progetto di recupero e valorizzazione di un'antica strada romana*: 61-72. Padua: Il Poligrafo

Parker, A.J. 1992. *Ancient shipwrecks of the Mediterranean and the Roman provinces*. (BAR International Series 580). Oxford: Archaeopress.

Parodi, A. 2013. *Le anfore di età romana (I sec a.C - V d.C-) dall'insediamento alla foce del torrente Prino, Imperia-Porto Maurizio*. Unpublished Master's by Research dissertation, Università di Pisa.

Patterson, H. (ed.) 2004. *Bridging the Tiber: Approaches to Regional Archaeology in the Tiber Valley,* Rome and London: British School at Rome.

Patterson, H. and Coarelli, F. (eds) 2009. *Mercator Placidissimus: The Tiber Valley in Antiquity: New Research in the Upper and Middle River Valley: Rome, 27-28 February 2004,* Rome: Edizioni Quasar.

Patterson, H., Di Giuseppe, H. and Witcher, R. 2020. *The Changing Landscapes of Rome's Northern Hinterland. The British School at Rome's Tiber Valley Project.* (Archaeological Monographs of the British School at Rome. Rome and London: British School at Rome.

Patterson, H. and Lapadula, E. 1997. Le anfore di Spello nelle Regiones VI e VII. *Papers of the British School at Rome* 65: 127-156.

Patterson, J.R. 2006. *Landscapes and Cities: Rural Settlement and Civic Transformation in Early Imperial Italy*. Oxford: Oxford University Press.

Peacock, D. and Maxfield, V. 1997. *Survey and Excavation— Mons Claudianus, 1987–1993. Volume I: Topography and Quarries.* (Fouilles de l'Institut Français d'Archéologie Orientale 37). Cairo: Institut franccçais d'archéologie orientale, Le Caire.

Pecci, A., Clarke, J., Thomas, M., Muslinc, J., Van Der Graaff, I., Toniolo, L., Miriello, D., Crisci, G.M., Buonincontri, M. and Di Pasquale, G. 2017. Use and reuse of amphorae. Wine residues in Dressel 2–4 amphorae from Oplontis Villa B (Torre Annunziata, Italy). *Journal of Archaeological Science* 12: 515-521.

Pedro Bernardes, J. and Viegas, C. 2016. Roman Amphora Production in the Algarve (Southern Portugal), in I.V. Pinto, R.R. De Almeida and A. Martin (eds) *Lusitanian Amphorae: Production and Distribution*: 81-92. Oxford: Archaeopress.

Pellegrini, G.B. 2004. Item ab Aquileia Bononiam: un itinerario di età romana tra La via Emilia ed il Po. *Atlante tematico di topografia antica* 13: 43-63.

Peña, J.T. 1989. P.Giss.69: evidence for the supplying of stone transport operations in Roman Egypt and the production of fifty-foot monolithic column shafts. *Journal of Roman Archaeology* 2: 126-132.

Peña, J.T. 2007a. The quantitative analysis of Roman pottery: general problems, the methods employed at the Palatine East, and the supply of African Sigillata to Rome, in E. Papi and M. Bonifay (eds) *Supplying Rome and the Empire: The Proceedings of an International Seminar Held at Siena-Certosa Di Pontignano on May 2-4, 2004, on Rome, the Provinces, Production and Distribution* (Journal of Roman Archaeology Supplements 69): 151-72. Portsmouth (RI): Journal of Roman Archaeology.

Peña, J.T. 2007b. *Roman Pottery in the Archaeological Record*. Cambridge: Cambridge University Press.

Pensabene, P. 2002. Il fenomeno del marmo nel mondo romano, in M. De Nuccio and L. Ungaro (eds) *I marmi colorati della Roma imperiale*: 3-68. Padua: Marsillo.

Pensabene, P. 2013. *I marmi nella Roma anticha*. Rome: Carocci.

Pensabene, P. 2015. Arco di Susa: forme della decorazione architettonica. *Anno 52*: 75-100.

Pensabene, P. 2015. Blocks and quarry marks in the Museum of Aquileia, in P. Pensabene and E. Gasparini (eds) *ASMOSIA X: proceedings of the tenth International Conference of ASMOSIA, Association for the Study of Marble and Other Stones in Antiquity, Rome, 21-26 May 2012*: 611-614. Rome: L'Erma di Bretschneider.

Perna, S., Antonelli, F., and Lazzarini, L. 2023. Archaeometric analysis of the 'greco scritto' marble slabs from the Edificio dei Triclinii at Murecine (Pompeii, Italy). *Archaeometry 65*: 1-16.

Perry, J.S. 2016. Sub-Elites, in A. Cooley (ed.) *A companion to Roman Italy*: 498-512. Oxford: Wiley.

Pesavento Mattioli, S. 1992. *Anfore romnne a Padova: ritrovamenti dalla città* Modena: F. C. Panini.

Pesavento Mattioli, S. 1998. *Bonifiche e drenaggi con anfore in epoca romana: aspetti tecnici e topografici*. Modena: F. C. Panini.

Pesavento Mattioli, S. 2011. Le anfore Schörgendorfer 558 e il commercio delle olive adriatiche, in G. Lipovac Vrkljan, I. Radić Rossi and B. Šiljeg (eds) *Rimske keramičarske i staklarske radionice; Proizvodnja i trgovina na jadranskom prostoru/ Zbornik I. Međunarodnog arheološkog kolokvija Crikvenica, 23.-24. Listopada 2008*: 165-173. Crikvenika: Institut za Arheologiju Muzej grada Crikvenice.

Pettenò, E. 2007. *Vasa Rubra. Marchi di Frabbrica sulla Terra Sigillata da Iulia Concordia*. Padua: Esedra.

Pettirossi, V. and Pistarino, V. 2008. Le Anfore, in A. Bacchetta and M. Venturino Gambari (eds) *La raccolta archeologica di Augusto Scovazzi*: 55-66. Genoa: De Ferrari and Devega.

Peyre, C. 1979. *La Cisalpine Gauloise du III au I siècle avant J.-C*. Paris: Presses de l'École normale supérieure.

Picco, L., Rainato, R., Mao, L., Delai, F., Tonon, A., Ravazzolo, D. and Lenzi, M.A. 2013. Characterization of fluvial islands along three different gravel-bed rivers of North-Eastern Italy. *Journal of Agricultural Engineering 44*: 117-121.

Piccoli, F. 2004. *Il vino nel Nord Italia in epoca romana: storia della coltivazione della vite, della produzione e del commercio del vino in Cisalpina*. Verona: Della Scala.

Picon, M. 2002. À propos des sigillées, présigillées et imitations de sigillées: Questions de "coûts" et de marché, in Sfecag (ed.) *Société française d'étude de la céramique antique en Gaule, Actes du congrès de Bayeux 2002*: 345-356. Marseilles: SFECAG.

Picon, M. and Lasfargues, J. 1974. Transfert de moules entre les ateliers d'Arezzo et ceux de Lyon. *Revue archéologique de l'Est et du Centre-Est 25*: 60-69.

Pieri, D. 2012. Regional and Interregional Exchanges in the Eastern Mediterranean during the early Byzantine period, in C. Morrison (ed.) *Trade and markets in Byzantium*: 27-49. Washington D.C.: Dumbarton Oaks Research Library and Collection.

Pisano Briani, A. 2016. Terra Sigillata. *Rivista archeologia dell'antica provincia e diocesi di Como 198*: 9-51.

Pitts, M. 2013. Pots and comparative history. The case of imported Roman fine wares and Chinese porcelain in NW Europe, in M. Fulford and E. Durham (eds) *Seeing Red: New Economic and Social Perspectives on Terra Sigillata*: 381-390. Chicago and London: Chicago University Press.

Pitts, M. 2015. Globalisation, Circulation, and Mass Consumption in the Roman World, in M. Pitts and J.M. Versluys (eds) *Globalisation and the Roman world: world history, connectivity and material culture*: 69-98. Cambridge: Cambridge University Press.

Pitts, M. 2017. Gallo-Belgic wares. Objects in motion in the early Roman northwest, in A. Van Oyen and M. Pitts (eds) *Materialising Roman Histories*: 47-64. Oxford: Oxbow.

Pizzolato, D. 2018a. Anfore africane, in L. Sperti, M. Tirelli and S. Cipriano (eds) *Prima dello scavo. Il survey 2012 ad Altino*: 154-166. Venice: Edizioni Ca' Foscari.

Pizzolato, D. 2018b. Anfore iberiche, in L. Sperti, M. Tirelli and S. Cipriano (eds) *Prima dello scavo. Il survey 2012 ad Altino*: 167-173. Venice: Edizioni Ca' Foscari.

Po River Basin Authority. 2006. Caratteristiche del bacino del fiume Po e primo esame dell' impatto ambientale delle attivitá umane sulle risorse idriche. Parma: Po River Basin Authority.

Poblome, J., Özden Gerçeker, S. and Loopmans, M. 2017. Different similarities or similar differences? Thoughts on koine, oligopoly and regionalism, in A. Van Oyen and M. Pitts (eds) *Materialising Roman Histories*: 85-100. Oxford: Oxbow.

Poblome, J. and Waelkens, M. 2003. Sagalassos and Alexandria. Exchange in the Eastern Mediterranean. *Publications de l'Institut Français d'Études Anatoliennes 15*: 179-191.

Poletti Ecclesia, E. 2019. Ricognizione sui più antichi manufatti in marmo di Candoglia ed elementi per l'individuazione della lavorazione lapidaria sul lago Maggiore nel I secolo d.C., in G.a.E.M.D. Mergozzo (ed.) *Le Vie della pietra: estrazione e diffusione delle pietre da opera alpine dall'età romana all'età moderna. Atti del Convegno in occasione del decennale dell'Ecomuseo del Granito di Montorfano (28-29 Ottobre 2017)*: 41-70. Mergozzo: Ecomuseo del Granito di Montorfano.

Ponsich, M. 1974. *Implantation rurale antique sur le Bas-Guadalquivir*. (Publications de la Casa de Velázquez. Série Archéologie. Madrid: Casa de Velázquez.

Preiser-Kapeller, J. and Werther, L. 2018. Connecting Harbours. A comparison of traffic networks across ancient and medieval Europe, in C. Von Carnap-Bornheim, F. Daim, P. Ettel and U. Warnke (eds) *Harbours as Objects of Interdisciplinary Research:*

Archaeology + History + Geosciences: 7-31. Kiel: Verlag des Römisch-Germanischen Zentralmuseums.

Prenc, F. 2002. *Le pianificazioni agrarie di età romana nella pianura aquileiese*. Trieste: Edizioni Quasar.

Previato, C. 2018. Aurisina Limestone in the Roman Age: from Karst Quarries to the Cities of the Adriatic Basin, in D. Matetić Poljak and K. Marasović (eds) *ASMOSIA XI, Interdisciplinary Studies on Ancient Stone. Proceedings of the XI ASMOSIA Conference, Split 2015*: 933-939. Split: Arts Academy: University of Split.

Previato, C. 2023. The Amphitheatres of Regio X – Venetia et Histria: The Impact of Stone Supplying Cost on Ancient Construction Processes, in S.J. Barker, C. Courault, J.Á. Domingo and D. Maschek (eds) *From Concept to Monument: Time and Costs of Construction in the Ancient World. Papers in Honour of Janet DeLaine*: 356-371. Oxford: Archaeopress.

Previato, C. and Mareso, N. 2015. Marbles from the Domus of 'Bestie ferite' and from the Domus of 'Tito Macro' in Aquileia (UD), Italy, in P. Pensabene and E. Gasparini (eds) *ASMOSIA X: proceedings of the tenth International Conference of ASMOSIA, Association for the Study of Marble and Other Stones in Antiquity, Rome, 21-26 May 2012*: 299-309. Rome: L'Erma di Bretschneider.

Previato, C. and Zara, A. 2014. Il Trasporto della Pietra di Vicenza in Età Romana. Il Relitto del Fiume Bacchiglione. *Marmora* 10: 59-78.

Previato, C. and Zara, A. 2018. Quarrying, circulation and use of stone during the Roman Age. A Database and GIS project about Regio X - Venetia et Histria. The case study of the Euganean Trachyte, in D. Matetić Poljak and K. Marasović (eds) *ASMOSIA XI, Interdisciplinary Studies on Ancient Stone. Proceedings of the XI ASMOSIA Conference, Split 2015*: 597-609. Split: Arts Academy: University of Split.

Profumo, M.C. 2005. Fronte di sarcofago detta "sarcofago del vinaio". in G. De Marinis (ed.) *Arte romana nei musei delle Marche*: 266-267. Rome: Poligrafico.

Purcell, N. 1990. The Creation of Provincial Landscape: The Roman Impact on Cisalpine Gaul, in T. Blagg and M. Millett (eds) *The Early Roman Empire in the West*: 7-29. Oxford: Oxbow.

Quercia, A., Semeraro, M. and Barello, F. 2015. Strevi, località Cascina Braida. Un insediamento rurale di età romana. *Quaderni della Soprintendenza Archeologica del Piemonte* 30: 143-172.

Quilici Gigli, S. 1998. Sulle bonifiche nell'Italia romana, in S. Pesavento Mattioli (ed.) *Bonifiche e drenaggi con anfore in epoca romana: aspetti tecnici e topografici*: 15-22. Modena: F. C. Panini.

Quilici, L. 2009. Land transport, part 1: roads and bridges, in J.P. Oleson (ed.) *The Oxford Handbook of Engineering and Technology in the Classical World*: 551-579. Oxford: Oxford University Press.

Quiri, E. 2009. Importazioni di anfore altoadriatiche a Torino, in S. Pesavento Mattioli and M.B. Carre (eds) *Olio e pesce in epoca romana. Produzione e commercio nelle regioni dell'Alto Adriatico, Atti del Convegno (Padova, 16 febbraio 2007)*: 293-300. Rome: Edizioni Quasar.

Quiri, E. 2014. Le Anfore, in M.C. Preacco (ed.) *Augusta Bagiennorum: storia e archeologia di una città augustea*: 201-211. Turin: Celid.

Quiri, E. 2015. Imports of eastern transport amphorae to Turin (Italy), in S. Demesticha (ed.) *Per Terram, Per Mare: Seaborne Trade and the Distribution of Roman Amphorae in the Mediterranean*: 161-180. Uppsala: Astrom Editions.

Quiri, E. and Spagnolo Garzoli, G. 2015. Imports of alum from Milos to Novara (Italy), in S. Demesticha (ed.) *Per Terram, Per Mare: Seaborne Trade and the Distribution of Roman Amphorae in the Mediterranean*: 181-188. Uppsala: Astrom Editions.

Radbauer, S. 2013. The Roman terra sigillata production of Westerndorf (South Bavaria, Germany): history, location and technology, in M. Fulford and E. Durham (eds) *Seeing Red: New Economic and Social Perspectives on Terra Sigillata*: 151-164. Chicago and London: University of Chicago Press.

Raepsaet, G. 2009. Land Transport, Part 2: Riding, Harnesses, and Vehicles, in J.P. Oleson (ed.) *The Oxford Handbook of Engineering and Technology in the Classical World*: 580-605. Oxford: Oxford University Press.

Ratto, S. 2014. Il vasellame ceramico da mensa e da cucina: vita quotidiana e indicatori commerciali, in M.C. Preacco (ed.) *Augusta Bagiennorum. Storia e archeologia di una città augustea*: 157-200. Turin: Celid.

Ravasi, T. and Barbaglio, F. 2008. Merci e Persone sui Fiumi. Le imbarcazioni monossili conservate presso il Museo Civico di Crema e del Cremasco, in M. Baioni and C. Fredella (eds) *Archaeotrade. Antichi Commerci in Lombardia Orientale*: 37-61. Milan: Edizioni ET.

Reddé, M. 1986. Mare Nostrum. *Les infrastructures, le dispositif et l'histoire de la marine militaire sous l'empire romain*. Paris and Rome: Écoles Françaises de Rome.

Reed, K., Leleković, T., Lodwick, L., Fenwick, R., Pelling, R. and Kroll, H. 2022. Food, farming and trade on the Danube frontier: plant remains from Roman Aelia Mursa (Osijek, Croatia). *Vegetation History and Archaeobotany* 31: 363-376.

Remesal Rodríguez, J. and Revilla Calvo, V. 1991. Weinamphoren aus Hispania citerior und Gallia narbonensis in Deutschland und Holland. *Fundberichte Baden-Württenberg* 16: 349-389.

Remesal-Rodríguez, J. 1986. *La annona militaris y la exportacion de aceite bético a Germania: Con un corpus de sellos en ánforas Dressel, 20 hallados en Nimega, Colonia, Mainz, Saalburg, Zugmantel y Nida-Heddernheim*. Madrid: Ed. de la Universidad complutense.

Remesal-Rodríguez, J. 1997. *Heeresversorgung und die wirtschaftlichen Beziehungen zwischen der Baetica und Germanien: Materalien zu einem Corpus der in Deutschland veröffentlicheten Stempel auf Amphoren der*

Form Dressel 20. Stuttgart: K. Theiss.

Remesal-Rodríguez, J. 1998. Baetican olive oil and the Roman economy, in S. Keay (ed.) *The Archaeology of early Roman Baetica* (Journal of Roman Archaeology Supplements 29): 183-199. Portsmouth (RI): Journal of Roman Archaeology.

Remesal-Rodríguez, J. 2002. Baetica and Germania. Notes on the concept of provincial interdependence in the Roman Empire, in P. Erdkamp (ed.) *The Roman Army and the Economy*: 293-308. Amsterdam: Brill.

Repetto, I. 2021. La via Postumia tra Genova e Libarna. La funzione Least Cost Path di ARCGis per una ricostruzione dell'antico percorso, in S. Giorcelli Bersani and M. Venturino (eds) *I Liguri e Roma. Un popolo tra archeologia e storia*: 345-353. Rome: Edizioni Quasar.

Reynolds, P. 1995. *Trade in the Western Mediterranean, AD 400-700: the Ceramic Evidence*. (BAR International Series 604). Oxford: Archaeopress.

Reynolds, P. 2018. The Supply Networks of the Roman East and West: Interaction, Fragmentation, and the Origins of the Byzantine Economy, in A.I. Wilson and A.K. Bowman (eds) *Trade, Commerce, and the State in the Roman World*: 353-396. Oxford: Oxford University Press.

Rice, C. 2012. *Port Economies and Maritime Trade in the Roman Mediterranean: 166 BC to AD 300*. Unpublished D.Phil dissertation, University of Oxford.

Rice, C. 2016. Shipwreck cargoes in the western Mediterranean and the organization of Roman maritime trade. *Journal of Roman Archaeology* 29: 165-192.

Rickman, G.E. 1981. *The Corn Supply of Ancient Rome*. Oxford: Clarendon Press.

Rieth, É. 1998. *Des bateaux et des fleuves. Archéologie de la batellerie du néolithique aux temps modernes en France*. Paris: Errance.

Rieth, É. 2014. Le chaland Arles-Rhône 3 dans la batellerie gallo-romaine: étude typologique et interprétation historique. *Archaeonautica* 18: 279-287.

Rieth, É. and Guyon, M. 2011. Les chalands gallo-romains du Parc Saint-Georges, in G. Boetto, P. Pomey and A. Tchernia (eds) *Batellerie gallo-romaine: Pratiques régionales et influences maritimes méditerranéennes*: 91-101. Aix-en-Provence Bibliothèque d'Archéologie Méditerannéen et Africaine.

Righini, V. 2004. Fra produttori e consumatori: I materiali fittili pesanti nella Cisalpina, in S. Santoro (ed.) *Artigianato e produzione nella Cisalpina: Parte I. Proposte di metodo e prime applicazioni*: 239-264. Florence: All'Insegna del Giglio.

Rizzo, G. and Molari, C. 2023. Adriatic imports to Rome: An insight from the wine amphorae, in I. Borzić, E. Cirelli, K. Jelinčić Vučković, A. Konestra and I. Ožanić Roguljić (eds) *TRADE - Transformations of Adriatic Europe (2nd-9th Centuries AD). Proceedings of the conference in Zadar, 11th-13th February 2016*: 248-277. Oxford: Archaeopress.

Robino, M. 2008. La ceramica fine da mensa: vernice nera, terra sigillata, pareti sottili, in A. Bacchetta and M. Venturino Gambari (eds) *Raccolta archeologica di Augusto Scovazzi*: 21-34. Genoa: De Ferrari and Devega.

Robino, M. 2017. Le ceramiche fini da mensa, le ceramiche comuni e le lucerne, in A. Bacchetta and M. Venturino Gambari (eds) *La città ritrovata. Il Foro di Aquae Statiellae e il suo quartiere*: 61-106. Acqui Terme: Sistema Museale di Acqui Terme.

Rodrigue, J.-P. and Notteboom, T. 2020. Transportation, Economy and Society, in J.-P. Rodrigue (ed.) *The Geography of Transport Systems*: 90-123. fifth ed. London: Routledge.

Roffia, E. 1991. Ceramica Africana, in D. Caporusso (ed.) *Scavi MM3. Ricerche di archeologia urbana a Milano durante la costruzione della linea 3*: 89-105. Milan: Edizioni ET.

Romanowska, I., Bobou, O. and Raja, R. 2021. Reconstructing the social, economic and demographic trends of Palmyra's elite from funerary data. *Journal of Archaeological Science* 133: 105432.

Romanowska, I., Brughmans, T., Bes, P., Carrignon, S., Egelund, L., Lichtenberger, A. and Raja, R. 2021. A Study of the Centuries-Long Reliance on Local Ceramics in Jerash Through Full Quantification and Simulation. *Journal of Archaeological Method and Theory*: 1-19.

Roncaglia, C.E. 2013. Client Prefects?: Rome and the Cottians in the Western Alps. *Phoenix* 67: 353-372.

Roncaglia, C.E. 2018. *Northern Italy in the Roman World: From the Bronze Age to Late Antiquity*. Baltimore: John Hopkins University Press.

Roncuzzi, A. 1992. Topografia di Ravenna antica: le mura. *Corsi di cultura sull'arte ravennate e bizantina* 39: 691-741.

Roncuzzi, A. and Veggi, L. 1967. Risultati di una ricerca dell'antica topografia nel territorio a Nord di Ravenna. *Bollettino Economico della Camera di Ravenna* 2: 287-292.

Roncuzzi, A. and Veggi, L. 1968. Nuovi studi sull'antica topografia ravennate. *Bollettino Economico della Camera di Ravenna* 3: 193-201.

Rossi, C. 2013. *Le necropoli urbane di Padova romane*. Unpublished PhD, Università degli Studi di Padova.

Rossiter, J. 1981. Wine and Oil Processing at Roman Farms in Italy. *Phoenix* 35: 345-361.

Rossiter, J. 2008. Wine-Making After Pliny: Viticulture And Farming Technology In Late Antique Italy, in L. Lavan, E. Zanini and A. Sarantis (eds) *Technology in Transition A.D. 300-650*: 93-118. Leiden: Brill.

Rousse, C. 2013. Opérations de canalisation dans les ports fluvio-maritimes de la Regio X Venetia Histria: réflexions sur l'urbanisme et les transformations du territoire à l'époque Romaine. *Antichità Altoadriatiche*

76: 123-140.

Royal, J. 2012. Illyrian Coastal Exploration Program (2007–2009): The Roman and Late Roman Finds and Their Contexts. *American Journal of Archaeology* 116: 405-460.

Rubio-Campillo, X. and Coto-Sarmiento, M. 2022. New Approaches to Old Questions: The Exploration of Large-scale Trade Dynamics Using Hypothesis-testing Frameworks, in T. Brughmans and A.I. Wilson (eds) *Simulating Roman Economies: Theories, Methods, and Computational Models*: 167-195. Oxford: Oxford University Press.

Rubio-Campillo, X., Coto-Sarmiento, M., Pérez-González, J. and Remesal Rodríguez, J. 2017. Bayesian analysis and free market trade within the Roman Empire. *Antiquity* 91: 1241–1252.

Ruggiu Zaccaria, A. 1969. Indagini sull'insediamento longobardo a Brescia. *Contributi dell'Istituto di Archeologia* 2: 110-150.

Russell, B. 2008. The dynamics of stone transport between the Roman Mediterranean and its hinterland. *Facta* 2: 107-126.

Russell, B. 2011. The Roman Sarcophagus 'Industry': a Reconsideration, in J. Elsner and J. Huskinson (eds) *Life, Death and Representation. Some New Work on Roman Sarcophagi*: 119-147. Berlin and New York: De Gruyter.

Russell, B. 2013. *The Economics of the Roman Stone Trade.* Oxford: Oxford University Press.

Russell, B. 2018a. 'Difficult and costly': Stone transport, its constraints, and its impact, in C. Coquelet, G. Creemers, R. Dreesen and É. Goemare (eds) *Roman Ornamental Stones in North-Western Europe*: 131-150. Namur: AWaP.

Russell, B. 2018b. Stone Use and the Economy: Demand, Distribution, and the State, in A.I. Wilson and A.K. Bowman (eds) *Trade, Commerce, and the State in the Roman World*: 237-264. Oxford: Oxford University Press.

Sacchi, F., Dell'acqua, A., Bugini, R. and Folli, L. 2011. I portici del foro di Brescia, in S. Maggi (ed.) *I complessi forensi della Cisalpina romana. Nuovi dati. Atti del convegno di studi, Pavia 12.-13. marzo 2009*: 115-129. Borgo San Lorenzo: All'Insegna del Giglio.

Salmon, E.T. 1982. *The Making of Roman Italy.* Ithaca: Thames and Hudson.

Salomon, F. and Rousse, C. 2022. Navigable canals in deltaic environments during the Roman period: deciphering location patterns, in A. Lasheras, J. Ruiz De Arbulo and P. Terrado Ortuño (eds) *Ports Romans. Arqueologia dels sistemes portuaris. Actes V Congrés Internacional d'Arqueologia i Món Antic Tarraco Biennal, 24-27/11/2021*: 173-195. Tarragona: Institut Català d'Arqueologia Clàssica.

Salomon, F. and Rousse, C. 2023. Geoarchaeology and Archaeology of Navigable Canals in River Deltas during the Roman Period. Technical, Methodological and Conceptual Approaches, in A. Tibbs and P.B. Campbell (eds) *Rivers and Waterways in the Roman World. Empire of Water*: 35-50. London: Routledge.

Sanesi Mastrocinque, L., Bonomi, S. and A., T. 1986. L'insediamento romano di Corte Cavanella di Loreo. *Quaderni di Archeologia del Veneto* 2: 25-30.

Sanesi Mastrocinque, L., Peretto, R. and Zerbinati, E. 1985. L'insediamento romano di Corte Cavanella (Loreo). Rapporto preliminare. *Quaderni di Archeologia del Veneto* 1: 11-23.

Sarabia-Bautista, J. 2017. L'acqua come elemento generatore dei paesaggi storici nella pianura sud-orientale dei Colli Euganei, in G.P. Brogiolo (ed.) *Este, l'Adige e i Colli Euganei. Storie di paesaggi*: 69-88. Mantua: All'Insegna del Giglio.

Sauer, E.W. 2014. Milestones - misunderstood stone monuments: displays of loyalty in times of instability. *Ancient Society* 44: 1-36.

Scheidel, W. 2009. In search of Roman economic growth. *Journal of Roman Archaeology* 22: 46-70.

Scheidel, W. 2012. Approaching the Roman Economy, in W. Scheidel (ed.) *The Cambridge Companion to the Roman Economy*: 1-21. Cambridge: Cambridge University Press.

Scheidel, W. 2013. Explaining the maritime freight charges in Diocletian's Prices Edict. *Journal of Roman Archaeology* 26: 464-468.

Scheidel, W. 2014. The shape of the Roman world: modelling imperial connectivity. *Journal of Roman Archaeology* 27: 7-32.

Schindler, M. and Zabehlicky Scheffenegger, S. 1977. *Die glatte rote Terra sigillata vom Magdalensberg.* Klagenfurt: Verlag des Landesmuseums für Kärnten.

Schindler-Kaudelka, E. 1980. *Die römische Modelkeramik vom Magdalensberg.* Klagenfurt: Verlag des Landesmuseums für Kärnten.

Schmidts, T. 2012. *Akteure und Organisation der Handelsschifffahrt in den nordwestlichen Provinzen des Römischen Reiches.* Mainz: Fast and Steiner.

Schulthess, C.D.M. 2020. Produzioni locali, importazioni e esportazioni dall'attuale Canton Ticino (Svizzera). *Rei Cretariae Romanae Fautorum Acta* 46: 139-147.

Scott, J. 2017. *Social network analysis.* London: SAGE Publications.

Sebastiani, R. and Serlorenzi, M. 2008. Il progetto del nuovo mercato di Testaccio. *Workshop di archeologia classica* 5: 137-172.

Secchi, L. 2017. Le anfore da trasporto, in A. Bacchetta and M. Venturino Gambari (eds) *La città ritrovata. Il Foro di Aquae Statiellae e il suo quartiere*: 107-123. Acqui Terme: Sistema Museale di Acqui Terme.

Sfameni, C. 2004. Residential villas in Late Antique Italy: continuity and change. *Late Antique Archaeology* 2: 333-375.

Shafie, T., Atkinson, P., Delamont, S., Cernat, A., Sakshaug, J.W. and Williams, R.A. 2020. *Social network analysis.* London: SAGE Publications.

Shennan, S. 1997. *Quantifying archaeology*. Edinburgh: Edinburgh University Press.

Sheppard, E. 2006. The economic geography project, in S. Bagchi-Sen and H. Lawton Smith (eds) *Economic Geography. Past, present, and future*: 11-23. London: Routledge.

Spagnolo Garzoli, G., Deodato, A., Quiri, E. and Ratto, S. 2007. Genesi dei centri urbani di Vercellae e Novaria, in L. Brecciaroli Taborelli (ed.) *Forme e tempi dell'urbanizzazione nella Cisalpina (II secolo a.C. – I secolo d.C.). Atti delle Giornate di Studio Torino. 4-6 maggio 2006*: 109-126. Florence: All'Insegna del Giglio.

Spagnolo Garzoli, G., Deodato, A., Quiri, E. and Ratto, S. 2008. Flussi commerciali e produzioni nei municipi di Novaria e Vercellae in prima e media età imperiale. *Quaderni della Soprintendenza Archeologica del Piemonte*: 79-109.

Stefani, M. 2017. The Po Delta Region: Depositional Evolution, Climate Change and Human Intervention Through the Last 5000 Years, in M. Soldati and M. Marchetti (eds) *Landscapes and Landforms of Italy*: 193-202. Springer International.

Steinmann, L. and Weissova, B. 2021. datplot: A New R Package for the Visualization of Date Ranges in Archaeology. *Advances in Archaeological Practice* 9: 288-298.

Sternini, M. 2019. The production centres and river network of Italian terra sigillata between the Arno and Tiber valleys: a geographical point of view. *Journal of Roman Archaeology* 32: 485-494.

Stoppioni, M.L. 1990. Appendice 2. Le Anfore, in G. Susini (ed.) *Storia di Ravenna I*: 457-467. Ravenna: Marsillo.

Stoppioni, M.L. 2008. La sigillata tarda di Sarsina, in A. Donati (ed.) *Storia di Sarsina I. L'età antica*: 713-762. Cesena: Stilgraf.

Stoppioni, M.L. 2021. Le anfore adriatiche a Rimini, in D. Rigato, M. Mongardi and M. Vitelli Casella (eds) *Adriatlas 4. Produzioni artigianali in area adriatica: manufatti, ateliers e attori (III sec. a.C. – V sec. d.C.)*: 281-300. Bordeux: Ausonius.

Surian, N. and Fontana, A. 2017. The Tagliamento River: The Fluvial Landscape and Long-Term Evolution of a Large Alpine Braided River, in M. Soldati and M. Marchetti (eds) *Landscapes and Landforms of Italy*: 157-167. Cham: Springer.

Taelman, D. 2022. Marble trade in the Roman Mediterranean: a quantitative and diachronic study. *Journal of Roman Archaeology* 35: 848-875.

Talbert, R.J.A. and Bagnall, R.S. 2000. *The Barrington Atlas of the Greek and Roman World*. Princeton: Princeton University Press.

Tartaron, T.F. 2014. *Maritime networks in the Mycenaean world*. Cambridge: Cambridge University Press.

Tassaux, F. 2004. Les Importations de l'Adriatique et de l'Italie du Nord vers les provinces danubiennes de César aux Sévères, in G. Urso (ed.) *Dall'Adriatico al Danubio: L'Illirico nell'età greca e romana: Atti del convegno internazionale (Cividale di Friuli, 25–27 settembre 2003)*: 167-205. Pisa: ETS.

Taylor, T. 2009. Materiality, in R.A. Bentley, H.D.G. Maschner and C. Chippindale (eds) *Handbook of Archaeological Theories*: 297-320. Lanhem: AltaMira Press.

Tchernia, A. 1986. *Le vin de l'Italie romaine. Essai d'histoire économique d'après les amphores*. Paris and Rome: Ecole Française de Rome.

Tchernia, A. 2011. *Les Romains et le commerce*. Naples: Publications du Centre Jean Bérard.

Tchernia, A. 2016. *The Romans and Trade*. Oxford: Oxford University Press.

Temin, P. 2001. A Market Economy in the Early Roman Empire. *Journal of Roman Studies* 91: 169-181.

Temin, P. 2012. The Role of Economics, in W. Scheidel (ed.) *The Cambridge Companion to the Roman Economy*: 45-70. Cambridge: Cambridge University Press.

Temin, P. 2013. *The Roman Market Economy*. Princeton: Princeton University Press.

Tempesta, C. 2011. Nuovo Mercato di Testaccio: dallo scavo archeologico allo studio dei materiali. I reperti ceramici dell'ambiente I degli Horrea, in A. Gallone and S. Zottis (eds) *L'archeologia con gli occhi di Silvia*: 189-200. Catania: Edizioni Prampolini.

Tempesta, C. 2013. Le Anfore, in C. Guarnieri (ed.) *Vivere a Forum Livi. Lo scavo di via Curte a Forlì*: 111-124. Bologna: Ante Quem.

Tempesta, C. 2018. Anfore da Trasporto, in C. Guarnieri and G. Montevecchi (eds) *Il genio delle acque: scavi nelle piazze di Ravenna*: 131-144. Ravenna: Longo Angelo.

Terpstra, T. 2013. *Trading Communities in the Roman World. A Micro-Economic and Institutional Perspective*. (Columbia Studies in the Classical Tradition Series 37). Leiden and Boston: Brill.

Terpstra, T. 2019. *Trade in the Ancient Mediterranean: Private Order and Public Institutions*. Princeton: Princeton University Press.

Terracina, F. 1991. Lastre Marmoree di Rivestimento, in D. Caporusso (ed.) *Scavi MM3. Ricerche di archeologia urbana a Milano durante la costruzione della linea 3*: 159-164. Milan: Edizioni ET.

Throckmorton, P. 1989. The ship of Torre Sgarrata. *Tropis* 1: 263-274.

Tibiletti, G. 1969. Problemi della romanizzazione della Lombardia pedemontana occidentale, *Archeologia e storia della Lombardia pedemontana occidentale*: 43-52. Como: Casa Editrice Pietro Cairoli.

Tiboni, F. 2009. Chioggia. Localit`a di Motta di Cavanella d'Adige. Le operazioni di scavo e primo studio di un relitto del II–I secolo a.C. *Quaderni di Archeologia del Veneto* 25: 82-84.

Tiranti, D., Rabuffetti, D., Salandin, A. and Tararbra, M. 2013. Development of a new translational and rotational slides prediction model in Langhe hills (north-western Italy) and its application to the 2011 March landslide event. *Landslides* 10: 121-138.

Tirelli, M. 1987. Oderzo: rinvenimento di un molo fluviale in via delle Grazie. *Quaderni di Archeologia del Veneto* 3: 81-85.

Tirelli, M. 2001. Il porto di Altinum, in C. Zaccaria (ed.) *Strutture portuali e rotte marittime nell'Adriatico di Età Romana*: 295-316. Trieste: Edizioni Quasar.

Tomber, R. 1993. Quantitative approaches to the investigation of long-distance exchange. *Journal of Roman Archaeology* 6: 142-166.

Tonc, A. and Filipović, S. 2020. Only the Best Olive Oil, Please: On New Amphorae Finds From Mursa. *Ephemeris Napocensis* 30: 273-294

Toniolo, A. 1991. *Le anfore di Altino*. Padua: Società Archeologica Veneta.

Tortorella, S. 1996. Considerazioni sulla sigillata tarda dell'Italia centro-settentrionale, in M.G. Picozzi and F. Carinci (eds) *Studi in memoria di Lucia Guerrini*: 323-335. Rome: L'Erma di Bretschneider.

Trapero Fernández, P., Carneiro, A. and Moreira, N. 2023. Transport and distribution of heavy loads in ancient times: Estremoz Marbles in the Roman province of Lusitania. *Journal of Archaeological Science: Reports* 49: 103962.

Trentacoste, A., Nieto-Espinet, A., Guimaraes, S., Wilkens, B., Petrucci, G. and Valenzuela-Lamas, S. 2021. New trajectories or accelerating change? Zooarchaeological evidence for Roman transformation of animal husbandry in Northern Italy. *Archaeological and Anthropological Sciences* 13: 25.

Trivini Bellini, M. 2021. La terra sigillata africana, in J. Bonetto, S. Mazzocchin and D. Dobreva (eds) *Aquileia. Fondi Cossar. 3.3. I materiali ceramici*: 301-350. Rome: Edizioni Quasar.

Trocchi, T., Marchesini, M., Marvelli, S. and Lambertini, F. (eds) 2014. *La villa nel pozzo. Un insediamento rustico romano a Sant'Agata Bolognese,* San Giovanni in Persiceto: Museo Archeologico Ambientale.

Trovò, R. 1996. Canalizzazioni lignee e ruota idraulica di età romana ad Oderzo (Treviso). *Quaderni di Archeologia del Veneto* 12: 119-134.

Uggeri, G. 1978. Vie di terra e vie d'acqua tra Aquileia e Ravanna in età Romana. *Antichità Altoadriatiche* 13: 46-79.

Uggeri, G. 1987. La navigazione interna della Cisalpina in età romana. *Antichità Altoadriatiche* 19: 305-354.

Uggeri, G. 1990. Aspetti archeologici della navigazione interna nella Cisalpina. *Antichità Altoadriatiche* 36: 175-196.

Uggeri, G. 1997. I canali navigabili dell'antico delta Padano in A. Coen and S. Quilici Gigli (eds) *Uomo, acqua e paesaggio: atti dell'incontro di studio sul tema Irreggimentazione delle acque e trasformazione del paesaggio antico: S. Maria Capua Vetere, 22-23 novembre, 1996*: 55-60. Rome: L'Erma di Bretschneider.

Uggeri, G. 2002. *Carta archeologica del Territorio Ferrarese (F. 76). Rivista di topografia antica.* Galatina: Congendo.

Uggeri, G. 2006. *Carta archeologica del Territorio Ferrarese (F. 77 3. S.E. Comacchio). Rivista di topografia antica.* Galatina: Congendo.

Uggeri, G. 2016. "La Romanizzazione dell'antico delta padano." 40 anni dopo: una revisione. *Atti dell'Academia delle Scienze di Ferrara* 93: 79-104.

Ugolini, F. 2015. The Roman harbour of Ariminum and its connections with the Aegean and the Black Sea, in G.R. Tsetskhladze, A. Avram and J. Hargrave (eds) *The Danubian lands between the Black, Aegean and Adriatic Seas (7th century BC - 10th century AD): proceedings of the Fifth International Congress on Black Sea Antiquities (Belgrade - 17-21 September 2013)*: 243-247. Oxford: Archaeopress.

Ugolini, F. 2021a. The Network of Roman Ports in North Adriatic Italy from the First to the Fifth Century AD: Development, Operation and Relevance. *Archaeologia Maritima Mediterranea* 18: 49-93.

Ugolini, F. 2021b. Shipping Adriatic wines in the Roman Mediterranean: a quantitative approach. *Babesch* 96: 83-100.

Ugolini, F. 2023. Quantifying Wheat at Production. Consumption and Export in Roman Adriatic Italy (150 BC - AD 250). *Agri Centuriati* 20: 91-111.

Vaccaro, E., Capelli, C. and Ghisleni, M. 2017. Italic Sigillata Production and Trade in Rural Central Italy: New Data from the Project 'Excavating the Roman Peasant', in T. De Haas and G. Tol (eds) *The Economic Integration of Roman Italy: Rural Communities in a Globalising World*: 231-262. Leiden: Brill.

Vaccaro, E. and Mackinnon, M. 2014. Pottery and Animal Consumption: New Evidence from the 'Excavating the Roman Peasant Project'. *HEROM. Journal on Hellenistic and Roman Material Culture* 3: 225-257.

Van Den Berg, J. 2012. Rare and exotic amphorae in North-West Europe: finds from the Roman fort on the Kops Plateau, Nijmegen. *Journal of Roman Pottery Studies* 15: 215-235.

Van Der Veen, M. 1989. Charred Grain Assemblages from Roman-Period Corn Driers in Britain. *Archeological Journal* 146: 302-319.

Van Limbergen, D. 2011. *Vinum Picenum* and *Oliva Picena*: wine and oil presses in central Adriatic Italy between the Late Republic and the Early Empire: evidence and problems. *Babesch* 86: 71-94.

Van Limbergen, D. 2016. A Note on olives and olive oil from Picenum (Marche, Northern Abruzzo). An obscured food product within the economy of central Adriatic Italy in Roman times? *PICUS* 36: 171-182.

Van Limbergen, D. 2018. The Central Adriatic Wine Trade of Italy Revisited: The Central Adriatic Wine Trade of Italy. *Oxford Journal of Archaeology* 37: 201-226.

Van Limbergen, D. 2019. *Vinum picenum* and *oliva picena*

II: further thoughts on wine and oil presses in Central Adriatic Italy. *Babesch* 94: 1-31.

Van Limbergen, D. 2024. Approaching Palaeo-terroir: Thoughts on How to Study the Geography of Wine in the Roman World, in E.K. Dodd and D. Van Limbergen (eds) *Methods in Ancient Wine Archaeology. Scientific Approaches in Roman Contexts*: 33-52. London: Bloomsbury.

Van Neer, W., Ervyneck, A. and Monsieur, P. 2010. Fish bones and amphorae: evidence for the production and consumption of salted fish products outside the Mediterranean region. *Journal of Roman Archaeology* 23: 161-195.

Van Oyen, A. 2015. The Roman City as Articulated through Terra Sigillata. *Oxford Journal of Archaeology* 34: 279-299.

Van Oyen, A. 2016. *How Things Make History: The Roman Empire and its terra sigillata Pottery*. Amsterdam: Amsterdam University Press.

Van Oyen, A. 2017. Agents and commodities: a response to Brughmans and Poblome (2016) on modelling the Roman economy. *Antiquity* 91: 1356–1363.

Van Oyen, A. and Pitts, M. 2017. What did objects do in the Roman world? Beyond representation, in A. Van Oyen and M. Pitts (eds) *Materialising Roman Histories*: 3-19. Oxford: Oxbow.

Vanetti, G. 1987. La terra sigillata di regione Maddalene, in Chieri (ed.) *Museo Archeologico di Chieri* 136-156. Chieri: Museo Archeologico di Chieri

Vanni Desideri, A. 2001. Gestione dello spazio urbano e del territorio in Val d'Aosta. Analisi archeologica nell'area del teatro, in S. Giorcelli Bersani (ed.) *Actes du Colloque Internationale "Les anciens et la montagne. Ecologie, religion, economie et aménagement du territoire*: 261-276. Aosta: L'Hartmattan.

Vecchi, L. 1999. Le anfore di Clastidium nell'ambito dei commerci padani, in C. Maccabruni (ed.) *Multas per gentes, et multa per aequora. Culture adriatiche in provincia di Pavia: Lomellina, Pavese, Oltrepo, Atti della giornata di studi (Gambolo, 18 maggio 1997)*: 205-218. Milan: Enerre.

Verboven, K. 2021. Introduction: Finding a New Approach to Ancient Proxy Data, in K. Verboven (ed.) *Complexity economics: building a new approach to ancient economic history*: 1-18. Cham: Springer.

Vezzoli, R., Mercogliano, P., Pecora, S., Zollo, A.L. and Cacciamani, C. 2015. Hydrological simulation of Po River (North Italy) discharge under climate change scenarios using the RCM COSMO-CLM. *Science of the Total Environment* 521-22: 346-358.

Vidal, J.M. 1999. Anfore e Relazioni Commerciali, in P. Braconi and J.U. Uroz Sáez (eds) *La villa di Plinio il Giovane a San Giustino*: 101-112. Perugia: Quattroemme.

Vidal, J.M. 2009. Mercantile Trade in the Upper Tiber Valley: The Villa of Pliny the Younger in Tuscis, in H. Patterson and F. Coarelli (eds) *Mercator Placidissimus:*

The Tiber Valley in Antiquity. New research in the upper and middle river valley. Rome 27 – 28 February 2004: 215-249. Rome: Edizioni Quasar.

Vigoni, A. 2006. Il canale interno di Iulia Concordia. Dati storici, archeologici e topografici, in D. Morandi Bonacossi, E. Rova, F. Veronese and P. Zanovello (eds) *Tra Oriente e Occidente. Studi in onore di Elena di Filippo Balestrazzi*: 451-468. Padua: SARGON.

Volonte, R. 1996. Le Anfore, in L. Passi Pitcher (ed.) *Bedriacum: ricerche archeologiche a Calvatone*: 189-208. Milan: Edizioni ET.

Volonte, M. 1996. Le Terre Sigillate, in L. Passi Pitcher (ed.) *Bedriacum: ricerche archeologiche a Calvatone*: 105-118. Milan: Edizioni ET.

Volonte, M. 1997. Ceramica terra sigillata: i servizi da tavola in F. Filippi (ed.) *Alba Pompeia. Archeologia della città dalla fondazione alla tarda antichità*: 432-450. Alba: Omega.

Volonte, M., Ravasi, T. and Nicodemo, M. 2008. Le Vie delle Anfore. Il commercio di derrate alimentari a Cremona attraverso i dati dello scavo di Piazza Marconi, in M. Baioni and C. Frenelli (eds) *Archaeotrade. Antichi commerce nella Lombaria orientale*: 285-303. Milan: ET Edizioni.

Ward-Perkins, J.B. 1980. Nicomedia and the marble trade. *Papers of the British School at Rome* 48: 23-69.

Ward-Perkins, J.B. 1992a. Materials, quarries and transportation (First Shuffrey Lecture), in H. Dodge and B. Ward-Perkins (eds) *Marble in Antiquity: Collected Papers of J. B. Ward-Perkins*: 13–22. Rome and London: British School at Rome.

Ward-Perkins, J.B. 1992b. The Roman system in operation (Second Shuffrey Lecture), in H. Dodge and B. Ward-Perkins (eds) *Marble in Antiquity: Collected Papers of J. B. Ward-Perkins*: 23-30. Rome and London: British School at Rome.

Whittaker, C.R. 1993. *Land, city and trade in the Roman Empire*. London: Variorum.

Whittaker, C.R. 1994. *Frontiers of the Roman Empire. A Social and Economic Study*. Baltimore: Johns Hopkins University Press.

Wickham, C. 2005. *Framing the Early Middle Ages: Europe and the Mediterranean 400-800*. Oxford: Oxford University Press.

Wilkes, J.J. 1979. Importation and Manufacture of Stamped Bricks and Tiles in the Province of Dalmatia, in A. Mcwhirr (ed.) *Roman Brick and Tile* (BAR International Series 68): 65-72. Oxford: Archaeopress.

Williams, J. 2001. Roman Intentions and Romanization: Republican Northern Italy, c. 200–100 BC., in S. Keay and A. Terrenato (eds) *Italy and the West: Comparative Issues in Romanization*: 91-101. Oxford: Oxbow.

Willis, S. and Capulli, M. 2014. Putting the pieces together. The laced timbers of the Venice Lido III assemblage. *INA Quarterly* 41: 10-15.

Willis, S. and Capulli, M. 2018. A Report on the late

1st–2nd-century-AD Venice Lido III Sewn Timber Assemblage. *The International Journal of Nautical Archaeology* 47: 343-336.

Wilson, A.I. 2009a. Approaches to Quantifying Roman Trade, in A.K. Bowman and A.I. Wilson (eds) *Quantifying the Roman Economy: Methods and Problems*: 213-249. Oxford: Oxford University Press.

Wilson, A.I. 2009b. Indicators for Roman economic growth: a response to Walter Scheidel. *Journal of Roman Archaeology* 22: 71–82.

Wilson, A.I. 2009c. Villas, horticulture and irrigation infrastructure in the Tiber Valley, in H. Patterson and F. Coarelli (eds) *Mercator Placidissimus: The Tiber Valley in Antiquity. New research in the upper and middle river valley*: 731-768. Rome: Edizioni Quasar.

Wilson, A.I. 2011. Developments in Mediterranean shipping and maritime trade from the Hellenistic period to AD 1000, in D. Robinson and A.I. Wilson (eds) *Maritime Archaeology and Ancient Trade in the Mediterranean*: 33-59. Oxford: Oxford University Press.

Wilson, A.I. 2011. The Economic Influence of Developments in Maritime Technology in Antiquity, in W.V. Harris and K. Iara (eds) *Maritime Technology in the Ancient Economy: Ship-Design and Navigation* (Journal of Roman Archaeology Supplements 84): 211-233. Portsmouth (RI): Journal of Roman Archaeology.

Wilson, A.I. 2014. Quantifying Roman economic performance by means of proxies: pitfalls and potential, in S. De Callataÿ (ed.) *Quantifying the Greco-Roman Economy and Beyond* 147-167. Bari: Edipuglia.

Wilson, A.I. 2022. Positioning Computational Modelling in Roman Studies in T. Brughmans and A.I. Wilson (eds) *Simulating Roman Economies: Theories, Methods, and Computational Models*: 308-324. Oxford: Oxford University Press.

Wilson, A.I. and Bowman, A.K. (eds) 2018. *Trade, commerce, and the state in the Roman world*, Oxford: Oxford University Press.

Wilson, A.I. and Bowman, A.K. 2018. Introduction: Trade, Commerce, and the State, in A.I. Wilson and A.K. Bowman (eds) *Trade, Commerce, and the State in the Roman World*: 1-24. Oxford: Oxford University Press.

Wilson, A.I., Schörle, K. and Rice, C. 2011. Roman ports and Mediterranean connectivity, in S. Keay (ed.) *Portus and the Ports of the Roman Mediterranean*: 367-391. Rome and London: British School at Rome.

Wiseman, R., Bulik, O., Lobo, J., Lodwick, L. and Ortman, S.G. 2023. The Impact of Transportation on Pottery Industries in Roman Britain. *Open Archaeology* 9: 20220286.

Zabehlicky Scheffenegger, S. 1992. Terra sigillata tardo-padana. *Rei Cretariae Romanae Fautorum Acta* 31/32: 415-443.

Zabehlicky Scheffenegger, S. and Sauer, R. 2000. Metodi di distinzione dei due gruppi di sigillata padana augustea trovati sul Magdalensberg, in G.P. Brogiolo and G. Olcese (eds) *Produzione ceramica in area padana tra il II secolo a.C. e il VII secolo d.C: nuovi dati e prospettive di ricerca: convegno internazionale, Desenzano del Garda, 8-10 aprile 1999*: 69-78. Mantua: All'Insegna del Giglio.

Zamboni, L. 2021. The Urbanization of Northern Italy. Contextualizing Early Settlement Nucleation in the Po Valley. *Journal of Archaeological Research* 29: 387-430.

Zanda, E. 2011. *Industria, città romana sacra a Iside. Scavi e ricerche archeologiche 1981-2003*. Turin: Allemandi.

Zanetti, C. 2011. I miliari di Valentiniano e Valente in Italia: alcune considerazioni sulle titolature imperiali, in P. Basso (ed.) *I miliari lungo le strade dell'impero. Atti del Convegno (Isola della Scala, 28 novembre 2010*: 115-140. Verona: Cierre Edizioni.

Zara, A. 2018. *La Trachite Euganea. Archeologia e storia di una risora lapidea del Veneto antico*. Padua: Edizioni Quasar.

Zidanšek, I.B., Vojaković, P. and Žerjal, T. 2022. The Amber route between Caput Adriae and Emona basin
the ceramic evidence on inner road – and water – communications, in G.L. Vrkljan, A. Konestra and A.E. Borzić (eds) *Roman Pottery and Glass Manufactures: Production and Trade in the Adriatic Region and Beyond*: 36-46. Oxford: Archaeopress.

Zucca, I. 1996. Le anfore romane rinvenute a Cremona e nel suo territorio, in G.M. Facchini, L. Passi Pitcher and M. Volonte (eds) *Cremona e Bedriacum in età romana I. Vent'anni di tesi universitarie*: 125-133. Milan: ET Edizioni.

Zulini, E. 2017. Terra Sigillata Africana, in P. Maggi, F. Maselli Scotti, S. Pesavento Mattioli and E. Zulini (eds) *Materiali per Aquileia: lo scavo di Canale Anfora (2004-2005)*: 115-135. Trieste: Edizioni Quasar.